31-1583

THE ECONOMIC MIND IN AMERICAN CIVILIZATION

1606–1865

VOLUME ONE

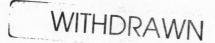

Also published in

REPRINTS OF ECONOMIC CLASSICS

BY JOSEPH DORFMAN

THORSTEIN VEBLEN AND HIS AMERICA [1834]

THE ECONOMIC MIND IN
AMERICAN CIVILIZATION

1606-1865

BY

Joseph Dorfman

VOLUME ONE

REPRINTS OF ECONOMIC CLASSICS

AUGUSTUS M. KELLEY · PUBLISHERS
NEW YORK · 1966

VOLUMES I AND II OF THE ECONOMIC MIND IN AMERICAN CIVIL-
IZATION 1606 - 1865 by Joseph Dorfman were originally published in 1946 and reprinted in 1953 by The Viking Press.

They are reprinted in 1966 by arrangement with The Viking Press.

AT THE END OF VOLUME II, JOSEPH DORFMAN'S ADDRESS

THE JACKSON WAGE-EARNER THESIS

ORIGINALLY PUBLISHED IN THE AMERICAN HISTORICAL REVIEW,

JANUARY 1949, IS REPRINTED BY PERMISSION.

LIBRARY OF CONGRESS CATALOGUE CARD NUMBER

64 - 7664

PRINTED IN THE UNITED STATES OF AMERICA
by SENTRY PRESS, NEW YORK, N. Y. 10019

TO THE PIONEERING SPIRIT

OF THORSTEIN VEBLEN

AND THE FIRST-BORN

OF HIS INTELLECTUAL HEIRS,

WESLEY C. MITCHELL

Prefatory Note

For this reprinting of volumes I and II of *The Economic Mind in American Civilization*, I have made only a few minor, verbal changes.

At the end of volume II, I have added the address which I delivered before the American Historical Association in December 1946, "The Jackson Wage-Earner Thesis," which originally appeared in *The American Historical Review*, January 1949. I wish to thank the editors of the *Review* for graciously granting permission to reprint it.

Joseph Dorfman

Columbia University
February 15, 1966

Contents

Preface

IN AMERICA as elsewhere, economic thought is an integral part of culture. Its richness and the reach of its relevance can be appreciated fully only when it is treated in its natural habitat of practical affairs and intellectual endeavor. It grows by constant cross-breeding with other species of learning and speculation. Since in the final analysis men's minds may be read most clearly in their actions, the practical ambitions and political interests of the molders of economic thought must constantly be kept in view by those who seek to understand what successive generations have put into the public record.

In any age then, economic thought shares the characteristics of the contemporary forces at play. And the history of economic thinking in the United States falls conveniently into two great eras separated by the Civil War. Both periods have a marked individuality.

The long span from the small beginnings of the nation in the seventeenth century to the close of the great conflict for the preservation of the Union is sharply characterized by the fertile force of commerce, the ideal of a stratified and hierarchical society, and the sophisticated culture of the then dominant groups with its traditional sanctions and rhetoric of religion and humanitarianism, which shifted gradually toward liberalism, democracy, and agrarianism.

The most potent determinant of economic action and thought was world commerce—the commerce that gave us treasure, the commerce that brought foreign goods and took our exports, that profited shipper, middleman, and speculator; the commerce, in short, that created the rich urban community and enlarged the money economy. Domestic trade and industrial production were important, but in the eyes of the articulate actors, they were merely adjuncts to the expanding and profitable activity in world trade. The domestic economy was animated by the larger economy embracing the old world and the new. The vast wild fertile lands of America might serve as a lure for the oppressed and discontented of the Old World, but in contemporary eyes they acquired value only as they promised to furnish profitable staples for commerce. Finally, around commerce swirled the never-ceasing experiments in monetary devices that were designed to secure treasure—the benchmark of national power and wealth.

Commerce implied elbow room for the individual in the achievement of his pecuniary purposes. When men's eyes were turned to the sea, and the foreign lands beyond, men's thinking and habits were cosmopolitan. They felt the breath of the contacts and collisions international relations engendered. The rising individual, however, while he dared to act more freely, not so much to exalt his dignity as to increase his wealth, comfortably thought along the old ways of aristocracy and authority.

It is little recognized how strongly the note of a strictly ordered society sounded on these shores. The idea of a society comprised of "orders" in which every man found his appointed place, almost his inherited place, was brought to this country by the "corporate" groups of colonists. It flourished mightily in the land and reached a climax in the intellectual appeal of the ante-bellum South for authority and force to maintain a slave society.

Such is the counterpoint of liberty and authority in our youthful days as a community trying to find itself.

Between the constriction of a social tradition which was hierarchical, and the strivings of ambitious individuals to attain distinction of wealth and position, democracy had a terrific struggle to attain a toehold. For the most part, the leaders of democracy viewed it as freedom and individualism within the specific framework of commerce and finance. All the great utopian and radical movements eventually succumbed to the pervasive and jealous environment of commerce. And the anti-democratic residue of the old hierarchical tradition was never banished.

Closely connected with democracy was the problem of the agrarian classes. City and factory labor were unimportant until well into the nineteenth century. But the farmers bulked large in numbers, and the freehold franchise so generally prevalent for the greater part of the period made them potentially an important political interest. But they generally yielded to the activity, agility, and leadership of the mercantile groups and the planters with business interests. Again and again the farmers as well as the relatively unimportant laboring class

appeared in the arena as the auxiliaries of rival business factions for
which they provided the bucolic pen names signed to "capitalistic"
pamphlets.

A highly urbane culture characterized the age under review. In
striking contrast to the specialists of today, reflective men thought
comprehensively but also systematically on a variety of subjects. The
chasm between men of affairs and men of thought had not yet opened.
Men of action were strikingly and joyously articulate, suave, and
learned. The ghost writer had no market. Clerics, politicians, business
leaders, and academic men did not stay put in their pulpits, forums,
market places, and cloistered halls. The four callings interacted intimately to the point of meeting often in the same person.

This integration of interests was genuine and yet paradoxical. As
men of action, the writers of our economic literature exhibited a
stark realism and materialism; as urbane men, they shone with the
polish of idealism and high purpose. With great agility they rode two
horses, which did not always willingly go in the same direction. It
was under the ingratiating guise of "Man of God," "Republican,"
"Agricola," "Philanthropos," that they made their appeals. Aristocratic academicians appeared as "Workingman," "Mechanic," and
"One of the Sovereign People." This phraseology of obeisance to
humanist, classical, and religious ideals misled only succeeding generations; hence the current fashion of scholars to describe the age
in terms of great struggles between "capital" and "labor," "farmers"
and "merchants," "debtors" and "creditors," "democracy" and "aristocracy." But predominantly the fierce intellectual controversies on
economic matters reflected the struggles of contending mercantile
groups, to which were occasionally added the factors of vested
political interest and prestige.

These contending factions played their roles on an ample stage.
Commerce was not a static and homogeneous interest. Enterprise
was at large in an adventurous and quickly changing world. Business
classes and individuals were reacting feverishly to sudden opportunity.

Here and there through the chinks of commerce flashed the flame
of idealism and human passion, and the authentic voice of democracy
strained through the hardness of social stratification. The allegiance
to these permanent values remains the ambient glory of the tradition
of Jefferson and his kind.

Such are the salient characteristics of the long period covered in these two volumes. The succeeding age has a distinctive quality of its own. Foreign commerce of course did not disappear after the Civil War, but with the great development of the railroad and other modes of transportation and especially of intensive industrial production, domestic business became the principal concern of thought and policy. A manuscript dealing with the post-Civil War age is nearing completion and will, I hope, soon follow these volumes into print.

But I have said enough by way of preface.

Let me add my thanks and gratitude to old friends and new. Especially would I pay my respects to Professor Wesley C. Mitchell. He has read numerous drafts, but even more precious to me have been his words of encouragement, backed by deeds, when the travails of the task grew too heavy. Professor Walter W. Stewart, remembering my earlier study of his great teacher, Thorstein Veblen, extended the hand of friendship to facilitate the completion of this inquiry. I must thank the Rockefeller Foundation for a liberal grant of funds.

I am under deep obligation to Mr. B. W. Huebsch of The Viking Press, who during the decade since the inception of the project has shown sympathetic understanding and great patience. My friend, Professor Solomon F. Bloom of Brooklyn College, has been extremely generous in helping me to revise various sections of the manuscript, and to clarify the drift and bearing of the whole. Mr. Sidney Hertzberg has applied his editorial skill to the entire draft.

My wife, Sarah Sorrin Dorfman, has been a loyal co-worker in the development of these volumes—and more than that. With her generous attitude toward human nature, she has enlarged whatever note of sympathy dwells here. And my little daughter Susan symbolized to me how much he who seeks to add to the world's knowledge is moved by the hope of the approval of posterity—people he will never see.

JOSEPH DORFMAN

Columbia University
August 20, 1945

BOOK ONE

Colonial America

CHAPTER I

The English Heritage

THE history of economic thought in the United States has its beginnings in the ideas current in England during the era marking the successful establishment of English colonies in the New World. It was the England of the early seventeenth century, the England of Elizabeth and the first Stuarts. The social structure conformed to a corporate scheme of status, class, and rank, animated by the almost interchangeable objectives of honor and profit. The observance of order was the keynote, and order meant the relations of superior and inferior. All swore fealty to the Crown as superior and absolute head in the church and state. The prince was "the life, the head, and the authority of all things." From him flowed the titles, honors, perquisites, and valuable offices. All worth-while activities, from learning to trade, depended on grants or charters of incorporation from him. Even the cities and towns—the boroughs— acquired their status as privileged places of trade and market by royal charter of incorporation.

The great aristocracy gathered in the House of Lords held positions of honor and rank in war and peace; their mere presence as heads and councilors of great trading companies was held to impute dignity and success to such enterprises.

After them came the lesser gentry and gentlemen in general. Gentlemen, wrote Sir Thomas Smith in his *De republica anglorum*, are "all those who can live idly, and without manual labor, and will bear up the port, charge and countenance of a gentleman." Next come the respectable yeomanry, who, holding freely disposable lands from the lords, are entitled to vote for members of the House of Commons. They are obedient to the gentlemen and rulers, "tend to their own business, come not to meddle in public matters, but when they are called, and glad when they are delivered thereof." The right to choose members of the House of Commons was also held by

3

the "freemen" of the towns; that is, those having the privileges of
the towns. The great mass being the "vilest sort of men" possess "no
voice in our commonwealth, and no account is made of them, but
only to be ruled."

Absolutism was easily reconciled with the familiar doctrine that
all laws lacking the public approval were tyrannical. Explained
Richard Hooker in his *Of the Lawes of Ecclesiastical Politie:* Public
approval is given not only by direct explicit consent, but also when
others do it in the public's name, "by right . . . originally derived
from them." So the command of an absolute monarch has the force
of a law whether his subjects approve or not, and what was long
received in silence and is now by custom established as a law we
may not transgress though we gave no explicit consent, "because
corporations are immortal; we were then alive in our predecessors,
and they in their successors do live still."

Of course the doctrine of absolutism was questioned. Sir Edwyn
Sandys, favorite of Hooker, turned his master's logic to defense of
the privileges of Parliament when it sought to check what it thought
were arbitrary acts of the Crown in matters of religion, commerce,
and taxation. Parliament's liberties, franchises, and privileges, it was
asserted, were the ancient birthright and the inheritance of Englishmen by grant of past sovereigns. However, this did not mean questioning the exclusion from the franchise of the masses of Englishmen, including many who possessed property but not a "freehold"
or freemanship of the town. Said Cromwell's son-in-law, General
Henry Ireton: The franchise can only belong to those "in whom all
land lies, and those incorporations in whom all trading lies"; in short,
in those who had "a permanent fixed interest in this kingdom."
Servants and the like certainly could not have the vote because, being propertyless, they would confiscate property.[1]

University instruction with the degree-granting power was restricted to the two incorporated universities of Oxford and Cambridge. Here as elsewhere class distinctions were rigidly maintained,
even in the records. The end was to train theologians, but gentlemen's sons and the sons of the nobility attended for a short period to
qualify properly as gentlemen. No degree could be granted unless
the candidate accepted the articles of the established church and the
political and ecclesiastical supremacy of the King. Instructors, let
alone students, who in the slightest manner questioned the abso-

[1] All bibliographic references will be found at the end of this volume.

lutism of the sovereign were expelled or imprisoned by the university authorities with or without a specific royal request. Books of a similar character were ordered burned.

As "order" ruled the political and social structure, so "order" ruled the economic structure. Dominating trade and industry were the powerful guilds, companies, or "mysteries." Their charters of incorporation gave them exclusive privileges and powers of coercion over members and interlopers. The general membership—the "generality," "commonality," or "freemen"—was itself exclusive; but even where the members still had the nominal right to choose the governing body and heads, the wealthier members usually held the powers, and the powers for the most part were centered in the governing body.

A similar practice prevailed even in the leading business activity, foreign trade, where the voting members of the companies were generally men of substance. It mattered not whether it was a great regulated enterprise such as the Merchant Adventurers Company where the participants traded on separate account with the Low Countries and Germany, or the great East India Company where the participants traded by joint stock. The board of directors of the latter once tried to conceal the company's liabilities by declaring that it was "privileged" above the "generality" and passing an order prohibiting members access to the accounts and correspondence except by its permission, on the ground that it did not intend to "exclude lords and gentlemen, but only such persons who on sight of accounts and letters raise dissension and debates." [2]

It was generally felt that the pursuit of riches might endanger virtue, but that riches were necessary. As Bacon put it in his essay "Of Riches," riches were to virtue like baggage to an army: they hindered the march but could not be spared or left behind.

But idleness was the root of all evil. Excessive inequality of wealth was deprecated, but high rewards to officers and even plural livings to high or favored clergy were justified by Hooker on the ground that men should be rewarded as they are in "quality and as their services are in weight for the public good."

In accordance with this doctrine of each man receiving an income according to his calling in the hierarchical scheme, was the notion of the "just price" of Aristotle and medievalism. But just price by now had been almost completely converted into the market price of a competitive market. As the merchant Gerard de Malynes stated in 1622 in his standard guide, *Consuetudo, vel, lex mercatoria:*

"Every man knoweth that in buying and selling . . . there is an estimation and price demanded and agreed upon between both parties according to a certain equality in the value of things . . . grounded upon the commodious use of things." Therefore, except for certain necessities for which the prince may fix a price including a reasonable gain, the seller should charge according to the "common estimation and course revealed" by the market. To avoid suspicion of selling unjustly, the seller should follow these rules: "First the buyer to be expert in the commodities he buys; secondly, that he be not too needy, or constrained to buy; thirdly, that persuasive reason be omitted, which cause the party to buy dearer."

Money is a public measure intended to eliminate the inconveniences and iniquity of barter, but if sufficient money is lacking, then the trade of the nation languishes though goods "be abundant and cheap."

Just "as the blood in the body containeth the soul which infuseth life," so money is the soul of trade, explained Malynes. Money obtained through a favorable balance of trade is even better for a state than an equal amount of treasure obtained from its own mines if it have any, for the money gained in foreign trade must be lost by some other nation. As Bacon put it in his essay "Of Seditions and Troubles," "the increase of any estate must be on the foreigner (for whatsoever is somewhere gotten, is somewhere lost)." Domestic trade is inferior to foreign trade, for in the former the nation as a whole neither gains nor loses. Exports of manufactures and shipping services are more valuable than export of produce, for the nation gains the difference because of "labor."

Since money is gotten through foreign trade, the merchant becomes the great instrument of national wealth and strength. Respectable Englishmen from the King down know that, in the corporation that is England, the clergy instruct, the noblemen fight, the magistrates defend, the husbandmen gather subsistence, and the artisans produce the wares; but to the merchant is reserved the function of enriching the nation. The farmer and the artisan are productive classes, but even their rewards are dependent on the skill of the merchants in finding markets. Of course, the merchants know that nobles, divines, doctors, and the like are unproductive but useful in preventing evils, and if they increase beyond a limited number, the wealth of the nation would be sapped in their support.

The government instead of restricting the merchant should grant him privileges and reliefs so that he is infected with the "radical moisture of gain," for what "makes the commonwealth but the private wealth?" [3] If the state is wise, its legislation for trade should make the customs of merchants permanent and enforceable, for these customs are of slow, imperceptible growth, the tried outcome of long experience.

The thinkers, however, had considerable difficulty with the problem of monopoly, despite the acts against it. John Wheeler, governor of the Merchant Adventurers, denied in 1601 in his *A Treatise of Commerce*, that the company was a monopoly. Trade must not be managed in a "dispersed, loose and straggling manner," lest English goods be sold at low prices and foreign goods in England at high prices. Since the company has a vast membership and, unlike joint stock companies, each one deals with his own stock, it is no monopoly. Its policy of determining how much each member should ship is not a price-fixing, but an anti-monopolistic measure, for it prevents the wealthy members from destroying the poorer ones.

The joint stock companies, pointing out that anyone can buy a share, quickly denied they were monopolies.

On the other hand, a group of critics headed by Sandys in 1604 demanded free trade on the ground that, as all free subjects "are born inheritable, as to their land, so also to the free exercise of their industry." Since merchandise was the chief and richest trade, restricting it to a few violated the natural right and liberty of the subject. True, the companies had a vast membership, but the governors by "monopolizing orders" and "plottings" had enabled a few Londoners to engross the trade at the ruin of the mass of their membership.

Free trade, its advocates claimed, would increase the national wealth because the greater number of merchants would increase the price of English goods, and so make the people more industrious. By preventing the concentration of wealth in the hands of a small group of Londoners, free trade would achieve a more equal distribution and thus eliminate discontent, the mother of innovation and trouble. The larger traffic would increase the Crown's profits. Finally, the destruction of monopoly would eliminate foreign animosities and so bring international peace.

However, there was no objection to the merchants' coming together voluntarily, for "provident men" would always consult and join together in matters concerning their common benefit and safety.[4]

Malynes explained that the problem of monopoly was confusing because of the many definitions of monopoly concocted by the jurists. Monopoly is a kind of commerce in buying, selling, changing, or bartering "usurped by a few" and sometimes by only one person, to their or his private gain, and to the detriment of others, "whereby of course, or by authority," the monopolist can set a price at his pleasure. Monopoly is displeasing because it commonly leads to an ill end by increasing prices in a "disorderly" manner. But monopolies, he held, should be differentiated into "reasonable, unreasonable, and indifferent." Monopolies are reasonable when they concern objects of pleasure—starch, cards, tobacco. They are unreasonable when they concern foodstuffs or other goods without which man "can hardly live civilly." It is a matter of indifference with such commodities as sugar, delicacies, dainties, curiosities.

Since abundance lowers prices to the discouragement of merchants and the overthrow of trade, it is better for the people to pay higher prices for commodities than to have them "overcheap," especially commodities serving the "back and not for the belly." Engrossing is especially commendable when companies of merchants are established in foreign trade, for this enables English manufactures to be sold at "reasonable" rates abroad. Underselling abroad by individual traders is vicious because it merely leads to a further loss of treasure and consequent disturbances at home. The companies must not abuse their privileges by too narrowly restricting their membership, as the powerful Merchant Adventurers Company has done; but those seeking to eliminate the companies completely fail to see the difference between government in a monarchy and in a democracy.

However, Henry Parker, an employee of the company, declared in his *Of a Free Trade* that the company's principles by providing "perfect order" accord true liberty, for liberty "includes not any wild condition, such as leaves us loosely to our own discretion."

The condition of the great propertyless laboring mass was reflected in their designation as the "laboring poor." Legislation ostensibly to relieve their grief and burden provided for the fixing of reasonable maximum wages by officials drawn from the employing class. Those refusing to accept the fixed wages were to be treated as vagabonds, the "true caterpillar of the commonwealth," to be jailed, whipped, and then bound out to a master for a term of years.

Pauper children could be bound out beginning at the age of five. Labor organizations to raise wages were severely repressed as involving felony and treason.

To the enlightened Englishmen the mass of propertyless laborers was not an organic part of the commonwealth; though its labor, they declared, was the source of the material gain of the classes that did constitute the commonwealth. So if laborers are worked to the utmost and given the barest subsistence, the wealth and power of the nation would be increased. Were their wages increased above subsistence, they would merely work less or spend their additional income in drink, to the further loss of the national productive power. Conversely, it was argued by some, high prices for foodstuffs are good, since they force the laborers to work harder. If more food be produced than expected and prices threaten to fall, wrote Sir William Petty, the surplus should be put in granaries instead of allowing it to be "abused by the vile and brutish part of mankind to the prejudice of the commonwealth." [5] An increase of population is desirable; by lowering wages it spells competitive advantage in foreign trade. But if laborers could not be employed, then their death "was nothing but an ease" to the commonwealth. [6]

One suggestion for providing employment was the growth of luxury among the wealthy and noble. Dr. Nicholas Barbon, enterpriser, argued in his *A Discourse of Trade* that the chief causes promoting trade are "Industry in the Poor and Liberality in the Rich" in spending freely to satisfy their desires. This great virtue of liberality has two extremes, "prodigality and covetousness." While prodigality is bad for the individual, it is good for trade. But "covetousness" is bad for both. "It starves the Man, and breaks the Trader; and by the same way the Covetous Man thinks he grows rich, he grows poor; for by not consuming the Goods . . . there ariseth a dead Stock called Plenty, and the Value of those Goods falls, and the Covetous Man's Estates . . . become less worth." Nevertheless, Bacon wrote in "Of Expense" that increase of estate is possible only if expenses for display be kept well below income.

Protest against existing evils was most articulate in the realm of religion. England is falling on evil days, was the cry, because of the decline of true religion. Many of the lesser clergy specifically complained against the "corruptions" of the Church of England—its clerical hierarchy with sinecures and plural livings for favorites, its nominations of ministers by lay patrons and ordinations by bishops, its elaborate ceremonials. As a consequence many ministers are dumb preachers lacking learning and godliness, while the learned ones are bereft of proper position and income. The "innovations"—man's "inventions" must be swept away by "reformation"; that is, a return to the church polity laid down in the Scriptures.

For a goodly part these "Puritan" ministers looked with favor on the polity of the Calvinistic Presbyterian Church, which had become the established church of Scotland. Authoritative absolute control of the churches was vested in a series of hierarchical councils composed of "elders," clerical and lay; but, as Milton said, the clerics are equal in rank, "an equal aristocracy." [7]

Going a step further was the strictly Congregational polity of those Puritans who declared it necessary to separate completely from the corrupt Church of England. They found temporary haven from persecution by the Established Church in the commercial republic of the Netherlands. The power was formally vested not in bishops or a college of Presbyters, but in the individual church as a corporate organization. This church did not comprise all who attended voluntarily or involuntarily, as in the Anglican and Presbyterian polities, but only God's elect or sanctified, united by covenant with God and each other to walk in the ways of God.

Loyal sons of the Church of England denounced the Separatists as believing in "community of goods" and in democracy, which "was the nurse of confusion, the mother of schism, the breeder of contention."

The great leader of the Separatists, John Robinson, Cambridge graduate and pastor of the Separatist church in Leyden, replied that the Congregational polity resembles Parliament, "the highest and most honorable court of assembly in the whole land," and also "the privileged . . . corporations in the kingdom." It combines all three forms of lawful polity—monarchy, aristocracy, and democracy. The Scripture, "like a gracious charter given to this spiritual corporation . . . by the king thereof, Jesus, do clearly plead the people's liberty and power of the choice of their ministers"; but the government was aristocratical, for it was to be administered by choice men. "The people freely . . . vote in elections and judgments of the church," but the elders "govern the people in their voting. . . . Let the elders publicly propound and order all things in the church. . . . Let the people of faith give their assent to their elders holy and lawful administration."

Since church officers are the servants of the church, they are not irresponsible rulers, as critics claim, and therefore do not require control by a hierarchy of superiors outside of the individual church. The civil magistrates, however, should repress public idolatry and might force the subjects to listen to the true Gospel for their instruction and conversion, but the magistrates must neither compel an unholy person to partake of the covenant nor force the church to accept him in fellowship; that is, as a member. The civil magistrates were the nursing fathers and mothers of the church, but not "procreant parents." The spiritual corporation, like more earthly ones, must be supported by the state, but the state must not interfere with its corporate independence.[8] To avoid the charge of schism by the Church of England, Robinson's friend and fellow Cambridge graduate and exile, William Ames, expounded non-Separatist Congregationalism. He asserted that the Congregationalists were not separating from the Church of England, but only from its corruptions. The Church of England churches are not as good as Congregational ones, but they are true churches, said Ames, for their "essence" is Congregationalist. The parish assemblies of England were not founded on an explicit covenant, the non-Separatists admitted, but if any members who were good Christians attended voluntarily, there was an implicit covenant which was just as substantial and real. Again, in the Anglican churches, the pastor is nominated by a patron and installed by a bishop, but he could consider himself as having been elected by the congregation as evidenced in their tacit consent through submission.[9]

On earthly affairs the Congregationalists were just as conservative as their critics, if not more so. The relations between magistrates and subjects, ministers and members, fathers and children, masters and servants, fall into the category of the relation between superior and inferior, wrote Ames. Inferiors owe superiors reverence and submission, not only for their eminence in degree, but also as being the cause of the inferiors' well-being. The maintenance of due order cannot exist without this subjection, any more than a relative in logic can exist without its correlative. Subjects should be wary of censuring magistrates because public business is very complex, and certainly light offense and infirmities should be tolerated for "public quietness sake." Thus not only all violent insurrections, but also contempt and disesteem by the subject is repugnant.

The relation between master and servant differs somewhat from that between child and parent. The end of the latter is the good of the child, not the father; but servitude aims directly at the good of the master, not of the servant. Servants should be faithful and obedient to bad masters as well as good ones. They should not aim primarily at the reward received of men, but of God, because the primary ground of the duty is not the merit of the masters but the ordinance of God, and if they run away from their masters they are thieves.

On both the "just price" and usury, the Puritans were clearly attuned to the commercial needs of the times. Buying cheap and selling dear is sinful, said Ames, unless bounded within certain limits. For most things the common rate of the market, the "common value," is to be followed. This is "natural price," for this "rate hath the force of a tacit law, and excludes the danger of any deceit to the damage of another." In this sense may be admitted "that rule approved in the Civil Law, and the manners of men: that . . . every saleable thing is worth so much as it can be sold for; that is, as it can be sold for commonly, not out of any affection, or for the profit of this or that man." The precise point cannot be determined, but operates within a range of variations or departures from the "normal price." Thus a merchant may still sell unjustly, though below his purchase price, either because he bought foolishly or afterward the rate changed. The just price may rightly fall when the ware seeks a buyer, for, according to the common proverb, "profferred wares stink." On the other hand, if the dealer is seeking wares, the price may justly rise, for then the store of buyers "augments the common value." In any event the common rate is to be followed.

The usury commonly practiced by the Banks of Italy is unlawful, said Ames, because it is a "catching art, has no regard to charity or equity and lays in wait for other men's goods." But usury, generally speaking, is lawful, since it is merely a share of the fruit yielded by the use of money. Gain is taken not simply for the use of the borrowed thing according to its substance, "but according to the value, or income remaining after the substance is consumed; and is oftentimes in things not consumed by use: as also for the office, and act of lending, from whence the borrower received profit." The return from moneylending stands on no different foundation of productivity than rent from land or the return of "labor or work."

Of course, the Puritans believed that there should be a limit to the individual accumulation of wealth. The limit was vague. It was best put by the great teacher and acknowledged intellectual father of both Robinson and Ames, the Reverend William Perkins. Wealth should only be accumulated, he said in his *A Treatise of the Vocations, or Callings of Men*, to the point of sufficiency. But sufficiency differs obviously for those of different degree. The measure or limit of wealth for any man "is the common judgement and practice of the most godly, frugal, and wise men with whom we live and that which they . . . judge sufficient to his place and calling, that is to be esteemed sufficient."

Riches, exclaimed Ames in *Conscience With the Power and Cases thereof*, are "rightly called the gifts and blessings of God"; but since by virtue of human corruption, they tempt "their possessors to pride, idolatry and luxury, we must strive by diligence as well as by prayer, to make riches our instruments of piety. Then if riches increase by God's providence, the mind is . . . fortified against those vices, which usually accompany them."

Poverty directly sought is especially wicked because the person is directly choosing the evil of punishment. Poverty not deliberately sought is generally joined with weakness or defect, but is not necessarily criminal because it is often sent by God to the godly either as a correction or as a trial, or both. Hence, miserable though they be, the poor must not "murmur against the providence of God, or use unlawful means to help themselves."

The duty of alms belongs not only to the rich, but also to those of a "meaner condition who get their living by their hands." Alms should be distributed in the order of the quality of the person; that is, those more profitable to the commonwealth should be preferred before those less profitable. Since beggars and vagabonds belong to "no civil society or corporation," they are "as rotten legs and arms that drop from the body."

Back of the Puritan emphasis on religion lay the common charge that in the absence of true religion men failed to observe true order and obedience each in their degree and became excessively worldly minded and self-seeking. The lower classes were the greatest sinners. "The meaner sort," exclaimed Perkins, spend their gains "in fine apparel and good cheer"; and thus "the House of God is less regarded; for every common man nowadays must be a gentleman, and it is very hard for a stranger sometimes to discern the master from the servant; and there is such an excess in all degrees, that the dress of the noblest is the plainest." There are other "common grievances groaning for reformation." The game of hawking, heretofore reserved for regality, nobility, and gentility—that is, for the better sort of ample possession and revenues—was spoiled and in disorder because "inferior populaire," especially handicraftsmen, engaged in it. Similarly, carriages and coaches were purchased by persons of "mean . . . quality and condition" instead of being restricted to the nobility and the like. Consequently "the ancient mystery and company of saddlers" is impoverished.[10]

Under these ideals of "order" and commerce is begun the great era of colonization.

CHAPTER II

The Virginia Enterprise

COLONIZATION could proceed only in terms of the ideals to which Englishmen were habituated. Permanent settlement began under the familiar corporate structure.

In 1606 James I granted to two incorporated companies composed of "knights, gentlemen, merchants and other adventurers" the exclusive right to colonize and trade in the vast area called "Virginia," stretching from what is now Maine to Cape Fear. The Virginia Company of London had the southern part; the Virginia Company of Plymouth, the northern.

Each company appointed the resident council vested with sole governing power in its colony; but a royal council in London, composed in good part of the members of both companies, controlled these local councils as well as political matters in general. Trade in each of the colonies was managed through a resident agent of the company—the "cape merchant"—who received and distributed all supplies and provided return cargoes. No distribution of assets or profits was to occur for five years, and during this period the actual colonizers were supported from the common stock.

The net result for the southern company was a starving settlement at Jamestown; for the northern, even less. In 1609 the promoters of the southern company succeeded in obtaining a new
charter vesting complete control of government as well as trade
in the company on the ground that otherwise people would not
supply the funds, the "sinews and moving instruments" in great actions. By the amended charter of 1612, the source of all power was
nominally in the generality of "freemen"—the "General Court"—
who were the shareholders, plus any others admitted to the right of
freemanship by the company. Voting was by person, "voice," not
by share. But, as in all companies, vast powers were given to or taken
by the officers; that is, the council and the executive officers—the
treasurer and deputy treasurer.

It became a typical joint stock company along the model of the
East India Company, with stock subscription and transferable shares.
The price of a share was based on the cost of transporting an equipped
settler, £12 10s. Those going in person at their own expense, the
planters or "adventurers," were to receive additional shares in the
eventual distribution now set for seven years instead of five. Such
shares were calculated in terms of the hierarchical scheme of values
of English society. As the regulation put it, "every extraordinary
man, as divines, governors, ministers of state and justice, knights, gentlemen, physicians and such as be men of worth for special service,"
were to be rated before going "according to the value of their persons." For the laboring mass the reward for seven years' servitude
was to be one hundred acres.

Some of the nation's most prominent men guided the company's
destinies. The first head, Sir Thomas Smith, was the leading merchant prince, the executive of the East India Company and a host
of other important trading concerns. Another supporter, the Puritan sympathizer Robert Rich, soon to become the second Earl of
Warwick, was one of the wealthiest noblemen and the greatest leader
of privateering. The most powerful figure in the company was Sir
Edwyn Sandys, the scholar in religion and politics, the leader in the
House of Commons against the royal prerogative and monopolies,
the friend of Puritans and a shareholder in the East India Company.

The leaders contributed relatively little, but hardly a man of
importance in business, politics, religion, and learning was absent
from the list of subscribers. In accordance with Malynes's doctrine

that plantations were in the category of "pious uses," the Crown granted the company the privilege of a lottery.

The ostensible principal aim of the company, according to the charters and authorized publications, was to bring the barbarous natives "to the true worship of God, civility and virtue." To meet the costs of the civilizing process only the heathen's superfluous lands would be taken. This would not violate their property rights, for they had no particular property in any part of the country, but only a general residency like wild beasts in the forest. Of course, the heathen were free to help in the task of their conversion, but if they obstinately refused, they should be treated as enemies of the commonwealth.

A second professed end was ridding England of "the unprofitable . . . increase in our people," the "superfluous twigs." The natural tendency of population to exceed its profitable use had caused all of England's evils, from enclosure and usury to robbery and rioting. The laboring mass is the blood of the commonwealth, but, like too much blood, overflowing multitudes bring plague and poverty to the community. With wars relatively absent, new employments must be found or the kingdom prostrated by an increase of robbers at home and pirates abroad. Even many of the most industrious laborers are forced to work long hours at starvation wages "because work is so hard to come by and there be so many of the same trade that they cannot thrive one for the other."

True, the excess is a base lot; but if compelled to endure a hard life of labor they should prove good members of a commonwealth. Children sent by means of funds of the philanthropic-minded would under severe masters "be brought to goodness."

Finally the investment would be profitable. Of course, ideally, profit should not be the aim of the stockholders or colonists. The former should remember that this is a holy enterprise; the latter should bear to heart that the pursuit of great wealth is a dissatisfying, never-ending pursuit. Contrary to reason, it is without limit, for no man is rich absolutely, but only relatively in comparison with one having less than he.

However, Virginia's prospects are such, they said, that mankind's greediness for profit would be amply satisfied. It would supply great revenues for the King, navigation for defense, relieve unemployment at home, and provide land for all, even the poorest prospective colonist. The territory must contain gold, and perhaps the long-sought Northwest Passage to the fabulous South Seas countries. Virginia would supply naval stores, other raw materials, rough manufactures, and luxuries which England at high prices and loss of treasure imported from other countries. Furthermore, the Indians when brought to civility would provide an outlet for the great but now depressed cloth trade. Thus the venture would prevent England from being eaten out of all the profits of trade by her more industrious neighbors of Europe.

The original venture had failed, the promoters explained, because the resident government had been "aristocratical," not monarchical. With the members of the council equal in power, every man wanted to command and refused to be commanded. Consequently the colonists became idlers and "covetous interlopers in the Indian trade." Thereby the "trifles" in trade with the Indians were cheapened and the Indian goods raised in price. The situation is to be remedied by sending a supreme absolute governor and installing martial law for a time in all phases of life. Severe penalties would even be visited on any who should utter "unseemly and unfitting speeches" against the company or publish such a book.[1]

With tobacco production, of all things, turning out to be the profitable staple, a new chapter opened. The King had long ago written a tract against the "smoky weed," and enlightened opinion agreed with him that it damaged the people's morals and wasted the nation's wealth. The company was of the same opinion, but it declared that its production would provide the funds for developing the really worth-while staples which would eventually replace it. The Crown resolved its dislike of tobacco and the need for revenue by placing a tax on the import; and, "for the better support of the colony," it prohibited the domestic production of tobacco. Tobacco even became the standard of value and medium of exchange of the colony.

Dominant figures in the company now argued that the company lacked the capital to stock the country with the necessary servants and supplies. So both for settlement and industry a vast program of joint stock ventures with transferable shares was sponsored by the company, but for the profit of the particular adventurers. They were given powers of government over their servants and trade almost as complete as those of the company over the colony.

"The liberty of marriage we dare not infringe," wrote the home

authorities to the cape merchant in regard to the joint stock for exporting women, but if any of the women should "unwarily or fondly
bestow herself" on one unable to pay the stipulated price, "this debt
was to precede all others of the spouse."

The manufacture of beads, the money in the Indian trade, was
by joint stock venture, but the company held a share. The colonial
authorities were ordered to prevent the secret of their manufacture
being discovered lest their value be reduced.

The profits of the undertakings, explained the home authorities,
belonged to particular men; but the benefit was to the whole colony.
Consequently colonial officials must aid them with any assets of the
company, human or otherwise. The local authorities had their own
interests also. They wrote to the home government that it was hard
to make a profit on commodities other than tobacco because labor
could not be obtained except at "intollerable rates." Such commodities can succeed only in populous countries like France, Italy, and
Spain, where thousands of women and children and idle people are
available at less than half the wages of the lowest-paid labor in the
colony. So all the more necessary in the eyes of the planters and
authorities was the increase in indentured servants for a general labor
supply.

"Our principal wealth," wrote home the learned John Pory, secretary of the colony, in 1619, "consists of servants." And the servants,
under long-term indenture in return for their passage, were rated as
property, payable for debts and even church dues. Their time was
subject to sale and transfer like a "damned slave." The import of
black servants soon led to the classification of "servants for life." [2]

Meanwhile, in 1619 martial law was replaced by a "laudable form
of government" in order to encourage migration. To the company-
appointed governor and council there was added an annual assembly
composed of members of the council and two burgesses chosen by
each town and "particular plantation" which was a joint stock. But
the assembly's measures were subject to the governor's absolute veto
power and were not enforceable until ratified by the General Court
of the company in London. And the assembly itself maintained the
English hierarchical scheme. Punishment for offenses was to be with
due respect to the "quality" of the delinquent. Vagabonds were to
be placed under a master until reformed. Measures were passed to
enforce servants' indentures and to prevent the "seducing" of servants from one plantation to another. Wages of artisans and their

servants were to be fixed by authority, each according to "the quality of his trade and work." The assembly also enacted the company's instructions to the governor, fixing the price at which the cape merchant should accept tobacco, limiting the profits to 25 per cent, and ordering all tobacco shipped by the cape merchant so that the price might "be upheld the better."

Meanwhile changes in the northern Virginia Company depressed the southern company's prospects. The northern Virginia Company became the New England Council, with a board of proprietors which read like "an abstract from the peerage" and included Warwick. The financing of its operations was to be through funds supplied by merchants in joint stock for trade and fishing, for "every reasonable man knows the difference of trading by joint stock under government and order; and the promiscuous trading without order and in a disjointed manner." At the same time the new organization was given the exclusive control of fishing off its coasts, whereas heretofore both companies had had the exclusive right of licensing fishing off either company's coasts. And these rights were valuable for promotional purposes, especially since Captain John Smith in 1616 had described to Englishmen the riches to be reaped from New England's fishing settlements. Laborers can earn handsome returns, since the ground is more fertile than that of England and "costs nothing but labor," Smith wrote in *A Description of New England*. Masters grow rich quickly, especially if they have large numbers of apprentices and servants, and in turn the latter do likewise after their term is over.

The southern Virginia Company protested that the New England Council was a vicious monopoly and demanded the retention of the old scheme on the ground of liberty of fishing, for the sea was to "all free and common as the air." The monopoly, it said, under pretense of reforming abuses really set heavy fines. The New England Council replied that it was not composed of merchants interested in immediate profit and that it was not a monopoly since "it was undertaken for the advancement of religion, the enlargement of the bounds of our nation, the increase of trade, and the employment of many thousands of all sorts of people." [3]

Worse still for the Virginia Company, its leaders complained, was the low price received for tobacco at home because of the competition of Spanish tobacco. Depression in England and in the colony, they informed Parliament time and again, could be eliminated by excluding Spanish tobacco, which drained the kingdom's treasure.

Money is both the mother and daughter of trade. Because money is lacking, rents are impaired, contracts broken, bonds forfeited, markets and farms deserted, "the better sort impoverished and the meaner . . . for want of means in the better" not employed. The ultimate cause of this "general distemper" is that English merchants trading with Spain take "smoke" in exchange for bullion. A "full and exact examination" plainly reveals that by the undervaluing of our native commodities to obtain ready money for the Spanish tobacco and by the money itself paid for the weed, the kingdom has lost its enormous return treasure. But the colony tobacco should not be excluded, because the colony takes English manufactures, not money, as returns. Furthermore, through the exclusion of Spanish tobacco, the "reasonable price" for Virginia tobacco would lure multitudes of people to the colony, and they will quickly find better commodities than tobacco. Otherwise the glut produced by Spanish tobacco will lead to the revolt of the plantations.

In 1621 the company warned the colonial authorities that no further supplies could be sent in exchange for their "darling tobacco" because the planters had not paid their debts to the cape merchant. It also complained that the local officials were abusing their authority for private gain in forcing the cape merchant to accept tobacco at the old fixed price, thus compelling him to sell his goods at "under values" instead of leaving him free to sell and barter his goods. The market for the sale of supplies was to be preserved open and for "all men freely or indifferently to buy and sell." Such "engrossing and forestalling" of the market deprived the particular joint stock from supplying the colony of its best commodities at low prices and forced the poor to pay excessive rates. At the same time to prevent a glut of tobacco in Europe production was ordered reduced to one hundred pounds per person.

An Indian massacre wiped out a good part of the population in 1622. The secretary of the company in London informed the public that this augured well for the colony because the Indians' cultivated places could now be seized. The "laborious mattocks" can be converted into "the victorious sword" which yields more "ease, benefit and glory" to obtain the fruits of other men's labor. The meanest inhabitant of the plantation could now employ himself exclusively in the more "generous arts and occupations" while the savages would be compelled to perform laborious tasks. But to the planters' pleas for food supplies the company replied that the massacre was God's punishment for their sins, especially in "enormous excesses in apparel and drinking." They would now understand that it would be necessary to pay their debts to the company and all the particular joint stocks. "Secure yourselves from . . . famine and nakedness by a just retribution of profit to your friends."

On being ordered by the Privy Council to send relief, the company authorities wrote to the colony that the adventurers in this new joint stock must receive speedy returns. Only 25 per cent profit is being charged, a "gain too high indeed in a certain and orderly . . . trade," but not in this hazardous one. All old debts must be collected and no one spared in the process, for the funds are needed to pay the company's debts.

When the massacre occurred, Sandys, attempting to solve his and the company's financial difficulties, arranged with the Crown's treasurer to get for the Virginia Company and the allied Bermuda Company a monopoly of all tobacco imported into England. This was to be done through two subsidiary or particular joint stocks, one for the tobacco from the English plantations, the other for the Spanish tobacco. In the list of "faithful officers to manage the business with salaries proportionable in some measure for their paines," Sandys appeared as the director—at a substantial salary, of course.[4]

Sandys's opponents—by now the Smith and Warwick interests— charged that the contract with the Crown had been ratified by the companies through Sandys's use of every conceivable device of manipulation, from holding meetings at night to suspending freemen on the ground of "premeditate intention to raise a combustion." Even if the measure had been ratified without manipulation, still the method of voting by "plurality of voice" enables those least burdened with the cost to pass the measure and, by depriving the owners of their property without their consent, violates the laws of England.

The King revoked the arrangement in 1623, after the old farmers of the customs offered to lower the duty on tobacco without reducing the King's income. The council in Virginia thanked the King for his action: The contract was "made wholly without our consents or privity." These sinister practices of principal persons of the company "who pretending their majesty's profit, but their own more, would have reduced us to the original state of starvation." But the King at the same time should keep open the market for plantation tobacco. Without it, we shall perish for want of English commodities which "our nature and breeding require." Things "of more real value and constant sale" than tobacco require more time for their growth than their present resources admit, but with this threat of enslavement by the monopolists in the company removed, our poverty will be relieved and desirable staples will be produced.

Sandys's opponents successfully called for a royal inquiry into the company's affairs. Captain John Smith, who had been in the local council under the 1606 charter, asserted that from the beginning, when Sir Thomas Smith was the head, the record of the company was a dreary tale of manipulation for the profit of the officers, with bankruptcy for the company and starvation for the colony. The officers made "religion their color" but "present profit" their aim. As a remedy he proposed that a royal council be in complete charge. The Warwick and Smith interests amplified their attacks on "plurality of voice" and charged that it made the government of the company "democratical and tumultuous." Voting should instead be by shares, for "experience shows that men are . . . careful ... . according to their particular interests," and the greater the interest "the more care for the common good."

Captain John Bargrave, who had long been irked by the trade monopoly of the particular joint stock, had originally charged in a suit against Smith that "this factious and popular government here by voice founded on joint stock will bring such disorders as to lead to the colony's independence of the Crown." Now he similarly charged that the Sandys group by the use of same device was attempting to establish a "free popular state" in Virginia. Had not Sandys offered a haven to the Separatists, those dangerous enemies of monarchy?

Lord Cavendish, speaking for the Sandys group, replied that it was gross slander to call the company government "democratical." The opponents "cry out against democracy" and call for oligarchy without making the government either better or more monarchical. Except by unanimity scarcely ever possible, the judgment can only be determined by "plurality of voice." This slight democracy in the company organization must be allowed because the plantation was developed at the cost not of the Crown but of the private adventurers, and they would never have ventured if they could not vote in the regulating and governing of their own business.

The King, claiming that all the contention had arisen from the change of government from a small council of his choice to a more "popular course" and among many hands, had the charter revoked and took over the company's power of government in 1624.

The colonial assembly and authorities came to agree that, for the sake of trade, "as the blood and life of a commonwealth," company government should never be re-established. "The freedom of our trade with England under the King's regulations" would again be monopolized under the guise of "managing" the trade, a word in every sense of it convertible into monopoly. A company form, as a "popular and tumultuary government, depending upon the greatest number of votes of persons of several humours and dispositions" would endanger their estates; whereas the monarchical form of government was their birthright.[5]

Virginia stood loyally by the Crown at all times. The trial and execution of Charles I and the questioning of the divine right of kings was denounced by the governor, council, and assembly as the treasonable practices of republicans and against divine law and the law of nature and nations.

Home and colonial thinkers were generally agreed as before that the plantations should be a spring of trade and wealth to the mother country, that they should work for the latter and so center their treasure in the homeland.[6] There was much disagreement, however, between the English and colonial statesmen and thinkers as to what would be most beneficial to England. Colonial measures regulating trade in a manner not deemed desirable by dominant home interests would be disallowed on the ground, among others, that "trade is to be courted not forced."[7]

With its policy of draining specie home, England would not authorize a colonial mint or allow export of English coinage to the colonies. Virginia, however, requested the introduction of specie money to relieve "the great wants and miseries which do daily happen unto us by the sole dependency upon tobacco."[8] Ostensibly to acquire and retain specie from the near-by Spanish colonies, Virginia turned to one of the devices denounced by the great majority of English mercantilists; namely, raising the value of money by law. The colony valued the Spanish pieces of eight—in metallic content equal to 4s. 6p.—at 5s. Attempts to raise it to 6s. in 1687 brought forth a pronouncement from the English authorities well versed in rephrasing the mercantilist logic for the purpose in hand that "trade is not balanced by notions and names of money and things but by intrinsic values." Such measures would hinder trade and damage the general good by enabling debtors to "defraud creditors." [9]

The colony argued that neighboring provinces and governments by enhancing the value of foreign coins drain away whatever Virginia obtains, "to our impoverishment and their great advantages." If Virginia is allowed to raise the value of foreign coin, encouragement will be given to its importing "as well as keeping the same to circulate and pass plentifully in this country." [10]

The play of conflicting interest under the accepted mercantilist logic was best revealed in *A Discourse and View of Virginia*, written by Governor Sir William Berkeley for the home authorities in 1663. There was no more ardent supporter of the Stuarts than Berkeley. But he was an equally ardent entrepreneur, ever seeking vast land grants in and out of the colony and directly interested in controlling such lucrative fields as the Indian trade to increase his income.

He thought it unwise for the English government to force tobacco to be shipped only to England. Tobacco production was a necessary evil. Other staples were not produced originally, he wrote, because in the corruption of those early times the governors supposed that, by satisfying this universal vice of tobacco, great wealth would be reaped. England would gain treasure at the expense of Spain. For many years this was the case, but increasing production in the colony and elsewhere has so reduced the price that the duties paid the Crown on tobacco are twice as much as the planter receives. A condition has been reached where the plantation can neither handsomely subsist with it nor do without it. Measures for limiting tobacco production and encouraging other staples are useless so long as they are not applied to other tobacco-producing colonies, notably Maryland. The most sensible remedy is to let the plantation sell its tobacco anywhere and not restrict it to export to England. No loyal subject would oppose the pressure and restraint of confining trade to England if the Crown or commonwealth gained, but the policy of restricting export to England only enriches the forty merchants who buy the tobacco. They in effect have the forty thousand inhabitants as servants at cheaper rates than slaves who have to be fed and clothed in any event.

At the same time a public stock should be raised to obtain skillful workers for such expensive undertakings as iron mines and mills.

England in return would get the desirable staples more cheaply, and tobacco production would decline. Public aid is required to entice skilled workers to migrate to Virginia because the poor planter just barely making a subsistence could not afford to pay the high wages required.

Thus the Crown should increase the customs on tobacco, but give the increase to the colony to meet its public charges—including, of course, the governor's salary—to purchase supplies to resist the Indians, to build mills for iron and planks, and to procure on "good salaries, able men for silk, cordage, mines and flax." The charges would really be paid by the planters, and that accords with the maxim that no community of people "has good done to them, but against their wills."

At the close of the century, Crown officials in Virginia reported that the economic defects of the colony flow from the lack of towns, markets, and money. Because of this lack, skilled artisans have no incentive to come and practice their specialties; consequently their labor is dear. True, the colony has attempted to establish towns and markets, but it has used compulsory measures. A money circulation would quickly exist but for the governor's forcing the use of tobacco as a medium of exchange in order to raise the rate of exchange in England where most of his salary paid in tobacco is deposited.

The policy of making large land grants to individuals is not wise, for it deprives ordinary planters of land for cultivation. These small planters are worth more to the Crown and to England than the large landholders, because their great number makes possible an increase of tobacco duties, ships, and seamen, and the maintenance of multitudes of people engaged in the manufacture of tobacco in England, or of goods sold to the planters.[11] Not least in the minds of these agents was the difficulty of collecting from the great landowners the quit rents due the Crown which might be used to pay their salaries.

As for labor, the promotional literature for foreign consumption gave the usual glowing picture of Virginia as the haven for the industrious poor. Berkeley, in the very same publication in which he painted the depressed condition of the planters to support his tax proposal, could declare that, whereas in England people engage in riotous living and behavior because they lack prospects of bettering themselves, in Virginia they know that if they are provident and industrious for a year or two they may provide for their posterity for ages. That servants live wretchedly is a base rumor, exclaimed John

Hammond in his *Leah and Rachel* (1656), because true labor cannot be either expected or exacted without sufficient subsistence, clothing, and lodging.

According to the statutes runaway servants were not only to suffer corporal punishment, including branding, but were also to serve long periods of additional time. Poor children were to be bound out until their majority to prevent youth from being corrupted by idleness. Poor children as young as seven were to be housed and fed in public houses and used to produce flax as a profitable staple; force might be used if parents refused to part with their children through "fond indulgence or perverse obstinacy." [12]

Slavery grew. So foreign at first was the institution to familiar English ideas that one of the standard treatises on the practices for merchants could only characterize its existence in the English plantations as unnatural.[13] On the other hand, the German social scientist Samuel von Pufendorff, whose works were standard in the Protestant world, declared that slavery is compensated "by the perpetual certainty of maintenance, which is often not the lot of those who work by the day, because of lack of employment, or their own laziness." Some declare, he wrote in *De jure naturæ et gentium libri octo*, "not without cause" that the elimination of slavery among Christians is one of the reasons why one meets everywhere such a "pack of wandering thieves and sturdy beggars." This kind of argument was to take time to develop in America. But already the Crown had chartered the Royal African Company on the grounds that the great profit in slaves would go to England, that the supplying of slaves to the plantations would prevent the drain of population from England, and that, with other nations engaged in the traffic to supply their own colonies, the growing English plantations would become useless to England through want of the usual supply of slaves from Africa.

Colonials defended privateering—often differing little from piracy —on the ground that it indirectly increased the slave supply in the colony. Directly, privateering increased the number of ships, kept employed artificers at "extraordinary wages," supplied necessary commodities at reasonable rates, including coin, in exchange for foodstuffs. With these the poor planters could buy more slaves.[14]

On the other hand, a press was forbidden, and as in England education for the mass was held undesirable on the ground that it would take them from their work and make them "too knowing to be obedient and submissive."

But of course there had to be a college for the children of the respectable. So in 1693 the King granted a charter for the College of William and Mary "to achieve the education of our youth, a constant supply of our ministry, and perhaps a foundation for ye conversion of our neighboring Heathen to the Christian faith." Despite money and land grants, and an export duty on tobacco and various other gifts, the college consisted only of a grammar school until well into the next century. But these youngsters quickly learned to manipulate the logic of mercantilism, or at least their teachers did it for them in the public speeches the students delivered. Said one student speaker in 1699: Virginians should patronize this institution rather than English schools, because the latter involves a loss of treasure to the colony.[15]

New colonies carved out of the old Virginia Company domains portrayed much of the same dominant economic thinking despite differences in origin and intention.

The Crown made huge grants called "proprietaries," or feudal domains, to favorites. Under the proprietary form of government the sovereign power as well as the ownership of soil were vested in the "proprietor," but there was always the stipulation in the charter that laws could be enacted and taxes levied only with the advice and consent of the freemen. But a qualification for freemanship was generally a substantial holding of land. The never-ceasing struggles between proprietor and the "people" generally meant a struggle between the proprietor and a powerful oligarchy dominating the legislature.

To the learned Catholic, Lord Baltimore, Charles I gave in 1632 a great section of the old Virginia territory as a proprietary. Ostensibly it began as a Catholic refuge but, bottomed like Virginia on tobacco, it soon followed Virginia's lead in practically all its institutions.

George Alsop, who claimed to be a former indentured servant in Maryland, wrote in a promotional work that without servitude the best of kingdoms would be unhinged. There could be no greater confusion in a monarchy or domestic government than when either the subject or the servant strives to be equal with him from whom he receives his subsistence. "Good servitudes are those colleges of sobriety" that restrain the giddy and wild-headed youth by a limited constraint. Without it thousands in most kingdoms would be unable to subsist, for it is in the nature of an apprenticeship in learning some trade, art, or science. If those ordained to be servants endure their time with patience, he declared in *A Character of the Province of Maryland*, then after their time is served they will quickly become masters and mistresses themselves.

However, obedience to superiors had a somewhat different content where English trade regulations were concerned. To the home authorities' requests for social and economic data, especially on trade and industry, Lord Baltimore replied that the scrutinies required would lead to insurrections and the depeopling of the province.[16]

Another large area in the old Virginia domains which was given as a proprietary to eight loyal supporters of the Stuarts, including Berkeley, had the benefit of John Locke's guidance. He supplied them with the short-lived "Fundamental Constitutions of Carolina" of 1669. Proceeding in the spirit of James Harrington's powerful utopia, *The Common-Wealth of Oceania*, its note was "all power and dominion is most naturally founded on property." It is essential so to arrange the distribution of land and correlative functions as to establish the interest of the Lords Proprietors "with equality and without confusion, to make the government most agreeable to the monarchy," and finally to avoid "erecting a numerous democracy." A literal re-establishment of the feudal hierarchy was provided. Lest the nobility and gentry overbalance the "people," it was provided that only two-fifths of the land should go to the former classes and three-fifths to the latter, but "people" meant manorial lords and freeholders as against proprietors. The social classes were made hereditary. Irrespective of whether the slave be a Christian or not, "every freeman of Carolina shall have absolute power and authority over his Negro slaves."

The Fundamental Constitutions were declared to be perpetual and unalterable. "Since multiplicity of comments serve only to obscure and perplex; all manner of comments and expositions on any part of these Fundamental Constitutions, or any part of the common or statute law of Carolina, are absolutely prohibited."

Controlling the entire scheme were the eight proprietors. By virtue of assignment, death, sale, and purchase, minors even became proprietors. The proprietors "cared but little for their property beyond the returns that might accrue from it and many of them were incapable of taking an intelligent interest in it; but because they had inherited, purchased or received by assignment certain of the proprietary shares, as of a joint stock, they maintained that they had a right to do what they liked with their own. Such was an Englishman's idea of a property franchise in the seventeenth and eighteenth centuries." [17]

Here as elsewhere the pamphleteers, from governor to colony clerk, pointed to the familiar economic advantages of colonization. Carolina, it was argued, has considerable advantages over other colonies. Because of its climate, it could supply foodstuffs more abundantly and cheaply than other colonies. Consequently it could turn quickly to developing manufactures, naval stores, and other useful staples for England.[18]

Dr. Samuel Wilson, secretary to the Lords Proprietors of the colony, explained in *An Account of the Province of Carolina in America* (1682) that a rational man would ask himself, "What commodities shall I be able to produce, that will yield me money in other countries, that I may be enabled to buy Negro slaves (without which a planter can never do any great matter)."

As the southern colonies went on their way of achieving an economic theory according with the ideals of order and commerce in an environment of slavery and agricultural staples, the northern area, which came under the New England Council, was being colonized by men with the same general social philosophy, but more directly bent on achieving a religious aim as well: a homeland for the true Puritan Church.

CHAPTER III

The New England Way

NEW ENGLAND, like Virginia, was settled on the current principles of joint stock company organization. The first enduring compact settlement was established at Plymouth in 1620 by members of John Robinson's Separatist church of Leyden, Holland. In going to the New World, they claimed that they were seeking relief from their plight as exiles. They complained that economic necessity forced them to be hard not only on their servants, but also on their children, who in Holland fell easy victim to the licentious example of the Dutch youth and to the temptations of the city.

With a group of English merchants possessed of a patent "for a particular plantation" from the Virginia Company, they formed a voluntary joint stock association. The terms of the association were in the manner of the Virginia Company's scheme of adventurers in purse and person, with distribution of assets at the end of seven years.

Pastor Robinson thought that the Pilgrims, as an incentive, should own the homes they built and the lands they improved, and be allowed two days a week for their private employment. Without these conditions, the poor would be adversely affected and the building of good houses and improving the lands hindered. Consider how unfitting you would find it to serve "a new apprenticeship of seven years and not a-day's freedom from task," he wrote to the partners in England. Besides, such a scheme renders it unprofitable to have servants and implies that all men are "of one condition."

The London agent of the Separatists, Robert Cushman, replied in a similar vein of contradictory arguments. True, the conditions would benefit the poor, but we should give more consideration to one that adventures his money and person than to one who merely adventures his person. The building of good houses for the present should be discouraged, for our riches shall not be in pomp but in strength, in more ships, men, ammunition. Commonwealths decay when fine houses and gay clothes appear. "Look to it, brethren, you that make profit your main end."

If by "condition" wealth is meant, then all are of the same condition; if "condition" means qualities, then those not content that their neighbors live as well as themselves are not of "good quality" and are unfit for any society. Some of the adventurers do not have an eye for profit, but others do, and "why not they as well as we?" Ventures are undertaken by all sorts of men, and we must try to content them if we can. Finally, the risk of the planters is, of course, greater than that of the merchants, but do they force us to it?

The Separatists acquiesced and finally in 1620 set sail for the New World on the *Mayflower*. Whether by accident or design, the ship found itself in Cape Cod, which was in the domains of the New England Council, not the Virginia Company. The leaders decided to settle on the shore of Plymouth, but before disembarking a civil counterpart of the church covenant, the famous Mayflower Com-

pact, was signed by all the "responsible people" aboard. They agreed
to render due submission and obedience to whatever laws, acts, constitutions, and offices should be thought most convenient for the
general good of the colony. "This was done," said their second governor and first historian, William Bradford, "because of the mutinous
speeches" of the "strangers" aboard—a majority—that none had
power to command them in the absence of a valid patent.

A patent was obtained from the New England Council. The company never held a charter of incorporation from the Crown, but it
took on all the powers and attributes of such a corporation, with
jurisdiction vested in the partnership.

As with the Virginia Company, the home partners demanded immediate returns, and the same tale of lack of supplies was repeated.
Cushman, sent to stop the planters' murmuring for a division, took
as his text for a sermon in 1621, "Let no man seek his own: but every
man another's wealth." "Self-Love" leads to destruction. Everyone
must look out for his brethren and share equally with them. Satan
brought "this particularizing" into the world "because he was not
content to keep that equal state with his fellows, but would set his
throne above the stars."

Not division but the provocation and example of the industrious,
while all worked together, would cure idleness and slothfulness. By
division "shall not gentry and beggary be quickly the glorious en-
signs of your commonwealth?" Though men are not equal in strength,
skill, and courage, is it not sufficient reward for the superior to reap
the glory and credit of doing their task well? The less able would be
punished by shame and reproach. But it is more to the point that
"before we think of gathering riches, we must . . . think of re-
quiting" the charge and labor of our friends in England, and "cursed
be that profit and gain which aims not at this."

The colony leaders in 1623, on the ground that supplies were short
and nothing was to be expected from the home partners, began to
establish the terms originally demanded by the Leyden Pilgrims.
With the advice of the "chief men," the governor ordered that every
man should plant on one-acre plots "corn for his own particular."
Bradford, writing long after the event, claimed this made for more
industry. He deprecated "the vanity of that conceit of Plato and
other ancients . . . that the taking away property, and bringing in
community into a commonwealth, would make them happy and
flourishing; as if they were wiser than God." Because of the inherent

self-regarding, corrupt nature of man, it causes confusion and discontent and retards employment. It is unjust that the weak should share equally with the strong. The aged and graver men hold it an indignity to be ranked and equalized "with the meaner and younger sort" in labor, food, etc.

The governor, in his *History of Plymouth Plantation,* reported that later in the year "the Lord seemed to blast their hopes and to threaten . . . more famine." Shortly afterward, the temporary possessors of the lands demanded and got permanent tenure, for yearly changes would lead to neglect of the holdings in order to prevent others from benefiting. A later editor of Bradford's *History* stated in a footnote that the demand for a permanent tenure arose from the higher price of the short crop resulting from the drought.

In 1625 the home partners explained that, since the shares of the company had fallen to almost nothing in the market, little aid could be sent the colony. The Plymouth stockholders arranged the following year to buy out the London stockholders and to pay the debts of the company over a nine-year term. To achieve the financing and to control untoward persons, the "associates" decided to take into partnership in the government those inhabitants "of ability, and free, . . . and able to govern themselves . . . and their affairs." This meant, of course, those of property, not servants. As "purchasers," or what became known as the "generality" of freemen, fifty-three of the planters were enrolled and five of the old London partners who were "sympathizers in religion." All the assets were divided among the shareholders except that the governor and the "special men" kept their houses, while the others made allowances to one another. Shareholders were to pay the debt by an annual charge in corn or tobacco.

Ostensibly to hasten the process, the governor, seven other Plymouth leaders, and four of the London partners organized a holding company to continue to "manage" the trade of the colony—primarily the Indian trade—for six years, after which it should be returned to the "generality."

To extend the fur trade monopoly, a patent was obtained from the New England Council for Kennebec, in what is now Maine. This monopoly was so zealously guarded that bloodshed resulted. Their Puritan brethren in Massachusetts Bay complained, "They have brought us all, and the gospel under a common reproach, of cutting one another's throats for beaver."

Bradford complained that others, envying the good fortune of Plymouth, paid the Indians higher prices. He wrote the New England Council about this "irregular living" of many who without either patents or license, order of government, trade with no intention to settle in the country but to skim it and leave. He also complained of "the inordinate course of fishermen" who trade instead of fishing. Such unprofitable consuming of foodstuffs not only prevents a worthy subsistence for the colony, but also hurts England, because otherwise the profits would be returned to England for other necessaries. Finally, if traders continue to undersell one another, the trade with the Indians will be completely overthrown and existing investments rendered valueless.

Not a little of the animosity of the Pilgrim fathers and other Puritan settlers toward Thomas Morton, a near-by trading English gentleman lawyer, was aroused by his interference with their profits from the fur trade. Morton, wrote Bradford, has committed many sins. He is licentious and atheistical. He offers a haven to runaway servants, and he supplies the Indians with guns. All sorts of punishments were visited on this "unscrupulous competitor," from burning down his settlement to banishment to England. Morton quite gaily explained in his *New English Canaan* that, while he gave the Indians guns to obtain furs, the Pilgrims gave them the more potent rum.

The undertakers dissolved the holding company in 1639, seven years after the original dissolution date. The Plymouth fathers complained that, despite the expanding business, not only had all the gains gone to their so-called "special friends," the London partners who had acted as factors, but their debts to these self-regarding "friends" had increased through devious practices and manipulations.

Though himself not a "gentleman" by birth, Bradford, like all good Separatists, recognized that order was the fundamental concern of political and economic life. Bradford's favorite citation from Seneca was that a great part of liberty is a "well-governed belly and to be patient in all wants." And Bradford noted in his eulogy of the ruling elder, William Brewster, the only "gentleman" in the original *Mayflower* contingent, that he was compassionate of those in misery and want, especially those who had been of "good estates and rank." [1] The governor and council distributed land according to the "quality of persons."

Plymouth never grew to much importance in terms of size and wealth and was finally swallowed up in 1691 by the powerful Massa-

chusetts Bay Colony that was set up by non-Separatist Puritans
who followed Ames.

The Massachusetts Bay Colony was unequaled in the number of
merchants and gentry who came to stay and in the galaxy of intellectual lights, at least the equal of any in England in university training and the ways of the world, that moved across its history. Its
influence far outreached its own domains. From the Bay Colony
came the great intellectual leaders, the theologians who became the
leaders or co-leaders in the establishment of colonies in the rest of
New England: John Davenport in the New Haven Colony, Thomas
Hooker in Connecticut, and Roger Williams in Rhode Island. Nor
was its influence restricted to New England, for its ideals and aspirations, stripped of their specific theological wrapping, became the
dominant influence in the development of the United States.

The influential phase of the colony's history began with the royal
charter of incorporation to the Massachusetts Bay Company obtained
in 1629 with the aid of none other than the Earl of Warwick. The
charter was that of a trading company closely modeled on the Virginia Company but with the charge of democracy apparently avoided
by the relatively high price of shares and the limited number of
assistants. With the absence of the usual provision requiring residence of the supreme governing body in England came a new note
in the literature of colonization—the wealthy should move en masse
across the seas with their base servants. That plea moved along the
level of religion and economics.

Commerce has opened new lands for the preaching of the gospel,
promoters wrote. But the godly who live in wealth and prosperity
must head the settlements, for a great work requires the best instruments, not a multitude of rude and misgoverned persons, the very
scum of the land.

In England there is little hope for the godly. The fountains of
learning and religion—the universities—are corrupted by "the licentious government of these seminaries where men strain at gnats and
swallow camels, use all severity for maintenance of caps" and other
ceremonials, but tolerate "ruffianlike fashions and disorder in manners."

The wealthy, if they stay, are threatened with the destruction of
their wealth, in any event. True, England is rich in the plenty of a
long peace: but as a consequence the earth has long grown weary of

her inhabitants so that "man, the most precious of her creatures, is here more vile and base than the earth they tread on" and of "less price . . . than a horse or sheep." Masters are forced by authority to entertain their servants; parents to maintain their children; all towns complain of the burden of poor relief.

The wealthy foolishly think that poor relief will save them from harm, but "to preserve life in the weaker you must draw blood from the stronger." They pointed to the result of the peasants' commotion in Germany. Those base people were soon punished or subdued, but then the rich were called to a reckoning which cost many of them their lives and estates.

Thanks also to that peace and plenty, things have reached such a height of excess in all intemperance and riotous expenditures that no man appears to have sufficient to keep "sail with his equals." "Whosoever can not do as other men do" lives in contempt. As a consequence all trades and arts must be conducted with fraud and deceit if a proper standard of living is to be maintained.

In England land is scarce, but in the New World one hundred acres can be cultivated at the labor and costs of one in England.

The justification of the Virginia Company's right to seize Indian lands was presented in a somewhat different form. God has given to mankind a "twofold right in the earth"—a natural and a civil right. The natural right existed when men held the earth in common, every man sowing wherever he pleased. But as men and cattle increased, they appropriated portions of ground by enclosure and cultivation, and this appropriation by their own industry created the individual's civil right in the land. Therefore Christians have liberty to live on the Indians' waste lands. For those more worldly-minded, there were the profits from fishing, naval stores, wood, and the cultivation of oriental products.

Other plantations failed, it was argued, because their ends were carnal, not religious. They aimed chiefly at profit. The merchants induced authority and nobility and all godly and well-disposed persons to contribute great sums by pretexts of "the honor of the Crown . . . the enlargement of God's church, . . . and the great good of the land, to employ so many idle . . . at home for trade and traffic," but they never mentioned "their own particular benefit." When the merchants did not see immediate gain, the promised supplies were sent rather tardily or not at all so that the settlements starved to death.[2]

In 1630 came the mightiest expedition in the history of English colonization, accompanied by the governor, deputy governor, a few assistants, and the sacred charter. In the New World the shareholding feature was in effect scrapped in favor of what might be called the regulated form of company.

Of course, everyone had to attend a Congregational church, but not everyone could be a member. Membership was important, for only those freeholders and gentlemen who were members of a church could have political rights. The freemen chose the governor, deputy governor, and assistants, who together composed the council of assistants or magistrates. Naturally these were gentlemen, and their powers were vast. In the General Court they could veto the measures of the representatives of the freemen from the towns. Their control was buttressed by the power to correct any church that departed from what they conceived to be the true faith, and by the need of any proposed new Congregational church to obtain their permission.

But, unlike Virginia, the Massachusetts authorities had great faith in education as a means of inculcating the true light in the people. Every township had to provide a schoolmaster, but this did not mean that elementary education was compulsory or free.

In 1636, Harvard, the first college in the British colonies, began functioning in accordance with English as well as respectable Puritan ideals. It was supported by the colony and controlled by the authorities. Schools, the authorities held, must depend on the magistrates to prevent the corruption of sound doctrines.

The Harvard of the seventeenth century was little more than a one-man college. But learning flourished. In that age the great theological treatises included detailed discussions of what constituted the content of the social sciences. A complete book of divinity was one that had everything a lawgiver should know—from logic to the ways of the market. The "word and scripture of God do contain a short . . . platform, not only of theology, but also of other sacred sciences . . . attendants and handmaids, thereunto, . . . ethics, economics, politics, church—government, prophecy, academy," explained Reverend John Cotton, the great spiritual leader.[3]

Logic was the divine instrument for revealing the proper meaning of the "written word" and the building up of all sciences. A textbook in logic was prepared even for the Indians. The important thing about logic as Ames taught it was "method," the "orderly" classification of doctrines with proper heads and subheads. Thereby the anatomy of the body of theology was so imprinted on the memories of the students that they became "exact and perfect in the definitions of heavenly doctrine." The great logical principle was that of relatives and correlatives of superior and inferior in the arrangement of phenomena, including human beings, so as to achieve an orderly classification and government. "Order" is the fundamental principle in all activities by the "received rules of logic," wrote the Reverend Thomas Hooker, the lawgiver and spiritual leader of Connecticut, in *A Survey of the Summe of Church Discipline* (1648).

This was especially worked out in elaborating the Congregational polity on the foundations laid down by Ames and Robinson. The safety of the church depends on the right and due ordering of the privileges and liberties of the brethren and the ministerial authority of the elders, wrote Cotton. The gospel reserves church authority wholly to the elders, but prevents their tyranny by the firm establishment of the liberties of the brethren. These can choose their officers ordained by God. They may join in passing censure, but the elders first of all have power to reject "careless and disorderly complaints," and before the matter is brought before the brethren the elders privately examine the offender, the proof of his error, "ripen the matter for the churches cognizance," and declare to the church the will of God therein. "Whereunto the people give consent, in obedience to the will and rule of Christ." [4]

As Hooker put it, in a more sophisticated form, when the "native and naked state of the controversy" has been presented by the elders, "even the meanest in the congregation will generally be able to see cause to join their judgments with the truth." Unless the people are able to convince the elders of errors and mistakes in the sentence, "they are bound to join their judgment with theirs, to the completing of the sentences."

Theoretically the church can proceed against an elder, but it cannot proceed against all the elders of the church, for if the church be without rulers, no act of excommunication is valid. As formulated by a synod of the Congregational churches in the Cambridge platform of 1648, no church act can be consummated or perfected without the consent of both the elders and brethren, which together constitute an organic church. As Hooker's colleague and disciple, the Reverend Samuel Stone, put it, the officers are "a speaking aristocracy in the face of a silent democracy." [5]

What was more, the very process of control by elders helped maintain that hierarchical ordered society so congenial to respectable

Englishmen of the seventeenth century. To be admitted to church membership, wrote Hooker, a candidate must first be scrutinized by the elders to determine whether he is likely to be a "visible saint." If the person, aside from being able to give a reason of his hope toward God, is not guilty of any known neglect of duty and is "effectual in his calling," the elders will believe that there is "something of God and Grace in the soul, and therefore fit for church society." Suppose it is discovered afterward that the individual is merely a conformist—in other words, a hypocrite? Only that hypocrite should be removed, answered Cotton in *The Bloudy Tenent, Washed* (1647), who "either walks inordinately without a calling or idly or negligently in his calling."

Everyone must stay in his due and proper place. Persons of differing endowments and qualifications "need a differing station to be disposed into, the keeping of which is both the beauty and strength of such a society," the Reverend William Hubbard in 1676 said in the annual sermon before the General Court prior to the election of a governor.

"Is it not found by experience, that the greatest part of mankind, are but as tools and instruments for others to work by, rather than any proper agents to effect anything of themselves?" They are but sheep always requiring a shepherd. In peace, left to themselves, they would destroy themselves by slothfulness and security. In war they would be destroyed by others except for the wisdom and courage of the valiant. Therefore "whoever is for a parity in any Society will reduce things into confusion." The magistrates are the animating force, continued Hubbard. "The foot moves not, the hand is not lifted up without the order and command of the head." Therefore the magistrates are the pins upon which the glory of the state rests.[6]

The dogmatic Cotton affirmed, in his *The Powering Out of the Seven Vials* (1642), that corruption always starts from the bottom, from the inherently corrupt, unstable "people," not from the top, the rulers. The charge that the Congregational form of church polity was a democracy was to him the height of absurdity. "Democracy . . . God did [not] ordain as a fit government either for church or commonwealth," wrote Cotton. "If the people be governors, who shall be governed?"[7]

Revolution on the part of the "people" as distinct from gentlemen and magistrates was, of course, never justified. But in the light of the civil war between King and Parliament in England and the rise of the English Puritans to power by the sword, the theologians found that, if the rulers commit atrocious evils, they may be opposed by others of the magistracy of gentlemen.

Thus Cotton wrote in 1644 in his *The Keyes of the Kingdom of Heaven* that, if some of the persons who have the spiritual guidance are also entrusted by the civil state with preserving the laws and liberties, peace and safety of the state, "and shall meet together in a public civil assembly . . . whether in Council or Camp . . . they may there provide by civil power" to protect their rights by strong measures.

Opposition to the earlier crudely disguised theory of the divinity of magistracy came even from within the respectable ranks of the Puritans, notably from Hooker. A scheme in which the magistrate's conscience was to be the sole guide meant tyranny to him: The safety of a community must be sought in the supremacy of impersonal law rather than in the discretion of the magistrate.[8] Rule by "judicial proceedings" rather than by "will" should be paramount. "The choice of public magistrates belongs unto the people. But this privilege of election must not be exercised according to their humours but according to the blessed will and law of God." So the differences between Cotton and Hooker were little more than those formal differences between two thinkers of the same school, but with one, Cotton, in high standing with the governor. Since "even the most conscientious governors may do some evil and that when he is most zealous, therefore we may not think the worst of a governor because of some weakness," said Hooker.[9]

The "Fundamental Orders of Connecticut," framed under Hooker's guidance, provided that the magistrates together with the governor and deputy governor constitute a "particular court" to run affairs and to "administer justice according to the laws here established, and for want thereof, according to the rule of the word of God." The governor had to be formerly of the magistracy.

It was the Reverend John Davenport who clearly reconciled the great authority of magistrates with the doctrine of all power in the people. Davenport was well versed in the art of casuistry. He it was who, in 1636 in his *An Apologeticall Reply*, skillfully defended the churches of New England as not schismatic: The churches of England are Congregational churches in essence because, while a patron's nomination cannot create a valid summons to a minister, "yet the consent of the people by acceptance and submission" make it good.

The "power of government," he now declared, is originally and radically in the people, but lies only virtually in the people, not *"formally."* The freemen were exhorted to choose good rulers—those who fear God—because "you must submit to their authority, and perform all duties to them whom you have chosen, . . . whether they be good or bad, by virtue of their Relation between them and you; so Wives to their husbands, . . . and servants to their masters though froward." [10]

A number of well-to-do non-Congregational colonists protested against the "New England Way" in church and state. They charged that their natural rights as freeborn subjects of England were being violated by the arbitrary Massachusetts authorities. By refusing civil rights to other than church members and forcing all to pay taxes for the support of the Puritan ministry, the authorities deprive men of property of their rights and tax them without their consent. All the evils, however, flow from the popular and democratical form of government in state and church. The logical outcome of the influence of the independent democratic church of New England or Old England has been, they said, the rising up of the Levellers. Actually the Levellers held to religious freedom, the abolition of exclusive corporations, the extension of suffrage to those not servants and able to pay poor relief, and the restriction of governmental power to the maintenance of the public peace, all in the name of the sanctity of property rights.

More of a nuisance to all Puritan New England was that mystic, Samuel Gorton. Gorton appealed to the Crown to restrain the magistrates from suppressing his own peculiar brand of religion and from violating the sanctity of contract by their interference for their own benefit with his land purchases from the Indians. Edward Winslow of Plymouth, representing.Massachusetts in England, declared in 1646 that Gorton was a "notorious disturber of the peace." Gorton and his sect "were unlearned men . . . yet they would interpret the most difficult places of Scripture . . . to serve their own turn." Winslow's first published defense of Massachusetts against Gorton was called *Hypocrisie Unmasked.* When the attacks on the Levellers began, the same pamphlet was immediately issued in 1649 with the new title, *The Danger of Tolerating Levellers in a Civill State.*

The Massachusetts authorities replied to all complaints that they adhered to their charter and to the laws of England "with as bare allowance for the disproportion between such an ancient, populous, wealthy kingdom, and so poor an infant thin colony, as common reason can afford." [11] The colonial authorities even questioned the right of the appeal to England. Said Winslow in his *New-Englands Salamander* (1647): "If the Parliaments . . . should impose Lawes upon us having no Burgesses in their House of Commons, nor capable of a summons by reason of the vast distances of the Ocean . . . then we should lose the liberties and freedome I conceived of English indeed." There was even a note of almost complete independence in one writing. No duties could be imposed unless expressly mentioned in the charter. The charter grants the colonists, as a company, the liberty of making laws, of governing themselves fully and absolutely, and of defending themselves against all attempts to damage them. The charter also secures them from the consequences of any act done and gives them a sufficient discharge even against the King.

With this social and theological background, Massachusetts and its Puritan neighbors developed views on economic matters that accorded with the fundamental principles of order and commerce. Theologians and lay leaders did not lack skill in handling economic problems and in expounding proper principles of economic conduct. They had a broad acquaintance with economic literature gleaned not only from the theological works, but also from such great books on government and economics as Jean Bodin's *Six livres de la république* (of which an English translation was published in 1606) and Hugo Grotius's *De jure belli ac pacis*. As in England, Malynes's *Consuetudo, vel, lex mercatoria* was a standard guide.

In economics, as in all other phases of behavior, Cotton laid down the basic philosophy. The swiftest men and horses won the race; the strongest were most able in battle; men of knowledge were most likely to win favor from the high; men of understanding were most likely to attain riches. Exceptions were meant to show God's sovereignty, "to prevent persons from abusing their talents, and to prevent discouragement of such as lack gifts or means."

Since the Lord allows no trust unless he directs it, oppression of the poor was for instructing the people, not an occasion for the breaking forth of discontent or discouragement. So, if a charge of oppression is made, first inquire whether the oppression be true; secondly, if true, see "God's hand in all"; and, finally, seek to "reprove and reform according to our place." [12] In his *The Soules Effectual Calling to Christ* (1637) Hooker added that he never knew a man "desperately poor, but his heart was desperately proud."

The great missionary to the Indians and translator of the Bible into the native languages, the Reverend John Eliot, in 1678 gave the notion a classical form in *The Harmony of the Gospels*. "Wealth is an exercise of the dominion of man, therefore it exalts a man in the world; poverty strippeth man of his dominion, therefore it lays him low in the world." His wretchedness must ever be an example of the price of sinful conduct. Rulers despise a poor man and the people think God despises him; and all can easily oppress him and inflict wrongs upon him.

The attitude toward poor relief was best evidenced by Hooker's indignant denial, in *A Survey*, that the poor, like the ministry, should be aided by the same treasury. To raise a common treasury for both the poor and the ministry is to confound justice and mercy. The treasury should be raised for the ministers alone, for the Word states: "Let him that teacheth be made partakers of all our good things," but no one else. Ministers are entitled to their wages, for laborers are worthy of their hire. An honorable and comfortable maintenance for them is a due debt. But "neither rule nor reason leads us or allows us to relieve the poor by all our good things."

Of course, wrote Cotton, the insatiable craving for wealth evidences the greedy eye. But when should a man consider himself satisfied? "We may desire wealth of God, partly for our necessity and expediency, and partly to leave to our posterity. Thus far a man may desire wealth. But we are never to desire more than we have good use of." [13]

Much as they spoke of the vice of covetousness, the ablest thinkers could describe the greatest activity of man—the desire for Christ—in no better terms than the insatiable desire for wealth. "A covetous man desires wealth, and would he have but a little?" remarked Hooker in *The Soules Effectual Calling*. "No, he cries more and more, and hath never enough. . . . So he that longs for the Lord Jesus, will have all Christ, and everything in Christ, and Christ in everything." Nor was there any better description of the ceaseless struggle of man with his Lord for salvation. "Be not fancy with the Lord, but in the sense of thy own baseness, as it were: catch the Lord Jesus, and strive with him; leave not till thou hast those comforts which he hath promised."

Desire is the great agent of spiritual and temporal wealth and goodness; but it must be sound desire. It must be constant and can only be accomplished by labor. But it is through the labor of others that substantial wealth is to be acquired. Men of good estates will prosper in New England, wrote one pamphleteer, William Wood, in his New Englands Prospect (1634), "if they go well accommodated with servants," for it is "the industry of the faithful and diligent laborer," well directed in useful industry, that "enricheth the careful Master."

That diligence under order be duly exercised was held in the Puritan colonies to be a function of the state, especially in the case of those classes which were mean, "turbulent, inferior"—laborers and artisans, servants. No person was to live "idly or unprofitably"; that is, idly without means.

There is no possibility of fastening "vagabonds, beggars and vagrant persons . . . to any employment or to settle them in any place," wrote Hooker in his The Application of Redemption (1659), "before they come under the eye of authority and power of the magistrates." They are like "our vagrant thoughts that have no stability or rest." So the magistrate must restrain the foot-loose, masterless men.

Serving the double purpose of reducing poor relief and increasing the supply of dutiful labor were the various settlement laws, apprentice regulations, and the like. Connecticut magistrates had the power of placing all persons with no definite or authorized settlement wherever was most fit for their "maintenance and employment." If any persons living on town relief did not employ their children toward getting a livelihood, or if any family could not or did not provide competently for its children, the authorities could place the children with "good families."

At the same time, the Massachusetts spokesmen pleaded with the philanthropic in England "to cloath and transport . . . poor children . . . which may be a great mercy to their bodies and soules, and a help to us, they being superabundant [. . . in England]" and "we wanting hands to carry on our trades, manufacturing and husbandry." [14]

Servants were in the class with children, requiring constant oversight by the masters lest they become rude, stubborn, and unruly. The Reverend Increase Mather thundered at his congregation: "You that are servants . . . have you been guilty of stubborn, disobedient carriage towards your Masters, though God in his word tells you that you ought to be obedient to them with fear and trembling?" [15] Those who for any reason rise up against their masters will have no peace of mind, never be prosperous, and will die before their time.[16]

Christ came as a poverty-stricken servant, wrote Eliot, for he came to atone for all man's sins; but he did not take the lowest degree of servitude, that of a bond servant for time or life, but only that of a hired servant—the artisan for daily pay. As a bond servant he would have been hindered from doing the will of "the Father that sent him."

Servants that prove "unfaithful, negligent or unprofitable in their service shall not be dismissed" after their term of indenture, generally seven years, until "they have made suitable satisfaction according to the judgment of authority," declared the Massachusetts General Court.

As in the other colonies, almost from the start the magistrates fixed wages, including artisan services, on the ground, as Hubbard put it in *A General History of New England*, that "men gotten from under the reins of government are but like cattle without a fence," apt to run wild and grow unruly. The first regulations were repealed in six months. In 1633 came new ones on the plea that scarcity of laborers caused by the increasing number of plantations enabled laborers to charge extortionate wages. Their immoderate gains led to "vain and idle waste" of time and thus to discord.[17] Worse still, it led to a reversing of the relations of status. Laboring men, recalled Captain Edward Johnson in his *Wonder-working Providence* (1654), "ill . . . recompensed those persons, whose Estates helped them to food before they could reap any from the Earth. Forgetting those courtesies, their excessive prices for worke," made "many File-leaders fall backe to the next Ranke" while the laborers advanced themselves in the meantime.

Prices were fixed in 1633 on the theory that otherwise wages would rise. The Massachusetts General Court declared that, lest workmen be discouraged by excessive prices for commodities necessary for their life and comfort, the "court would set order" in the prices of the all-important imports. The prices are to be one-third higher than the prices in England. But perishable goods are to be sold at such rates as the seller and buyer might agree upon, "provided they be moderate." It appears that this vague legislation soon went into abeyance.

In 1636 John Cotton declared in his proposed code of laws that, in order to avoid all oppression in buying and selling, judges in every town are to appoint certain selectmen to set reasonable rates on all commodities and to limit wages proportionately. The governor and assistants are to do the same for prices throughout the country.

The General Court acted as far as wages were concerned, but in 1638 complaints were again voiced in the court that wages, especially those of smiths, and the rates of cartage and teams were oppressive. Three years later, when a great depression was on, the General Court called on the towns to cut wages because the scarcity of money and fall of the prices of corn and other products make it impossible to pay the old wages. Since many would retire from business rather "than spend the small remainder of their estates for the maintenance of others in such a way as will not offer them some equal recompense," all servants, laborers, and workmen should "lower their wages according to the fall in the price of the commodities wherein their labors are bestowed," and that they should be paid in the commodities of the country. They must be content to share the suffering of the present scarcity, for they have had their advantage by the plenty of former times.[18]

In 1670 and 1672, bills presented in the General Court stated that farmers suffer because of small crops, low prices, and slow markets. Their difficulties have been greatly increased by the excessive dearness of labor by artificers, laborers, and servants "contrary to reason and equity." These oppressive gains are spent for extravagant apparel "altogether unbecoming their place and rank, and in idleness." A great part is spent viciously in taverns and sinful practices. A committee of the General Court reported that the trades of tanners, glove makers, and shoemakers are oppressed by the high wages demanded by workmen; that the excess of pride of mean people has led them to demand the most recent fashions and the highest priced shoes, with the result that they refuse to work except at wages as "maintain them in this profuse expensive manner." Therefore the price of shoes should be fixed, and so also other artisans' commodities where the rule of equity has been exceeded.[19]

During the desperate Indian War of 1675 the General Court passed a series of laws to reform "provoking evils" that had brought God's wrath down on the colony. It emphasized with italics that the colony was beset by "oppression" not only by merchants and shopkeepers, "but *also by mechanics and day labourers.*" Complaints as to prices were directed to the grand jury, but those against extortionate wages were handled in more summary fashion. Selectmen heard the complaints and could force offending laborers to make double restitution to their employers and to pay a fine of double the excess value.[20] The New England Confederation, composed of commissioners from the Puritan colonies of Massachusetts, Plymouth, New Haven, and Connecticut, passed a regulation providing for the return of runaway servants and called on the colonies to end speedily the oppression in wages.[21]

Almost any evil was attributed to the oppression in wages. Massachusetts granted to an iron manufacturing company exclusive privileges, land grants, and exemptions from taxation, and called on those with funds to invest in the enterprise as one of sure gain both to the investors and the commonwealth; but its failure after a number of reorganizations was attributed by contemporary local historians to high wages. Emanuel Downing, lawyer, merchant, and assistant of the Massachusetts Bay Company, pessimistically wrote that he despaired of ever having labor at reasonable wages because of the available land, unless black slaves could be obtained in exchange for captured heathen Indians.[22]

Of course, when complaints against high wages and idleness threatened to deter investment and migration by Englishmen of substance, a less bellicose tone was taken in the literature. It has been erroneously reported, declared Wood, that servants and poor men grow rich and masters and gentry poor in New England, but the diligent hand makes rich. The laboring men have good pay and live well and contentedly, but the employers have no less riches. However, the fundamental attitude remained that expressed by the governor of Connecticut to the English home authorities—that the colony suffers from "expense of labor" and from "want of capital"; that is, "men of estate." [23]

Price regulation for other than artisans' products received little attention compared to wages. The leaders believed in the just price as presented by Ames.

A number of cases were tried under the general act that charging extortionate prices might be punished by the court, but the circumstances and outcome of the most celebrated case illustrated the difficulties. In 1639 Captain Robert Keayne, a successful merchant in Massachusetts, a deputy and a brother-in-law of the co-pastor of Cotton's church, was tried by the General Court for extortion; namely, charging more for certain items than did other tradesmen. Keayne claimed that, according to his books, his prices were approximately a third above original cost, which had been the limit assigned in the original short-lived act. But his books, the General Court felt, had been altered. Keayne, on the advice of influential friends, pleaded guilty to having been misled by false principles of trading and threw himself on the mercy of the court. The magistrates held that the fine set by the deputies of £200 was too severe, and they forced its reduction in effect to one-half. They declared that no law existed limiting profits; that it was common practice in other countries "for men to make use of advantages for raising the prices"; that Keayne was not the sole offender; and, finally, that a "certain rule" could not be found for an equal rate between buyer and seller, though much labor has been bestowed on it, and various laws have been made, which, upon experience, were repealed, as not being "safe and equal."

Having been penalized by the court, the captain was still to be tried by the church. Cotton took the occasion to lay down the principles of "commercial ethics." No one should sell as dear as he can and buy as cheap as he can, "for a man may not sell above the current price, i. e., such a price as is usual in the time and place and as another (who knows the worth of the commodity) would give . . . if he had occasion to use it." However, where the commodity is scarce, he may raise the price, for "the hand of God [is] upon the commodity."

Having presented the "sound" principles of trade, Cotton declared that "neither the habit of covetousness. (which is in every man in some degree), nor simply the act . . . declares a man to be such, but when . . . a man sins against his conscience, or the very light of nature, and when it appears in a man's whole conversation." Keayne was not such, but had merely erred in his judgment through being led by false principles. Besides, "he is otherwise liberal as in his hospitality, and in church communion, etc. . . . So the church consented to an admonition." [24]

Keayne later explained in his lengthy will of 1653 that the church, despite the feelings of all the elders and of the magistrates that he had been unjustly treated, could do no less without some offense, "considering what had passed in Court . . . against me. . . . Courts may err and a faction may be too hard and outvote the better or more discerning part." He felt, however, that by 1653 people had become accustomed to commerce and its laws. Indeed, he said, his supposed offense was common now in every shop and warehouse, and in fact was generally true at that earlier day, but he had been the victim of personal spite.[25]

By 1680 the ministry were complaining that prices had gotten out of hand and attributed the trouble to the difficulty of determining what was reasonable gain. Hubbard recalled the early era as the "golden age" of New England when "vice was crushed . . . especially oppression and extortion in prices and wages."

Of course, there could be opposition to "under prices" of domestic goods, especially if the great leaders are adversely affected, as during the great depression of 1640. Until then New England had been prosperous, the leaders wrote, because of the great inflow of dissenters of means fleeing from persecution in England. By the sale of cattle and corn to immigrants at high prices, the old planters with stock began to grow rich. But the civil war in England brought a cessation of migration, and prices fell suddenly. Winslow complained that cattle were "under their true worth." This is aggravated by the lack of money, whereas in England it is easy "to turn any valuable commodity into money." [26]

In 1640 the General Court of Massachusetts declared that because of the scarcity of money many debtors could not meet their obligations though their goods be sold for half their worth. But on an "equal valuation" they could not only pay their debts but live comfortably on the remainder. Therefore the assets of debtors are to be valued by three "indifferent men." [27]

Such a device, however, could only be justified by the greatest emergency of a universal character. It was not to be considered normal. Hooker's most effective illustration, in his *The Application of Redemption*, of the heinous notion of pursuing the life of faith only when it is to one's convenience was the trader who insists that his creditors need not be paid punctually when "straights lie upon him, and he cannot pay, but with much prejudice to his estate, either to part with that which is profitable, or upon low rates, and for loss."

Imprisonment for debt was so much a matter of common sense that Hooker used it to illustrate the damnation of man through the impossibility of obtaining the means of redemption after too frequent departures from the continuous pursuit of grace. "The debtor hath borrowed so much money, which he may improve, and is bound to repay at such a day appointed; if he through his prodigality and riot, shall vainly misspend, the funds that he cannot pay to satisfy, may not the creditor . . . punish or imprison? No nation ever questioned it."

Monopolies, according to the Massachusetts *Lawes and Libertyes*, were not to be granted except for inventions for the public good and then only for a short time. But inventions had the broad meaning of the old country. The granting of exclusive privileges to private individuals for such public utilities as grist mills, bridges, transport, was so much a matter of common sense that it called for no particular comment.

The granting of exclusive privileges in the Indian fur trade was not the granting of odious monopoly, but the orderly regulation of trade whether done by one company in the colony or by dividing the trade into zones with the payment of a tax by the beneficiaries. One Massachusetts governor went so far as to hold: The English colonies can only achieve success in the beaver trade if there be a company to order it in every colony and all the companies agree on general principles of trade; otherwise the trade will be overthrown and "the Indians will abuse us." [28]

The strongest opposition to state grants of monopoly came from the man who already had the monopoly which the state wished to bestow on him under restraints and taxes. This was William Pynchon, who was a wealthy landowner in England and New England and an assistant of the Connecticut colony as formerly he had been in Massachusetts. As an enterprising merchant with an effective control of the fur trade in his strategic settlement of Springfield, he saw little reason in any state-authorized monopoly arrangement, especially when such authorization entailed the payment of a tax.

In 1638 the Connecticut authorities "gave" him the monopoly of the fur trade in his area and provided that he pay a tax of so much a skin. He protested that it was against "the public goode and the liberty of free men to make a monopoly of trade. . . . I hope the Lord in his mercy will keep me from coveting any unlawful gaines; or [consent to] any man's hindrance where God doth not hinder them." [29]

At the same time, the authorities, facing a scarcity of corn and fearing that "if every man have liberty to truck with the Indians" the Indians would charge "unreasonable prices," gave Pynchon a monopoly of the trade for corn up the Connecticut River. In return he was to sell the corn at a fixed maximum price. Pynchon justified his fail-

ure to deliver the corn on the ground that the owner of the sup-
posedly only available canoe had rightly refused to lend it, lest he be
prevented from carrying on his own industry. Hooker, however,
felt that Pynchon had failed to use his power as a magistrate for the
public good in order that he might monopolize the trade and "so rack
the country at his pleasure." The Connecticut magistrates rined
Pynchon for "unfaithfulness" in breaking his contract. But Pynchon
replied with Hooker's theory of government: "If magistrates in New
England should *ex-officio*, practice such a power . . . [over] men's
proprieties, how long would tyranny be kept out . . . Truly the
King might as legally exact a loan *ex-officio* of his subjects by a dis-
tresse on men's proprieties (because he pleades as great necessity) as
to presse a canoe without a legall order." While governments are
ordered "by the lawlesse law of discretion, what is transient in particular men's heads may be of dangerous consequences." [30]

So Pynchon, dissolving the covenant between Springfield and
Connecticut, placed the area under the jurisdiction of Massachusetts
and returned to his position as assistant in the Massachusetts colony.[31] However, when in 1650 the Dutch authorities of New Netherland (New York) complained to the commissioners of the New
England Confederation that Pynchon was endangering trade by paying the Indians excessive prices for furs, the commissioners replied
that "trade is free." [32]

Naturally the colonies felt the same way when it came to the English Navigation Acts. Apprised of her error at the restoration of the
Stuarts, Massachusetts informed the Crown that at first she had not
thought that His Majesty's laws applied to Massachusetts because
Massachusetts was not represented in Parliament, but she was willing to acquiesce in the restrictive Navigation Acts in the hope eventually of "liberty of trade." [33]

The question of the acquisition and distribution of lands was
handled in accordance with the conceptions of order and contract.
When land is appropriated, they continued to say, "it must be improved," for this alone "gives a theological right unto any possession." [34] The doctrine of improvement applied primarily as a justification of acquisition of Indian lands. Since the Indian lands they took
had been for the most part used as a pasture, and thus were in effect
vacant, the Massachusetts Bay Company justly acquired them by way
of "reasonable purchase and free consent" or "free assignment,"
explained Cotton. So far as distribution is concerned, he added, we

follow the practice of England, where the King and noblemen possess greater territories than other men because they do greater service to church and commonwealth. They employ their parks and forests not only for hunting, but for timber, the nourishing of tame as well as wild beasts, and "also for habitation to sundry Tenants." [35]

The justification of rent from land as from any capital in the presumed costs and pains of the original cultivator was considered so obvious that it was used by Hooker in his *The Saints Dignitie, and Dutie* (1651) to drive home the meaning of the crucifixion of Christ. "A certain man . . . planted a vineyard, and set a hedge about it, and digged a place for the wine vat, and built a tower; (here was much pains, and a great deal of cost bestowed). Well, he let out this vineyard to husbandmen, and went into a far country, and at the season, he sent to the husbandmen, that he might receive of the fruit of the vineyard. Did he receive any . . . ? No." They beat and stoned the messengers. "Certainly, says God, *they will reverence my son*" and "stoop at his commands," but instead they slew him.

As in the southern colonies, New England eventually turned to the heretical principle of raising the "value of money" by the familiar device of giving a higher rating in shillings to the Spanish pieces of eight. Where Massachusetts went further was in establishing a mint in 1652, under private management and without authorization from the Crown, and coining the famous pine-tree shillings at a properly "depreciated" rate in English shillings and a heavy seigniorage charge to the mint master. The measure, it was argued, would create a uniform standard, prevent counterfeiting, and retain specie.

The colonial writers argued just as the English mercantilists did, that with sufficient money, or at least an increasing proportion, exports would not be undervalued in relation to imports. On this ground the export of pine-tree shillings was prohibited. "Greedy importers might raise the price of English goods to correspond with the reduced bullion value of the Massachusetts shilling. This doth bring an undervalue upon all commodities raised among ourselves, and so utterly frustrate the end and use of money amongst us." [36]

Strenuous demands were made for abolition of the seigniorage charge. All money passing to the mint, said one group of petitioners in 1680, returns to the owner at least six and a quarter times lighter than it entered. And the impress adds nothing to the intrinsic value —a Spanish cross (on the pieces of eight) in all other places being as well esteemed as a New England pine. The loss for the mere stamp is so considerable that "nothing but necessity makes it tolerable; those who are able choosing rather to lay up, or send their plate, bullion, and pieces of eight abroad." Thus little is coined, and of this much is sent to other colonies to the damage of trade. John Hull, the mint master who was paid the seigniorage, declared, however: If our coin is being carried out, this is an indication that it is not as light as it should be. Injustice to existing creditors should be prevented by provisions to pay them at the old rates.

Hull, who was a successful merchant in slaves and other commodities, was certain that many evils existed, but that the mint was not among them. In his diary he noted that the churches are lax; judgments of synodical councils are not acknowledged by churches; and members are not obeying ministerial judgments. The people begrudge adequate support to magistrates and the ministry. Gaudy display, pride, worldliness, idleness, now abounds. Self-interest is too predominant in many. There is a want of subjection of inferiors to superiors. Servants are unruly, declared Increase Mather in 1677 in *A Discourse Concerning the Danger of Apostacy*.[37] The child behaves proudly against the ancient, and "the base against the honorable." The spirit of New England has changed from a religious to a worldly interest; trade is almost ruined and everything is down; a great and general reformation is in order, but this can only be achieved if the civil magistrates forward it. Mather together with the other ministers at a synod in 1679 maintained that, first of all, the magistrates are to take care that ministers have "due encouragement and maintenance."[38]

The restored Stuarts and the English economists continued to view New England, especially Massachusetts, as a thorn in the flesh. They never ceased to feel that Massachusetts was heading toward independence from England. The conservative leaders were charged with being factious republicans. Her Puritan religious qualifications were a bone of contention; but equally bad, if not more so, to English leaders were her violations of the Navigation Acts, her establishment of a mint, and other "unsound" financial and economic practices, let alone her harboring of pirates. She was a business competitor instead of an obedient servant.

Sir William Petty, most liberal and tolerant of economists, could state in his *Political Arithmetick* that the "government of New England (both Civil and Ecclesiastical) doth so differ from that of His

Majesty's other dominions that 'tis hard to say what may be the consequence of it."

Sir Josiah Child, head of the powerful East India Company, argued in his *A New Discourse of Trade:* The frugality, industry, and temperance of New England are unexcelled, but they are lacking in that paramount duty of every good man to regard the welfare of his native country as the first consideration. The exports of the other American plantations are not competitive, but New England's cattle and corn are. New England inhabitants participate in the Newfoundland fisheries, to the prejudice of the inhabitants of old England. They make returns to England in the commodities of the more valuable sugar and tobacco plantations, by sale to the latter of food commodities, but these would otherwise be purchased from England. This prejudices the rise of land values in England.

Their charters do not strictly tie them to the enforcement of the Navigation Acts, and so they assume at times a liberty of trading contrary to the Acts. Thereby many American commodities, especially the tobacco and sugar of the southern and West Indies possessions, are surreptitiously transported by New England shipping directly to Europe without first landing in England and paying duties. This not only loses the King revenue and prejudices the navigation of old England, but totally excludes the English merchant from selling commodities where New England merchants trade. Most prejudicial and dangerous to the mother kingdom is New England's aptness for building ships and breeding seamen.

The southern plantations producing tobacco and sugar are the valuable ones; for, with their great number of slaves, every Englishman in the plantations employs four at home; whereas ten Englishmen sent to New England do not employ one man. Thus New England drains England of population, whereas Virginia and the British West Indies make possible an increase of population in old England.

But England gains in direct trade with New England. We export to them ten times as much as we import from them. Therefore, if any reformation of the government is attempted, it will require great tenderness and circumspection.

The Crown, beginning in 1684, had the charters of the New England colonies revoked, and along with New York and New Jersey they were formed into the Dominion of New England. Political power was vested in a Crown-appointed governor and council.

Spokesmen for the restoration of the charters defended New England in the name of the rights of liberty and property of Englishmen. To collect taxes without the people's consent violates the Magna Charta. Violations of various English acts and regulations have been merely in the nature of circumstantial measures, but do not touch the essence. Besides, has not obedient Massachusetts passed laws prohibiting the violation of the Navigation Acts? asked Increase Mather, preaching Massachusetts' cause in London as the colony's agent. Where trade flourishes a poor people becomes rich and great, he continued. England should make up its mind either to encourage trade or let it drop, and in the latter event, do as some country gentlemen advise: prohibit all operations with strangers, force the colonials to eat and wear their own products and so turn savages. Thereby England will keep its money circulating within itself, make wool dearer, and consequently make land yield a greater price. But if trade is to be encouraged, do not take away privileges, but give more privileges and liberty. He pointed to the powerful Dutch East India Company. which is lord of India but a servant of the Netherlands.

The cry that New England is a republic and intent on breaking away from England's control of trade is ridiculous, said Mather. Its so-called republican privileges are merely those of a great trading company. Trade and tyranny will never agree; trade must be regulated, but by men experienced in trade. Some manufactures exist in New England, but since they can only supply one-half the country's needs, New England imports considerable from old England.

New England is more profitable to the Crown than the other American plantations. The West Indies cannot exist without New England. England's distance is too great to supply them with provisions, timber, etc.; but near-by New England, by providing these, makes them prosperous and beneficial. The King gains from the customs on the goods exported to New England and the returns made for the purchases. But the royal colonies suffer from debauched, indigent governors and a people in consequence lacking industry and virtue. In them a rich man would not be safe even in partnership with the government.

Not only should the charters be restored, but also the mint. Massachusetts, the colony spokesmen declared, stamps silver because it has no staple commodity with which to pay debts or buy necessaries but fish and corn, which are too troublesome and cumbersome.

But more definite was the colony's argument that "debased" coinage is essential to provide sufficient money for the colony's growing production and trade, and consequent increase in property values. Scarcity of money holds down the prices of staples and property. Since money is the measure of value, therefore the value of money depends on the ratio between the stock of goods and the stock of money. But "the stock of lands and goods in every country is a hundred times more than the stock of money; therefore the value of money . . . must depend upon and be governed by the value of goods." Had not England herself frequently changed the content in order not to choke her growing trade? Certainly if the mint were forced to issue money at the English valuation, the rise would benefit the landlord and creditor but ruin the debtor and tenant, destroy the trade of the country, and injure the King's customs.

The English authorities replied that property does not determine the value of money; instead, money determines the value of property. True, England has altered the content from time to time, but this does not justify differences in content between different parts of the realm. Altering the standard in any one of the Dominions would adversely affect the rest. Finally, lowering the standard coin would draw silver from England to America.[39]

The new King William might as a good Dutch Calvinist be a sympathizer of the Puritans; still, he also knew as the former leader of the commercial Dutch republic that colonies, like children, have a natural tendency to go their own corrupt, independent way if not closely supervised. He knew, as every good English mercantilist knew, that colonies had the role of being instruments for the achievement of the prosperity of English merchants; and so, with a general supervisory body on trade containing the names of such able mercantile-minded economists as Locke and Pollexfen, home policy became somewhat more systematic as regards the need of keeping the colonies in their place.

Connecticut and Rhode Island were allowed to retain their old charters on the ground that they had never been legally annulled; but that of the most powerful colony, Massachusetts, was modified. The General Court was still composed of two bodies: a Council and a House of Representatives, but no longer were the freemen to choose the governor and magistrates, or councilors. The Crown appointed the former; the latter were elected by the House of Representatives and the previous Council and subject to the approval of the governor. The governor could veto all acts of the General Court, and the Privy Council exercised an ultimate veto power. By the new charter, said Increase Mather in his sermon *The Great Blessing, of Primitive Counsellours,* in 1693, "property and liberty are confirmed."

The old families still controlled. The old Puritan religious qualifications for the franchise were replaced by a stringent property qualification, but the Congregational church here and in Connecticut remained in effect a state church through taxation for the support of the ministry. Harvard was still a Puritan college duly supervised by the state and the Congregational clergy. As in English colleges, the students were classified according to social status.

A writing of Latin and a reading of Greek is required for admission, wrote President Mather in 1689 in his *A Brief Relation;* and the curriculum consisted of "Logick, Natural and Moral Philosophy, Metaphysicks, Geography, Astronomy, Arithmetick, Geometry, etc."; or, more accurately, theology, the classics, and elementary mathematics.

The theses for public orations of the candidates for the all-important master's degree—three years after the B.A.—reveal that medieval tenets still played an important role in the intellectual foundations of the new world. "Is there a stone that makes gold? Affirmative." "Does Extension belong to spirits? Affirmative." [40]

The theory of church and state organization was propounded more definitely in terms of the danger of democracy. Among the *Thirty Important Cases of Conscience, Resolved With Evidence of Scripture and Reason* discussed by a synod in 1699 was that "taking away the negative of the Elders, or other necessity of their consent to church acts," would destroy all government and turn the church into a "mere democracy." [41]

Persons of public station should be supported in the more noble fashion befitting their place at the public expense, explained the Reverend Samuel Willard, vice-president of Harvard.[42] They should not be allowed to ruin themselves and their families for the public, nor let their indigency force them to be corrupt. At the same time, said Increase Mather in a sermon at the election of the councilors, councilors should be men of estate to support the place and dignity of a ruler, lest government be held in contempt.[43]

The accumulation of wealth has a limit determined by "exact rule," declared his son, the Reverend Cotton Mather. This rule is seen in the principles of some great dealers who "stint their estates at a moderate and competent elevation." These resolve "that they will never be richer than just so far," and will devote the excess to the "pious uses" of paying and lending, giving and forgiving. But if any fail to provide for his own and his posterity, he has denied the faith. Charity begins at home.

Paying consists in meeting public charges, including adequate stipends for the civil officers and ministers. These, he said in *Durable Riches* (1695), are not alms deeds, but debts "which honesty rather than charity" binds us to pay. The overseers of souls must be handsomely provided so that "they may be neither discouraged nor contemptible in their Work."

Lending as a pious use consists in aiding those without means to engage in a trade who "are likely thereby to come into a way of what they may call their own."

Giving consists in part of supplying the necessities and relieving the calamities of the indigent when they have a manifest need of them. But "don't misapply your charity." For the poor "that can work and won't, the best liberality . . . is to *make* them." A method, exclaimed Mather, must be discovered whereby the idle persons may obtain their bread. This is the best charity to them. But it is up to the authorities to find the method. In any event, as for the idlers, common beggars, and the like, here we must follow God's command, "Let them starve." "Our beggars . . . shamefully grow upon us, and such beggars too as our Lord Jesus Christ hath expressly forbidden us to countenance." Not long ago the lack of beggars made New England Utopia, but now the story is different. More spiritual is giving for propagating the gospel, dispensing the Bible, and providing an endowment for educating poor scholars at Harvard.

Forgiving of debts is only to occur when the "pure frowns of God" have brought a debtor low. But if debtors have become insolvent by their "bad courses," by being too greedy for riches, then they should undergo "whatever lash the Law will help their creditors to inflict upon them"; for they are in effect cheats and thieves.[44]

So important was the question of the validity of usury that of the thirty cases of conscience before the synod of 1699, usury was the only non-theological question discussed. Usury is justified by necessity, utility, and equity, the ministers declared. If all usury were denied, "human society as now circumstanced would sink." Since the borrower gains from the loan, it would be sinful and uncharitable for the borrower not to share his gain. Since money is an "improve-able" thing like any other commodity, a return on it is as justified as that on any other good. Therefore, "the severe declamations of the ancients against usury, must be of no further account with us." How-ever, rates should not be carried to a biting extremity.

The community was also open to the notion held by a minority of the English mercantilists that lowering the rate of interest by law was legitimate. This was evidenced by the lowering of the legal rate from 8 to 6 per cent in 1693 in Massachusetts on the ground that reductions benefited trade and agriculture.

As for slavery, New England was willing that Negro slaves have religious services under proper rules and auspices. According to the *Rules For the Society of Negroes*, prepared in 1693 by Cotton Mather, should any be "disobedient and unfaithful to their mas-ters," they would admonish them and exclude them from the meet-ing. "We will . . . set ourselves to do all the good we can" to the other Negro Servants in the Town; "and . . . if any of them should run away from their masters, we will afford them no shelter. But we will do what in us lies, that they may be discovered and pun-ished." [45]

Judge Samuel Sewall, Harvard M.A. and a leading merchant and moneylender, did, however, object to the institution of slavery. Sewall saw no moral or economic justification for it. All men are sons of Adam and therefore co-heirs of all the earth. "Originally and naturally, there is no such thing as slavery," and it is forbidden by divine law. The end to be sought, however, is the elimination of blacks from the population through the substitution of white serv-ants.

Because their color prevents their assimilation, they are not suited for peopling the country. Instead, they remain in "our Body Politick as a kind of extravasat Blood." They are useless for defense. They are undesirable servants, for they are "much addicted to stealing, lying, and purloining." Their constant longing for their forbidden liberty renders them unwilling servants, and they seldom use freedom well when given it.

On the other hand, white servants would increase desirable popu-lation and provide a constant stream of liberated servants to settle the frontiers. Sewall attempted to show by a detailed computation how much more profitable servants were to a master than slaves. The risk is much less, for the capital investment is not heavy. Three years' interest on the price of a Negro will almost purchase a white manservant. The death of forty-four Negro servants in Boston in one year, Sewall pointed out, destroyed a capital investment that would have supplied more than 500 servants in four years' time. Thus it would even be desirable to pay a bounty on the importation of white servants.[46]

Defending slavery was an equally prominent political figure and merchant, John Saffin, who "imported Negroes clandestinely from Guinea." [47] He declared that slavery was the means of bringing the heathen black savage to civility and Christianity. Slavery is merely a form of servitude, and servitude no one questions. To declare that all men have "equal rights to liberty and all outward comforts of life" goes against the divine wisdom, for God has ordained different degrees, "some to be high and honorable, some to be low and despicable; some to be monarchs, Kings, Princes and Governors, Masters and Commanders, others to be subjects and to be commanded, servants of sundry sorts and degrees bound to obey; yea some to be slaves, and so to remain during their lives as hath been proved." Otherwise "there would be mere parity." True, every member of the body is useful, but this does not mean that they are of "equal and like dignity." Each has an office in the duly arranged hierarchy that constitutes the social organism. Good manners as well as prudence dictate that one is not to treat the prince and the peasant alike.

But even the proponents of slavery agreed that white servants were preferable; they simply questioned that slavery was unlawful.[48] The practical consequence of Sewall's work was that Boston's representatives to the General Court were instructed to "promote the encourageing the bringing in of white servants and to put a period to Negroes being slaves." [49]

That New England's economics as well as politics should be highly conservative was in good part due to the great statesmen who shaped its destinies, notably John Winthrop and Roger Williams.

CHAPTER IV

Molders of New England

JOHN WINTHROP AND THE CORPORATE STATE

T HE man who most effectively shaped dominant sentiment in New England was John Winthrop. He was its most powerful figure for twenty years, from the beginning of the Massachusetts Bay Colony to his death. For most of that period he was governor. No one was more gifted in all the arts of political strategy.

Winthrop deeply felt that he was of the "elect" both in church and state, and that the "inferiors" must be constantly shown their place; but he had a respect for learning that called for explanation of his acts extending beyond biblical citation or an outright appeal to the light of nature.

The sense of authority and superior class had been Winthrop's birthright. In old England he was lord of the manor of Groton, with the usual rights of magistracy and appointment of the minister. His grandfather had held the highest post of master in the powerful Clothiers Company of London. When Henry VIII broke with the Pope and seized the church properties, Winthrop's grandfather had sufficient wealth and importance to be a beneficiary. Winthrop's father was a lawyer and in addition held the important position of auditor of two Cambridge colleges.

John Winthrop entered Trinity College, Cambridge, in 1602, at the age of fourteen, and stayed the usual two years considered proper and sufficient for a gentleman's son. There he acquired the use of the Aristotelian syllogism, and became deeply interested in theology of the Calvinistic Puritan brand with which Cambridge was saturated. In 1606 he "made a new convenant with the Lord." He would re-form both in God's service and in "my calling," and the Lord would on his part forgive his many sins and "strengthen me against the world, the flesh, and the Devil." [1]

Winthrop had planned to enter the ministry but instead was persuaded to enter the law, the road to high position and wealth. Through influential friends and relatives, he obtained in 1623 one of the inferior magistracies in the Court of Wards and Liveries in London, where the dealing with "wards, widows and lunatiques" strengthened Winthrop's sense of authority and patriarchal outlook. The post was one of dignity and made possible valuable contacts; but Winthrop, who had rather high moral standards, found the office an added expense, since it involved living in London. So in 1629 he left it. He was dissatisfied with the state of England in general and with his own in particular, especially since his income, reduced by allotments of his estates to three sons now of age, was insufficient for the standard of living required of a member of his class. Just then came the offer to head the Massachusetts Bay Company.

Winthrop was methodical in setting down his reasons for accepting the offer. The "general considerations" that moved the Puritans, he of course knew. The "particular considerations" for himself were also somewhat familiar. There was first the religious consideration of devoting the small remainder of his life to the services of the church. Secondly, "the welfare of the plantation depends upon my assistance" for its main pillars, "the gentlemen of high quality" refuse to promote the project if he deserts them. Finally, his means were so shortened that he could not continue in his present place.[2]

Winthrop did not treat the perils lightly. While on ship he sketched in *A Modell of Christian Charity* the moral principles that should guide the saints by calling.

In accordance with the medieval Christian tradition, Winthrop held that every man after the fall is born with the principles of self-love. But with Christ taking possession of one's soul comes the principle of love to God and one's neighbor to restrain self-interest within bounds. This works out in the necessary division of every society into two classes: the rich, eminent in power; the poor, mean and in subjection.

This division creates dependency of every man on others, and their harmonious working together evidences the spirit and love of Christ, so that the community of saints becomes "the most perfect and best proportioned body in the world." This principle of love restrains the rich and mighty from devouring the poor, and induces the inferior and despised to render obedience to their superiors. Only the unregenerate poor and despised would rise against the rich and honorable, for the latter are merely stewards of God. No man is made more honorable than another or more wealthy for any particular respect to himself, but for the glory of his Creator and the common good.

The two rules that should guide men are justice and mercy. They are distinct, but they may concur in the same subject. There may be occasion of "showing mercy to a rich man, in some sudden danger of distress; and also of doing mere justice to some poor man in regard of some particular contract."

The duty of mercy falls into the categories of giving, lending, and forgiving. As for giving, ordinarily we should first lay up for our posterity and children, and he is "worse than an infidel that provideth not for his own." Indeed, only by accumulating wealth can we provide for those occasions when the "Lord shall call for them from us."

In lending, the rule is first to observe whether "thy brother has present or probable, or possible means of repayment." If so, the act is not to be judged by the law of mercy, but by way of commerce where "thou arte to walk by the rule of justice."

After the company landed, Winthrop's problems began. A limited number of additional freemen were immediately created at the insistence of the "planters," but these "freemen" were to Winthrop of no higher character and possessed of no more power than the generality of a craft or liveried company, or of the mass of tenants of a manorial lord. Holding that the charter was the bulwark of religious freedom and the warrant for "absolute power of government" of the company, and treating the company and himself as identical, Winthrop practiced what might be called in effect absolute rule for a number of years. He and the few assistants constituted themselves the sole government authority to make laws and ordinances, raise money, distribute lands, and punish offenders at discretion.

When in 1632 the pastor and elder of the Watertown church protested that the imposition of a tax by the Court of Assistants violated the charter and that such action would bring themselves and posterity into bondage, Winthrop was aghast at such insolence.

Two years later came another outburst against the rule of the magistrates. The freemen of each of the towns without any leave of the magistrates sent two deputies to the General Court to demand to see the charter and assert their powers, usurped by the Court of Assistants. Winthrop explained away the violations by arguing that when the patent was granted, the number of freemen was supposed to be, as in like corporations, so few that they might well join in making laws; but now they had become too numerous. Eventually they must choose a select company for this purpose, but for the present there was an insufficient number of men qualified for such a business, and furthermore the commonwealth could not bear the loss of so many from their ordinary business as must attend.

The freemen, backed by some of the oligarchy, successfully insisted, however, on what they conceived to be their charter rights. Winthrop was not re-elected, but only a few years passed before he was in his old post with a series of elaborate defenses of oligarchical control in the name of church purity, the liberty of the corporation, and the general welfare. In 1643 he defended the "negative voice," or veto power, exercised by the magistrates over the deputies' measures on the ground that to deny the veto would be "to establish a meere Democratie." Democracy is the worst form of government, a monster; and history records that it is always temporary and "fullest of troubles." [3] He explained that the veto is a means not of infringing the people's liberties, but of preserving them from their violent passions.

In 1645, after having just been acquitted of exceeding his power as deputy governor by the General Court, Winthrop sent to the deputies his most finished analysis of the nature of liberty. "There is a twofold liberty, natural and civil or federal." Natural liberty is a wild beast which "it is the end and interest of all God's ordinances to subdue and restrain." Civil liberty means the right to be good, just, and honest. This liberty is maintained and "exercised in a way of subjection to authority." Thus the woman's own choice makes a man her husband; but, having been chosen, the man becomes her lord and she subject to him. On the other hand, where the people choose magistrates, as in Massachusetts, "they are taking people from among themselves with the same passions as themselves. Therefore when they see infirmities in the magistrates, they should reflect on their own, and be more tolerant of those of the magistrates."

If Winthrop conceived of "freemen," though they be godly freeholders, as in the category of unruly children, it was to be expected that he would entertain the respectable Englishman's attitude toward the artisan and laboring classes. When, in 1633, the General Court —which then meant Winthrop and the few assistants—set wage maximums, Winthrop explained in his journal that the scarcity of labor, especially in the building trades, incited workmen to raise their wages excessively. The general complaint against high prices was somewhat misplaced, he felt, because it was the "excessive wages" which caused the high prices. The "excessive wages" were bad because workmen were enabled to idle a good deal of their time or spend their surplus income for tobacco and strong drink. These were not only bad in themselves, but as imports they were a further drain on the commonwealth specie.

Later he explained the difficulties of wage-fixing. The General Court had found by experience that no law could restrain "excessive wages," for the workmen would either go elsewhere or else, being able to live by planting and other employments of their own, they would not work for hire. Therefore, fixing rates was left to the towns individually. "This took better effect for a while, so that in a voluntary way, by the counsel and persuasion of the elders, and example of some . . . they were brought to more moderation than they could be by compulsion. But it held not long."

Winthrop found another way to solve the problem, and that was by limiting land grants not only to reserve land for future colonists, but "to prevent the neglect of trades." [4] He bewailed in his diary in 1645 that the civil war in England kept servants from coming to the colony. Those who served their time could be hired only at unreasonable wages. This threatened to turn masters into the servants of their former servants.

Under Winthrop's reign the foundations of Massachusetts and New England in general were firmly laid, but these foundations rested on the logic of the medieval corporation. Time was to render Winthrop's terminology obsolete, but the substance of his views was to remain a basic element of American culture.

Winthrop was a zealous Puritan, and he knew how to utilize the machinery of the Puritan church organization for whatever he deemed to be for the public welfare. Whenever necessary he saw to it that a synod of elders was called to show that the Word of God supported his practices. As he put it, the matter would be sketched beforehand for the guidance of the elders. Should perchance a governor be chosen with whose views he disagreed, like Sir Henry Vane, he was sufficiently adept at parliamentary practices to obtain his way eventually.

As governor he regarded any opposition to his policies, vocal or otherwise, as seditious. However, when he was out òf office, he viewed his own criticisms as necessary to preserve fundamental principles. Changes there might be; but they must not occur in what he called "fundamentals." So any violation of the charter that he perpetrated was held not to touch the substance, though it might strike at what respectable Englishmen called their inherited rights and liberties, notably in matters of taxation.

Men of his class might accuse him of being arbitrary, but he would dismiss the critics either as exponents of vicious democracy or as "wise and godly men misled by their own invention." Of course, most of his critics did not disagree with his governing principle that the "best part [of a community] is always the least, and of that best part, the wiser part is always the lesser"; [5] but they did object to Winthrop's operating on the principle that he alone constituted that lesser part. In a broad sense Winthrop was right. It had never been intended by the Crown that the accident of the relatively liberal privileges of freemen in a powerful trading corporation should be applicable to the mass of property holders. Winthrop knew that a successful godly plantation must operate on the same principles that guided the relations between lord and tenant on a manor, masters and commonality in the great guilds, the liveried companies, and even the trading corporations. They were organisms, corporations in which each part had its place of superiority and inferiority. The parts were bound together by a contract tacit or explicit, guided by these deeper relations. So conceived, every man must love his brother, in the sense of not attempting to change places but of achieving the welfare of the corporate or organic whole by performing to the full the place or function assigned him.

The Massachusetts scheme owes much of its rigidity as well as its stability to the forceful personality of Winthrop. But it should not be forgotten that Winthrop befriended Roger Williams at critical times, even though the Massachusetts proceedings against Williams had their origin in principles of political and social organizations that Winthrop established.

That friendship between the outstanding exponent of the conservative corporate state and the great exponent of liberty of conscience raises the question as to whether there were any significant differences on matters economic and political between them.

ROGER WILLIAMS AND CORPORATE FREEDOM

The one New England colony that was outside the pale as far as the Puritans were concerned was Roger Williams's colony of Rhode Island. Even then, fellow Calvinists of New Netherland called it the "sink of New England." The only substantial difference between that colony and others, however, was that here church and state were completely separated.

The guiding spirit and founder of the colony claims attention as one of the most significant intellectual figures of the seventeenth century, especially for the influential economic doctrines implied or specified in his pleas for liberty of conscience.

Like any great disturbing figure, Roger Williams (1603–1683) was the product of complex forces. The forces that created the Puritan revolution enveloped him and sent him on to New England. But where others adjusted themselves to the "New England way," Williams pushed one stream of the Puritan logic along a line of development that made him a nuisance to the respectable authorities of the Puritan commonwealths and a contributing factor to the later phases of the Puritan revolution in old England.

By birth Williams was just outside the fringe of the powerful classes of England, but sufficiently connected with them to feel constantly the pain of thwarted hopes. His father and oldest brother were members, but only members, of the powerful autocratic guild of the Merchant Taylors Company which "regulated" the woolen and linen trade. His mother was a distant relative of some of the Puritan leaders. In 1621 he was made a scholar at Charterhouse, an endowed school for "persons exceedingly well connected but really poor." From there, with scholarships provided by the school, Williams went to Cambridge where, in the rigorous classification of students, he ranked as a "pensioner." He was just above the lowest, the "sizars," who did menial tasks for the others as a means of obtaining their education; and above him were the "fellow commoners" composed of the sons of the gentry and the wealthy.

In 1627 Williams obtained the intermediate, or "imperfect," degree of B.A. He had already completed two years of the three for the M.A. at Cambridge when his Puritan leanings or, as he put it, his "tender conscience," forced him to leave Cambridge and his scholarship to take a not very profitable post as private chaplain to a member of the Puritan gentry, Sir William Masham, who was a parliamentary leader and shareholder of the Massachusetts Bay Company.

Having been bred a gentleman, Williams had high ambitions, but he was shown his place when his lack of wealth and status proved a bar to marriage with a Puritan daughter of quality. This failure was too much for Williams, so he warned the girl's guardian of the dire consequences that would befall her for having tampered with the will of the Lord. "He with whom we deal excepteth not the persons of princes, nor regardeth the rich more than the poor for they are all the work of his hands. Those having greater birth, more ample maintenance, more plentiful means of grace, must have at the same time greater duties and responsibilities." [6]

It was perhaps ironical that the successful suitor, another future Massachusetts minister, William Hooke, should bless the Puritan revolution in a more equalitarian ideology than Williams ever used or would approve. "Liberty is more precious than life . . . servitude is the portion only of men destined to misery." [7]

Williams had already received a "call" from New England; and, "godly and zealous" as he was under the circumstances, he was in no mood for any restraint in what he considered the role of the ministry. He arrived in Boston in 1631, just after the Massachusetts Bay Colony got under way. He refused to join with the Boston church because it refused to abjure the non-Separatist tenet that it was separated not from the Church of England but from its corruptions. The church at Salem was apparently willing to subscribe to the conditions, so Williams was willing to accept its call; but the Bay magistrates requested further consideration before he was "called." While matters hung in the balance, Williams betook himself to Plymouth, where he exercised the office of minister. He freed himself from any material dependence on the church by acquiring lands and becoming a successful trader as well as missionary among the Indians.

Williams, however, became convinced that the Plymouth church, too, was guilty of the same heresies as the Boston church, and he returned to Salem to head its church in 1634. He held the church to the strict Separatist pattern. But the central authorities and the clergy of the Bay agreed, with Bradford, that Williams was "divinely mad." Though he had the "root of the truth in him," his boisterous manner would rock the civil peace of the colony. Pressure was brought to bear on the Salem church by the General Court's temporarily refusing a land grant to the town. Williams, in turn, with the consent of the Salem church, sent letters in the church's name to the others charging the magistrates that were members of their respective churches, of "sundry heinous offenses," and he at the same time informed the members of his church that, unless they would separate from the churches of New England as well as old England, he would separate from them. But Salem wanted the land. So Williams carried out his threat and refused to have any dealings with his congregation, including his own family, who continued to attend. He maintained a meeting in his home, where he preached to the few faithful.

The able Hooker could not convince him of the error of his ways; neither could his good friends, Cotton and Winthrop. The General Court finally decreed that since, among other things, he had "broached . . . new and dangerous opinions, against the authority of magistrates," he must depart from the jurisdiction of the colony.[8] Hearing that he planned a separate colony near by, the magistrates secretly ordered that he be seized and sent to England. But warned, perhaps by Winthrop, he escaped with the aid of some Indians to the area that became Rhode Island and founded Providence. Here, by a compact resembling the Mayflower Compact, he established a government modeled on New England governments, except that liberty of conscience was provided. Quite naturally, he carried over the feudal pecuniary notions of government.

He wrote his "pious and prudent" friend Winthrop, that he had purchased the place at his own expense, with those desiring to enter paying him a proportionate part, until the full cost had been met. The question is "whether I may not lawfully desire . . . of my neighbors, that just as I . . . shall not bring . . . any person into the town without their consent; so . . . against my consent no person be . . . received." He aptly summed up his position in stating: "I desire not to sleep in security and dream of a nest which no hand can reach. I cannot but expect changes and the change of the last enemy death, yet I dare not despise a liberty which the Lord seems to offer me, if for mine own or other's peace."

Political rights were originally vested only in the propertied masters of families. Heretofore, he wrote Winthrop, the masters of families have consulted together and passed measures by "mutual consent." But to appease the demand for political rights of some propertied younger men of whom "we had much need," an additional compact was drawn up whereby the younger men promised to obey the rules passed by the greater number of the present masters of families and "such as they shall admit into the same fellowship and privilege." [9]

To prevent Massachusetts from taking Rhode Island as its own, Williams went to England and obtained a charter from Parliament during the civil war. The charter was the most liberal of its day. The "inhabitants," which meant those already having the rule, were granted a "free and absolute charter" of incorporation, with full authority to rule themselves and such others as shall inhabit the tract by "such a form of civil government as by voluntary consent, of all, or the greater part of them, shall find most suitable." At the first general court of election, the Rhode Island freemen stated that their form of government was "democratical"; that is to say, a government held by the free and voluntary consent of all or the greater part of the free inhabitants. But it was the democracy of a limited number of freeholders, and to all intents and purposes Winthrop's description of Massachusetts' frame of government as a "mixed aristocracy" would have applied just as well to the Rhode Island "democracy."

What is important is that Williams derives his notions of the liberty of conscience from the principles of order and commerce. While in England, if not before, Williams had decided that he could not be a minister; and instead had become a "seeker," because no ministry could show due warrant or "lawful commission" from the "rightful supreme authority." The Church of Christ had so fallen into apostasy as to lose its right form and the due administration of the ordinances, which could only be restored by a new apostolic or specially commissioned messenger from above. "The apostacy of anti-Christ hath so far corrupted all, that there can be no recovery out of that apostacy, till Christ shall send forth new apostles to plant churches anew." No man, regardless of how wise and good he is, can attempt the work of conversion without "a Word, a Warrant, and Commission, for matter and manner from God himself," he wrote in *Christnings make not Christians* (1645). There can be no preaching "without a true sending," but Williams proclaimed that he knew not "where the power and authority of sending and giving that commission now lies."

He even felt that something of the same situation existed in England's civil state during this period of civil war and parliamentary rule. "Is it not, in this present storm of England's sorrows, one of the greatest queries 'who are the true officers, true commanders, true justices, true commissioners; which is the true seal?' " The officers' actions might be noble, excellent, yet "not persons fit, but also truly authorized are true officers."

Williams did not allow these doubts in the political realm to interfere with his obtaining a charter from Parliament, though doubtless in the light of his abhorrence of the execution of Charles I he felt less troubled in his own conscience about the security of his colony when Rhode Island obtained a charter from the restored Stuart, Charles II.

But in any event, the verdict of a majority in any sense of that term meant nothing so long as it did not accord with a "lawful commission." Thus he justified himself for not listening to the voice of his church at Salem and the voice of the synod. The argument from multitudes was a "popish argument." "David himself and the Princes of Israel and 30 thousand Israels, carrying up the Ark, were not to be hearkened to, nor followed in their . . . holy rejoicings and Triumphings, the due order of the Lord, yet being wanting to their holy intentions, and affections." They were a type of God's best servants reforming yet not after "due order." [10]

His great exposition of the doctrine that civil power derives from the people was not developed in connection with expanding the scope of popular rule, but in proving that, since the Massachusetts government and all government derives from the people, a state's control over the church would place the company of saints by calling under the dominion of the corrupt, unregenerate mass. The Massachusetts clergy, he wrote in *The Bloudy Tenent, of Persecution*, in 1644, had declared that the civil power may enact any form of government deemed most wise. From this, said Williams, it follows that the "sovereign, original and foundation of civil power" lies in the people. Such governments can have no more power and no longer term than the people bestow. Now, if the magistrates receive their power of governing the church from the people, then the people have "fundamentally and originally" a power to govern the church and correct the church in its errors. But this would be pulling "God, and Christ, and Spirit out of heaven" and subjecting them to "natural, sinful, inconstant men; and so consequently to Satan himself, by whom all peoples naturally are guided."

Conceiving of religious opinion as not involving the security of the state, Williams argued that the chief purpose of the state is security lest men devour each other.[11] Among the things written in the heart of men, "is that until matters come to a settled government no man is ordinarily sure of his home, goods, land, cattle, wife, children, or life. Hence the ancient maxim: better to live under a *tyrant in peace*, than under the sword or where every man is a tyrant." [12]

Anarchy would be prevalent if all men were equal politically. Not individuals but families were the foundation of government for a commonweal is only a "commonweal of families, agreeing to live together for the common good."

From the beginning of the world God has armed fathers, masters, and magistrates to judge and punish evildoers for the public safety, Williams reiterated in *The Bloody Tenent Yet More Bloody* (1652). "The father hath power and authority over his child, the husband over the wife, the master over his servant."

Just as there were degrees of Christians, so there were "equals, superiors, and inferiors" in the social and political order. In the civil order as in the spiritual order there was a sharp distinction between the people and the rulers. The magistrates were the most important because on them as pilots depended the safety of the people. On the one hand, there were "the more high and honourable at the helm of government"; and on the other hand, there were "the more inferiour, who labour and sail" in the ship.

So obvious was it to Williams that the poor lacked the qualities to be magistrates that it served as a postulate for one line of reasoning to prove that magistrates need not be Christians. Few Christians are "wise and noble and qualified for affairs of state," said Williams, because of the few "who receive the Gospel" God has ordained the poor and mean to be the bulk.

Just as Williams appealed to the current political practices based on status to justify liberty of conscience, so likewise he appealed to current economic practices based for the most part on the "freedom" of the market place.

Cotton, in defense of Massachusetts' action, had argued that Williams, in separating from the New England churches and refusing to administer the Word to all, was refusing to sell God's corn, and was in the position of a monopolist cursed by the people for withholding the staff of life. Replied Williams: "Corporal or spiritual corn may not be lawfully sold or bought without consent and authority of the owner." In fact, a good reason for not taking literally the statements in the Bible in support of the forcible repression of the ungodly is that many of the economic practices there condemned are now lawful.

"In Israel the not selling or the withholding of corn presumptuously was death." But Cotton cannot prove that any state in the world now prescribes the death penalty. In Israel, lands, fields, houses, vineyards, were sold with the proviso of returning them again in the year of jubilee to the "right owners." Such provisions are not now enjoined by God, nor is such jubilee or redemption to be expected. The very materials, the gold and silver of the idols of Canaan, "were made odious to the people of Israel," that they might not desire it and become accursed. "Whereas we find not any such accursed nature in the materials of idols or images now." The idolatrous forms being changed, the silver and gold may be cast and coined, "and other materials employed lawfully."

Usury, too, Williams justified on grounds drawn from the defense of the liberty of the merchant. Of course usury is a disease. But, just as the state attempts to eliminate the ungodly, so a physician permits "noisome humours, and sometimes diseases, when the cure or purging would prove more dangerous." Thus the state allows usury in order to prevent greater evils—"stealing, robbing, murdering, perishing of the poor, and the hindrance or stop, of commerce and dealing in the commonwealth."

Not least of the defenses of liberty of conscience was that it increased trade and commerce. Persecution, especially of Nonconformist merchants, hurt the markets. The confluence of the persecuted in the Dutch towns "by God's most gracious coming with them, drew shipping trade, wealth and greatness, honor."

Perhaps most significant of all was his defense of the freedom of the church company from state oversight on grounds that implied the freedom of great chartered companies from state oversight. The church, or company of worshipers whether true or false, is like a college of physicians in a city, "or like a corporation, society or company of East Indian or Turkey merchants or any other society or company in London." These "companies may hold their courts, keep records, hold disputations, and in matters concerning their society may dissent, divide, break into schisms, and factions, sue . . . each other at the law; yea, wholly break up and dissolve . . . and yet the peace of the city not be in the least measure impaired or disturbed; because the essence or being of the city, and so the well being

and peace thereof, is essentially distinct from those particular societies; the city courts, city laws, city punishments distinct from
theirs." He also held that the rights of property are so sacred that,
though the king and the nobles use their great parks merely for
occasional hunting, "no man might lawfully invade" them.

The problem of the Indians bothered him a little—at least more
than the lot of the poor with which he seemed to identify them tacitly.
The Indians had befriended him in his hour of peril, and they trusted
him. They were, however, "Adam's degenerate seed." Adhering to his
conception of property, he helped to return runaway captive Indian
slaves to Massachusetts. Enemy Indians, Williams informed Winthrop, might be lawfully despoiled of all comfort, including wife and
children, but he queried whether "after a due time of training up to
labour, and restraint" they might not be set free, provided there be
no danger of their joining the enemy.[13]

He wrote the Massachusetts General Court that by "their councils
and command" the Indians might be forced to forsake their filthy
nakedness and keep cattle so that "civility may be a leading step to
Christianity." [14] The Indians, he felt, should be especially trained in
sound economics. They are poor because "they endure not that life
of labour and endeavor wherein that plenty and better state is
found." [15] Instead they harbor the erroneous notion that the English
traders labor to deceive them, and so they waste considerable time
trying all markets and places to get the best bargain. The evil partly
flows from their failure to appreciate the principle of money and the
great law of supply and demand. Beaver has fallen in England; consequently wampum, the Indian bead money used in the trade with the
Indians, has fallen in terms of English shillings; and the commodities
sold to the natives must be sold at a higher price in their money. But
the natives, "not understanding the cause . . . say that the English
cheat them though I have laboured to make them understand the reason of it."

Broadly speaking, there was a harmony in the economic universe,
though on the face of it there were some discrepancies. Thus, while
God "hath so advanced Europe above America" so that every hoe,
hatchet, knife, or rag of cloth in all America comes from Europe,
"and yet that Europe be not proud, nor America discouraged, what
treasures are hid in some parts in America, and in our New English
parts, how have foul [Indian] hands (in smoky houses) the first
handling of those furs which are after worn upon the hands of

Queens, and heads of Princes?" [16] Naturally in his wrath against the attempts of the Puritan neighboring colonies to acquire Rhode Island territory, he could exclaim that land had become "as great a God with us English as God Gold with the Spaniards." [17]

Williams granted that the avid pursuit of wealth for its own sake is vicious, but the pursuit and acquisition of wealth takes on a proper Christian way, he wrote in *Experiments of Spiritual Life & Health, and their Preservatives* (1652), if we "beg grace from heaven, that we may use earthly comforts as a stool or ladder, to help us upward to heavenly comforts," profits, pleasures. The true Christian meditates upon his assured spiritual victories, "as the soldier meditates upon the glory of his victories" and "the merchant on his gains." But "in things civil," reiterated Williams, "nothing is lawful but what is according to law and order. Do not all civil men throughout the world forbid all building, planting, merchandising, marrying, execution of justice, yea all actions of peace and war, but by a true and right commission and in a right order?" "Order" as understood by a Puritan English gentleman came before all else in Williams's scheme.

Even Williams's belief in liberty of conscience was sorely taxed when the Quakers invaded Rhode Island and disturbed the sense of order. Their simple religious faith—guidance by an "inner light" and the progressive betterment of all mankind—was too much for his Calvinistic view of man in eternal enmity with his Creator. "The Spirit of their religion," he said, "tends mainly to reduce persons from civility to barbarism." Their usages are worse than those of the Indians. They employ women preachers. They are irreverent to superiors, they refuse to "bend the knee or bare the head, signs of English reverence and civility" from a "horrible . . . pretence that Christ's amity (even in civil) things respecteth no man's person." So Williams felt that a "due and moderate restraint and punishing of these uncivilities (though pretending conscience) is . . . far from persecution (properly so called)." [18]

The Puritan clergy were willing to forgive Williams much after these denunciations of the Quakers. Fortunately Williams's earlier and greater works in behalf of liberty of conscience had gone to feed mightier streams of thought. Perhaps not altogether clear gain was the fact that the notion carried along with it, by virtue of its context, political and economic ideas that bespoke an unmitigated system of order and commerce.

CHAPTER V

Commercial New York

INASMUCH as the Dutch domain of the New Netherland had been originally the possession of the exclusive Dutch joint stock West India company, it had been operated primarily from the standpoint of obtaining profits from the Indian fur trade. The company had complete control of government and trade; self-government was hardly known; but vast grants of a feudal character were made to principal members of the company on the stipulation that they stock their feudatory patroonships with servants. In the commercial center, New Amsterdam, only those possessed of "burgher's rights," obtainable at a fee, could practice a trade.

As elsewhere, there were criticisms of company management, but they came in good part from the spokesmen or possessors of the great patroonships, such as Adrian van der Donck. They demanded more local self-government, freedom from the exactions of the company and its control of trade, and an increased importation of farmers and servants. Each side charged the other with being monopolists and extorting huge gains.

Both sides criticized the small traders. The company authorities attempted to curb "the petty traders who from time to time come over from the Fatherland" and aim solely to "spoil trade and business by underselling." The critics denounced "the petty traders, who swarm hither with great industry, reap immense profit and exhaust the country without adding to its population and security," while in the meantime agriculture is neglected.

The critics demanded free trade in the sense of exporting where they saw fit without the expense of inspection and duties. The company authorities replied that trade was free to those who engaged in it by proper contract and orders with the company.

Some English settlements in the colony sided with the company-appointed director of the colony, Peter Stuyvesant. They wrote to the home authorities in 1651 that frequent changes of government or "the power of electing a governor from ourselves . . . would be our destruction by reason of our factions and the differences of opinion which prevail among us." Such self-government is satisfactory in old countries, for they are "established and settled by long and well experienced laws and fundamentals, . . . best agreeing with the condition of the people." In our infant community composed of different nations many things occur for which there "are no rules or examples" and "consequently must be fixed at discretion by the governor." In this way the community will develop as a "blooming republic." Besides, at present we lack sufficient qualified people to establish the scheme. Every man would do as he sees fit, and the "strongest would swallow up the weakest."

Private individual traders were the oppressors of the people. Therefore the settlements should be allowed to hire vessels in Holland to bring over farmers and laborers, "provided the directors would permit their ships and no other to trade thither." But if the company would import more slaves, it could reap a double profit for itself in duties and cargo, as well as benefit the community.[1]

When it suited their fancy, the company authorities expressed a disapproval of grants of monopoly on the ground that, in a new and budding state, "the population and welfare can only be promoted through general benefits and privileges, in which every one who might be inclined to settle in such a country, either as a merchant or a mechanic, may participate." [2]

The Dutch traders soon learned that the Indians had little appreciation of metallic money. A clergyman tried vainly to explain to an Indian chief the value of the Dutch silver *rixdollar*, but the latter laughed to think that the Dutch should set such a high value on what he termed a piece of iron. The Dutch therefore used wampum, which they introduced throughout New England. The authorities found that, like all money, it was subject to many complexities. They declared that a great deal of "nasty, rough," bad wampum was circulating, while "good, splendid wampum, was out of sight or exported." If this were not prevented, the country would be ruined. So they placed different valuations in terms of Dutch money on the different kinds of wampum.[3] On the pretext of providing an adequate supply of wampum, they on occasion raised its "value." The company critics in 1649 demanded that the "loose," as against the stringed, wampum be prohibited, but the local authorities justified its retention on the ground that there was no coin in circulation, "and the farm laborers and other common people having no other money would be great losers." [4]

In 1664, during the war with the Netherlands, the English seized the province, and Charles II gave it to his brother, the Duke of York, as a proprietary. When the Duke became the sovereign in 1683 it became a royal colony. But for the most part it retained the characteristic features of the Dutch scheme with the Presbyterian Dutch Reformed Church claiming the affection of a good share of the respectable citizenry.

The merits of "orderly trade" were set forth in a continuous controversy on whether or not the making and packing of flour for export should be confined to New York City, as was done previous to the passage by the assembly of the Free Bolting Act in 1695. The learned spokesmen of the city claimed: The manufacture of flour and biscuit in New York City is the chief support of New York trade and keeps up the price of grain for the farmer. It is necessary to confine these operations to one place so that by proper inspection the reputation of the flour can be maintained. This Act violates all sound principles of trade. Through this "libertism of trade and confusion of market the whole Government is reduced to an anarchy, every man doing what seemeth good in his own eyes." Those bolting flour outside of New York City have corrupted it with a mixture of Indian corn that has spoiled its reputation in the valuable West Indies market. As a consequence New York's grain, which used to command the highest prices over grains from other British colonies, has fallen below the others and the colony is deprived of the valuable returns of Spanish money. If the Act is not repealed, the revenue and navigation of the colony will decrease, money will pass to other colonies, the government will be embarrassed by poverty, and all things reduced to confusion even to the dissolution of the province. The greedy farmers are behind the Act. The husbandmen grown rich from the high prices given by the New York merchant for their produce under her old privileges clamor now for the ruin of the city and for every homestead to become a market.

Despite the statement of these petitions, the evidence appears to indicate that the clamor came from other commercial communities, notably Albany.[5]

The Anglican chaplain to the British forces, the Reverend John Miller, reported in 1695 in his *A Description of the Province and City of New York*, that merchandising English goods yields anywhere from 100 to 400 per cent and that anyone who will take pains can have lands enough to gain an easy livelihood. But unfortunately not only the poor and inferior people, but also young merchants, drink and have other vices, so that they and their families starve. The real cause is the absence of a properly organized and sufficient Anglican clergy. The other ministers are "pretended ministers," for, being dependent on their congregations for salaries, they must "delight the fancies of their hearers" instead of "preaching up true religion and a Christian life. . . ." The effective remedy is to send an Anglican bishop. He should also be made governor of the province, to which should be added New Jersey, Connecticut, and Rhode Island. He should come with a small force to subdue Canada and "five or six sober young ministers, with Bibles and prayer books."

New York, unlike New England, could boast no distinguished thinker who typified its ideals and contributed to the stream of development. But in William Penn, of adjoining Pennsylvania, who was the close friend of James, as Duke of York and later as James II, the middle states could hold up their heads with the best that colonial America produced.

CHAPTER VI

William Penn: Feudal Lord and Man of Commerce

WITHOUT much question, the greatest intellectual figure that trod colonial soil in the seventeenth century was the Quaker, William Penn. Actually, Penn spent little time in the New World—altogether less than four years in two visits. But as the outstanding Quaker leader next to George Fox, the founder, he commanded respect among the Quakers in America as well as in the Old World, and Quakers were a powerful force in more colonies than Rhode Island. As proprietor of Pennsylvania, he exercised an important influence on what soon became a leading colony.

Penn was born in 1644 in the midst of the Puritan revolution and grew to manhood as England returned to the old Stuarts. His family had originally been of little account as such things went in England. His mother was a Dutch merchant's daughter. His father had started as a captain of an armored trading vessel, and the civil war gave him the opportunity to rise to the high rank of vice-admiral under Cromwell. The Stuarts, grateful for his assistance in helping in their restoration and for his naval successes, gave him more honors and vast estates in Ireland, profitable offices, and a knighthood.

The role marked out for young Penn by his father was that of man of the court. So in 1660 Penn was sent to Oxford to get the polish proper to a gentleman. As befitted his aristocratic status, he was ranked as "a gentleman commoner." But Penn balked at observance of the Church of England ceremonials required at the two universities. Before two years passed, he was expelled from Oxford. His father thought the customary European tour for "finishing" an aristocrat would cure his son, but young Penn spent four months at Paris acquiring polish and two years at the Huguenot College at Saumer making up deficiencies in his education and deeply studying history and Protestant theology. A year's training in the law at Lincoln's Inn gave him legal knowledge useful not only in managing his father's great Irish estates, but also in defending the Quakers, whose faith he zealously embraced.

The Quakers preached not Calvinism, but the opportunity of every man to be saved provided he is sufficiently humble and obedient to the Lord so that he might follow "the light of Christ within man." Religion is the fear of God and its demonstration good works; and faith the root of both, wrote Penn.[1] The Quakers opposed tithes, a salaried ministry, war, ceremonials, flattering salutations, and demanded "plainness of speech, apparel, furniture." Naturally their tenets for the most part were anathema to the important dissenting sects of the Calvinist persuasion as well as to good Anglicans. The severe penalties of the Parliamentary acts against Nonconformists to the Anglican faith were more sharply enforced against the Quakers.

However, the polity and discipline of the Quakers as laid down and enforced by Penn was as oligarchical, if not more so, than those of the Puritans. The elders controlled, and criticisms of their rule Penn could trace to some weakness in the critics. "Those by whom the Lord has eminently appeared, and who were the first instruments of his several dispensations to the sons of men, have always exercised that authority among the people they have gathered, and have been constantly preserved from falling away, though some . . . have risen against them with the clamour" that they were self-appointed, have departed from the true path and gone beyond their lawful powers. It was never heard of "in the dealings of God with the sons of men, that he varied or changed his ·dispensations in the life time of the instruments of any of them."

"The compliance of a society to such methods of order as the elders thereof have exhorted to, and the generality . . . have embraced," are "expedients of order, and methods of rule about things universally agreed upon." If, instead of viewing these expedients as a discipline for the sake of the young and weak, "you . . . mistake liberty . . . imposition . . . formality . . . the nature and end of things, and the intention of your ancient friends and brethren in them, you will judge carnally and be ready to think as if outward rule, and lordliness were aimed at . . . even whilst our care . . . is . . . in reference to the young, the weak, and such as may be careless and ready to fall asleep. . . . For their sakes, a discipline, as to conversation must be. . . ." [2] In language that every good Puritan could understand, he exclaimed: Liberty "is not to commit sin innocently, . . . but to be freed from sin." In the church, as in the state, each has his place and function.[3] There are diversities of gifts in the church. To everyone a talent is committed, and the usefulness and happiness of each individual depends on his filling the measure of his duty. A good servant, wrote Penn, should be "more tender of his master's honor and interest than of his own profit." Should they be obedient and not neglect their masters' desires and work, they may expect double wages for their work; "to wit, here and hereafter, because a good servant serves God in serving his master." Country-bred servants are superior to those trained in the city because the city kind are proud and conceited; they will not take direction and overrate their qualifications.

So deep was the sense of "order" in Penn that one reason he gave for eliminating flattering titles was that they were certainly unbecoming to common people. "Monsieur, sir, and madame, were originally names given to none but the king, his brothers and their wives, both in France and England, yet now the ploughman in France is called Monsieur, and his wife, madame; and men of ordinary trades in England, sir, and their wives, dame." [4]

Likewise luxurious living, he declared in *An Address to Protestants*, is vicious first of all because it is living beyond one's station; that is, living beyond one's rank or degree and thus confounding "all reasonable distinction and those civil degrees that are amongst people." Of course, luxurious living brings misery and poverty while avoidance of it would increase the wealth of the kingdom by enabling individuals to increase their estates and enlarge their trade.

Were the "generality" content with less luxurious expenditures, according to their rank, the price of labor would fall, manufactures would be cheaper, and a greater market provided. Where now we are the debtors of foreigners, "then they would be debtors to us for our native manufactures." So "the temperance I plead for is not only religiously, but politically good." Should any of the producers of luxuries rendered unemployed be poor, Penn had a solution. Public workhouses would be effectual correctors of all these lazy and lustful distempers with more profit and a better conscience.

Penn, like every Puritan moralist, denounced the evil of accumulating excessive wealth without being very specific as to the limit to be sought. But the most monstrous case of avarice was the person who simply accumulated, spent practically nothing, and refused to give anything for alms to the aged, sick, widow and orphans. Those that loved wealth strongly and spent it liberally in luxurious expenditures were guilty of sin, but this was more commendable, he wrote in *No Cross, no Crown*, than the mere love of money for its own sake; for then expenditure did good to some. The miser by hoarding his money in vaults or placing it in bonds and mortgages was an "enemy of the state," for he spirits their money away, "obstructs the circulation of the blood" of the body politic.

Penn found any number of serious economic evils that must be rectified. As an owner, and especially as an absentee owner, of large Irish estates, he had good reason to deprecate England's treatment of Irish agricultural exports. England, he informed the authorities on one occasion, should remove her prohibition on the import of fat Irish sheep and her heavy duty on the import of Irish wool; instead, she should impose a sufficiently heavy duty on the domestic manufacture of woolens in Ireland so as to bring "the woolen trade of both kingdoms upon a balance abroad." England would thus absorb more Irish sheep; Irish manufacturers would confine themselves to making coarse cloth, while English sheep raisers would profit by the larger market and increased demand for Irish sheep.[5]

The great evil of England was the persecution of dissenters in general and Quakers in particular, for this violates the first and fundamental right of free-born Englishmen, that of the right of property, namely, that "what I possess is *absolutely mine own*." [6] By rendering property rights insecure, persecution endangers the prosperity of England, for trade, "which is the greatness of this kingdom," was primarily in the hands of dissenters.

In times of danger, men "draw in their stock and either transmit it to other banks, or bury their talents at home for security. . . . Either is fatal to a kingdom"; but if mildness prevails, every man being at ease, every man will be at work; and the stock of the kingdom employed, like the blood that hath its due passage, will give life and vigor to every member in the public body.

Stated another way, persecution must ruin the dissenters, and in this case at least one-fourth of the trade and manufactures of the kingdom sinks. If to avoid this, wrote Penn in *A Perswasive to Moderation*, they go with their estates into other governments, "nay, though it were to any of the king's plantations, the numbers were far too great to be spared from home. So much principal stock wanting to turn the yearly traffic, and so many people too, to consume our yearly growth, must issue fatally to the trade one way, and to the lands and rents of the kingdom the other way."

If toleration to dissenters is granted, England instead of losing people will become a haven for persecuted foreigners, who will make her mistress of the arts and manufactures of Europe. Their number will increase the prince's subjects, their labor and consumption, the trade and wealth of his territories. "For what are all conquests, but of people?" And by indulgence it obtains a victory without charge. What is more, compulsory uniformity of religion makes for a poor city, whereas "they become great and *opulent* by the admission of trading hereticks." [7]

Even land and population moved into an inferior category to trade as Penn pleaded the cause of dissenters. The dissenters are equal in "strength and value," though not in numbers to the conformists, for the revenue lies not as of old in "tenures and in lands," but in trade, which is controlled by the dissenters. [8]

Practically any form of government would be acceptable to the "people," so long as the fundamental absolute right of ownership, as he conceived it, was upheld. The doctrine found its most extreme statement in Penn's defense in 1681 of the assertion of the "prerogative" power by his friend Charles II against Parliament. Parliament's demands that the King's Catholic brother be excluded from the succession and restraint be placed on the King's "arbitrary" dissolutions of Parliament, had been met by another dissolution. As England appeared on the verge of another revolution, Penn in an anonymous "impartial" pamphlet calling for "moderation," warned the electorate and the parliamentary leaders that the civil war had been more pernicious than any despotism. Cromwell's "Geneva Republic" had evidenced the tyranny and faction of a commonwealth and all history's lesson that democracy is the worst type of government and leads to despotism. Nothing was as wicked as for a private subject like Cromwell not only to "exalt himself above, but to trample upon all his equals and betters."

To petition continually for the calling of Parliament after the King has shown his dislike of it is uncivil. Monarchs in the past were more direct in upholding their rightful prerogatives and took severe action against any parliamentary interference. The factious Parliament oversteps its powers in demanding the right to determine how long and when it may sit, free of the King's right to dissolve and call. The King represents God; Parliament, the people. "The consultative power by the King's permission is in Parliament, but the commanding power remains inseparable in him; the results and productions of parliaments, at best are but bills, 'tis the King's breath makes them laws; which are till then but dead things. . . . The Lords advise, the Commons consent, but the King ordains"; they mold the bills, but the King makes them laws.

The critics of the King were "either lovers of popular applause" or necessitous and beggarly persons of broken fortunes, extremely in debt. Even if the subject is reduced to extremity under a tyrannical regime, conscience and interest command his obedience. "No plea is sufficient to bar the Lion of his right. If it be no dishonour to submit to a stronger party (though of thieves) when fallen into their hands, then let not the example of a few fools . . . tempt you to oppose your felicity against the Imperative power; under which the disposure of your person doth wholly remain, and therefore madness to deny it words."

To the leaders he cried out: Do not place your faith in the rabble. It is most dangerous to be the pen or mouth of a multitude. Hearken to the words of Machiavelli: "He who builds upon the people, builds upon dirt." The rabble's zeal "is not so soon heated by the real oppressions of their Rulers but may be as easily cooled by the specious promises and breadth of authority." The leader against oppression "adored by the mob one day is torn in pieces by the same the next." [9]

Behind this outburst in support of the Crown lay more than Penn's close friendship with the Stuarts, a friendship that earned for him the title of "Quaker courtier" from enemies. He hoped not only to obtain toleration for Quakers in England, but also to provide a secure home for Quakers in America through his great Colonization Scheme.

Penn had been and continued to be deeply involved in the affairs of New Jersey. The colony had been ceded originally by the Duke of York from his proprietary of New York to a company of royal favorites, but through purchase and the validating of the purchase by the Duke, the Quakers exercised the dominating control. While Penn as one of the leaders possessed large landholdings there, the proprietary right of government of one part of New Jersey, West New Jersey, was vested in one Quaker; and the proprietary right of the other part, East New Jersey, was vested in a company composed of Quakers and others. But Penn was extremely anxious to have a great colony of his own where he could try out a holy experiment in ideal government, and incidentally recoup his declining fortune. Just before the outburst in 1681, Charles II made him the "true and absolute proprietor" of soil and government of the great domain to be called Pennsylvania in honor of Penn's father, and not long afterwards the Duke from his holdings ceded to him the adjoining territory which later became Delaware.

The King stated in the charter that he granted Pennsylvania to enlarge the empire, "to promote such useful commodities as may be of benefit to us and our dominions, as also to reduce the savage natives . . . to the love of civil society and Christian religion." But Penn claimed he was given Pennsylvania as payment of a £16,000 debt owed by the King to his father for provisioning the Navy.

New Jersey had already given Penn experience in preparing alluring descriptions for prospective investors and laborers. Now he had a greater field for such talents. One great objection he had to meet was the ever-growing complaint of English economists and statesmen that colonies were causing a decline in England's wealth by draining it of people. Penn himself had used the argument before, and he used it again later when declaiming against the economic evils of the persecution of dissenters; but he found no difficulty on this occasion in "proving" that colonies increased the population of the mother country. Colonies, he informed prospective "adventurers," are the seed of nations begun and nourished by the care of wise and populous countries as the means of increasing the human stock and benefiting commerce. The cause of "the decay of people and wealth" is not the plantations but the luxury and corruption of manners. The

ancient discipline of husbandry, virtue, and industry is no longer rewarded, consequently population declines. In the olden days gentry
and nobility remained on their lands, rents were easy, and under their
masters' favor the servants married early and population increased.
But now the Lords live in towns and the servants they draw either
do not marry or, if they do, pine away their small gains in a petty
shop for, being so many, they prey on one another. What is worse,
the state of affairs gives the lazy an occasion to turn beggars. The
remedy is a vigorous execution of our laws against corruption of
manners. But, in any event, colonies are not to blame for England's
decline in population. Instead they contribute to the greatness of
England by increasing her trade as well as the King's revenue.[10]

The emigrants are worth more to England in the plantations than
at home, for the fertility of the soil and the type of commodities—
sugar, tobacco, etc.—yield a higher value than they could have produced at home. The product comes home and is paid for by English
growth and manufacture. Those unable to marry here can easily do
so there, and the increase further increases the market for English
goods. Should one of these formerly poor return to England with
his wealth, he is able to "buy out twenty of what he was when he
went over." Furthermore, the plantations employ much shipping and
thereby increase the wealth of England by supplying activity as well
to all the subsidiary trades and merchants involved. Finally, consider
how many thousands of blacks and Indians are accommodated with
clothes, tools, utensils from England and their labor brought to England and thus added to England's wealth and people.

Penn issued further literature on this subject and arranged for trans-
lations to be distributed on the European continent. The propaganda for colonization—that is, for investment and labor—was carried on all over Europe on a scale never before equaled. The familiar
arguments were presented but with some new variations. "The poor
are the hands and feet of the rich," he wrote. Their labor improves
countries. So that many poor may be transported to the profit
of the "rich that help them," Penn presented the great benefits of indentured servitude and similar devices not only to the laborers but
also to capitalists. No one complains of the labor of clearing land,
but desires more hands for the greater profit to plant what they have
already cleared. Artisans' wages are extraordinary, and the same may
be said for day laborers until the country shall be more developed.

Wages are three times those in England, wrote one of the later pamphleteers, Gabriel Thomas. The wages of servants are high because of the great fertility of the land and profitable price for the products, the little cost of the land and the cheapness of provisions. If wages were not high, laborers would themselves take land. Women's wages are high because they marry early and demand servants.[11]

But while the propaganda mill ground out seemingly endless literature, the actions of Penn and his fellow Quaker leaders soon showed that they held to traditional notions as regards labor and the need for a better discipline to encourage industry and frugality.[12] During Penn's first stay, 1682–1684, the council approved measures empowering the justice of each county court to set the wages of workmen and servants "at a just rate." [13] During his second stay, 1699–1701, a law against "clandestine marriages" was passed, "that people might not be deprived of their children or servants without consent." The Anglican clergy now raised the charge of infringement of religious and personal liberty. They argued that by their "oath of canonical obedience" they had to marry any couple requesting it, provided they be not too close of blood, above twenty-one, and thrice asked. Penn replied that, not only did the law strengthen their oath, but according to "American good sense . . . bound servants are minors and are not of age to marry without manifest injustice to their masters" unless they consent. "Servants are the best leg America has to stand upon." It is "an ill consequence to plead conscience against the security of property, and such are servants." Penn sought the co-operation of governors of other colonies to establish a uniform law regarding "run-away servants and debtors" who shift not of poverty but knavery.[14]

Penn and the Quakers accepted the institution of slavery. He felt that slaves might be more desirable than other servants because then "a man has them while they live." [15] However, a sharp protest against slavery came from the Dutch Quaker settlement of Germantown, headed by Penn's friend Francis Daniel Pastorius, who had been trained in German universities. He and his group sent a petition to the Quakers' monthly meeting in 1688 demanding freedom for the blacks. Slavery violates Christianity and constitutes dealing in stolen goods. Liberty of body must accompany liberty of conscience. Europe has heard reports that the Quakers deal in men as in cattle, and many have been dissuaded from coming. The petition was carried eventually through the hierarchy of meetings to the "yearly" meeting, which forbore judgment on the ground that the case had "so General a Relation to many other Parts." [16]

Penn recognized chartered companies with monopoly rights as useful for many purposes. So at the start he chartered the "Free Society of Traders," a joint stock company with a capital stock of £10,000. It was given 20,000 acres to be erected into a manor and was to enjoy all "services incident to the said tenure." Its members had certain exemptions from the jurisdiction of the colony courts and from the payment of various fees. It planned to go into almost every branch of industry, from the fur trade to manufacturing.

The prospectus for the sale of shares stated: "It is a very unusual society, for it is an absolute free one, and in a free country, a society without oppression, wherein all may be concerned that will, and yet have the same liberty of private traffic as though there were no society at all"; so that it promotes both public and private good. "It is no small convenience and ease to . . . planters (happily unacquainted in trade) that they may have some part of their estates improving in a united way and care, whilst they thereby may with less distraction, and more freedom . . . apply themselves to their particular plantations, for here a few hands do the work of the whole." This union of traffic prevents destructive emulation. "The profit must be greater and surer and navigation, manufacture, and arts better improved, than by force of private and divided stocks." As a permanent concern, it is the friend of the widow and orphan.[17]

Complaints were made soon enough that monopoly was written in the charter, and the enterprise eventually proved a failure.

Penn thought that one way the colony might supply his "proper maintenance" would be for the colony to grant him the Indian trade, but his agent, James Logan, wrote him that the merchants would not countenance this.[18]

Penn had his hands full defending the colony before the home authorities on charges of encouraging piracy and violating the Navigation and Trade Acts, while at the same time he was castigating the colonial authorities for these violations. He informed the home authorities that piracy had been wiped out; besides, all the money the pirates brought into the province, England received "to make up the returns due . . . upon trade." [19]

The rigorous enforcement of the Navigation Acts, he informed the home authorities, by discouraging the industry of the people would destroy trade, and trade alone makes America valuable to

England. With trade crushed, the people would be compelled to become only "planters, or farmers endeavouring a self-subsistence." Thus would come to an end the value of the colony to the Crown.[20] If trade were allowed with the Spanish possessions, as was done during war periods, England would be the gainer, for trade is merely an indirect means of obtaining goods, especially money, and of paying for English goods. For want of returns to England, Pennsylvania and all the other colonies will lose all their money to England. While this flow of money and not goods might be a condition that England would like, it would meet opposition from the colonies and was not for the good of England; for the colonies, lacking coin to circulate among themselves, must dwindle in trade.

Penn felt that free trade would not be enough to relieve the scarcity. In addition, the British market for timber should be reserved to the colonies by placing an impost on "foreign" timber. Also a mint to coin small coins of silver should be allowed in the colonies, preferably in New York.[21] But he sharply criticized the colonial practice of overvaluing English and foreign money, and in particular he was incensed at the Pennsylvania legislature's fixing a rate higher than that of the other colonies. The local assembly had justified such overvaluation as the means of preventing the exportation and encouraging the importation of money in order to promote trade and ease the people. Penn argued that he himself did not suffer by the overvaluation because his quit rents were payable in sterling or wheat at a fixed price, but it was bad economics.[22] The practice, he said, could not achieve the end desired by the colony, increasing the supply of money. Instead they merely cheated themselves.[23] In his ideas of overvaluation Penn was at odds with his colonial agent, the equally conservative aristocratic James Logan, who sympathized with the practice.[24]

Penn's antipathy to overvaluation was so strong that he even used it in his *A Perswasive to Moderation* to illustrate the foolishness of the Church of England in attempting to force all to obey its principles. "To overvalue coin . . . beggars any country; and to own them for sons she never begat, debases and destroys any church." As a remedy, Penn proposed that the Crown establish once and for all a uniform valuation for foreign coins in all the colonies.

While Penn and the colonials agreed that there was a scarcity of money and lack of returns, the propaganda literature told a different story. Pastorius, in *A Particular Geographical Description of the*

Lately Discovered Province of Pennsylvania, prepared for the home folk in Germany in 1700, declared: At first the settlers were forced to obtain provisions from the Jerseys for money at high prices, but now have a surplus that is marketed in the West Indies. To prevent the draining away of money, he continued, the colonists are developing woolen and linen manufactures, and established fairs where people can barter and trade.

Again while Penn and the Quaker colonial leaders pleaded for free trade, they were not adverse to local legislation aimed at "unprofitable trade",with neighboring colonies. Thus the legislature complained in 1701 that the import of cattle from East New Jersey to supply Philadelphia drained the colony's coin and was bad for its "self-subsistency." It passed a series of acts ordering the landholders to raise sheep and regulating the slaughter and sale of cattle.[25]

All the while near-by proprietary Maryland was passing acts ostensibly to prevent Pennsylvania traders from draining the colony of coin. Thus, in 1694, the Maryland Assembly declared that Maryland's specie was being drained to Pennsylvania to "purchase beer, rum and other liquors to the great discouragement of husbandry" in Maryland. So it placed an extra duty on beer and rum imported by land from Pennsylvania.[26]

Penn was always in danger of losing his proprietary right. On the overthrow of his friend James II, his rights to the government but not to the soil were temporarily suspended. Penn protested: "I am an Englishman and that country and government of it inseparably my property, dearly purchased every way and much indebted to me and my children yet." It is the support of my family.[27]

Penn's rights were restored, but at the turn of the century the English authorities were intent on eliminating all proprietary and corporate colonies. That proprietary colonies are more profitable and civilized than royal ones, Penn pointed out, is evidenced by the fact that they all have larger towns than the royal ones, and towns are the centers of education and traffic. Seizing the proprietary rights of government is violating the sacred right of property. "The power [to govern] is as much our property as the soil. . . . Without it the soil is but as the ring without the stone; that worth twenty shillings, this worth one hundred pounds." [28]

At the same time Penn had to defend his "property" rights against the "people" of the colony, more accurately, resident Quaker leaders. He had devised any number of sets of irrevocable fundamental laws for the colony, based on Locke's model for South Carolina, but the upshot had been in the end a colonial assembly chosen by the substantial freeholders as the freemen. Penn when resident, and his deputy governor in his absence, ostensibly had a veto power over any legislation; but the Quaker leaders of substance in the legislature refused to recognize such a power. They had been brought up in the discipline of "order" of the Quaker faith, but they saw no reason to view Penn as their superior. The lesson that he constantly preached in behalf of toleration in England—namely, that liberty and property are the fundamental rights of Englishmen—was turned by them against any "interference" by Penn in colonial affairs.

Penn complained that his lands were being occupied, that quit rents were refused or in arrears, that the legislature refused to take care that he receive a reasonable return on his huge investment, that it failed to provide him with a suitable income for his position whether at home or in the colony. Even in Philadelphia he had been forced, he said, to live too simply, with only a nurse, three maids, and three or four men for himself, wife, and child.[29] He complained that they had given him more than sufficient cause to revoke his grant of government to them. His critical fellow Quakers in the legislature and at large "were a rude and base people." They had that "excess of vanity" that comes from having got out of the crowd in which they were lost in England. "Upon every little eminency there" in Pennsylvania they "think nothing taller than themselves but the trees, as if there were no after superior judgment to which they should be accountable." These sturdies should be obliged to take turns in visiting England, "that they might lose themselves again amongst the crowds of so much more considerable people at the custom-house, exchange, and West Minster Hall." They would thus be "humbled and made more pliable." But "with the distance and scarcity of mankind there, they opine too much."[30]

The Quaker leaders—the "people"—in turn accused Penn of being an oppressor, interested in fleecing the country and destroying their liberty and property in order to satisfy his greedy desire for exorbitant gain.

Financially embarrassed and fed up with the chronic "highly disaffected character" of the people and assembly, Penn offered to sell to the Crown his right to the government for a "great sum of money" and be satisfied merely "with the rights of landlord and lord of the manor of the country."[31] In the bargaining between the parties as to the pecuniary worth of the colony, Penn reduced his price, but the deal was never consummated. Instead, the proprietary government became a flaming political and economic issue in the colony.

Penn, like all thinkers moving in the world of action, was a complex figure. He loved best to view himself as a kindly feudal lord living on his estate and supervising his tenants for their welfare. So the agricultural life of the country with its due order and subordination became for him the one true life; commerce and cities were to be avoided, he wrote in *Some Fruits of Solitude*, as the source of disorder and greed.

But actually living in the country on an estate was for Penn something he always looked forward to in his retirement. It was an unrealized dream rather than something he actively practiced. Only by conceiving of England or Pennsylvania as a vast estate did the ideal acquire some reality for him.

As a cultured and learned man of the world, with vast interests at stake in his church and in his own financial affairs, Penn found London far more inviting than his Irish estate or the wilds of Pennsylvania. Moreover, as a seventeenth-century English gentleman as well as an active trader in his own right he knew that cities were the center of commerce, and therefore of national wealth and power.

Needless to say, Penn quickly established a town, Philadelphia, to be the great trading center of his province. He managed to reconcile his sentimental love of rural life by expressing the hope, in the advertisement for prospective investors in Pennsylvania real estate, that it would always remain a spacious "green country town." [32]

But Penn's working theory as to what the future should be was best stated in his being "overjoyed" to hear in 1685 that his close friend and adviser, Sir William Petty, the economist, had predicted that the earth and Pennsylvania would be fully peopled in 124 years. Penn desired, wrote a mutual friend to Petty, that it might not be contradicted.[33]

Of course, with this increase of population, as Petty and all economists taught, came lower wages and rise in lands to their "intrinsic value," as indicated by the most fertile English and Irish lands. By recourse to the vague doctrine that the good man should always avoid excessive wealth, Penn easily found that occupations making for the accumulation of wealth were to be viewed as necessary evils, not as devices of the devil.

If anything, Penn was more insistent on the sanctity of property rights than were the Puritans. The right of property remained the fundamental human right. "What civil right, hath any man in government besides property, at least without it?" exclaimed Penn.[34] But that right became rather elusive in Penn's hands. He used it in the famous Penn-Mead trial in 1670 to establish the great principle that a judge must not dictate the verdict to a jury, for trial by jury is the protection of a man against unlawful invasion of his property rights, including his right to life and liberty. But Penn believed that on the same level stood the sanctity of an individual or company's proprietary right of government.

There was no question for which Penn could not find an answer in his blend of the ideal of "ordered" property and trade. His loyal friend Pastorius moaned:

> "War begets Poverty, Poverty Peace
> Then People will traffic & Riches increase
> Riches produceth Pride, Pride is War's ground
> War begets Poverty, So we go round." [35]

But the resourceful Penn saw a way out of the dilemma. He wrote in *An Essay towards the Present and Future Peace of Europe:* Peace makes "our trade . . . free and safe. . . . The rich bring out their hoards, and employ the poor manufacturers; buildings and divers projections for profit and pleasure go on; it excites industry, which brings wealth, as that gives the means of charity and hospitality."

The aristocratic Quaker never forgot that the national welfare was based on the animation of trade and commerce through the increased flow of money as the measure of trade.[36]

The problem of increasing the money supply received an answer in the closing decades and constituted a unique development in monetary literature—namely, the introduction of paper money.

CHAPTER VII

Monetary Reformers

PROPOSALS for paper money were advanced by conservative and highly respectable leaders in the political and economic life of the colonies. The writers were mostly English born and trained. They were influenced by English monetary ideas, but they developed these ideas along lines they thought accorded with their adventures and speculations as well as the general good of the colonies.

The first scheme that appeared in print was that of the Reverend John Woodbridge. He was trained for the ministry at Oxford but refused to take the oath of conformity and came to Massachusetts in 1634. By marrying a daughter of Governor Thomas Dudley, he became related to the leading families. He soon acquired extensive landholdings, was appointed to minor judicial offices, and was even elected deputy to the General Court from Newbury. In 1643 his financial fortunes seemed none too good, for he began schoolteaching in Boston, and later, in 1645, was ordained pastor of the church at Andover. With the Puritans dominating England, Woodbridge returned to the mother country and took over important pulpits. But, losing his lucrative posts on the restoration of the Stuarts, he returned to Massachusetts, where he became assistant to his uncle in the Newbury church. However, a decade later he was forced to resign from his ministry because of opposition of the congregation, who declared that Woodbridge was an "intruder" and had been brought in by artifice. He returned to civic and economic pursuits, and the "remarkable blessing of God upon his own private estate," wrote Cotton Mather, more than repaid the public stipend that he had been forced to give up as a minister.[1]

While in the ministry, Woodbridge had developed his ideas on banking and even put them into practice in a tentative way. In England, according to his account, he had discussed with his "intimate friend" William Potter the latter's scheme for relieving the lack of a sufficient medium for commercial transactions. Potter's scheme, elaborated in 1650 in his *The Key of Wealth*, was a bank to furnish credit based on personal credit, "by a considerable number of able men engaging," or upon the depositing of goods.

In the course of his discussion with Potter, Woodbridge said, he developed his own ideas of a bank based on land. When he returned to New England and saw the distress due to lack of an adequate medium for commerce, he imparted his scheme to a public-spirited merchant. The council became interested, and a merchant "well read in the nature of banks," on being asked about the scheme by a magistrate, said in support that banks founded on hard money are threatened with the danger of a break, but not those based on land. Finally, with the aid of some enthusiasts, he began to issue bills, and in six months "a considerable number espoused the design." In order to show the "safety and benefit to all prudent and unprejudiced men," he consented in 1682 to publish the scheme under the title, *Severals relating to the Fund*.

Money, he declared, is the medium which answers all things. When it is plentiful no buyer is bound to one person or market. He is not forced to purchase credit at the grantor's price or compelled to become the servant to the lender. Money quickens trade, increases manufactures and farming, promotes settlement in new areas, lowers interest, and raises the price of land. It eliminates the iniquities, higgling, and vexations of barter and encourages heartless idlers to work. But where coin is scarce, business is in depression, indebtedness increases, payments are slow, extortion prevails, litigation increases, and merchants and shopkeepers are forced to undersell.

A specie money unfortunately derives its "esteem" not from use, but from its "intrinsic value." This is not essential for the purpose of money, which is merely to "procure what one wants, that another abounds with." A specie money is subject to serious inconveniences: the danger of fire, robberies, mistakes, and especially of being "covetously hoarded up." On the other hand, a fund or deposit in land could be established instead as the basis of "credit" to perform the functions of money. That is, a "company" such as he had already started would give individuals credit on the security of mortgages, and this credit would be passed among the members or any willing to agree to the scheme, by "book entries" and "bank bills" in the adjustment of accounts.

Unfortunately little is known of the scheme in actual practice, except that the "fund" was in existence for a time and that such prominent men as Winthrop's grandson, Adam Winthrop, were involved in it. That Woodbridge was not considered unorthodox was evidenced by the facts that he was chosen an assistant in the following two years, and he temporarily occupied a pastorate again during the incumbent's illness in 1684.

The movement for a bank continued. The next public statement came in 1685 from Thomas Budd, a prominent Quaker merchant, landowner, and political figure of West New Jersey and Pennsylvania. Budd, like Woodbridge, was English born and was continually shuttling between England and America. While carrying on his business ventures, he engaged in theological controversy with his fellow Quakers. In fact, most of his published writings were on theology. Early in the 1690's he joined George Keith in criticizing the "looseness" of the original Quaker faith, was eventually read out of the faith and fined for calling a Quaker magistrate an "impudent, presumptuous and insolent man." Finally he joined the Baptists and preached among them.[2]

In the meantime, in 1685, he published a promotional pamphlet, *Good Order Established in Pennsilvania & New-Jersey.* Basing his work on Andrew Yarranton's *England's Improvement by Sea and Land* (1677), he sketched a comprehensive program for the development of agriculture, manufacture, and commerce. The labor supply would be provided in good part by the importation of indentured servants and the employment of children as part of their education. Central to the program were a number of related schemes for establishing "a Bank of Monies and Credit." The legislature would first fix the rate of interest at 8 per cent. Then all bills and bonds would be entered on a "public registry" and be transferable by assignment. Consequently a bill or bond would become in effect a bill of exchange, and one "bond or bill would go through twenty hands, and thereby be as ready monies" for the benefit of trade.

At the same time all lands and houses should also be entered on a public register with an account of their value and how occupied and tenanted. Then a borrower could obtain a loan of approximately two-thirds of the value of the property. Such an "Anchorage, Fund, and Foundation," he said, "will then bring out the moneys unimployed . . . in these Provinces, even People of all degrees will put in their moneys, which will be put out again into Trade to Merchants."

Public storehouses of flax, linen, and hemp and granaries for corn should be established. The owner of the deposited commodities would receive transferable bills from the storehouse keeper specifying the quantity, quality, and value. Until used to claim the deposited goods, these notes would pass from hand to hand and facilitate the exchange of goods between farmers, manufacturers, and merchants without the use of money.

The banking proposals were rather vague because they appear to have been set forth to show the prospective investor, tenants, and servants that the great future of America need not be obstructed by a lack of specie. No wonder Penn wrote enthusiastically from England that the "book is universally liked as to American matters." [3]

Penn, too, was deeply interested in a bank of credit and knew that his friend Petty in his "General Cautions Concerning Pennsylvania," doubtless written for Penn's benefit, already had stated: "Decline the use of gold and silver for money, but use small brass pieces [copper tokens], printed parchment and bank books." [4]

JOHN BLACKWELL: PURITAN THEORIST

And just at that time, in Boston, began appearing concrete proposals for a bank of credit from a man with the right background and speculative temperament for such ventures—Captain John Blackwell, Jr. His career covered England, Ireland, New England, and Pennsylvania, and included a variety of occupations, from military adventure and administration to land speculation and promotion of currency schemes. His father was a man of such substance and social position as to be a "gentleman of the Board of Green-cloth," the Treasury to Charles I. Both father and son, however, supported Parliament from the start of the civil war.

Young Blackwell became one of Cromwell's most ardent followers. With his leader he embraced the cause of the "Independent," or Congregational Church. He earned a good military reputation on the field, especially as a disciplinarian in the "new model" army. He early showed talents as a first-rate publicist with the publication in 1645 of his letter to his father called *A More Exact Relation of the Great Defeat Given to Gorings Army in the West*. At the same time he apparently showed great talent in finance, for he was made a treasurer of war and a receiver general of assessments.

Blackwell's duties kept him mostly in Ireland during the rule of Cromwell and his son, but this sphere of operations promised him handsome financial returns, especially through certain old investments. Originally, in 1641, Parliament had set out to suppress the Irish rebellion by turning over the whole matter to what constituted in effect a joint stock company of contributors or adventurers. These would not only raise the funds but also supply the military force. The adventurers were to be repaid in lands confiscated from the estates of the rebels. The force raised was used instead by Parliament in the English civil war that broke out shortly afterward. But the claims of the adventurers remained outstanding, and with Cromwell's conquest of Ireland the adventurers received handsome land dividends. Blackwell's father was one of the Committee of Adventurers which sat in London and made the regulations regarding the allotments in different baronies in Ireland.

Through "assignment" from original adventurers, Blackwell too became an adventurer to the amount of around £2700 and received lands estimated later by a Crown official to be worth £80,000.[5] Of course, with officers and men being paid their arrears in pay in debentures redeemable in confiscated land, Blackwell came in for additional substantial amounts of real estate.

His enterprises were by no means confined to Ireland. In 1650 he was one of the twenty-six patentees who were given the Bahamas by Parliament.[6] By 1656 he was sufficiently prominent to be sent to the House of Commons from Surrey County, England.

But with the restoration of the Stuarts in 1660, Blackwell lost his government offices and most of his lands. However, he managed to retain some of his wealth by the use of a familiar device—namely, "assigning" his grants to a person sufficiently powerful or friendly with the Stuarts—the Irish Lord Kingston.

For a while Blackwell was even threatened with execution for regicide on the ground that he built the scaffold for the beheading of Charles I. But he was able, or at least powerful friends were able, to convince the Crown authorities that he had nothing to do with the matter except as treasurer to pay the expense of building the structure. Lord Kingston, who owed Blackwell a considerable sum, vouched to the Crown on the occasion of a somewhat similar danger to Blackwell some years later: "He has not been criminal since the King's restoration, and is, I know, penitent for what he did before." Blackwell acquired a reputation with landlords both in Ireland and England of being a good appraiser of land values and an excellent manager of estates with recalcitrant tenants.[7]

In 1685 Blackwell came to Boston, commissioned by some English and Irish dissenters ostensibly "to inquire if they may be welcome there and may reasonably expect that liberty they promise themselves and others"; that is, a township under their own immediate jurisdiction.

Blackwell was welcomed. He was known to good Puritans to be "a gentleman of much piety and worth." He was a distinguished Cromwellian. In addition, he had taken as his second wife a daughter of one of Cromwell's generals, John Lambert. So well was he thought of that he barely failed of being chosen an assistant when he had been in the colony hardly a year. The General Courts of Massachusetts and Connecticut both made extensive land grants to him, and he became involved in large land transactions in the other New England colonies.

What was more, despite the fact that Massachusetts' charter had been revoked and a Crown-appointed council with a president was given all executive, judicial, and legislative functions in 1685, Blackwell remained on excellent terms with the authorities. In fact, under the wider jurisdiction of the council as the council of the Dominion of New England, Blackwell took advantage of new opportunities to obtain extensive land grants in behalf of himself and "divers others his Majesty's loyal subjects in England as well as in this . . . dominion." [8] He was even given important judicial and administrative posts. That this man, with his Cromwellian past as a "violent commonwealth's man," should be "consulted with in all public affairs" by the government, was, to the Crown-appointed secretary of the council, evidence that "the Independent faction prevails" and a general governor must be immediately sent from England to save New England for the Crown. A governor came late in 1686, but Blackwell was by no means out of favor. On the contrary, he was bringing to fruition, with the support of the council, his scheme for a land bank.

Behind this scheme, besides Blackwell, were the leading figures in the colony's business and political circles. They included Joseph Dudley, who was Woodbridge's brother-in-law and then leading member of the council; John Saffin, the defender of slavery; Adam Winthrop; and another grandson of John Winthrop, Wait Winthrop.

According to the account Blackwell and his associates presented at the time, the council considered the "present scarcity of coin as the cause of the great decay of trade, obstructions to manufactures and commerce in this country." They listened in 1686 to the proposal presented by Blackwell on "behalf of himself and others, his participants, as well in England as in this country," for a "bank of credit,

Lombard and Exchange of moneys by Persons of approved integrity and prudence and estates in this country." They referred the scheme to a committee of divers eminent and worthy persons, "merchants and others," and the committee reported that it would conduce "to the encouraging of trade, navigation, manufactures, planting and improving of lands and estates, increasing his Majesty's revenues, facilitating the payment thereof and of other debts, and removing the present greatest obstructions thereto."

The council accepted the report. It declared that the scheme was a "public and useful invention." The "countenance of his Majesty's authority, respect and assistance" was promised and the government engaged "not to molest, hinder, or interrupt the said bank or managers thereof in any of their lawful doings therein according to the said constitution." It was even proposed that its notes be legal tender. They were "to be esteemed as current moneys and payments as well as for his Majesty's Revenue, by the Treasurer and Receivers thereof as any other occasion for moneys whatsoever in common trade and dealings." Under the scheme an elaborate system of offices was set up and there was even a provision for an agent at the Court of England. The elaborate scheme, in fact, seemed to fit London better than the small town of Boston. The expected profits were to be divided into 112 parts, 100 of which were known and were to be received by the officers who were, of course, the promoters. The other parts were to be paid to unrevealed "friends to the bank." As regards these beneficiaries, Dudley thought that "further speech about the matter" was not convenient until a "very good and large dividend of profit" was made.[9]

Blackwell got ready for publication a prospectus of the scheme for public support, under the title *A Discourse in Explanation of the Bank of Credit*. There is a scarcity of money throughout the world to meet the increased trade, he wrote. Since money is merely a measure of value to remove the inconvenience of barter, there is no reason why bank notes properly secured could not perform its functions.

The foundation of the bank will not be specie, which the country lacks, but "real and substantial lands and goods of unquestionable title and value (which this country hath)." This bank therefore will be a bank of credit, not a bank of moneys.

Each of the partners is to deposit moneys and other estates in the bank as a stock or fund for further security of the undertaking. To achieve the circulation of the notes, "a considerable number of persons, some of each trade, calling and condition (especially in the principal places of trading in this country) agree voluntarily to receive as ready moneys, of and from each other and any persons in their ordinary dealings, bank-bills of credit," signed by the partners. The bills would be issued against land mortgages and staple unperishable goods and merchandise, to one-half or two-thirds of the value of the mortgage and goods deposited, and an interest rate of 4 per cent instead of the legal rate of 8 per cent would be paid.

These bills need not be convertible into specie because their advantage and convenience over specie are such that they will command a premium over specie. Bank bills are superior to specie because of their "ease of counting and carriage" and their "safety in travelling or hoarding up." Of course, with the guarantee of the company, the notes are better than the notes of individuals.

By this scheme "the trade and wealth of this country is established upon its own foundation, and upon a medium or balance arising within itself": viz., its lands and products, and not be dependent on specie which may be withheld, prohibited, or enhanced "at the pleasure of foreign nations."

The bank, by converting men's estates and goods into purchasing power, will stimulate and quicken all economic activities. Production will be increased; oppression and extortion of prices will cease; fishing and navigation will develop. The great beneficiaries, he wrote, will be landowners. The value of lands and rents will naturally rise because of the lowering of interest rates and "the plenty of money or what is a valuable credit equivalent thereto," the bank notes. Merchandising and trade will be increased and quickened. The banks will facilitate the better sale of goods, since the "storehouse" or places of deposit will serve as ever-open markets. Manufacturers can therefore buy materials advantageously, while abundant working capital will be provided by credit. With the resulting increase in manufacturing, exports will increase and thereby give rise to a "return of bullion, moneys or other useful goods." The development of manufacturing along with the other industrial developments will afford a comfortable subsistence to many ingenious and industrious persons at present without employment; and this will draw more inhabitants and planters. By providing for employing the poor in mining and manufacture and other economic activities, it enables the poor to buy necessaries and pay debts. This helps "the consumption of, as well our own manufactures as other imported goods and merchandise." This in turn helps to "civilize the ruder sort of people, and encourages others to follow their example in industry and civility." Thus all sorts of persons become enabled to live handsomely and out of debt.

The payment of all public taxes is facilitated, and naturally the great development will yield to the Crown increased revenues. None of these multifarious advantages, of course, can be expected from that small pittance of cash that must ever be the maximum in the country, unless assisted by the aid of the bank. Thus, the less need there is of money by such current credit, "the more will be the increase of money itself, as is manifest in Holland, Venice and all places where Bank credit supplies those species."

Of course, when it came to financing the poor directly, through small loans to the poor in the form of pawnshops, the *mons pietatis*, as advocated by Malynes, Blackwell shied away. There is no such necessity for them in this country as in others. The country has so few poor people that, given the bank credit, not only can they be fully employed, but more can be provided for at such "moderate wages as would enable them to live comfortably without exposing their employers to like poverty with themselves."

But the prospectus, it seems, was never printed. Though Blackwell had gotten together the necessary equipment, including a rolling press and plates and had bills printed, his associates refused to continue with the scheme, doubtless in part because of the fear that the council had no legal right to authorize a company.

Blackwell was naturally annoyed and in July 1688 complained of the funds he had expended, but he was willing to cancel the articles of agreement. He hoped in that case that his associates would let him have the rolling press and plates, which "will do nobody else good, and possibly may never do me any."

Blackwell was not dismayed. He removed from the manuscript all direct references that it was intended to promote a Boston institution, polished it up, and had it published anonymously in England the same year under the title *A Model for Erecting a Bank of Credit: with a Discourse in Explanation Thereof.* But where the original subtitle referred to a bank for Boston, the subtitle now was *Adapted to the Use of any Trading Countrey, where there is a Scarcity of Moneys: More Especially for his Majesties Plantations in America.*

Of course certain original statements in favor of the bank as a Boston institution had to be adjusted. What may explain in part the breakdown of the Boston plan was the reference to the objection that it must have the "public approbation" or sanction of the authority of a country. Blackwell answered that this part of the "merchant's calling is in every respect, as free and lawful for any to undertake, and needs no more of public encouragement or countenance than that part of buying and selling . . . with or for ready money, time, or barter which they better understand and practice. And the managers . . . may as well expect a benefit by it as the others," for it takes up a considerable time, improves the trade of any country, and has its risks.

There was, however, one significant addition to the manuscript. In the printed pamphlet there was an appendix which the evidence indicates Blackwell had printed in New England and then had added to the sheets of his London publication.[10] This supplement was devoted to denouncing the other and more familiar proposal for relieving the scarcity of money—namely, raising the value of coins. This proposal had in the meantime won out in Massachusetts. The royal governor, Sir Edmund Andros, had been forced in 1687 to let the "pine-tree shillings" as well as the Spanish pieces to pass at the old overvalued rate rather than according to weight. This measure doubtless also played a part in the breakdown of the Boston bank scheme.

In the appendix Blackwell appealed to the King for his own benefit and the benefit of the colonies not to allow this overvaluing, especially in Massachusetts, but to force all the coin to pass at valuations of English money in accordance with their weight. He explained that the overvaluation leads to the confusion of world trade. It is unjust to all classes receiving fixed income, rents, or any form of long-term contractual income because it raises prices. Finally, since, like any "debasement," it compels a general all-round rise in prices, it will not relieve the money shortage, he explained both in the main text as well as in the supplement, because the scarcity is caused by an unfavorable balance of trade which drains the country of its specie. In the earlier manuscript he had given the balance of trade as only one cause, but at that time apparently the authorities had not yet agreed to the overvaluation measure.

The remedy was simple. His bank, through supplying a necessary proportion of credit for trade as good as money, would encourage the growth of manufacture and the like. The exports would then exceed the imports, and of course specie would flow in. In this connection he was willing to allow the colonies to pass sumptuary and trading laws for balancing "the importations of such commodities as are most useful, with the exportations of manufactures and products of the country that may be best spared, after the utmost improvement made of them."

Blackwell's views on overvaluation did not conflict with those of Andros and with English opinion as well, especially Penn's. What was more, Blackwell had dedicated the treatise to Penn, so he told Penn a year later. The publisher or those who managed the affair for Blackwell in England apparently thought it best to omit the dedication because James II was being driven into exile and Penn, as a supporter of James, was in bad repute.

In the meanwhile, Penn made Blackwell, who was a kinsman, his deputy governor in Pennsylvania. True, Penn had not long ago denounced the Cromwellians in general, and he had referred in particular to Blackwell's father-in-law as "Lambert and his levelling party," but these outbursts were after all for the occasion and were never intended to interfere with his business ventures.

Penn explained to influential Quaker leaders that he had not appointed a Quaker but a stranger "that he might be impartial and more reverenced: Blackwell is in England and Ireland of great repute for ability, integrity and virtue." What is more, he is experienced and has formerly commanded men. "I have a rough people to deal with about my quit rents," and with his "talent to regulate and set things in method," he will be just the right man for the job.[11]

The problem of a bank soon came before him. A group including Budd and two members of the council in February 1689 presented a petition to Blackwell and the council of "their design in setting up a bank for money, etc. and requesting encouragement from the governor and council for their proceeding therein." Blackwell told them that he had proposed something of this nature and dedicated it to the governor "some months since, out of New England, to which he believed he should receive his answer by the first shipping hither out of England." Blackwell thought there might be one serious objection to what appears to have been one of the petitioners' proposals— namely, to give their personal bills to such as would take them as money to pay, as merchants usually did bills of exchange." It might be suspected that "such as usually clipped or coined money would be apt to counterfeit their bills, unless more than ordinary care were taken to prevent it," and this might ruin them as well as the people who should deal with them.[12]

What bothered Blackwell most of all was the great overvaluation of money in Pennsylvania, greater than in any of the colonies, despite Penn's supposed injunctions. He wrote to Penn that there is one great evil that threatens to prevent the blessings of God on the prosperity and trade of the province. This is the "excessive extortion . . . wherewith the poorer sort of people are oppressed by the wealthier traders; and those again ruined in God's righteous judgment and retaliation upon their impairing their estate unavoidably by the same means. The ground whereof is laid in the altering of the rates . . . of coins from the king's standard, which seems to be a paradox,. and little understood by most men" in America. This is all occasioned by "a fundamental error imbibed; viz. that the raising of the values of coins brings and keeps in moneys amongst them." All imported commodities to the poor ultimate consumer are at excessive rates of three or four times the first cost because of the raising of the value of money and the additional profit and charges to cover the increase. It may be said "surely the shopkeepers and merchants (who are the great improvers of the lands) must thrive," but the cost of labor rises, and in some cases higher wages must be paid than in New England. For instance, sawers of pine boards get at least £3 per 1000 feet, while the price in Boston·is 20 to 25s. This concerns all builders and drains away the specie. And this sinful practice affects not only the poor, the merchant, and importers, but also Penn as proprietor, the recipient of rents.

"O what's become . . . of the spirit of the old puritanes of England, who made it a case of conscience in London (within my memory) whether they might lawfully and with a good conscience receive above one penny in the shilling [equal to 12 pence] profit in their tradings . . . I have said as much in New England amongst the traders there, where 'tis not altogether so bad, though too highly covetous (even to Extortion) for which God charged his people of old and told us in the New testament, 'tis Idolatry." He added that in this matter "I formerly imparted some things to you by way of Appendix to a small treatise I dedicated to your self touching a Bank of Credit proposed to have been Erected in New England." [13]

Blackwell became exasperated with his thankless job. The Quaker leaders in the legislature were too much for him, as they were for Penn. They had gone merrily on their way passing acts that Penn had not liked in matters of trade and money; and, though Penn had insisted that in his absence all legislation must have his approval before becoming law, they had just ignored him. Blackwell could do little with them, for they even denied that he had any real authority. He even had trouble getting his salary. He found, he wrote Penn, that he could not govern a people who had not the principles of government amongst them nor would be informed. Not least of his grievances to Penn was that goods were so costly in Pennsylvania that he could live in London at half the charge.[14]

But Blackwell saw eye to eye with the leaders that the Navigation Acts restraining exports to England would ruin the province, for it would have no markets for its goods. He also agreed with them as to the need of suitable provincial courts to reduce the country to sobriety and "support the government authority thereof in the lower people's respect and obedience," but in lower people he included the Quaker leaders.

Penn reluctantly accepted Blackwell's resignation, but he wanted Blackwell to remain and manage his interests. So Penn offered him the position of register general of the province and receiver general of his estates. He held out as an inducement to the register general's place that he left great room for a bank in it, and "It will be the foundation for thy desirable thing, and many things may be with time grafted upon it." He even sent along a banking proposal of Blackwell's old comrade-in-arms, Edward Roberts, who had served as auditor general in Cromwell's armies while Blackwell was treasurer. The prosperity of the bank of credit would be in "laying the foundation of trade and in the increase of corn, cattle, whale oil, skins, etc."

Apparently the object of the scheme, as of almost all the other bank proposals, was to prevent "the unjust usage of factors and correspondents." But Penn pointed out a general objection that doubtless applied to Blackwell's original scheme—namely, that it was so elaborate and so full of checks that it was unsuited in its original form for "our nonage" and "early time of ye day." [15]

But he thought Blackwell could modify it to suit the exigencies of Pennsylvania. Blackwell, however, would have nothing to do with Pennsylvania and after little more than a year in the colony, he left in 1690 for Boston with a parting shot at Philadelphia Quakers: "Each prays for his neighbor on First Days and then preys upon him the other six." [16]

The agitation for a bank of credit continued in Massachusetts. Cotton Mather, in an election sermon on *The Serviceable Man* in 1690, could refer to the recent action of the "governor" in calling a General Court and promising the relaxation of difficulties, as in effect erecting a "Bank of Credit" among them, and rendered "credit so passable, that the indigent people might still enjoy their livings, and yet have *credit* enough" to demand from one another what their exigencies called for.

Later in 1690 the discussion over paper currency took another line. The Massachusetts authorities, who were operating without a charter, had sent out an expedition to conquer French Canada with the expectation of paying off the temporary loans and soldiers' wages with the expected plunder. But the expedition was a disastrous failure, and in its plight the General Court resorted to a device found in French Canada. It issued non-interest-bearing bills of public credit, payable for all public dues, to be redeemed by tax levies. The General Court stated that the bills had been issued because of the "present poverty and calamities of the country and (through the scarcity of money) the want of an adequate measure of commerce, whereby they are disadvantaged in making present payments as desired." [17] But the bills soon depreciated amid cries that they were not real money and had no legal warrant. The poor soldiers and seamen, wrote a contemporary, could at best get only half their value for them.[18]

Both Cotton Mather and Blackwell rose to the defense of the bills in 1691. "Bonds or bills . . . of exchange were paper too," exclaimed Cotton Mather in *Some Considerations on the Bills of Credit*, "and yet they are as valuable as so much specie if the security of payment be sufficient." The security of the public paper is the best, for it is the credit of the whole country. As metal, money is a commodity like other merchantable things, said Mather. But as money it is only "a counter or measure of men's proprieties," a medium of exchange. Money as a medium of exchange has its origin in "a general ignorance of Writing and Arithmetick." Since these arts are now commonly known, specie money may "well be discharged from the conceited necessity thereof in human traffic," and paper in various forms, from negotiable private bills of exchange and notes to bills of public credit, may be substituted. The bills facilitate the payment of taxes as well as animate trade.

The contention that the necessary taxes could be paid in corn, at an overvalue, as of old is unsound. The losses entailed in collecting and storing corn would be too large; as for using specie, silver will always be scarce because of the unfavorable balance of trade. So taxpayers can provide silver only by ruinously "undervaluing the fruits of their labours and their lands." Paper, however, unlike specie, can never leave the country and thus returns would have to be made in the native growths instead of specie, to the country's advantage. Should the public paper be made current, the credit of the country would rise to the utmost height of its ability on extraordinary emergencies. Otherwise the country will be distressed because if the bills be dead upon the merchant's hands, buying and selling on credit must end, and so trade cease.

Depreciation—that is, taking the bills at underrates whether in money or in excessive prices for commodities—is a horrible crime against the soldiers. Those engaging in the practice are like avaricious parasites who in the civil war in England purchased soldiers' debentures at low rates, and used them to purchase great estates from Parliament. Those not accepting them at full value should be forced to pay higher taxes and in silver, and be forbidden to pay the bills out. Furthermore, if the General Court should pass a law requiring that they be acceptable for all debts at full face value, those not complying should not have the use of the courts for recovering their debts until the public debts are paid. Should they resolve to make no more debts in fear of this law, they will find their trading will be dull. And, what is more, irrespective of any change of government in the country, debts must be paid.

Mather easily disposed of the objection that the taxes to be levied to redeem the issue and thus maintain their value were illegal and unjust, and that they who ordered the expedition should be compelled to meet the costs. Mather appealed to the doctrine that all power is in the "people." All of a sudden he found that the gentlemen administering the country are only "the country's agents," and therefore it is the country, not they, who must meet the burden. All the inhabitants, taken as one body, are the principals who reap the benefits and must bear the burdens. The gentlemen only get a return for their pains and not a little obloquy. If any murmur at their management as having needlessly brought on the expense, the answer is simple. "So long as they enjoy the choice of administrators, they must bear what's past, and right themselves for the future, by choosing better next, if they know where to find them. So merchants do with their factors."

Blackwell, in *Some Additional Considerations*, also denounced unwillingness to pay taxes. This refusal arises from the sin of covetousness, which prevails too much in New England. The great complaint is "our venturesome Expedition to Canada has run us into debt." But "the voice of the people everywhere called for it." There can be no settled peace as long as Canada is in French hands. Under the colony's necessities the bills of credit is the best solution.

Silver we can never have enough of, and we can easily do without it, like the other colonies, for what is the use of coined specie but to furnish a man with "credit, that he may obtain from his neighbors those commodities which he hath occasion for?" In fact, the more sensible part of mankind have thought banks of credit preferable to silver in their pockets. Though more portable than coin, they will not be exported or hoarded but "inspire our whole trade with such a vigor as hitherto has not been seen." Until we can discover something equivalent to coin that "may run amongst us in such a quantity as may agree with our affairs, and yet not bleed away . . . by every vessel that goes to foreign parts, we shall always have a consumption upon us." With an eye to his land bank Blackwell added that, if the dealing in these bills were "more improved and refined," it would be easy to propose a certain method by which this poor country could be immensely enriched in a short time and great sums commanded by the authorities with only a fraction of the vexation that every tax occasions. Certainly the paper money is just as good as tobacco money, potato money, sugar money, corn money.

Debasing the bills—that is, forcing them to pass for less than their nominal value in silver—is a horrible crime. But the merchants cannot be accused of depreciating them, though an unthankful community has so charged. Having taken bills in payment for their loans to the province, they are interested in maintaining their value.

To establish the credit of the bills, let the taxes be raised greatly so that in one year all the bills will be in the treasury and canceled. The people will then find it to their advantage to have bills. Furthermore, if only a competent number of men who deal much would jointly agree to give a just reputation to the bills, the whole country must join with them.

After all, Blackwell had no trouble adjusting himself to bills of public credit, for he was acquainted with the history of the debentures given to the soldiers in the civil war in England, a history which Mather had so sharply criticized.

By 1692, the bills had been made current pay and equivalent to money in all transactions, and payable for taxes at a 5 per cent premium; the depreciation appears to have disappeared. Cotton Mather, writing in his *Magnalia Christi Americana* in 1702, of the early history of the paper, said, "The government in its extremity had found an expedient which may be useful to countries whose distresses may call for a sudden supply of money to carry them through any important expedition." In the absence of a charter, many people had feared the existing government would be overturned and the bills would consequently be waste paper. So their credit was much impaired at first. Had the government been settled, and therefore no question entertained as to the taxing power, the bills of credit would have been better than so much ready silver, "yea the invention had been of more use to the New Englanders," than if all the mines of Peru had been moved to New England. "The debts of the country have been its riches," he enthusiastically exclaimed later.[19] The bills became a permanent feature of Massachusetts, and other colonies soon enough followed suit.

Blackwell, meanwhile, after making his defense of the public bills, returned apparently for a temporary visit to England to see among other things about recovering some of the lands he had lost originally with the restoration of the Stuarts.

On paper he was successful in recovering for his Irish lands. Blackwell claimed that, by the seizure of his lands under Charles II, he had lost £10,000, and the Crown authorized in 1693 that, "in consideration of adventures, deficiencies and damages . . . and as a special mark of royal favor" he be given land of a clear yearly income of £1000 from any lands which could be discovered to have been originally appropriated by Parliament for the adventurers.[20] Because of these complications and the maze of assignments involved in his early transactions, Blackwell died without recovering any lands.

But before he died he presented to the English public a treatise on how to raise revenue for the perennial wars with the French. The answer, of course, was paper money. Blackwell declared: The recent establishment of the Bank of England is further evidence of the truth of his idea that bills are so necessary that many desire them rather than money. On this ground banks of credit have been multiplied since the erecting of the Bank of England, but most of them are merely for private advantage and of no use in supporting the "parliamentary funds and credit given by them" or in raising the necessary war funds. He proposed that Parliament give legal tender bills of credit within limits to useful companies in export trade, especially the chartered Royal Fisheries Company, which was at-tempting to organize a bank of credit; also to those providing guard ships and convoys for trading vessels. Furthermore, bills were to be given to those who would pay their own and others' taxes in advance. Even the deficiency in taxation could in this way be balanced. Thus taxes need only be moderate; but ample funds could be raised to prosecute the war and invigorate trade at an insignificant cost, since the bills cost nothing. They would bring specie out of hoarding and increase the nation's supply by increasing the favorable balance of trade. Taxes were the fund securing their payment if desired.

As in the colonies, so in England, Blackwell argued against the current proposal to raise the value of the money in connection with the recoinage. He utilized his old arguments and even recalled the "experience" of New England and Pennsylvania. In the New World, he said, the overvaluation raised wages so that many masters were impoverished and, contrary to the true order of things, their chil-dren became servants to their former servants.[21]

The career of the most eminent of Blackwell's seventeen children, Sir Lambert Blackwell, came to a climax on a note in keeping with the paper-money tradition of the Captain. He became a director of the notorious South Sea Company and, along with the other di-rectors, was forced to turn over all his assets when the "bubble" burst in 1721. Among the items he listed in his inventory were: "I have a claim from the Crown for lands in Ireland belonging to my father as an Adventurer for suppressing the Rebellion there, which claim has been renewed and received in several reigns, at a great ex-pense, without the desired success. I have likewise title to some lands amongst the Indians in New England left me by my father, which at present is of no value." [22]

Blackwell's friend Penn continued, on the other hand, to promote almost every monetary device except overvaluation. In 1701, while in Pennsylvania, he wrote the royal Council of Trade and Planta-tions: "The Whole continent labours under the want of money to circulate trade in the respective governments, which has put Boston herself upon thinking of tickets to supply ye want of coyn; and New York as well as this province are following." [23]

Two years later, calling forth a general monetary program for all colonies, he wrote the council that, along with a colonial mint and a "uniform" valuation for foreign coins, a bank might be helpful if practicable, and paper credit thereby might serve in place of specie which was being drained to the mother country.

Then in 1705 came the pushing of another familiar device in Pennsylvania. Penn was using the bonds given him by purchasers of land to pay his debts. So he called on his colonial agent to have all sums due him, whether for purchase of land or quit rent, put under bond and then have the assembly make "bonds assignable and current pay, whether the assignee live or die," on the ground that money was so scarce.[24] But in addition to the request for this form of legal tender paper, he expressed the wish that the province have a "land bank" so that payment might be made easier to all parties; but the lands which are to be the "fund" of the bank should not be overrated.

So the seventeenth century bequeathed to the eighteenth an enduring controversy on the problems of money and trade, and around these would center, as before, all other economic issues. But it passed on more than that. The paramount importance of order in the hierarchical sense would still vigorously control thought and action.

CHAPTER VIII

Political Economy of the Eighteenth Century

AMERICA was following closely the upper-class English pattern, at least in form. Primogeniture was permitted in the Carolinas, New York, Massachusetts, Pennsylvania, Virginia, Maryland; and entailed estates in all the southern colonies, in Pennsylvania, and in New York. The councils were generally composed of office holders who often held multiple positions. Voting was usually restricted to substantial freeholders or possessors of equivalent personal property.

All believed that gentlemen must rule, and that intellectual inquiry was a pursuit for gentlemen of leisure and learning. The calling devoted to inquiry, declared the popular Reverend Jonathan Mayhew in his *Christian Sobriety*, is restricted to those few "whom God has blessed at once with riches and with large sagacious minds," for these may devote the greater part of their time to study, observations, and discoveries in the "word and works of God."

So highly were learned gentlemen venerated that the Georgia authorities treated with considerable respect their polished German-born communist prisoner, Christian Priber, who had taught the Indians how to avoid being exploited by British traders. In the prison where he died, every gentleman in the vicinity had visited him for conversation because he was "adorned with every qualification that constitutes a gentleman." They agreed that he "had read much, was conversant with arts and sciences; but in all greatly wedded to system and hypothesis." [1]

Educational facilities and requirements accorded with this scheme of status and order. A "liberal education" for a boy of the "middling rank" was to stay at school until he had "attained perfect vulgar arithmetick and other branches of the mathematicks as is most taking to him." A girl was to learn to "read, write and cipher, and the use of her needle." [2]

The other colonies followed the lead of Massachusetts and Virginia in establishing colleges. They were small, often with a president and a tutor or two, and generally had elementary schools attached. Educational standards were such that Yale records one student's passing the simple entrance examination at the age of seven. Provision was made for gentlemen's sons having no desire to know the long fatigue of turning books. With the nominal exception of "The College, Academy and Charitable School of Philadelphia" [3] (now the University of Pennsylvania), chartered by the Proprietors in 1753, all were founded under sectarian auspices. All received grants from their respective colonies. All sought funds from England on the ground that the colleges, by spreading the accepted civil and religious notions among the colonists and Indians, would strengthen the Protestant interest and help make the colonies profitable to the mother country. [4]

The classics, moral philosophy, and theology, along with rhetoric, logic, and eloquence, still dominated; mathematics and the sciences were at best incidental features of the curriculum. Locke was the great name in philosophy. But in 1769 the Reverend John Witherspoon of Scotland became president of the Presbyterian College of New Jersey (now Princeton). He brought with him the first echo of the philosophy that was to dominate all America—the Scotch school of Common Sense. The philosophy had been developed by the Reverend Thomas Reid, professor of moral philosophy at Glasgow, in response to the need of Presbyterian Scotland for a speculative philosophy which would justify as immutable and eternal the prevailing common-sense beliefs against the skepticism of David Hume.

Hume, carrying to the logical end Locke's position that knowledge is derived from our experience of particular facts and sensations, declared that all so-called primordial truths, whether of religion, morality, or the universe, are simply impressions and ideas associated by custom. They are expectations, developed in individuals by experience—that is, by habit—and, although of great practical usefulness, they cannot be rationally established. The existence of fundamental truths assumed the rationality of the causal principle, which Hume denied because it required the connecting of two concepts, an event and an antecedent cause, between which no necessary connection of any kind can be detected in the mind. Reid appealed to the common sense of mankind for justification of fundamental truths. They were "principles which the constitution of our nature leads us to believe and which we are under a necessity to take for granted in the common concerns of life, without being able to give a reason for them." They were "self-evident truths," and "anything manifestly contrary to them is what we call absurd." [5] In Witherspoon's language, in his *Lectures on Moral Philosophy*, "they can be no more proved than you can prove an axiom in mathematical science."

The philosophy was easy to teach. Fundamental beliefs were self-evident truths, questioning of which was an irrational act. In the course of moral philosophy the students were duly indoctrinated in a dogmatic and integrated fashion in the orthodox principles of politics and economics, along with whatever psychology, philosophy, and theology happened to be accepted by the clerical president.

The colleges remained very conservative throughout the colonial period. Even Witherspoon, who was the one college head unreservedly to embrace the American Revolution, once the die of war had been cast, wrote as late as 1772 to an English nobleman that he was instilling in his students "a love of order and an aversion to that . . . sedition into which the spirit of liberty when not reined, may degenerate." [6]

The Reverend William Smith, provost-head of the College of Philadelphia, explained in 1755 that infant settlements flourish fastest if the government is a "republican or popular form" because it immediately interests every individual in the common prosperity and settles itself at once on a broad basis. Since the people are few, and public office of small profit, the government of such a state may be administered without the faction and anarchy incident to popular forms. But in proportion as a country grows rich and prosperous, increasing checks on the power of the people are necessary.[7]

Learned Crown officials had, of course, the characteristic conception of authority. Any criticism of the controlling power or its representatives they traced to the vulgar nature of the populace, even though these critics might be men of substance. Such views came not only from the outright politicians, but even from men of distinction in science and letters who held office. Most outstanding of these was Cadwallader Colden of New York. Colden had a good family and university background in Great Britain. He had been a doctor, but became a merchant in Philadelphia, and then managed to become a judge, surveyor general, and lieutenant governor in New York, reaping the gains of multiple offices and land grants. At the same time he became a distinguished figure in the physical sciences.

The only proper government, he declared, is one based on the principle of the balance of power, with its monarchical, aristocratical, and democratic elements. History shows, however, that a mixed government runs more danger from an "overpower" in the democratic than from the monarchical element because people "are always jealous of the monarchy but fond of everything that increases the democracy. . . . Ambitious cunning men . . . by means of increasing the democratical powers . . . have always . . . been able to establish the tyranny at which they aimed." Here in America the inhabitants unfortunately "are generally educated in republican principles and great numbers of them (perhaps the greatest number in some of the colonies), foreigners who know nothing of the English constitution and can have no esteem for it." In a characteristic appeal, signed "Freeholder," he called on fellow voters to elect assemblymen favorable to the governor on the ground that "the middling rank of mankind, being the most honest, must be more cautious of ill-using their good qualities than some" rich men who know the force of money and have powerful or rich relations to prevent inquiries into their conduct.[8]

In Massachusetts, holding high the banner of prerogative, was the descendant of that Mistress Anne Hutchinson whose exile Governor Winthrop decreed lest his colony be run by theologians. Thomas Hutchinson was a Harvard M.A. and a historian. The son of an eminent merchant, he was bred a merchant and participated in land promotion and other business enterprises. He believed that "gentlemen of principle and property" must have control of government; and this belief was strengthened as he acquired various royal offices, including the governorship. He viewed all opposition as coming from "plebeians," and if there were merchants among them, and generally the opposition was composed of such and the like, they could not really be merchants as he saw things, but at best small shopkeepers or bankrupts. In his eyes all the ills of the colony, including opposition to English restrictions on colonial trade and commerce, flowed from its "democratical government" and its lack of a "balanced government." Democratic government is vicious because in it "number rather than the weight of the inhabitants," quantity rather than quality, is decisive.[9]

The critics, however, in asserting the doctrine of "popular rights" were primarily concerned, as Winthrop had been before them, with the freedom of the colony in its corporate capacity from outside control. They, too, were not concerned with the liberty and equality of mankind. Although they started with the latter as a point of departure, they ended up as an aristocratic republic under the guise of a self-governing dominion.

Ablest and most radical of this group was James Otis of Massachusetts. He was one of the most learned men of the day, and a member of a well-to-do and politically prominent family. He was a Harvard M.A., student of literature, the classics, and political and economic theory. He was one of the leaders of the "popular" party which opposed the assertion of power by the Crown and by Parliament. As an able lawyer he was an effective spokesman for the merchants in the struggle against the English Trade Acts. Otis reminded Hutchinson that the talk of a need for more balanced governments came with ill grace from a man who held at the same time the posts of lieutenant governor, chief justice, and other royal offices.

However, he agreed with Hutchinson that democratic government is biased toward numbers rather than weight. But this is true only in speculation. It cannot be examined in practice because no government is strictly democratic. The only equitable way is to "set quantity against quality, and to keep an exact balance as between debtor and creditor as the nature of the thing will admit," by placing the legislative, executive, and judicial departments in different hands.[10]

But, of course, the common people should have little to do with the government. Those laboring in the fields and in mechanical arts are not men of liberal spirit, of true courage, by virtue of their occupations, he stated anonymously.[11] "The incomparable Harrington," he said in a public address, "demonstrated in his *Oceania* and other divine writings, that Empire follows the balance of Property," and it is also certain "that property in fact generally confers power." [12] As "Rusticus" put the Lockian tradition, men entered society to preserve property, for "Liberty without Property is like a Man's having a good appetite, without anything to satisfy it." [13]

The Reverend John Wise, defending the independent Congregational Church polity against the Mathers' advocacy of a Presbyterial form, became enthusiastic about the superiority of democracy over every other form of government in *The Churches Quarrel Espoused* (1710) and *A Vindication of the Government of New-England Churches* (1717). But his democracy meant nothing more substantial than the freedom of each church in its corporate capacity from the "foreign" aristocratic rule of the synod. He accepted completely the central doctrine that the consent of both elders and brethren is essential to a church act, and what Cotton with more relevance had eulogized as non-democratic, he now called "democracy."

The great cry of no taxation without representation, raised by the colonials against the Stamp Act and duties on colonial trade, rested in the last analysis on a matter of geography and not on the right of all taxpayers to elect the people who levy the taxes. "Though nine-tenths of the inhabitants of any country should not be entitled to vote," exclaimed Maurice Moore, educated in New England, a member of the legislature, and associate justice of North Carolina, "yet, they are a part of that country, and as such, may be virtually represented by those elected to represent the whole country." Its inhabitants intimately reside together; the interest and circumstances of those not voting for representatives is the same with the non-voters, "and are equally well known to and understood by such representatives." The virtually represented can never be subject to any imposition that will not equally affect the electors. But the colonies are too distant from Great Britain to have any influence with the electors or elected. Therefore, if Parliament insists on taxing the colonists, as their virtual representatives, then are they stripped of that constitutional right on which their liberty and property depends and reduced to the most abject slavery.[14]

Luxury was deprecated, but luxury had reference to status. Those guiltiest of giving way to the vanity and luxury of the age were the poorer sort of people, said Increase Mather in his sermon *Burnings Bewailed*. "They will go above their quality, above their parentage, and above their estates. . . . Such pride is enough to provoke the Lord to kindle fires in all the towns of the country" such as that which just visited Boston.

There was general agreement, however, that sumptuary laws are directly opposed to the interests of a trading country, for they discourage industry, hinder the progress of manufacture, stop the growth of trade and the advancement of both public and private wealth.[15] Certainly when not all the people need be employed in supplying necessaries, the surplus labor should be "employed in innocent arts more for ornament than for necessity," because any innocent business that yields "an honest penny is better than idleness." Therefore if the rich pay for needless curiosities, "chiefly to employ and maintain the poor, it's noble and generous of them, better than if they had given them the cost thereof for nothing." [16]

At all times the respectable complained that the wages of labor were too high. " 'Tis the poor that make the rich," one writer frankly admitted in John Peter Zenger's *New-York Weekly Journal*.[17] Logan complained to Penn in 1705 that Pennsylvania was in depression because England with its cheap labor could undersell Pennsylvania in the provision trade in the West Indies. If only more people could be brought in to "lower the prices of labour," the colony would prosper.[18] There were but few thinkers who did not believe that high wages meant only extravagance, luxury, intemperance, idleness on the part of the poor, to the ruin of themselves and the country. "It is really a misfortune to be vicious when the wages they receive for the labour of one day will support them in intemperance for three days," reported a correspondent of the *Maryland Gazette*.[19]

The Reverend Samuel Willard, vice-president of Harvard, declared in his *Compleat Book of Divinity* that the laborer's wages must bear proportion to his labor, but, as was too common, they must not turn oppressors and demand "unconscionable wages." The *"levelling"* spirit which this would prompt is not to be indulged. Their wages should not be so high as to enable them to live on the same standard with the rich. They should have "food and raiment, suitable to the order in which God's providence has placed them." This does not, of course, mean that all are entitled to the common sufficiency at all times. "Common equity decrees that the same labour requires the same hire," and if a person cannot support his charges with it, he is the object of a public charity. Should an employer foolishly give him more than the common wage, he would be giving it to him not for his work, but for his poverty.

Migration from the settled areas was sharply attacked. Those on the frontiers, complained the Reverend Thomas Barnard, were not the most profitable to society, and migration prevented the growth of manufactures.[20] Benjamin Gale, Yale graduate and Connecticut physician and landowner, quite frankly stated that the migrations depopulated the Connecticut towns, impoverished their inhabitants, and lowered the values of local lands.[21]

Penn's view of indentured servants as property was still retained. The influential Quaker preacher, Thomas Story, exclaimed in 1741 that bought servants are as much "the property of their masters, as their lands, goods, money, or clothing." Without them the masters "could not cultivate their lands or maintain their families." Therefore the governor is "infringing the just liberty and property of the people" in allowing the servants to enlist in the war emergency.[22]

The assembly and council added that this "unconstitutional" practice injures the masters whose servants have not enlisted, for they "must humour them in everything lest they be provoked to enlist." Thus they grow "idle, neglectful, insolent and mutinous."

The enlightened Mayhew of Massachusetts envied Pennsylvania her mass of German indentured servants. These, he declared in an election sermon in 1754, made Pennsylvania as rich and populous in a few years as the greatest and most opulent of colonies. Even Washington, endeavoring to people his frontier lands for his own gain and his country's protection in the cheapest, most effectual manner, thought strongly for a time of obtaining a "parcel of these people." [23]

The area of slavery expanded in the South. Georgia had been founded in 1732 with the stipulation that slavery be barred, but the colonists argued that indentured servants were so much more expensive than the cheap slave labor of neighboring colonies that the neighbors were capturing Georgia's foreign markets.[24] Even the evangelist George Whitefield, who had originally supported the prohibition for Georgia, agreed that slavery would propagate the Christian religion. Besides, "Liberty is a sweet thing to such as are born free, yet to those who may never know the sweet of it, slavery . . . may not be so irksome." [25]

The slaves, argued Southerners, are better off than the laboring poor in England because the owner naturally takes good care of them as a valuable property, and the slaves have no worries. Compared to the hovels of the Irish and Scotch peasant, declared Arthur Lee in *An Essay in Vindication of the Continental Colonies* (1764), the slaves' habitations are palaces and their livings luxurious. Considering that God has established for the good of all that "some must toil and drudge for others, . . . this kind of connection between a master and a servant is perhaps not less liberal, and less advantageous, than the venal and mercenary one of compact and hire," explained the Reverend Jonathan Boucher of Maryland in his *On American Education* (1773).

There was some opposition to slavery, however, even in the South, and especially when tobacco prices were falling. Resolutions were passed in various Virginia counties against the African trade on the ground that it prevented manufacturers and other useful migrants from settling in the colony and instead increased the colony's unfavorable balance of trade. In the North the Pennsylvania Quaker John Hepburn, in his anti-slavery tract *The American Defence of the Christian Golden Rule,* said: "When the country grows full of people and also abounds with Negroes, poor people will want employ, and must either beg or steal for their living." Eight years later, in 1722, the Pennsylvania Assembly was petitioned by "labourers" to prevent the hiring out of slaves to do "the servile work" in Philadelphia, for this debarred the "petitioners from being employed." [26]

The charge of land engrossing was raised in practically every colony, but the declaimers had generally in mind some great promotional venture rather than an escape for the laborer. For example, in 1772 Samuel Wharton, powerful Philadelphia Indian trader and land speculator, appealed to the Crown with the aid of Benjamin Franklin in behalf of what came to be known as the Grand Ohio Company, for a vast proprietary grant in the Ohio Valley. In his appeal he declared that in the middle colonies—New Jersey, Pennsylvania, Maryland, and Virginia—there is hardly any vacant land, "except such as is monopolized by the great landholders, for the purpose of selling at high prices." But "the poor people of these colonies, with large families of children, cannot pay these prices," and so they will be "forced into manufactures." Therefore great areas of the West now closed by the Crown to settlement should be opened, but under the management of men with sufficient funds to do it in an orderly way. [27]

Much effort was made to impress on the youth that the accumulation of wealth and a pious life did not conflict. The scriptural warnings regarding riches were not intended, exclaimed Mayhew in his *Christian Sobriety*, that riches should be disregarded. The Scriptures mean that "you ought to be industrious in some honest course of life," and to be thankful to God if he bestows riches upon you, yet you are to regard this world "and its perishing riches" in due subordination to the greater and better things promised by God. Wealth is a gift of God, a worldly blessing. Therefore, though it is a trial, it is a real good and not to be despised. Harvard masters answered in the affirmative to: "Is wealth more conducive to virtue than poverty?"

The Reverend Joseph Morgan of New Jersey (1674–1740), close friend of Cotton Mather, described the avid pursuit of riches as a slavery undergone by the rich for the benefit of the poor. Morgan's treatise, *The Nature of Riches* (1732), was not out of place in a career that included lawsuits, charges of practicing astrology, and temporary suspension from the ministry for intemperance.

Each man coveting to become rich achieves the public good, wrote Morgan, for men can only gain wealth by helping others. Thus God turns our wickedness to the public benefit. The most covetous and envious man cannot prevent riches from being devoted to the public good. Unless others share, he cannot gain or keep his riches. Be he honest or knave, the rich man can consume only a limited amount of what he produces and acquires. "Thus it is not the good intentions of men, but their covetousness that makes for the public good." The merchant animated by gain hazards his life and property for the welfare of the country by buying the surplus of some lands and exchanging it for the surplus of other countries which the first need more.

He leads, in fact, a miserable life with his cares and worries. The poor man with his simple fare and clothing has no griefs over losses and has the comfort that, if illness disables him, the rich must provide for him. Having no expectation of rising high, he sleeps with a cheerful mind.

Cotton Mather, in his *Lex mercatoria, or the Just Rules of Commerce Declared*, exclaimed that all New England businessmen were being unjustly maligned for the sins of a few. Still, he felt that there was need of laying down sound rules of business practice. The basic rule was: Let "my dealings be such that I should not be ashamed, of their coming to the knowledge of other men, able to judge of the honesty of my dealings." The light within all men is a very poor, insufficient guide in things concerning the worship of God, but it "enlightens all men for the most part in things that concern their dealings with one another." True, the rich oppress the poor; but the poor oppress one another and the rich also.

Witherspoon simply declared in his *Lectures on Moral Philosophy:* "Value is in proportion to the plenty of any commodity, and the demand for it. The one taken in the inverse, and the other in the direct proportion." Any attempt to fix maximum prices would simply prevent the forthcoming of supplies to the community.

Though a city be suffering a famine and a ship or two should arrive with grain, the owners of which would not sell it but at a most exorbitant price, "perhaps equity might admit that they should be compelled; but if any such thing were done, it would prevent others from going near that place again."

Much earlier, in 1710, the Reverend Ebenezer Pemberton exclaimed that, if the poor cannot afford the price of corn and start trouble, this merely shows that they are not "God's people but the Devil's . . . if they had not impoverished themselves by rum they might buy corn." [28]

Price regulation in the Indian trade was finally eliminated as the Board of Trade in 1764 declared that the policy was "doubtful in its principle, and difficult in its execution," since it is in its nature inconsistent with, and might, in its operation, be restrictive of that freedom, which is one of the first principles of commerce, and cannot either in justice or reason be fixed without the mutual consent of parties having adverse and contradictory interests. [29]

One of the "cases in conscience" was: "Did we any wrong to the Indians in buying their land at a small price?" It was answered in the negative by Harvard's librarian, the Reverend Solomon Stoddard. "We came to their market and gave them their price. . . . Our dwelling on it, and our improvements, have made it to be worth." [30]

Though price fixing by authority on the whole was frowned upon, regulations affecting prices indirectly were advocated. Thus the Reverend Benjamin Colman of Boston early in the century demanded an organized central market for the sale of country produce on the ground that city gentlemen are placed at the mercy of petty hucksters, and "mean people" live so high and are so free with their money that sufficient goods are not available for their superiors. That all the country people be compelled to sell all in the market did not violate natural rights and liberties. Only they who come into order can live "free and easy." [31]

A number of shopkeepers, it was held, is always necessary to supply the community with goods in small parcels and save time and expense of traveling distances, but they should be limited to those bred to the business or having a stock with which to begin, not empty-handed artisans and tradesmen with "an itch after living by their heads rather than their hands." [32]

The classic case of "orderly trade" was the great staple of tobacco which had to be shipped to England and yielded the Crown a handsome revenue. Professor Hugh Jones of the College of William and Mary argued, in his *The Present State of Virginia* (1724), that the excessive production of tobacco spoils the market. Too much tobacco is worse than too little for the planter, the merchant, and the public.

To restrict tobacco production, various devices were advocated and utilized. The old scheme of the "stint," of directly restricting production, was tried, but Lieutenant Governor William Gooch of Virginia informed discontented planters that the practice did not remove the chief cause of low prices—namely, the existence of "trash" tobacco. The direct limitation of production would work if Virginia were the sole producer of tobacco; otherwise it would merely mean that other colonies or countries would seize Virginia's markets. Suppose that in England, on the complaint of dullness of trade by the clothier, every farmer should be limited as to the number of sheep he could keep, and that every laborer in the manufacture should work only six hours a day, would not the French and Germans further capture their markets? Just as the only way to improve the wool trade was to make enough cloth of better quality than their rivals, so with tobacco. [33]

Gooch had the assembly pass an act in 1730 "for amending the Staple of tobacco; and preventing frauds in His Majesty's Customs." This was a revival of earlier measures. Under the scheme all tobacco for export was stored in public warehouses where it was "inspected" and "trash" tobacco burned. For the tobacco deposited the owners received transferable notes signifying the quantity deposited. These notes, said Gooch, provide a good internal circulating medium. The people thereby have a ready cash to pay debts; and goods (imports) would be cheaper, for storekeepers would know the tobacco is good.

Gooch primarily defended the act to the planters in an anonymous treatise, *A Dialogue Between Thomas Sweet-Scented, William Oronoco, Planters,* in 1732, on the logic of the pernicious effects of a "debased" currency. The dull-witted planters foolishly complain that burning of the "trash" destroys the fruits of their labor. On the contrary, the price of the remainder yields a greater total than that at the old price, for "bad tobacco destroyed, stamps a value on the remaining good which will forever be depreciated by a mixture."

Gooch informed the home authorities that the act, by preventing frauds, would benefit English merchants and the Crown. Consumption would not decline since tobacco has become a necessary especially to the English mechanics. True, the act has led to burning of the warehouses in Virginia, but this was done "by disorderly" people, ex-servants and jailbirds, who hoped thereby to dispose of their "trash" tobacco again. If the Act were disallowed, tobacco prices would decline, and the planters forced to enter manufactures.

Critics, on the other hand, complained that the act was intended to give a monopoly to Virginia's great planters, would hurt the poor sort, especially tenants, and force them to turn to manufactures. It was in line with Virginia's policy of forbidding transit to North Carolina tobacco and thereby forcing North Carolina, too, to turn to manufactures. Gooch answered that forbidding the entrance of North Carolina tobacco was merely a device to prevent North Carolina's "trash" tobacco from being mixed with and thus depreciating Virginia tobacco.[34]

Maryland followed with an act like Virginia's, and the supporters there added that the act did not raise the rents of tenants, for it was not to the landlord's interest to exact an exorbitant rent in a counry where land may be had on easy terms.

The act does not fix a price for tobacco. The price of no commodity can be fixed, they asserted, but the quality of a commodity can be established. Every commercial state imposes regulations for the better sale of its staples. Not every regulation of trade is destructive of property, not every "control of licentiousness" an "invasion of liberty."

The act restrains not property, but the abuse of property. People can do what they will with their own, provided they do not injure their neighbors. That the majority produce good tobacco is not enough, if a few from their shortsighted interest sell "trash." [35]

The supporters finally declared the scheme would bring in the money economy. With a good circulating money available, imports would be cheap and exports high in price, mechanics and artisans would be attracted, towns created, a powerful wealthy local merchant class established, treasure accumulated; and the great tobacco colonies would achieve that freedom from sole reliance on tobacco that had prevented their growth.[36]

Another step must be taken if towns are to be achieved, said the vigorous exponents of the inspection law. This step, long advocated both in Maryland and Virginia, should be the restriction of trade by the legislature to a few centers. Otherwise neighboring colonies with large towns have a competitive advantage. They pointed to Philadelphia, where the opulence, the compact manner in which the trading men live, and the ease with which they can communicate their opinions and assist one another enables them to form sound judgments on policy.[37]

A good-sized town cannot arise in the absence of such regulations because the numerous navigable rivers allow for a straggling, dispersed trade, to the great loss of planters who are forced to deal with the extortionate, excessive number of petty shopkeepers.

But if the trade were concentrated, men of large fortune would invest in it. When opulent men engage in trade, those tilling the earth or manufacturing from its materials receive a good price for their labor, whereby they are encouraged to work incessantly, and so the general stock of the province is increased.

These towns would become the seats of learning as well as commerce. Academies can only be established in an opulent trading center, for only these can supply a sufficient number of rich pupils to support the instructors with the decency suitable to their character. Thus the towns would become centers of culture and commerce.[38]

Another way southern opinion envisaged the growth of commerce and commercial towns was by developing internal navigation with government aid. Most significant for future developments was the Potomac navigation project. Thomas Johnson, a large landowner on the western Maryland side, called for subscriptions to develop the navigation of the Potomac. This, he said, would facilitate the commerce of Virginia and Maryland with the back inhabitants, who now must use a long land route to a seaport. More important, by affording communications with the waters of the Ohio, the project would give to Maryland and Virginia the commerce of the great western country. With Alexandria and Georgetown on the Virginia and Maryland sides of the Potomac as the villages destined to be the proper ports, Maryland and Virginia will acquire, said a writer in the *Maryland Gazette*, the very lucrative skin and fur trade which Pennsylvania now monopolizes.[39]

Leaders in western land companies, especially of the Ohio Company, which included members of the Washington family, saw a great future for the scheme, provided that, in addition to public aid and subscriptions from interested landowners, the two legislatures granted privileges that would attract other investors. Washington informed Johnson that, as far as Virginia was concerned, the object could never be accomplished on public account alone. Of course, the improvement would be the means of giving to Virginia and Maryland as against the other colonies the great commerce between Great Britain and the immense western territory at a relatively small expense. Even if Virginia's finances were in better shape, the people would still be too divided in their interests and too confused in their views to appreciate that a tax on the whole community for the purpose is not really for the advantage of a part, but for all of Virginia and Maryland. Through ill-timed parsimony and supineness, the natural advantages of the Potomac route "may be wrested from us" and the trade be "conducted through other channels, such as the Susquehanna . . . the Lakes, etc.," and thus the northern port towns. What the two states should do is jointly charter a company and allow it to charge such high tolls that the distant moneyed gentry "would be tempted by lucrative views." [40]

To a proposal that the profits be limited through readjusting tolls from time to time as in England, George Mason, treasurer of the Ohio Company, answered that such adjustments were not administratively possible; and even if they were, investors would be deterred—especially those at a distance would not and should not invest upon so great a risk but "with views of great and increasing profit." [41]

With Washington as the prime mover, the Virginia Assembly passed the necessary measures, including the granting of a lottery to the company. But Maryland refused to grant incorporation, according to Washington, because of the opposition of selfish Baltimore merchants who feared loss of the land traffic.[42]

As the period closed, the merchant mind in its appeal to the politically powerful gentry for privileges and grants, including the encouragement of importation of labor and the elimination of what it conceived to be burdens on trade, had worked out a philosophic position that made the merchant the instrument of high wages as well as high rents and land values. It accomplished this feat without surrendering in fact the older doctrine of low wages, and it made the benefits of high wages accrue to the landlord.

Best of the statements was that of "Philopatris" in the *Maryland Gazette*, March 1762, a performance which the influential *Boston Weekly News-Letter* reproduced without acknowledgment in September under the title of "The Great Advantage of Trade and Commerce to a Province Considered": There is an unfortunate prejudice that commerce hurts agriculture, but in fact agriculture is the foundation of commerce, and commerce incites agriculture. Wherever is that pleasing object of the poor, full employment, thither will they most certainly migrate. "Like birds of passage, they will explore every unknown region to reach the necessaries and conveniences of life. Hunger, and the various sufferings of their faithful wives and tender infants plead with eloquence irrefutable." But commerce creates the employment and provides the routes.

It quoted Hume on wages rising because of the increase of trade and money: Though the rise reduces a nation's export advantage, it is the effect of the public wealth and prosperity "which are the end of all our wishes." Better still was another author who said: "Countries where trade is most effectually extended, and has the greatest influence, there the poor thrive best and their wages are highest." This leads successively to the greatest consumption of provisions and the highest prices for them, and finally the highest rents.[43]

Witherspoon went so far as to say in his *Lectures* that, if men lived entirely by agriculture, a vast proportion of property would center in a few hands, and they would soon seize all power. Therefore an agrarian law would be necessary to maintain liberty. But trade and commerce make the agrarian law unnecessary "because the great and sudden fortunes accumulated by trade cause a rotation of property."

As Logan's ideal citizen or "countryman" put it in 1725 in his anonymous *A Dialogue Shewing, what's therein to be found*, "I always judged the opulency of towns to be the advantage of every industrious and frugal countryman," for these contain the great merchants who can bear losses without discouragement.

So well did the merchant exemplify the dominant ideals of colonial America at the end as well as at the beginning of the period, that Mayhew used his behavior to illustrate the need of making haste and taking advantage of every opportunity to seek salvation. He wrote in his *Practical Discourses* in 1760: "The discreet merchant, the object of whose attention is worldly gain and profit, acts in conformity to the same prudential maxim of observing times and opportunities; which being once slipped, may never return. Does he not carefully observe the rise and fall of stocks, and of interest? Does he not diligently inquire into the state of foreign markets; and into a hundred other things and circumstances, which are in their nature fluctuating and changeable, that by improving his opportunities, at the critical time he may make sure of something; and promote his interest to the utmost? Will he neglect a present favorable opportunity, when he knows not but delaying a day or two may not only put it out of his power to make great profit to himself, but prove ruinous to his fortunes, and reduce him to bankruptcy? Certainly a cautious prudent merchant will not be guilty of such negligence; but improve every fair opportunity that presents itself, while it is in his province."

The tax policies of the colonies unleashed controversies that embraced the whole arena of economic problems. These controversies revolved around the ubiquitous but ambiguous doctrine of the balance of trade and the requirements of the logic of status.

The colonies varied somewhat in their objects of taxation. The list included poll taxes, taxes on "estates" on the estimated "profits" of professions including the laborers', excises, and export and import duties including the importation of slaves. Unimproved lands usually were not taxed, and the poll tax was the most common and often the chief tax.

Hermon Husband, the leader of the North Carolina "regulators," in his complaint that the "Sons of Liberty" denounced oppression from abroad but practiced it at home, uttered in good biblical manner the old cry that the poor man is taxed as high as the richest. But "there ought to be some regard . . . to the strength of the beast, for all asses are not equally strong. We ought to be taxed according to the profit of each man's estate." [44] No one disagreed in theory with this principle or its equivalent form that taxes should be "rationally laid on in proportion to every man's ability"—estate.[45] There was also the principle that the slothful as well as the richest should pay the most,[46] lest others rebel; and this meant that no tax was desirable if it prevented the growth of a colony's wealth, treasure, or claims on treasure.

The most elaborate presentation of local taxation was in Colden's anonymous pamphlets of 1726 while he was, among other things, surveyor general of New York. Claiming at first to be a man of the "country," a farmer as against the "city" and the merchant, he attempted to "prove" in *The Interest of the Country in Laying Duties* that a tax on "luxury" imports and foreign shipping is the soundest method of taxation since it will provide for the support of government, promote the industry and manufacture of the people, and restrain idleness, luxury, and unnecessary expense. Thus the duties would make the people richer than they would be without them.

At present the "country" people work hard for a bare subsistence, he wrote. They bring to town their best dainties for the rich townsmen, the merchants, in order to obtain a little money for bare necessities. On the other hand, the town is full of idle rich constantly gambling, drinking, and consuming wastefully. Therefore the latter should be taxed on their superfluities by taxing the imports of consumption goods. No one would question the duty on Madeira, which drains New York of specie or bills of exchange on England. Country people might object to a duty on West Indies rum because they claim rum invigorates labor in our climate. But homemade cider could replace it without lessening the profits of the industrious. The "country" would get a better price for its domestic drinks; their manufacture would increase our skill in making them, so that eventually they would become an export and so increase the colony's specie holdings. Molasses from the West Indies is consumed by the people to make their coarse diet more palatable, but local products like honey could with advantage replace it.

Finally the duties on drinks, by preventing excessive drinking, increase the labor time and industry of many inhabitants who would otherwise impoverish themselves and their families. Many good tradesmen and laborers earn in two days enough to keep them drunk four days. If the price of strong liquor were doubled, they would have to work as many days as they could be idle and drunk, so that the country would save half the consumption of a foreign commodity and gain double the labor. By such taxes on expense, the Hollanders have become frugal, hard-living, and pinched in the belly, and so protected from usury and debauchery.

He praised the recently enacted duty on "foreign" tonnage. Even if the measure, by discouraging foreign shipping, reduces the demand for native produce, this is more than offset by the encouragement to the manufacture of ships and the retention of treasure for the use of our own shipping and sailors.

If the duty were removed, not only would artisans immediately concerned suffer, but also many others now gainers by these tradesmen would be damaged, and "so by degrees we shall find the loss to be general." Finally the reduced employment would lessen the demand for people, and so hinder populating the province.

Whether the affected foreign area is a British possession or any other is irrelevant, for "every inhabitant of New York would rather contribute to make New York rich and flourishing than any other place, and if it is shown that a British possession" acquires money for freight that would otherwise remain here, the case is proved. We stand in the same relation to other British colonies as Britain, France, and Holland, each struggling to outdo the other in trade.

On the other hand, the tax on slaves is bad because it is a tax on labor and manufacture and thus reduces our competitive power. True, the tax discourages the use of Negroes; and Negroes, unlike freemen, have no interest in promoting the country's good. But the want of hands and dearness of servants makes slaves necessary. The tax is an unequal one because it hurts the poor and industrious rather than the rich and idle. The former improve their lands by the aid of slaves at great privation to themselves. They "save out of their bellies and off their own backs" to support Negro children so that in their old age they can have laborers for their support. On the other hand, few rich possess more than two slaves, and most of them give away the infant Negroes as not worth the charge. Thus the poll tax is designed to excuse the rich at the expense of the poor and industrious on whom the rich live.

A land tax is undesirable because, with few renting the lands they cultivate, this would fall on the farmers, laborers, and manufacturers; whereas in England it has a justification because, the mass of farmers and laborers being renters, the gentlemen, the owners, pay the tax from the rent.

An anonymous "critic," in *The Interest of the City and Country to Lay No Duties*, claimed that the interest of both "city" and "country" is to lay no duties on trade, for such duties are paid by the "country" in higher prices for imports, or reduce the demand for country produce. Rather than tax trade, why not raise the revenue by a tax on men's estates in both city and country, especially land? The burden would not fall on the poor because, having little, they would pay little; whereas under the present or proposed scheme some, having much, pay nothing.

With his customary astuteness, Colden thought of entitling his anonymous reply *The Second Part of the Interest of the Country in Laying Duties*, but he got a better idea. Why not give the impression of an impartial third party seeking to reconcile both the "city" and the "country" spokesmen? So he rephrased it and called the anonymous reply *The Two Interests Reconciled*.[47] The most significant portion was his adroit handling of the income-tax issue. The critic, he said, is theoretically correct in insisting on discouraging the engrossers of great land tracts who neither sell nor improve them, by a general tax on the value of men's estates, whether land or money. Lenders can better afford to be taxed than borrowers. Those having money may enjoy a high interest rate at the cost of the borrowers' hard labor and often imprisonment. But the high interest is bad because it discourages trade through requiring too great a profit to pay the interest. This explains why the Spaniards have lost their trade to the English and Dutch.

Those refusing to sell or improve their lands might also be taxed according to the value of their lands; for, thanks to the industry of their neighbors and the increase of people in the province, this value rises continually, as fast as money does by interest. The great engrossing, especially the refusal of the engrossers to sell lands at reasonable rates, has hindered the material growth of the province. "A stranger could not believe that some men . . . own above two hundred thousand acres . . . which neither they nor their great grandchildren can hope to improve," while others "are forced to send their children into another province, to buy and cultivate land at a dear rate." Thus the colony loses great sums of money and people.

The land engrossers are more dangerous to the public than usurious lenders because the latter make some circulation of their estate, though at an immoderate profit; but the former, having a dead treasure which they cannot spend, are absolutely useless. Thus the proposal of the critic is reasonable. However, it is not practicable.

Even granting that the value of the estate could be determined, the tax would discourage industry and cause riots, as happened with the introduction of the income tax in absolutist France. If, of two men with the same annual income, one spends it all in drink and other vices and the other uses it to improve a piece of land, should not the former pay more to support government than the other? The latter, being industrious, feeds many laborers and increases the produce and the trade of the country. Furthermore, a young country should follow the example of countries of long standing, especially that of the mother country, rather than try novel measures, for "experiments are always dangerous, especially in politics."

The critic rightly argues that the burden will hardly fall on the poor, and he might have added that the day laborer and tradesman will often pay nothing; for, "as they generally live merely from hand to mouth and commonly spend before they get, their estate is nothing." But this is the greatest objection to the scheme from the practical standpoint: did the critic ever hear of a country where the whole burden "was taken off the poor and laid on the rich? Is it not generally the rich that lay taxes, and do they not constantly take care not to overburden themselves?"

It would not be surprising if future research should reveal that the "critic" was Colden too. The critic's pamphlet and Colden's were all printed by the same individual, none other than Zenger, to whose newspaper, the *New-York Weekly Journal*, Colden was a contributor. Colden himself, as Crown officers often did, argued for a tax on land from time to time and increasingly so in later years as a means ostensibly to prevent land engrossing, but actually to secure a substantial revenue for the Crown without being dependent on the local assembly, where the powerful gentry and merchants, often indistinguishable, made things difficult for the Crown officials or their interests.[48] As Colden's like-minded friend, Archibald Kennedy of the New York Council, put it in a learned treatise, *An Essay on the Government of the Colonies* in 1752, the rich have engrossed the lands, not with a view of settling them, but of parceling them out to the best bidders. This parceling prevents payment to the Crown. Let a gentle tax on land be levied so that officers of the Crown will become independent of assemblies, trade relieved, and the extravagant landed gentlemen forced to pay a proportion.

In Massachusetts the controversy over the excise measure of 1754 to provide funds for frontier fortifications furnished the finest opportunity for so-called "city" spokesmen to use all the stratagems. Previous to 1754, in Massachusetts as practically everywhere else, in addition to an import duty on wine, rum, and other spirits, there was an excise paid by the retailer; that is, by the seller of small quantities. This meant that those who purchased in large quantities were exempt from the excise. But in 1754 the General Court passed a measure whereby all consumers must pay an excise on all such drinks consumed above that purchased from the retailer. If the collectors were suspicious of the excise payer's statement, the latter must take an oath as to its accuracy. The legislature declared that the bill was passed to prevent "the polls and estates of the province from being overburd ed."

Immediately the cry went up that the landed interest was oppressing the trading interest. Governor William Shirley said that such a manner of levying a tax—forcing every private family to render an account, under oath if demanded, of the excisable liquors consumed by their private families—violated the "natural rights of every private family." It was consequently, in his opinion, unconstitutional. Besides, the true policy of government required that the people pay their taxes in an imperceptible manner and not in a way "as would have a tendency daily to remind them of their burden." Therefore he suggested that the representatives gather the opinion of their constituents on the question through the familiar town meetings.[49]

One group of objectors declared that they were not criticizing the duties, for taxes should be laid as much as possible on luxury rather than industry and frugality, but the manner of laying it made it an inquisition and opened the way to despotism: A man's home is inviolate except in criminal cases, but what is the real value of this right if he must account for his most innocent transactions, that of his private economy, his family? True, only a few articles are so taxed at present, but eventually we will be called upon "to give an account of every transaction, and these will be exposed to public view and remark" and so destroy man's most essential natural right of protection of person and property. Therefore it is inaccurate to assert that the opponents are the few large consumers of rum and wine, who pay no excise.

"It is the opening wedge into the constitution," wrote the Reverend Samuel Cooper, colleague and successor to Benjamin Colman in Boston's wealthiest church, in *The Crisis*. "You who are now poor may think to obtain relief by the excises, but it will be only partial and temporary. . . . And if through earnest industry, you should reach affluent circumstances, you must go through all the fatigue, self-denial and patience required for a posterity of slaves." And when once the popular voice shall be for it from a pretext of easing the poor by this imposition on the rich, a precedent will be established for excising any other article of our constitution. Although wine be esteemed by some an article of luxury, our wine is chiefly purchased by our exports of lumber and fish, and the latter is the kind that cannot be sold except in the islands whence the wine comes. So even if the excise as laid before was unequal, the remedy, "my country brethren," is worse than the evil.

"You think that your superior interests in the House will secure you as long as any trade be left to be taxed, but if instead of being tender to the interest of trade, you destroy it," and merchants and tradesmen are forced to leave you, "then, farewell to the country. Many a country has grown rich by trade alone, no country without. . . . 'Tis as easy to lose trade as to lose reputation, and 'tis equally hard to recover either." [50]

Others attempted to prove that the excise tax violated the postulate of taxing according to estates. The tax would be good if confined only to rich persons. But it burdens the poor half-starved frontiersmen, fishermen, and laborers who need the rum to carry on their arduous labors. On the other hand, it relieves the mass of opulent farmers who live in settled plantations. They need no rum but have even a surplus of domestic drinks of malt and cider to sell abroad for money. Therefore the domestic drinks should be taxed for the sake of equity. It is claimed that malt and cider are our own produce and therefore should not be taxed. But rum is also in effect a domestic product, the very blood of the men engaged in the lumber and fishery trades.[51]

Presenting most effectively the other side of the issue was a member of the legislature who had part of his speech published because the rumor had spread abroad that it had "grossly reflected on the character of merchants." He declared that he has as much reason as any man to oppose oppression of trade, since he is a merchant. But a great difference exists between oppressing trade and regulating it.

Merchants are the best judges of the proper seasons for carrying out and bringing home the commodities of a country and for buying and selling the same, for practice makes perfect in everything. The business of a merchant as a merchant with all justice is to discover what trade will yield him the greatest profit. It never enters his mind when two legal branches of trade lie open before him which one is the greatest good to the country. So a merchant may engage in a trade beneficial to himself but ruinous to the country, or the reverse. So this legislator would not leave "entirely in the breast of gentlemen in trade, to point out the channels in which it ought to be put." In fact, as the merchant is necessarily prejudiced in favor of the trade yielding him the greatest profit, "I have thought that a Gentleman no way interested in Trade" is more capable of "judging of it, as a science, than the merchant himself." Having no bias in his mind, he views the matter with a "degree of evidence which the merchant himself never thinks of."

The legislature's business is to discourage every bad trade and en-courage every good one in such a way that the merchant will find his interest in pursuing the trade most desirable for the country. Discour-aging the importation of wine or any other unnecessary article does not damage trade. That these luxuries are objects purchased with the country's product of fish and the like, which have no other market, would only be a valid argument if the imports were re-exported. If there is not as much money or re-exports brought into the country as the value of the fish exported, we should stop the fishery and cul-tivate our lands. Consequently we should raise the duties still higher on these useless imports.[52]

An answer in part was supplied by the Pennsylvania Assembly's reply in 1753 to the Proprietors' assertion that increasing excise duties was more equitable and preferable than taxing the unimproved land of the Proprietors, which yields no product. While the excise is paid voluntarily, it is a tax on the subsistence of labor, it said; and, "since the laboring men must live, . . . he generally finds ways to get more for his labor." [53]

There was general agreement in the colonies that bounties were legitimate for the encouraging of staples, but there was sharp opposi-tion and division as to bearing the tax burden. The situation was summed up in the protest of the town meeting of Boston against bear-ing any share of the taxes for such bounties: The bounty might be for the general good, but the immediate advantage is to the country, not to Boston.[54]

Commerce still directly held the primacy or, as that merchant sup-porter of the Massachusetts excise measure put it, since "trade being as it were, the oil to the springs of government, it ought to be our principal object." But there was hardly a field of enterprise in which there was not sharp disagreement over what constituted the interests of trade. Overshadowing or at least complicating these conflicts were the requirements of colonial dependency on the mother country.

THE ECONOMICS OF COLONIAL DEPENDENCY

All formally conceded that the colonies were "junior branches" of the empire and that their profits should inure to Great Britain. In increasing the stock of the elder branch, the whole empire was strengthened. The colonial thinkers always had to cope with the necessity of proving that the measures they proposed would increase England's profitable trade and commerce. This never proved difficult, though at times it puzzled the English authorities.

Except by way of threat, few dared go as far as Hugh Jones, who in 1724 declared that it would be to England's interest to let the colonies develop any manufactures they found profitable: The plantations, especially Virginia, can produce several things with less labor and more plentifully than England. Things involving great cost and toil forced from England's barren ground and bad climate, might be produced cheaper and better in the colonies and the people and land of England occupied in more profitable business. At the same time the profits would center in England through the carrying and re-export trade.

The colonial mind, however, was adept in proving that colonial manufactures could not be competitive with those of England. The destiny of the colonies is agriculture, wrote Stephen Watt, M.A. of the loyal College of Philadelphia, in a prize essay, because the small population relative to the land makes land cheap and labor dear. Therefore any crude manufactures arising from this pursuit should not be viewed as competing with English manufactures, but as providing, through the funds obtained from their export, a market for England's finer and more valuable manufactures.[55]

There was at all times general agreement that England should grant temporary bounties for its importation of essential raw materials and semi-finished manufacture, such as naval stores and iron; but conflicts generally arose as to who were to be the beneficiaries. Explained Captain Thomas Banister, important Boston merchant, in 1715 in a letter to the Lords Commissioners of Trade and Plantations: New England pays for its immense purchase of British manufactures in commodities that "serve your necessities and not one that increases your luxury and unnecessary expense." England, therefore, should give a good bounty for the importation of naval stores from New England. Otherwise, because of the unfavorable balance of trade, England will suffer a double loss. We shall be forced to manufacture and in so doing employ the hands that would otherwise be used to produce naval stores and the like.

On the other hand, Colden argued in 1723 that the bounties are essential because without them people cannot be persuaded to leave their common means of agriculture to adventure on new methods, which in the beginning are always expensive and of uncertain profit. England could not lose by offering a bounty, or better still by taking the goods at a price above their "intrinsic value" temporarily, because the whole industry, frugality, and trade of the province is employed to balance the trade with England. By the naval-store trade the colony can return more money and goods to England and thus consume more English manufactures.[56]

John Rutherfurd of North Carolina in 1761 argued in *The Importance of the Colonies to Great Britain* that England should grant a temporary bounty to home merchants to import not only naval stores, but also cotton, iron, and timber from the colonies. This would eventually provide England with cheap materials, and at the same time the colonists could purchase British manufactures at an "advanced price."

He even thought that a bounty for the importing of skilled labor should be given for the benefit of iron production. Because of wartime conditions, labor in Sweden, from which England imports a good share of her iron, is dear, and so England must pay a high price for the product. But if means could be found to import the poor distressed miners of Saxony to North America as servants, then with the assistance of the Negroes, the price of labor could be lowered and England could import her iron cheaply.

The objection was made that, if iron manufacture were encouraged, the colonies might go on to finished iron and steel products. This was ridiculous, replied Joshua Gee, English merchant and economist and the Pennsylvania agent to whom Penn once mortgaged his province, because where land costs little the workers demand wages much higher than those in England.[57]

Equally important to the substantial colonial leaders was the lifting of English duties and restrictions on trade and the prevention of new ones. Banister, as he argued for a bounty on naval stores, requested that England should not listen to the demand of the British West Indies sugar islands that the trade between the continental colonies and the foreign West Indies sugar islands be restricted or prohibited. The foreign West Indies, he said, take for their cheaper rum and molasses New England's refuse fish and other products which have no other market. This traffic employs many ships, and in addition the rum and molasses which are distilled and then exchanged provide many good livings and goods or money for returns to England. If England should grant the demands of the British sugar islands, then the continental colonies, "because of their unfavorable balance of trade would be forced to manufacture for themselves and they then would be on their way to political independence as well."

The move for legislation became especially serious in 1731, as the British sugar islands pleaded that prohibiting trade between the continental and foreign plantations would make it unprofitable for the French West Indies to export their competing sugar, rum, and especially molasses, and thus not only increase the wealth and strength of Great Britain as against the other powers but especially cripple the hereditary enemy. At the same time they demanded that England lift the requirement that all sugar had to move through England, for this reduced the returns to the sugar planters and thus the market for English goods.

From Virginia to New England came protests against the proposed restrictions. Lieutenant Governor Gooch of Virginia wrote to the Council of Trade and Plantations: The continental colonies supply the West Indies with flour, bread, beef, pork, fish, and lumber in return for sugar, molasses, and rum. Since the continental colonies produce more than the British sugar islands consume, they cannot be prohibited from "seeking a market where they can find one." On the other hand, the British sugar islands cannot supply all the rum and molasses the continental colonies need for their great fishery and Indian trades. In any event, the gain must center in Great Britain.

The continental colonies can make remittances to England only by their exports to the foreign West Indies and the "foreign" sugar they ship to England. Whether the returns be "British" or "foreign," sugar is irrelevant to the mother country, for she remains the market and staple for both and pays in British manufactures. Such legislation would place the continental colonies at the mercy of the British sugar planters by obliging them in effect to sell their goods and take the product of the British West Indies at whatever price suits the latter.

In any event, New England, with its vast shipping, would either engage in the trade or in outright piracy, "since it is morally impossible that such a number of stout fellows as are now employed in that trade, can content themselves to starve on shore."

From the northern colonies came amplifications: Great Britain has a favorable balance of trade with the northern colonies but an unfavorable one with the sugar islands. English exports of woolen manufactures to the northern colonies are far greater than to the sugar islands, and thus the northern colonies employ more tradesmen in England. The legislation would strip the inhabitants of the northern colonies of the means of subsistence and of purchasing necessaries and conveniences from Great Britain. Without liberty to dispose of their surplus produce above consumption, the Pennsylvanians, for instance, cannot undergo the great expense of developing the country, for without a market for lumber and provisions the country will not be cleared of its forests and placed under cultivation.

To give the British sugar islands a monopoly of the sale to the northern colonies of sugar, rum, and molasses would be to take away the birthright of English subjects—"liberty and freedom of commerce"—and make them slaves and bondmen of their fellow subjects in the sugar islands. It would aggrandize a few opulent subjects in those islands at the expense and ruin of many thousands who are as useful though not as wealthy.[58]

The spokesman for the sugar islands replied also in terms of the balance of trade. John Ashley, holder of large estates in the islands, deputy surveyor and auditor general of the islands and member of His Majesty's Council in Barbados, reminded the Crown that New England's inhabitants have wrested the fishery from the mother country, engrossed in great measure shipbuilding, violated the Navigation Acts, and established a host of competing manufactures so that Great Britain does not get their money. But in the British sugar islands there is not one trade or manufacture that competes with England.

As for the charge that the British sugar islands are monopolized by a few planters, he replied that the many sugar islands and many independent planters render a monopoly much more impracticable than among "tobacco planters or our farmers or manufacturers at home where a combination never occurs."

The northerners unfairly insinuate that, if the planters would curtail the luxuries, the prevailing price for sugar would be ample. But these plantations were bought at the old level of prices, and were the critics to engage in planting, they, like the present possessors, would still lose heavily even if they and their families went as naked as Indians, worked as hard as slaves, and ate nothing but New England refuse salt fish, with their hams and potatoes.

If the legislation raises the price of the island products in the northern colonies, it would prevent many people in America as well as Indians from dying of excessive use of rum, and possibly end Indian wars. Still better, with "living prices" the Britᵢₕ sugar planters would spend their surplus in money in Great Britain, in the education of their children, or otherwise; but if they are kept poor, they might be forced to go the northern continent, where they may live more cheaply upon their small fortunes than in Great Britain.[59]

In 1733 Parliament ordered the levying of duties on the importation of "foreign" West Indies sugar, rum, and molasses into the continental colonies, but it was not until the end of the wars with France in 1763 that England felt free to attempt to enforce the Navigation Acts strictly and especially make the tax on the importation of "foreign" sugar products by the Sugar Act of 1764 yield a substantial revenue for the support of the English authority in the colonies.

The uproar in the colonies was tremendous. Harvard masters in 1765 gave the affirmative to the question: "Can the new prohibitory duties which make it useless for the people to engage in commerce be evaded by them as faithful subjects?"

Otis, pointing to Lord Coke's dictum that trade and traffic "is the livelihood of the merchant, the life of the commonwealth," asked if the merchants of British America were not entitled to a livelihood also. "Are they not British subjects?" Then, of course, he threatened that the colonies would enter manufactures despite British regulations if their trade were cut off. The country has the natural means of every manufacture in Europe and even some that are not in Europe's power to make or produce. It will scarcely be believed a hundred years hence that American manufacture could have been brought to such perfection as they will then probably be in, if the present measures are enforced. In fact, he exclaimed as he waxed warm: "Can anyone tell me why trade, commerce, arts, sciences and manufactures, should not be as free for an American as for an European? Is there anything in the laws of nature and nations, anything in the nature of our allegiance that forbids a colonist to push the manufacture of iron much beyond the making of a horseshoe or a hob nail?"

However, as far as manufactures were concerned, he added quickly enough in another protest, England need never fear their growth in the colonies if only trade were not restrained. "I can never hear American manufactures seriously talked of, without being disposed to a violent fit of laughter. My contempt is inexpressible, when I perceive statesmen at home amusing the mob they affect to despise, with the imminent danger from American manufactures." [60] As for smuggling in of foreign manufactures, Otis said, this was done not by the merchants but by the customs officials and was the result of the too strict patrolling.

Oxenbridge Thacher, another lawyer and leader of the "popular" party, explained in *The Sentiments of a British American* (1764) that "trade is a nice and delicate lady; she must be courted and won by soft and fair addresses." Consequently the regulations must break the heart of the colonial trader. Worse, they will create a vast unemployment in England and bring her down, as is now happening.

Even ardently loyal institutions took much the same attitude. Dr. John Morgan, M.D., Fellow of the Royal Society and professor in the medical school, in the prize essay of the College of Philadelphia on "The Great Advantage of the Union between Great Britain and the Colonies," declared "it was not wise policy to prevent the colonies from enriching themselves by trade at the expense of their neighbors." For these are the only channels through which the riches of foreign countries are poured into the coffers of Britain. But "commerce, once forced from her wonted course, is seldom or never brought into it again." Foreigners will soon usurp our trade, and thrive in proportion as we decline.[61]

Parliament reduced the duty on sugar products, but included those coming from the British sugar islands as well as from the foreign ones, and replaced the obnoxious and recently repealed Stamp Act with new duties—the Townshend Acts—on various colonial imports.

The outcry was vigorous. The taxes might seem light, said the Boston merchants in their *Observations on Several Acts of Parlia-*

ment in 1769, but merchants operate on such small margins that the tax means a loss. They do not, they said, complain "of their trade being confined to Great Britain for such goods as are manufactured there, so long as they can be imported duty free"—that is, the collecting of duties on imports in the colonies by Crown-appointed officials should cease. With their elimination, of course, was to go what the colonial merchants felt was the too rigorous anti-smuggling machinery controlled by the Crown. All duties on goods imported into the colonies for purposes of revenue should be repealed as inconsistent with the rights of the merchants "as free subjects," and as prejudicial to the trade of Great Britain.

In 1770 the Townshend Acts were repealed with the exception of a small duty on tea, but this did not do away with the main objection of the strident commercial interests opposed to the strict enforcement of the general Navigation Acts which they formally lauded.

CHAPTER IX

The Role of Paper Money

THE pivotal problem within and between the colonies and between the colonies and the mother country remained the problem of the money supply. There was general agreement with Cotton Mather's statement in *The Christian Philosopher* (1721) that the love of money is the root of the evil, but where "money has not been introduced, men are brutish and savage, and nothing . . . good has been cultivated." There is perhaps no greater sin, he declared in his *Essays to Do Good* (1710), than preventing the circulation of money by hoarding it. Harvard masters in 1761 gave an affirmative to the question: "Is the man who has an ardent passion for accumulating riches a greater injury to the state than a spendthrift?"

Though "commodities" at fixed or "current" prices were still extensively used as money, no one in the last analysis questioned that at best this was a necessary evil and that specie was the only sound money. To obtain specie the old device of competitively raising the value of foreign coins and bullion was continued for a time, but when the Crown followed Penn's suggestion and proclaimed in 1704 a uniform overvaluation of approximately one-third, paper money became the great panacea and the center of monetary discussion.

Contrary to the tradition that historians have perpetuated, a critical analysis of the contemporary literature indicates that the proponents as well as the critics were not poor debtors or agrarians, but for the most part officials, ministers, merchants, and men of substance and learning in general. Involved in the discussion were the questions of cheap money, avoidance of and shifting of taxation, conflicting and changing business interests, the pecuniary interest of officials both at home and in the colonies, and finally the drive by each colony to achieve the commercial and social grandeur of England. Not the least striking feature was the shift in position of some of the participants from time to time, depending on the exigencies of their affairs.

All the colonies, following Massachusetts's lead, issued paper money of one kind or another. The legal-tender feature, whether qualified or complete, raised a storm of controversy from the start. Massachusetts in 1712, on the ground of preventing "oppression to debtors," made the public bills legal tender in payment of debts except for "specialties and express contracts in writing" (documents under seal). This action aroused Judge Samuel Sewall, himself a merchant, to exclaim that bills should never have been issued and that the merchants unjustly complain of a scarcity of money, for they have exported and continue to export the real money.

Vigorously leading the opposition to the judge's views was Jonathan Belcher, who on later occasions was to use the judge's arguments. He had not only a Harvard M.A. and the polish of contact with royalty on the Continent and in England, but also the wealth of a successful firm that imported Madeira wine, among other choice goods, furnished supplies to the colonial armies, participated in provincial loans, invested in copper mines, and speculated in Maine lands. The judge, Belcher declared, "should do well to be out of the way rather than hinder so great a good" as the Tender Act.[1]

At the same time came the reprinting of Blackwell's original treatise—that is, the one without the appendix—criticizing overvaluation. As in the earlier phase, there were appeals both to the Crown and the colonial government, and proponents as well as opponents were leading citizens, including ministers and merchants. The great exponent who was to push this scheme for over a quarter of a century was John Colman, brother of Benjamin Colman. He was a leading citizen and prominent merchant engaged among other things in the sale of Negroes, male and female. But as before the scheme faced opposition from other powerful groups.

The outstanding opponent was the learned attorney general, Paul Dudley, who like Colden claimed that he spoke for the "country," for the "husbandmen." His father, the governor, had strenuously backed Blackwell in the eighties, but now both felt that such a private bank would overpower government, and its bills would sink because it intended to charge an interest rate lower than the market rate.

The only sound banks, wrote Dudley in *Objections to the Bank of Credit* (1714), are money banks like the Bank of England with specie reserves behind its convertible bills, and with Treasury support in emergency. Real money is scarce because the "ordinary sort" of people live beyond their circumstances, especially in consuming vast quantities of rum and wine. This has led to an unfavorable balance of trade. However, until people can make adjustments, some paper must be issued to enable people to pay taxes and engage in trade. Therefore the colony should lend individuals a limited amount of bills for five years at interest, ostensibly on land security. The profits at least would go to the public rather than to private adventurers.

The issue of such public bills or loans is constitutional, Dudley continued, because the charter grants the colony the right to tax for the necessary defense and support of the government and the protection of the inhabitants, and bills are required for the preservation of the people in trade and business.

Proponents of the private bank also appealed to the "country." They agreed that the lower classes have engaged in extravagant consumption and thereby increased the colony's indebtedness to England. But the scarcity of money is the cause, not the effect, of the unprofitable direct trade with England; for the laboring men, forced by the lack of money to take their pay in notes on shops, spend more than they want or should on imports. At the same time the necessary resort to barter in internal trade and the consequent "bad pay" raise the price of labor, to the loss of export markets.

Public bills are desirable to a limited degree. They might be issued to build granaries for the prevention of gluts in foreign markets and to provide bounties for naval stores, manufactures, and especially for importing indentured servants. The debts contracted by these emissions would be the country's real credit and strength. Therefore heavy taxes need not and should not be levied to redeem them.

But the loan of public bills to individuals for trade and commerce is not granted by the charter. If the government had this power, it could create a despotism, for it unites the purse and the sword. Thus a private bank must be used. But land banks are preferable to specie banks, for silver constantly fluctuates.[2]

When the proponents found their efforts being blocked in the colony, they appealed to influential friends in England to help them obtain a Crown charter. Cotton Mather wrote two knights of importance that the public bills have been a great boon, but with their continual redemption the country is being left with insufficient circulating medium. Even at that, they are never adequate to the country's increasing business with the growth of the people. Consequently the people are being distressed. "The blood in our veins is much of it exhausted; and what little is left, is by some wealthy people, stagnated." The proposed further issue of public loan bills, many think is inadvisable and unjustifiable. But to relieve adequately the colony's difficulties, a number of our more "ingenious gentlemen" have proposed a private land bank. The persons concerned are of "superior circumstances. From all parts of the Land they pray to come into the partnership; their interest is very potent, and very much carries the new elections for our general Assembly." But this worthy project is opposed by some "who can do what they will in our government," and so the "gentlemen prostrate themselves before the King for his royal favor."[3]

Over in England, Banister, in the very same letter in which he appealed for bounties on hemp and other naval stores and the continuation of "free trade" with the "foreign" sugar islands, called for a Crown charter for the bank. He reiterated Mather's point that, with the public bills being called in, men of substance, if they owed any money, were being forced to sell their assets at sacrifice prices. To free themselves from this "big-belly'd evil," the inhabitants have projected a bank of credit founded upon land security and request a royal charter of incorporation. In return they offer the Crown a small percentage of the profits. What is more, they propose a proper encouragement—premiums—for such as shall raise a certain quantity of hemp. In this manner the colony would be extremely serviceable to the Crown, for it would free England from its frightful and costly dependence upon the northern continental powers in the Baltic for commodities essential to our trade.

Public bills won out in the contest, and along with issues for government expenditures came the first issue of loan bills in 1716, with borrowers paying 5 per cent. But the depreciation of the public bills brought an outcry. Prices have risen not because of the scarcity of commodities, wrote one critic in 1719, but because of the "mean opinion people have of the current money." Like any other commodity, the more issued, the less it is valued. Notes or bills of credit are not money, but a security that payment shall be made at a specified time. The shorter the date of redemption, the greater their value and esteem in people's mind, for everyone desires present pay. To postpone the redemption of bills, as has been done, violates the government's engagement with the holder, sinks the credit of the bills, and so raises prices. This hurts not only fixed income receivers, but also tradesmen and day laborers, for their wages remain relatively fixed. Full legal tender for the public bills would not stop their depreciation, for human laws cannot "change men's minds about things."[1]

Governor William Burnet, who claimed to be an expert on monetary theory because of experience gained through his heavy losses in the South Sea Company, attributed the depreciation in 1728 to a lack of a balance in the Massachusetts government, for with the governor's office denied a permanent salary there was no check on "the sudden and unadvised measures of former Assemblies."

As governor of New York and New Jersey, he had pleaded with the home authorities in 1724 to allow the issue of legal-tender public bills in his colonies. The home government has failed, he said, to understand the value of "compulsive paper credit." Since there is no proportion between specie and bank bills, the Bank of England in emergencies, instead of relieving government, must rely on government for support. Consequently convertibility is a "fashionable bubble," and the government, instead of making its exchequer bills legal tender, foolishly pays interest on them and allows the Bank of England a profit to circulate them at par. Paper money saved Carolina and Massachusetts from being conquered. Paper keeps up the country, occasions an increase in trade and business, and a consequent increase of specie exports to England. The measures are sponsored by the merchants here; the evils are imaginary ones, the misrepresentations of merchants in England.

Now Burnet informed the Massachusetts House that England's public credit is high despite heavy charges and debts because its exchequer bills are only a tender for taxes and the Bank receives a profit to circulate them at par. To make the Massachusetts bills legal tender for specialities would depreciate the bills further, for "liberty is the life of credit," and force its greatest enemy. Therefore it is beyond comprehension "to find you arguing for compulsion to force Englishmen to take paper against their will instead of money." [5]

Meanwhile John Colman re-entered the fray. The evil of the public bills, he said, is not their excessive quantity, but their scarcity. This ruins the "middling sort" of people, the enterprisers, but enriches the usurers. If government would support a private land bank with its authority, all industry and business would be stimulated. The fatal defect of the increasing deficiency of the public bills will be avoided because the supply will not fluctuate. Otherwise, to prevent the stagnation of business and the unemployment of the poor, the government must engage in some of the great public works with public bills, and so achieve a favorable trade balance.[6]

As another supporter put it, in *Trade and Commerce Inculcated*, in times of peace government must make fortifications, colleges and other expenditures for great public works; for the "common ordinary demand for labor is insufficient to prevent idleness, especially among a people not given to advancing their worldly grandeur in the expense of labor."

Colman was immediately answered in newspaper and pamphlet by a "country man" who was as much a rustic as Dudley, the Reverend Edward Wigglesworth, later professor of divinity at Harvard. Along with Dudley and now also Cotton Mather, he saw the trouble in overtrading, in an excess of imports over exports, which was in turn both the cause and the effect of the extravagance of the poor. One would hardly think that Boston is in distress, he said, if bridges and fortifications and other ways of spending money are proposed. This would increase, not reduce, the province debt. Such matters, if profitable, should be left to private parties rather than government to take the risk and benefit. To encourage manufacture is wise, but manufactures cannot develop as long as labor is dear; and as long as bills are cheap, labor will be dear.

In the absence of bills, prices would fall and sufficient specie would return to carry the trade at the reduced price level. But, since the trading community will not be convinced of the soundness of the proposal and since the traders are the only ones who can bring in silver, the province might eliminate the bills gradually by lending a large sum of differently designated bills without interest to traders, but the traders must repay in silver to the same nominal value, a certain per cent each year.[7]

Public bills and particularly the land bank received support from the great opponent of the Mathers on ecclesiastical polity. The shrewd and witty Reverend John Wise had borrowed public bills and dedicated his treatise, *A Word of Comfort to a Melancholy Country*, to the merchants as the "principal steersmen," the greatest benefactors. It is as foolish, he said, to speak of overtrading among merchants as overthreshing among men whom God teaches to thresh corn. Since we are not only a dependent government, but also a "dependent merchandise of Great Britain," we cannot reduce imports from Great Britain and thus prevent the draining of our specie unless we want to live like savages.

A country grows rich not by "the sprinkling of money" always unpatriotically on the wing, like silver, but by diligence, frugality, and the circulation of the produce with a profit to every man, especially the farmer, whereby he is recompensed for his prime stock, labor, and risk. The tyranny of money and moneyed men has been in lowering the price of our export goods to the ruin of the farmer. The bills, on the other hand, have raised the price of the country's goods to a "due rate or estimation." True, salaried men, especially ministers, have been hurt; but government should raise their salaries proportionately.

The bills can do still more good. By bills, the number of settlements, towns, and peoples might be tremendously increased. The bills might be lent especially to societies of adventurers to cultivate their vacant ground, and "buy stock and servants."

But where was the province to obtain the people? We "will invite our good brethren" at home, who will bring with them "a superior ingenuity and skill in manufactures." Besides, many of our old towns have too many inhabitants for husbandry. Also many of our people marry late for lack of settlements, whereas in old countries they marry without such precaution and so increase infinitely.

When all the land is fully occupied and the towns full of specialized craftsmen, manufactures for a foreign vend will develop, but not until then. Witness old, overcrowded countries, where great numbers must beg, steal, or fight for their living, or work for starving wages. Therefore we should encourage settlement speedily, "so that we may put things into some good forwardness and leave a wise model for the next age."

For the present, with the help of plentiful bills of credit to vend and circulate our own produce and effects, we can buy goods from our merchants cheaper than we can make them, and so save our time for more profitable business.

But for preventing depreciation a private land bank issuing legal-tender bills is preferable to a public one. The maintenance of the value of public bills depends on the principal men and traders accepting them as such. But, guided as all men are by self-interest, these men will depreciate the bills because they do not profit from their management. This explains why the South Carolina bills suffered heavy depreciation. Therefore the bank should be a private corporation composed of principal and suitable gentlemen; of great landed men and merchants, rich farmers and mechanics influential in their communities.

Since they are men of differing functions mutually checking one another and forced to accept the bills at par in their own transactions, self-interest will induce them to act rightly. By their wisdom, caution, and example, they can regulate all prices and so prevent "the wild and insulting prices of things." Thereby they act as though absolute masters of the market and yet hurt no man's property and liberty, to the end that everyone receives reasonable gain. The profit seems a "booty to particular men," but the bank, by maintaining the medium for all business, would be just as beneficial to all as though done by the government.

That the paper money was essential at this time, few denied. The Harvard masters' theses list for 1728 gave the affirmative to the question: "Does the use of paper money contribute to the public good?" The depreciation was generally attributed to the merchants. In order to obtain the colony's specie for returns to England, wrote the eminent theologian, Solomon Stoddard in *An Answer to Some Cases of Conscience*, they give thirty shillings for twenty in silver. They can afford the high rate because they sell their goods at excessive prices. However, they need not have done this "for they have the command of the market, and might buy the produce of the country at such prices, that they might make as profitable returns," as at present.

Beginning in the next decade, the situation became more tense. Royal instructions were given the new governor, none other than Jonathan Belcher, that all outstanding bills were to be called in punctually according to their specified dates, which meant by 1741; that an annual issue of £30,000 would be permitted for current, ordinary expenses, but this should be at any time the maximum outstanding.

As Massachusetts bills were being restrained, Rhode Island made large issues of bills for expenses and loans, ostensibly to provide fortifications, bounties, and other aids to the fishery and manufactures non-competitive with the mother country. All the rest of New England accepted them, though not as legal tender. Supporters in Massachusetts declared that, with New England's traders requiring more circulating media, the Rhode Island issues prevent the havoc being wrought by the royal instructions. Rhode Island gains a profit, but this is of little consequence if the public is profited at the same time. At "our risk and venture" the inhabitants of the rest of New England are supplied with a proper medium, said a Rhode Islander.[8]

Governor Belcher, who had so strongly supported the original issues, now complained that the debtors, as the majority in the New England legislatures, were endeavoring by constant emissions to depreciate the bills to "cheat the honest, kind creditors." New England has departed from the simple frugal ways of the founding fathers.[9]

However, the Boston town meeting, that unparalleled aggressive organ of mercantile opinion, informed its representatives in 1736 that, in the interest of the province in general and the trade and business of the town in particular, they must demand the issue of more paper and so prevent that "rigorous execution" of the royal instructions which is jeopardizing their "laws, liberties and properties," their "natural rights" and "chartered privileges." [10]

The Massachusetts House of Representatives in 1739 asked the public for schemes for supplying a medium of exchange of invariable value. The Colman group came forward with a slightly modified version of the land-bank scheme, in the form of a manufactory company. Subscribers and other borrowers were to pay off the interest and principal in the bills of the company or in specified produce and manufacture suitable for developing export industries and reducing the imports, and the bills were to be redeemed in the specified goods in twenty years. At approximately the same time a group of merchants, including Judge Sewall, proposed a so-called silver bank. Like the Colman group, it argued that England had drained the colony of specie in payment for manufactures, that business in the province had been transacted by bills of credit, and that in a short time all the bills would have been called in. But specie was the only basis for a bank. Since specie could not be obtained suddenly, the bank notes were to be redeemed in fifteen years at a small appreciating rate. Proponents of each scheme described the other as a disastrous experiment. Both were unsuccessful in obtaining charters but, pleading the right of "liberty and property," they began operations.

The manufactory had "popular" support. It had around 900 subscribers at the beginning, including among others some leading officials, members of the legislature, and even members of the governor's family. But the governor and the council after some hesitation denounced the scheme and used every possible device to end it, from barring its lawyers from the courts to jailing the purported leaders of what the governor claimed was to be an organized march of this self-styled Patriot Party in Boston to see why the bills would not circulate there. Finally Parliament was asked to dissolve the Colman bank.[11] Parliament went further and also ended the silver bank by extending the "Bubble Act" to the colonies.

The great controversy that culminated in the ending of the private land bank produced two able pamphleteers, Hugh Vance and William Douglass.

Vance's family connections were of the best. His wife was the daughter of the Reverend Ebenezer Pemberton. The mercantile code of the day he knew well. In 1728 he joined with the Boston merchants in an agreement not to purchase dried codfish from the Marblehead fishermen above a certain price. Boston appreciated his talents by making him a member or chairman of the committees that formulated the town's position on currency and taxation. But in 1758 he was judged bankrupt.

In all the current literature, so shot through with polemics and denunciation, Vance's pamphlets came the closest to being dispassionate. He even made detailed mathematical calculations as to the efficacy of various proposals. Vance was a close observer of conditions at home and abroad. His pamphlets, especially *An Inquiry Into The Nature and Uses of Money*, reveal a mind familiar with the best mercantile literature, not only "the great Mr. Locke," but also John Law, who wrote "admirably well on money in the year 1705," many years "before the fatal Mississippi scheme fathered upon him, but more likely . . . the device of the then regent of France, I mean the iniquitous part." Vance used Locke skillfully to suit his purposes, though his conclusions ran counter to Locke's.

Vance built on the familiar argument presented by Wise—the inability of a dependent colony to rectify the "shameful balance of debt" with the mother country by reducing its imports of finery; that is, "its mode of living." But Vance was more systematic in his thinking. He felt that he must present the general theory of value before he could present his theory of the value of money. From this exponent of the land bank and public bills came the most elaborate presentation of the theory of value to be found in colonial literature: All things in use have their value or estimation either from "craving necessity or . . . from voluntary choice of mankind." The first have real, unchangeable, intrinsic value; the latter have an accidental or circumstantial value. In the first class are air, water, necessary provisions; in the second, precious stones, metals, and finery—in short, every article of provision or clothing upon which more cost is bestowed than needful.

The changes in the comparative value or price of things in the market arises either from the plenty or scarcity of the commodity for sale or from the greater or smaller number of buyers; that is, a change in the proportion between the quantity to be sold and the demand for that quantity. The former is the present quantity of goods with which the sellers are inclined or forced to part; the latter is the amount which the buyers are obliged at the time to purchase.

Exportable commodities common to the world in general change their value by means of any change in the proportion between the quantity and demand in the whole trading world, but non-exportable goods change their value from the same cause within any particular country.

The true proportion between quantity and demand is rarely known because no man can tell what obligation or disposition other people may have to buy or sell. We can only form a general judgment of the circumstances of the market; but in any event a price change can occur only as result of a change in the proportion. Many incidents may contribute to vary the demand for a commodity besides its own "natural and common circumstances." Shortages in corn and rye may be overcome by good wheat crops; consequently the demand for the latter will be increased. A plenty of fresh fish or wild pigeons will tend to lessen the demand for beef and thus lower its price. But these "and all other like circumstances are included in the notion of quantity and demand." The rents of house and lands are governed by the proportion of quantity and demand, and the purchase value is governed by the rent.

Now, gold, silver, paper obey these fundamentals. Gold and silver have their value not so much for their usefulness as metals as from the common consent of mankind in choosing them as money. "Money is any one commodity or a number of commodities . . . received either by the trading world in general, or any community in particular, more readily than all other commodities passing in trade and that for which contracts or agreements are usually made." Just as the willingness to receive silver, not the act of government, gives value to silver, so common consent gives value among the trading community to the bills of credit in the market. Government can rightly declare the bills lawful tender where money is promised, but they have "justly excepted special contracts, for otherwise they would strike at the root of trade." But convertibility even in the future into specie is undesirable, for this reduces the paper from the status of a money to merely that of a promissory note and is consequently subject to a discount depending on date of redemption.

Variations in the value of money can be judged in two ways: First, by comparing it with other things in the market; but this is practically impossible to determine objectively. Though many things have risen in value in proportion to the increase in silver, the common money in Europe, yet many things have also fallen. For, although money is the cause of a greater demand for many things, yet its vastly quicker circulation than other commodities animates "the invention and industry of mankind, and so becomes also the means of increasing the quantity of many things." A second and more serious difficulty with the method is that it is hard to tell whether the change in value is in money or in the things money measures.

The other and more satisfactory way of judging the value of money is by the variations in the yearly increase, or natural interest, which is the market rate. With reference to houses and lands this return is called rent. Just as a variation in rent varies the purchase value of a house, so the change in the natural interest is infallible evidence of a change in the value of money, for the rate of interest is governed by the proportion of the quantity and demand of money. Since the rate of interest is increasing, there must be a scarcity of money. But, as the essential tool of commerce, money ought to be, proportionately to the countries with whom we trade, the cheapest commodity—that is, at a lower rate of interest than our neighbors'.

The scarcity of money arises from adherence to the precious metals as money. They should be reduced to a commodity and not used as money.

Gold and silver are extremely useful as treasure, for they are universally the chief encouragement and reward for industry. Having universal acceptance, they are the best commodities for paying balances between nations. To meet such demands every trading country must have a sufficiency; otherwise the price of silver rises, to the ruin of the country. But universal commodities such as gold and silver cannot serve as "money." Every country must choose a special or local one, a non-exportable commodity, for universal commodities cannot have the basic prerequisite of money, stable value. Stable money requires that the quantity fluctuate with the demand for the needs of trade. But the price of silver, as colonial experience shows, cannot be fixed despite laws, for it will always be rated according to the course of trade without regard to the necessary proportion between quantity and demand within a country.

Any commodity left free to its course in the market must always fluctuate in value, for "no assigned quantity of any one thing will long continue precisely equal to an assigned quantity" of anything else; even silver and gold do not naturally hold an exact proportion to one another, and every community must change the proportions whenever the maritime nations or the majority of them do, on risk of losing the more valuable and receiving the less valuable metal.

Some have thought that the rate of labor might be the standard measure of value. True, the labor cost is often the chief cost in production, but the goods must be sold in the market according to the proportion of quantity and demand, consequently wages vary from occupation to occupation.

The bills of public credit would be a perfect measure of value if they were fixed to an assigned rate of interest from, say, 3 to 6 per cent, and at this rate emitted and called in in proportion to the demand every day. They could not change their own value, nor could they fix the rate of any commodity, for this can only be done by the common consent of a community or by special agreement among private men.

The advantage of such bills is seen from Rhode Island's great gains from paper. That colony used to purchase considerable European goods from Massachusetts. Thereby Massachusetts "gained the carriage, merchants' and often the wholesalers' profits." Massachusetts obtained not only gold and silver and other commodities for direct returns to the mother country, but also articles "capable of additional improvements" in Massachusetts, and at the enhanced value serving as returns to England in a more remote way. But now the roles are reversed. Rhode Island will continue to gain if she continues to provide enough bills at low interest and reduces the term of issue so that the quantity can be varied as trade requires. Her great advantage of money at a low interest will eventually create a balance of debt against us, in her favor. This might be worse than the debt to the mother country, for after the payments of produce and treasure to her she will require our lands to make up the balance.

We have not lost by the use of her bills, for without them the scarcity of money would have been greater and Massachusetts' plight worse. But our industrious neighbor has gained on us, and we must follow her example. But in the light of the royal instructions against public bills, "private notes of the same nature (having the common consent of the trading part in the province) might be circulated in trade, and by a due regulation be of the same or greater benefit to the province." The manufactory scheme, backed as it is by principal "men of judgment, of integrity and of sufficient estate," is the most practicable solution.

On the other hand, for the country to attempt to return to silver or to embrace schemes of notes redeemable in silver at certain fixed rates in the present or in the future would ruin trade and industry, for then these would raise the price of silver and thus increase the scarcity of money.

There have been sufferers from the change in the measure of value, but only a few have a legitimate right to relief; namely, officials with fixed salaries. The others have been at all times at liberty to make contracts in specie at fixed rates. As for the officers, the standard of readjustment should not be the rate of silver, but "the different circumstances of the office on the one hand, and the change of mode of living on the other." [12]

In reply to Vance came the customary "The Countryman's Answer to his Friend the Merchant in Boston." He felt that the "employers abroad" of "you merchants and factors in Boston" must be greatly nonplussed by Vance's theory.[13]

The great opponent, however, was William Douglass, a native of Scotland with an extensive medical training at leading European centers. He took a great interest in the physical sciences and engaged in correspondence with the American scientists of the day to advance that realm of knowledge. A man of strong opinions, he did not hesitate to engage in vigorous polemics, whether on smallpox, where he first opposed inoculation, or on military affairs, where he turned out equally wrong.

In the course of time Douglass acquired large landholdings and tenants, and during his lifetime a town in Massachusetts was named for him. He felt that he had lost much by the "fraudulent" public paper and frankly stated so in his publications. He was also bitterly opposed to the private land bank, but he was sympathetic to the silver bank. He was none too careful in collecting his facts, and his knowledge of the literature was narrow.

Douglass accused Vance of being as much prejudiced against "matters of fact as against silver." But that he was hardly a match for Vance in matters of technical, detailed knowledge, he was aware. "I shall forbear any idle criticism upon his calculations, figures, and technical, commercial words as being out of the question" was all he could say on this level.

Silver, Douglass declared, is the only true money. It has universal acceptance among merchants because its value varies least. It can only depreciate to an insignificant degree because, being in universal demand throughout the world, continued additions are like throwing drops of water into the ocean. Consequently it is the one commodity of which a country can never have too much.

Douglass contended, however, that European countries have learned that a paper credit well founded and not larger than what the silver currency will bear is a good expedient for business and leaves silver free to be used as merchandise and for petty occasions. But if paper credit exceeds a certain proportion of the concomitant silver currency, then all the evils of depreciation follow. But the proper proportion is to be learned only by experience. Private notes like those of the silver bank are better than public notes because in the latter case no recourse can be had in case of breach of the public faith.

Because of the excessive issues of public paper, silver has risen in value and disappeared. A base currency will always drive out the better. But, just as some countries destroy a part of their staples to raise their value, so if Massachusetts would reduce its paper, the value of the remainder would be equal to the value of the whole paper now current or proposed to be added.

The supposed scarcity of bills is the result of the great issues. The greater the issue, the greater the rise in prices, the greater becomes the demand for more paper to carry the same amount of goods. The effect of currency depreciation in causing the rise in general prices is obscured to many by the fact that particular goods fluctuate according to quantity and demand.

With the reduction of paper, imports will be fewer and cheap. If we add to our exports by industry and reduce our imports by frugality, a favorable balance arises, and consequently the country obtains sufficient specie.

Likewise the great rise in the rate of interest is not evidence of usury or scarcity of bills, but of excessive issues of bills. If the natural medium, silver, is plentiful, interest falls, but with the excessive depreciating paper the lender to save himself is obliged to lay the growing loss of the principal on the interest. If bills were to depreciate at a definite rate, justice might be done by imposing the loss which the principal might sustain upon the interest of a bond or price of goods, but depreciation is uncertain, and great confusion in dealings is the result.

A land bank in any form is pernicious. Land can hardly be used as returns and cannot be transferred by bills of exchange. Produce, in addition, is too perishable and unwieldy. Besides, of the three great branches of business—trade, manufacture, and produce—trade is the most profitable, but agriculture the most necessary though the least lucrative. "People of genius for trade grow rich by the labor of peasants, and the peasants or laborers happy by being employed." If land bank schemes be tolerated, this province noted for trade will soon become a habitation for rustics.

When Douglass began delineating the classes that grievously suffered from the depreciation, the laborers and tradesmen became for a moment "the heads which feed the belly of the commonwealth, and therefore deserve our chief regard." They suffer because their wages lag behind the rising prices.

The greatest sufferers are the industrious and frugal, the large foreign traders composed of the English merchant adventurers to New England, and the rich moneyed men. They are defrauded by the landed men and the shopkeepers. The former purchase land on credit or mortgage their existing estates and call for more paper emissions to reduce the debts to insignificance. The latter purchase goods on long credit from the merchant, sell them at the proportionally higher prices caused by the emissions, and repay in the depreciated money. At the same time, the emissions, shop notes, and long credit encourage laborers and tradesmen to buy goods above their condition. Thus the party for multiplying a paper currency is the idle, the extravagant, and the fraudulent debtors. It includes "some men of substance," but these are of a "natural improbity and depravity of mind."

The Paper Party includes the majority, for the majority are debtors. But as debtors they cannot have the interest of the country at heart; for, having nothing to lose, they will surrender the country to the first invader. Thus in Great Britain the peers, by reason of their great estates, are deemed "the natural and standing council of the king and country." The firmest supporters of the colony are the great foreign traders and rich moneyed men because of the great substance deposited here. If paper-money schemes were for the general good, would they be opposed by the gentlemen of large interests?

Since the majority have the most votes, they elect men of their stamp. So the infatuation for paper has had a mutinous effect in several of the colonies. Thus the peoples' representatives, the democratical part of the constitution, have frequently refused to provide for the necessary charges of government, especially the governor's salary, because the governor and council would not violate the royal instructions on paper issues. The "democratical spirit" has abused English liberty and property and has given rise to "levelling and licentiousness" and the denial of subordination.

He pointed to Rhode Island, where both the legislature and the executive are chosen by the people, and government therefore becomes worse than a state of nature. If this "tyrannical system" of popular control continues, farewell to dependence on Great Britain.

In Massachusetts the projectors of the Massachusetts manufactory scheme have instilled in the unthinking multitudes the idea that common consent or the humor of the multitude, the *vox populi*, ought to be the *ultima ratio* in everything. This principle if logically pushed would, like the depreciating public bills, result in the equal division of all property among the people, "because we are all born equal."

The permanent remedy is for the legislature to sanction a private society like the silver bank group, to emit bills on a good silver bottom continually appreciating at a rather small rate, say 3 per cent per annum above the present value of paper, in order to prevent the hoarding of the bills. Its bills, like the public ones, should be accepted by the government.

Previous experiments in silver banks in the colony were defective because they could not effectively bring the bad currency under a discount. Consequently as silver rose the notes, becoming more valuable, were hoarded. Therefore as a circulating medium they are worse than the depreciated public bills, for the latter circulate in business. But the debtor's party malignantly seeks to persuade the multitude that the private silver-bank project and the governor's opposition to the land bank are impositions upon "liberty and property." [14]

Douglass, in temperament, family, educational background, and social philosophy, closely resembled his boyhood friend, Cadwallader Colden. But where Colden always ran off "sound" economics and politics under the guise of opposition to merchants and in support of country gentlemen, Douglass ran off the same politics and economics under the unusual guise of opposition to the rustics.

Basically Douglass differed only slightly from Vance, for in the last analysis he stood against "hard" money, even as he presumably called for it. Much of the difference turned on the old battle between "foreign" and "native" merchants, or more precisely between different groups of merchants. But the land-bank opponents could utilize a popular appeal, while the others could and did appeal to "authority" and "order."

Douglass got sympathy and information from his friend Colden in New York, where the governor had approved a large issue of public loan bills on the ground, among others, of encouraging ship-building and relieving trade of the taxation land should bear.

The New York Assembly's action in declaring the bills equal to specie and a tender in all payments, Colden wrote Douglass, shows that we have little security in our constitution against "despotic power, I mean by the mixture . . . of the Democracy in it." But New York's bills have maintained their credit better than neighboring provinces because of its merchants' interest to do so. Since they dealt generally on their own stock, and only slightly on consignment from abroad, a rise in exchange, said Colden, would proportionately reduce all debts due them.[15]

After the battle over the land bank was formally over, Belcher, of whom Douglass thought highly, was transferred to the less lucrative governorship of New Jersey and there, as he had originally in Massachusetts, pleaded with the home authorities to approve an issue of bills on the ground that New Jersey paper was superior to that of the other provinces, and its treasury was empty.

On his arrival in 1741, the new governor of Massachusetts, William Shirley, followed his predecessors in lecturing the House of Representatives on the great evils of paper money. But he explained to the home authorities that he had consented to additional issues because it was impossible to suppress the paper completely. Rhode Island bills could not be prohibited from circulating in Massachusetts because the trade relations between the two colonies were too intertwined.[16]

With the outbreak of war between France and England, Shirley called for emissions of public bills to finance expeditions against French Canada. Finally the assembly declared that, if they issued more bills, a great impairment if not the loss of public credit would follow.

With the depreciation in terms of sterling exchange reaching twelve to one, the outcry against depreciation in Massachusetts and Connecticut was tremendous. The New England Congregational clergy in fast-day and election-day sermons wailed that the circulating medium was "as unstable as water" and as "variable as the wind." "We trade and traffick, buy and sell" with these false weights and measures and "so we daily oppress one another." It is a matter of indifference whether the medium be "coined metal or stamped paper," provided it be of invariable value.[17]

The Reverend Charles Chauncy said it was practically impossible for a dependent government without real money to prevent its substitute from "varying in its real worth," but it could fix some "certain standard, to which the current medium may be so related so that the true value, at different times, may be . . . ascertained." [18]

Meanwhile Massachusetts passed acts for adjusting debts in depreciated paper, but controversies arose over determining depreciation. As a first standard the price of silver and sterling bills of exchange was taken, but in 1747 the legislature ruled that the value of the bills could not properly be estimated by the value of any one or two commodities, or merchandise, as silver and bills of exchange are at present. These prices are liable to be "very suddenly and immoderately increased" by a few self-seeking persons, with the result that the bills depreciate in respect to these two commodities, though they maintain their value with respect to all other commodities. Therefore the courts, in calculating depreciation, must consider not only the prices of silver and bills of exchange, but also of provisions and necessaries and the plenty and scarcity of the articles.[19]

At the same time the negotiations for the Crown's reimbursing Massachusetts for her war expenditures threw into the limelight the closest approach to a hard-money man in New England. This was aristocratic Thomas Hutchinson, Speaker of the House of Representatives.

A "great frailty of human nature," he said, "is an inability or indisposition to compare a distant, though certain inconvenience . . . with a present . . . delight." True, an emission of bills brings prosperity for a time, but it is an illusion. With the exchange fluctuating every day, possessors of large sums of bills for even a few days, could not fail to perceive the difference in their value in the period between their receipt and their disposal. "The apprehension of their depreciation tended to increase it, and occasioned a quick circulation.' . . . Nobody kept them long." Consequently "business was brisk, men in trade increased their figures, but were sinking in the real value of their stock, for peoples will not cut expenses as long as they imagine their wealth is increasing and so the unfavorable balance of trade grows ever worse."

He did admit one advantage to paper money: As it depreciated, the wages of seamen did not immediately rise in proportion to the rise of silver. Since this enabled Massachusetts vessels to be hired more cheaply than those of any other colony, Massachusetts vessels became the carriers from many parts of the continent, the West Indies, and Europe. "The advantage in this particular instance, of the reduction of the price of labour shows us what improvements might be made in other branches of trade and manufacture, if ever it should be reduced to the price in Europe, compared with the price of the necessaries of life."

In accordance with the Crown's wishes, he demanded that the expected bounty be used to eliminate the paper. But the paper is to be redeemed at its current rate, not its nominal rate, for the latter would give an "unreasonable profit" to the possessors. This policy was adopted—the bills were redeemed in silver at only a slightly higher rate than the current one, after British merchants protested to the Crown "that many persons in the administration have bought up the depreciated bills and hope to receive double the sum they paid." [20]

On the other hand, Douglass, whom Hutchinson classified among men with good sense, violently opposed complete immediate redemption and demanded that the bills be gradually reduced lest there be a stagnation of business, confusion, and uproars.[21]

The most demagogic appeal for gradual redemption came from an anonymous writer who, judging from the wealth of learned quotations, must have been a college graduate. He appealed to the people as "the voice of God" against the machinations of the rich and high-born who threaten "the liberties and properties of the middling and common people." Complete immediate redemption was the scheme of base greedy merchants.

"To make the commonality slaves and vassals and themselves Lords of Mammon and sole possessors of our lands, liberties, etc.," they have induced the vain and silly majority to exchange their paper which is the reward of their industry for trifles and gewgaws, and now they await the silver bounty which they will export to England to build up estates.

Instead, the bounty should be left at the Bank of England as the fund or security for the province bills, and the interest could be used to redeem the bills gradually. This would make the notes in effect sterling money, which is the invariable and just standard in all business affairs. The bills would then in reality be measured by profitable labor which is the true basis of money.

After the redemption had been ordered by means of the bounty and short-term interest-bearing loans in 1750, the proponents of the Bank of England scheme exclaimed that the bounty would have been more profitably used if it had been devoted to building warships or ships to import poor but able-bodied laborers, presumably indentured servants. This would have employed many laborers, whereby the money would have freely circulated.[22]

In Connecticut the Reverend Samuel Johnson was certain that Connecticut would fritter away its bounty money in idle projects of trade instead of providing for a certain and valuable currency unless its "democratic constitution" was radically revised to give the governor a negative and make the council not so "absolutely" dependent on the people.[23]

But in 1755 Douglass, in his *A Summary . . . of the British Settle-ments in North-America*, complimented Connecticut as a government of "sagacious husbandmen," managed by "men of wisdom and prob-ity," for they allowed three years to cancel the bills gradually, and in-stead of bringing the silver to the colony they saved the expense and drew bills on their English agent—bills which readily purchase silver for currency.

Rhode Island, the great supplier of paper currency to all New Eng-land, furnished the occasion in 1751 for ending the legal-tender issues in the area. To Parliament its issues were denounced as "frustrating the good intentions" of the act providing for a uniform fixed rate for foreign coins in the colonies, for using paper as money alters the rates of silver and gold. It was even contended that men of substance had been prevented from coming to live in England because the depre-ciated paper rendered them incapable of paying their English debts. However, the Rhode Island evil could only be cured by eliminating legal-tender issues in all New England, for bills of any one New England colony promiscuously circulate in all.

The agents of the New England colonies vainly argued that such action would violate the natural rights and liberties of Englishmen in those colonies as embodied in their charter rights. These charters were contracts; the consideration was the blood and labor that had gone into making them profitable to England.

By the parliamentary act of 1751 the New England colonies were forbidden to issue new legal-tender bills, and the old ones were to be retired at the dates specified in the emissions. Non-legal-tender bills could be issued, but provision must be made for their redemp-tion through taxes in a short period. Rhode Island's agent wrote home that the Act would "probably . . . prevent any further depreciation of the paper money," and should not prove any great injury to the colony, since all the other New England colonies are "put on the same bottom." [24]

In Massachusetts in 1761 the discussion over money returned to the days of Blackwell and his opposition to raising the value of silver. The controversy arose over legislation to make gold as well as silver ex-plicitly a legal tender and at its present fixed rate. It was argued that otherwise, with silver being exported because of the rise of its price in England, debtors might be oppressed.

Heading the single-standard silver forces whose supporters were primarily in the council was Hutchinson, who was now, among other things, lieutenant governor and chief justice. Heading the forces of bimetalism were Oxenbridge Thacher and James Otis of the House of Representatives. As in the later stages of the paper-money controversy, the council group was dubbed the Court party; the other side the "country" party. The controversy became so heated that the governor dissolved the General Court, but the contestants transferred the battle to the newspapers. Hutchinson cited Locke and Isaac Newton as authorities; the opposition granted that Locke might be in favor of silver, but Newton was not. However, James Bowdoin, Harvard M.A., scion of a wealthy merchant family and "gentleman commoner" of Oxford, threw in the weight of his travels in England to claim for the Hutchinson side that Newton was being misinterpreted.

Hutchinson argued that gold had never been a legal tender, and, even if it were, two metals cannot both be the measure and both be fixed because, as Vance, his earlier great opponent had doubtless taught him, they are frequently changing their proportions to one another. Therefore gold should be a merchandise like copper. If gold were made a tender, silver would leave. Therefore the rate at which gold coin should pass should be reduced to the proportion existing in Europe. But, as one metal was made the standard and the only lawful tender, government should not regulate the other but "leave it to chance."

In the last analysis, the only way both silver and gold can be kept is by lessening our imports. We shall not do this sufficiently until compelled by a real scarcity of money. "The plenty of money has produced luxury; luxury naturally tends to poverty; poverty will produce industry and frugality." This will lessen the proportion of imports to exports and will bring money, but before this revolution is finished the "mischiefs from the disproportionate rates" must occur unless the rates are changed.

As with other ills, the great cause of the evil has been the "democratical government." The ignorant majority, unrestrained by a superior class, has always sought to tamper with real money. Since they are primarily debtors, they have continually sought to establish some form of "ideal money" to lighten their burden, but whether it was raising the pieces of eight, using "country pay" at fixed rates, or issuing paper, the effect was necessarily a heavy depreciation of the "ideal" money as reflected in the rate of exchange.

His opponents, Otis and Thacher, agreed with him that the "depreciating and detestable paper currency" had led only to confusion and disorder. But demonetizing gold was a breach of good faith and economics. They cited law and custom to prove that gold was a legal tender. Demonetization was not only a breach of faith with those who by custom if not by law had thought gold a legal tender, but it would result in a reduction of the supply of money, to the damage of trade. None would lose by maintaining the existing ratio, but if gold were lowered, "debtors or what is the same thing, traders and others will lose, because they have nine-tenths of the money." Finally, said Thacher, the truth is both metals have been rising; therefore, if a change must be made, the value of the silver dollar (Spanish) should be raised, not the gold coins lowered.

Raising the value of silver, retorted Hutchinson, brought the evils of paper. Proponents claim that traders want this, but the traders are foolish to do so, for every trader will lose 40 or 50 per cent of all debts due him, without reducing his debt in England. The province in general will be the losers because large sums are due the inhabitants from other colonies.

It was Otis's answer to Hutchinson's underlying social philosophy that revealed how much they agreed, even as Otis thought they disagreed. Hutchinson's deprecation of luxury, Otis said, was unwarranted. Luxury is a vague and loose term. If it means the importing of many foreign commodities, then the more we have, the better, provided we export enough to pay for them. Poverty is not the basis of industry and frugality, but the occasion of vices directly opposite. "I should be glad to see here, as in England, tradesmen and yeomen worth their tens and their hundreds of thousands of pounds," for not until then shall "we have gentlemen and merchants worth . . . their millions."

Unfortunately the local tradesman and the husbandman, in demanding a cramping trade, a restriction of imports, are killing a faithful servant who is toiling night and day, eating the bread of care for their good as well as his own. That trade once diverted seldom returns to its former channel; that multitudes of people, constant employment and quick pay, whether they agree to take silver, paper, or cockleshells are the riches of a country; that domestic improvements, and consequently the commodities raised and manufactured, are the surest measure of the wealth of a people, "are observations never the less true for being old." [25]

The General Court in 1762 ordered that gold be a legal tender at the old rate, regardless of the "varying prices of gold and silver bullion." The silver monometalists later explained that the measure did no damage because the price of silver bullion fell shortly.

New England's contribution to monetary discussion was the most elaborate and extensive and revealed most of the issues and answers that were to be brought forth time and again on the matter.

The southern colonies faced the problem in a somewhat similar fashion, but the analysis was slightly different in detail. South Carolina was, in fact, the first to issue public bills of credit as loans to individuals. In 1712, four years before the first similar Massachusetts measure, its legislature ordered an issue and stipulated that borrowers were to provide security to twice the value in lands, slaves, and other personal property and pay 12½ per cent annually for twelve years in discharge of the principal and interest.

The assembly declared that the public debts of the province have become so large that the province's public duties and income cannot pay them in a "tolerable time," and that the "ordinary method of imposing a tax on the estate, stocks, and abilities" of the inhabitants would be oppressive at present. Therefore the province would follow "the example of many great and rich countries" who in similar emergencies established "funds of credit which have effectually answered the ends of money and thereby given a quick circulation and encouragement to trade and commerce." [26]

Critics of South Carolina paper complained that paper money payable for debts violated the rights, liberty, and property of the British subjects; that by these "despotic . . . proceedings, the British merchants and traders who had given the planters large credits to stock themselves with Negroes, etc. lost immediately half their debts." [27]

Supporters for additional issues proved equal to the occasion with arguments to fit the southern scene. The evils of barter were sketched in a manner reminiscent of the previous century. One spokesman for a new issue of public loan bills in 1732 declared in his *An Essay On Currency* that a barter trade tends to ruin all towns. The people live scattered, with only a few trading houses, to the great discouragement of foreign trade and foreign traders. "By barter you can neither sell nor buy, but once a year" except from the oppressive country stores. Because of the latter, many families who formerly had many slaves now scarce have one. Thus barter oppresses the poor and leads to the concentration of wealth in a few hands. But paper money performs specie's function in eliminating the evils of barter. The bills should be loaned at a low rate, say 10 per cent, for a high rate makes the rich, who should be promoting improvements, lazy.

On the other hand, if the existing paper were called in, the poor— that is, the poor slave owners—would suffer greatly. They would be compelled to sell their slaves. Furthermore, the people finding the sale of their produce—pitch, tar, rice—uncertain, would turn to manufactures and their export. So England would not only lose a market for her manufactures, but be forced to pay more for the materials formerly obtained in the colony. At the same time he warned the northern colonies that they should not oppose paper issues in South Carolina; for their traders, like the English, exchanged manufactures for the produce of the colony as returns to England.

Among the ablest of the colonial documents was a committee report of the assembly in 1737 which advocated an emission of loan bills to facilitate trade, especially by providing "poor protestants from Europe with tools and supplies." It pointed out that the English merchants protesting against the proposed issue had requested previous ones. It cited the "received maxims" of trade from the "immortal Locke." The adverse trade balance, it said, drains the colony's specie. It is objected that, if this unfavorable balance continues, the province will be bankrupt, but the greatest part of the imports, Negroes, is not consumed but converted into permanent stock, and their labor redeems the debts of the preceding year.

It is objected that the increase of paper money raises exchange and the price of produce, to the prejudice of profitable tradings here and British merchant creditors. But the cause of the rise of exchange and produce cannot be paper, for at times when paper issues increased, the price of exchange fell; at other times when bills were redeemed, exchange rose. Exchange and produce have risen because of the great import of the "grand Article," Negroes. The profits are so large that Negro merchants and factors can afford to give large prices for country produce and high rates for bills of exchange.

It is objected that land cannot be a "fund," for if bills depreciate the fund will not help the possessor. Only the nominal amount must be met. But the objection also holds against specie. "Can the lender of an ounce of silver worth at the time of lending a bushel of wheat or 100 pounds of rice, when he is repaid demand a security that the ounce of silver . . . should be worth the commodities?" He may, and may he not with equal justice complain, if at the end of the period, through the scarcity or overdemand of these commodities, the ounce will procure only a portion of them? Whatever truth there is in the objection can be achieved by something in the objector's power; that is, stop importing Negroes for the next five or seven years.

The great gainers from a paper issue would be the British merchants, for if the province has a sufficient medium in trade the planter can buy British manufactures with ready money in the commercial center. The scarcity of currency, on the other hand, enables a few large debt-free planters to distress the market.[28]

From North Carolina came a contribution echoing that colony's constant cry of vassalage to other colonies. It was from the Quaker, William Borden (1689–1748). Borden was originally a shipbuilder in Rhode Island, where he had been a beneficiary of the colony's public bills to the extent of long-term loans and bounties for the manufacture of cloth for sail. But, not prospering, he moved his business to North Carolina in 1732. Here he achieved some success, and his "due bills," known as "Borden's scrip," were widely circulated in lieu of the heavily depreciated public paper which at one time reached the exchange rate of a hundred to one for sterling. Apparently using his treatise on currency as a campaign document, he won a seat in the assembly in 1745, but he never sat because as a Quaker he refused to take the oath.

Borden, like the rest, held that North Carolina suffered from an unfavorable balance of trade, but it was an unfavorable balance of trade with other colonies. Lacking a satisfactory circulating medium as well as transportation facilities, the planters are "a prey to the commerce of New York and neighboring colonies"; consequently they receive less for their exports and pay more for their imports than neighbors do. The poor North Carolina planters, he argued, have to pay a dear rate for the worst goods because the latter are burdened with the expense of navigation in the neighboring colonies and the profits and livings of many merchants and traders there.

Under "our wild and rude manner of trafficking," the laborer's returns would hardly purchase enough to cover his nakedness unless the employer suffers loss. The poor man becomes a charge on the landlord and the King is deprived of his quit rents. Even those having six or eight Negroes and equipment have "rather a scrabble to live." Neither foreigners nor fair traders would settle in the colony.

Borden "proved by arithmetick" that the remedy was £100,000 of non-interest-bearing loan bills of credit, or any sum for which there was a necessary demand. The borrower was to pay annually one-tenth of the principal to trustees in "merchantable"—exportable—commodities deposited in public warehouses and valued at the prices ruling in the great port towns. The trustees were to sell the goods to shipmasters and merchants and receive in payment one-fourth specie and three-quarters "West India" goods—sugar, rum, and molasses—and other merchandise at wholesale prices. The trustees, in turn, were to dispose of their purchases to the inland traders and inhabitants for the exportable commodities. At the end of a reasonable number of years, the treasury should have specie equivalent to the amount of the bills to maintain their value.

Should the Crown disallow such paper, the same result could be achieved by the planters' depositing in the public warehouses such a proportion of their goods as the legislature deemed sufficient to obtain the foreign "necessaries," including specie; and the returns would be distributed among the planters in accordance with their contribution. "Out of their nothingness the province is enriched with sufficient gold and silver which in itself has intrinsic worth." [29]

In Maryland the issue of paper was linked with the problem of restricting the "excessive" production of tobacco. In 1733 Maryland authorized the issue of £90,000 of paper to enable the people to meet their taxes and other engagements now payable in tobacco and to destroy the "trash" tobacco which "clogs the market and depreciates" good tobacco. A substantial share of the bills was allotted for a governor's house, repairs of the capital buildings, a prison in every county; but the bulk was to be a bounty to planters for destroying "unmerchantable" tobacco.

The bills were by no means full legal tender. Officers' fees, proprietary quit rents, and the poll of forty pounds of tobacco for the clergy were exempted. One-third of the issue was to be redeemed in fifteen years, the remainder in thirty-one, by a sterling tax on tobacco exports. Meanwhile the tax money was to be invested as a "fund" for the notes in the Bank of England stock, which, as has been noted, the Massachusetts radicals wanted to do with the bounty from the Crown.[30]

Pennsylvania appeared in the eyes of contemporaries as the most successful in issuing public loan bills. The story began with the depression of 1722. Various cures were proposed to the assembly: to prohibit the hiring out of slaves, to encourage the manufacture of beer and distilled spirits from local produce, to make the country's produce legal tender, to reduce the legal rate of interest from 8 to 6 per cent, to suspend the execution of debts, to raise the rate of English and foreign coin, to prohibit the export of specie, and to issue paper money. The latter received the most discussion.

Penn had sympathized with such land-bank schemes, but his heirs and their representatives, including Logan, at first bitterly opposed the issue. Supporting the issue was the assembly, composed of substantial Quaker traders backed by the governor, Sir William Keith, learned in law and history and heavily involved in promoting the iron industry.

The governor used the familiar argument of the need for more money to check the monopolists and rich usurers who are "grinding the face of the poor." He pointed to New York as evidence of the successful use of bills to create a better and faster sale of products. The bills must be loaned at less than common interest to encourage their circulation. Of course, unfrugal people will be hurt by borrowing, but thereby they will be succeeded by industrious ones. A small issue may not meet the needs of those having good security. A tooshort term such as five years may prevent some persons from effecting what they might accomplish for their own and the country's advantage in more time.[31]

Supporting the governor with treatises as well as political power was Francis Rawle, wealthy land promoter and trader. Rawle declared, in *Some Remedies Proposed, for the Restoring the sunk Credit of the Province of Pennsilvania* (1721), that the money must be full legal tender, for otherwise it would depreciate by limiting its uses and crippling its ready currency.

The proprietary group—the gentlemen and merchants—submitted a petition which showed an intimate acquaintance with Pollexfen's *Discourse of Trade, Coyn, and Paper Credit*. The petition declared: The stamp of authority cannot create intrinsic worth. To the degree that bills are issued on easier terms than specie would be, by so much at least the bills will fall, meaning the rise of specie and commodities, "for credit has its own laws as unalterable . . . as those of motion and gravity are."

The cure for the depression is new markets for our goods. But the proponents of public bills for long-term loans at low interest are being misled by the "spirit of malignity." With few rich men in the province, with money scarce on any terms, the proponents abuse the few rich, return reproaches for what has been obtained by prayer, and "under the endearing appearance of popularity . . . strike at the very sinews of a country's strength and the means of its prosperity," in which all would, according to their ranks, more or less partake.

However, some paper money is necessary for a circulating medium. But the issue should be a small one, just sufficient to pass from hand to hand as a currency. Its term should be short, for the sooner it expires, the more easily will people take it. Most of the issue should be used to pay the province debt and build a prison and workhouse.

The upshot was the lowering of the legal rate of interest from 8 to 6 per cent and the relatively large full legal-tender issue of £15,000, primarily for the purpose of loans, on the security of real estate from two to three times the principal. The loans were made for eight years at 5 per cent, with principal repayable in eight annual installments. No loan could be less than £12 10 s., nor more than £100, by no means small sums.

Six months after the first issue the assembly declared that the paper had given new life to business, but that the quantity still was insufficient to circulate the colony's trade. So more paper, on twelve-and-a-half-year loans, was issued.

In 1728 the "inhabitants of the city and county of Philadelphia" successfully petitioned the assembly for an increase, on the ground that the beneficial effects of the original issues in increasing trade and population now required more bills, lest the trade be reduced, "the manufactures lie on hand, the navigation discouraged." [32]

The opposition vigorously expressed its sentiments from the start. Isaac Norris, then of the proprietary group, wrote that investment in Pennsylvania was unsafe and should not be undertaken by Englishmen.[33]

Logan, like Hutchinson later, was willing to grant in an anonymous treatise that paper created a temporary but specious business prosperity. At first, trade does boom, he said; but it is the false joy of a drugged body. Foreseeing that the paper must depreciate, people willingly invest in various enterprises and goods while the project, especially shipbuilding, is young and before prices are altered. The critics of paper rightly argue that all will subside again and the future "be governed by proportion, and the encouragement or discouragement which may arise from freights and markets, etc."; that as foreign goods rise in disproportion to our produce, the burden which at first seemed to be thrown on others will fall upon the planter and tradesman.

The trouble is that the politicians and city idlers, seduced by the faithless governor, Keith, are inflaming the people, whereas they should follow the example of good countrymen and be hard-working, frugal, industrious citizens, keep out of politics, and avoid taverns.[34]

Rawle could match this type of reasoning. The riches of a country, he wrote, consist of a favorable balance of trade, but as "riches is the mother of luxury and of idleness," so "the daughter devoured the mother." As the province grew more populous and demands from England increased, the country consumed more West Indies rum. Thus the colony lost markets and suffered gluts. The balance of trade became increasingly unfavorable as the price of produce fell. If people had not imported spirits, paper money would have been unnecessary, but in the present state of affairs, paper money, though only nominal riches, is the force which will encourage agriculture and commerce.

The interest on the loan bills might be used by the government to establish insurance offices, for these are the best device for finding new markets, and new markets with a consequent rise in produce prices is, of course, the ultimate remedy for the depression.[35]

Successive issues, mostly in the nature of reissues, were made from time to time, the issue of 1739 with its ten- and sixteen-year loans becoming the model. Some of the old critics, like Norris and Logan, had early changed their opinion of the bills. The Proprietors were willing to allow issues, provided there was some return to them in the way of tax exemptions and bonuses.

But in such disputes the assembly viewed the bills a little less enthusiastically than the Proprietors. The assembly, in demanding the taxing of unimproved proprietary lands in 1753, declared that the interest paid on the paper money borrowed from the colony was a tax, since it was paid for by the labor of the borrowers. But the Proprietors answered that the interest was not a tax because the borrower could not take the paper unless he received a benefit. So, while they would not allow their lands to be taxed, "we shall be induced from the state of your trade . . . to consent to an increase of your paper currency" to raise a revenue.[36]

The assembly, guided by the skillful Franklin, was quite dexterous in answering complaints of British merchants. The English merchants should not complain against the issues, declared the assembly in one report, for they have been the great beneficiaries. They sell more and at higher prices than before, while our valuable commodities of wheat and flour remain at the old prices, and all tradesmen, hired servants, and laborers are paid at the old rates.

This type of argument was naturally modified when exigencies required. Thus the assembly declared in 1752 that the limited loans for a long term, on easy interest and repayable in yearly installments, enabled many to acquire estates and raise families where otherwise they would have remained single and laborers for others or left the colony. Because of the ease of acquiring land, thousands have come from Germany and Ireland where they could never hope to rise above the tenant state. True, their acquiring land keeps up the price of labor and prevents the old settlers from obtaining working hands, but the old settlers achieve a net gain in the rise of the value of their lands because of the increase of people. The Dominions of the Crown are strengthened and extended; Proprietors dispose of their wilderness territory. Best of all is the unavoidable increased demand for British manufactures. "So long as land can be easily procured for settlements between the Atlantic and Pacific Oceans, so long will labour continue dear in America; and while labour continues dear, we can never rival the artificers or interfere with the trade of our mother country."

The ablest theoretical argument in defense of paper and the prevention of its depreciation came from John Webbe, the shrewd Pennsylvania journalist and lawyer who developed Vance's argument of determining the requisite amount of money by the natural rate of interest.

Through newspaper, magazine, pamphlet, and petition, Webbe pushed his scheme in the early 1740's. He presented an able summary of the importance of money: The riches of every country are derived from the labor and industry of the people, but unless money is sufficiently plentiful these will not be fully developed. Instead the community remains in the barbaric stage of barter. The population will remain unduly scattered, many will be unemployed, and the employed will work only under necessity. But with an increase of money, closer settlement will result, with its economic and social advantages. The people can more easily assist one another, necessaries will be produced more cheaply through each man's being able to follow a single trade, and a greater market will result for England's manufactures.

Money is governed "by the same rules and laws of value that govern the vent and price of other merchandises which rise and fall in the proportion to their plenty and scarcity, supposing the demand for them to be always equal. . . . The current cash of a nation . . . is always worth the quantity of the commodities in that nation which such a sum can at once purchase or command." The value of paper money, like any money, depends on its general employment in trade. Its employment will be in proportion to the "intrinsic worth" of the movable commodities exchanged by it. When these commodities increase in quantity without diminishing in goodness, or increase in quality without diminishing in quantity, their intrinsic worth increases.

If the quantity of money were equal to the demand, the same number of shillings would always purchase the same quantity of labor, assets, or necessaries of life. The value of money would be invariable in comparison not with a few commodities, but with all commodities. Thus perfection would be achieved so far as this is possible without attempting the impossible and undesirable objective of making invariable the natural and constantly variable relations of commodities to one another.

Webbe's specific determination of the proper amount of money took the form of Petty's old analysis. It should be in proportion to population, but account must be taken of the differences of the degree of industry of people in different places and the degree of close settlement, enabling a greater amount of goods to be produced and exchanged. The difficulty is, he declared, that none of these things—population, skill, production—is known.

However, as Vance had argued, the natural rate of interest provides an automatic regulator. Let a bank be established to lend any sum requested, on real estate, at the natural rate of interest—say 5 per cent; but let the bank pay an equivalent rate on any bills deposited with it. The rate on deposits should be lower than on loans because of the depositors' advantages—absence of risk and the prompt withdrawal of funds for opportune investment. Should trade not require the available money, the redundant supply would tend to be deposited.

Setting the difference in rates between loans and deposits would not be left to the discretion of the managers, but "regulated by a perpetual table that the men of figures will easily form on the data" supplied by one year's experience. On the same data rules may be determined for discovering at all times the hire of money at market, and as that decreases, so must the bank rate be reduced. But there

can never be any occasion to increase it, "for natural interest between man and man (which . . . can never fall too low) will be
always falling until every branch of trade be fully supplied with
money. Thus the scheme is as easy in practice as it is true in theory." [37]

On the other side stood Tench Francis with a qualified support of
paper, provided it was limited in quantity and not legal tender for
foreign debts and previous contracts. Francis, Irish-born and educated in Great Britain, came to Maryland in 1720 as attorney for the
Proprietor. There he held various offices and was for three years a
member of the Maryland Assembly. In 1738 he migrated to Philadelphia, where he soon became the leading lawyer in the province
and was appointed attorney general of the province and recorder of
Philadelphia. He was, of course, conversant in matters of money,
"both as a lawyer and a merchant."

His systematic, mathematical mind, like Vance's, demanded that a
preliminary discourse or value theory be presented. The value of
things arises from their fitness or power to answer or procure the
necessary conveniences or pleasures of life. There are two categories of value. Absolute value is our esteem of anything without
referring to any other, but the problem of money is concerned with
relative value, the value of an object as compared with another. Men
can discover the qualities giving an object value, and by laws, customs, or fashions they can greatly increase its value; "but to know or
fix its worth on price compared with other things, *a priori*" is beyond
human capacity because we are unable to foresee and control all the
circumstances. Those which are in, or follow, the nature and order
of things in general "may be foreseen and judged of with some certainty, but others consist of the innumerable incalculable passions,
prejudices and misapprehensions of mankind."

From the natural order of things, the worth or price of any object will always be as its uses among mankind directly and its quantity inversely. Water is as necessary as anything, and a diamond perhaps as little; yet the superfluous plenty of the former makes it
worthless, and the scarcity of the other gives it an extravagant power.

Variations in quantity or use cause a change in price, but not in
proportion to the variation. "The prevalence of men's appetites for
a scarce commodity, under the dreads and apprehensions of wanting
it, with their different abilities to procure it, on the one hand, and
their great contempt of useless excess, on the other," renders "more
probable, that the difference between the means and the extremes shall

not be the same in the prices as in the quantities." Merchants have discovered by experience "that lessening a commodity one-third from the mean quantity, *ceteris paribus*, nearly doubles the value; that adding a third, subtracts one-half." Though it is extremely difficult if not impossible to investigate these proportions mathematically, still "events springing from use and experience have equal certainty in them, and to all practical purposes are as much to be relied and depended upon."

These rules of estimating the value of things give the principles of sound policy on paper. If a nation's money supply is equal to its commerce, then land, commodities, and labor will bear "a middle price," the best condition for enriching the people. Should paper be added, the value of money will fall, the price of lands and rents rise, and labor and commodities be rated higher than elsewhere. Since this rise in men's fortunes is nominal, not real, the resulting idleness, expense, and poverty cause the real money instead of commodities to be exported. On the other hand, if their commerce or use of money exceeds the quantity, then the land, labor, and commodities will sink below their worth in other countries to an even greater degree than the decrease in quantity. The results are monopoly, a few great fortunes, and the desertion of the inhabitants to places where their labor will be better rewarded. In these circumstances paper money strikes the fetters of the poor, multiplies merchants, raises the price of labor and the fruits of the earth, and thereby the value of lands. An equal distribution of gain and profit succeeds and destroys the partial accumulation of wealth. These marks of the value of the lands, labor, and commodities compared with their worth in other countries are the only infallible means for determining a country's money needs.

The quantity of paper, if paper is to be the only money, ought to be adequate to its uses; in other words, to all commerce, foreign and domestic. It is easier to grasp the truth in speculation than to reduce it to practice because the number and extent of the uses of money in a populous and industrious country are beyond our knowledge and comprehension. But from the circumstances of other places, the quantity of money current before using paper, and the value of their exports, rational conjectures may be formed. "Experience alone can teach what sum will suffice." However, the inevitable erring at the start should be on the side of deficiency rather than excess, for, after the emission, additions are easy to make, but subtractions difficult.

Inconvertible paper money can never have the value of specie money. Some say that money is merely a counter representing to the possessor's mind a quantity or degree of power, and that no receiver ever examines how or whence it acquired that power. Therefore they argue that a piece of paper, under distinguishable characters and impressions, affixed by law and common consent, should have the power of an English coin. But silver by virtue of its use in foreign commerce has one more use than paper. Consequently we cannot esteem them equally, for that "would be to control the different virtues and influences of things over the mind of man, which necessarily depending upon the things themselves, no laws or consent can . . . vary or direct."

This does not mean that paper might not in certain cases be a tender to the nominal amount. It can be for all domestic contracts made after a tender law has been passed, for then the creditor or seller has been informed of the medium of payment and is not obliged to exchange more for the paper than he thinks equal to the real unit. This type of law falls within the doctrine that the community can prohibit the exercise of a "particular natural right inconsistent with the welfare of the whole." However, for payments due abroad on contracts previous to a tender law, while the paper should be a tender, the debtor must pay a "sum of paper equal with the foreign money" or the silver. Otherwise foreign credit and international commerce would be destroyed.

It is argued that such provisions for old contracts and foreign payments would lessen the current value of the paper and damage society. However, not legislative fiat but the opinion of the possessor of the commodities for which the paper is exchanged sets the value of the paper, unless the lawmakers can limit the prices of all commodities. The latter, however, is neither practicable nor consistent with the order of things.[38]

In 1764 Parliament prohibited the further issue of legal-tender bills by any colony. The Board of Trade reported that legal-tender bills cause the export of gold and silver from every colony to its ruin, "that the prohibition has been beneficial in New England, that every medium of trade should have an intrinsic value," but paper can never possess it; "that debtors in the Assemblies, make paper money with fraudulent views; that merchants trading to America have . . . lost by it"; that even in the middle colonies, where the credit of the paper money has been best supported, the bills have constantly depreciated when the quantity has been increased.[39]

Some of the wealthiest and most conservative leaders in the colonies spoke against the regulation. John Dickinson recapitulated the familiar arguments in defense of the Pennsylvania scheme as ideal for all the colonies. Paper money for loans not only helps the prospective farmers, but enables others in distress to carry on some business when otherwise they would be crippled, for no private person would lend money on such favorable terms. From the borrowers the currency passes to other hands, increases consumption, raises the price of commodities, quickens circulation, and after communicating a vigor to all kinds of industry returns in its course into the possession of the borrowers, to repay them for that labor which it may properly be said to have produced. They deliver it, according to their original contract, into the treasury, where the interest raises a fund for public uses without the imposition of taxes.[40]

While efforts were being continually made to lift the prohibition, schemes were presented within the colonies that paid credit to the dominant spirit of enterprise. In 1769 in Maryland came the proposal to issue loan bills to prevent "the exactions of labourers," provide for the "correction of the dissolute and the idle," and supply money for trade. The paper was to be distributed among the counties for building workhouses. The counties were to repay the loans by taxes, but until the loans matured the tax money was to be lent to individuals.[41]

On the eve of the Revolutionary War, Thomas Johnson informed Washington that, along with a charter of incorporation, Maryland must issue loans bills to the prospective subscribers to the Potomac scheme on the Maryland side. Money was so scarce that these men, including himself, he said, could otherwise only raise funds, despite the best security, "by selling a part of the very Estate to be benefitted by the scheme, on very low terms." [42]

The opinion of the shrewdest of the pre-Civil War historians, Richard Hildreth, on all these and subsequent schemes was not far from the mark. They were contrivances, he wrote, "for raising out of the public at large a fund to be lent out as a trading capital to the more active and adventurous" businessmen, "a class numerically small, but whose superior activity and sagacity have given them always a decided and generally a controlling weight in our public affairs." [43]

All the schemes easily found justification in the dominant principle that a nation grows rich by the difference between the value it carries to market and the value it buys, which it "either lays by or lends out upon interest to its more improvident neighbours." [44]

The cry for paper throughout the era furnished the occasion for throwing into the limelight the outstanding figure of the period— Benjamin Franklin.

CHAPTER X

Two Disciples of Penn

BENJAMIN FRANKLIN: GENTLEMAN OF COMMERCE

OF ALL the figures that rose to prominence in the eighteenth century before the Revolutionary War, Benjamin Franklin was the most characteristic of that enlightened opinion which was to dominate in the succeeding period.

In an age where great flexibility of mind and action was called for, he was without a peer in moving with the course of events. His inconsistencies were many, but they were the inevitable accompaniments of his diverse loyalties and his journalistic habits.

Franklin had little to begin with. His family belonged to the class denoted as independent artisans and tradesmen. His formal education was of the elementary sort Boston provided for the sons of this class. But Franklin was an omnivorous reader, and he early acquired a fluent style. As an apprentice on his brother's newspaper, he broadened his education, learned the limits of the patience of authorities, and felt the public pulse. It was fortunate that his brother treated him not as a younger brother, but as a servant, for young Franklin got tired of the treatment while he was still learning about the world and before the crust of Boston had encased him. He ran away in 1723 at the age of seventeen to try his luck in a different jurisdiction.

Philadelphia was another Boston, but before he settled down permanently in the Quaker capital in 1726, he saw the brilliant life of London, if only from the distance of a journeyman printer, for a year and a half. When he returned, his ambitions were not limited to those of the colonial tradesman.

Like others of the day, his Philadelphia print shop dealt in slaves, indentured servants, imports from the West Indies and elsewhere, and a variety of other items as well as printed matter. Before long Franklin had a successful newspaper, had acquired that most lucrative field of the printing business—the public printing—not only in Pennsylvania but also in neighboring colonies, and through partnerships was operating a chain of print shops and newspapers in various provinces. His postmastership in Philadelphia and his clerkship of the Pennsylvania assembly were adjuncts the usefulness of which Franklin fully appreciated.

When just past forty and in business less than twenty years on his own, Franklin acquired sufficient wealth to retire from active management of his print shop and leave behind him the taint of a shopkeeper. He had his investments, but he now had more time for politics, for experimentation in electricity, and for vast land speculations that stretched from Nova Scotia to the Ohio Valley. As assistant postmaster general for the colonies and as a member of the assembly with an able pen, he was so outstanding a figure that in 1757 he was sent by the assembly as agent to present its grievances against the Proprietors to the Crown.

His march to political greatness had begun in 1729 over the question of a new issue of loan bills. Using as a guide Petty's theories of value and interest almost verbatim, Franklin sketched the beneficence of more paper money as animating trade and developing a money economy in Pennsylvania. All important classes would benefit, from the Crown and Proprietor to the landowners and the merchants. The paper was to be at one and the same time the substitute for the absent specie and the instrument by which specie would be accumulated as the sign that the balance of trade was favorable and Pennsylvania on its way to achieve the great prosperity of England. Like so many other pro-paper money treatises, *A Modest Enquiry Into the Nature and Necessity of a Paper-Currency* called on the "country" to support the "city." It started with a labor theory of value and ended with paper as merely the representative of labor.

Labor is the just measure of the value of silver and all other things, for trade in general is nothing but the exchange of labor for labor. Suppose one man raises corn and another digs and refines silver. Then for any given period of time, "the complete produce of corn and that of silver are the natural price of each other," and if one be twenty bushels and the other twenty ounces, then an ounce of the silver is worth the labor of raising a bushel of the corn. Should more easy or plentiful mines be discovered so that the same labor yields double the silver, then the bushel of corn "will be as cheap at two ounces as it was before at one, *ceteris paribus.*" Therefore a country's riches should be valued by the quantity of labor its inhabitants can purchase, not by the quantity of specie it possesses.

The rate of interest is set by the other "natural" factor, land, in the same pecuniary fashion. The natural standard of usury is the rent of so much land as the money lent will buy, when the security is undoubted. "For no man will lend his money for less than the rent it would earn if invested in land, the most secure property in the world." But if the security is casual, then to the simple natural interest is added a sort of insurance payment which may rise to any height.

Usury laws cannot fix a maximum rate of interest because those needing money will find ways to pay the market rate when they cannot have it for less. But both the wealth of the nation and a declining interest rate as a means thereto depend on a sufficient proportion of money to carry on the country's internal trade. In a trading country a scarcity of money in the first place occasions a high interest rate because the security for debts becomes precarious. A high interest rate lowers the price of land, for few will invest in land where more can be made by lending. Trade will be discouraged for the same reason, and in addition those countries with a lower rate of interest will capture markets from those with a high interest rate.

Furthermore, the scarcity of money reduces the price of the country's produce entering into trade. With trade declining, local manufactures, especially shipbuilding, is discouraged, and so the unfavorable balance of trade is exaggerated and the country rendered less able than ever to retain necessary specie.

Finally, the scarcity of money discourages "labouring and handicrafts men (which are the chief strength and support of a people)" from settling in the province, for they must with difficulty get their wages under barter arrangements.

The bills issued on a money security by European banks are very advantageous to traders, for they increase in effect the amount of running cash. Bills based on land security are equally as good if not better. "For as bills issued upon money security are money, so bills issued upon land, are in effect coined land."

Since the security of the Pennsylvania paper is undoubted, and since the device merely permits the people by law to coin their own land, which costs the government nothing, the interest rate on the paper loaned should not be more than 4 per cent. The lower the rate, the more money will be borrowed and thus the common usury in which security is more dubious would be brought down to the legal rate.

Foreign creditor merchants might fear the increase in paper because, by increasing the demand for our exports, it will raise their price, and so they will get less returns in goods, but they will be paid their debts more easily and punctually.

Franklin's pamphlet was influential. It helped Franklin obtain the contract for printing the new issue in Pennsylvania, and it was reprinted in conservative newspapers in other colonies, including wealthy William Bradford's *New-York Gazette*.

Of course, Franklin never intended that his deprecation of specie should mean that the colony should refrain from obtaining it; on the contrary, the very use of paper in place of specie as a currency was for the purpose of increasing the supply as treasure. Labor in industry and manufactures—that is, exports—will yield, he wrote in the Philadelphia *American Weekly Mercury* at that time, that treasure of specie that men with great loss generally seek in attempting to dig for it. Thus the Newfoundland fishery is more valuable than Spain's mines in Potosi, for the fish can be coined into "Spanish pieces of eight," not to mention the national profit of fitting out and employing the ships and men. "Poor Richard," of Franklin's famous almanacs, along with the country, became rich by his industry and frugality because, by avoiding useless expense in foreign superfluities and increasing exports of commodities, he produced a "growing plenty of money." [1]

Trade restrictions by other colonies, Franklin did not approve on administrative grounds, though he granted the soundness of the logic. Of a Connecticut act of 1747 taxing imports into or via Connecticut, he declared that the tax was really paid by the consumer. But "if you can make some of the goods imported," he wrote Jared Eliot, the noted Connecticut student of agriculture, "the higher prices will encourage your manufactures," and in time Connecticut will have the advantage of not needing the imports. But meanwhile smuggling is difficult to prevent; consequently, under the tax measure, fair traders will be undersold. Besides, the affected colonies will retaliate. [2]

In 1751, when the British sugar colonies were demanding that Parliament impose more stringent measures to reduce the trade of the northern colonies with the foreign sugar islands, Franklin prepared a paper on the theory of population that followed the mercantilists' conception of the labor supply as the wealth and strength of the nation. *Observations concerning the Increase of Mankind* was a masterly paper in its attempt to prove that the trade-restriction policies of the English government were against England's interest. It attempted to show at one and the same time that the colonies did not drain England of population, that any growth of colonial manufactures could not endanger England's hold on the colonial market for manufactures, that the continental colonies were preferable to the sugar islands, and finally that it was to England's interest to acquire more adjacent territory for the benefit of the American colonists. All this was demanded in the name of increasing the English population because population was the wealth and strength of a nation.

Europe, being fully settled with manufacturers and husbandmen, cannot increase much in population. But America's position is different. With land plentiful and thus cheap, the laboring man can quickly earn enough to purchase sufficient land for himself and a future family. Consequently population has doubled itself every twenty-five years. But this great increase does not mean that labor will be cheap. On the contrary, it will remain high because many ages must pass before the great area of land can be fully settled. Therefore Great Britain should not fear that the colonies will interfere with the mother country in trades depending on labor, manufacture, etc. In proportion as the colonies increase, so the market for British manufacture and the population of England increase. In fact, so great will this market become in a short time that England will be unable fully to supply it. "Therefore Britain should not too much restrain manufactures in her colonies. A wise and good mother will not do it. To distress is to weaken, and weakening the children weakens the whole family."

Besides, should British manufactures by virtue of the American demand rise too high in price, foreigners will drive the British out of foreign markets. The foreigners will be encouraged in manufactures, become England's rivals in power, grow more populous and more powerful; while England's "own colonies kept too low, are unable to assist her, or add to her strength."

But some have foolishly argued that slavery will provide the colonies with the cheap labor supply necessary for manufacture. Slave labor, however, is in fact more expensive than free labor in

England. There is the interest charge on a heavy investment, the insurance or risk on the slave's life, his support when sick and idle, and finally the heavy costs of indolence, carelessness, theft, and supervision 'flowing from the fact that he has no property right in his labor. The only reason slaves are purchased is because hired men are continually leaving their master, often in the midst of his business, and setting up for themselves.

Slaves decrease a people. Franklin pointed to the decrease of whites in the English sugar islands. The poor are deprived of employment while a few families acquire vast estates and spend them on foreign luxuries. An income that supports one would otherwise maintain a hundred. The idle slave owners, being enfeebled, are not prolific. The blacks, being overworked and ill fed, have a higher death rate than birth rate.

Trade increases population. Exported manufactures draw subsistence from foreign countries. But if a nation loses a trade and no new employment is found for the unemployed, population decreases. Similarly, if a nation has a fishery, it not only employs a great number but makes food cheap. Consequently, should another nation become master of the seas, as the French may, people will diminish.

On the other hand, the import of foreign luxuries—that is, manufactures—decreases a country's population but increases the population of the exporting country. Therefore laws preventing the importation and encouraging the exportation of manufactures are generative laws.

But "home luxury in the great, increases a nation's manufacturers" —artisans—by providing them with employment, and it diminishes only the few families indulging in it. Since the greater the common fashionable expense of any rank of people, the more cautious they are to marry, luxury should never be allowed to be common.

So Franklin concluded that "fathers of their nations" are the prince who acquires new territory if he finds it vacant, or removes the natives to give his own people room; the legislator who makes effective laws for promoting trade, increasing employment, improving the land, developing the fishery; and, finally, the inventor of new trades, arts, manufactures, or agricultural improvements.

The strength of a nation might be in industrious numbers, but for the laboring mass as such, bereft of a competency, Franklin, at least in his private writings, retained the verities that went back to the days of John Winthrop. Though English laborers, said Franklin, are much better paid in the colonies than in England, still, here their in-dustry decreases in proportion to the higher wages. On the other hand, the Germans, with their traditions of frugality and hard work, become rich. The source of the evil is the English poor laws, which "compel the rich to maintain the poor." Such relief laws, or even relief foundations as in Catholic countries, lessen the incentive of the poor to provide for old age and lead to extravagance and idleness, for human nature is only by necessity compelled to labor. He pointed to the Indians.[3]

In 1757 Franklin prepared the assembly's report of the colony's grievances for submission to the Crown. The Proprietors, through the veto of their governor, have successfully refused to bear their share of the tax burden and have likewise forbidden the issue of paper money, which the internal commerce of the colony requires. At the same time, for the sake of the trade and commerce of England, the Crown rather than Pennsylvania should repay the masters whose servants have enlisted and confirm the title of masters over servants so that enlistment cannot occur in the future. Finally, the Crown for the same reason should contribute financial assistance to protect Pennsylvania frontiers, especially since Delaware, New Jersey, and Maryland are beneficiaries without bearing any of the burden.[4]

What better man to send to present the grievances than Franklin himself? So after a lapse of thirty-one years Franklin once again en-tered London, where he remained until 1775, except for a short period in America.

Then he had come as a lowly journeyman printer. Now he was an important political figure as well as a scientist with an international reputation, more particularly a scientist who had a substantial in-come and good prospects. Few doors of the great were closed to him. Oxford and St. Andrews awarded him honorary degrees. With Hume and Adam Smith he dined and conversed, and he even con-vinced them of the relative soundness of the Pennsylvania variety of paper money.

That the life of cosmopolitan, brilliant London was the ideal one, he all the more accepted when he was temporarily at home in 1763. To a close friend he wrote: "That little island enjoys in almost every neighbourhood, more sensible, virtuous and elegant minds, than we can collect in ranging a hundred leagues of our vast forests."[5]

There was much to hold his loyalty to the Crown. His illegitimate son, William Franklin, was appointed governor of New Jersey in

1762. He was interested in obtaining for himself and his associates huge land grants. His office of assistant postmaster general in the colonies was a Crown office, and he drew its emoluments while living in London. And there was always the prospect that he would obtain a post in the ministry. Lord North, who became head of the English government during the Revolutionary War, informed Franklin that he would do his best to make it sufficiently attractive for Franklin to remain in England.[6]

But Franklin was agent not only of the Pennsylvania assembly, but also of other colonial governments, including Massachusetts, New Jersey, and Georgia. He had many roles to play at the same time, roles which often got in each other's way. And there was always, of course, the complication of his own personal interests.

He generally treated great questions of constitutional government and social amelioration from the standpoint of those in authority, at least so long as they did not immediately adversely affect the various agencies and responsibilities with which he was entrusted

The celebrated case of John Wilkes involved such basic questions of liberty as the freedom of political criticism from prosecution, the publicity of legislative debates, the protection of home and property from unreasonable search and seizure, and the right of a constituency's duly elected choice to sit in the legislature unless disqualified by law. But Franklin was dismayed in 1768 that this penniless "outlaw and an exile, of bad personal character" should again win an election, and his feelings were outraged at what he called mobs forcing "gentlemen and ladies of all ranks, as they passed in their carriages to shout for Wilkes and liberty." Even the courts of justice, he bewailed, were afraid to give judgment against Wilkes. "All respect to law and government," he wrote his friends in Pennsylvania, "seems to be lost among the common people, who are moreover continually inflamed by seditious scribblers, to trample on authority and everything that used to keep them in order."[7]

In an anonymous article, "On the Labouring Poor" (1768), he described the claim that the rich were oppressing the poor as unjust. The literature of protest, he wrote, merely makes the poor uneasy and leads to insurrections which cost the poor their lives. Violent censure of the rich for their expensive and luxurious living while the poor are starving is pure malignancy, for these expenditures provide employment for the poor. Besides, the laboring poor receive "the whole revenue of the nation, . . . I mean not only the public revenue, but also the revenue or clear income of all private estates, or a sum equivalent to the whole," for everything used and consumed is the work or produce of the poor. So even if wages seem too low, where is the additional fund to pay them higher wages? Only by giving less employment could wages be raised. Besides, the increased cost will prevent exports and so reduce the fund.

The basic cause is that wages obey the fundamental law of value. As other things are cheap because of their plenty, so the cheapness of labor is generally owing to the large number of laborers and their underworking one another to obtain employment. The ultimate cause of low wages is that St. Monday is generally as dutifully kept by our working people as Sunday; the only difference is that, instead of employing their time cheaply at church, they are wasting it expensively in the ale house. In no country are the poor more idle, dissolute, drunken, and insolent than in England, thanks to public poor relief. Repeal the poor-relief legislation, and St. Monday and St. Tuesday will cease to be holidays.

On similar pecuniary grounds Franklin in another anonymous article supported the gentry's claim that an export embargo on grain was ill advised. The corn trade should be free. Short harvests on the continent bring a good price for England's grains and make us flow in money at the expense of the foreigners. But government forbids its export at the mob's insistence that it be sold at less than market price.[8]

In fact, the higher the price of provisions, as Petty taught, the better, declared Franklin. The common people do not work for pleasure generally, for the acquisition of more wealth whereby to employ more people, as do the rich, but from necessity. If provisions are cheap, workers are more idle; less work is done. But "dearness of provisions obliges the manufacturer to work more days and hours; thus more work is done than equals the usual demand; of course it becomes cheaper, and the manufactures in consequence." [9]

So, as Franklin watched the disturbances of the Wilkes group for liberty, and of laborers for higher pay, he complained to correspondents at home: What the outcome will be "God only knows. But some punishment seems preparing for a people who are ungratefully abusing the best constitution, the best king [George III] any nation was ever blessed with." They are intent on nothing "but luxury, licentiousness, power, places, pensions and plunder." As for his mission, he wrote home that "the ministry intent in securing popularity in case they should lose favor" naturally have little time or inclination to attend to the remote and what is to them the small affairs of America.[10]

Among those American affairs were his land promotions. Though Franklin might be sent by the assembly to get rid of the proprietary form, still he was not averse to having that same form established in effect in the vast area of the Ohio Valley, the source of a rich fur trade over which England had fought the Seven Years' War with France.

Franklin, along with Wharton, was a moving figure in the most important of the companies. At one stage his associates gave him the power "to add such gentlemen of character and fortune" in England as could help to promote the project. Involved were not only American land speculators, but also influential nobility and great London bankers. Even Hume played a role.

Franklin had already presented the theoretical basis for such acquisitions in 1760, when he had pleaded in *The Interest of Great Britain Considered* that England take Canada rather than the French sugar islands as compensation for the war. Canada is essential to provide security for our present settlements and—perhaps more important—for our claim to the Ohio Valley east of the Mississippi River. It is claimed that if the danger of French Canada is removed, America will become independent and engage in manufactures. But the greatest security to English manufactures is precisely the new Ohio Valley area, for this will keep the people in agriculture for centuries. "Manufactures are founded in poverty. It is the multitude of poor without land . . . and who must work for others at low wages or starve, that enables undertakers to carry on a manufacture, and afford it cheap enough to prevent the importation of the same kind . . . and to bear the expense of its own exportation." On the other hand, with masses of settlers furnished with a livelihood and able to marry, the demand for British manufactures must increase, and consequently England's people and profit. On the other hand, if Canada is not taken by the English and the Ohio Valley remains unsecured, then, as the density of population in the colonies increases, the price of labor will fall, manufactures will become profitable, and the colonies eventually will become independent.

As for the area's ability to furnish returns for British manufactures, if the poor Indians there can pay for the manufactures traders now furnish them at prices "loaded with all the impositions, fraud and knavery can contrive to enhance their value, will not industrious English farmers . . . be much better able to pay for what shall be brought them in the way of fair commerce?"

At about the same time Franklin also argued against a proposal of the English government that prices be fixed in the Indian trade for the sake of peace with the Indians. Franklin contended: It is "contrary to the nature of commerce, for government to interfere in the prices of commodities. Trade is a voluntary thing between buyer and seller; in every article of which each exercises his own judgement, and is to please himself. . . . Where there are a number of different traders, the separate desire of each to get more custom will operate in bringing their goods down to a reasonable price. . . . Therefore . . . trade will best find and make its own rates." [11]

Naturally, too, even the objective of lifting the restraining act on legal-tender issues Franklin handled in the light of his ambitions as well as the interests at home he was supposed to represent. For a while he thought the answer lay in a scheme concocted by himself and Thomas Pownall, former royal governor of Massachusetts and an associate of Franklin's in the Ohio Valley scheme. Pownall, like Otis, questioned first of all that an unfavorable balance of trade was bad for a young developing country. The progressive improvement of a commercial country of settlers, he wrote in *The Administration of the British Colonies*, creates an unfavorable balance of trade and a decreasing silver currency.

The settlers are necessarily in debt because of their continual want of money and other materials for trade and business. These very things, applied to their improvement, will on return not only pay the debts, but create a surplus for further improvements. Thus, money "lent upon interest to settlers, creates money." It will create gold and silver in principal while the interest meets the government charges. This currency is the "true pactolian stream which converts all into gold that is washed by it," as was evidenced by Pennsylvania's success. But, whereas Pennsylvania issued limited amounts of paper and provided that foreign creditors be paid according to the exchange rate, the other colonies, guided only by the necessities of their inhabitants, issued excessive amounts of legal-tender paper. Therefore the majority of the men of business and property in the colonies demanded that Parliament restrain the issue of legal-tender paper. But the businessmen deem some paper necessary, and if the colonies lack sufficient money to drive their trade, England will lose the profits, and the price of labor in the colonies would be sufficiently reduced so that the colonies could turn to manufactures.

The Pownall-Franklin proposal was a combination of the ideas of Webbe, who had worked for Franklin, and those of Francis, whose tract Pownall described as having "the most exact and decisive sentiments on this subject." It proposed a bank managed from England, but a loan office was to be established in every colony to issue the bills on ten-year loans at 5 per cent and secured by a double value in real estate. A person might borrow any sum, but to prevent a redundancy of currency 4 per cent interest would be paid on deposit of the bills in the loan offices. The bills were to be legal tender, but this would not be dangerous, the authors felt, since Parliament would control their issues.

By this scheme all the specie acquired by the colonies would eventually be sent to England, but the colonies would have sufficient currency. The settlement and improvement of new tracts of land would be greatly encouraged and promoted, population increased, trade extended.

"It will operate as a general tax on the colonies," wrote Pownall, "and yet not actually be one," since the borrower will reap a gain. This tax will in effect spread itself more equally on all property than any other, since everyone, during the period he retains the money, virtually pays the interest of it, "the first borrower having received the value of it (to use for his own profit) when he parted first with the original sum." Thus, the rich, who handle most of the money, will rightly pay most of the tax. At the same time the plenty of money will prevent wages from falling and thereby prevent the apprehended danger of interfering manufactures. Also, the interest will provide a great annual permanent revenue to the Crown for expenses in America and relieve the governor and other Crown officials from pecuniary dependency on the colonial assemblies.

Franklin's advocacy of the scheme might have spelled trouble for him at home, but his connection with the scheme was not public knowledge at the time, and he made it known only to those substantial Pennsylvania leaders who placed the real or imaginary need for legal-tender paper above any mere question of freedom from irresponsible "foreign" control over the colonies.

The authors suggested the scheme to the government every year for the three years of 1764–1766. First it was turned down in favor of the Stamp Act. By the time the failure of the Stamp Act and similar measures had turned the government to serious consideration of the proposal, the issue of "taxation without representation" had taken such a turn that anything conceivably like a tax imposed by the English authorities on the colonies had little chance of colonial acquiescence. Franklin reported to the ministry in 1767 that no colony would take the money on the terms proposed.

When the original Franklin-Pownall plan for a bank appeared unacceptable to the colonies, Franklin had an alternative plan to which few conservatives in America could have found objection. Each colonial legislature could issue any sums necessary for the revenue, trade, business, and agriculture of the colony. These bills would be a legal tender, but all "debts, specialties, etc.," were to be paid at the current price of gold and silver. The bills issued for expenditures were to run for six years, in wartime ten years, a proportional amount to be called in every year by a tax on all estates. The legislature could also lend bills on securities at 4 per cent interest.[12]

But with the explosive situation continuing and with Franklin engrossed in matters of more immediate interest, he thought it unwise to push the matter too strenuously and even began to wonder whether legal-tender paper was necessarily good, at least so he wrote to friends in Pennsylvania.

To Joseph Galloway, wealthy merchant, land promoter, speaker of the assembly, and ardent proponent for lifting the restraining act, he wrote in 1767 that the prevailing luxurious mode of living in the colony had drained the province of all its money, including the vast amounts brought in by the war with the French. If the colony did not return to industry and frugality, prosperity would never return. In fact, if the scarcity of cash continued, the people would be driven to industry and frugality, and this would result in the accumulation of sufficient real cash. "But I suppose our people will scarce have patience to wait for this." So the merchants, traders, and principal people of all sorts "ought to petition the assembly for a moderate emission" and, though it could not be a legal tender, still its small quantity along with the petitioners' agreeing to accept it in all dealings at rates fixed by law, should maintain its value. Perhaps, he added, "a bank might be established that would answer all purposes." [13]

But on one issue neither Franklin nor any other colonial agent could avoid engaging in some energetic action. This was the opposi-

tion to the new restraints placed on colonial commerce. The Townshend Acts of 1767 had resulted in the formation of non-importation
agreements in the colonies, as with the Stamp Act. The Boston town·
meeting in particular aroused the fury of the English authorities by
its call, enforced by all the weapons that shrewd, learned Boston
merchants and lawyers knew, for a boycott of British imports and
the promotion of local manufactures. At that time Franklin found a
new faith to add to his old ones of mercantilism and free trade, that
of Physiocracy.

Franklin seems to have picked it up first on a visit to France in 1767,
and since the Physiocrats were ever on the alert for worthy disciples
they showered Franklin with attention and pamphlets. In turn Franklin, though he might view France as an intriguing nation, claimed they
alone knew the real truth, and he even got Turgot to provide him
with a summary of Physiocratic views on· taxation, which meant in
effect the general principles of the school as well.

Physiocracy's basic doctrine of agriculture as the sole productive
occupation and source of wealth was by no means foreign to colonial
or English traders, certainly not since the days when Locke originally
used it to prove that all taxes must rest essentially on land, and therefore the landowners should pay all the taxes in the first place rather
than attempt to tax trade. In the hands of Franklin the new faith was
a combination of what he had already written on free trade and mercantilism, plus the rhetoric of Physiocracy. His labor-time theory of
value now took the variant form, also presented by Petty, of labor in
agriculture as the standard.

Writing early in 1768 to a Philadelphian incensed at colonial
temerity, Franklin said the Boston people, pretending to interfere
with the manufactures of England, have caused a great clamor in
England against America in general. He had therefore endeavored to
palliate matters with several little public papers. But England, he declared, "is fond of manufactures beyond their real value, for the true
source of riches is husbandry."

Manufactures only change the form; and the increased value they
impart to the material is merely an equivalent for the value of subsistence consumed in manufacturing, for the manufacturer, the artisan, does not obtain from his employer for his labor more than a mere
subsistence. But manufactures enable provisions to be more easily
carried for sale to foreign markets. Should the latter prove difficult,

the provisions should be transformed for our own use as well as foreign sale, and this can be done easily in the odd moments of freedom
from customary tasks.

England, on the other hand, has increased the number of manufactures beyond reasonable limit. The price of provisions has risen
exorbitantly because she must now import to supply her multitude,
and the rise of food prices raises the price of manufacture. Thus the
manufactures can be made cheaper where the provisions are raised
and the mouth will go to the meat.[14]

Fair commerce, he informed the English in *Positions to be Examined, concerning National Wealth* (1769), is where equal values
are exchanged; that is, where the commodities are exchanged in proportion to the amount of labor and charge necessary to produce them.
The advantage of fair commerce is that each party increases the number of his enjoyments. But the bargains will be generally equal only
if the labor and expense of producing both commodities are known
to both parties. Thus, the exporter of wheat will generally obtain
more profit by converting the wheat into manufactures because most
purchasers, not knowing any of the expediting and facilitating methods and assuming more labor has been employed, will be induced to
pay more than the goods are honestly worth.

Therefore, of the three ways a nation can acquire wealth—war,
commerce, and agriculture—the first is robbery, the second is generally cheating, but the third is the only honest way, wherein a man
receives a "real increase of the seed thrown into the ground, in a
kind of continual miracle, wrought by the hand of God in his favor,
as a reward for his innocent life and his virtuous industry."

The concrete objective grew clearer in letters of approval to the
leaders of the non-importation movement in America. To the Reverend Samuel Cooper, who supported non-importation with the same
ardor that he had criticized the province excise act, Franklin wrote:
"The perseverance in industry and frugality, will pay your debts,
improve your farms, increase your real wealth, in a plenty of every
useful home production, and all the true enjoyments of life, even
though no foreign trade should be allowed you; and this handicraft,
shop-keeping State will, for its own sake, learn to behave more civilly
to its customers." [15]

To the Philadelphia "Committee of Merchants" he added that farms
will become more productive through the use of money formerly
wasted in superfluities; artificers will be able to carry on their business

more advantageously; gold and silver will become more plentiful; and trade will revive and grow after things are settled, "for an industrious, frugal people, are best able to buy, and pay best for what they purchase."

Franklin could even write to his philosopher friend, Lord Kames, that if the colonies were wise they would not ask for repeal of the restraining act on paper, for the scarcity of money "will work with our other present motives for lessening our fond extravagance in the use of the superfluous manufactures of this country, which . . . grudges us the enjoyment of common rights, and will tend to lead us naturally into industry and frugality." [16]

On the questions of migration, investment, and land speculation Franklin now took a position that he would have characterized formerly as "seditious." Writing to one acquaintance in 1772, he said: Great Britain is composed of a small number of extremely opulent landlords and gentlemen and a mass of poverty-stricken tenants and laborers living in hovels and clothed in rags; whereas in America the people follow the most honorable, useful, independent employment —that of the farmer. Every man is a freeholder; votes for the public offices, has plenty of food, and goes well clothed in home manufactures. If ever they come to envy the trade of European countries, let them, like the Irish, live on potatoes and buttermilk and go without shirts so they can export beef, butter, and linen. Let them, like the mass of the Scotch, go barefoot so that they can export shoes and stockings; and, if content to wear rags, like the spinners and weavers of England, they can make textiles for all the world.

If the people want an enormously wealthy gentry, let them sell their farms and pay rackrents. As the landlords rise in the scale, the tenants will become depressed into abject, servile, dirty creatures. Said Franklin, if he had not been resident in the American colonies but had only his experience of Great Britain by which to judge civil society, he would not advise a nation of savages to admit civilization. Compared to these people, every Indian is a gentleman. The effect of British society is to depress the multitudes below the savage state in order that a few may be raised above it.[17] He took a look at high death rates in the manufacturing towns of England and concluded that "farmers who manufacture in their own families what they have occasion for and no more, are perhaps the happiest people and the healthiest." [18]

English critics of colonial demands against British restrictions looked at slavery and indentured servitude and charged colonial spokesmen with hypocrisy in talking about liberty and freedom. But Franklin had answers. England brought slavery to America. Furthermore, slaves are better off than laborers in Great Britain. In general, the working poor are in effect slaves, for the law compels them to work long hours at low wages, denies them liberty of bargaining, and imposes imprisonment in the workhouse if the terms are refused. In addition, "the poor ingenious artificer" is forbidden to migrate though offered better wages in foreign countries.[19]

When a bill was pending before Parliament in 1774 to prevent migration to America, on the ground that the country thereby lost men and money, Franklin, signing himself "A friend to the poor" and using Penn's arguments, held that some of the avaricious noble lords no longer live on their estates in honorable independence among their respecting tenants but have chosen instead a life of luxury and dependence upon the Court. So they have callously rackrented their tenants to support the expense. No one has complained of the consuming of the rents in London, which is equally prejudicial to the area from which they are derived, but now loud protests are heard against the departure of the oppressed tenants. The remedy is not to abridge British liberty, but for the lords to return to their country seats and so "patronize and cherish" their tenants.[20]

So in the end, without sacrificing any mercantilist or Physiocratic tenets, Franklin argued, as always, that all English restrictions on trade should in effect be abolished. No nation was ever ruined by trade, even seemingly the most disadvantageous, wrote Franklin in 1774 in his contributions to George Whatley's *Principles of Trade*.

Wherever desirable superfluities are imported, industry is excited and plenty is produced. If only necessaries could be purchased, men would work no more than necessary for that purpose. Even in wartime the contestants should not molest traders. Since trade is mutually gainful, a contending prince by interfering with commerce "hurts himself as much as the enemy."

It was left to Whatley in this performance to combine clearly the logic of mercantilism with that of free trade. In many cases, said Whatley, individuals may engage in a trade seemingly injurious to the public, and yet it may be beyond the power of the state to hinder it without breaking in upon the freedom of trade. Thus the Dutch magistrate who gloated in selling the besieging Spaniards munitions and provisions was not as wrong as seemed at first sight. His country would gain if his goods were captured by his countrymen, and if he successfully sold the goods to the enemy, the transaction brought profit to him, and in consequence to the state of which he was a member. After all, the enemy can always obtain necessary supplies elsewhere. Therefore why should we not receive the profit from supplying them?

In 1774 Franklin's career in England became dark. He had sent to the leaders of the Massachusetts House of Representatives letters of Governor Hutchinson in which Hutchinson called for "an abridgement of what are called English liberties." The House demanded that the Crown remove the governor; instead the Crown dismissed Franklin from his post of assistant postmaster general. With his downfall came the end of his prospects for the great land grants which were then close to fruition. But at least Franklin was freed of some of his conflicting roles, and his shrewdness became available in the councils that were to call the United States into being as an independent nation.

Franklin was typical of the enlightened eighteenth-century cosmopolitan figure. Religion sat lightly on him, but he frankly supported and justified Whitefield's evangelical type on the ground that it instilled in the people respect for the existing social order.[21] In his writings he reiterated, of course, the principle that he and every respectable citizen knew was axiomatic truth: without wealth we could hardly be virtuous. However, the familiar catalogue of economic virtues that Franklin preached was at least free from that tone of aristocratic condescension that pervaded Cotton Mather's sermons, which he early imbibed. The aristocratic Logan had earlier run off a similar tale of "Poor Richard" when he had fought the issues of paper money, but his ideal citizen began as an indentured servant where Franklin's began as an apprentice.

Franklin, with inspiration supplied by land speculation and controversies over monetary and trade regulations, drew a glowing picture of America that became so deeply imbedded in American consciousness as to be almost an unquestioned reality. "Poor Richard" with his "industry and frugality" was to become a symbol of what America could promise, but that character and his traits were to reveal in the course of time the varying meanings and inconsistencies that ran through Franklin.

Here and there was a voice that challenged the picture with the hope of realizing the professed idealism. Such a one was John Woolman.

JOHN WOOLMAN: QUAKER HUMANITARIAN

John Woolman (1720–1773) was a gentle Quaker from New Jersey who struck a critical note in terms of Quaker theology and practice. He came of a family "of a middle station between riches and poverty." His father had lands and considered himself a planter, but, as was characteristic of this Quaker middle class, he was also a master craftsman, a weaver with his own looms in his own home.

The implied ideal of a self-sufficient community with moderate foreign trade, and a servant and an apprentice here and there, stood out in sharp contrast with the life of the wealthy Quakers, who were the richest men in Pennsylvania and New Jersey; great powers in politics, trade, and finance; possessors of vast estates and servants, even slaves.

John Woolman's world was not narrow. Like so many Quakers who in the great tradition of the founders responded to a "concern," he would leave his business and make long journeys, with whatever hardships they might entail, to uplift himself and his fellow men. Woolman visited New England, the South, the West Indies, and finally England. As a member of what was in effect the great directing body of American Quakerdom, the Council of Ministers and Elders of the Annual Meeting of Philadelphia, Woolman was at the center of things.

He read books, but he also observed and noted closely. He wanted to understand slavery thoroughly so he went on journeys to the South, stopped at plantations and conversed with the slaves as well as the masters. As he traveled through England he noted wages, costs of necessaries, and the general treatment of labor.

In his community his manifold activities brought him face to face with most problems. He was a schoolteacher and even wrote a primer; he surveyed lands, wrote wills, acted as an executor of estates, kept accounts for tradesmen, and wrote announcements of sales for farmers. But his main occupation was that of a tailor, an independent artisan. He had learned the craft in the expectation that such a useful occupation, with a little shopkeeping on the side, would provide him a "plain" living, a sufficiency of useful goods, but not great wealth and luxury, with their temptations to lead men astray from the path of righteousness. However, his "natural inclination for merchandising" resulted in the shop business increasing greatly, though he even convinced customers to avoid superfluous goods and debts. But the more successful he was in shopkeeping, the more he was disturbed. So he gave up shopkeeping after vainly trying to reduce the business by discontinuing various lines. He was by no means a poor man, for he had inherited some lands and he acquired other property in his shopkeeping days and even had an apprentice later; but he had set his limits, never completely specified, and he knew that no one could really get rich who stuck primarily to a craft, certainly not one who spent much time in finding out about the world.

Such a man was bound to have deep convictions which he would do all in his power to achieve within the bounds set by the peaceful tenets and procedure of the Quakers. His friends numbered the wealthy, powerful Quakers, but that did not prevent him from raising questions as to whether they had not departed from the tenets of the faith they professed. They listened, since he used the effective Quaker instruments of simplicity of style and humility.

He had some "singularities" that troubled his wealthy Quaker brethren. He traveled steerage because he felt that patronizing the better quarters of ships merely encouraged ostentation by the ship companies. He wore undyed clothes because the dyes were made by slaves. He would not write into wills provisions bequeathing slaves. In England, because of the ill treatment of the post boys, he refused to use the post for travel or for mail.

In great part Woolman's general point of view sprang from the complaint nowhere voiced more often than in New Jersey—that the evils of the community flowed from the importation of luxuries —a complaint which in Woolman's time was being used even by conservative merchants as a tactic to obtain the lifting of English restrictions on trade; but Woolman's use of the argument went far beyond anything the mercantile element would have found pleasing.

Woolman acknowledged in passing that servants should obey their masters, but "the present concern of my mind," he wrote in his posthumously published *A Plea for the Poor* (1793), "is that masters . . . demand nothing of servants, which is unreasonable, or that in the performance of which they must necessarily act contrary to universal righteousness."

There was little in his work on the obligations of the poor, but much was devoted to the obligations of the rich to mend their ways. His "standard" by which men should guide their conduct was the familiar vague "loosely watchful attention to the leadings of Him who is the light of life." With this standard "we are content with a little," but the admonition was directed to the rich. His typical rich man was the moneylender and his typical "poor man" the tenant, but his discussion included here and there the hired man as well.

Woolman's starting point was the starting point of all the great Quakers and Puritans: Worldly wisdom and conformity to customs are necessary to a certain degree, but they have insensibly supplanted righteousness or the guidance of the inner light. Deep-rooted customs are not easily eliminated. Bad customs when they become general are so powerful that people emboldened by the example of one another have been unmoved at the most serious warning. Worldly wisdom grows so insidiously into custom and convention that by the time it has completely overpowered righteousness, it is assumed to be the righteous way. With the conduct of their parents and neighbors before them as to what is proper, the passing generations glide more and more from pure wisdom to conformity, until their hearts are immune to the gentle movings of "uncreated purity."

What are the customs and conventions that are so dangerous? These are embodied in the love of luxury and superfluities. Luxury enters whenever the slightest departure is made in the use of an object or creature from that intended by the Creator for the welfare of mankind, whether it be slavery or costly furniture.

The roots of custom are in the selfish, not the divine, aspect of man, in man's "natural love of superiority," power, and distinction. It gives rise to that pursuit of wealth for the sake of power that "cloathes itself with the name of justice" and leads to all the injustice and culminates eventually in bloodshed. Thus, to satisfy the customs, men grasp after wealth, and the acquisition of wealth feeds luxury, until the sense of human usefulness is completely overwhelmed in the avaricious and ambitious.

The immediate spring of luxury is trade and traffic—that is, commerce—for commerce provides the luxuries, and the desire for luxuries makes possible an expansion of commerce beyond the limit of the exchange of useful objects.

The customs are mixed with every trade and employment, and though small in their beginnings they grow as they expand business and masses of men become dependent on the traffic. Thus arises all the great evils, from oppression of labor and high interest, to slavery and war. The man rich in money—that is, the moneylender or the great trader—charges heavy interest in order to maintain and expand his luxurious standard of living. Landowners in order to meet the interest are forced to rackrent tenants, and these in turn must oppress their laborers, in low wages, excessive hours, and robbing the soil to meet the rent charge.

The rich man argues that if he were to reduce his expenses, many of the poor would be without employment. But, said Woolman, it is a consequence of large wealth in selfish hands that few are employed in useful things and these forced to labor hard, and others would be unable to earn their bread if employments having no real usefulness were not invented to produce objects to satisfy the vain mind of the rich and their imitators. Thus the money acquired by the wealthy from the poor who do more than a proper share in raising it, is paid to other poor for business which is alien to the true use of things. If the rich lived plainly, tenants would not be forced to pay excessive rents, the laborer could receive equitable wages, and his hours could be reduced so that labor becomes, as it was intended, agreeable. But, where rich men gather money through the toil of husbandmen and circulate it by trading in superfluities and employing people in vanities, the poor are oppressed by poverty and want and are entangled in employment about vanities.

Now, if interest were lower, grain lower and kept more plentiful in our country, wages of hired men might with reason be lower also. This would encourage husbandmen to raise more sheep and flax and promote means for employing more poor people. Since wages would be lower, employers might be satisfied with having less done in a day or week.

The thrifty landlord is also subject to similar vices, whether it be to meet the interest charge or his own desire for a luxurious standard. The landlord takes advantage of the increasing number of landless laborers to lower wages; and at the same time the demand of cities and towns and foreign markets raises the price of foodstuffs, to the damage of the laborers. If the inhabitants of the area to which we send grain should apply themselves more to tillage and less to trade, sufficient food would be available for all, and labor would be easy for all tillers; laboring people would have grain in proportion to their labor, and "in the plentiful produce of our country, . . . rejoice with the landlords," he wrote in *Considerations on the True Harmony of Mankind* (1770).

The landholders argue that, in return for the surplus grain exported, gold as well as merchandise is obtained. But the real use of gold is only a slight fraction of the cost of labor in extracting and circulating it. Its use is as a currency, and if trade were limited to what is consistent with pure wisdom, trade might be carried on without gold.

To make grain scarce for the sake of getting as a currency a little fine metal which is not worth its weight in steel, not only distresses the poor laboring people, but is often 'a snare to the inner state of people's minds. Certainly in cultures where gold does not have the importance it does in ours; the people would be astonished at the high value we place on it in terms of necessaries.

Thus the love of money, so understood, is the root of all evil. Gold, where the value fixed thereon is agreed to, conveys a certain degree of power, and where men get much of this power their hearts are in danger "of being lifted up above their brethren, and of being estranged from that meekness and tender feeling of the state of the poor, which accompanies the faithful followers of Christ." Those with plentiful estates have power over those having only their hands to labor, and if they misapply the power, "the joints and bands of society are disordered." In this love of money and outward greatness the wants of one may require as much labor to supply as would supply ten with useful goods.

When people are entangled with the spirit in which men receive honor of one another, the resulting competitive expenditures are at the cost of the poor. Thus when people love money their hearts are encased with imaginary greatness to run as high as their acquaintances or higher. The disease easily spreads from one to another, and indulged children often drive their parents into financial difficulties in order to live up to expensive customs. A man may intend to accumulate wealth for himself or for his children, but not by oppressing others. However, in the fixed intention to increase his estate, the working of his designs may cause starvation and want among the poor, and at the same time their hardships may remain unnoticed by him.

Agreements among employers to fix wages, Woolman declared in *On Loving Our Neighbors as Ourselves*, are dangerous. They "therein have regard to a profit to themselves answerable to unnecessary expense in their families, which the wages of the others on a moderate industry will not afford a comfortable living for their families. . . . This is like laying a temptation in the way of some to strive for a place higher than they are in, when they have not stock sufficient for it."

Inequality of wealth and income is not necessarily bad, for poverty is no virtue and slothfulness is not as desirable as frugality and industry; but this does not preclude every man's right to make a living.

By the contracts of our fathers and predecessors and by our own acts, "some claim a greater share of the world than others." This is equitable so long as possessions are used for the general good, but every person living "answerable to the design of our creation" is entitled to a "convenient subsistence." Any contracts agreed to by the poor by virtue of their poverty and the power of the wealthy, constitute a violation of trust and an invasion of their rights. In a thickly settled country there is a variety of useful employment besides husbandry, and so the amount of landholdings may rightly vary, but where anyone by virtue of the strength of his possessions demands more interest and rent than moderate labor by the payer can supply, useless employments are promoted.

Some may equitably obtain greater profits than others, yet the poorest people, so long as they are honest, are as much entitled to a certain portion of these profits as those inheriting much. "A right of propriety" implies that the claim must accord with righteousness; and so any claims, irrespective of their legal authentication, must rest on the ground that the lands and profits are used for the general good.

Suppose twenty free men occupy a hitherto unknown island, divide it equitably, improve it, and multiply. Suppose nineteen leave instructions for equitable division and arrangements for the common good, but the twentieth leaves everything to only one child by a duly authenticated legal instrument. To maintain his great distinction, the heir demands from his tenants income to support him in luxuries. Having absolute disposal and providing numerous employments, his power is so great that in all conferences on public affairs, the plain honest men on the island have great difficulty in achieving equitable arrangements.

Suppose each heir in turn leaves all to one heir to continue the grandeur of his name. Thus for many ages over a twentieth part there is one great landlord, and the rest are poor and oppressed. The burdens of the mass are further increased because some, in virtue of the manner of their education and a notion of the greatness of their ancestors, find labor disagreeable and successfully get a living from the rest. But we cannot believe in our hearts that the one Great

Claimer had a right to so great a share of land, after such a numerous increase of inhabitants, whose nature required sustenance thereof. These people, despite the lack of legal instruments, had a right to a part of the possessions of the Great Claimer. "Thus oppression in the extreme, appears terrible; but oppression in more refined appearances remains . . . oppression; and where the smallest degree of it is cherished it grows stronger and more extensive."

The inheritance of wealth in general seemed to Woolman to require investigation. If a person could be fully peisuaded that his children could use his fortune better than others, it might be desirable to leave them all. But this is hard to know. Rather, the heir may use the fortune to live in idleness and luxury and oppression instead of useful labor. Further, this very desire to pass on a fortune to children may easily lead to oppression. Parents may feel justified in acquiring great wealth for their children after seeing what befalls poverty-stricken children, but generally extreme poverty is the result of oppression in acquiring wealth; and secondly there is a tendency for parents to acquire more wealth for their children than they really need to shield them from any undesirable poverty. After all, every generation must produce its own subsistence, and some labor is desirable for all people. So just as much should be left for one child as accords with "pure wisdom" and the rest devoted perhaps to the children of the poor, who might be worthy of it on impartial consideration.

Woolman thought that, if the life of the poor came directly under the observation of the rich, the latter would be compassionate; but the life of the poor is hidden from the rich. He suggested that, if the rich were to change places with the poor and enslaved, they would be greatly aroused against their own ways and "the ill use of religion." The rich man, instead of looking upon himself as superior, should view his riches as an unmerited favor that his way through life has been made easier. Therefore he should employ every opportunity of "leading . . . out of those vicious customs which have entangled the family" to the oppression of the poor. He should occupy himself in looking into the wants of the poor and furnish a perfect example of humility, "that the pure witness may be reached in many minds, and the way opened for a harmonious walking together."

To the poor, Woolman held out the policy of non-violence and persuasion. If, under the harsh treatment of the rich, the poor are industrious and frugal and humbly present their case to their oppressors, they may "reach the pure witness in their minds . . . and though we should remain under difficulties as to outward, yet if we abide in the law of Christ all will work for our good."

But if poorer people instead murmur in their hearts because of their poverty and "strive in the Wisdom of this World to get riches for themselves and their children, this is like wandering in the Dark."

Selfish-minded men may hold their riches in a selfish way, depending on the strength of the civil power, but they will always be ill at ease in the reflection that the poor might rise and pay them in kind for their oppression. Thus selfish men, he declared in "An Epistle to the Quarterly and Monthly Meeting of Friends" in 1772, may possess the earth, but "the meek inherit . . . [it] free from all the defilements and the perplexities of unrighteousness."

On slavery, however, Woolman was very definite. In the first place, it violates natural right and bespeaks luxury in the wide sense of using a creature in a manner not conforming to God's intent. Men taking on the government of others, he said in *Some Considerations on the Keeping of Negroes* (1754, 1762), may intend to govern wisely and make the subjects happy, but absolute command belongs only to him who is perfect.

Men generally want slaves that they may live conformable to the customs of the times which have some luxury in them. The institution is not for the benefit of the slaves but for the gain of the masters. On the one hand it releases the master and his children from the God-given necessity of useful labor and plunges them into all the vices of an idle, luxurious life, and on the other hand the slaves are forced to labor beyond their strength.

The claim that the slaves were well treated Woolman received with considerable skepticism. He had seen the overseers in action and the naked Negro infants about. Besides, masters and slave traders, he said, are hardly impartial judges of the institution since their interest biases them against a candid opinion.

In the last analysis slavery violates that great rule of equity, of paying the laborer the wage he earns. Woolman even made calculations as to the debt, including compound interest, that masters owed the slaves in withholding their wages.

The crude frontier life and Indian wars were likewise the outgrowth of the adherence to customs of luxury in settled areas. Plain living was most desirable, but the living of the frontiersman was coarse rather than plain. Woolman's apology in his famous *Journal* is revealing: "It is the poorer sort of people that commonly begin to improve remote deserts with a small stock; they have houses to build, lands to clear and fence, corn to raise, clothes to provide, and children to educate." Consequently Quakers visiting them should sympathize with them in the wilderness. The best entertainment they can give "may seem coarse to some who are used to cities or old settled places," but visiting disciples of Christ should be content under the circumstances.

However, frontiersmen very often settled unlawfully on Indian land, and by cunning have acquired the land and furs of the Indian at ridiculously low prices. The result is that the Indians feel cheated and Indian wars occur. But the poor people who are the cause of this have been forced to leave settled places and colony territory in order to live more independently of the wealthy, who often set high rents on their land. Thus again, if all our inhabitants lived "according to pure wisdom . . . and ceased from every inordinate desire after wealth, and from all customs which are tinctured with luxury" even a greater population than now could comfortably live on honest employment instead of being tempted to outrage and oppress the Indians.

The funds that men devote to make war with the Indians, Woolman felt, might with better advantage be used in doing justice to them. War in general has no other cause than men's love of luxury and gain. "In the love of money and outward greatness, the mind is perplexed with selfish devices; how to keep; how to defend from the crafty designs of the proud and envious; and from the desperate attempts of the oppressed."

At the age of fifty-three, on the eve of the Revolutionary War, the gentle Quaker passed away.

Woolman and Benjamin Franklin were neighbors for a good part of the time and doubtless occasionally met. In fact, Franklin published one of Woolman's works, but it has been well said that "their views of life, present and future, were too radically different to permit of any common standing ground, and Woolman would naturally shrink from the brilliant social circle" in which Franklin and his Tory son moved.[22]

CHAPTER XI

The Revolutionary War

THE conflict was inevitable. Most enlightened Englishmen believed that the colonies should be drained of their wealth for the benefit of the mother country.

Among those with access to the ruling classes, there was no greater sympathizer of the colonial viewpoint than Pownall. But he insisted in his *Administration of the British Colonies* that the principles of the Navigation Acts must be retained, for these were the palladium of British commercial success.

Their principles are that the colonies shall import from and export to a British market only. Their application, of course, might be modified in the commercial interest of England. Thus, having all goods pass through England is a waste of labor. Therefore, except for such exports as are the materials for British manufactures and such imports that interfere with British manufactures, the colonies should be allowed to trade directly with any country they please. However, these goods should pay the duties they would pay if landed in England, and they should be handled through British houses located in the foreign countries. In this way colonial exports would be encouraged and smuggling reduced and the two points of commercial policy achieved—namely, that the profits of the labor of the colonies should center finally in the mother country and the colonies be customers exclusively of England.

Pownall's views might follow from the premises and objectives formally entertained by enlightened colonial merchant opinion, but colonial opinion had never entertained the notion that British merchants were directly to receive the profits of colonial commerce. They were to flow there by leaving trade absolutely free, except possibly for British manufactures qualified by smuggling.

Harrington's thesis that property gave power was common sense to Englishmen, and so the increase of wealth in the colonies must lead to independence; but Harrington's thesis was also common sense to the colonials. And both looked at the rapid increase of population in the colonies, believing that numbers were the index and source of wealth and power. The students of "political arithmetick" pointed out that the doubling of the colonial population in twenty-five years because of frugal living and available lands meant that in fifty years they would have more inhabitants than Great Britain and Ireland.[1] Men like Franklin drew what was to them the happy conclusion that eventually the seat of the British Empire would be in America. Englishmen shivered at the idea.

Their fears were hardly allayed when the Reverend Charles Chauncy of Boston explained in 1772 to Richard Price, English philosopher, economist, and friend of the colonies, "that half a century will so increase our number and strength, as to put it in the power of New England only to tell any tyrants in Great Britain in plain English, that they will be a free people in opposition to all they can do to prevent it."

The torch that finally started the conflagration was not slaves, molasses, or furs; it was tea. In 1773 the British government, acting on a suggestion of Thomas Wharton, Franklin's associate in the Ohio Valley enterprise, granted the East India Company the right to ship and dispose of tea in the colonies under its own auspices. Heretofore it could only dispose of the tea by auction in London. This meant the end of a substantial number of merchants, whether "fair traders" who had previously bought their tea in London, or smugglers who had dealt in teas which had not passed through England.

The colonials raised the cry of monopoly. Once competition has been driven from the market by undercutting, the monopolist can charge extortionate prices, they declared. Worse still, they added, the tea monopoly is the first step in a systematic scheme to grant exclusive monopolies to English companies. The upshot was the famous Boston Tea Party. This in turn led to punitive measures by the British government, including the closing of the port of Boston until the tea destroyed was paid for.

Professor John Winthrop of Harvard exclaimed to English sympathizers: What must be the feelings of men "when they see themselves treated like a parcel of slaves . . . who are to work just as they are ordered by their masters, and the profit of whose labours is to be appropriated just as their masters please." [2] "Our contention," exclaimed the Reverend Gad Hitchcock in the Massachusetts election sermon of 1774, is "not about trifles, but about liberty and property."

"Sons of Liberty" organizations came into being again through-

out the colonies, and a Continental Congress was called. Loyal supporters of the Crown at first hoped for much good from the Congress.
Since riots and disturbances must all be due to farmers, mechanics,
and tradesmen who have forgotten their place in society, full confidence should be reposed, wrote one Anglican clergyman, "in the
wisdom, the prudence, and patriotic spirit of our representatives
at the congress, who are generally men of property, and have much
more to risk than most of their constituents." [3]

But Congress proceeded to enforce a boycott on all British trade
through the use of extra-legal associations. Prices were fixed and embargoes established to prevent speculation. "We will, in our several
stations," encourage frugality, economy and industry; promote agriculture, arts and manufacture, eliminate extravagances, especially
"cockfighting and funeral expenditures," read the articles of association prepared by Congress in 1774.[4]

Eventually colonial merchants will gain, said one supporter under
the signature of "Atticus" in the *Maryland Gazette*, because we will
easily be able to undersell England. There the price of labor has risen
because luxury pervades all classes. The shortage of labor for manufactures, explained Dr. Benjamin Rush of Philadelphia, will be eliminated by using labor-saving machinery and the great number of
women and children otherwise employed in agriculture.[5]

On the opposition side, the most outspoken were leaders of the
Anglican clergy. Boucher declared that to deny the supreme authority would be to bring on anarchy, slavery, tyranny, luxury, and
conflicts between rich and poor. He warned that England could start
Indian wars and slave insurrections. Should England lose, the southern states would be enslaved by the northern states. Therefore, let us
"revere the laws of the land, the collected wisdom of ages." [6]

The Reverend Samuel Seabury, under the pen name of "Farmer,"
wrote that the city people, especially the merchants, have contempt
for the country people. The non-importation agreement will hurt
the poor by causing unemployment and higher prices for goods. The
people let themselves be dictated to by the Congress, who take their
property without consent. Merchants suffer themselves to be bullied
by a congress and cowed by a committee on penalty of being pub-
licized in the newspapers. "That men who exclaim so violently for
liberty and the rights of Englishmen should ever voluntarily submit
to such an abject state of slavery!" [7]

John Randolph, Loyalist attorney general of Virginia, likewise warned against the boycott. Randolph appealed to the public, but when "I mention the public, I mean to include only the rational part of it," not the ignorant, vulgar, or giddy multitude and those lacking "a serene mind and sound understanding." If trade is stopped, we shall deny men the fruits of their labor. "What benefit will the planter receive from a crop, made by the sweat of his brow, if he be deprived of the liberty of sending it to a proper market? How is his family to be supported but by the profit of his estate?" [8]

The battle of Lexington began the resort to arms. The familiar doctrine of obedience to authority was easily made consistent with the taking up of arms against the British: All are to render obedience to rulers, but tyrants are not ordained by God. In its final statement the colonists were not the rebels, but the King and Parliament. They had broken the compact and invaded the rights of persons and property of the colonists. They were merely stewards with no more rights than the people gave them. "Who is to determine when a ruler is guilty of oppression and tyranny?" asked the Reverend Samuel West in the Massachusetts election sermon of 1775. "I answer the public. Not a few disaffected individuals, but the collective body of the state must decide this question." John Cotton's doctrine had come in handy.

In 1776 came the cry no longer for a restoration of the "old order," but for independence. Critics declared that the colonies should not want "absolute independence," but "constitutional independence." A system of "absolute independence" would burst asunder the band of religion, laws, language, blood, and of interest and commerce, of all "those habitudes in fine which unite us under the influence of the common parent." The colonies would be unable to agree on a common government. They would be jealous of one another; and the diversity of laws, the inequality of riches, variety of possessions, would sow the seeds of discord. There would be no way of adjusting their relative rank or proportion. The fact that the King is 3,000 miles away should not be an objection, because thereby he can exercise less personal influence in colonial affairs. [9]

On the other hand, Witherspoon tried to prove to the English that American independence was good for England. True, England loses the exclusive trade of the colonies, but an exclusive trade is not easily preserved and when preserved is generally hurtful. "Trade is of a nice and delicate nature," and is founded upon interest. It will force its way wherever interest leads and can hardly be made to go in another direction by an act. An exclusive trade makes a people less careful to work as well and as cheaply as others to procure voluntary purchasers. It tempts and enables great merchants in the capital to import from other nations what they can export to such a forced market to advantage instead of benefiting England's manufactures. A few private individuals gain, but no essential service is done to the British people, and the ultimate profit goes to that country where the goods are produced. If England's balance of trade is unfavorable with every country except Portugal, as her writers say, the cause is the exclusive trade with the American settlements.[10]

The higher learning felt the impact of the war. The heads of the two crown-chartered colleges—King's (now Columbia) and William and Mary—were forced to flee after repeatedly denouncing the colonials for their disloyalty to God as well as to the mother country. The Pennsylvania Assembly decided that the only way to eliminate the Loyalist influence of the trustees of the College of Philadelphia and the stipulation of the charter of allegiance to the English authorities, was by transferring the property to a new corporation, the University of Pennsylvania. But the trustees of the old institution and the former provost, the Reverend William Smith, complained that the transfer was a violation of their property rights.

On the other hand, the mere fact that Catholic France and Spain were our allies was not allowed to interfere with the delivery of the Dudleian Lectures at Harvard against the papacy. Harvard students were warned by one Dudleian lecturer that our "alliance with popish powers" should not blind us to the errors of the Papacy.[11]

The colonies became independent states. They remodeled constitutions, but for the most part they retained the old political arrangements, except for the elimination, in good part, of feudal institutions of entail, primogeniture, and state church. The franchise was broadened, but it was still surrounded with pecuniary qualifications. In the pages of the *Maryland Gazette*, wealthy and well-educated Charles Carroll of Carrollton informed the public that the only bright spot in the otherwise wicked life of his former associate in western land speculation, Samuel Chase, was that he had successfully opposed a "democratical form of government" for Maryland.[12]

The differences in status were recognized even in governors' proclamations calling for the help of all in the cause of independence.

Proclaimed Governor William Livingston of New Jersey: "Let us . . . of every rank and degree, remember our plighted faith and honor." [13]

James Madison, graduate student under Witherspoon and son of a substantial Virginia planter, suggested that regiments of Negro slaves be raised and be offered their freedom; but the dominant sentiment, expressed by his fellow Virginia congressman, Joseph Jones, was that it would drain off immediately some of the best agricultural labor. The result would be the ruin of the individual, the distress of the state, and perhaps loss of the war, for food production would be reduced.[14] Congress in January 1776 ordered that no "bought indentured servants" were to be accepted in the Army or Navy without the "consent of their masters." The draft was often used to fill the armies, but the wealthy could provide substitutes, in accordance with the general notion that the poor assist with their persons, the rich with their loan of money.

Congress spent months wrangling over whether officers should after the war receive half pay for life. The measure was passed after General Washington declared that otherwise the "officers will moulder to nothing, or be composed of low and illiterate men void of capacity for this, or any other business" for the good men are resigning to make more money in outside lucrative employment.[15] However, Congress turned down a proposal that officers' commissions be vendible as in the British Army, so that the Army could be "kept officered by gentlemen." [16]

From New England to Maryland came pleas that trade be pushed by means of a Navy. The great essential is full employment. The country instead of sinking into poverty would be enriched by the gain of individuals, for the public stock is increased by private profit. The poor would be employed and the farmer receive his proportion of the gain.[17]

Trading with the enemy was by no means uncommon. It was even urged in Congress on the Whatley-Franklin principle that, since the enemy could obtain supplies elsewhere, the treasure the colonies would obtain from the enemy would drain England and animate America. Congressman Joseph Jones of Virginia declared that the ports must be opened to provide an outlet for surplus agricultural production, for otherwise the collection of heavy taxes would be oppressive and produce discontent. It could not be taken off by internal demand and consumption.[18] Madison was pleased with Spain as an ally in Florida and the West Indies, for she took American flour and sent specie. As the French and Continental armies joined for the final assault on Cornwallis in Virginia late in 1781, Madison expected prosperity for Virginia even if the objectives were not achieved. "It would," he wrote, "leave the militia men more at leisure to pursue their occupations," and the demands of the armies will afford a sure new market for the surplus produce of the country. It will diffuse among them the gold and silver of our ally, and the ships of the French in the Chesapeake will revive trade, reduce the price of the imported necessaries, and raise the staple of the country again to its proper value.[19] States competed for prisoners' camps, since the prisoners were provided with specie by the English government.

As for labor, Franklin doubted the wisdom of government restraints to encourage manufactures on the ground that duties allow workmen to tax the home consumer by greater prices, while the wages the workmen receive makes them neither happier nor richer, since they only drink more and work less.[20]

The wealthy Massachusetts merchant, James Bowdoin, in his address as first president of the American Academy of Arts and Sciences, in Boston, declared in 1780 that "the balance of advantage" which yields a national superiority in riches, influence, and prosperity will always be in favor of the people whose skill, industry, and cheapness of labor induces them to manufacture and export the greatest amount of goods whether manufactured from their own rough produce or that of other countries.

On the other hand, complaints were heard that artisans, especially in the superior crafts, were demanding high bounties from the parents of prospective apprentices. An anonymous "mechanic" retorted that bounties would be taken only from people who could afford them.[21]

Few doubted that America had within herself the material resources for waging war, but just how to call them forth by a monetary expedient was the question. The colonials had faced wars before and regretted later some of the financial practices used; but this war was no exception to the rule that men refused to learn from experience. The men in power, whether in the state governments or Congress, were well educated, students of the best learning England as well as America had to offer. They knew the latest theories of economics and politics, but by the pervasive mercantile logic they could

hardly reconcile the conflicting interests among the respectable. Fortunately the enemy was habituated to the same logic.

All insisted on the wisdom of taxation, but found it hard to agree
on concrete proposals. So the first and chief reliance in obtaining
revenues both by Congress and the states was the old, simple device
of legal-tender paper money. The formulator of the Congress policy
was a wealthy New York lawyer, twenty-four-year-old Gouverneur
Morris.

Only a few years previously he had been an active participant on
the other side in a paper-money controversy in his home colony
in New York. He was graduated at the age of fifteen from Kings
College in 1767, and two years later he was opposing in the press a
proposal in the colonial legislature for an issue of loan bills, though
the measure was expected to have royal approval. Morris had presented the familiar objections. He claimed that debtors were attempting to pay their debts at a lower rate of interest, at the cost of
the province and posterity. "A multiplied currency is a never failing
source of national debt . . . there are no bounds to national debt
but national ruin," he had claimed.

Now, in 1775, he declared that the crisis demanded an extraordinary supply of money which could not be raised by taxation.
Therefore the Congress should issue $2,000,000 in bills to be liqui-
dated in seven years. Such a currency would "be a new bond of
union to the associated colonies." [22] So began the pouring forth of
the famous "continental." Government loan offices were afterward
established to "prevent" the depreciation of the paper by issuing loan-
office certificates bearing interest payable in bills of exchange drawn
on France in return for the paper or specie. At the same time Congress and the states issued certificates of indebtedness for the payment of troops, bounties, goods, and various services, and so
contributed along with land warrants to further issues of paper for
circulation and speculation.

On the Tory side a similar state of affairs existed. During the British
occupation of Philadelphia, the Loyalists continued to use the old
Pennsylvania legal-tender bills to relieve the "scarcity of money."
Those refusing to accept them in trade at full value were accused of
lacking confidence in the ultimate success of British arms.[23]

On the American side, as prices rose, a great outcry was made
against "monopolists, engrossers and forestallers." But Pelatiah Webster, Yale graduate and Philadelphia merchant, explained in 1776 that

the general rise in prices was due to uncontrollable war circumstances, to the greater risk involved in imports, and to the scarcity of laborers. The high prices could not be attributed to the paper money because the amount of paper issued was hardly sufficient to supply a necessary circulating medium, which he assumed as did others to be $30,000,000.[24]

In celebrating the first anniversary of the Declaration of Independence with a sermon on *The Separation of the Jewish Tribes* . . . the Reverend William Gordon declared: "The nature of the time must unavoidably make goods dearer than formerly." Consequently all the price advances cannot be attributed to oppression and extortion. Critics of trade and merchants forget that, except for trade and merchandise, the country would never have been settled by their forefathers but would have remained the uncultivated abode of Indians. Without trade and merchandise we would have been enslaved by now, for only by these means do we obtain the necessary military supplies and drugs from abroad. Finally, it should not be forgotten that the president of the Continental Congress is a merchant.

In 1777 the Reverend Jonathan French devoted a whole sermon to *A Practical Discourse Against Extortion,* aimed, it appears, primarily at the farmers. There was no worse sin than extortion, but all were to blame. "You will plead . . . that the merchants began first and therefore you are not to blame." Many will argue that, as they "are obliged to pay exorbitant prices for what they purchase, there is no inequity in asking the like for what they sell." But this attitude is unjust as long as there are more purchasers than vendors. Suppose the authorities should encourage the extravagant demands of the merchant, but at the same time "force your commodities from you at the former usual prices, would you not cry . . . oppression? . . . Equal injustice is now practiced by the merchant and farmer both and yet you do not feel it, or, if sensible of it, do not reform."

But how shall the evil be reformed? It must be a general reformation, but, like any reformation, it must begin with individuals. Each individual reformation would be a little drop and would be added to other drops until a mighty torrent would be created and the reformation completed.

The demand for price-fixing and similar measures was widespread, and the states began to take action. Connecticut led the way in November 1776 with a comprehensive price-fixing act. It attributed the "rapid and exorbitant rise of prices" to monopolizers. But it rec-

ognized that the problem could not be solved by each state individually. A convention of New England states was called to devise
means to prevent the "oppressing of soldiers and inhabitants" by extravagant prices. The committee took into account "the most extravagant price of labour in general." Farming labor was fixed and
made the "standard," and the "labour of mechanics and tradesmen and
other labour" was ordered "computed according to the usages and
customs that have heretofore been . . . practiced in different parts
of the several states compared with farming labour." Practically all
domestic prices were fixed. Imports, asserted the committee, were
500 to 600 per cent of the prime cost, and they retailed at the "unreasonable profit" of 40 or 50 per cent or more in addition. Therefore wholesale mark-ups of imports were ordered cut in half and
retailers limited to 20 per cent mark-ups. But military stores were exempted from any price regulation. Finally, the states were to stop
issuing paper and resort to loans if necessary.

At the same time Congress was called on to provide a uniform
measure for all the states. Said Samuel Chase, who not long afterward took up active merchandising as a sideline and was accused of
attempting to corner the wheat supply, price regulation must be
resorted to, for the mines of Peru would not support a war at the
present high prices of the necessaries. It was admitted to be a temporary measure but would serve as a stopgap until a more permanent
remedy could be devised.

Critics in Congress insisted that price rises were due primarily to
the scarcity of commodities and excessive paper issues and declared
that price-fixing was an attempt to raise the value of money, an
experiment which had failed even in absolutist France.[25]

Witherspoon thought that even recommending the measure to the
states for consideration was bad, because it would spread further the
impression of distress. In a letter signed "A New Jersey Farmer," he
even lectured General Washington on the inexpediency and injustice
of attempting to fix prices for provisions for his Army. Price-fixing
must aggravate the evils they intend to cure and end in starvation for
the Army. The determination of prices is among those things that
depend for success on inward inclination, on interest, not on law
and authority; on immediate sensible personal interest, not national
interest. No man can be compelled to bring goods to market at
prices he considers unreasonable. A reasonable price can only mean
that "which is proportioned to the demand on the one side, and the

plenty or scarcity of goods on the other," but this price will fix itself by the consent of the buyer and seller, better than it can be done by any politician, for if the fixed price is not agreeable, no goods will be forthcoming.

How can authority fix a reasonable price when the determining circumstances are so numerous that they cannot all be attended to or even ascertained? Differences in the quality of the goods, in the relative supplies, in weather conditions, in distances—all these and a hundred other circumstances which can never be foreseen actually govern and ought to govern the prices of goods at market. But if prices are left free, the various circumstances restrain and limit one another. "He who is nearest and has goods in plenty will by selling cheap, moderate the demands on him who comes far." If a high price is paid one day, the news spread abroad brings in prodigious quantities, and the price falls. Finally, the "persons concerned, buyers and sellers, will use every art to defeat . . . [price-fixing] and will certainly succeed." [26]

Some superficial reasoners, he declared later in an *Essay on Money* (1786), have cited the familiar regulation, among others, of the price of chairs, hackney-coaches, and ticket porters in cities and public ferries. But these instances are different from laws regulating prices in voluntary commerce. The persons in the former activities solicit the privilege, obtain a license, and come under voluntary engagements to ask no higher prices; consequently there is as complete a free contract as in buying and selling in open shops.

As another Congress member summed up: Prices cannot be regulated as long as the quantity of money and the articles of life are fluctuating. Since this must always be so, prices can never be regulated.

Respectable merchant opinion was summed up by General Nathanael Greene, who engaged in business on the side. Price-fixing, he asserted, is founded in "public covetousness, a desire to have the property of a few at a less value, than the demand will warrant to the owners."

In February 1777 Congress merely recommended that the states hold regional conventions to discuss price-fixing. In August another northern convention recommended the repeal of all price-fixing legislation as unworkable; but at the beginning of the year still another convention declared for price-fixing. Independence, it declared, depends on the success of the Army; the latter depends immediately on the credit of the currency. Officers and soldiers cannot support themselves at the present prices, and the community cannot afford to increase their pay, since the bills with which they are paid must eventually be redeemed in specie at the nominal values.

Therefore the rate of all expenses must be reduced to their original standard. Congress is taking measures to reduce the amount of currency, and so appreciate it, by resorting to foreign loans and taxes, and these in time may work the remedy; but temporarily price-fixing must be used. We cannot complain of "partial infringement of liberty" to save the community. "Must the lunatic run uncontrolled to the destruction of himself and his neighbours merely because he is under the operation of medicines which may in time work his cure?"

Labor was ordered limited to a 75 per cent rise over 1774 prices, but maxima for commodities ranged from 75 per cent upward, and retailers were allowed 25 per cent. However, military stores and various other imports essential to the Army and people were exempt because the charges and risks of importation were too great, various, and uncertain. But they hoped that these prices would be so far governed by the estimate of other articles as to preserve a due proportion.[27]

But in 1778 Congress recommended that the states repeal all price-fixing acts. Experience demonstrated that they were ineffective and produced evil consequences and oppression. States which had enacted such acts in conformity with Congress's earlier recommendations should lift them because a change of circumstances in commerce rendered them unnecessary and the measure had not yet been adopted by all the states.

More paper was issued. Washington complained bitterly of the high prices and their effect on the Army, but Gouverneur Morris explained to him that paper money was the great engine by which the resources of the country were drawn forth for the war effort. True, the paper will necessarily depreciate, but this is not as bad as it seems. The debt does not increase, for a certain sterling sum which would have paid it one year ago will pay it now. The depreciation in the interim has operated as a tax. It is too bad that the tax falls heavily on those who have served and continue to serve their country, but to relieve fully their suffering is not in our power.[28]

The general apparently remained unconvinced. "Speculation, peculation, engrossing, forestalling with all their concomitants, evidence the decay of public virtue." These have caused the depreciation of the currency; and this, aided by stock jobbing and party dissensions, has fed the hopes of the enemy and kept their arms in the country. "We should be . . . devising ways and means to appreciate the currency, on the credit of which everything depends"; but not price-fixing, "for this . . . is inconsistent with the very nature of things, and impracticable in itself." [29]

Benjamin Franklin worried from time to time about the paper; but he convinced himself, or at least tried to convince correspondents both at home and abroad, of Morris's argument that, though the depreciation was an evil to particular individuals, yet it was an advantage to the public at large. Paper is a wonderful machine, he wrote the Reverend Samuel Cooper. "It performs its office when we issue it; it pays and clothes troops, and provides victuals and ammunition, and when we are obliged to issue a quantity excessive it pays itself off by depreciation." It was the most equal tax, since it depreciated in the hands of the holders "in proportion to the sums held and the period held, which generally is in proportion to a man's wealth." [30]

Chauncy, who had uttered the customary denunciation of the unstable paper medium in colonial days, informed Price likewise that the continentals were not as bad as they might seem. Notwithstanding the vast depreciation and the excessive rise in price of necessaries, the American states are richer in reality as well as in name than ever before and better able to prosecute the war; our freeholders and farmers by means of the plenty of paper money have paid their debts and extended their farms. But one great fault is that the people have "almost universally been too attentive to the getting of gain." Otherwise we would long ago have driven out the British.[31]

Nathaniel Scudder, a physician, summed up the mystification of Congress on matters of finance in 1778. Much time has been spent on finance, he wrote while in Congress, "All I have found out is what will *not* do for the support of our public credit and the prevention of a general depreciation. When I shall be happy enough to determine what will do, Heaven only knows." [32]

Even the sages of the past were nonplussed. Roger Sherman, important Connecticut merchant and member of Congress, had chastised public paper in his popular almanacs, but in 1778 he declared: "We can't lessen the quantity much while the army is kept up." [33]

A Virginia writer declared in 1779 that the value of money can only be appreciated by a free trade. The news of cargoes has already frightened the forestallers and monopolists with ruin. Therefore the laws should let them alone.[34]

Later in 1779, Congress declared that it had set the limit for emissions at $200,000,000 and that the paper would be redeemed at full value in specie. John Jay, wealthy conservative New Yorker and president of Congress, prepared the circular. It set forth the familiar advantages of a non-exportable medium of circulation based on "the natural wealth, value and resources of the country." The causes of depreciation are either "natural" or "artificial." Natural depreciation is in proportion to the excess of the issues beyond the requirements of commerce. This can be cured easily by loans and taxes. Worse is artificial depreciation, which arises from lack of confidence. But the paper will unquestionably be fully redeemed in specie. There is no reason to "apprehend a wanton violation of the public faith," for Congress as the representative of the people has no more power "to annihilate your money than your independency." The honor and pride of America would revolt against violating our national faith and sacred contracts.

The paper can easily be redeemed because of the nation's increasing population, wealth, and trade. The country is still ours. Great areas remain to be cultivated, and vast lakes and rivers are "yet to hear the din of industry, become subservient to commerce, and boast delightful villas, gilded spires and spacious cities rising on their banks." [35]

Only weak and designing men, added "Meanwell" in the *Maryland Gazette* in November 1779, have argued that the public debt should be paid at a discount. These claim that, because great sums were paid for a trifle of produce or merchandise, large sums are owed to or possessed by engrossers, and consequently the public debt has grown too large for redemption at full nominal value. But the money is chiefly possessed by or owed to planters and farmers. Speculators have realized their money by purchasing lands or produce. Finally, it is impossible to distinguish the virtuous and innocent from the monopolists and engrossers.

The general sentiment of the respectable, from Charles Carroll to General John Armstrong, was that taxation was the ideal and ordinary solution, but the disease had run too long to be overtaken by a common cure. The increasing of taxes, it was argued, would start murmurs and investigations. All efforts should instead be made to obtain foreign loans.

With prices rising faster than the issue of the bills, the uproar was tremendous for price-fixing and other measures "appreciating" the currency. One member of Congress reported on May 24, 1779, that prices had doubled in three weeks in Philadelphia. "This has made those vermin the speculators, become the object of resentment and a mob has assembled to regulate prices. What will be the issue God knows." [36]

The "mob" was a committee of respectable citizens headed by General Daniel Roberdeau, wealthy merchant and former member of Congress, and William Bradford, eminent lawyer and later attorney general in Washington's cabinet. Prices are higher than they ought to be in proportion to the quantity of money, stated their manifesto. Every new cargo instead of lowering prices, raises them. The prices of rum, tea, sugar, flour, coffee have risen without any real cause. The tax laid on us by forestallers and monopolists the last six months has been sufficient to prosecute the war for a year. The only way to make good our money is to reduce the prices of necessaries and provisions. It has long been said that trade will regulate itself, but experience shows that the maxim is not true in all cases. By stepping in between importers and retailers, monopolizers can introduce a scarcity when they choose and, by transporting goods from one state to another, create a scarcity in one or all; and the retailers are practically free to add what profits they please. Consequently trade "becomes clogged with a disease, which left to itself, will destroy it." The great remedy is to follow the practice of the monopolists, in reverse—that is, bring prices down week by week to the old levels—and there will be money to spare for paying taxes.

The capital of Virginia, Williamsburg, in July followed suit. A professor of the College of William and Mary and the clerk of the House of Delegates called a meeting presided over by a clergyman to consider similar measures. Prices have advanced so far beyond what the difficulty of obtaining the goods or the quantity of money in circulation would occasion, that the public expense cannot be supported. The remedy is to reduce by easy steps first the prices of domestic commodities and then of imports.[37]

Through the pages of the *Connecticut Courant*, "Unbiassed Speculator" commented that these price measures were silly, for only by reducing the quantity of money and paying taxes could the money be fixed.

Pelatiah Webster outdid Witherspoon in insisting that "freedom of trade," or "unrestrained liberty of the subject to hold or dispose of his property as he pleases," was absolutely necessary for national prosperity in wartime as well as peace, for "gain is the soul of industry," and the hope of reward sweetens labor. In essays on "free trade and finance" in 1779 and 1780, he declared that every man will be satisfied with the market price; for, though he may not obtain the price he expected, he has had "the full chance of the market." Consequently he can blame nobody. Given this liberty, every industrious man will procure to his utmost the greatest quantity and best quality of goods for the market, for thereby he gets the most money. He will supply the most scarce commodities because these have the largest demand and the highest price. With goods high in times of general scarcity, every man will be impelled to use goods most economically, and great distress and total destitution will be prevented. The high prices and great demand by their natural operation will induce the producing and bringing to market of further supplies. The price cannot exceed the degree of scarcity, for otherwise supplies will be quickly forthcoming at lower prices.

Besides, under price regulation there are the insurmountable administrative problems of deciding who shall be the proper purchasers and of preventing hoarding. Must the seller or producer "have his house searched from top to bottom for concealments? Even the lodging rooms of his wife and daughters! I must beg to be excused from any further description of these horrors which too many know are not mere creatures of the imagination. . . .

"Laws ought to conform to the natural course of things." So remove all obstructions to our market, all fetters and restraints and discouragement of business, such as embargoes, tender acts, limitations, regulation, etc. "Let every man be at liberty to get money as fast as he can" and be put under every natural advantage for doing it. Likewise privateering should be encouraged by more liberal rewards.

With trade unrestrained, the circulation of money is brisk, the price and demand for goods high. So money may be raised and taxes paid more easily than in periods of business stagnation resulting from fettering trade. In fact, in such periods of business prosperity, the payment of taxes and their return into the circuit of trade would be such that the gains to the producing classes would pay most of their taxes.

Those arguing that price-fixing will appreciate the currency are ignorant of the principles of money. The value of money is nothing in itself, but a mere relation between the medium of trade and the objects of trade—everything for which money is paid. Money varies in value according to the variation in its quantity and the quantity of the objects of trade.

Both appreciation and depreciation are undesirable, for the fluctuations alter contracts. But of the two, appreciation is worse because it involves the hoarding of money. The depreciated paper has achieved the benefits Gouverneur Morris and Franklin claimed for it. Its great evil flows from the legal-tender feature.

The remedies lie in the devaluation of the paper and taxation, Webster declared in 1780. Devaluation is no breach of the public faith any more than any other promise which, however "properly made at first, is become by a change of circumstances, either impossible or highly improper to be performed."

When the presses are stopped, which must take some time yet, and an effective method of supplying the Treasury with taxes is devised, the continental will make for itself an exchange or gain a fixed value. It is impossible to say what that value will be, but however it fixes itself it will be right. Then the exchange is to be fixed according to that value by directing that hard money shall be paid and received in the Treasury at this rate.

All payments from or to the Treasury are then to be paid at the exchange which existed at the time they were contracted. For this purpose Congress should set up a table or rate of exchange, to be continued from the first depreciation of continental bills up to the date of the fixing of the currency. Taxes need not be levied immediately for sinking any of the bills, for the quantity circulating will be no more than necessary for a medium of trade. When the war ceases, the country will easily pay off both the foreign debts and domestic loans and sink the bills if necessary.[38]

James Madison took another line of reasoning toward the same goal. His approach was the anti-quantity theory of the last of the great mercantilists, Sir James Steuart, as expressed in *An Inquiry Into the Principles of Political Oeconomy:* The depreciation is not due to the quantity, for the quantity of money never directly determines the value of money. If the money is paper, the value depends on the date of redemption into specie and the government's credit. Quantity affects the value only as people think it will postpone or endanger the redemption. Therefore it is the lack of public confidence that reduces the value, and the very discredit of the money begets further emissions *ad infinitum*.

Now, considering that Congress expects to eliminate all the $200,000,000 of paper money in eighteen years, the rate of interest to be 6 per cent, the "intrinsic depreciation" of the paper money according to the rule of computation by date of redemption should be less than three to one. Even by the rule of quantity, with $30,000,000 assumed to be the supply of money requisite to the needs of the community, it should not be more than seven to one. But the market rate is between thirty and forty to one.

On the basis of his principle, he also argued that the domestic loans, through the use of loan-office certificates, merely increased the burden of the community by the interest payment. They circulate as money, and thus by making the date of redemption of the paper more remote, they help to lower instead of raising the value of money. "We think it a piece of dexterity in finance, by emitting loan office certificates, to elude the necessity of emitting bills of credit." [39]

The most radical, and highly unacceptable, suggestions came from "Agricola" in the *Virginia Gazette* in 1779: "Take the whole trade of the continent out of the hands of individuals and let it be carried on for the benefit of the public by persons authorized by the legislature under stated but liberal salaries."

Finally, in March 1780, Congress took Webster's advice and with his blessing devalued the continentals at forty to one for specie in payment of state quotas of taxes. Congress explained that, in view of the country's exigencies, more bills had to be issued than were required as a circulating medium. This, along with a lack of a specie fund or other valuable security on which to guarantee their eventual redemption, depreciated them. Inasmuch as they now passed by "common consent" in most areas at one-fortieth of their nominal value, steps must be taken to stabilize their value at this rate. Continental bills paid in were not to be reissued. But up to one-twentieth of the nominal amount of the old bills, new bills might be issued bearing 6 per cent interest and redeemable within six years in specie or bills of exchange. Following to a certain extent another of Webster's suggestions, it further provided that for loan-office certificates issued after March 1778, a scale of depreciation based on their value at date of issue be established for eventual redemption. In this way the holders would be paid the "full current value" of the paper when loaned.

A year later, with both kinds of bills heavily depreciated, Congress forbade the circulation of the continentals.

The states likewise began to devaluate their paper and set up scales of depreciation for the settlement of various public dues and transactions. In 1779 representatives of the Massachusetts battalions complained that the great decline of the purchasing power of the paper constituted an infringement of the government's contract with the Army. The state promised to make good after the war to them "and the heirs of such of them as shall then be dead" the wages stipulated in the original acts of enlistment. Under the Act of 1780, it set up a table of depreciation based on averaging for each month the price of beef, Indian corn, sheeps' wool, and sole leather, and officers and soldiers were paid the balance due them in long-term interest-bearing notes.[40]

South Carolina provided for the adjustment of all contracts, including those of public creditors, according to a scale of depreciation composed of the average of two other tables, the "British specie depreciation table" and the average of the prices of rice, indigo, and Negroes.[41]

Before the war was over the legislatures repealed their legal-tender acts. The Massachusetts legislature in an *Address* informed the people in 1781 that "the value of money which is but a representative of property will ever be regulated by the common consent of the people at large"; hence, as long experience proves, attempts of the legislature to regulate it must prove futile. The paper currency is to be a tender "according to the value established by yourselves in your mutual commerce."

Opponents of paper like Witherspoon declared that the states should resort instead to loans from private individuals in anticipation of taxes. This is the case in England, Witherspoon added, for all their taxes would be too late if monied men did not advance in the meantime the necessary funds.

In accordance with this idea came the proposal in Congress for a government specie bank to finance the war by loans in anticipation of taxes. Spokesmen argued that the country abounded in more specie than before the war because the war had prevented the payment of British debts, forced the country to manufacture, cut off luxury imports, and brought in a heavy inflow of specie to supply the British and French forces. But the specie had not gotten into circulation because of the fluctuating paper currency and the tender laws.

People could lend the specie to the bank because the bank's reserves would be in specie raised by taxes. At the same time, with Hume as the authority, it was held that by locking up a good deal of the specie in the bank, prices of imports could be prevented from rising; consequently the country would drain other nations of specie instead of losing it.[42]

William Barton (1755–1817) of Pennsylvania came forth with a bank proposal early in 1781 that attracted considerable attention. Barton came of a leading Pennsylvania family. His father was a distinguished Tory and Episcopal clergyman, and one of his uncles was the astronomer David Rittenhouse. As befitted his social position, he had gone to England in 1774 to get education and polish, but five years later in the midst of the Revolution he returned to side with the colonials. A man of varied talents, he served for a while as an army officer, and then became a lawyer. Honors came to him quickly from the learned. In the year he issued his plea, the University of Pennsylvania awarded him an honorary M.A.; later the College of New Jersey awarded him a similar honor. The American Philosophical Society, the Massachusetts Historical Society, and what might be called the Royal Economic Society of Spain enrolled him in their select membership.

Barton's scheme, presented in his *Observations on the Nature and Use of Paper-Credit* (1781), was a national specie bank with notes convertible on demand, but the specie was to be raised by a lottery and all profits for the first four years were to go to "fifty gentlemen most conspicuous for integrity, fortune, ability and attachment to the country," who were to be chosen by Congress and incorporated as the "Governor and Company of the American Bank." At the same time all tender laws were to be abolished; all public non-interest-bearing paper eventually eliminated; and the states were to sell their vacant and unappropriated lands at "reasonable" prices to ease the burden of taxation. The only kind of public paper to be allowed would be that of interest-bearing public debt.

In 1781 another of Webster's suggestions—that a superintendent of finance be appointed to give system to government finances—was accepted. The choice was none other than Robert Morris, whose ruling principle was to connect "the public service and private interest." He stipulated that he was to be allowed to continue his private business. As his assistant he chose Gouverneur Morris. He knew that the solution lay through a private commercial bank chartered by the government and supplied with government funds and powers. Morris argued successfully in favor of a scheme of a group of Philadelphia merchants and financiers which had already been rejected by the Pennsylvania Assembly. They proposed a bank with a specie capital of $400,000, with notes payable on demand but receivable for all government dues and taxes. No other private group was to be allowed to issue paper.

Morris declared: The country's exigencies require anticipation of revenue, but confidence is lacking to call out for the purpose the funds of individuals in the form of loans. The private bank, however, will aid the government by its money and credit. It will gain from individuals that credit which property and ability never fail to command, and supply the loss of paper which is so depreciated that there is an insufficient amount for trade and taxation. Able to borrow abroad, it could prevent the drain of specie if an unfavorable balance of trade should occur. It is absolutely essential if the government debt, especially to the Army, is to be paid. Best of all, it "would attach many powerful individuals to the cause of our country by the strong principle of self-love, and the immediate sense of private interest." [43]

Many felt that Congress had no power to charter a bank, but they concluded with Madison that, though they are aware of the "poisonous tendency of precedents of usurpation," still it should be tried in the absence of anything better.[44] By the time the bank commenced operations in 1782, the war was practically over. Only $70,000 in specie had been supplied when it began in January 1782, but Morris deposited in it more than $400,000 in specie borrowed from the French.

The bank hardly lived up to the expectations held forth by the promoters, and Morris informed Congress in 1782 that the bank had limited resources; therefore we must resort to additional foreign loans. Expressive of this common attitude was the Reverend Hugh Williamson, the former professor of mathematics at the College of Philadelphia and bitter opponent of Franklin, but at the time a merchant in North Carolina and congressman from that state. Congress, he informed the governor of North Carolina, is rightly seeking to obtain loans from her allies rather than resorting to taxation. The peculiar quality of our staples and the scarcity of money in North Carolina is a good reason for North Carolina to support this policy. We are rich enough to deserve credit, but at present we are unable to pay taxes because tar, pitch, turpentine, lumber, corn, and our other staples are too bulky to bear transportation in wartime. We can pay with these in times of peace.[45]

A Congress committee agreed with Morris that it was absurd to continue to pay interest on the loan-office certificates issued before March 1778, in bills drawn on France. Witherspoon, in behalf of the Committee of Finance, prepared in June 1782 the proposal to suspend such payments. But so loud was the protest that Witherspoon turned around in August and September and lectured Congress on the sanctity of contract. If creditors are treated in this manner, how can we obtain a loan from Europe? If, on the other hand, our security and credit are good, public obligations could always be turned into money at par or slightly less. Congress should learn a lesson from Britain. By punctually fulfilling all engagements of interest, she has supported an enormous debt. She is "not wholly without experience of depreciation. Navy debentures have been frequently sold . . . at a third of their value; by that means they seem to be held by that class of men called by us speculators. Did that government ever think of presenting the holders . . . when they came to be paid, with a scale of depreciation? The very idea of it would knock the whole system of public credit to pieces." [46]

However, Congress did go on record in favor of an import duty in 1781 to be collected by its own agents in order to provide the "fund" for paying the debts contracted or to be contracted in the future. Since taxation was a power not granted to the Congress, the consent of all the states had to be obtained.

But the Rhode Island Assembly unanimously rejected the first measure and discountenanced subsequent ones. Virginia did likewise later, and other states specified qualifications. Supporters of the Rhode Island action presented all the objections that had been brought against England's Trade Acts, ranging from violation of the rights of person and property and absentee control to the entering wedge of despotism. But they chiefly emphasized the argument that the burden would fall heavily on commercial states and benefit agricultural states.

Benjamin Franklin entered the controversy to assert that the claims of creditors could not be disallowed by any appeal to property rights. They object, he said, to giving Congress "a power to take, as they call it, the people's money out of their pockets, though only to pay the interest and principal of debts duly contracted." But this would over-throw society. He informed Robert Morris: "Money justly due from the people is their creditors' money and no longer the money of the people, who if they withhold it, should be compelled to pay by some law."

All property beyond that required for a person's subsistence is the creature of public convention, and therefore the public has the right of regulating "descents and all other conveyances" of property, and even of limiting its quantity and uses. More specifically, all property necessary to a man, his conservation and the propagation of the species, "is his natural right, which none can justly deprive him of." But the excess is the property of the public who by their laws have created it, and who may therefore by other laws dispose of it whenever the public welfare so requires.[47]

Congress, in circulars prepared by Madison and Alexander Hamilton, vainly attempted to convince Rhode Island that the import duty would not give the agricultural states an advantage because an import duty is ultimately paid by the consumer, not the merchant. Such a tax is the fairest tax because it promotes frugality and taxes extravagance. Even if it discouraged imports it would be advantageous to commerce, for it would incline the balance of trade in the country's favor.

The principal object of advantageous commerce is promoting exports. Thus taxes on possessions and articles of the country's own growth and manufacture, whether a land tax, excise, or export duty, are bad because, by tending to increase the price of exports, they enable others to undersell us. After all, the fund is being used to pay the debts of a revolution "from which an unbounded freedom has accrued to commerce."

Pelatiah Webster attempted a more theoretical defense in 1783. With his customary frankness, he later explained the circumstances of the essay. The peace was expected; but peace, though the most desirable thing, was clothed with terror. Soldiers were threatening mutiny, for they were to be disbanded without money available to pay them. Unliquidated debt accounts both of the Army and the creditors were paid merely in interest-bearing certificates. At the same time the merchants had imported heavily from Europe. Therefore the tax was necessary not only to supply the Treasury, but also to maintain the price of goods and save the merchant from great losses from falling prices entailed by peace. At the same time the impost, by preventing a deluge of imported goods, would prevent the draining of the country's cash.

Webster declared that the tax reduces the competitive level of ostentation and increases the industry of the country. Treasure saved is thrown into circulation again and "becomes a clear saving, or balance of increase of the circulating medium, and consequently of realized wealth in the country." The whole country would be alive since business would be brisk instead of stagnant, and so the individual would gain more than the tax will cost, as he had already argued in his demand for unrestrained freedom of trade.

The enforcement of the Tax Act should be entrusted to the merchants, for they have a "professional honour" in the matter. Two of a trade cannot cheat each other as easily as either of them might cheat a stranger. It is both needless and cruel to subject the persons and fortunes of merchants, "the great negotiators of the nation's wealth," the handmaidens and servants of the great staple industries, "to the insult of custom house officers. . . ." After all, they are the most important class or, as he put it later: "The parson lives on the sins of the people, the doctor on their diseases, and the lawyer on their . . . quarrels . . . but the merchant lives on the wealth of the people." The richer his customers, the more they can purchase and the better they can pay. Consequently the merchant has every inducement to seek and promote the wealth of the state.

Webster began to think that if a proper national government were established, an integral feature should be a chamber of commerce composed of merchant delegates from the trading towns. The body would have charge of the revenue, and its advice would be asked and admitted on all measures concerning trade. The chamber of commerce would give dignity, uniformity, and safety to our trade, establish the credit of the bank, pacify discontent, unite the interests of the country, and thus cement the union and finally relieve Congress from the pain and trouble of deciding many intricate quirks of trade which it does not understand.[48]

As peace was declared in 1783, the debt situation was summarized in the Lexington sermon of the Reverend Zabdiel Adams, *The Evil designs of man Made Subservient by God to the public good:* "When the heavy debts contracted by the war, will be paid, the wisest politician cannot tell."

SAMUEL GALE AND THE EQUILIBRATING POWER OF PUBLIC DEBT

From the Tory side, just as the war was formally ending, came the ablest discourse on how a public debt could be manipulated to achieve prosperity. The author was Samuel Gale (1747–1826), an "Englishman, a gentleman of good education and possessed of high notions in favor of his native country." [49] He came to Philadelphia around 1770 and issued there a prospectus of a proposed book, *The Complete Surveyor*. Colden, then lieutenant governor and surveyor general of New York, among other things, took an interest in him. Gale obtained the clerkship of Cumberland County and a deputy surveyorship of which, he asserted, "the incidental advantages were of more value than the pay." At the same time he acted in the area as agent for the settlement of land, for which he received 5 per cent commission. [50]

But his life in Cumberland County was hectic from the beginning, for the county was in the disputed "New Hampshire Grants," where New England speculators fought with New York speculators for possession. The Allen brothers with their armed supporters even chased him away in 1773 as he tried to make surveys of land patents.

On the outbreak of the Revolutionary War, he was arrested by the American forces and taken to Connecticut. He complained to the New York revolutionary Provincial Congress that he was being treated in confinement like a "felon of the degree of shoeblack" and not according to his station. He demanded a parole to finish his "intended publication on surveying which is . . . allowed by all parties to be a matter of great . . . actual service to America."

Fortunately Gale had the friendship of the revolutionist James Duane, a great New York landowner and a power in New York politics. The Provincial Congress, with one eye on the Revolution and another on the disputed territory, had him released on parole, but only a short time elapsed before it ordered his rearrest for "dangerous correspondence with the enemy." Gale joined the British forces on their arrival at Sandy Hook in 1776, and from then on until the close of the war he served as a cashier and assistant paymaster with the British armies. [51]

While with the British forces in South Carolina and East Florida in 1782–1783, he began to write a series of four essays (*An Essay* [*Essays 1–4*] *On the Nature and Principles of Public Credit*, 1784–1787) on how the British government should handle the public debt.

Gale began the study partly to satisfy himself on a subject that "seemed to be more and more mysterious, the more it had been viewed," but also "to keep disagreeable reflections from my mind," for he was then "separated from his family and his little property near seven years by the troubles in America."

Gale's arguments were in large part drawn from the controversies over paper money in the colonies both before and during the Revolution. His essays bear traces of intimate acquaintance with the works not only of Locke and Hume, but also of such men as Pelatiah Webster. His work belonged to that aspect of current British literature which saw in what he called the "progressional power" of the sinking fund, the automatic redemption of the public debt. By a proper handling of the sinking fund, the debt would increase in an arithmetical progression, but would be repaid in a geometrical progression. Consequently repayment must eventually overtake the addition.

Gale's general thesis was that in wartime a public debt is not only the proper way of financing, but also produced savings as against the full use of taxes because of the effect on the interest rate. But the argument also held in large part in peacetime within limits, and the taxes were to be substantial.

The problem, let alone Gale's occupation, made him emphasize mathematics. The investigation, he said, "is of a mathematical nature and the theorems are likewise illustrated . . . by argumentative deductions and numerical examples," for an "investigation purely mathematical" is the one "unerring probe which God has vouchsafed to man."

The main design is not "historic inquiries" except incidentally, but to trace out the effects that flow, according to "the natural course and order of things from given causes"—that is, "to trace by fair deductions, those unerring paths of nature, by which causes and effects are . . . inseparably connected." But if history is unfolded the deductions "presented will be supported in every part."

Gale started with the familiar sort of principles, which he called "axiomatic" postulates or "definitions," especially as concerns value and interest. The "comparative value of commodities of all kinds, for the time being, whether considered with respect to exchange, purchase, or rent, must be governed by the demand . . . for such commodities respectively and the ease or difficulty with which such demand may be supplied."

Production is anything "honestly acquired," irrespective of the occupation. The expectation of profit is the mainspring of industry, and money is the flowing matter which sets the mechanism of industry in motion. Money includes any representative of money applied as an instrument with which to buy. Money need not be specie exclusively. A man receiving money in specie views it only as an instrument which he may pay away again for goods he wants to buy. It has its representative quality from the faith and credit which everyone entertains of being able at any time to obtain any other articles for it, and the continual demand for it is the only thing that supports this faith and credit. Therefore, so far as the same faith and credit shall extend and be actually supported with respect to obtaining any desired article in exchange for a circulating paper, so far the paper will produce the same effect as specie.

Paper should only be legal tender in the payment of charges to the Treasury; otherwise it would be fraudulent and result in all the well-known evils of paper money. In the same way, and for the same purpose, he answered the argument of those proponents of price-fixing who claimed that prices had risen higher than was justified by the amount of paper money in circulation. "The comparative value between money and other property is not as the quantity of the circulating money, but as the product of the multiplication of the quantity by the force or velocity of the circulation." So conceived, "the circulation of money and the circulation of other property" is "in effect one and the self same thing."

Gale's general argument was concise as it moved in summary fashion from men's desires to the beneficence of a public debt. To supply men's wants and necessities, commerce and industry must be encouraged. To promote and increase commerce and industry, the capital therein employed must be increased. This can only be done if the means of bringing capital into motion are rendered more easy. Therefore the rate of interest must be decreased, but the rate of interest cannot be reduced by law below the real rate naturally determined by the current demand. To produce a falling rate of interest, an additional proportion of money raised by taxes must be thrown regularly into the immediate channels of the lenders. Since the public debt is a wheel of the commercial machine by which to throw money into the particular channel of circulation, endeavors to increase the commerce and industry of a state must be directed solely to this particular wheel.

The want of money for the public service, said Gale, gives rise to the public debt. The punctual payment of interest and transferability of the stock makes possible the re-employment of money after leaving the hands of its lenders. This naturally brings into circulation funds that used to be dead and thereby raises banking to its proper high rank in the scale of commerce. The regular influx of money into the hands of the bankers and lenders naturally lowers the rate of interest and increases industry and commerce, for the industrious can now, on the same given real resources as before, increase the capital in their undertakings. When the lower rate does not make the periodical expense less to the industrious occupant, as with rent of land, it makes the capital value appertaining to the proprietor greater. Consequently even a small alteration in the interest rate has enormous effects in animating industry.

Thus England's public debt, by producing a decrease of more than 4 per cent in the rate of interest, increased England's prosperity and wealth during the first half of the eighteenth century to a degree never known before.

Paper money and public debt are not to be confused with real wealth, but their ill or good use determines whether industry is to be clogged or animated.

The rate of interest is not governed simply by the quantity of circulating money, but by the "circulation thereof whereby the quantity to be lent shall bear a lesser or greater proportion to the quantity circulating." The brisker the circulation of money (or of commodities) the greater will be the proportion to be lent, and "of course the lower . . . the rate of interest."

The critics, said Gale, argue that the use of paper and transferable stocks cause a loss of specie. They even argue that a nation should not allow all its specie to circulate, let alone issue paper, but instead should impound specie during the peace preceding a war. If a nation has a favorable balance of commerce, the influx of specie would otherwise raise the price of provisions, materials, and wages. Consequently other nations would be enabled to undersell us in foreign markets.

The other side agrees, he said, that an increase in the quantity of circulating money will produce a decrease in "the ratio of its representation" with respect to other commodities; but, as Hume had said, in the necessary interval of time between the increase in the current medium and the consequent alteration in the prices, the natural desire of acquiring wealth, "or that love of money . . . implanted in the human heart" will be so animated by the increase that the increase in industry will balance the inconveniences of the subsequent rise of prices. It will be a case of "the hindmost wheels of a chariot pursuing continually the foremost wheels without being able to overtake them." On the other hand, if the money were impounded, it would operate as a continual check to industry; and, though prices would be lessened, this advantage would always be behind.

Moreover, with taxes levied only for the interest and not the whole expense, the effect is the same as lending to industrious individuals their respective proportions, and the capital employed in productive industry is not reduced thereby. By providing for the temporary investment of idle funds, the public debt enables the industrious individuals to sell goods for smaller rates and yet obtain a greater aggregate profit than before. Therefore, to the extent that the profits shall exceed the interest, the nation's resources and riches are increased by the public debt.

Furthermore, great political benefits are reaped from a public debt, for the holders become a bulwark against "that unhappy spirit of opposition and revolt."

Gale agreed with the opponents of a public debt that variations in the quantity of circulating money will produce some effect on "the ratio of its representation" with respect to other commodities, but not an equal effect. The velocity with which the money may circulate and the manner in which internal commerce is carried on must be considered. If circulation is brisk, the same commerce can be managed with less money—that is, with a given quantity of money, the demand for money will be supplied with more ease than if circulation were slow. Furthermore, to the extent that barter exists, the less is the demand for money; and, as the comparative value of money or prices of commodities is governed by the demand and the ease or difficulty of supplying the demand, the changes in prices cannot be simply a change in quantity.

Finally, the use of both transferable public stocks and paper acts to moderate the tendency of either to excess. "The former is a commodity to be bought and sold, the latter is a commodity with which to buy and sell." The transferable public debt remedies the inconvenience that would otherwise attend a too great increase in money; the latter remedies the inconveniences attending such a demand for money as would otherwise be excessive in proportion to the amount previously circulating and "the force or velocity with which it might circulate for supplying such demand." Each contributes to the support of the other. Each operates to prevent the evils which too great a quantity of either might by itself produce, and each in turn contributes to the preservation "of a par or equality in the value of money considered in its representative capacity, as a commercial medium."

History contradicts the critics. If the critics be correct, the price rise in nations having public debts should be greater than the increase of circulating specie, but ever since the discovery of the mines of the Western world the amount of specie has increased faster than prices. Moreover, history reveals that an impounded treasure is unimportant, for government will sometimes spend in one year of war almost the whole supply of money in the country. Thus not the quantity of money, but the force of the circulation enables a nation to finance a long war.

It is difficult, however, to determine the precise point to which a public debt should be extended for the needs of commerce because not all people are disposed to industry and some prefer to live in idleness on the income of stock. But in any event all those investing in public stock increase the demand, and by the rise in price the rate of interest is reduced. This causes a larger capital to be obtained from a smaller revenue. Therefore a public debt must even make the lazy beneficial to the state, although not to the degree it would if they were industrious.

If the debt is too small, the demand for the stocks will be more than proportionate to their quantity, and the price will rise higher than par. Thus the effective rate of interest falls. Since the interest on the debt is accordingly reduced, the quantity of money circulating in that channel will be decreased, and consequently demand and value will fall and par or equilibrium be restored.

If the public debt is more than sufficient for circulating the excessive money, more money will be needed to preserve equilibrium. In order to throw in an additional quantity of money, taxes must be increased and therewith establish a sinking fund. The increased taxes are a burden on the public, to be sure, but the burden is counteracted by the beneficial effects of the decline in the interest rate.

As additional taxes cause a rise in commodity prices, so also the additional vigor of the circulation produced by the application of the taxes checks the increase. The actual burden of the additional taxes will be no more than the excess of necessary profits on commodities which goes hand in hand with the fall of the rate of interest occasioned by the acceleration of circulation.

Suppose that necessary profits, including a premium against bad debts, is three times the rate of interest. Suppose also that the interest is 6 per cent and a new tax at first produces a 5 per cent rise of prices. If the application of the revenue produced by the tax reduces the interest to $5\frac{1}{2}$ per cent, the burden will be only $3\frac{1}{2}$ per cent. If interest rates fall to $4\frac{1}{2}$ per cent, the burden is $\frac{1}{2}$ per cent; at 4 per cent, a benefit emerges. Thus the tax for the purpose of rendering money cheaper is like a tax to build roads, bridges, canals, but is more extensive. In fact, in countries with a high rate of interest the additional taxes might yield a net benefit.

As an incidental statistical proof of his theoretical doctrine, Gale drew up elaborate tables of calculations and compared these "computative values" deduced from general principles with the current prices of the public stock. Many of the lesser causes affecting the value of stocks, he said, are not capable of being reduced within any regular system of computative investigation, such as "temporary demand from foreign countries, temporary influxes and effluxes of wealth, temporary fortunes and misfortunes in war and commerce, together with the temporary speculations that are naturally attendant on every one of these considerations." Now, considering the many lesser factors that are not subject to computative investigation, "the agreement is so much greater than could have been imagined that no . . . doubt can be reasonably entertained with respect to the truth of the general principles."

At the same time the effects flowing from panic or envy cannot be provided against, but in view of the "close" correspondence between actual prices and what "mathematically and infallibly" follows from the principles, they will seldom be either great or lasting when "counteracted by those natural principles of private interest which are inseparable from a regular circulation of property."

The requisite taxes must be allocated with reference to the velocity of circulation if depreciation and inequitable burdens are to be avoided. That is, the taxes are not to be levied simply according to the visible "abilities" or the "estate" of the people—i.e., the apparent value of their estates—but according "to the product of the multiplication of the apparent value of such property by the force or velocity with which it shall actually circulate or be bought and sold."

The depreciation of the American paper money was caused by failure to follow this principle, he argued. During the first war year the paper money held up because of the natural demand for a circulating'medium, but once the channel overflowed and taxes could not be collected because of the disproportionate and unsystematic arrangement, the paper quickly depreciated.

Had the people of America enjoyed the same degree of personal freedom as under English rule, it would have been reasonable to expect that the terrific depreciation would have overturned the government in a short time, but the people of the Confederation enjoy such a small degree of personal freedom that the expected effect was not produced. However, "I aver it mathematically" that the government under the Articles of Confederation, cannot draw forth the resources from the states in due proportion, and this alone must produce a total insecurity. They can only save themselves by "a reunion with the mother country."

The great and sudden fluctuations of the price of public stock Gale attributed to the parasitic idle class of stock jobbers. These wager on their speculative opinions with respect to the prices of stock in the future. These idlers naturally propagate false rumors and engage in fictitious sales in order to vary temporarily the prices one way or the other, depending on their objective. Consequently prices are often affected by these "discommendable" practices of the market rather than by the principles of actual reason, and the public debt ceases to be a substantial'axle for beneficial circulation.

However, legislative action against the pernicious stock jobbery has proved futile. The remedy is to attempt to preserve a par on equality in its value as with any other commodity through preserving the proportion between the quantity of the commodity for disposal and the demand for it.

The basic elemental principles—both theoretical and practical— for making the public debt an instrument of national prosperity are, he summarized in his treatise and also in a private communication to his friend Duane, as follows:

"First, that in order to avoid the maladies and to attain the benefits with which a public debt may be attended, it is especially necessary that the value of the public securities . . . should be preserved from depreciation; and that, in order thereto, an extra proportion of revenue should be . . . applied to that channel of circulation (in addition to the interest) during the time of the advancement of new loans equal to the premiums.

"Secondly, that a public debt should consist of redeemable annuity stock, transferable, bearing a rate of interest higher than the ordinary rate, and subject to a limited tender for the periodical redemption of the capital equal to the annuity therefrom periodically flowing." [52]

Naturally, by themselves these principles do not indicate, he added, what scheme should be established by a given nation. The practical system should include both these principles "compounded," but the manner of compounding them must depend on the financial state of the country in question.

Equally significant in Gale's treatment was that, on the basis of the doctrine of the dependence of "industry" on the pecuniary "capital" wherewith to employ labor, he espoused "free trade." Regulations of commerce by positive laws—prohibitions, monopolies, bounties, drawbacks, exemptions, etc.—turn industry from its natural channels, with the inevitable loss of the expense of the ejectment, for commerce and industry can be increased only by increasing the capital so employed. The regulations may encourage particular branches, but they divert capital from others. This has a natural tendency not only to distress the latter branches, but also to cause excessive production in the favored branches to exceed the natural proportions and so create a general glut.

If any particular trade is more profitable than the others, a preference must be unnecessary; and if it is less profitable than others, it is not worth a preference. The incentive to the improvement of commerce and industry therefore ought to be general and free, not partial or confined. This ought to be directed to the reduction of the interest rate by the free and open competition of the market.

The British *Monthly Review* thought Gale personally was entitled to some consideration as a "distressed Loyalist," but found that the only really valuable thing in all the four essays was an appendix to Essay IV "containing tables of the comparative values of Redeemable Annuity Stocks." [53]

The English government gave Gale a pension for his services, and he spent his last days in obscurity in Canada. One hundred and fifty years later such views as Gale expressed were to become worthy of discussion in orthodox circles.

Meanwhile the British, after the surrender of Cornwallis late in 1781, became convinced that there might be considerable truth in the argument that independence and free trade for the colonies might be economically advantageous for England.

BOOK TWO

From Independence to Jackson

PART I

The Emergence of Traditions
of "Free Enterprise"

CHAPTER XII

The Problems of Adjustment

THE announcement of peace brought an outpouring of sermons and the like proclaiming the future glory of the United States. Even the old paper money was now viewed as having been an instrument of salvation. "Faithless depreciating currency" is one of the worst things with which a people has ever been scourged, said the Reverend Joseph Huntington in his Connecticut election sermon of 1784, *God ruling the nations for the most glorious end.* But "Providence has so ordered, that it has answered the end of a mighty tax on us, and has made even filthy rags a cord for the necks of our enemies."

Witherspoon, in a Thanksgiving sermon, declared that it financed the war, blinded the enemy, and disappointed their expectations. However, he feared that liberty would become license. The manners or habits of the people are more important in free states than in monarchical ones because in the latter "a principle of honour and subordination of ranks, with the vigor of despotic authority, supply the place of virtue, by restraining irregularities and producing public order." But in free states, especially in a republic, where the body of the people has the supreme power, confusion and anarchy result from a general corruption of manners. Consequently the people must choose as rulers men of religion and learning who have financial skill. "Is it reasonable to commit the management of public revenue, to one who has wasted his own patrimony?" [1]

Benjamin Rush felt that the Revolution was not over: We must have a revolution in our principles, opinions, and manners so as to accommodate them to the form of government we have adopted. By a universal common education, the people must be taught that, while all power is derived from the people, they possess the power legitimately only at election time. Afterward it is the property of their rulers.

Universally popular and influential throughout learned circles was a new English work, *The Principles of Moral and Political Philosophy*, by the Reverend William Paley. With a philosophy ostensibly based on "utility" and consequences, instead of natural right, he declared that the splendor of the English constitution lies in "the balance of interest" which accompanies and gives efficacy to "the balance of power" of King, Lords, and Commons. A monarch gives vigor, dispatch, and secrecy to the government. The House of Lords with its wisdom from experience and education is an effective check over a factious popular assembly, for it disdains to receive laws and opinions from its inferiors. Since the House of Commons seems to be all-powerful through control of money bills, Paley justified what was euphemistically called the "King's influence" in selecting and attaching members of the House of Commons through offices and pensions. If the King had used such patronage in America, no revolution would have occurred, said Paley, for he could then have checked that "restless arrogating spirit which, in popular assemblies, when left to itself, will never brook an authority that checks and interferes with its own." The system of rotten boroughs is also wise because it infallibly secures a great weight of property to the House of Commons by rendering many seats accessible to men of great fortune. Purely popular elections are uncertain. In times of tranquillity the "natural ascendancy of wealth will prevail, but when the minds of men are inflamed by political dissensions, this influence often yields to more impetuous motives."

In Paley's scheme property, particularly large property, was the beginning of moral and political philosophy and the principal subject of justice. Paley declared that the "institution of property" superficially presents the spectacle of ninety-nine out of a hundred "toiling and scraping together a heap of superfluities for one; getting nothing for themselves all the while, but a little of the coarsest of the provisions, which their own labour produces; and this one too, oftentimes, the feeblest and worst of the whole set, a child, a woman, a madman or a fool; looking quietly on, while they see the fruits of all their labour spent or spoiled; and if one of them takes a particle of it, the others join against him, and hang him for the theft." But, while the inequality of property, abstractly considered, is an evil, it is an incidental evil that flows from those rules concerning the acquisition and disposal of property by which "men are incited to industry, and by which the object of their industry is rendered secure and valuable."

Opposition to slavery increased, but enlightened General Otho Williams of Maryland felt that there was no contradiction between his purchasing slaves and hoping for the elimination of the institution: Buying is different from selling them, for by the former operation we make sure that our slaves are well treated. Some by freeing their slaves have often thereby given liberty to a number of ignorant, ill-disposed barbarians and thus injured society more than they have helped it. Therefore, though abolition is the goal, the process must be gradual.[2] The Reverend Ezra Stiles, president of Yale, expressed the opinion, in *The United States elevated to Glory and Honor*, that the slaves like the Indians if left to themselves will diminish.

The participants in the discussion of the great controversial economic issues were adept at citing the latest literature in Great Britain. All seemed to know Sir James Steuart. Adam Smith's *An Inquiry into the Nature and Causes of the Wealth of Nations* would often be cited along with Steuart, but always within the framework of that variant of mercantilism to which the author adhered. There were even exponents of a mathematical variety of mercantilism which went back more directly to the methods of Petty and his *Political Arithmetick*. Notable among this group was Colonel James Swan.

Swan had left Scotland as an obscure apprentice, but in Boston he managed to rise to wealth and distinction, aided by marriage with an heiress. He took an active part in the "Sons of Liberty" and was one of the famous "Indians" of the Boston Tea Party. He saw service in the Revolutionary Army, the Massachusetts legislature, and civil posts, and all the while managed to be involved in a host of enterprises including, along with traditional mercantile ventures, toll-bridge corporations, privateering, army contracts, insurance companies, speculation in continental securities, Maine lands, Boston real estate, and confiscated Loyalist estates.[3]

From the start Swan's literary productions showed the temper of the enterpriser. In 1772 he informed the public that the way to end slavery would be to let the blacks stay in Africa to produce commodities, especially gold that Americans want, in return for American products and manufactures. Therefore let exclusive trading companies of the regulated sort be organized to manage the traffic, but the government should supply funds for defense posts in Africa.[4]

In 1786 he published his comprehensive *National Arithmetick*, which covered the ills of the Confederacy in general and Massachusetts in particular, and the "proper" remedies. The book was ostensibly based on that "easy, but sure way of proving by mathematical . . . rules, for while words may mislead and volubility deceive, figures never can err." But the mathematical rule was of a kind that Gale and Morris had used in elucidating public finances and led to conclusions in keeping with Swan's proposals on slavery. In his *National Arithmetick* he said that Massachusetts' policy is to discourage the importation of indentured servants. Pennsylvania has increased in wealth and numbers in a much greater ratio than Massachusetts because she not only welcomes indentured servants from all countries, but facilitates the process by tax exemptions. As a consequence the Pennsylvania farmer can undersell others and pay his taxes better, and the state of Pennsylvania can maintain her public payments and credit.

Problems of finance raised more controversy. The clergy claimed that the failure to settle the public debts of the war threatened national prosperity. Refusing to pay the just public debts, said the Reverend Samuel Wales of Connecticut, in *The Dangers of our national Prosperity* (1785), is taking property without the consent of the owner. If the country looks poor, it is only because we have engaged in luxury and extravagance. In all wars, despite the increase of the public debt, England has obtained all the resources she needs because of her faithfulness in meeting obligations. The Reverend Huntington added that should we refuse to pay, God will be on the side of the foreigners as they resort to arms to collect their debts.

Bitter disagreement arose among the respectable, however, over what constituted full value and who were the rightful creditors. Pelatiah Webster said that justice and sound economics called for discrimination in the payment of all certificates between original creditors and present holders. The speculators paid only the commercial value of the certificates. Consequently they are entitled only to this sum plus interest. The difference between the nominal value and the sum received by the original holder remains an unpaid debt due original holders. It is a matter of public notoriety, exclaimed Webster, that almost all the widows, orphans, soldiers, and other distressed public creditors have been forced to sell their certificates to speculators.

Some say that the speculators are entitled to the gain because they supported the public faith by giving something for the certificates when others would give nothing. But in fact, said Webster, they decried the public faith until they persuaded the poor soldiers to sell their certificates at a fraction of their nominal value rather than trust the public any longer.

Europe's fatal experience should be a warning. Ever since the invention of the blessed scheme of funding, every nation has had a race of stock jobbers and speculators in the public securities who never fail to appear in plenty whenever a state is distressed and the public faith falters slightly. "Like flies about a sore, or crows around a carcass," these vermin have no design to "heal the sore, or restore life, but to feed themselves." [5]

Non-discrimination would take an immense property from those who have earned it and who would probably make the best use of it. It would impoverish the great body of the people to aggrandize a few and thereby not only weaken the state but destroy that equality essential for maintaining our republican government.

The heavy tax burden required to pay the speculators the full nominal value retards the increase of our trade and population and lessens the value of lands, and above all things damages the country area for the benefit of the city. The mass of farmers who must pay the taxes will receive no benefit from the circulation of the payments; for the holders, the speculators, live in the city. Finally, it draws people from the honest and painful method of earning fortunes by industry and "encourages them to obtain wealth by sleight of hand."

Some pushed Webster's logic further and returned to Gouverneur Morris's statement during the war, that debts would be settled at their current value in the postwar period. In Massachusetts proponents of this procedure declared: This has been "the usage in all governments" which have resorted to the temporary expedient of a paper money, and the usage of this state, so well evidenced in 1650. Present holders are entitled to what Webster allows them, but the original creditors should not get the difference, for in selling they have alienated their rights.

In the Massachusetts General Court the proponents of "full value" to present holders declared that the charge of speculation was irrelevant. Speculations in the funds of every country are encouraged by government. "They are the barometer . . . of modern power; and explain the strength of a community beyond the calculations of arithmetic." [6]

Colonel Swan, who invested heavily in the certificates and was interested in foreign trade and investment connections, suggested in his *National Arithmetick* that whenever the treasury has surplus cash, it should purchase the public notes in the market at their current value. It could best be done by the state's accepting taxes in kind and arranging for their disposal by consignment to opulent houses abroad. By allowing the latter 5 per cent interest, it could anticipate half or two-thirds of the value and consequently import specie to that amount a year before the taxes are collected. With a small amount of specie a good part of the whole state debt, including the state's share of the continental debt, could be purchased. This at the same time would reduce the interest rate to 3 or 4 per cent.

As always, the central consideration was commerce and its encouragement. Harvard masters answered in the affirmative: "Is commerce in a republic worthy of the attention of the aristocracy?" They replied in the negative to: "Although commerce produces luxury, should it be restricted in a rising republic?" And Rush thought the fact that Philadelphia's commerce was the avenue for the wealth of the state would alone justify the systematic teaching of commerce along with the principles of money in Pennsylvania's colleges.[7]

The ideal system, said Madison, is "perfect freedom" of trade, but before this system can be possible for the United States we must be out of debt, and before the system is really attainable all nations must concur. So long as other nations impose disabilities on American ships and seamen, we must either retaliate in kind, on the principle of reciprocity, or renounce both our just profits and hopes of achieving real independence.[8] The Revolution has robbed us of our trade with the British West Indies—the only trade yielding a favorable balance —without opening any other channel for it.

There were appeals to England to let America have freedom of trade with her colonies. This type of reasoning was best elaborated by aristocratic and opulent William Bingham (1751–1804), a leader in Philadelphia social and financial life and son-in-law of Thomas Willing, president of the Bank of North America and partner of Robert Morris. He had served from 1770 to 1776 as commercial agent for the British government in the French West Indies and then acted for the next four years in a similar capacity for the Continental Congress. In the meantime he acquired a considerable fortune from trade and privateering and became one of the great enterprisers of the day, with interests in lands, public securities, bank stock, as well as general mercantile enterprise. As was customary, from time to time he held high political office, serving in the Continental Congress, the Pennsylvania Assembly, and later in the United States Senate.

His address to the English authorities in favor of "free, unrestrained commerce" between the two countries, especially the West Indies, was reminiscent of the petitions of colony agents before the war. The state legislatures will take retaliatory measures, he wrote, especially when "it is considered that they are selected from those who are the best versed in the interest of the states, as relative to those of other commercial powers, and who will embrace every advantage that nature has given, or art can procure, to the improvement" of their competitive positions.

If England continues her "selfish contracted system, founded on extreme cupidity," and fails to appreciate the reciprocal advantages that each country will derive from a "free, open, unrestrained connection," the states will enter manufactures. This will ruin England. The luxury and extravagance of her people have already advanced to the "ultimate point of abuse" and cannot be sufficiently increased to augment the home consumption in proportion to the threatened loss of foreign trade. The starving British manufacturers will be forced to come to America.[9]

The concept of "free trade" again acquired somewhat different meanings in the conflict over the question of forcing Spain to allow free navigation of the Mississippi. Southern leaders, especially Virginians, prodded by the inhabitants of its then district of Kentucky, complained that the eastern merchants, in the interest of a "free liberal system of trade" with Spain, were willing to let Spain close the Mississippi to free navigation. Eastern merchants and political figures, headed by Gouverneur Morris and Rufus King of Massachusetts and later of New York, claimed that the resulting development of the West would be at the expense of the East. The settlers beyond the Appalachians could never be attached to the Union. Nature has by the mountains severed the two countries, and interest and convenience will keep them so. Every immigrant would be lost to the Confederacy. The states situated on the Atlantic "are not sufficiently populous and losing our men, is losing our greatest source of wealth." Colonel James Monroe of Virginia wrote that these Easterners desire to "keep the weight of population eastward . . . to appreciate the vacant lands of Massachusetts and New York," [10] whereas all good Southerners know that the population of the West must inure to the commercial benefit of southern centers.

Madison tried to convince Spain in particular and Europe in general that Spain should allow a free trade on the Mississippi. Spain would, of course, be the greatest gainer especially in that New Orleans would become a great flourishing city. Europe in general would gain because more European manufactures would be consumed and at higher prices, and the production of American export staples would be extended and their prices reduced in favor of the mass of European consumers. But if the navigation is prevented, people will not settle in the West; and, lacking the means of purchasing foreign manufactures, they must turn to home manufactures, to the loss of European manufactures.[11]

Washington, however, felt that until his proposed canal project tied the western territory to the Atlantic states, Spain's obstruction to Mississippi navigation might better remain since free navigation of the Mississippi would break the bond between the East and West in spite of blood. Only "interest binds one country or one state to another," and with the inhabitants most likely to be foreigners to a great degree, "a commercial connection is the only tie we can have upon them." Some "management may be required to quiet the restless and impetuous spirits of Kentucky." [12]

On the other hand, Madison pleaded that Virginia should restrict her foreign trade to two ports and so achieve that commercial empire in Maryland and Virginia promised by the advocates of the canal policy before the Revolutionary War. Otherwise we shall continue on the old plan of "British monopoly and diffusive credit." The critics, he said, are enamored of the old scheme of having the ships come up to the docks on their plantations. Consequently they are busily decoying the people into believing that "trade ought in all cases to . . . regulate itself." To confine trade to particular ports, the critics say, is to renounce the boon with which nature has favored our country. It must render trade more costly, for what is now handled by one set of hands will require three different sets, with each taking a profit —importers and exporters, carriers between the mouth and head of rivers, and finally retailers.

But goods are much dearer in Virginia than in states where trade is drawn to a general market. Goods brought directly from Europe

to western Virginia are retailed at a higher price than if imported indirectly via Philadelphia and Baltimore, and Virginia products sell
higher in Philadelphia, where, being as far from their ultimate market,
they cannot be worth intrinsically more. Ships of all nations visit other
ports; only British ships come to Virginia ports, though all the ships
come to buy the staples of Virginia. But, while the planters are dissatisfied, "they enter little into the science of commerce and rarely
of themselves combine in defense of their interests." [13]

The Virginia legislature agreed with Madison that commerce
should be restricted to a few points, but there was disagreement as
to which should be the ports. Madison wanted Norfolk and Alexandria, the village at the head of the Potomac in which Washington
had sufficient faith to invest heavily in its real estate. Other members
wanted additional ports, and the measure finally fell through.

Tied up again with the discussions over foreign commerce were
those on inland commerce. The general point of view was that inland
commerce, like anything else, was important from the standpoint
of creating advantageous foreign commerce. But here as elsewhere
were to be found business conflicts.

The basic ideal was reflected in the exhortation of the governor of
North Carolina shortly after the peace: If our rivers be made more
navigable and roads opened, industrious planters can have their goods
carried more conveniently. Thereby "more merchants of opulence
would be induced to settle in the state, and open new resources of
industry among our inhabitants." With the latter's labor "being fully
compensated," their wealth would increase and in proportion also the
state's revenue. [14]

The episode that threw into boldest relief the nature of respectable
thinking on this matter was the revival of Washington's Potomac
project for an exclusive incorporated company with state aid and
privileges, a project that eventually was to come to little despite
the enthusiasm of its sponsors and the privileges and aids which were
granted to it.

Jefferson had in 1784 urged Washington to revive the project.
Washington was glad to find that such a financially disinterested man
of "discernment and liberality" views the public benefits of the project "as I do, who have lands . . . the value of which would be enhanced" by the project. He agreed with Jefferson that "from trade
our citizens will not be restrained, and therefore it behooves us to
place it in the most convenient channels, under proper regulations,

freed as much as possible from those vices which luxury, the consequence of wealth and power, naturally introduces."

Shortly after visiting his western lands, Washington informed the governor of Virginia of the immediate necessity of pushing the project. Pennsylvania, he said, is planning to capture the prize by developing the Susquehanna, and despite the heavy cost such "a people . . . possessed of the spirit of commerce, who see, and will pursue their advantages, may achieve almost anything." That New York will also attempt to capture the trade by means of the Hudson "no person who knows the temper, genius, and policy of those people as well as I do, can harbour the smallest doubt."

But in Virginia, he said, there is jealousy lest one part of the state obtain an advantage over the others, as "if the benefits of trade were not diffusive and beneficial to all." It is foolishly argued that the people are already heavily taxed, that a sufficient spirit of commerce does not pervade the citizens of this commonwealth, "and that we are in fact doing for others, what they ought to do for themselves."

There might be some question whether foreign trade is advantageous to a country; but this state, as part of a Confederacy of states, all of whom are moved by the spirit of commerce, must adopt the spirit "or submit to the evils arising therefrom without receiving its benefits." Unless the spirit of commerce is totally eradicated in all the states and every man forced to become a cultivator of the land, or a manufacturer of such articles as are prompted by necessity, such stimulus should be employed as will force the spirit "by showing to our countrymen the superior advantages we possess beyond others, and the importance of being upon a footing with our neighbours." [15]

With Washington and Madison as prime movers, the Virginia Assembly passed the required measure for a company to develop the Potomac. Maryland, where Charles Carroll gave his support to the movement, passed the necessary identical act. Each state agreed to purchase 10 per cent of the stock of the company. Virginia purchased another 10 per cent for a gift to Washington as one of the tokens of the state's gratitude for his war service. Washington left it as an endowment for the development of higher education.

In the *Maryland Gazette* of April 1785, "Planter" questioned the wisdom of the state's contribution. He was answered that the state bought shares in order to have legislative control over it and share in the tolls. Without the project "the western trade will go down the Mississippi."

Washington was active in soliciting subscriptions from friends and acquaintances everywhere, including England. He even attempted to entice Robert Morris, the greatest promoter of the day and interested in the "rival" Pennsylvania project, to Philadelphia. He attempted to convince Morris not only of the great financial prospects of the company, but also of the additional profits Morris could make by being the first great trader to set up a branch of his mercantile house at Alexandria.

Alexandria, Washington informed Morris, would by means of the cheap water transportation provided by the canal obtain the great traffic of the surrounding area on which Baltimore on the land route now lives. But a large capital—that is, capital houses, large wholesale stores, as well as a commercial spirit—is required in the town. The local traders cannot compete with the great towns because they are small traders forced to import or purchase their goods in the country areas on credit; consequently retail dealers in the interior go to Baltimore and Philadelphia for the purchase of their imports and the sale of the staples.

Washington could even feel that the Potomac and related James River project would be a blessing to oppressed humanity everywhere. He informed Lafayette: "I wish to see the sons and daughters of the world in peace and busily employed in the more agreeable amusement of fulfilling the first and great commandment—*Increase and multiply*; as an encouragement to which we have opened the fertile plains of the Ohio to the poor, the needy and the oppressed of the earth. . . . The ways are preparing, and the roads will be made easy, through the channels of the Potomac and James River." [16]

Rented slaves as well as "purchased servants," Johnson informed Washington, are to be preferred if they can be gotten, because "their labour will be more valuable than that of common white hirelings." [17]

Intimately related to the expansion of commerce was the emphasis on encouraging domestic manufactures. Thus Hugh Williamson, then in Congress, stressed domestic manufactures in good part as a strategic argument to be used to obtain the lifting of British restrictions on trade with Britain and her possessions, especially the sugar islands; to promote inland navigation companies; to obtain power for Congress to regulate commerce, especially the levying of import duties to pay the debts; and, finally, as an answer to the proponents of paper money.

Writing under the pen name "Sylvius," he declared that if we turn to manufactures our staples will rise to their proper value and specie will come in. Let the manufacturer demand what he pleases for the produce of his labor; the farmer can easily settle the account by selling his provisions accordingly.

The citizens of the East should set the first example of manufactures. Producing little fit for exportation, they cannot pay for their imports. But their climate as against the heat of the South allows year-round work for whites. They are free of domestic slavery, which is unfriendly to manufactures, but they live close to one another in contiguous small towns, which are the proper nurseries of manufactures. Moreover, they are naturally industrious and tractable. As the manufacturing towns increase, provisions may become scarce in the East, though the South's fertile soil will always supply sufficient foodstuffs as well as raw materials.

But the mechanics against their own interest have the habit of raising their prices to correspond to the tariff. However, the 5 per cent duty to pay the war debt, plus the saving of freight and the like, would be a sufficient bounty.

Under our present policies we are like the "idle and thoughtless debauchee" who neglects the improvement of his farm and spends his time and estate in a tavern supporting the family of another while his own perishes. Thus we become slaves instead of becoming really independent by enticing industrious tradesmen here, discharging our public and private debts, encouraging the use of American vessels and merchants, and forcing an opening into the West Indies.

Perhaps the most significant passage in the essays, though not particularly relevant to his objectives, was the reference to luxury as necessary to "mature" countries. In old nations where manufactures flourish and where wealth is unequally distributed, some of the inhabitants being exceedingly rich and the great body desperately poor, government was wise in encouraging luxury. By it "the wealth of the rich circulates through the hands of the manufacturing poor." But the policy would be madness for an infant nation like the United States, for the "luxuries" come from abroad, and so encouraging their consumption "enriches another nation and impoverishes ourselves." [18]

Among the most comprehensive writers on "balanced economy" was William Barton, then secretary of the Pennsylvania Society for the Encouragement of Manufactures and the Useful Arts. To Barton "the grand desideratum in commerce of a nation is to maintain a favourable balance in foreign trade" in order to achieve the commercial prosperity and consequently the real independence of the American states.

The growth of manufacturing towns along with internal improvements, he explained in *The True Interest of the United States, and Particularly of Pennsylvania, Considered* (1786), is for the benefit of agriculture because a certain profitable home market is created instead of the extremely fluctuating one dependent on the "precarious operations of the foreign nations." Prohibitions, bounties, and duties are required for manufactures until our rapid increase of population reduces wages to a level to meet English manufactures.

The carrying trade also should have protection, said Barton. The country abounds with naval stores, and shipbuilding is or may be one of its most beneficial employments. This species of manufacture demands the imposition of navigation acts. We should impose extraordinary duties on dutiable commodities imported from foreign countries in vessels built or owned abroad, especially on articles of mere luxury. But in some instances goods ought to be free of all duties, irrespective of the ship. These cases are hard to designate, for they depend on circumstances. In other cases exemptions might properly be restricted to American vessels, as in the East India trade. True, imports from the East Indies are generally considered luxuries. But habit has made many of them necessaries. Therefore, instead of constantly importing them via Europe, we should encourage Americans to carry on a direct trade. The profits now enjoyed by strangers would center in our citizens; while the new channels of commerce would employ additional American shipping and furnish an outlet for an article, ginseng, of domestic growth much esteemed there.

The internal communications between the various parts of the country should be facilitated by improving roads, opening canals, and removing all obstructions to river navigation.

A great problem is to obtain uniform commercial regulations for all the states. At present the states damage one another with their regulations. A power must be lodged somewhere for adjusting the commercial as well as the political interests of the Union to one general scale. According to the principles underlying "our Federal Constitution," this ought to be "vested in the Supreme Head of the Union," the Continental Congress, "in order to establish the commerce of the United States on the solid basis of the national system."

Foremost exponent of a "balanced" national economy was Tench Coxe, also a member of the Pennsylvania Society. He had a distinguished ancestry which went back to the proprietary family of New Jersey. He attended the College of Philadelphia until the Revolutionary War disturbances sent him into his father's mercantile house in Philadelphia. Coxe participated in all the leading types of enterprise, including land speculation, trade, and banks; but he never quite managed to reap what he considered great financial success, or at least an income to which his ancestry, position, and services entitled him.

Much of his time he devoted to seeking government positions. His political career was ambiguous and shifting, shot through with that streak of opportunism common in that generation of able young men of little means. A suspicion that he had been a Loyalist during the British occupation of Philadelphia always clung to him. His changes in party allegiance seemed to be in the nature of moving with the wind. He came closest to being the Defoe of America.

He was ever interested in new projects, and men in high office on opposite sides were willing to use him as an "expert" at the same time. He had not only extensive business experience, a wide knowledge, and a good pen, but an interest in details that gave his accounts more substance than was characteristic of those of his contemporaries.

Agriculture, he informed the friends of manufactures in an address, is the paramount interest of the community. But manufactures would not only provide a certain market and incentive for the increasing produce of our land and fisheries, but also necessary supplies in wartime.

Manufactures further will accelerate the improvements in our internal navigation, and this will help to keep the British and Spanish out of the lucrative trade with the West and at the same time maintain the contact between the West and the older regions.

It would keep from crime those poor that cannot find other honest means of subsistence and relieve such states as Massachusetts from the unemployment resulting from the British restrictions on navigation. But manufactures should not be attempted in states where the people are fewer, tillage more profitable, and provisions dearer than in others. Thus the North should foster manufactures, but the South should diversify its agricultural production, produce cotton and other raw materials for the North in exchange for manufactures.

Theoretically, agriculture can absorb all labor; but many of our citizens are too poor to reach and settle in the waste lands. To the more inclusive argument that the high price and scarcity of labor precluded manufactures in the United States, Coxe answered that these difficulties can be easily overcome by factories utilizing "water mills, wind mills, fires, horses, and machines ingeniously contrived." In England a few hundreds of women and children, kept from the mischief of idleness, perform the work of thousands of carders, spinners, and winders there. "In short, combinations of machines with fire and water have already accomplished much more than was expected from them by the most visionary enthusiast." In fact, such machines, while of immense advantage to the United States, are "dangerous to the manufacturing nations of Europe." Should they continue to use and improve them, their people may be driven to us from want of employment; and if, on the other hand, they should return to manual labor, we may underwork them by these invaluable engines."

As for the objection to manufactures on grounds of health, not only is employment in domestic manufactures less dangerous than in a number of important agricultural pursuits, but the question is irrelevant to the modern large manufactures using machinery, because horses, and the potent elements of fire and water aided by the faculties of the human mind, would be our daily laborers.

As for outright tariffs, Coxe advocated the familiar doctrine that the Congress impost of 5 per cent, if passed, along with the other differential advantages possessed by American manufactures, would operate as a bounty of 25 per cent while it would provide revenue for paying the public debts and expenses. Further aid might be given by allowing the free importation of raw materials, which he held would be safe and expedient for the agricultural interests since they are producing increasingly less for a foreign market.

A navigation act like the English one, which excludes from commerce the ships and merchants of countries that do not carry their native products, should be enacted; for this would end English tyranny over our carrying trade and commerce with the West Indies. Best of all, it would end the present deplorable situation of the remains of the excessive importations of preceding years being constantly offered for sale at prices lower than their cost in Europe or at home. But these measures require that Congress have the power to regulate commerce and to veto the commercial measures of the states.[19]

The complexities of the promotion of manufactures were revealed in the activities of the Pennsylvania Society. To achieve "the better employment of the industrious poor," especially women, and to render the society as useful as possible by means of factories, it organized in 1787 a subscription to a short-lived manufacturing fund with transferable shares and profits to the subscribers. A cotton factory was set up as an experiment. A year later Coxe and George Clymer, a merchant, as a committee of two, reported to the Society on the difficulties of the factory. They declared that spinning and weaving would be less expensive when private operators enter the business in the future. Since the factory was established partly to employ the poor, the directing committee has been less particular about wages than a private person would be. More economy of day labor and less waste of raw materials would occur in a private factory than in the public one, where each member of the committee has his individual, private business to watch. The directors, continued the report, have appointed a person at "constant wages" to sell the goods. Since the private manufacturer would do this himself, these wages would be added to his profit; or, if the factory were ten times larger, the selling operations might still be done by the one person. Machinery, accomplishing the great object of saving manual labor, will raise the manufacturer's profit exceedingly.

The factory's use of cotton yarn from India is another instance where foreign commerce is benefited by the development of domestic manufactures. Although the project has been profitable, new subscriptions are required to continue the work until a "knowledge and due sense of its value shall induce some person, either citizens or foreigners to undertake it." [20]

The following year the state was induced to subscribe to the project in order to prosecute the plan "upon that extensive and liberal scale" which is the state's interest to promote. The project soon failed.[21]

In more prosaic fashion, the greatest American of the day, as the period closed, had the same comprehensive vision as Barton and Coxe; but the scheme was to center around the Potomac, and Alexandria was to be the seat of empire.

The greatest object of public interest is encouragement of manufactures and inland navigation, Washington informed fellow enthusiasts in the Potomac Company. Of course a great manufacturing town would grow close to Alexandria because of its many fine mill seats. Already representatives of French cotton manufacturers are convinced, he wrote, that cotton manufactures may be prosecuted here with greater advantage than in Europe. They have been training the planters of Georgia for a long time to raise the new product. Cotton may prove the most profitable crop for Georgia and South Carolina. "The increase of that new material and the introduction of the late improved machines to abridge labour, must be of almost infinite consequence to America." [22]

For almost every thinker the objective was, in the last analysis, the reduction of the unfavorable balance and the obtaining of a favorable balance of debt. This raised the eternal question of the money supply.

The cry became vigorous for state issues of paper money for loan and expenditures, for bills of full legal tender, and for bills as a tender only in the payment of public dues. Much the same arguments that were heard before the Revolutionary War were advanced. Proponents cited Sir James Steuart as the great authority, and critics had by now learned to use the arguments of the old defenders. As before the war, time found men shifting sides.

Madison, repeating Hutchinson almost verbatim, successfully fought paper issues by Virginia. He declared that paper issues disgrace republicanism and, by creating dissension between the states, is anti-federal. The right of coining money, said Madison, has been given by the Articles of Confederation to Congress to prevent fraud by the states toward each other and toward foreigners, and issuing paper is coining money. As scarcity of specie is the child of extravagance, so it will become the parent of economy and restore to us our due share of the universal medium, provided no bills be issued. So certain was he of this result that he suggested that Jefferson, then minister to France, might profitably borrow funds in Paris to join him in speculation in New York lands because the rate of exchange would fall later.[23]

Williamson, in his "Letters of Sylvius," informed the country in general and North Carolina in particular that England had encouraged colonial paper issues to discourage manufactures and consequently keep us dependent and poverty-stricken. Thus we have become accustomed to paper issues. The only way to relieve the scarcity of money is domestic manufactures and the expansion of advantageous commerce in other ways as well.

From South Carolina, whose government was distinctly "for the rich, well born," came issues of paper money, moratoria laws, and the like; but these measures were attacked as though they were the product of an ignorant rabble. A grand jury complained against the many interferences of the legislature in private contracts between debtors and creditors. These destroy credit, especially foreign credit, the very thing that has converted this howling wilderness into a fertile, well-peopled country. "Better that a few individuals should suffer . . . than that a whole community should be distracted, distressed, and stigmatized for want of faith, and a total disregard to national honour." [24]

The unsuccessful struggle in Maryland in 1785–1787 to issue non-legal-tender loan bills on real estate, led by Chase for the paper side and the prewar proponents Carroll and Johnson for the opposition, revealed that as elsewhere the struggle was in good part a "factional dispute within the ruling oligarchy" of planters, lawyers, and merchants who, by the prestige of their "superior wealth and economic power" and the closely restricted franchise and aristocratic political structure, controlled the state.[25]

Handbills were circulated calling on the people to overthrow the "aristocratic junto" by electing paper-money men to the legislature.

Said the House of Delegates: The current money ought always to be in proportion to trade, industry, consumption, alienation, and taxes. But the state's circulating specie is insufficient even for commerce alone. Thus the country's staples, tobacco and wheat, cannot command a reasonable price; land, houses, and Negroes do not sell for more than one-half their true rates; only at an exorbitant premium can specie be borrowed to carry on trade or manufactures, to build roads, or to cultivate and improve our lands.

Back of the difficulties is the unfavorable balance of trade or debt. Though the property of the citizens be many times the debt, still, with the circulating specie less than the debt, a great balance is due. Thus, to prevent general bankruptcy, citizens' property equal to the deficiency of the medium must be melted down and made to circulate in the form of paper money. The need for tax payments alone is sufficient to take up the quantity so as to maintain their value.

Since the state can pay its share of the general debt in public debt certificates, and since these will continue to sell for some time at one-sixth or one-eighth of their nominal price, it would be to the state's interest to use part of the issue to buy up the certificates at their depreciated rate. The Senate proposal that the bills be turned over exclusively to the holders of certificates would only help the speculators in certificates.[26]

Ablest of the pamphleteers on the critics' side was A. C. Hanson, who wrote under the pseudonym of "Aristides." He had the temper of Douglass and, like Douglass, devoted considerable space to the evils of an unconstrained popular will. Fortunately, he argued, Maryland has a Senate which protects the people, in spite of themselves, by checkmating their representatives in the House who demand paper. As for English works, especially Steuart, cited by proponents of the House measures, he declared that he would be ashamed to quote foreign writers on bills of credit because "they can reason only on speculation."

There was justification for issues before the war when the state was a vassal colony and burdened with a balance of debt in favor of England. Now we are independent, and specie will find its level among us as it has in other independent nations, without impolitic, forcing measures during peace.

We must be ignorant, obstinate, or biased by superstitions against our real interest if we cannot distinguish between a time when opinion favored bills and a time when it distrusted them; between a time of vassalage and severe restrictions on our trade and a period when we have taken our just place in the world and our commerce is courted by the world; between the period of infancy of a country and its ripe age.

The clamors for the loan paper as a tax medium are really being raised for the benefit of the rich, not the poor. The rich declaim against heavy impositions, complain of the want of a medium and the necessity of postponing collections. They are ordinarily unwilling to pay the necessary taxes, and they withhold payments.

The strongest argument for the emission is that the state can thereby redeem its share of the Confederation's debt cheaply. But, since this involves using the bills to purchase export staples, the state as a trader would be overwhelmed by a host of problems as regards prices and trade. Furthermore, since the other states would be competitors in the process, the price of the certificates would rise. The House cannot object to the Senate plan of turning over the loan issue to the certificate holders, for under the House plan the adventurers would also be the great gainers. Do not the adventurers hold the bulk of the debt?

Hanson had his own remedy. Let the state obtain a ten-year specie loan from England at 8 per cent and buy up the certificates at four or five to one. Bills drawn against the loan could be sold in Philadelphia for specie, and state commissioners or agents of the loan could make their annual payments by tobacco. Government can go further in good work. It can encourage home manufactures, prohibit certain imports, or impose a duty, and thereby increase the revenue, decrease imports, and discourage luxuries.

With the balance of trade in our favor, we can pay off the British debt. This will be helped by making a fair composition, such as payment on installments, with British creditors. This procedure would be thought a violation of contract if creditors did not universally consent to the measure.

But if the state issues loan bills, we shall continue our luxuries; our imports will be increased or, worse still, "we shall get merchandise from a neighbouring state." Thus we shall lose our hard cash, and at the date of redemption money will be scarce, and the people's debts increased.[27]

In Pennsylvania the issue was complicated by the existence of the Bank of North America with its exclusive privileges. This bank had been so successful, with dividends running from 12 to 16 per cent, that banks were established in Boston and New York in 1784. The president of the bank did not mind banks elsewhere. In fact, President Willing informed the promoters of the Massachusetts Bank, who sought advice on how to run a bank, that "the world is apt to suffer a greater mystery in this sort of business, than there really is. Perhaps it is right that they should do so, and wonder on—but you may proceed without fear."[28]

But when others in Pennsylvania desired to share in the profits of the "mystery" and petitioned the Pennsylvania Assembly for a charter for an additional bank in Philadelphia, there was an outcry. Many sensible members, complained Gouverneur Morris, believed it would be good to have two banks, "two shops, to go to," especially since this foolish doctrine "was laid down by some in high stations, for whose sentiments they had acquired a habitual respect."

The directors of the bank, added Pelatiah Webster, another stockholder, realized that two banks would be fatal "because they might act in opposition to each other and of course destroy each other." So, with much trouble, they prevented formation of the new bank by increasing the capital and allowing some of the promoters of the proposed new bank to purchase shares, not at $500, their market rate, but at $400, their par value.

But in 1785 the assembly issued bills for loans and for expenditures to relieve the "scarcity of money" and make the payments of interest on the state debts. The bills were a tender only in the payment of dues and debts to government. Their proponents were soon delineating the great advantages of the measure. With the bills the state could pay the long-suffering public creditors; the poor settlers who had bought Pennsylvania public lands on installments could pay the purchase price to the state; the value of the public debt certificates would be raised; a revenue would be yielded to the state, a spring given to circulation, and the amount of specie in the state increased.

A protest petition of "merchants and traders," of which only two signers were not stockholders or directors of the Bank of North America, declared that the old Pennsylvania loan office had been fine, but people then had faith in the state's promises. The people had not forgotten the repudiation of the currency both by Congress and the states in their devaluation measures. Better let the state make a loan from the bank, declared Robert Morris, and let the state revenue be mortgaged to the bank to assure that the revenues are paid to Pennsylvania creditors of the United States.

After the issue, petitions were presented to the assembly requesting the repeal of the bank's charter on the ground that the bank was ruining the "fair trader" and mechanic, preventing agricultural improvements and the equal circulation of money, and charging excessive interest.

In the heated controversy the opposition to the bank blamed the bank for the current depression and threw in all the arguments that had been used against the private land banks. Importers have obtained a fictitious credit by a temporary punctuality at the bank while they have drawn on their honest neighbors to trust them with their property or to pledge their credit as security. By the temporary use of money and credit they have "overtraded"—that is, increased importations—with the result that specie is exported and the business community and the state distressed, said the self-styled "farmer" spokesmen, William Findley and John Smilie. Time and again the stopping of discounts by the bank has operated on "the trading part" with a degree of violence scarcely less than that of a stagnation of blood in the human body. It has forced the wretched merchant to resort to grasping usurers to meet loans and has thrown the husbandmen and mechanics into bankruptcy. The bank discriminates in favor of speculators as against fair traders, mechanics, and husbandmen. The directors may give preference in trade by advancing money to themselves and their favorites.

Moreover, the bank's large profit attracts foreign investments and leads to a further drain of specie. Worse, the foreign influence would reduce the American people to dependence on European courts and their intrigues. Even if stockholding were restricted to Americans, the bank's accumulation of wealth, its capital practically unlimited, and its perpetual duration would destroy freedom. Instead of the bank's being dependent on government, it would control the government, and its directors would dictate legislation. Already the bank has shown its power in its attempt to destroy the state paper money by refusing to accept it; and the people have been forced to acquiesce.

Its monopolistic character flows from its charter with its exclusive privileges, including limited liability. Its limited liability features enable moneyed men to increase their gains without having either their person or estate upon the same level of responsibility as other citizens. The bank can break, but its directors gain. The voting for directors by shares or property rather than persons allows a few men or their representatives to control the bank during their lives. By virtue of its corporate character, the many stockholders are dominated by one point of view—that of acquiring wealth; and its directors, in carrying out the trust, must obey its sole guiding principle of avarice and relentlessly pursue its soulless pecuniary object without deviation. The special monopolistic temper of the institution pervades all its operations; and this, like a snowball perpetually rolled, must continually increase its dimension and influence until it engrosses all the power and wealth of the state. None of its enormous profits go to the government which bestowed the valuable privileges it enjoys, nor will it allow access to its records by the government's investigating committee.

The government can repeal the charter on the ground that it endangers the welfare of the state. In annulling the bank charter, no property would be taken, for the charter is not a property. The actual property is as safe as it ever was. There is nothing to prevent the stockholders from establishing a private bank without the exclusive privileges granted by the charter.

In the final summation, the general sentiment of the opposition was, however, that all would be well if the charter were amended to limit capital and eliminate the bank's exclusive monopoly and perpetual term. Thereby it was expected that the bank could render aid in bringing about the immigration which would reduce the price of labor. As William Findley put it in his polemic against the "moneyed aristocracy" of the city, "to cultivate these now jarring interests [of farmer, mechanic, and merchant] and render them mutual, we must first propagate or import a greater number of people that we may have labour cheaper."

To the defense of the bank and all its rights came a group of able Pennsylvanians, most of whom were stockholders or in debt to the bank. It had the services of James Wilson, American army officer, eminent student of constitutional law and banking with an Edinburgh training. He was prominent in Congress and was an active land speculator. At this time he was in debt to the bank for $30,000. He prepared a paper for which the bank paid him $400, "proving" that by virtue of its Congress charter, any repealing act passed merely by the Pennsylvania Assembly would be unconstitutional. To the claim that the Pennsylvania Assembly merely wants the directors to agree to reasonable changes in the charter, Wilson replied that the bank owes a trust to all the states; consequently the directors cannot agree to any changes without Congress's approval.

True, said Wilson and Pelatiah Webster, the Articles of Confederation state that powers not expressly delegated to the United States in Congress assembled are retained by the states, and no such power to charter a national bank is literally given. But any power which the individual state is not competent to handle must necessarily belong to the Congress. Now, a *national* bank is beyond the power of any state to charter, but Congress has the right, as a means of doing what it is expressly empowered to do: to finance, defend, and promote the liberties and general welfare of the states. Congress is empowered to borrow money on the credit of the states, which implies a power to find or procure someone who will lend the money. This was effected by the bank. Even granting that Congress had no power to incorporate a bank, this defect was remedied by the states' acquiescence in the bank. Furthermore, since the Pennsylvania charter formed a contract between the legislature and the company, one side cannot break it without the consent of the other.

Since the charter vests "a right, privilege and interest, i.e., a valuable property right," in all the stockholders of the bank, Webster bluntly said, its repeal would be depriving citizens of their property. "Charters have ever been considered . . . a sacred thing, not to be vacated by a bare holding up of a few hands." Attempts to destroy them "have only happened in times of great corruption of government and dangerous encroachments of arbitrary power."

To repeal the charter would deprive Pennsylvania and the United States of all the advantages, public and private, of a bank in both peace and war, declared Wilson. The independence and almost the existence of the present political establishment must depend on the bank in case of invasion, for the necessary defense could not be made under a depreciating currency or without the anticipated revenue the bank can supply. He cited impartially Sir James Steuart and Adam Smith on the usefulness of a bank in increasing circulation, credit, and commerce, and saving the expense of specie. These truths hold especially in a young country with a great extent of land to be developed.

Pelatiah Webster's defense on the economic side was more detailed. A bank of deposit, loan, and discount which issues convertible bills and provides for the use of bank checks is of the greatest benefit to the state, for it can aid business and government to a number of times its real cash without incurring a depreciation of its notes. On the other hand, the destruction of the bank must mean a calling in of loans and a reduction of the circulating medium, which would bring ruin and chaos.

A private bank is the best antidote against tyranny in government because of the rich owners' influence. "The rich have an interest in their poor fellow citizens, and (as some men use their wives) however tyrannical they may be themselves, they will not suffer anybody else to tyrannize over them." Wealth creates influence, but it is the safe kind. The bank is a mercantile institution, and the influence of merchants is the safest that can affect a government.

In any event, a banking company is least likely to be dangerous. The stockholders are so numerous and scattered, their sentiments and convictions so different, that they balance each other's influence and thereby prevent the bank from becoming a tyrant. But if a state bank is well managed and grows rich, it will lead to despotism in government because the head will have a rich treasury.

Let the true type of private and state bank be joined together, as they are in the Bank of North America. Let the state revenues be deposited in the bank and all public payments be drawn by check on it, and let the state become a stockholder. Thereby the bank could supply the state with any loan required and increase the aid to private citizens and companies.

As for overtrading, true, said Robert Morris then a member of the assembly, after the peace an inordinate increase in importations occurred; but "we shall have no more of those wild adventurers" because, with industry and frugality returning, the balance of trade will be favorable. Besides, the people really do not understand the doctrine of the balance. As another leading merchant member and supporter, Thomas Fitzsimons, added: "The Balance of trade is the metaphysics of commerce, which few understand and which serves no other purpose than to disturb the imagination."

Banks, instead of facilitating the export of specie, prevent the drain, declared Gouverneur Morris; for when the bank realizes that cash is being exported it lessens or stops discounts in self-defense, and this not only stops the export but causes an inflow of money.

The argument that the dividend payments to foreigners will drain the country's specie, he said, is like telling a farmer not to borrow to improve his ground lest the interest drain his cash. Of course, if these foreign wealthy men would migrate to Pennsylvania, the country would greatly benefit. They will do so if good laws protect property. But if solid establishments can be overthrown by every capricious breath, the wise and good will avoid us like a pestilence, and then wealth will be constantly drained from the country.

From a political standpoint foreign investment, instead of being a threat to our government, is a support; for the foreign investors will be our advocate with their governments in case of trouble. As for any unfair advantages in trade the directors may have, the annual election provides the only reasonable check because every stockholder becomes "a sentinel, bound by his private interest to discover unfair practices, and sound the alarm, when undue advantages are obtained." For government to share in the profits directly without investment is reprehensible, since this would be putting charters up for sale.

Any control by the government savors of despotism, said Robert Morris. The state cannot invade the secrecy of accounts between individuals and the bank, for the depositors would not want their deposits, any more than the cash in their chests, made known to the public. Much less would debtors want their accounts known to others than their creditors. As superintendent of finance, he said,

I have received a daily statement of the accounts of the bank but never felt that this should extend to the accounts of individuals.

Some foolishly claim, added Gouverneur Morris, that if the bank's term and capital be limited, as with the Bank of England, the danger of its wealth and influence would be removed. But this would be worse than directly abolishing it, for the bank directors would naturally be forced to corrupt the great men of the assembly in order to obtain a continuance of the charter and extension of capital when either was required.

But if the charter is held sacred, as all charters ought to be, applications for aid by the state will be "plain and manly transactions, not dirty jobs." The bank could then disapprove firmly of any undesirable financial actions of the assembly.

The bank charter is not a monopoly, said Robert Morris, but merely a right of the stockholders to lend their own money to whom they please. Any set of men might apply to the legislature for the same purpose, provided the legislature's hands are not tied by the one they have already granted. That the bank has bitterly fought the chartering of another bank is justifiable because the directors consider it injurious to the private interests of the established bank.

The perpetual character of the charter is no monopolistic device because the stockholders are constantly changing. The bank is common to all the citizens. Anyone can easily buy a share. If voting were not by share but by persons, people would not invest in the bank.[29]

John Witherspoon jumped into the fray with an anonymous *Essay on Money*, written, it was said, at "the urgent request" of the very group of members in Congress who had originally favored government paper but "had lived to see the error of their ways." [30]

Since he was more of an academician than a man of commerce, he said, commercial men might question his right to discuss the theory of money, but he possessed great knowledge of history and fundamental principles of human nature. Besides, commercial men are too closely bound to their business to appreciate the underlying wider theory.

After a thoroughgoing defense of the bank, he concluded that those who prevent the circulation of doubtful paper by refusing it are "not enemies but friends to their country."

Franklin, having become a stockholder in the bank, lost his faith in his old paper schemes and was now arguing that those complaining of a scarcity of money were the few idlers who have nothing to give in exchange for money.[31] But the supporters of the state paper reprinted his old tract and cited Pownall also. At the same time both sides in the paper-money controversy in Maryland agreed that the Pennsylvania paper was only slightly depreciated, but Hanson attributed this to its moderate amount and the general demand.

Among the bank's critics was William Barton, who in his *True Interest of the United States* viewed the old paper money as the ideal monetary instrument for turning the resources of Pennsylvania into the channels of gainful commerce. Unlike loan bills, the paper money of mercantile banks and that of the state for expenditures are both undesirable because they are based on mere confidence. There is a tendency of the managers to overissue by overrating the productiveness of those anticipated funds on which that confidence is grounded.

Under a favorable balance of trade, the credit of the paper of a mercantile bank may be rendered sufficiently stable by the prudence and foresight of the managers. But the bank operations are liable to extension beyond proper bounds in countries with an unfavorable balance because the bank managers' interest will lead them to circulate as much fictitious money in their paper credit as they think consistent with their own safety. This credit acts to accelerate the trade already prejudicial to the nation.

But paper based on "land" is different because the security has a real existence. The credit represents the value of the funds. By increasing alienation—that is, the transfer—of property, and thus exciting industry, such a bank has a direct tendency to increase the country's specie. Since such paper cannot raise the price of labor and commodities as long as it does not exceed its uses, the price of exports will not be excessive.

The attempt to have Congress uphold the validity of the Congress charter when Pennsylvania revoked its charter fell on deaf ears, but after the Pennsylvania state elections of 1786, Rush wrote Price that "an important revolution" has occurred "in favor of the wisdom, virtue, and property of Pennsylvania. . . . Robert Morris is at the head of the Party that will rule our state. . . . This gentleman's abilities . . . and integrity place him upon a footing with the first legislators and patriots of ancient and modern times. It is expected the charter of the Bank of North America will be restored and that the College of Philadelphia . . . seized by fraud and force . . . will be given back to its original and just owners." [32]

In 1787, with a new legislature and Franklin as president of the state, the bank received a new charter from Pennsylvania but with the modifications which, if accepted in the first place, might have prevented the repeal. It no longer was to have a monopoly of banking; its term was limited to fourteen years, its capital to $2,000,000; it was prohibited from trading in merchandise, except bullion and bills of exchange. Finally, it was to deposit with the state authorities copies of all bylaws it passed. But demands for rotation in the holding of directorships and the abolition of plural and proxy voting were defeated.

New England still retained its primacy in vigorous discussion of monetary and related questions. In Rhode Island the judges in 1786 declared that the legal-tender features of the state's loan bills were unconstitutional. The assembly ordered the dismissal of the judges. Supporters of the judges pleaded that judges are bound by the law of nature in preference to any human laws because they are ordained by God. They are likewise bound by the principles of the constitution in preference to the acts of the General Assembly because the former were ordained by the people prior to it and created the powers of the General Assembly. Had not Locke taught that people surrender a part of the natural rights to obtain the rest? Finally, they declared, although the court has refused to grant that the bills are legal tender, the bills circulate more widely and business prospers knowing they could be refused or accepted.[33]

In Massachusetts various towns in 1786 sent petitions to the General Court complaining that taxes are grinding the people, that government salaries are exorbitant and judges and lawyers are living in magnificence and growing more insolent. Paper money should be issued to relieve the scarcity of cash.

Behind the movements for "relief" legislation to cure the business depression were some of the leading businessmen of the community, such as James Warren.[34] But the General Court in special session declared: Paper money causes an export of specie, corrupts morals, and ruins the widows and orphans. Money is scarce, but the people are to blame because we have bought foreign gewgaws and neglected home manufactures.

Judge James Sullivan (1744–1808), who was also a leading if not the leading entrepreneur of Massachusetts and whose economic views were like those of James Swan, father-in-law of one of his sons, informed the people of the disaffected areas that "the fair daughters of America, who were once contented to sit down and sing all day to their spinning wheels, who were proud of their ability to appear in the modest apparel wrought with their own hands, are now ambitious only to be flaunting in their lutestrings and brocades; and Columbia's hardy sons, who knew not the source of their corruption, but boasted of their independence in being able to feed and clothe themselves with the fruit of their own soil and the labour of their own hands, are ignobly sunk into venality and idleness." [35]

Fisher Ames (1758–1808), foremost advocate of the "conservatives" and a leading lawyer, declared: It is a sign of decadent government that the General Court should devote time to the protests of the local conventions, and that it should pass some relief measures such as Winthrop's old measure of commodities as a tender in payment of private debts.

The movement of protest finally culminated in the organization of bands to close the courts. This move was led by a former Revolutionary War captain, Daniel Shays. Madison suspected that the leaders aimed at a division of property and were plotting with the British.[36] Congress ordered the raising of troops to crush the discontents under cover of meeting "the hostile intentions of the Indians in the Western country." The governor of Massachusetts, none other than James Bowdoin, successfully appealed to "gentlemen of fortune and ability" for funds to suppress the revolt.[37]

Harvard masters had by now traveled a long way from the support of paper money in the twenties. In 1787 the masters gave an affirmative to the question: "Is paper money the root of all evil?"

The election sermons of New England began to ring with denunciations of the "rebellion." "The multitudes were under the clouds of God's anger and were sadly forsaken of restraining grace." The object sought in the tumult was "most faulty." They wanted a legal-tender paper, "a measure wholly preposterous" and at best an opiate, for the public should be discharging its debts instead of acquiring new ones, exclaimed the Reverend Joseph Lyman in the Massachusetts election sermon. And in near-by Connecticut the Reverend Josiah Whitney declared in the election sermon: The leaders are restless persons of broken fortunes and characters "who call for the redress of pretended grievances, with a view to gratify their avarice and ambition." [38]

Madison wrote that the malcontents are turning to the polls, and if they can manage sufficient votes their "wicked measures" are to be sheltered under the forms of the constitution. Governor Bowdoin has been replaced by John Hancock, first president of the Continental Congress and eminent merchant, but his "acknowledged merits are a little tainted by a dishonourable obsequiousness to popular follies." [39]

However, Noah Webster, the great lexicographer and conservative, though he disapproved of paper money and of the uprising, asserted: The rebels were not a rabble but "the substantial yeomanry of the country" and had justice on their side. As Pelatiah Webster had prophesied, their property is being sold for taxes to pay the speculators in the metropolis. If the Webster scheme cannot be effected, better the whole debt be wiped off at once, wicked as that might be, rather than that injustice be perpetuated. [40]

After the suppression of the "rebellion," Ames called for a stronger "energetic" government. In administration of government, he said, the fixed rule and standard of conduct must be "the greatest permanent happiness of the greatest number of people," not the wild projects so fascinating to the multitude.

The source of the trouble lies in the speculative views advanced by leaders in the Revolutionary War. The people have turned against their teachers the doctrines which were inculcated in order to effect the late revolution. These philosophic teachers viewed the contest with Britain as involving the fate of liberty and science. They anticipated a system of government too pure for our state of imperfection. These speculative sons of science failed to realize that, under a popular form of government, the legislators themselves feel, and too often fear and obey, the sudden passions and ignorant prejudices of their constituents.

The rulers have done their duty but much remains to be done; for, with the state in depression, sedition has fertile ground. We have heavy foreign and domestic debts; manufactures are destitute of materials, capital, and skill; agriculture is depressed and commerce bankrupt.

Experience demonstrates the need for new maxims of administration, but not of the kind exemplified by "six-penny retrenchments of salaries," by levying war against any profession of men, or by giving "substance" to the frothy essences and fantastic forms of speculation; more specifically, by paper money, abolition of debts, or by "implicit submission to the insolence of· beggarly conventions" of the advocates of democracy. If public and private credit is to be revived, the Articles of Confederation must be amended.

"In spite of national beggary," moaned Ames, "paper money has still its advocates." In spite of national dishonor in the non-payment of the public debts, the continental impost is still successfully opposed. The federal government is refused the necessary powers to "extort commercial treaties from rival states or to establish a national revenue." [41]

If reason will not bring about a strong federal government, said Rush, "force will not be wanting to carry it into execution," for "not only all men of wealth but all the military men"—that is, the officers associated in the Society of the Cincinnati—are "in favor of a wise and efficient government." But "we are travelling fast into order and national happiness. The same enthusiasm now pervades all classes in favor of *government*, that actuated us in favor of *liberty* in the years 1774, and 1775." [42]

The outcome was a meeting in Philadelphia in May 1787 of delegates from the state legislatures that ended in a new instrument of national government, the Constitution. The call for the meeting owed its original stimulus to the exigencies of commerce, domestic and foreign; but the fact that all the states except Rhode Island, which had issued paper money and opposed the continental impost, were represented was due not a little to the fear that Shays' Rebellion had instilled in the "men of principle and property."

The convention was naturally composed of men of wealth and position, of men who had played leading roles in their states and in Congress. But the feature that stood out was the great influence wielded by relatively young men of learning. For them the grandeur of empire was alluring.

There was hardly any disagreement with the postulate that the mass of the people are, by nature, not addicted to enlightened self-interest, but are creatures of emotion and passion; and consequently that the commercial evils of the country could be traced to the existence of too much democracy. But there was sharp disagreement over the form of federal government that would curb the excesses and make possible commercial prosperity and national strength. These struggles were essentially like the contest between the Congregational and Presbyterian polities, with young Madison at one extreme and the elderly Roger Sherman at the other.

Madison had already sketched the defects of the Articles at great length. Under them, the United States is merely a league of sovereign powers and Congress has no coercive power to enforce its acts. The Congress could not raise money nor regulate commerce. It could not prevent its members from violating treaties and the law of nations. It could not prevent the abuses of interested or misguided majorities in the states in the matter of money and sanctity of contracts, witness paper money and stay laws, which stayed collection of debts in whole or in part.[43]

"In framing a system which we hope will last for ages, we must consider the changes age will produce," he informed his fellow delegates. An increase of population will necessarily increase the proportion of those laboring under the hardships of life and who "secretly sigh for more equal distribution of its blessings." These may eventually outnumber those who are "placed above the feelings of indigence. . . . Symptoms of a levelling spirit . . . have sufficiently appeared in a certain quarter to give notice of the future danger." In other words, when in future times the great majority becomes propertyless, they may under the influence of their common situation combine and consequently subvert the rights of property and public liberty through their votes. What is more likely, "they will become the tools of opulence and ambition," as the state will abound in the not distant future with mechanics and manufacturers who will receive their bread from their employers and consequently have their vote dictated.

Since to Madison and to his type of commercial mind the great evils arose from the state legislatures, he wanted the states reduced to little more than administrative units. Where they had selected the delegates to the Congress, he now proposed that the "people," limited by a proper pecuniary qualification, should elect the members of one House and then these in turn choose those of a second body, the Senate; and so on.

The discussion became slightly fantastic as John Francis Mercer of Maryland declared that the state governments are "all ready aristocracies" and the only way this could be checked is to allow the executive to appoint the administrative officers from members of the legislature, as in the royal colonies.

The slave trade also became an issue. Mason, after a passionate criticism of slavery, declared that the general government should have the power to prohibit the slave trade. The right is one of those rights along with many others that the states should properly surrender. "The infernal traffic," he said, "originated in the avarice of British merchants"; and he lamented that some of our eastern brethren have, from a lust of gain, embarked on it. Maryland and Virginia forbid the traffic, but their action is nullified by the fact that Georgia and South Carolina allow it. The western people are already calling for slaves, and they will get them through the latter states.

But C. C. Pinckney of South Carolina bluntly declared that Virginia demands a prohibition in order that her surplus slaves should rise in value. It would be unfair to require Georgia and South Carolina to confederate on such unequal terms. That the importation of slaves was to the interest of the whole union, he "proved" by the same type of argument Mason used to have slaves counted in determining representation. "The more slaves, the more produce to employ the carrying trade; the more consumption also; and the more of this, the more revenue for the common treasury."

Oliver Ellsworth of Connecticut felt that if, as Mason argued, slavery is to be viewed in a moral light, we should emancipate slaves, rather than simply stop their importation. They multiply so fast in Virginia and Maryland that it is cheaper to raise than import them in those states, but in the sickly swamps importations are required. If we go no further than Mason urges, we should therefore be unjust to Georgia and South Carolina. But "let us not intermeddle" with slavery. As population increases, poor laborers will become so plentiful that slaves will be useless.

The upshot was that Congress was forbidden to pass any measure prohibiting the importation of slaves for twenty years.

Mason argued that acts to regulate commerce with foreign nations and between the states should require a two-thirds vote of each house; for if a bare majority was allowed, the northern interest would oppress the southern interest. A navigation act, said Mason, would not only enhance the freight, but would enable a few merchants in Philadelphia, New York, and Boston to monopolize the staples of the southern states and sharply reduce their value. But his fellow Virginian, Madison, declared that, while a navigation act might cause a temporary rise of freight, the end result would be an increase of southern as well as northern shipping, the emigration of northern seamen and merchants to the southern states, and the removal of the existing injurious retaliation between the states. The upshot was that Congress got power to regulate commerce but was forbidden to levy export duties.

With Wilson to lead the fight, state issues of paper were absolutely forbidden, but the question of a national issue was left open. "The committee on detail" reported that the federal legislature should have the power to issue paper, but Gouverneur Morris said that "the moneyed interest" would oppose the plan of government if paper emissions were not prohibited. Madison thought, however, that non-legal-tender bills should be allowable. Mason went further and argued that, "though he had a mortal hatred to paper money, yet as he could not foresee all emergencies," he was unwilling to tie the hands of the legislature. The late war could not have been carried on had such a prohibition existed. The upshot was merely a deletion of the proviso.

The original proposal forbidding the states "to interfere in private contracts" was changed to "impairing the obligation of contracts" after Gouverneur Morris and Mason declared it went too far and would interfere with the smooth running of business. They said that the original proposal would prohibit necessary state legislation "relating to bringing actions, limitations of actions, etc."; for example, the "case of limiting the period for bringing actions, on open account—that of bonds after a certain lapse of time." [44]

The conflict in the states over adoption of the Constitution was bitter. Both sides in general appealed to the yeomanry and claimed to be the supporters of the middling class, the class between rich and poor that constituted the "people." Both sides had much the same social philosophy. There was little disagreement with the viewpoint of one anonymous supporter that in a "society where the acquisition and secure holding of property is one of the first and most darling objects of Government, and in this at least we are more than copyists of the Europeans," one of the first intentions of the government ought to be to make property perfectly safe in the hands of the rightful possessor. [45]

Madison emphasized in that greatest of defenses of the Constitution, The Federalist, that the power to regulate commerce between the states must be granted to the federal authority, for without it "the great and essential power of regulating foreign commerce would have been incomplete and ineffectual."

Noah Webster wrote that the great benefit of the Constitution is the elimination of the pernicious policy whereby certain states take advantage of their situation to tax the commerce of their neighbors, as New York with the goods of Connecticut. Williamson reminded his state of North Carolina that she should not object to the prohibition of any state levying export duties in view of Virginia's use of this weapon to North Carolina's detriment.

Jay of New York declared: The depression is the result of Congress's lack of the power to regulate commerce. Our fur trade has gone to Canada because of the British garrisons remaining in the West. Our shipyards are closed and our seamen and skilled shipwrights are in foreign lands and foreign pay. We permit all nations to fill our markets with their merchandise, but their best markets are closed to us. To no island can an American vessel carry a barrel of flour for sale, and the Algerians exclude us from the Mediterranean.

Oliver Ellsworth, the merchant, under the pseudonym of "a landholder," informed the yeomanry: "You were told that Peace and Independence would reward your toil, and that riches would accompany the establishment of your liberties by opening a wider market and consequently raise the price of America's export commodities." These rewards have not been yours because of the lack of a strong central authority to deal with the exactions of foreign states on our commerce. The present state of America limits the majority of inhabitants to agriculture, but our surplus earnings can be devoted to a better purpose than purchasing the labor of European nations. The general belief that, where the price of land is low and that of labor high, manufactures are not profitable was true of some but grossly false of other manufactures. New England can rival Great Britain in some of the latter's principal manufactures, especially woolens. Hartford gentlemen have formed a fund to establish a manufactory. As the manufacture of cloths is introduced, "opulent farmers" could advance their property by the raising of flax, and the country would thank them.

Criticism as well as defense turned in the last analysis on the question whether damage to local pecuniary interests would outweigh the gains. Governor George Clinton of New York, under the pseudonym of "Cato," went back to Montesquieu's view that large republics cannot succeed because they cannot provide security for property.

"You have already observed the feeble efforts of Massachusetts against their insurgents; with what difficulty did they quell that insurrection."

On the critics' side in Massachusetts stood the descendant of John Winthrop, James Winthrop, former librarian of Harvard and an entrepreneur, among other things. Writing under the name of "Agrippa," he argued that the unlimited power over trade granted Congress would injure free enterprise. Massachusetts' great prosperity is due to the freedom of enterprise, to the lack of shackles, which has given her a favorable balance of trade.

The greater part of our increase in people is employed in settling the new lands while the older settlements enter largely into manufactures. Our immense country can produce the necessary raw materials, and the restrictions on our trade in Europe necessarily oblige us to make use of them, and "the high price of labour operates as encouragement to mechanical improvements." Thus we are rapidly achieving economic as well as political independence. But the excises that Congress may impose may destroy the growth of manufacture, which is encouraged by the import duties.

If we surrender the right of taxation and commercial regulation, the landed states to the southward will drain our resources, for the planters will save whatever the imposts on our trade and the excises on our manufactures will yield. Such savings ought to be made in favor of our own state. Consequently "we ought never to surrender the unlimited powers of revenue and trade to uncommercial people."

True, Massachusetts tolerates such vicious practices as a "tender act," but "what government has not some law in favor of debtors?" It would be hard to find a government "that is not more unfriendly to the creditors than ours." Such laws, like any favoring a part of the community, are wrong in principle, but the states should not be forbidden to issue non-legal-tender bills of credit.

Finally, no single legislature can legislate for both the northern and southern states, for many circumstances make the southerners essentially different from us; for example, their unequal distribution of property, the toleration of slavery, the ignorance and poverty of the lower classes, the softness of the climate and dissoluteness of manners.

In the South, Richard Lee of Virginia, wealthy planter, likewise set against congressional control over commerce, warned that it would be a consolidated government, that the northern majority would carry everything against the scattered rurals. Congress would establish pernicious land and poll taxes, for import duties are limited by what commerce can bear and by the danger of smuggling.

One who utilized an extreme form of the demagoguery so common to supporters as well as critics was Hugh Brackenridge, the Princeton graduate and "radical" Pittsburgh journalist. His criticisms of the Constitution included the claim that no security was given that the President would be a white man. He might be a "vile Negro"! In fact, there was no guarantee that he need even be a man of property. "Who knows but the electors at a future period, in days of corruption, may pick up a man-servant and give him dominion." [46]

With the men of "principle and property" thus divided, the Constitution was ratified only with considerable difficulty. Time and again Madison was to assert that the instrument was called forth by the exigencies of commerce. That it was accepted in those "oligarchies" that constituted most of the states was evidence that it was believed to make for expansion of "profitable commerce." But it could hardly be expected to end controversy as to what was profitable commerce.

Just how complex the question might be was revealed by the anonymous author of the *Observations on the Agriculture, Manufactures and Commerce of the United States* (1789), addressed to a member of the new Congress, about to assemble.[47] He attempted to work out a harmony of their great interests along the lines laid down by Barton, Williamson, and Coxe.

Agriculture is the foundation of the nation's wealth; but, since the value yielded from manufacture of raw materials is four times that of raw stuffs, a nation forced to choose between agriculture and manufacture should encourage manufactures and obtain its subsistence from abroad.

A more profitable commerce can be supported by manufactures than by natural production, for in return the nation obtains not superfluous and unprofitable merchandise, but circulating specie, or what leads to specie eventually, "something capable of improvement, something productive and accumulating, something in short which will increase the wealth of the nation."

At the same time manufactures increase the strength of the nation by allowing a great increase in population, which in turn creates wealth. Thus Connecticut, with its 200,000 people, has reached its

limit of growth under its present agricultural economy, but if manufactures be developed it can support four times the number.

Farmers should raise produce that could be used by manufactures.
Government should encourage manufactures by a tariff, bounties,
and prohibitions. The import of goods which we produce in sufficient quantities should be prohibited; those which we could produce
in such quantities should have a small preference by a tariff. Exports
of raw materials which might be wholly manufactured in the United
States should be prohibited, and on the other hand, the importation
of raw materials such as cotton and wool, machines, instruments
which are not yet produced in sufficient quantities at home, should
be free. At the same time the new manufactures might get tax exemptions and other special aids.

Eventually, with sufficient capital devoted to manufacture, with
their number and production increased, with the growth of "habit
and use in the manufactory arts," their price will be reduced to "a
reasonable standard," become cheaper than imports of a similar kind,
and consequently create the valuable surplus. A tax on imports is
one of the best because it protects domestic manufactures, takes the
money from the rich, is optional, voluntary, and the effect is not
seriously felt.

Of course, he also advocated an excise on country-distilled liquors
so that imported drinks should be on equal footing. If the liquors
are exported, the excise is to be returned; just as in the case of imports re-exported, a "drawback," or rebate, would be allowed.

A free and open trade would be the best for the happiness of
mankind at large; but, since practically every state aims at engrossing
an unequal share of commercial advantages, each must protect its own
interest by acquiring more circulating property or goods which tend
to increase circulating property. The purpose of commerce is to
dispose of surpluses, but the surplus is determined by the nation's
"industry," its capacity to acquire a balance of debt in its favor.

The objective should be profitable commerce, not "licentious commerce." Profitable commerce means obtaining advantageous markets
to obtain necessaries not produced at home; to give employment to
domestic merchants, mechanics, and mariners; to increase the circulating property; and, finally, to establish a basis for a national
revenue.

The first aim of profitable commerce consists in obtaining the
greatest price for our products. This aim is to be achieved by treaties

of commerce, the removing of obstructions to new markets, helping merchants to establish a new trade, and enacting various regulations for maintaining the price of our productions. It might be advisable to establish exclusive companies of the regulated type in foreign trade.

Only the native merchants should be encouraged, for a country will eventually lose the foreign merchants and their money. The foreign merchants, notably English, drain the country's wealth and leave our people the hewers of wood and drawers of water for England because of our debtor position.

The worst effect is that the nation's merchants cannot make a living from commerce. An excess of merchants and traders beyond the number necessary to obtain support from it creates the licentiousness of trade by disturbing the regularity and relative permanency in the mode of business and price of merchandise. Therefore regulations discouraging the mass of people from entering trade would be for the public benefit.

Steps should be taken to prevent Nova Scotia from being a competitor in shipbuilding and the whale-oil industry. Our carpenters' supplies and provisions enable her to reduce the price of labor and outstrip us in shipbuilding. She constructs ships beyond her need to provide employment and carry her products. Likewise, if we prohibit the emigration of whale men and provisions for the Nova Scotia whaling industry, England would be forced to remove her prohibitive duties on our whale oil.

Finally; the country should provide proper military strength. Our disposition is now pacific but, like all peoples, our ambitions will be excited by and increase with our increasing power. We shall rest content with the Mississippi on the south, the St. Lawrence on the north, and with the West Indies. But the country's growth in wealth and population will drive England to attempt to form a hostile confederacy. Consequently the nation should have a strong militia. Since our growing navigation and commerce will increasingly tend to rival the commerce of the great European powers, a navy is also essential.

So the new government fell heir to old problems.

CHAPTER XIII

The Decade of Federalist Power

AFTER the establishment of the new government, complaints were still heard that the old evils had not been completely eliminated. Coxe agreed: "Property may be almost called the palladium of the communities," but many restrictions still exist upon it in the United States. Paper-money issues are outstanding in some states; so are valuation and stay laws.[1] But these undesirable features will quickly disappear.

Barton informed the American Philosophical Society that, with our good government, the rapid increase of population is the best evidence of our great destiny. A country whose population is rapidly increasing, is increasing in wealth and strength with proportionate speed despite transitory disturbances in the public economy of a state that may, for the interval, give "an appearance . . . or even an actual existence, in some degree . . . of public debility and distress." The chief factors in the country's unequaled rapid increase are the good climate, the virtuous and simple manners of the mass, and the great resources.

Data on the rate of increase are not available, "but a laudable spirit of inquiry is gaining, so fast that great regularity and precision in arranging data will be introduced in the several departments of public economy" as will lead to further useful knowledge and particularly to improving that branch of science.

After making his investigations by the highly speculative methods of "political arithmetic," he concluded by asking: "Must not the mind of every American citizen . . . glow with . . . pride, when he reflects on the blessings his country enjoys?" It has "every advantage which nature can bestow." It is "inhabited by more than three millions of the freest people" and possesses "territory amply sufficient to maintain for ages to come many additional millions of freemen, which the progression of its population is supplying with wonderful celerity."[2]

Slavery was disappearing from the North. The rector of the Swedish churches in America told the American Philosophical Society that the introduction of "mechanism" in the southern states would eliminate the need of slaves; but the invention of the cotton gin led to the opposite result.[3]

Defenders of slavery declared it was a necessary evil that would eventually cure itself. The slaveholder could not be held guilty of crime because slavery as a very common thing is due to the state of society, for which the slaveholder is not responsible. Slavery in America is preferable to liberty in Africa because the slave gets better care and acquires the Christian religion. In fact, the underlying reason for importing slaves is to further the Christian religion.

Restrictions in the southern states against manumission were defended on the ground that it would lead to the freeing of the old, decrepit, and sick, and to the infecting of slaves with notions of freedom and running away as well as creating general disorder. "A man has almost as good a right to set fire to his own buildings though his neighbor's is to be destroyed by it, as to free his slaves." [4]

In the new state of Kentucky, proposals to the legislators for gradual emancipation and pecuniary compensation to owners were thwarted. The wealthy ex-Virginian, John Breckinridge, denounced them as a first step by the "envious, the discontented or the needy, . . . to extinguish our land titles, for both are held by rights equally sacred." [5]

Respectable opponents, generally in New England, questioned the argument that slavery is a curse of society, not of the individual. It is no more valid, they said, than the notion that drunkenness and adultery are not delinquencies of the individual. Whether the slave is better off here than in Africa is for the slave to decide, for every man has a right to judge concerning his own happiness and to choose the means of obtaining it or promoting it. Would we feel it just, they asked, if Africans carried us into slavery because they thought it would be better for us? The greatest evil is that the slaves will eventually outnumber the whites, and this must lead either to the most horrible event, intermarriage, or the destruction of the whites.

For the most part, the critics looked for remedies in the abolition of the slave trade, the growth of voluntary manumission, and even the growth of trade and commerce with Africa in the manner pictured by Swan. It was agreed that pecuniary considerations were the most important barrier to voluntary manumission, but the slaveholder was told to trust to the Lord for his recompense.[6]

The general attitude was best expressed by the Baptist clergyman

Samuel Jones of Philadelphia: The slave trade is abominable; the possession of slaves is not profitable except in newly settled regions where the costs of labor are very high. But the slave owners are innocent inheritors of the institution and not obliged to free their slaves, "at least not until they shall be fully reimbursed the full amount of their cost on equitable principles." [7]

The attitude toward lower classes was the same as it was in colonial days. The morals of the lower classes here, said Noah Webster, schoolmaster of the nation, are less pure than in Europe because of the nature of our government and the price of labor. Despotic governments have an advantage over other kinds in that "people in general have less wages, and of course are compelled to labour more hours and days for subsistence, than in our country." Consequently "they have less time and less means to indulge themselves in vices, and after all . . . industry does more to preserve morals than laws or sermons." [8]

Writing under the signature of "Patriot," he claimed that he saw everywhere "an abundance of poor children wandering about the streets, clothed in dirty rags, illy educated in every respect." But they would be trained to usefulness both for themselves and the community if they were placed in textile factories.[9]

Robert Coram, Delaware journalist, schoolteacher, and opponent of ratification of the Constitution, felt that society could meet its obligations of providing everyone with the means of subsistence by the establishment of public schools to teach "the rudiments of the English language, writing, bookkeeping, mathematics, natural history, mechanics and husbandry," and of apprenticeship regulations by which "parents and others having authority over youth, should be compelled to bind them out" to trades or professions.[10]

The usury laws came under heavy fire. Noah Webster, drawing his arguments from Bentham, declared that a man has the same natural right to exercise every act of ownership upon money as upon other property. Usury laws involve the absurdity of attempting to fix the value of money. Its value depends wholly on the quantity in circulation and the demand. In this respect it resembles all other articles of trade, and whoever thought of fixing the price of goods except a few foolish legislatures during the war? It may be said that the price of bread is legally fixed in all cities, but it is a question whether the citizens of our large towns would be supplied with bread at a cheaper rate without such regulations.

On the other hand, Webster declared that the public support of preachers in New England, though it meant taxing the inhabitants, did not constitute a restraint upon natural right. Rhode Island's "turbulence" furnished conclusive proof of the need and usefulness of such a clergy.[11]

The literature of land promotion was succinctly summarized in the London prospectus of Robert Morris's North American Land Company of Philadelphia, with lands almost anywhere to sell, as well as the stock. Land is a species of property which benefits every possessor, it read. It is a well-known fact that many entered very largely into the speculation and purchased of the states to an amount that would appear astonishing to Europeans. Their system was simple and reasonable. When the increasing population had conferred an increase of value, they sold to others at an advance, proportioned to the time they had occupied the land. These did likewise "till that which was a wilderness approached, by cultivation and improvement, something towards its intrinsic worth. In many instances the value of these lands have doubled in . . . five or six years." [12]

Of course, it was also not unusual to depreciate areas other than those in which the promoter or promoters had interest. So Rush informed wealthy English that Pennsylvania land had the benefit of the labor already performed by the shiftless pioneers who moved west. The first settler in the woods is generally a man who has lost his credit and fortune in the cultivated parts. On his plantation of three to four hundred acres he builds himself a wretched cabin. Being lazy, he cultivates merely a little corn, but nature is bountiful. During the first year he suffers from cold and hunger, but he does not complain. He adopts the manners of the near-by savages and enjoys long periods of repose in his filthy cabin after a little violent labor; he finds pleasure in fishing, hunting, and drinking by himself. Because of his licentious manners, he is opposed to religion.

But in a few years, as population increases, his troubles begin. Taxes and laws become necessary, but the independent settler considers these shackles, and rather than sacrifice a single natural right for the benefit of orderly government, he leaves for the wilderness to begin again. If the first settler is the owner of the land, he sells it at a considerable profit to his successor, but since he is more often a tenant of some rich landholder, he abandons it in debt. But the small improvement he leaves generally makes it an object of immediate demand to a second species of settler.

In this second type, the Indian manners are more diluted. He generally has some property. He makes some improvements, but he too is a bad manager. "With high ideas of liberty," he refuses to bear his proportion of the debt contracted to establish civil government in our country. He is fond of company, drinks excessively, and passes much time at political meetings. Thus he contracts debts, and if he is unable to discharge them in a depreciated paper currency he is forced to sell out and depart further west.

The final buyer is the third and last species of settler. He is a man of property and good character, "sometimes the son of a wealthy farmer in one of the interior and ancient counties of the state." Only in this type is civilization completed; its members alone should be called farmers. He brings in all improvements, builds an elegant stone house, more completely diversifies his production, and fully and thoroughly cultivates all his land. "His very kitchen flows with milk and honey." Beer, cider, and homemade wine are the usual drinks of his family. In proportion as he increases in wealth, he values the protection of law. Consequently, he pays his taxes punctually and supports schools and churches.

The western part of Virginia, the Carolinas, and Georgia have been settled by inhabitants from Pennsylvania because their soil and climate more easily support lazy farmers than does the stubborn and durable Pennsylvania soil. Thus Pennsylvania is the great outpost of the United States for Europeans, and after functioning as a sieve by detaining those with the stamina of industry and virtue, it allows the rest to pass to the states which are accommodated to their habits of indolence.[13]

Of much the same character was the literature extolling canal and navigation projects. In 1791 the two-year-old Pennsylvania Society for Promoting the Improvement of Roads and Inland Navigation, of which Robert Morris was president, asked the state to aid inland navigation in the interest of "the internal trade, manufactures and population" of the state. Washington's argument as to the need of connecting the interest of the West with the East was used, but the port town was not to be Alexandria or New York; it was to be Philadelphia. The state must act quickly lest the channels of trade go elsewhere; and, even though our route be the natural one, enormous expense will be required to restore the channel of trade to us once it is forced.

The memorial called for a comprehensive development of internal improvements, including both roads and canals. But the work should not be done on public account if the improvements will admit of a profit. Of course, the state should lend public money to the companies or invest in their shares to help toward their completion. The companies are to be granted incorporation with all its privileges, including transferable shares. The state is to fix tolls, but if the revenues fail to yield 6 per cent on the investment, the state could make up the deficiency or annul the contract by repaying the capital sums with interest. The state is to be restrained for a period to be determined from allowing turnpike roads or toll canals which would destroy or diminish the income of the first companies.

With Bingham as a leading member of the body, the legislature quickly saw the wisdom of the Society's proposals. Funds were made available, and three large navigation companies were chartered with Morris president of all three, and with boards of managers including Bingham, the Reverend William Smith, and that "celebrated philosopher and mechanic," David Rittenhouse, Esq., LL.D.," as the company literature described him.

The charters provided that every three years the companies were to lay before the state an abstract of their general financial accounts. If at the end of any ten-year period the investments yielded more than 25 per cent, tolls could be reduced.

Before the companies had gone far, the promoters requested further "liberal benefactions." They pointed to the large sums invested in the various stocks of this state and of the United States, such as banks, insurance companies, roads, canals, and other companies, and the growing demand for capital for the increased domestic and foreign trade. Because of this, they said, there is little prospect of additional investment or "prompt payment of a considerable number of the shares already subscribed according to law." Twice as much capital as already invested is needed.

The state's finances are really in a flourishing condition. An enlightened legislature could use the public money to no nobler purpose, even if the state never obtains a moneyed return from its investment, for can an interest of 8 or 10 per cent "on the moneyed capital of a great commonwealth be considered as an equivalent for suffering the improvements of a happy and fertile country to languish and decay?"

The state, though refusing direct financial aid, granted the companies the right to raise $400,000 by a lottery on the ground that companies from "the novelty of such extensive and arduous undertakings in a young country experienced numerous difficulties beyond those contemplated." The expedients did not succeed, and the projects practically ended as failures, as did most of the other large-scale schemes, including the Potomac project.[14]

The men of enterprise in general welcomed the French Revolution in its first phases. In 1793 conservative James Bowdoin, son of old Governor Bowdoin, wrote that it would tend to convert the absolute monarchy into a government appreciative of "the spirit and principles of commerce." This in turn would mean lifting of navigation acts and the like, and there is also the expectation that England would be forced as a result to conform to the "new order of things" of the "revolutionary spirit" of commerce.[15] Others even more respectable and conservative saw in the revolution that aristocrats and men of wealth in England and the continent would be more appreciative now of opportunities to invest in American lands and securities.

The great controversial discussions were mostly over national policy as men with varying outlook and interests attempted to give concrete meaning to what constituted profitable commerce.

Madison in the House sketched the broad philosophy to which all agreed in general. He was a friend of the "great principle of interest" as the regulator, and consequently of a "free and liberal commerce." Commercial shackles are generally unjust, oppressive, and impolitic. If industry and labor are left to take their course, they will generally be directed to the most productive activities. Just as the shoemaker gains no advantage by making his own clothes, so nations do not gain by restricting trade. Ideally there should be perfect freedom of trade. But there are exceptions. There are cases in which certain fictitious advantages possessed by a nation divert industry from its natural course and render it artificial. To overcome these barriers and turn the stream of industry their way, nations often necessarily impose restraints and grant special aids.

Suppose two countries are so related that one, by discouraging the manufactures of the other, "might not only invigorate its own, but transplant the manufacturers themselves. Here the gain would be a clear one and the effect evidently consistent with the . . . theory." In some cases a perfectly free competition would be fatal to a fair competition. For instance, if there is competition between two commercial cities and one is possessed of great wealth and long habits of business, but the other is superior only in natural advantages, the latter cannot acquire its due proportionable share of business and must finally succumb.

What holds between cities holds between nations. Paramount among the exceptions is the need of discriminatory tonnage duties in favor of nations "friendly" to our ships and merchants, as against the monopolistic British. Britain's carriers have more than their natural or proper share of the trade; and the commerce between the two countries has consequently exceeded its "natural boundary." If the United States imposes discriminating tonnage duties, Britain would be compelled to remove her pernicious restrictions. Otherwise British merchants in American tobacco and rice would sustain immense losses on their capital, and American manufacturers would develop at the expense of British ones. Britain could not retaliate by further restrictions on our trade with the British West Indies, for the latter need our cheaper supplies and our market for their staple rum on which they depend for the profits of their labor. As Madison put it later, we as the exporters of necessaries stand to Britain in the relation of an "opulent individual to the labourer in producing the superfluities for his accommodation." We can do without those luxuries the consumption of which gives bread to the latter.

When it came to a protective tariff, Madison grew circumspect: As an exception to free trade, the national government cannot abandon industries which flourished under the protection of the now-outlawed state tariff laws, for men cannot immediately shift from one industry to another without serious loss. Furthermore, where industries capable of achieving perfection have not done so, legislation may be necessary. Another exception is that articles necessary for war should be protected. But these exceptions may be carried too far; national interest may be forced to give way to local interests.

If Madison, with his doctrine of free trade and exceptions, supplied the general logic, the vigorous financier mind typified by Bingham sketched the concrete outlines of national policy whereby the nation would acquire the maximum of treasure in accordance with the latest practical principles of British thinking. Madison, as a product of Virginia planterdom and older types of mercantile thinking, could never fully comprehend those devices of finance that were familiar to a product of the financial capital, Philadelphia, aided by experience in London.

Following lines laid down by Gale, Bingham presented his scheme of converting the public debt into an engine for creating prosperity. In 1789 he wrote to Alexander Hamilton, the first Secretary of the Treasury, that to take advantage of the necessities of public creditors is to lose the future financial aid of a substantial part of the moneyed interest. So in any funding measure the holders of the present debt must be given securities the market value of which would be equivalent to their claims, which he calculated should be funded 6 per cent securities.

The landed interest would be the great beneficiaries; for a funded debt, being negotiable, acts like an increased supply of circulating media to raise the price of land. When "confidence is restored and the representative medium is augmented by a more extensive circulation of paper," the increasing wealth and commerce of a country will force a natural decline of the interest rate, and then the government will find that the holders voluntarily take in exchange new securities at a lower rate rather than their capital. However, if the government attempts to take advantage of creditors by reducing the rate of interest, public credit will be destroyed.

Proponents of reduced interest argue that the present holders paid little for the securities, but the purchaser resembles a "dealer in a lottery, where there are many blanks to a prize. Would it be just to contest the payment due to the fortunate ticket, because it had comparatively cost a trifle?"

The country must provide for discharging the debt by means of appropriations to a sinking fund. It is inconceivable how speedily such appropriations eliminate the debt by the operation of compound interest. His friend Price, the propounder of the doctrine, had just "proven" that were the Americans to reserve annually £100,000 and employ it at 10 per cent profit, in ninety-seven years it would amount to £10,000,000,000.

Pitt's action of raising taxes not only to pay the interest, but also to provide for a sinking fund worked like a charm, said Bingham. People then knew the debts would be paid. New taxes were laid, and unfunded debt being funded was raised to a value proportioned with other stock. Sufficient money then flowed into the country to supply the demand of every channel of industry.

Objectors to a sinking fund argue that it increases taxes. But, said Bingham, if taxes are skillfully employed, they will in some measure beget the means of paying them. Thus taxes, inducing increased labor to obtain necessary subsistence, increase the capital stock of the country. "Taxes when used for this stimulating purpose, do not impoverish a country by diminishing the common mass of property," but "only interrupt the circulation to the extent of the sum drawn from the people, combined with the time that elapses, before it returns to the common mass." Thus England's revenue has more than kept pace with her increasing expenditures despite the great increase of taxes since the Revolutionary War. Too high import duties, however, will cause a clamor by the merchant against the unequal burden and damage the fair trader.

"As an accumulation and increase of taxes forces money out of its natural circulation, as representing industry, and carries it into a new channel, towards other objects of exchange, which the system of public contributions opens to it (thereby saving interest and occasioning a diminished production and consumption)," the statesman resorting to taxes to increase revenue must increase the quantity of circulating medium.

This could best be done by having paper replace the expensive specie as a circulating medium, by means of a bank with sufficient capital to satisfy all demands and with its notes receivable for government dues. The bank could be achieved by increasing the capital of the present "national bank"—that is, the private Bank of North America—by means of subscription, five-sixths in government securities and the remainder in specie or bank notes. Should the government's revenue be insufficient to pay interest on the debt, the bank would for a "reasonable" compensation agree to circulate interest-bearing treasury notes, provided that only the amount of such notes as the bank thinks proper are issued.[16]

The Secretary of the Treasury, as a product of the Robert and Gouverneur Morris school, had long been convinced of the soundness of Bingham's logic, and it only remained to make such recommendations and additions to the Bingham scheme as would strip it of obvious features of personal aggrandizement to its promoters.

The upshot was a funding scheme which provided for no discrimination and practically no scaling down. The revenue was to be raised from an excise on spirits and moderate import duties and sale of land to men with large funds or credit. Along with this went the establishment of a privately controlled national bank with branches throughout the country, with capital composed primarily of the public debt, but with government supervision of the general character that Robert Morris had exercised over the Bank of North America during the war.

Closely attuned to the funding and banking measures were Secretary Hamilton's proposals for the development of manufactures. These were embodied in Hamilton's famous *Report on Manufactures*, where he argued that the federal government under the "general welfare clause" of the Constitution should grant bounties and other aids as well as impose tariff duties to develop large-scale manufacturing companies. This report evidenced the assistance of Tench Coxe, who had become Assistant Secretary of the Treasury.

Coxe still operated along the lines of his variant of the mercantile theory, or "balanced" economy. He agreed that imports from foreign countries should be reduced to equal their consumption of our goods. This, however, should not be attempted by precipitate measures, but by establishment of the country's mercantile credit abroad through the growth of capital and commercial and manufacturing enterprise. Thus what may appear at first sight an unfavorable balance would be in reality a favorable one. The balance of trade has been aptly called the "metaphysics of commerce." It requires as accurate and elaborate investigation as any great metaphysical question because of the existence of invisible items such as land and ship sales abroad, freight, and the like. In the country's present undeveloped condition (as Pownall and Otis had argued before) we should have little or no favorable general balance for the country's raw materials and instruments of production in preference to specie. Should our considerable export balance, outward freight, sales of land and ships be returned in these imports, the country would in fact have an immense favorable balance.[17]

At the same time Coxe warned the British through the press that if they continued to follow "an over driven spirit of monopoly" and impede the country's fisheries, shipping, and foreign commerce in violation of the doctrine of perfect freedom of trade, the United States with the aid of the surplus capital and labor of Europe would develop great manufactures.

The government, however, instead of burdening the nation with a general system of heavy protective duties, should encourage one branch of manufactures at a time. It should be an industry where much labor-saving machinery can be used and little manual labor needed.

The first European capitalist to establish manufactures by labor-saving machinery would rapidly make a fortune because the peculiar quality of such machinery is that it yields its greatest profit in countries where the price of labor is the highest. And if European countries should continue to fail to realize their opportunity, appreciation of our public stocks will entice some of our own creditors or capitalists.

Let a group of holders of the 6 per cent public debt be granted a charter of incorporation with transferable shares. The capital stock of public debt could be used as collateral for a foreign loan of specie at an interest rate lower than the stock. A large area of land should be purchased for a town well situated for receiving duty free imported materials and exporting fabrics. Thereby the investors would not only be successful in manufactures, but would help to raise a profitable town and support the value of the public debt.[18]

Coxe tried to sell the idea to Hamilton's great opponent, Secretary of State Jefferson, with the argument that, since agriculture is the "most natural employment" and since manufacturers are often "an intemperate and disorderly class, . . . modes of manufacture which do not require them, and which indeed in a certain degree supersede the occasion for them . . . appear to be very desirable." [19]

Finally, a definite prospectus that showed the handiwork of both Hamilton and Coxe appeared in the newspapers. It was a self-evident proposition that communities which cannot completely supply their own wants have not reached the highest political perfection. Theory and experience prove that, without extensive manufactures, a nation cannot possess much active wealth. The capital required would be supplied by using the public debt; the labor supply necessary for the labor-saving machinery would be composed of women and children and emigrants obtained on "reasonable terms in countries where labor is cheap." For proper policing of the inhabitants of the place, the principal seat of the factories was to be incorporated.

The result was the incorporated New Jersey Society for Useful Manufactures at Paterson, New Jersey. Stock could be purchased only with the funded public debt, and the latter could be invested only in the national bank stock. Voting was by shares, though in the *Report on the Bank* Hamilton had declared such an unlimited right made for conspiracy, and Coxe had considered such a provision as the one great blemish on the Bank of North America. However, if the federal government or a state subscribed, its votes were limited. The directors were vested with practically all the power; they, not the stockholders, chose the governor and deputy governor. (The governor, Colonel William Duer, trained in finance in Britain, the Revolutionary War, and the Treasury, was the country's leading speculator with operations in lands, public debt, bank stock, and other securities.)

According to its charter, the company could manufacture or make any commodity not prohibited by law. It was given the right to hold a lottery and also the power of eminent domain to construct canals. The state granted the company various privileges such as exempting its employees from military service and payment of taxes. "Upon the exercise of these generous privileges, the state imposed hardly any restriction." Aside from the submission of some general abstracts of accounts, "no reports to the state, no 'external' publicity, and no accounting for or limitation of profits was stipulated." [20] The company proved a failure in a short time.

The one feature of administration policy that raised a "rebellion" originally met little opposition in Congress. This was the excise on distilling of spirits from domestic produce. Madison had asserted that he was against any excise in theory, as a most odious tax, but since additional money had to be raised and the majority of the people, or at least the majority of the House, was opposed to direct taxation, he thought that the excise on ardent spirits would be "the least exceptionable." Theodore Sedgwick, Massachusetts merchant and bitter critic of Shays' Rebellion, praised the duty in Congress as the best form of taxation. Import duties are already as high as practicable, he said. Direct taxes are the most unequal and oppressive, whether imposed on capital or income, because a man's ability to pay taxes should not be based on his capital, property, or income, but on that part of his income in excess of the necessary standard of living for persons of his "degree" in the community. Direct taxes would especially oppress the country areas because money is so scarce in those areas that the inhabitants could only pay the taxes by a great sacrifice of property. Finally, the scattered nature of the American population renders collection expensive.

But in western Pennsylvania the distillers refused to pay the tax. Almost all the politicians in the area were behind the opposition: Findley, the well-known leader of western Pennsylvania "agrarians" and member of the House of Representatives; Brackenridge; and Albert Gallatin, an impecunious, ambitious, but learned youth from Geneva, Switzerland, interested in land speculation.

Gallatin in a petition to Congress declared that the excise was unequal and immoral: It would tend to heavy duties on everything we
consume and the obnoxious inspection of a host of officers. Because
of the distance of a permanent market, we are "distillers through
necessity, not choice, that we may comprehend the greatest value in
the smallest size and weight." Another circumstance rendering the
duty ruinous is the scarcity of cash to pay it.[21]

More effective than petitions was the sentence of excommunication
passed on those men "lost to virtue" by accepting the post of collectors of the duty. By 1794 violence led the federal government to
dispatch troops. The leaders outdid one another in attempting to
prove to the authorities that they had been the unwilling victims of
the mob or had attempted to prevent violence by joining with them.[22]
Coxe, who had been appointed commissioner of revenue, proposed
as a remedy a Pennsylvania Society of Useful Manufactures, modeled
on the Hamilton–Coxe New Jersey scheme, placed on the route of
Robert Morris's canal projects and connected with Philadelphia by
a good road.[23]

In the meantime the whole Hamiltonian program had created great
controversies among the respectable citizens. Madison began to have
doubts as to the wisdom of those policies which he had strenuously
advocated.

Madison, reversing his earlier opinion, created a furore by favoring
Pelatiah Webster's proposal for discrimination between original holders and speculators. For once Madison and his teacher, Witherspoon,
disagreed. Discrimination, wrote Witherspoon, "is totally subversive
of public credit. Such a thing registered and believed on the exchange
of London, would bring the whole [British] national debt to the
ground, in two hours." [24] Noah Webster changed the other way, too,
and went back to the arguments that Pelatiah Webster had fought.[25]

But Rush claimed that non-discrimination would create an aristocracy. "It will change the property of nine-tenths of the freeholders . . . and it will be a lasting monument of the superiority of idleness, speculation and fraud" over "industry, economy and integrity
in obtaining wealth." But the real cause is the ignorant mass. "The
funding measure clearly establishes this proposition, that revolutions
like party spirit, are the rage of many, for the benefit of a few." [26]

On the bank, Madison argued in Congress in 1791 that the Constitution did not empower Congress to grant charters of incorporation. Adam Smith, one of the "most enlightened patrons of banks," ad-

mitted that banks banish specie. True, the money is exchanged "for something equally valuable," but under the present habits of the country the returns would not be of "permanent" use. Furthermore, the people would be exposed to the evil of runs. Besides, the government ought to have a share of the profits. Finally, its presumed advantages might better be obtained by several banks properly distributed.

Pelatiah Webster also had to modify some former assertions. In an open letter to fellow stockholders he expressed indignation that the president of the Bank of North America should be publicly promoting subscriptions at the bank quarters for a rival which will "monopolize all the favors of government." The chartering of the new bank infringes on the rights of the old bank under the Congress charter by reducing the latter's profits and advantages.

All the uses of a bank for negotiating, circulating, and supplying the revenues of the country can be furnished more safely by the old bank along with the various state-chartered banks than by the new bank controlled by a few irresponsible speculators of sudden overgrown wealth.

The Bank of North America is far safer than the new bank. Its capital is composed of specie, while that of the new bank is primarily composed of an explosive public debt that must constantly fluctuate in value and be useless in times of national emergency. But the immense stock of the new bank will constitute an addition to current cash that will be more than the country's business requires. The result would be the evils of inflation—speculation, luxury, idleness, and finally the destruction of industry.

Its branches are a further source of weakness, Pelatiah Webster continued, because it is impossible to operate such a divided system spread over fifteen hundred miles with the uniformity, prudence, and integrity required of a complex institution like a bank. The principal shareholders will be the great speculators in the public debt. The nation's wealth will be monopolized in a few hands, and the liberties of all abridged for the benefit of the few. Since the institution is the tool of a junto and merely an aspect of the design of the managers of the general government to absorb all the wealth of the nation, they will have a thousand ways to get any spurious issues of their brains legitimated and funded under the sanction of the law.

The bank, finally, is an attack on the sovereignty of the states. Under our Constitution, the federal government is rightly allowed to handle only such matters concerning the general welfare which the states are not competent to manage. But we should have some check on it, more accurately to keep its managers within the legal bounds of their powers; for unchecked power will always be misused. Witness that, if there is only one tailor, shoemaker, or tavern-keeper in a district, his "demands will be excessive" and his "deportment haughty."

The great check on the general government and its agents is the state governments; but if the state governments, by the establishment of the bank, are restrained in their financial resources and their means of self-defense and improvement, they will soon lose their influence and be like lions without teeth.[27]

Coxe, on the other hand, defended the bank and argued that branches are a good thing because they prevent the accumulation of excessive banking capital in one place.[28]

GEORGE LOGAN: PHYSIOCRATIC SPOKESMAN FOR COMMERCE

Marking a clean sweep of all the administration measures was the Quaker doctor, George Logan (1753-1821). Logan was the grandson of the great James Logan and inheritor of the large Logan estates and investments both in Philadelphia and the country. He had received a thorough training in commerce as an apprentice to a merchant, but he preferred medicine as an active occupation and received a medical degree from the University of Edinburgh in 1779. He visited the Continent and came back to the United States in 1780 especially impressed with the works of Adam Smith and the Physiocrats. In the best traditions of a gentleman farmer, he devoted much of his time to agricultural experiments.[29]

In the current political struggle his "zeal, influence, and large inherited property," wrote the historian Hildreth, "contributed not a little to carry Philadelphia over to the opposition" against Hamilton and in favor of Jefferson.[30] His influential pamphlets, signed "An American Farmer," were addressed to the "yeomanry." Logan called on the country to observe the wisdom of equal rights proclaimed by the revolutionary French National Assembly, "the heaven born French philanthropy" in general philosophy, and the Physiocrats in political economy; but his philosophy and economics were more native than French, and he spoke in the spirit of Pelatiah Webster for the most part.

"We are indebted," he said, to a few enlightened Frenchmen "for the importance of political economy." This science is simple and certain. Its immutable principles cannot be frustrated or diverted by the false opinions of speculative men. Political economy means that natural order appointed by the Creator which gives security to men, and makes the "proportion of every man's happiness . . . depend upon his benevolence and service to others." It teaches that a nation can only acquire great riches and power by dependence on "the physical order of cultivation."

He followed Franklin's formulation rather closely in laying down the axiomatic truths: Cultivating the land is the only productive employment, for it alone furnishes a surplus above the expense of subsistence. This surplus varies according to the ability or independent situation of the farmer in regard to his investment in equipment and the like, for agriculture requires great expense of money or "moveable expenses" to make it productive. It is the net produce of such property, together with a very small part naturally arising from fertile soil, that constitutes the nation's real wealth and the source of its revenue. The proportion of produce is generally in proportion to the expense of investment.

Farming is unprofitable because, lacking sufficient funds, farms are too small. Large farms, not small ones, have superiority of management and improvement because the possessors of large estates have the independency, "conversation," and ready information to think and act without prejudice. But would-be farmers should not be discouraged by the large investment needed, for their produce will be in proportion to the expense. The interest of all classes is to make the quantity of produce the largest possible; for the lower the price, the greater the portion necessary to pay the expense of production. But this requires a perfect freedom of property and commerce.

In the natural order of political economy, Logan continued, the duties and rights of persons are equal. The right corresponding to our duty to satisfy our wants is the full liberty of our persons and property. Our rights over other species of property arise from the labor we have bestowed in acquiring them or from the bounty of others. This property can be alienated because its existence does not depend on the life of the original proprietors.

The first right derived from nature is full liberty of our faculties and the enjoyment of all property arising from their use. Our sensations drive us to pursue such advantages, to seek pleasure and avoid pain, to support our existence and satisfy our wants by means of productions we can only acquire by the full employment of our labor.

When the natural inequality of riches arises, a sovereign power is created, either by tacit consent or expressed convention, to protect all in their use of property. Government's only object is the protection of the "sacred law of property."

This right of property is absolute and without limit. The holder may use or destroy it at his pleasure without being accountable to any human being. "Should you desire to cut down a tree which you planted, should you wish to consume or even destroy the produce of your farms, what right has government to interfere to prevent you?" Civil law may interfere to compel the execution of contract, but it should not regulate the conditions or limit the price, for the industrious man will be discouraged from increasing his fortune by the most productions for his and the country's good. Free circulation produces the just value for every commodity. A fair competition occurs, for the price is regulated by plenty or scarcity, by causes "purely natural." Perfect free trade will always insure the farmer "the highest prices by bringing numerous purchasers to his door."

This happy natural order of perfect freedom is inverted by arbitrary commercial regulations. The farmers and merchants, no longer obliged to submit to the common law of competition, treat each other as enemies. Thus, for instance, the Navigation Acts, by excluding foreign shipping, give the merchants a legal monopoly and destroy a "just competition for the produce of your farms."

The history of civil society does not furnish an example of legislators interfering with and directing the occupation of its citizens except injuriously. Solon, to ingratiate himself with the "licentious Athenian citizens," ordered that husbandmen should sell their produce only to Athenians; but the result was the oppression of husbandry, the decline of agriculture, and high prices for food. On the other hand, Holland, by free commerce, not only got sufficient food for herself at all times, but also during the late convulsion in France was able to relieve the distress of the French through corn supplied by the banking house of Hope at Amsterdam.

Indirect taxes, whether excise or tariff duty, are vicious. Not being limited to a definite amount of the net produce, they may consume the entire gross produce of the farmers, out of which they are inevitably paid, by a rise in prices. In the last analysis the great evil is that they raise the price of labor and thus damage our industry. England's heavy duties would have long ago destroyed her foreign markets except for her great investment and the perfection of her manufacturing machinery.

On the other hand, if "moveable property," the real source of wealth, is taxed, men will not devote themselves to making improvements in agriculture and manufactures.

A public debt is a serious evil, in part because it gives rise to the extensive use of indirect taxes. The funded debt does not constitute an addition to capital, as its proponents claim, for the moment the first creditor advanced the money to the government a certain portion of annual produce was turned from serving as capital to serving as revenue, from maintaining productive labor to maintaining unproductive labor, as Adam Smith argued. When a revenue is raised annually from free and unmortgaged expense, the accumulation of new capital is, of course, hindered. But a loan causes the destruction of actually existing capital.

Funding and the bank paper increase the quantity of property in "idea," not in reality, to the damage of a nation's trade and manufactures and the loss of the valuable specie. Worst of all, having mortgaged its revenue and in large part to foreigners, the state will be at a considerable disadvantage when faced with internal difficulties or foreign negotiations in times of war or other international maneuvers. Has not the French monarchy fallen because of inability to meet its debts?

Finally, Logan argued, the incorporation of the New Jersey Society for Useful Manufactures tends to aristocracy by destroying the livelihood of thousands of mechanics and farmers to increase the gains of a few wealthy.

Inequality of wealth is inevitable because property alone can stimulate to labor, but excessive inequality is the great malady of civil society. In all countries the wealthy will necessarily administer government, for they alone have the skill and leisure for this function; but, as the French National Assembly and Burke have declared, laws should not fortify these conspiracies against the general interest by allowing exclusive corporations, whether of artisans or of the wealthy.

The grant of vast and exclusive privileges for manufactures to a few wealthy men will ruin thousands of useful citizens engaged in infant manufactures, and the result will be, as in England, starving, dependent manufacturers on the one hand, and on the other hand the principals living in indolence and luxury.[31] Worst of all, it leads "to the profligacy of manners" among workmen concentrated in large manufacturing establishments.[32]

"Freeman," who may have been Coxe, answered Logan. The United States has nothing to learn from France on freedom, for the French revolutionary leaders, like Lafayette, were first the pupils of America and then the distinguished champions of French and European liberty. France has everything that "Farmer" dislikes in America: navigation acts, excise and duties, a funding system and bank. Besides, he had never heard "Farmer" attack the Bank of North America.[33] This was a neat way of recalling that Logan in the bitter struggle in the Pennsylvania Assembly in 1786 over restoring the charter of the Bank of North America, had testified that "as a farmer he had experienced the good consequences" of the bank, and he had ardently defended it on the familiar constitutional and economic arguments.[34] Thus Logan's general position was not unlike that of Pelatiah Webster.

James Sullivan, the Attorney General of Massachusetts, at the very same time that he was acquiring exclusive charters for canal and bridge companies, also ostensibly attacked the stock jobbers and speculators in connection with the national measures, but in a manner that illustrated how apparent opposition was in reality effective support of these measures and of even more speculative operations. He delivered his views in a treatise deprecating man's excessive desire for riches.

Except for conquest, he wrote in *The Path to Riches* in 1792, commerce is the only way to acquire great estates. Successful commerce requires money as a medium of exchange. The real money is specie, but difficulties in transporting metal from country to country have given rise to bills of exchange and other forms of paper as the representatives of real money. These instruments have their value from being payable on demand or with interest if payable at a future date.

The Bank of England is the pivot of English prosperity, for its notes are payable on demand in specie. The Bank of the United States is formed on this principle, and the honor and safety of the nation depend upon it.

But whereas England, to safeguard the Bank, restrains and regulates even private banks, in the United States the states compete with one another in establishing private bank companies for the benefit of the few. If this continues, bank bills will suffer the fate of the "continentals," and the Bank of the United States may be rendered insecure and useless.

This vicious spirit of the individual states for banks arises from the nature of free and popular government; for the ruling powers being dependent by frequent elections on the will of the people and the people being liable to be influenced by party interests, many pernicious measures are passed.

Greatest of sinners is the exclusive Massachusetts Bank, owned by a few families with its notes acceptable for taxes due the state. By virtue of its unlimited power to issue paper, it controls trade and prices, both of public securities and goods, so as to obtain all the advantages and the exorbitant profits of the greatest monopoly. Trade has been perplexed by an unsteady medium. The bank's rigid insistence that payment of loans be made punctually has forced debtors to sell at a loss great quantities of property, especially of public securities. But the bank itself could not be punctual if a run occurred.

The bank charter should be repealed, for the state constitution expressly forbids granting exclusive privileges to any men or body of men. The charter violates the doctrine of equal rights. It is not like an incorporation to build a bridge or cut a canal, because in the first case the government grants a property in a river which is owned by the state, and in the last it "is only a grant of power to use the property and soil which they have bought or may buy of others." The state should charter a new bank in which all the members of the state should be interested and thus accord with the doctrine of equal rights.

Paper banks are an evil, he said, but they are necessary. In the first place, the public taste demands a bank, and "we must take mankind as they are." Secondly, the commonwealth as a sovereign state should have resources independent of any other government. Should the state in case of an insurrection or any adventitious distress be forced to anticipate taxes by a loan, a state bank would prove a savior.

The new bank should be chartered for fifty years and have a capital of $1,000,000 in ten thousand transferable shares. The state should supply half and could raise its share by a direct tax on polls and estates. No shareholder should have more than five votes. The state is to guarantee the credits of the bank and accept its notes for public duties. No other bank or corporation for banking is to be allowed, nor are a number of persons to associate for the purpose of banking.

Loans to farmers by the bank will be inadmissible. This has never been tried in any country except for the establishment of the "monstrous" Massachusetts land bank in 1740. Every loan to farmers is of no advantage to them. In the first place, new land purchased at a low price and rising in value through improvement and near-by settlement may yield 6 per cent; but not old land. Secondly, easy loans will lure the farmer into ruinous extravagances. Finally, the limiting of bank companies will prevent an excessive amount of capital being devoted to banking companies. Consequently this excess in the hand of private individuals can be lent to farmers.

Should the Massachusetts Bank not be abolished, it would still be a good policy to establish the new bank to act as a check on it. The branch of the Bank of the United States is no check, for it is controlled by much the same people who control the state bank.

At the same time merchants of Alexandria, after failing to obtain a branch of the Bank of the United States, successfully petitioned the Virginia legislature in 1792 for the first Virginia bank. They naturally tied up the project with the Potomac Canal scheme. By virtue of their banks, Baltimore and Philadelphia are draining almost all the trade of the fertile and extensive back country of this state and also of Maryland and of all the western country which nature intended should be carried on through the channel of the Potomac and James Rivers. Thus the wealth which ought to center in this state is diverted from its natural course and enriches the neighboring states. If the bank is not established, large sums of money will necessarily be expended by the merchants of Alexandria and the neighboring towns in negotiations at the Baltimore bank, which are most convenient. Consequently this part of Virginia will be impoverished.[35]

Washington naturally became a stockholder, but he left most of his stock to found a free school.

But John Taylor of Virginia (1750–1824), a Jeffersonian, opposed, at least formally, all banks as well as the other aspects of Hamilton's program. Taylor had the benefit of an education at William and Mary. Except for short periods in the Senate, he spent his time on his extensive Virginia plantation with its many slaves, engaged, like Logan, in writing on improvements in farming and attacking the Hamiltonian program in general as creating a new aristocracy from paupers.

But in detail his arguments were directed against the bank as the source of all the other evils. This ostensible "agrarian" likewise used for the most part the type of argument presented by Pelatiah Webster.

The accumulation of honest industry is seldom dangerous, and Providence shows its displeasure of both excessive or fraudulently obtained wealth by "raising up an extravagant heir to dissipate such wealth." But just as the old legal aristocracy attempted to counteract the natural effect by "artificial regulation" and perpetuities, so the new moneyed aristocracy does the same thing in the form of perpetual public debts and a national bank and other corporations with exclusive privileges that violate in effect the doctrine of division of intestate estates.

The public-debt measure, however, is irrevocably passed. Though it is compounded of materials originally honest and consisting even now in great part of such materials, it is probably impossible to unravel and remedy the intermediate frauds. The public debt would not have been dangerous if the commercial, mechanical, and professional interests—that is, the useful interest—had been publicly cautioned by the government to hold their public paper for the rise; the public debt, like other property, would have remained considerably dispersed. But the royal ministry (the administration) wanted to erect an enormous aristocracy or moneyed interest.

The national bank as well as the state banks of issue reap their enormous profit by defrauding the industrious, especially the mercantile interest; for the notes represent merely an idea, not substance, and they yield tremendous gains by forcing the export of specie and substituting its notes as the circulating medium. The propertied class become tenants, at the mercy of the monopolistic banks, and the gains become a perpetual rent charge on the product of the industrious. The calamities of the war resulting from the banishing of specie by paper are at least as great as those produced by the sword.

Bank debts are different from private loans. The latter must consist of money or money's worth. They are limited within reasonable bounds because they are founded on real wealth which cannot be even doubted by impressing hieroglyphics on paper. The former, based on "idea" not substance, may be infinitely multiplied by a printing press so long as the notes can pay £6 for every £100 of "idea" emitted.

By banking, labor is forced to pay an interest on the essential life-giving circulating medium, whereas if only specie circulates, "the medium in passing among the rich, often lies in the pocket of the aristocracy without gaining an interest."

Of course, specie, like paper, is only a representative of real wealth; but, unlike paper, it is an equivalent because it can transfer real wealth to us from a foreign nation. If capital is to be raised at public expense, it is best for commerce that the capital be bestowed on agriculture and manufactures for improvement because these alone create the real fund for exciting commerce for exports. Since the bank's dividends are not coextensive with their enormous profit, the people lose the chance of having all payments thrown back into circulation by the extravagance or luxury of individuals.

The trouble is that the power of legislation has been transferred from the natural interest of the country to an artificial interest. The natural interest includes whatever may subsist without the direct aid of municipal law, such as agriculture, commerce, manufactures, and art. An artificial interest is whatever is immediately created by law, such as public debt, public offices, and incorporated banks. The domination of the natural interest by the artificial interest is in the essence of slavery. The income of the natural interest is derived from industry; the income of the other by legally created monopolies and privileges.

Such paper acquisitions are "political" property rather than "natural" property, like land, which cannot be increased by law, and it is permanent in value. More broadly, the indefinite expansibility of paper property through legislative enactment must destroy liberty and the acquisitions of the industrious, for power follows property.

The holders of paper, however, are justly entitled to a return. But through its vast influence the stock-jobbing party in the legislature can in effect violate both the right of the majority—that is, of numbers—and also the right of property—that is, real property. The five million of the natural interest are oppressed by the five thousand of the artificial interest.

The machinations of the "paper" influence in government is best seen in the treaties with the Creek and Cherokee Indians in 1790 and 1791. These treaties dismembered states and annulled the rights of the citizens by ceding to the savages land that really belonged to Georgia and North Carolina. To consummate the system, all that is needed is to relinquish the right of pre-emption to the Indians beyond the Ohio so that the Indians and British can prevent the growth of republicanism in that quarter.

The dangers and difficulties with which our frontiers are extended generate an intrepid republican spirit in the frontiersmen, Taylor wrote. So a paper aristocracy forever attempts to obstruct mankind in the pursuit of competency and happiness by compressing people within the locality covered by its devices.

Instead of encroaching on the barbarians, we suffer them to encroach on us by treaties that supply them with arms and clothes wrung from the people by taxes. These treaty makers forget that a violation of charters and the endeavor to prevent population were two of the indictments against the Crown.

The working of the corrupt paper influence is also shown in its opposition to a republican navigation policy. A truly liberal policy for emancipating the nation from dependence on foreign nations is by simultaneously securing the regular exportation of the bulky commodities of the South and encouraging the shipping of the North. But the stock-jobbing paper interest fears that reduced import duties would jeopardize the value of their holdings of paper.

The effective check lies in the state legislatures' electing republican senators. As a sort of afterthought, he concluded that if two or three of the larger states should forbid the circulation of bank notes, they would acquire the Union's specie. Other states would be so distressed that they would take similar action. The United States, as a member of the commercial world, would then speedily occupy a "familiar pre-eminent status, for specie will ever flow where it can find employment." [36]

A great battle began again in Congress in 1794 over Madison's famous resolutions to have discriminatory duties imposed on the ships and goods of nations without a commercial treaty with the United States. This, as all understood, was aimed at Great Britain in order to force her to lift restraints on American commerce and goods. Madison repeated his familiar argument about free trade and the exceptions, but, he added, the discrimination would develop valuable trade with republican France, for this trade would yield specie whereas the trade that England allows us is losing trade because it loses us specie.

John Nicholas of Virginia went into a most elaborate analysis to show the benefit of such trade by questioning the beneficence of "free trade." It is not always true, said Nicholas, that the commodity purchased for the least money is the best bargain. The means of payment must always be considered. If a man will accept an article in exchange that others will not buy, it would be profitable to deal with him even though his prices are higher than others. So it would be wise even at an immediate loss to deal with countries that can become great consumers of American produce on terms of reciprocal consumption, if we have difficulty in selling that produce. Thus, if French manufactures were granted a preference, French agriculturalists would be drawn into workshops and a market would be opened for American produce. At the same time, by making French manufacture dependent on American agriculture, France might be forced to end some of her foolish practices that at present greatly depreciate American commodities—namely, the use of public granaries to supply food in times of scarcity. This "destroys the competition that raises everything to its just value."

The aristocratic Ames admitted that the measures were originally demanded in the days of the Confederacy by almost everyone, and he might have included himself at the time of Shays' Rebellion; but "a sober judgment on the tendency and reasonableness of the intermeddling of government often does, and probably ought still oftener to change our impressions." So he attacked the resolutions and declared: The theory of balance of trade is among "the exploded dogmas . . . refuted by the maxims of science and the authority of time." We follow experience too little and visions of theorists too much. In trade as in other matters we have too many laws. We should leave the management of trade to merchants. They will find the best markets for the nation sooner than legislators can. The great amount of British shipping in American trade does not arise from her restrictions on our trade, but from causes connected with the natural competition of capital and industry, from a lower rate of interest and seamen's wages.

The great object of the contest to force England to throw open the British West Indies trade to American carriers would endanger our far more valuable trade with England. The repeal of England's Navigation Acts, which are cherished as the palladium of her safety, which time has rendered venerable and prosperity endeared to her people, "is not to be extorted from her fears of a weaker nation."

A commercial treaty with Great Britain was successfully negotiated by John Jay in 1794, but the Jeffersonians, led by Madison, heartily denounced it as a betrayal of our commercial and financial interests and of our alliance with France. Administration supporters seem to have been privately agreed that it was a poor treaty, though better than nothing.

The Boston town meeting declared that no article was honorable to the United States. Ames in a private letter was indignant at the "blindness and gullibility of the rich men, who had suffered themselves to be made tools of" at this meeting by the opposition leaders.[37] But in Congress he asserted in 1796 that the people want the treaty, that the merchants almost unanimously support it. "Their sense is not so liable to be mistaken as that of a nation."

The election campaign of 1796 between Jefferson and John Adams as respective heads of the Republican and Federalist parties started the fires of political controversy, but there appears to have been little difference, once the polemics were stripped away, between the candidates on social philosophy or broad economic objectives. The polemic controversy reached a point where Adams was charged by some of the Jeffersonian opposition with being an enemy of Hamilton's policies.

Ostensibly on this ground, Coxe, though in the Administration, supported Jefferson rather than Adams for the presidency. He wrote anonymous articles signed "The Federalist" in the Federalist organ, the *Gazette of the United States*, which in a "revised" form were distributed among the public as a pamphlet, *The Federalist: Containing Some Strictures Upon a Pamphlet, Entitled, "The Pretensions of Thomas Jefferson to the Presidency, examined, and the Charges against John Adams, refuted."*

Coxe declared that the Bank of the United States is necessary, that no civilized nation can avoid the excise mode of revenue, that the funding of public debts which cannot be paid off when due "is as much a matter of justice and prudence" as giving a common bond for private debt and recovering it by mortgage. But Adams's disapproval of the funding and banking systems threatens disaster.

Jefferson's "ablest and most influential friends" in the House and Senate, said Coxe, rightly voted in favor of the excise. Likewise Jefferson's friends supported the most important act of Congress for the efficiency of government—namely, that which allows the president to remove the officers of the executive government at his own discretion. By strengthening our elective chief, they felt, we diminish the plea for making him hereditary, which is central in Adams's thinking.

The more responsible Gallatin presented a "critical" study of the finances of the United States that was rather convincing of the "soundness" of the Jeffersonian party's financial expert. His approach to Administration policies was not so much in terms of the rhetoric of opposition to "overgrown wealth" and the "corrupt squadron," but rather in terms of the greater success that might have attended the policies had it paid more attention to balancing the budget instead of increasing the debt. He did not object to funding but thought that it might have been done with greater benefit both to the creditors and the government through less careless methods. He objected formally to a public debt, or more accurately to its unnecessary increase, on the traditional ground that a large debt is an index of insolvency and thus offers an invitation to other countries to treat us unfairly in commerce. No expenditure, not even for a navy, would give us the external security and respectability that paying the debt as rapidly as possible would, for we would have our resources free of charge. However, its repayment must be gradual because the heavy taxes required for immediate repayment would entail a reduction of the capital of individuals, and this would be aggravated by loss of the use of the foreign capital repaid.

The funding measures have the support of public opinion as well as the majority, as evidenced by the debt's rapidly appreciating when the measures were announced. After being funded, the great objective was rightly to raise the price of the stock to the nominal value as quickly as possible to circumvent foreign speculators. This was quickly reached through establishing the sinking fund and the bank. In any event, refusal to pay the debt would be a "flagrant and pernicious breach of public faith and national morality."

The bank is beneficial in other respects. Its financial accommodations to government are necessary. Like all other banks, it is of great commercial utility by bringing into circulation otherwise inactive moneys and especially by increasing the rapidity of circulation.

Aside from taxes, the public lands offer a great resource for paying the debt. Congress provides for their sale both in small and large tracts at a minimum price of two dollars, payable one-half down and the remainder in a year. But actual settlers will be unable to buy because of the too-short credit, and the speculators requiring the usual profit in buying land to sell again to settlers will be excluded because of the minimum price.

So Gallatin proposed that the land be divided into lots of 900,000 acres each, then opened to sale successively beginning with the most valuable. Each purchaser was to subscribe for a tract of at least 640 acres in the lot at $2.00 per acre payable in cash or public debt certificates in ten annual installments at 3 per cent interest, but with liberty to discharge the debt at $1.50 an acre in specie at any time. The public would, of course, gain in the gradual extinguishing of the debt. Subscribers would make enormous gains without any labor on their part except to sell the land to actual settlers, as the price of land increases from the natural increase in population.

But land sales will not provide completely for the public debt or for current expenses. Taxes must still be used. Import duties are preferable to excises on manufactures because of ease of collection. The most extensive manufactures are carried on by a large number of persons, many of whom, "from their situation in life," would be unable to understand the complex regulations of revenue laws and consequently be "oppressed by subaltern officers." Furthermore, taxes from manufactures are very limited because manufacturers lack capital to pay it and the income drawn from manufactures is as yet inconsiderable.

Little is reaped from the excise on whisky distilled from native produce. The defect in the whisky excise might be remedied by a license fee on stills according to capacity, which is now only optional. This would not only cut expenses of collection and prevent evasion of the duty, but also free distillers from vexatious, inconvenient, but necessary inquisitions, and from "keeping correct books and accounts." It might be objected that such a scheme would fall more heavily on small stills, for the latter are generally owned by men of less capital and used in less advantageous situations. But reducing the immense number of distillers and leaving the field to large distillers would favor national wealth and morals. "The same quantity of labour produces perhaps a double quantity of spirits in large than in small distilleries," and "though the latter may sometimes fall under the favorable denomination of manufactures" this is overbalanced by their becoming nothing but tippling houses.

But import duties are as heavy now as they can be without causing smuggling, and the growth of the country will not yield from this source the increased revenue required. This type of taxation has been carried as far as prudence admits. Every increase of population diminishes the relative quantity of land and promotes manufactures. Consequently relative to population our exports of raw materials, our imports of manufactures, and the revenue raised on them will be reduced.

The only other substantial source of revenue is a direct tax. This tax is laid on property in proportion to either its capital value or its income. The general rule is that land and houses are the only proper object of direct taxation; other species of property must be reached through taxes on consumption by way of import duties. In England direct taxes fall exclusively on lands and houses and have never given any just cause of complaint. The tax is easier to collect on real than on personal property. Where the direct tax is laid rather upon the person's revenue, his profits and not his capital, the most odious excise would be less oppressive and unequal.[38]

The victory of Adams by no means ended controversy. The conflict over what constituted profitable commerce had yet to be settled. James Bowdoin in 1797 supported Jefferson but had his own variant of Jeffersonian tenets. He sought protection for "native" merchants against the "alien" British and their agents. Although he possessed large amounts of the funded public debt as well as land, he made the customary denunciations of the funding and bank schemes as a paper-money system. This raises the price of labor and other necessaries, he said, and thus of course discourages our manufactures. The Jay Treaty surrenders the true principle of commerce as defined by the doctrine of the balance of trade.

If the people are fully employed, if the several professions and callings find ready vent for their labor, a favorable balance of trade is indicated. True, Hume, he said, has attacked the doctrine of the balance of trade on the ground that the precious metals are only merchandise; that if a country loses the greater part of the circulating medium the remainder still is a means of transferring property at a proportionally lower price, and consequently if a nation only attend to its industry, trade will balance itself. That "excellent writer," Adam Smith, concurs with Hume in some points. But, while Hume may be right in the abstract, every nation is rightly apprehensive of the depreciating of the value of property in relation to specie, for such changes produce injustice and disorder. Was not the decline in the value of property due to the balance of debt to England, and export of specie, the cause of the suspension of public and private credit and disaffection of government in Massachusetts in 1786? Had the old situation continued, English commerce would in a few years have absorbed most of the country's personal property.

Attempting to liquidate the unfavorable balance with one country by favorable balance with another is too precarious, for the latter country will take action as soon as it appreciates the situation.

Since the profits of labor generally center in commerce, it follows that American merchants are the great source of the nation's wealth and strength. They are the nation's rich citizens and as such supply the best outlet for a nation's productions. They not only maintain the poor; but also drive them to improvement in arts and manufactures to supply the tastes of the rich. But by allowing alien resident merchants the same right as natives the nation must be beggared because these aliens will spend the profit of labor abroad. He pointed to the English and Scotch merchants engrossing the commerce of the southern states and returning to their native land to spend their wealth.

Therefore let the Navigation Act be strengthened, Bowdoin pleaded, and along these lines naturalization should be surrounded by heavy barriers as in England. Of course, domestic manufactures ought to be protected, but this should be done effectively by prohibitions, not by laying duties for the sake of revenue. Government should stand neuter between its commerce and revenue and not suffer the interest of the latter to encroach on the rights of the former. Do not levy duties on goods handled by American merchants.[39]

Complicating matters for all parties were the antics of promoter economists like James Swan. After taking up arms to help suppress Shays' Rebellion, he found that "the wickedness and relaxed state of government" were turning his numerous and great speculative ventures into a mass of unpayable debts and sending him to bankruptcy. So he went to France in 1788 to promote schemes for Franco-American commerce that would benefit both nations and himself. He would only deal, he said, with people of the first rank, for this accorded with the position which he had at home, and "which I shall have again after my return disencumbered from the shackles and perplexities of deranged business and a want of money." He was ever ready to put the principles of his *National Arithmetick* at the service of whatever government happened to be in power, whether the monarchy or the successive revolutionary governments, Robespierre or Napoleon. His variegated operations ran from speculation in the American debt and plans to convert the debt owed France, to commercial speculations and operations in the narrow sense.

To Robespierre's *Commission des Subsistences*, which controlled foreign trade, he presented a series of memoranda detailing how France could effectively obtain supplies from abroad. France needs foodstuffs and materials from the United States and other neutral countries, said Swan. Though she lacks specie and her credit is poor, France can pay by exporting non-essential luxury goods from the former mansions of royalty. Silk taffetas, though scorned by French republicans, might be sold in America, along with wines, brandies, and silk stockings. But if the merchants are to be encouraged in this trade, the government should fix the prices in advance and as high as possible. By thus avoiding the mistakes of appealing to the merchant's patriotism, "you are sure to get everything you need, even from the inhabitants of the enemy's country."

Claiming extensive connections for his firm in Spain, Hamburg, and London, as well as agencies with numerous American captains, he declared that he knew all the ways of "neutralizing" cargoes to avoid seizure by the British. The government thought sufficiently well of his talents to give him, along with other ex-American Revolutionary War officers, a good deal of contract business.

Under the conservative government which followed Robespierre's fall in 1794, Swan's firm was made one of the four to which all foreign business was designated. It was given the agency of obtaining supplies in the North American region with money advanced by the French government. The American minister to France, the Jeffersonian James Monroe, warned Madison and others that he had discovered that Swan was a "corrupt, unprincipled rascal" whose only interest was to monopolize trade by any sort of double dealing, but Swan knew how to maneuver the interrelated worlds of trade and politics.

With his headquarters in the United States, he evolved an elaborate, far-flung organization for eluding the British. He had an attorney in London to handle seizure by the British, a Danish correspondent to handle the insurance, and the French end was handled by John Higginson, Paris merchant and son of a leading Boston Federalist. He even converted the American debt due France into a liquid asset by having the American government exchange it for American domestic bonds, a good share of which was sold to France's enemies, the British.

Since the "British pay well" in the way of gratuities and subsidies to newspapers to present their case, he suggested that the French do likewise. He even wrote articles for the press, as was customary with both sides, especially at the time of the agitation over the Jay Treaty.

After the treaty was ratified, Swan advised the French government that France should demand from the United States a renunciation of the treaty, an alliance with France, and a huge loan. Until the American government consents to these terms France should suspend all negotiations regarding losses and seizure of cargoes by French ships or the government. Finally, the French government should remember that members of the American government are avid for money. Just "give the means to the minister and he will be able to do what you wish." These, he said, are "the observations of a man who knows his country and who is a friend of both nations." [40]

In 1798 the French Directory followed some of Swan's suggestions in its demands on the American government; Adams's Administration answered with an unofficial naval war. The contending political parties naturally utilized economic arguments that would suit their purposes, even if they constituted a temporary reversal of former theoretical positions. Thus Noah Webster, who was something of a journalist hack for the Federalists, had ardently defended every feature of the Jay Treaty but now he found that free commerce justified the naval action. Our citizens, he wrote, have imbibed a love and a spirit of commerce. Their habits are commercial, and no speculative advantages will induce them to renounce their opinions or alter their habits. Therefore it is impossible to remove protection from commerce.[41]

In the midst of the difficulties Logan lived up to his high pacifist Quaker role by going to France as a private citizen to attempt to bring about an understanding. He informed the Directory that if it recognized the true principles of commerce harmony would be restored between the republics. Since France is not a "mercantile nation, but more attached to the manly pursuit of agriculture," her interest is to place the neutral flag on the most respectable footing. The resulting competition in her ports would be to her advantage in the exchange of the surplus of her agriculture and manufactures for that of foreign countries. Since no people can so well assure these advantages to France as American citizens, "the commerce of the United States in a peculiar manner demands her protection."

Instead of being complimented for his peace efforts, Logan was denounced by the Administration and Federalist press. The Federalist Congress, which had already passed the notorious Alien and Sedition Acts, enacted the "Logan" law in January 1799. This law provided in effect that no citizen shall, without government permis-

sion, carry on any correspondence, verbal or written, with the officers of a foreign government. Logan asserted in his defense that, if
arrangements were not speedily made with France, negotiators from·
the northern European neutral powers would obtain advantages
whereby their countries might become the carriers of even American produce.[42]

But the cessation of actual hostilities came quickly enough as the
representatives of both nations satisfied each other's principles of
etiquette and got down to the advantages of commerce.

With England's restrictions remaining a sore spot, with the Federalists divided among themselves but agreed both in public and private that the people did not appreciate the principle of order, the
election of 1800 sent Jefferson to the White House, with Madison
and Gallatin respectively as Secretary of State and Secretary of the
Treasury.

Noah Webster complained later that the arch-Federalists had
ruined themselves by fighting the Adams Administration. Before
1798 the Federalists denounced every critic of the executive authority as a Jacobin and demagogue, but the moment President Adams
adopted measures that displeased "particular men," the Federalists
turned their animosity on the Administration. If one of their friends,
for the sake of consistency and the prevention of the ruin they faced,
called in question the propriety of their proceedings, "they fell upon
him like wild beasts, ready to tear him to pieces." [43]

Even in New England, if not the majority at least a goodly number of those who were generally termed men of "principle and
property," were in Jefferson's party as the men of commerce became
increasingly exasperated with English interferences with American
commerce. Of course the die-hard Federalists, including the New
England state-supported Congregational clergy, still denounced Jefferson as the vile opponent of religion and property, as an ardent
Democrat, solely relying on reason and speculation and believing
in the perfectibility of man. But Coxe and Barton, those two ardent
defenders of strong national government and "balanced economy,"
with emphasis on manufactures, were openly carrying the banner of
Jefferson.

Coxe, having been dismissed from office by President Adams, was
now emphatic that Adams went further than Jefferson in his dislike of the Bank of the United States. The bank, he was sure all good
Republicans believed, is the great moneyed organ of the country in

which "the blood of the body politic" is concentrated. The only serious objection is the preponderant amount of foreign holdings.[44]

Barton dedicated to Jefferson his *A Dissertation on the Freedom of Navigation* (1802), in which he said: Just because the United States is and will continue to be for ages an agricultural nation, foreign commerce must be an important branch of our trade. The surplus of our native productions, together with some articles of wrought materials, will be exchanged with the transmarine countries for those manufactures and other commodities our consumption requires. Thus the general interest requires that we have our own navigation, to which the government should grant "peculiar privileges." Furthermore, for the protection of "our maritime rights under the law of Nations," the government must insist on free commerce on the seas. Interference with this right leads to "the oppression of the many by the few—the poor by the rich."

Thus at the close of the eighteenth century the primacy of commerce asserted itself more forcefully than ever as the dominant strain in American economic thinking.

CHAPTER XIV

The Victorious Republicans

AS Thomas Jefferson took office and proclaimed a glorious revolution, the distinction between parties appeared to turn on nothing more substantial than the question of how many Federalist officeholders were to be removed. Noah Webster saw suddenly the wisdom of the new Administration's keeping in office opposition appointees and found precedent easily enough.[1]

Since Jefferson did not overthrow the bank and continued to meet the debt charges, he must be a hypocrite, the Federalist group felt at the end of his first term. Taylor answered that Jefferson had respected the national good faith and the "eternal mandates of justice." By eliminating the Hamiltonian measures, Jefferson could have lowered taxes and crushed the rising aristocracy, but he had gallantly refused to listen to "this spirit of unprincipled ambition," or "demoniacal revenge." [2]

At the same time the northern group of Federalists, protesting against the political supremacy of Virginia, called on the North to combine to protect the commercial interests against the vicious slave-holding democrats of the South. Because of the need to preserve slavery, every southern politician, be his party Federalist or Republican, must and will sacrifice every view to this interest. Every young man then will be educated in his duty to support this interest as the palladium of all that can render life desirable in that ardent and debilitating region. He will perceive nothing inconsistent in the democracy among masters and the despotism over the slaves. He will be a national republican and a local despot, using the terms liberty and equality as the custom of the country decrees.[3]

Commerce, as ever, gave rise to the most serious disputes. After Spain's secret cession of Louisiana to Napoleonic France in 1802, the Spanish authorities withdrew the right of deposit at New Orleans granted Americans by the treaty of 1795. A furore was, of course, raised not only by the Westerners, but also by the more influential eastern merchants involved in navigation and commerce with the area and adjoining foreign possessions. There was little question that France intended to obtain as much carrying trade to France as possible.

President Jefferson had his regular minister, Robert Livingston, plead the American cause for "freedom of commerce." He also used, in an unofficial way, his Physiocratic friend, Dupont de Nemours, who had just returned to France, ostensibly for a temporary visit to bring out an edition of the great Turgot's works. But French Physiocracy had always been a doctrine that had as its objectives the "freedom" of French commerce from restraint, just as Logan's Physiocracy had as its objective the freedom of American commerce. So Dupont informed the French authorities that the aim should be to favor French commerce.

New Orleans should be made a free port for France and Spain, "whose commerce shall enter and depart through the delta of the Mississippi," but "that of the United States shall only enter from above, and depart by the same embouchure of the river." Navigation shall be free throughout the whole course of the river on the condition that the United States shall exempt from all duties Spanish or French merchandise entering their territory by the Mississippi or Ohio. Thereby "we shall have conquered for the benefit of our manufactures, our silks, ironmongery, and glass of every description, and for the consumption of our wines, vinegar, oil, and dried fruits, all the commerce of the five states of the West, as well as of the new states, which in this country multiply so rapidly. The interior of America, from the Allegheny on the one side, to the . . . mountains beyond the lakes on the other, will only be populated and supplied by the means of the manufacturing industry, the agricultural prosperity and the commercial riches of France." English manufactures will be unable to compete because they would be forced to use the expensive land route and pay in addition duties from 12 to 15 per cent. In this way France's enemies will be hit at their most vulnerable point and the "good will of our friends will be advantageously confirmed." [4]

Livingston, in transmitting the copy he received from Dupont to Secretary of State Madison, naturally commented that the plan was impractical. The reasons, he informed Madison, "were too obvious to render it necessary to state them." Instead, Livingston suggested to the French that the area of New Orleans be made an independent state under the government of the three powers with a right of deposit to each, subject to an import duty of 1½ per cent in lieu of storage, wharfage, and other charges. France would gain from being the only manufacturing nation of the three. He explained to Madison that the advantages to "our American carrying trade (while it left our revenue untouched) are obvious." And, he added in an incidental fashion, in such a treaty "arrangements might be made extremely advantageous to the western people." Naturally, the "new nation must always feel its dependence on us, and of course respect our rights." [5]

There was hardly any disagreement that the country must have Louisiana and Florida eventually as parts of its natural empire. But spokesmen of the affected western peoples, along with the Administration, said they preferred first to seek the restoration of the rights of free commerce by negotiation. War, they held, was expensive, would increase the national debt and taxes, and subject American commerce everywhere to seizure. Besides, the western area would have to supply the troops, and the French and Spanish fleets could easily blockade the mouth of the Mississippi. "Peace and commerce" was the policy, and peace was only to be sacrificed if negotiations failed. While negotiations were going on between the contending Physiocrats, demands for immediate war were made.

Loudest were the eastern arch-Federalists and those who heretofore had thought the West was a threat to the commercial maritime East. Most outspoken was Gouverneur Morris, then a senator from New York. Morris, while in the Continental Congress, had expressed the opinion of his group that the West must eventually separate from the Union, and in the Constitutional Convention he had pictured the horrors that would befall the nation if the poverty-stricken western area joined the Union on equality with the eastern commercial states. But now Morris, with his customary skill, demanded that the President seize the territory first and then negotiate, for the sake of the western people and national honor. If France retains the affected area, he claimed, the flood of emigration to the fertile western regions must cease. The debts incurred in the hope of advantageous sales must remain unpaid, the debtor's distress must recoil on the creditor, and "from the common relations of society, become general."

War has advantages. "It calls forth the energies of character, it favors the manly virtues, it gives elevation to sentiment, it produces a national union, generates patriotic love and infuses a just sense of national honor. . . . Let the hour of trial . . . find us a band of brothers." At the same time the enslaved peoples of Europe will rise and overthrow Napoleon.

The equally fiery Ames added that the trouble is that our great wealth has made us avaricious and willing to take kicks.[6]

President Jefferson solved the problem, though with qualms over the constitutionality of his procedure, by purchasing the whole Louisiana Territory.

Immediately after the purchase, Gouverneur Morris, Ames, and their group were sure that the Administration was seeking to destroy the republic and establish an imperial dynasty. Talleyrand is close to the truth in saying that we "are phlegmatic, and without passion except that for money getting," declared Ames. Paying such a huge sum to a belligerent is a breach of neutrality, especially since Britain "is fighting our battles and the battles of mankind," and France seeks to enslave and plunder the world.[7]

Hardly had this controversy died down when the official renewal of hostilities between Napoleon and England in 1803 led to an equally if not more serious one over free commerce. England with her powerful fleet was, of course, in a better position to "interfere" with the commerce of neutrals. Adding further to the flame was the British impressment of seamen from American ships on the ground that they were British subjects. But, as Gallatin put it, if the United States were not to employ British seamen, our navigation would be worse hit than any restrictions the English "could lay upon our commerce."[8]

From practically all the American seaport towns came memorials of merchants to Congress praying for vigorous action to protect the carrying trade against the English regulations. New York's petition was typical and copied by a number of others: Because of the country's great agricultural surplus, free commerce is of especial importance. To acquiesce to Britain's regulations would deprive "us of many advantages connected with our local situation, enterprise, wealth and fortune." It would "require us to divert much of our capital and industry to new employments" away from commerce. "It is not on account of our pecuniary losses alone we complain. The constancy and valour of the American seamen are justly themes for patriotism. Our feelings are indignant at the recital of their wrongs; and we request in addition to the protection of a naval force, . . . that our brave countrymen be permitted to display their energy in their own defense. . . . We pledge our united support in favor of all measures adopted to vindicate and secure the just rights of our country."[9]

Ames agreed that a navy should be constructed and vessels armed to stop French depredations, but he held that the merchants were unwarranted in protesting against English acts and orders. Of course, it is hard for people who love money to believe that those who get it by their loss may have justice on their side, but the British are right. To quote learned authorities of the past who laid down the doctrine that "free goods make free ships," is irrelevant. "The whole modern system of commerce and naval power *is so recent*, that these principles have not been long enough applied under a great diversity of circumstances, to make their application familiar and precise." Since England's life depends on naval power, she has the right to utilize this to the full to achieve her object.[10]

But in 1806 Ames stood almost alone. Noah Webster, in answering Ames, was struck with horror that any American writer should deny a principle over which the American Revolution was fought: True, the British regulations of neutral commerce and extension of contraband accorded with the doctrines accepted by the Jay Treaty, which he had approved. But that recently lapsed treaty was really an unfortunate, novel departure from the traditional doctrine that free ships make free goods. On the authority of elementary writers, he had erroneously believed that the English measures were authorized by the general law of nations. Further investigations, Webster said, satisfied him of his mistake "and of the extreme danger of trusting to the opinions of modern elementary writers, without a careful inspection of original authors and documents." [11]

Secretary of State Madison laid down the tenet that "every belligerent's right to control neutral commerce, must, as an exception to the general freedom of trade, be positively and strictly proved"; and, after studying all the writings "most generally received," the evidence of treaties and the practice of nations including Great Britain, he found that the British restrictions were no valid exception.[12]

But Madison, along with President Jefferson, wanted to avoid war or what would lead to war—the building of a navy and arming merchant ships, as the merchants wanted. He turned instead to the old device of retaliatory restrictions in the form of non-intercourse and finally complete embargo of trade in 1807. But these measures to force the warring powers to return to the true principle of commerce caused an explosive controversy. Jefferson's own party was split. Gallatin disliked war because it meant debts and taxes, but he preferred war to an embargo from every point of view, for "governmental prohibitions do always more mischief than had been calculated; and . . . not without much hesitation . . . a statesman should hazard to regulate the concerns of individuals as if he could do it better than themselves." [13]

John Randolph of Virginia, former leader of the Jeffersonians, declared in the House that the embargo is merely for the benefit of the carrying trade, a parasitic trade, at the expense of southern agriculture. The Shylocks are the supporters of the embargo. If things be restored to the old channel, any loss would be borne by those best able to bear it—the men of great capital. Even granting that an embargo policy is best, no practical statesman would attempt to change a people's habits overnight. "Great change to be beneficial must be gradual, not forced upon the people." Nature might be coaxed, but she would not be coerced with impunity. Should the embargo be continued, a direct tax on land would be required to obtain a revenue, and this would raise a revolution.

This fiercest of southern "agrarians" was joined by Federalist opponents of Jefferson and leaders of the carrying trade in opposing the restriction measures. Hildreth, who had no sympathy with such measures, later explained that the merchants, too, were divided. Even some of the wealthiest applauded the government's embargo measures, but the Federalist protagonists explained away these sinners by saying that, being wealthy, they could wait for the renewal of trade and in the meanwhile "buy up, at a great discount the ships and produce of their poorer neighbours." [14] The measure, as the Administration intended, is giving an unfair advantage to wealthy merchants, exclaimed a Vermonter, but it will ruin the honest industrious young men with good prospects who contracted debts to purchase agricultural produce to carry it to profitable markets. "There is too much of Virginia money aristocracy in this for a Yankee." [15] But more to the point was the comment of John Adams's able wife, Abigail: "The youth of our country have no alternative but to till the land for bread to eat." [16]

Meanwhile, the issue was taken into the courts. Attorneys for the merchants declared that the embargo annihilated commerce and was not warranted by any express provision of the Constitution. The spokesmen for its constitutionality declared that the embargo and the like were means of executing an express power of Congress— namely, the power to regulate commerce; and they had the same constitutional justification as the Bank of the United States. But most surprising is that "men of such grave counsel and eminence" as the merchants' attorneys should attempt to excite the turbulent passions of the multitude with such loose talk about annihilating commerce, for after all the purpose of the act is to promote the nation's commerce.[17] Pointedly, added New York Republicans, an administration which has avowedly placed its whole reliance on trade for revenue, would certainly never designedly destroy the chosen foundation on which its own resources are built.[18]

The court decision in favor of the embargo did not end the controversy. Josiah Quincy, Federalist senator from Massachusetts and later president of Harvard, defiantly exclaimed in Congress that it was one thing to decide a question before a court of law and another to decide it before the people. "He did not threaten insurrection," but if there "is nothing but your law to stand between a man and bankruptcy on the one hand, and rapid fortune on the other, the temptation is too powerful to be withstood." "Those . . . denominated Federalists," commented Abigail Adams, "under the first two administrations, have now taken the ground of their opponents and rise up in opposition to government and the laws and [they] style those apostates who will not join with them." [19]

President Madison blandly wrote that the cry of the New Englanders that they will secede rather than submit to having their commerce suspended longer, did as little credit to their interest as to their sense of national honor. That a body of intelligent people with few native productions and an object of increasing jealousy to Great Britain on account of their commerce and navigation should think of abandoning the southern states, for which they are merchants and carriers, in order to ally themselves with Britain, is the height of absurdity. The difficulty of making an advantageous treaty between the United States and Britain "arises almost wholly from the patronage by the former of the maritime . . . interests of the Eastern states." [20]

The ultra-Federalists enrolled in their ranks the impecunious Charles Brockden Brown, who took time off from writing novels full of high-sounding slogans of virtue, honor, and denunciations of the French Revolution [21] to write an *Address to the Government of the United States on the Cession of Louisiana to the French* in 1803. He called vociferously for seizure first and then negotiations with the French. Did not the Revolutionary War show "that the passion for gain could not deter us from repelling encroachment on our liberty at the cost of every personal advantage?" Not "vulgar gain," but a "generous spirit" animates the nation in the demand for conquest.

But when the Jeffersonians put through the embargo on American shipping to compel Britain to lift its restrictions on neutral American commerce, Brown, like the rest of the ultra-Federalists, promptly forgot the chivalrous language and opposed the measure on strictly "materialistic" grounds. All embargoes, non-intercourse acts, and the like are "absurd, unreasonable and inexpedient," Brown now argued in 1809 in *An Address to the Congress of the United States on the Utility and Justice of the Restrictions Upon Foreign Commerce*. Acquiescence to the British regulations will restore commerce with a considerable part of the world.

"The phantoms of tribute and submission" will not prevent the American merchants from attempting to evade the foreign regulations or acquiescing in them, "provided they can grow rich by the adventure. . . . The most fiery patriot in your own body," he informed Congress, "would not be deterred from doing this, by the fear of humbling and disgracing his nation; because when things come home thus directly to his feelings, he sees that all these declarations about honor and tribute mean nothing."

Of course, the instigator of the restrictions, Jefferson, is not a student of the "science of politics" or a true statesman, but an irresponsible schemer because he questions "established truths" and assumes that "mankind can be governed by reason." As for Madison, he has been corrupted by Jefferson. On the other hand, Brown found that the Federalists were men of "high and honourable sentiments." [22]

The embargo was repealed as ineffective. But with Napoleon's agreeing to lift his restrictions on neutral commerce while England insisted on regulations that left commerce unrestrained only with Great Britain, came the passing of the Non-Intercourse Act with Britain. President Madison said that "experience warns us of the fatal tendencies of a commerce unrestricted with Great Britain, and restricted by her pleasure and policy elsewhere." The limited market would continue overcharged with American exports, and the disproportionate quantity of imports would drain the country's specie, endanger its moneyed institutions, arrest its internal improvements, and strangle promising manufactures. Ship owners, shipbuilders, and mariners would suffer also with American commerce and manufactures. [23]

Napoleon was still a problem. The "late licentiousness" of the French privateers in the Baltic, Madison warned in 1811, will lead to armed collisions. The American government would long ago have sent frigates there, except that the British have superior vessels in the vicinity. Madison attributed Napoleon's seizure of American ships in French harbors to "his want of money, and . . . ignorance of commerce." His "continental system" was "anti-commercial." [24]

President Madison sent a special envoy to Napoleon late in 1811 to obtain reparations for seizure of American vessels and the opening of his ports to American vessels on a "fair and liberal scale." American commerce should be placed in French ports on a footing "as to afford to it a fair market, and to the industry and enterprise of their people a reasonable encouragement." The interest of France and her allies is to avail themselves of the industry and capital of American merchants, to supply their people's wants and increase their revenue.

If France wishes to profit from neutral commerce, she must advo-

cate neutral rights in practice as well as in theory. She must therefore allow free entry to American ships carrying American produce.
True, the British have seized some French colonies, but France must
not be indifferent to them in their present distress by treating goods
from these colonies as enemy goods.

The act requiring that an equal amount of French goods, especially
silks, must be taken in return for American cargoes is unjust. The
duties imposed on American commerce, especially the great staples,
should be reduced as low as possible if not eliminated; otherwise they
depress the articles and discourage the trade. American goods must
be allowed transit through French ports to inland markets.

France "overrates our desire of her commodities," and the present
footing of commerce is intolerable to the United States. American
commerce with France "will be a barter of foods and raw materials
for superfluities, in great part, and altogether so (with the temporary
exception of colonial re-exports) as long as a balance in money is
prevented by the existing policy of France and a return of useful
fabrics by the war."

Napoleon's spokesman, the Duke of Bassano, argued that for the
most part American demands would interfere with Napoleon's continental system and were not for the real benefit of the United States.
He pointed to the United States tonnage duties on foreign ships and
to its tariff. The French duties, he said, affect only the French consumer. Since the goods are primarily tropical luxury products, the
duties can have no effect other than to raise their price without injuring the commerce in them. But he agreed that a commercial treaty
based on the principle of perfect reciprocity would be advantageous
to both countries.[25]

No wonder Madison hoped that Napoleon's reprehensible con-
fiscations and the "effect of the English monopoly on the value of our
produce" would break "the charm attached to what is called free
trade, foolishly by some, and wickedly by others."[26]

"Protection" of domestic manufactures received increasing attention in the literature as the relations with England became increasingly tense over England's "interference" with the freedom of American commerce.

Late in 1803, as war in Europe began again, there was an avalanche
of memorials to Congress calling for protection. The "artists and
manufacturers" of Philadelphia declared that most of the European
goods imported could be produced at home if Congress took proper

action. What prevents their production is the unjust competition of foreign manufactures, the necessary expense attending the commencement of complicated manufactures, the laying of injudicious duties on raw materials and goods partially manufactured, and finally addiction to foreign fashions, especially in clothing. Some contend that coarse goods and those of the first necessity only should be protected, but we should continue the importation of luxury goods. This action would give the most profitable branches to the foreigners.

As for the prevalence of vice among manufacturers, some of the memorialists have visited Europe and found in the manufacturing towns the greatest amount of virtue. Ten times more crimes are committed near courts and seaports. Oppressed as they are, the manufacturers are the most virtuous and the most intelligent class in civil society. Whatever republicanism is to be found in the constitution of England and France is to be accredited to the manufacturing class. In all ages the peasantry have been too ignorant to understand their rights and too remote from each other to be able to withstand oppression.

It is said that manufactures will prevent the populating of the western wilderness, but is the prosperity of the citizens in old established situations, especially the landholders, to be sacrificed to the whim of projectors and land speculators? Every migration east to west is a loss, not a gain, to the nation at large by the very act of migrating because of the inconveniences of a change of climate and other things.[27]

The Republican Congress was sympathetic but not too enthusiastic. The House Committee of Commerce and Manufactures, with Samuel Latham Mitchill of New York, formerly a Columbia professor, as chairman, reported in 1804 that the domestic tradesmen and artists of practically every denomination have asked Congress to "patronize their respective employments, and to increase their profits." Their requests are that various imported raw materials be exempt from duties, that import of manufactures be subject to heavier or prohibitive duties, that drawbacks be withdrawn from articles of foreign manufacture exported again, and that direct bounties be given.

Congress has already rightly given much aid along these lines to encourage domestic manufactures in many coarse articles. If we do not excel in the manufacture of the finer articles of cotton, silk, wool, and the metals, we "may felicitate ourselves that, by reason of the ease of gaining a subsistence and the high . . . wages, our fellow citizens . . . are not doomed to the wretchedness of a strict discipline in . . . manufactories of the finer articles."

In a country devoted to agriculture, the cluster of arts and trades which minister to its wants spring up naturally. The plainer, coarser, and more useful fabrics are manufactured with tolerable skill; whereas the more fine, costly and high wrought articles of those several kinds can be obtained more conveniently from abroad. Furthermore, if the manufactures of foreign countries were prohibited, we should have no market for our produce, and thus industry would lose one of its chief incentives at home. Consequently the report recommended such measures as would help, on the whole, coarse manufactures.[28]

Spokesmen for "fine manufactures" were incensed at the report. A member of the Society of Artists and Manufacturers of Philadelphia, which had just been incorporated with Rush as president and Coxe as vice-president, was aghast at the committee's "ignorance of political economy." They said:

The first progress of men toward the perfection of the social system is from a hunting to a pastoral life, but the progress is brought about not by the nature of things nor by necessity, but by the enlightened rulers of a nation. "Hence, if no enlightened statesman appears . . . the people may continue, as the aborigines of this country have done, hunters and warriors for thousands of years. . . . The same may be said of a nation [which] has progressed to a state of agriculture, and that cluster of necessary arts which minister to its wants. No step further can be made by them in the finer arts, which administer to the comforts of polished society, but by the direction of the legislature." Thus Connecticut, when inhabited by hunters, could not be as populous as at present, and she cannot increase until the government protects her home manufactures. Therefore the committee errs in saying that agriculture is the great occupation, setting in motion manufactures.

Of all things, the political economist will attend to the proper employment of the fair sex. In the United States at least a million women doing little or nothing might be employed in the different branches of the cotton manufactory without oppression or the wretchedness of a strict discipline.[29]

As trouble with England increased, Coxe, who now called himself a "Pennsylvania Democrat" and held the important federal post of purveyor of public supplies in Philadelphia, declared that the promotion of domestic manufactures was good in itself and would force England to restrain her restrictions on the freedom of American commerce. However, he was attacked later by the radical Republican *Aurora* as a traitor to domestic manufactures. He was accused of purchasing English goods for the Army, especially buttons, instead of domestic ones, and of using his role as a "great statistical inquirer" to undermine domestic manufactures.[30]

By 1809, as the Republican Administration struggled desperately to retain "retaliatory" measures against Great Britain, the tone of the Republicans had become decidedly more favorable but with important qualifications. The House Committee on Commerce and Manufactures now reported that manufactures should be given the support necessary to withstand foreign competition, skill, and capital without "fastening on the community oppressive monopolies." The protection of manufactures is a "delicate, difficult subject. Men of, great science and experience, have supported, and do still support, diversity of opinions." But additional duties ought to be laid on cotton manufactures imported from the East Indies, for the latter compete not only with domestic cotton manufactures, but with the European ones using American cotton.[31]

While Federalist Hartford reprinted Adam Smith's *Wealth of Nations*, the Republican Congress ordered the reprinting of Hamilton's *Report on Manufactures* and directed Secretary of the Treasury Gallatin to collect information on American manufactures and report it to Congress together with a plan best calculated to "protect and promote the same."

Gallatin, in his *Report on American Manufactures* in 1810, declared that the raw materials used and the foodstuffs and other articles consumed by the manufacturers create a home market not very inferior to that arising from foreign demand. The growth of manufactures has been more favorable than might be expected in view of the "natural" limitations of abundance of land compared to the high price of labor and lack of capital. But the introduction of machinery has nearly superseded manual labor in many important branches; a great capital has been accumulated, and the violation of our neutral commerce has broken inveterate habits and given a great impulse to manufactures.

Furthermore, the import duties, though designed for revenue, have given a preference to American manufactures. But the great prosperity of America is due primarily to the lack of internal restrictions or monopoly which disfigure European societies. Industry is perfectly free and unfettered. Every type of trade, commerce, art, profession, and manufacture is open equally to all without any previous apprenticeship, admission, or license. Consequently Americans have not only improved agriculture, but also developed commerce even in branches where monopoly has been deemed essential. The same principle has accelerated manufactures and will decidedly give this country superiority over Europe. The only serious disadvantage facing American manufactures at present is the great superior capital of England, which enables her merchants to give long credit, sell on small profits, and make occasional sacrifices. But the government might create a small amount of circulating stock bearing a low interest and lend it to manufacturers at par, on principles formerly used by New York and Pennsylvania in their loan offices.

Young Senator Henry Clay, an ardent Republican who had migrated from Virginia to Kentucky and married into a wealthy family interested in various enterprises in hemp manufactures, successfully demanded that the Navy purchase the domestic product. He frankly admitted that he spoke for a local Kentucky interest, but he thought that domestic manufactures sufficient to satisfy our needs were desirable. He did not propose to change the habits of the nation from agriculture to manufactures, he said. The vicious degrading effects of the factory system might follow if we became the manufacturers for other nations, but if we limited our efforts to our own wants, no evil could result. He hoped that the "yeomanry of the country, the true and genuine landlord of this tenement, called the United States" would continue to reform until the country was clothed at home. "Others may prefer the cloths of Leeds and of London, but give me those of Humphreysville," he said.

Humphreysville happened to be the company town near New Haven established in 1806 by the arch-Federalist, Colonel Humphreys. It was to be a model factory town free from the kind of demoralizing influence of factory industry that had disgraced England. It was "staffed mostly by unpaid apprentice boys, some of them orphans from the city of New York, and by women at wages of fifty cents to a dollar a week." In this way Humphreys felt that he was rescuing from poverty and possible crime many boys of New York City, training them to work and educating them.

At his behest the Connecticut legislature passed an act "constitut-
ing the Selectmen of each town in which manufacturing establishments should be erected, visitors to those institutions, with power to
enforce the proper care of the persons employed." Proprietors were
to control the morals of their workmen and to educate their children
as other children in plain families throughout the state were educated.

In 1808 the legislature commended Humphreys' introduction of
labor-saving machinery and employment of children. By this combination he overcame in a degree the "embarrassments resulting from
the dearness of labour" and at the same time in a "mode very honourable to himself and useful to the State" he converted into "an active
capital the exertions of persons who otherwise would be idle, and
in many instances a burthen to the community." It viewed with
"much satisfaction the exertions of Colonel Humphreys to render
the exertions of women and children more useful, and those of the
latter more nearly useful. Nothing is drained from tillage and yet the
funds of national industry are increased."

To encourage him, his superintendents. foremen, and apprentices
were to be exempt from the poll tax and assessments, from military
duty, and from working on highways; his textile establishment was
exempted from taxes and assessments for ten years.[32]

Party lines made no difference in the common opposition to labor-
union efforts to raise wages. In the case of the Philadelphia journeymen shoemakers in 1806, the Federalist court denounced the union
as a conspiracy because it tended to destroy the trade of the city.
This position was also taken by an ardent Republican, Robert Addis
Emmett, in presenting the views of employers in a New York case in
1809. "Such combinations," he said, "must in every country impede
and interfere with its manufacturing prosperity." [33]

As for domestic transportation, the Republican Administration
regarded sympathetically what its leaders had criticized in the days
of Federalist control. Gallatin, in his *Report on . . . Public Roads
and Canals* in 1808, thought that the national government should encourage canals and roads by purchasing substantial stock in the companies. Without this aid, these beneficial works for developing American commerce will not be prosecuted, for the demand for capital
is so great in America that little of it will be applied to such objects
yielding "remote and moderate profits." Furthermore, so little is subscribed at first compared to what "is actually needed that the work

proceeds slowly, and the capital applied remains unproductive longer than necessary and the accruing interest is an injurious addition to the real expense."

But in New York agitation had already begun for a canal under state auspices connecting Lake Erie with the Hudson, ostensibly to make New York the great commercial center and beneficiary of the western traffic. Leading the movement was the arch-Federalist, Gouverneur Morris, who had immense landholdings along the proposed route. "Some of the stockholders of the defunct Western Inland Navigation Company," stated one sympathetic account, find "that their stock was not as productive as they expected." So they took measures to promote the state canal "with a view of being remunerated by the State for the sums they had expended."

The state legislature appointed commissioners, including Morris, to report on a canal. In 1811 they declared that the canal would encourage agriculture, promote commerce and manufactures, and tend to consolidate the Union. The emphasis was now not on the question of New York's outdoing other commercial centers for the western traffic, but on the need to outdo Montreal's possibilities of capturing the traffic through the St. Lawrence. By winning over Canada we would avoid the danger of foreign influence. They protested, they said, against a grant to private persons or companies. "Too great a national interest is at stake. It must not become the subject of a job, or a fund for speculation." The reasons adduced for grants to individuals in Europe apply inversely here—namely, that few citizens "have more money than they want; and of the many who want, few find facility in obtaining it." But the public can readily command any reasonable sum at a fair interest. Moreover, such large expenditures can be more economically made under public authority than by the care and vigilance of any company.[34]

In the South, where attempts at turnpikes and private canal companies had been unsuccessful, praise of public construction of such ventures was also heard. Henry Banks, Virginia merchant promoter and journalist, declared that if Virginia by taxation should build roads connecting with the Southwest, especially Kentucky, she could capture the western trade and thus show that "a true and mercantile spirit was about to supersede the practice of shaving and other means of unrighteous gain that have long predominated."

Let the works be prosecuted on public account, and let individuals and companies submit propositions for their construction. The landowners are, of course, to be amply compensated. Land on both sides of the road may be condemned and resold to settlers agreeing to build houses to accommodate travelers. Competition in the area traversed by the roads will convert it from a howling wilderness into a continuous village.[35]

On the other hand, Superintendent of Patents William Thornton proposed in his pamphlet, *Political Economy* (1804), that the government repay the investors in the internal improvement companies, so large a number of which were defunct, and expand the program. At the same time he combined the internal improvement scheme with a plan to end slavery. The government was to buy the slaves and use them for a number of years on the public works to repay their cost and then free them. This would, of course, involve a heavy increase in the public debt, but, said Thornton, aside from the removal of a moral blot, the economic benefits in increased land value and business prosperity would make the debt burden insignificant and more than repay the costs. Certainly nothing is more foolish than continually to reduce our insignificant debt while the country has a crying need for internal improvements.

Land speculation still furnished the greatest drama. Most notorious were the "Yazoo Companies." In 1795 the Georgia legislature granted to four related companies for $500,000 thirty-five million acres lying west of the present boundaries of the state and stretching to the Mississippi. Most of the great land promoters in or out of public life, including Supreme Court Justice James Wilson, were stockholders in the companies. The state's title was questionable because the federal government claimed the territory, but this did not disturb the promoters. Gallatin declared, after a study of the case: "Even if considered as a contract," the original grant as such is null and void, for all the members of the legislature who voted for the sale, "that is to say the agents who pretended to sell the property of their constituents, were with the exception of a single person, interested in and parties to the purchase." [36]

But he and other cabinet members appointed as a commission to settle the matter justified a settlement on the ground that the sale by the original grantees had been to "innocent" purchasers. Congress hesitated to settle; and Sullivan, then Republican governor of Massachusetts, listed Congress's ill treatment of the Yazoo claims as but another evidence of the domination of self-interest over morality, threatening to break up the Union.[37] Finally, in 1810, Federalist

Chief Justice John Marshall, speaking for the Supreme Court, held that the rescinding act violated the constitutional provision forbidding the states to impair contracts. But Congress was still unconvinced.

The radical Republican organ,, the *Aurora*, opposed the proposed reduction of the price of public lands on the ground that it would encourage land jobbers and exaggerate the already excessive speculative fever that was ruining the country.[38]

The promotion of banks became almost as outstanding an enterprise as land speculation and was often engaged in by participants of the latter. In this, as in most of the new enterprises of the day, the promoters were among the outstanding men in the economic, social, and political life of the states and nation. Charters had to be obtained from the legislatures, and leaders of all parties and factions participated jointly or as rivals in this lucrative pursuit. Where Republican legislatures dominated, it became the fashion to insist that new charters were needed for Republican banks in order to counteract the political influence of the Federalists, who controlled the existing banks or increased the danger of speculation or foreign influence.

The need of a charter to engage in banking was often circumvented by obtaining a charter ostensibly to engage in a non-banking business, but which contained a provision allowing the privilege of note issue. The yellow-fever epidemic in New York in 1799 furnished the occasion for chartering the Manhattan Company in New York ostensibly to provide the city with a water supply. But the charter contained a provision that the company might employ its surplus capital in the purchase of stocks or any other moneyed operation. Shortly afterward its business was exclusively banking and insurance.

The first banking company west of the Alleghenies, the Kentucky Insurance Company of Lexington, arose through a substantially similar clause in a charter granted by the Kentucky legislature to an "association of patriotic gentlemen" to encourage the raising and exporting of the country's produce by devoting their funds to insure boats and cargoes on the Ohio and Mississippi rivers. But a clause was inserted in the charter reading, "Such of the notes of the company as are payable to bearer shall be negotiable and assignable by delivery only."

Among its directing spirits was Clay, who was also its attorney. Its dividends of nearly 19 per cent set off a demand that the banking privilege be revoked as having been fraudulently obtained from the innocent-minded legislature. The opposition was led by another shrewd lawyer, Felix Grundy, who like Clay had migrated from Virginia and had great political and economic ambitions. Interestingly enough, Grundy had dominated the legislature at the time the charter had been passed without opposition. Grundy denounced banking in general as a dangerous novelty which would destroy free government and enslave the people. Clay, elected to the legislature to fight the unprincipled demagogues, denounced critics as ignorant of constitutional law and the principles of money and credit: Repeal of a charter would be unconstitutional on the now familiar grounds of violating the right vested by the state in the company. On the other hand, the bank is the instrument for making Kentucky a great and powerful commonwealth, for, with her commerce expanding and her agricultural produce being exported to all parts of the world, she needs sufficient circulating media.[39]

At the same time, the Clay forces put through a charter for an additional bank, the Bank of Kentucky. The measure provided for branches, a nominal capital of $1,000,000, state subscription of one-half of the capital, and appointment of half the directors by the legislature. When $20,000 of the capital was paid in, the bank could begin business; its notes and other debts were limited to the customary three times the nominal capital over and above the deposits. Clay was chosen as one of the state directors. Some of Ohio's enterprising gentry, seeking a bank in their state, now argued that Kentucky, because of its bank, would receive specie for lands sold in Ohio, and that specie would cease to leave Kentucky because it was no longer dependent on the bank notes of other states.[40]

Over in Virginia, Henry Banks called for more banks in the state in addition to the state system and the branches of the Bank of the United States. He said: The general question of banks or no banks might be a matter of discussion if banks were to be established for the first time. But more than a hundred banks now exist in the nation, and some of the states get large revenue from them. Unless every state and all individuals with unexpired charters could be persuaded to relinquish their advantage, it would be folly for Virginia to follow a different scheme. Fortunately "the minds of men have received or soon will receive correct impressions upon this truly important question in political economy."

Last of his new bank projects was one for a "Mechanics Bank" as part of a scheme of internal improvements. The majority of directors shall be, or shall have been, employed in some mechanical calling; no director, private individual, or corporation should get a loan of more than $10,000 at one time. Most revealing as to the object of the promoters was his statement that those capable of supporting a bank should not be compelled to purchase shares of existing banks at their high price.[41]

North Carolina illustrated a case where Federalists supported practices that they generally attributed to vicious Republicans. The state's first two banks were chartered in 1804. Ardently supporting these two banks at all times was a Federalist national leader of great learning, William Gaston, a Princeton graduate and president of one of the banks. The banks refused to redeem their notes in specie, but instead paid in the state's paper money, which, having been issued in 1783 and 1785, was not subject to the constitutional prohibition of state issue of paper currency.

Complaints were made early that, because of excessive issues, the bank notes were heavily depreciated. The notes were denounced as a "cheat upon society" and as having driven specie from the state and prevented the growth of the state's commerce. In 1810 the legislature proposed to redeem the state's paper money and eliminate the inconvertible bank notes by chartering a new state bank with state investment, branches, and convertible notes. The other two banks were to be merged with it on the expiration of their charters in a few years. The supporters of the old banks argued that a new bank was not needed in a state which lacked commerce and which was almost exclusively agricultural, and cried out against the threat to the state's paper money and the injustice and impossibility of attempting specie payments.[42]

In the "non-partisan" *Raleigh Star* appeared the most striking defense of this position. All the old arguments in favor of an inconvertible currency were brought into play: That the premium on specie is not due to paper money but to the unfavorable trade balance is evidenced by the fact that even the notes of local branches of the Bank of the United States in the southern states are at a discount. Since the southern states are debtors of the northern, few northern people have occasion to send money South, and the premium naturally rises by the ordinary law of supply and demand. Thus the continuing unfavorable balance of trade of the state dooms any bank with convertible notes.

The new bank cannot have the advantages and income of large

deposits, as expected. In great commercial towns like Boston, the merchants utilize bank checks more than bank notes, but the trading capital of the North Carolina towns, like country areas everywhere, is too small for such operations. The townsmen neither make deposits nor desire bank credits, for the merchants borrow to pay the farmer and the farmer neither borrows nor collects money to leave in the bank. The existing banks, though not paying hard money, have doubled the circulating medium without impairing its quality, given activity to business, and improved the habit of punctuality in their areas. But when the present charters expire and all bank credit is at the mercy of a single institution, the monopoly will be in effect another Yazoo plot. The proponents of the new bank adopt the old Yankee's advice to his emigrating son: "My son, make money—honestly if you can, but at all events, make money."

The beneficiaries of a convertible currency would be the Yankee peddlers. That able and wealthy men are behind the bank is irrelevant, for they must be ignorant of the essential principles of "the science of banking" and of the complex interrelationships of society, to think of setting up such a hard-money bank. No problems in political economy require more patient thought than those relating to money and banking, but the projectors of the new bank have not deliberately examined the peculiar conditions in this state.

Every projector, irrespective of his understanding or integrity, as he seeks patronage for a supposed discovery of perpetual motion or a bank for supplying the state perpetually with hard money, attempts to convince others that his scheme is for the public good. Thus empires have been deranged and citizens ruined by schemes plausible in appearance. The author pointed to the South Sea Bubble in England and John Law's Bank in France.[43]

A legislative investigating committee found later that the two old banks had practically from their beginning been adept at the worst practices of an era known for its loose banking morals, and that the two joined with the new state bank to continue them.

From men of promotional talents came attacks on the authorities in economic theory. The Federalist Robert Hare of Philadelphia, an eminent chemist who later became professor of chemistry at the University of Pennsylvania, attacked Madison's Administration in 1810 for not building a navy to protect commerce. He complained in his *A Brief View of the Policy and Resources of the United States* that the ignorant majority fail to appreciate that if the public debt were used to build a navy, provide private subscriptions for banking and insurance companies, and other public objects, it would become the great engine of national prosperity. By a false association or analogy they presume that the insolvency of a government must entail 'the same evils of individual insolvency. But so long as the interest is paid, government insolvency is only apparent. Furthermore, they are unaware that credit is under some circumstances equivalent to capital, and as much may be lost by not employing credit as by not occupying capital. The erroneous view on credit and public debt arises from the influence of the authority of Hume and Adam Smith. The writings of these great men are now in the hands of almost every well-educated politician, and "have on our economical speculations, an influence which though in general well deserved is . . . very injurious, so far as it creates opposition to the employment of national credit." Despite England's financial experience to the contrary, these eminent writers contended that this engine would be ruinous if used to an extent much less than it has already been strained by England. This error arises from their notion that credit in its favorable operations on public wealth is merely subsidiary to specie, of which it has been considered the mere representative, and more especially when brought into circulation in the form of notes, bills, bonds, or certificates. But in reality credit constitutes "an original and . . . a peculiarly beneficial medium of interchange in trade," even more so than specie. "These metals are not represented by it, but are merely the measure of its value, or medium of exchange in which respect that they are . . . subsidiary to credit," rather than the reverse.

Consider how much profit would be afforded to the farmer, the landholders, the mechanic, or the manufacturer in expending ten or twenty millions in constructing a navy. From the whole amount thus expended, however, must be deducted all those profits or wages which would not have been earned except for extra demand. In addition, we must deduct the material resources which would have remained useless in the forest or in the mine, and those hours of idleness which would have occurred had not the stimulus of the national credit incited industry to unusual efforts. "For . . . a people are not made poorer or less happy by a system, which causes considerable expenditure; if at the same time it occasions an equivalent increase of the demand for produce and stimulus to industry." It is not true that the country produces as much as it can. "The prodigious amount of our exports during periods of extraordinary foreign demand, sufficiently proves that in ordinary times, we have not full employment for our means of production."

Disturbed by the proclivity of the immigrants to support the Republican Party, Hare called for barring them from citizenship. The worst, not the best, he said, have expatriated themselves. He was ever willing to forget his theory of the great productive effect of credit as he returned to an old argument Franklin had used in a somewhat similar opposition to the German immigrants in Pennsylvania. Said Hare: In view of the rapid native increase, "the period is not very remote when America will attain that acme of excessive population, which . . . is followed by an incurable wretchedness and degradation among the poorer classes." The daily admission of needy foreigners, along with the general ignorance of the people, demands giving more influence to wealth in the government, he said; otherwise power is given to spendthrifts and beggarly outlaws from abroad to command the earning of those who have spent their lives in in-. dustry. In Hare's eyes immigrants were desirable as laborers, but not as citizens.

Characteristic of the learned type in the business of promotion and speculation was Samuel Blodget (1757–1814), son-in-law of former Provost Smith. Blodget grew up in colonial New Hampshire. After serving for a time in the Revolutionary War, he resigned his commission in 1777 and obtained some wealth as an East India merchant in Boston. As Philadelphia definitely became the financial capital with the establishment of the Bank of the United States, Blodget moved there in 1792. Among other things, he became a director in an insurance company and designed the first building of the Bank of the United States. Like Robert Morris and other great speculators, he had visions that the new federal capital, then merely agreed upon as to location and not even named, would quickly become another London. So his primary interest became speculating in its lands and associated enterprises. He got himself appointed superintendent of buildings in 1793 and set out on a grandiose development program with the aid of lotteries. He promoted a bank and a bridge over the Potomac; he took an interest in the canal companies and similar enterprises affecting the new federal district.

Blodget did not even forget to include in his promotions a national university at the capital to train prospective legislators. He cited from a 1787 proposal that the head should be a professor of politics. The successful candidate "must understand morals, war, finance, commerce, manufacturing, agriculture, politics, philosophy; he must have a perfect view of all the great affairs of a nation in their whole extent and intimate connection. His republican heart should be equally noble with his understanding, animated with rational piety, warm philanthropy and sublime patriotism, infinitely above the narrow sentiments of sects and parties." For this task the specialist is useless. The political economist is not fit to hold this chair because he is "so narrow in his view of property, as to forget the proprietors, and in his pursuit of national wealth he thinks little of that liberty, honour, wisdom, valour, without which it cannot be enjoyed and preserved." Besides, political economy itself is divided into ridiculous sects; each is "blindly attached to a system . . . one doats on agriculture, another on manufactures, a third on commerce."

As for the studies, the science of war should be taught and also belles lettres and elegant literature, for such a program of "sublime learning is a powerful antidote against that excessive love of property" which exists in the present mode of civilization. "A man who has read the best political and military authors, who is well acquainted with the best poets and historians, who has often sighed on the select scenes of heroic tragedy, such a man cannot have low thoughts and mean sentiments" in the legislature.

Blodget's speculations, especially his vast holdings of real estate in the capital, soon got him into financial difficulties. Unable to raise loans to meet his commitments, he was imprisoned for a time.

Thanks to his interest in land speculation, the country was benefited with the first crude attempts to present statistical data in some detail in his *Thoughts on the Increasing Wealth and National Economy of the United States of America* (1801), and *Economica; A Statistical Manual for the United States of America* (1806).

Adam Smith was a poor guide, Blodget declared, for Smith stressed labor as the spring of national prosperity and deprecated the importance of specie holdings. But Shays' Rebellion was caused by the inattention of the rulers to the scarcity of money.

Labor as a merely latent power must be excited. Money and the whole of the arts and sciences that follow in the busy train of commerce are the most congenial stimuli. Since men are by nature rebellious and querulous, social ties are necessary to bend men's selfish propensities to the general welfare. In arbitrary government all this is done by compulsion. In republics it is more effectively done by pecuniary enticement, especially by voluntary joint stock companies. These moneyed commonwealths or public associations, with their free election to give a concerted direction to the employments of funds, might be called golden chains. These little, moneyed republics are things held in common for mutual benefit by affording frequent and profitable dividends. Furthermore, by the division of the whole into small shares, the people of all classes and descriptions, rich and poor, are united to oppose any revolution. At the same time, these republics of negotiable shares operate as an equipoise to the feudal monopolizing anti-republican tendency involved in the great holdings of private English money and landlords in the United States—the Barings and Pultneys—and many resident wealthy citizens as well. In other words, they obviate the need of an agrarian law to maintain the glorious freedom of America. True friends of the republican course should therefore do all possible to extend the system of companies like banks, insurance, canals, with small shares to embrace the poorer classes.

As the remedy for the crisis of 1808 he added to his list of desirable companies, manufacturing ones, especially in cotton. Since Arkwright's invention, he said, the joint stock company is better suited to the cotton branch than unconnected individual exertions.

To establish these minor republics in the interior towns, it is sometimes necessary to unite with each of them a bank or insurance company until the town becomes sufficiently large to support separate industrial enterprises. Government, both state and general, should have nothing to do with their direction. But government should heavily invest in these enterprises, especially around the federal district. The state would in due time obtain sufficient income without the need of taxes, and yet government would be so allied and thereby so dependent on the people that it would not dare to infringe their rights in the "minor republics."

At the same time the government should not listen to the engrossing land speculators who want to lower the price of western land. A low price of land—that is, below the "fair" or intrinsic value—makes common labor too expensive. No freeman will work for another if he can buy good land sufficiently cheap to provide him comfortable subsistence with two days' labor a week. Hence the back country people are more idle than is good for their health and the happiness of their family. If labor fell to a fair or natural price, slavery would end.

But the scarcity of money is also an important cause of the low price of land. The scarcity of money as well as the government's financial needs could be relieved by a "proper" use of the western public lands as a foundation for paper money. The government would issue transferable interest-bearing certificates redeemable in public lands. The public lands would sell at their "real value" of eight dollars; in fact the circulation of the notes to facilitate the payment for land would increase the demand for land in a greater ratio than the increase of money, and so lead to an ever-increasing price. The government would use these certificates for investment in the companies and in other "public works" such as colleges and warships.

Closely related to this plan was Blodget's proposal that the government borrow enough on the land security from Europe for these investments. The government would make a tremendous profit from the difference between the low rate of interest on money borrowed from Europe and the high returns on the investments. Should an excessive amount be borrowed, it could do no more harm than if a little more oil than necessary were applied to a creaking wheel. No loss could result, for it would have raised the value of our land pledged for the redemption of all loans, in a compound ratio of increase for any attainable size.

Loammi Baldwin, Harvard graduate and eminent Massachusetts engineer, decided in 1809 that the answer to all the raging economic problems was the study of political economy by statesmen in the light of the data to be revealed by the census of 1810.

Political economy has recently become systematized, he declared in his *Thoughts on the Study of Political Economy*. It combines the investigation of natural objects with the study of human passions. It is the "association of physical qualities with moral affections, which makes the great object of statistical researches" so as most effectively to aid the progress of national happiness. The handling of the problems in political economy must be left to the sovereign body. The mass of citizens must be satisfied with its consequences and corollaries, for in statistical questions the reasoning and evolution of correct results must necessarily be confined to a few having the necessary intimate acquaintance with all the facts of the situation.

The study and application of political economy deserves the encouragement, patronage, and assistance of government, which like "the faithful steward of a great household should carefully investigate the character of the inmates, watch them in their employments, ascertain to what purpose, they are employed, and scrupulously attend to the collection, application and management of its finance. . . . But what should be done by statute and what should be left to good sense is always difficult." However, this country cannot go by European models and experience, for its situation is different, especially with our federal compact and diversity of employments. Therefore everything in relation to political economy must be original.

A simple enumeration of numbers will not satisfy the statesman in his inquiries. Unquestionably there is in a new country a certain point from which different species of industry will diverge. In a new society such as the United States, the passionate ambition is to own an estate in land. This prevails over all other ambitions and until all the lands are occupied manufactures will be delayed. But once the population reaches a certain number, manufactures will enter.

On the other hand, Baldwin hailed as wise policy Gallatin's proposal for government grants to companies in public improvements because they abridge labor and bring literally incalculable benefits.

The results of manual labor can be precisely calculated. But the operation of canals, bridges, turnpikes, machinery, or any principle designed to magnify or gain power, or as a substitute for manual labor, is extremely subtle and must evade anything like a correct estimate. Their good effects are visible in all parts of the country, but it is impossible to measure the value at any one point. The labor one man or a given number can perform and the value of their industry can be ascertained as exactly as men can be counted. But a canal, for instance, secretly affects the convenience and labor of the community, even at a distance not apparently in its sphere, through the reduction of price in the market. How the labor withdrawn by the use of canals and the like from the old occupations is to be employed "is a question, a little embarrassing to cold phlegmatic sticklers for ancient habits and usage but easily resolved by enlightened liberal minds."

Baldwin complained that there were too many banks, especially in the country areas. The latter's bills are at a discount in the cities because of their excessive issues. These private bank companies promote speculation. Disrupting the standard measure of value, their fluctuations disturb the equilibrium between the price of labor and products. Consequently they hurt domestic trade and eventually foreign trade. The government should never let the circulating medium be the sport of petty corporations and private speculators. One remedy for irregular currency might be a consolidation of state banks, but the charters of some are perpetual. The other remedy is the extension of the capital of the Bank of the United States.

As the period closed, the great struggle over rechartering the Bank of the United States occurred. As usual in the great controversies, both sides claimed to be upholding the interests of the yeomanry and the commerce of the nation, but—also as usual—the struggle involved primarily conflicts of financial interests and personal political ambitions. Men of great wealth were to be found on both sides. They included on the opposition side, for instance, these stanch Republicans and merchant princes, Senator Samuel Smith of Baltimore and John Jacob Astor of New York.

The great Republican Party in its days of opposition had contended that the bank was unconstitutional, but now it was split. The party's financial expert, Secretary of the Treasury Gallatin, proposed that the bank be rechartered with a larger capital, but government was to receive a bonus. The bank, he said, provided a uniform currency, made possible the easy transmission of government funds from one area to another, and provided loans and other aids to government. State banks, he said, were not suitable for federal purposes, if for no other reason than that government has no control over state banks.

Leading the anti-bank forces in Congress was Clay. Using the old arguments of the critics of his Kentucky Insurance Company, he denied the usefulness of this "splendid association of favoured individuals invested with exemptions and surrounded by immunities and privileges." He denounced the Republicans supporting the bank as renegades who, seduced by the bank lobbyists, had joined Federalism's "Macedonian phalanx." Greatest of the objections was the foreign influence through the preponderantly British ownership of the stock, an argument that perhaps came with little grace from Clay, since the Kentucky Insurance Company was in the same situation.[44]

Findley, who had led the bitter opposition to the Bank of North America in 1785, in defending the Bank of the United States in Congress now spoke as if he had been on the other side in the earlier issue. He said that the people had been impressed with its incidental hardships rather than with its not yet fully developed advantages. The foreign ownership of bank capital furnished America with an effective weapon against any mischief by foreign countries. Even if Bonaparte should purchase the whole stock, it would be a good thing.

Senator William H. Crawford, Republican from Georgia who had humble Virginia origins, cried out against the state legislatures' instructing their senators to oppose recharter, as happened in Virginia, Maryland, Pennsylvania, Massachusetts, and Kentucky. These great influential states, "seduced by avarice and ambition," favor dissolution of the bank because they are the ones where the principal part of the revenue is collected. Thus the whole benefit of the public deposits is to be engrossed by the three or four great Atlantic commercial states. These will naturally monopolize the government, and the small states will be forced to accept a consolidated government.

The Republican, Mathew Carey, formerly a director of one Pennsylvania bank in which the state had an interest, declared in 1811 that he has lobbied and written in defense of the Bank of the United States because of the criminal neglect of its more powerful citizens, men of "splendid talents and conspicuous rank in society," to do so. As for the charge that the bank refuses to take the notes of branches from its customers, it ought, said Carey; but the state banks likewise refuse to receive the notes of their branches until compelled to do so by the legislature.

Those claiming that a national bank will be the engine of an intriguing administration may be right, but the Bank of the United States is not really a national bank. If Pennsylvania were an independent nation, the bank in which the state has investments and appoints some of the directors would be national, but the Bank of the United States is free of government ownership and government directors in accordance with the reply made by a wise merchant to Colbert's inquiry as to what government could do for trade and commerce—"*laissez-nous faire*—leave us to ourselves."

Finally, if the bank should be dissolved, the credit and honor of the United States, particularly in Europe, will seriously suffer, for Sir Francis Baring purchased the government shares in 1802 at a 45 per cent. advance, which will naturally disappear with dissolution of the bank.[45]

The Jeffersonian state senator, Nicholas Biddle, university graduate, littérateur, lawyer, and diplomat, defended the Bank of the United States in the Pennsylvania legislature. Citing Steuart, he declared that banks are the natural source of obtaining money in emergencies, because in emergencies individuals do not have the resources to lend the government. Government, of course, can issue bills of credit, but this device was ruinous during the Revolution. A loan through a privately run bank, however, provides a check; for a bank can lend to government only in proportion to its means, and its means are its loans to individuals. It can issue notes only when a demand exists for them, for any excess will be returned to the bank for specie. To suppose an indefinite issue of bank notes is to assume that the bank would force the people to take them gratuitously. This is like saying that coal-mine owners would constantly work their mines and send their coal to market with no thought of purchasers. The capacity of the government to borrow from the bank is therefore measured by the demand of notes from the bank and the people's confidence in it. But the government issue would be determined by its own needs and therefore would overflow the channel of trade. On the other hand, the government acts as a check on the bank through its power to remove the deposits instantly if it discerns any extravagance in the bank. Thus the bank and the government mutually check one another, and both are ultimately regulated by the "people."

If the government were to borrow from the state banks, it would become dependent on the states. Government, instead of being popular and one of majority rule, would be at the mercy of a few states whose money would overbalance territory and population. As for the constitutionality of the Bank of the United States, the mere fact of acquiescence for the past twenty years is sufficient. Pennsylvania should therefore support recharter.

If the bank were dissolved, specie would immediately be required, and the state banks would be forced to call in loans in self-defense. The trading community would be distressed, not because it lacks wealth, but because its assets cannot be turned quickly into money. Debtors unable to obtain specie would be forced to sacrifice their property, and the whole structure would collapse. Every fiber of society would feel its influence. No one would purchase land and produce, and they would fall at least to half their value.

Amid the general distress, the demand for specie would place the poorer classes, the small traders, at the mercy of money lords. Pennsylvania would lose the profit from her investments in the state banks. Arrears on her public land sales would not be paid, and instead of being able to continue appropriations for making canals, turnpikes, provide for educating the poor, and encourage manufactures, the government would be bankrupt.[46]

Recharter just barely failed of success. The trustees of the Bank of the United States sent a lobby to the Pennsylvania legislature for a charter for a bank of $5,000,000 capital. Finding that its original bonus offers were not considered "proportionable to what other banks have paid," it finally offered $500,000 to the state in the form of subscriptions in specified recently organized private turnpike and bridge companies to "induce subscriptions by individuals in the companies and to increase the emolument to the state for her interest in them." In addition, it would lend the state $500,000 at 5 per cent interest for internal improvements.

The directors declared in their memorial that the state's other financial institutions cannot remedy the evil of decreasing circulation, for they cannot acquire the bank's real capital of specie. This will not remain in Pennsylvania without a charter for a new bank; for, much as the former stockholders love Pennsylvania and would like to benefit her, they will obtain a charter in some other state, and thus Pennsylvania's rivals will be advanced at her expense.[47]

In addition to the opposition of various interests, Stephen Girard, Republican Philadelphia merchant prince, after originally supporting the move for a state charter, decided to enter the private banking business himself. The charter was not obtained, and Girard took over the bank building for his enterprise.[48] The sponsors finally turned to the New York legislature with a request for a charter for a "Bank of America." As in previous cases, with the political leaders of both parties not above the "temptation to enlarge their fortunes," a charter was obtained, and Hamilton's friend and successor as Secretary of the Treasury, Oliver Wolcott, was made president.[49]

CHAPTER XV

The War for "Free Trade and Seamen's Rights"

DESPITE the internal growth of the nation, the exigencies of commerce remained paramount in influential thinking. President Madison wanted peace, but he found that free trade had become such a raging passion with the strident leaders of both parties that the question was no longer one of war or peace, but whether to fight England or France. England's mighty fleet still made her the greater nuisance. Under the guidance of the ostensibly anti-commercial Republican Party and with the cry of "free trade and seamen's rights," the nation again took up arms.

The Republican war leaders, notably John C. Calhoun of South Carolina, Clay of Kentucky, and his former rival Grundy, now resident in Tennessee, turned the arguments which the Federalists had used in the Louisiana issue to their own use; but against England rather than France. Acquiring Canada and Florida would end Indian outrages on the western inhabitants, they said.

The Federalists opposed the war against England. They declared that it was not for the interests of commerce, as the Administration claimed, but for the interest of the southern slave aristocracy and western agrarians.

The most vociferous opposition was in New England. Its keynote was sounded by the Reverend Elijah Parish of Massachusetts in a fast-day sermon in July 1812. "Proclaim an honourable neutrality; let the southern *Heroes* fight their own battles, and guard . . . against the just vengeance of their lacerated slaves. . . . Break those chains, under which you have sullenly murmured, during the long, long reign of democracy; . . . and once more breathe that free, commercial air of New England which your fathers always enjoyed." [1]

Humphreys, as he engaged at Humphreysville in "promoting our agricultural and manufacturing interests and more especially the cause of morality as connected with the latter," was unconvinced by President Madison's protestation that the Administration was not aiming at the "systematic exclusion of commerce." Taking up arms to protect the sovereign state of Connecticut against all enemies in or out of the Union, he denounced the war as a selfish one for adding new states of heterogeneous population, for acquiring wild lands, as unbounded as they were unnecessary and unprofitable.[2]

With Noah Webster lending his skill and pen to give the movement an appearance of popular origin, a series of New England town-meeting resolutions culminated in the famous Hartford Convention which threatened New England's secession from the Union if the ruinous war did not cease and the Constitution were not amended along extreme states'-rights lines. The Administration had deceived the people by flattery and inflamed them by passion to carry out its knavish policy of ruining commerce and installing a southern despotism.[3]

Robert Goodloe Harper of Maryland, who had started his public career as a Republican South Carolina congressman and then become a Federalist and married a daughter of wealthy Charles Carroll of Carrollton, attempted to substantiate the thesis by an economic interpretation. He declared before an Annapolis celebration of Napoleon's defeat, that both the Revolutionary and the present war had been instigated by the southern debtors to English merchants. It had its roots in avarice and ambition and its leadership in the Virginia slaveholding aristocracy, headed by Jefferson. The enterprising wealthy southern slaveholders, especially the Virginia aristocrats, were ever seeking to increase their holdings of land and slaves and engaging in luxurious living. Consequently they were heavily indebted to the British merchants.

"The influence of such a state of things in fostering the spirit of resistance and the desire for separation [from England] cannot be doubted, unless we . . . doubt the operation of self interest and passion on human conduct." In the northern and eastern states these circumstances hardly existed, for the people were far less indebted, and with few exceptions their debts were due to each other.

This southern debtor party, continued Harper, fought the peace treaty of 1783 and the Constitution because these entailed the payment of British debts. Then they sought to have the United States support revolutionary France against England because they quickly realized that its English debts would be expunged with French success. The "debtor party, nursed in the arms and nourished with the milk of Aristocracy," thus became a leveling "democratic party." But, the better to cloak its real views and promote its plans, it assumed the name of the "Republican Party" and was finally successful in starting the present war to help Napoleon. But, thanks to Czar Alexander, who is self-sacrificing and above the popularity-seeking "vulgar great," Napoleon has been defeated.[4]

Gouverneur Morris denounced the French for their dastardly rebellion against the just and merciful Louis XVI, gave thanks to divine mercy for the restoration of the Bourbons, and, forgetful of his Louisiana performance, called on all the northern and eastern states —the "commercial" states—to secede, for the purpose of the war was to enable their masters, the West, to seize Indian lands at the expense of the blood and treasure of the East.[5]

Logan, the most ardent of Jeffersonians in the nineties, tried to convince the Administration that, in continuing this unjust war, it was retarding the progress of humanity. At no period of her history has England been "more powerful, free and respectable." The continental powers venerate her because she destroyed the tyrant of Europe. At home her leaders are taking the most effective steps for social reformation in the interest of the liberty and prosperity of the country. Since these depend "on the correct habits and information of the people," princes, nobility, and patriotic citizens are organizing societies "for the purpose of educating, and by a general distribution of the holy scriptures, giving moral instruction to the destitute."

There are, of course, defects in the English domestic picture. One great effect of her large-scale factories is that the working manufacturers "are united into Jacobinical clubs against their employers, and in opposition to the laws of the land." These frequently require a military force to suppress them. But in spite of the evils, the nation's energies appear "to increase in proportion to the difficulties." [6]

To raise military forces, money and land bounties were used increasingly; but the Federalist opposition denounced them as enormous, wasteful burdens and as withdrawing labor from useful employment. Even an attempt by the Administration to convert the militia into something more than a local body for three months' service within each state's borders was denounced by the Federalists as the first step toward conscription, "a plan which will never and ought not to be submitted to by this country while it retains an idea of civil freedom." Said Federalist Senator Robert H. Goldsborough of Maryland, of a measure providing two years' military service for the militia: It will fall heaviest on "the middling ranks of society—the tenantry, mechanics and manufacturers, the men who constitute the very bone and muscle of your population"—the poor—for men of wealth can procure substitutes.

A measure allowing the enlistment of apprentices was bitterly opposed as unconstitutional, for in effect it authorized the apprentice to violate his contract with his master. If apprentices can be enlisted in defiance of their masters, said Daniel Webster, then a Federalist representative from New Hampshire, Congress may deliver a slave from his servitude.

Legislation to prevent trading with the enemy was reluctantly passed by the Republican Congress. Necessary enforcing measures requested by President Madison were voted down, and before the war was over the prohibition of the importation of British manufactures and the export of all goods, including specie, was repealed. President Madison, in originally supporting the repealed acts, had thought they hindered the enemy by destroying her monopoly of commerce and preventing the drain of specie to England, rather than that they crippled the enemy's material resources directly. Operating on the same pecuniary logic, a large section of the Administration forces, including Gallatin and Calhoun, opposed the measure.

The Republicans as well as the Federalist Party argued that duties on British goods would yield revenue to prosecute the war and avoid recourse to the politically dangerous internal taxes. Besides, the restraining measures are impossible to enforce because of the many devices for smuggling and collusion. And with Napoleon defeated, England has not only a market for her manufactures but could get foodstuffs easily elsewhere, to our pecuniary loss. Finally, the lifting of the embargo would drain specie from the enemy and make the war prosperous.

In the end there was general approval of the proposition of the die-hard Federalists, Senator Christopher Gore of Massachusetts and Representative Gaston of North Carolina: As "all writers on political economy" agree, commerce is basic to increase a nation's population, riches, and power; and capital adjusts itself to the community's wants by continually seeking the most profitable employment, not by government interference.

The handling of finance followed a logic similar to that of the Revolutionary War. On the eve of war Gallatin bewailed that the Bank of the United States had not been rechartered. If this had been done, internal taxation would not be required; for taxation must be used in proportion as the ability to borrow is diminished. Since foreign loans are unattainable, the government must depend on the nation's own resources. But at all times the public credit must be maintained, for otherwise people will not lend at all; and to this end Gallatin religiously sought to meet payments on the public debt even to enemy holders.

Congressman Charles J. Ingersoll, Pennsylvania Republican, declared that considerable funds can be raised by borrowing, but only at an ever-increasing rate of interest. Consequently taxation should be used. Economic theory should provide an answer, but the "science of political economy is of very modern date. . . . The most authoritative treatise . . . the work of Adam Smith—did not appear longer ago than the first year of the American Revolution. . . . Since Smith wrote, a host of writers . . . have appeared for our instruction." But, after laboriously consulting all the theories, he felt that "these doctors disagree so much among themselves, as to defy the adoption of any one system from all their commentaries. They are like the members of this House. Each one has his own favorite fund of finance, and each one combats all the rest with ability." He himself, philosophically speaking, preferred an income tax, as introduced by Pitt, for all economists agree that it is the best. But, in view of the different circumstances in this country, including the difficulties of collecting it, the Administration program of a variety of taxes is the most suitable. The proposed tax on successions will be fair, profitable, and easy of collection. But a heavy excise on domestic whisky is not preferable to a land tax. It would involve hateful "domiciliatory interruption and superintendence." Had not Adam Smith declared that the excise falls on the consumer? It burdens the poor and the agricultural areas, but a land tax would fall equally on all real property and on all sections of the country.

Zebulon R. Shipherd of New York, ardent anti-war Federalist, declared, on the contrary: The land tax will break the spirit of the many enterprising immigrants who have purchased land on installments, and they will become disaffected to the government. On the other hand, the absence of a heavy excise would violate the doctrine of equality of burden, for under the existing system the seaboard pays heavily on imported liquors, while the more remote areas pay nothing.

With taxation a difficult recourse, the government continued to attempt to raise loans. Great merchants, especially Girard and Astor, contracted for considerable amounts of 6 per cent stock at a heavy discount; so did British financial houses and merchants. Banks outside of New England took portions in return for their bank notes, but the loans were not fully subscribed, and their market value was "depreciated." Short-term loans in the form of one-year interest-bearing treasury notes were issued to make up the deficiency.

The Administration's financial expert in the House, John W. Eppes of Virginia, Jefferson's son-in-law and disciple, proposed early in February 1814 to raise a new loan of $30,000,000, based on existing banking practice. The ability of a community to lend must depend on its income—on the value of the productive industry—and its circulating medium. Eppes, with "some diffidence," estimated the national wealth at $2,567,480,000, composed of lands both improved and unimproved, dwellings, houses, "other personal property including slaves," the capital in prewar commerce "allowing for exports and imports," bank capital, and turnpike, canal, toll-bridge, insurance stock, etc. He arrived at the income on this capital by taking varying rates of profit, from 4 per cent on personal property to 15 per cent on capital in commerce, and to the total he added the product of all other occupations, including manufactures, as stated in the none too accurate census of manufactures of $172,000,000, or a total of $237,649,600. He checked this against an estimate of $168,000,000 made in 1797 on the principles of "political arithmetic" and based on a population of 4,500,000. Since, on the basis of the present population, the estimate would be more than $300,000,000, Eppes felt some confidence in his smaller estimate.

The next question, said Eppes, is the amount of circulating medium required to circulate this productive industry, or national income. Writers on political economy differ as to the proper ratio, from as low as one-thirteenth to as high as one-fifth. Taking conservatively the highest percentage of one-fifth, or $47,569,120, as sufficient for actual circulation, the remainder of the circulating medium sum might be withdrawn from circulation without producing inconvenience or pressure. If the government gets the surplus, it is not withdrawn from circulation but is instantly returned to the community and becomes a part of the general circulation.

The question is, then, what is the amount of the outstanding circulating medium? He calculated that, on the estimated bank capital of $75,000,000, a circulation in notes and discounts of $100,000,000 may safely be deduced. Deducting the rate of one-fifth of the national income as necessary for actual circulation, or $47,569,120, the remainder of $52,430,880, or much more than the requested loan, constitutes the ability of the moneyed capitalists to lend. The final question is, will it be to the interest of the moneyed capitalists, especially the merchant with idle capital, to lend to the government? Since the loan combines all the advantages of safety, profit, and a command at will of the capital invested, it is a far better investment than banks or manufactures.

Timothy Pitkin, a statistician as well as a Federalist Massachusetts congressman, was astounded at Eppes's novel view of including bank deposits in the circulating medium.

Joseph Pearson, a Federalist representative from North Carolina, contended that government has already borrowed directly from the banks, or indirectly through individuals who use the banks, as much as the banks' fair and honest ability warrants, unless the government stock is considered a safe fund for paper issues. If this is so, the whole system is a tottering fabric, the government relying on the credit of the banks and the banks resting on the credit of the government. If this confidence really exists, why does not the government issue paper directly and save the enormous interest it pays to banks? He did not mean to advocate public paper, he added, but to show that the present system must fall because it is based on credit.

Federalist Congressman Samuel Sherwood of New York argued that the British would not invest since they knew the country would fall because of internal division.

However, Republican Congressman Nathaniel Macon of North Carolina reminded the opposition that the financial doctrine the Federalists now assert as "Democratic was formerly published as Federal by high authority."

Charles Ingersoll declared: The truth is that "finance is still a political secret. I have taken some pains to become at least a theorist in the science; but, after consulting most of the treatises . . . I have not been able to arrive at any more satisfactory conclusion than that the whole matter remains yet to be developed in its genuine effects." When Sir Robert Walpole introduced the funding system into England, he declared that, beyond a certain limit, the national debt would entail national ruin. Though the debt has been quintupled, ruin still holds off. Walpole used to say, when alarmists envisaged national bankruptcy and convulsion, that it had never been ascertained how much ruin there was in a nation, but that there certainly was a great deal. Pitt, unquestionably like Walpole one of the greatest of England's financiers, also subscribed to the doctrine of a limit, and his ministry was almost avowed to be a system of expedients. Yet the debt has left far behind the imaginary limit, and the system of expedients has been crowned with success.

England's debt has increased enormously, and her currency has depreciated; but what has conquered the gigantic power of France? asked Ingersoll. The subsidy system of England did this, but only a small part of the subsidies was paid in specie; the great share, in English endorsements and discounts. "Neither the frosts of Russia, nor the discipline and enthusiasm of all Europe combined in arms," could have beaten France without the reinforcement of English paper. Napoleon was beaten not by wealth or arms, but by the sword of finance, by that paper money which he deprecated as the greatest enemy to social order—"as to his social order, it certainly is." With paper his confederates were seduced and with "paper arms his enemies drove him behind the Rhine."

John Forsyth, Republican from Georgia, declared: "On the subject of finance we have witnessed much labour and experienced much fatigue. It has tended to make confusion worse confounded. In my researches, I, too, have met with a principle as true as any we have here heard, and infinitely more convenient. . . . The celebrated [Johann von] Herrenschwand lays it down as a most valuable discovery 'that a regular and constant increase in the expenditure of the Government, is the only true means of insuring a constant progression in the intelligence and enjoyment of the people.' The grand secret, then, for increasing the happiness of the people, is for its rulers to spend as much as possible. I cannot say I agree entirely . . . with this profound economist, although he is announced to the world by Arthur Young as one of the greatest political geniuses of the age. All I intend is to show that the subject of finance is intricate; that the greatest men are puzzled and that the gloomy predictions and dull calculations of the . . . [opposition] are to be listened to with much doubt and circumspection."

Promoters in practically every state successfully called for more banks. The reasons given included relieving the scarcity of circulating medium and providing various loans for the federal government. Leading citizens in many areas simply followed the old practice of not waiting for a charter, but setting up a banking "association" with all the powers and immunities of a chartered bank and transacting business while they waited, sometimes years, for a charter. In the capital district, which was under the supervision of Congress, the Bank of the Metropolis demanded a charter on the ground that Congress had evidenced its purpose to eliminate all monopolies in banking by the numerous charters it had already granted. The oversubscription for the stock showed that there was a need of additional banks in the district.[7]

The New York legislature in chartering the New York Manufacturing Company in 1812 for the production of the items necessary to the manufacture of cotton and woolen cloth, stated that it granted the concern the banking privilege because of "the difficulty of inducing persons to invest money in untried enterprises however important to the general welfare." [8]

On the other hand, the learned Republican lawyers, Alexander Dallas and Ingersoll, protested in behalf of Girard the action of the Pennsylvania legislature in prohibiting private merchants such as their client from issuing bank notes. This is "to place the civil rights of an individual, derived from the Constitution, upon the same footing with the artificial rights of a corporation created by a legislative grant." [9]

By 1813 business and financial expansion had reached a point where businessmen were complaining of restricted bank credit, and the possibilities of suspending specie payments in the leading commercial centers were being canvassed. Just at the time, a theoretical defense of such action tied up with government financing was presented in *An Inquiry Into the Nature of Value and of Capital, and Into the Operation of Government Loans, Banking Institutions, and Private Credit*, by the English-born Alexander Bryan Johnson (1786–1867). Johnson had no college education but had an amazing variety of intellectual interests, including physiology and speech. He came to know commerce early in life through working in his father's store in Utica, New York. While hardly more than a youth, he promoted an extensive glass corporation in western New York. He came to New York City just before the outbreak of the war to study banking, both as an investment and as a branch of "speculative political economy."

His treatise maintained that the financial problems of war as well as peace can be solved by the unrestricted extension and operation of banks and expansion of public debt.

Banks increase capital by increasing the issue of notes beyond their specie holdings to borrowers who can make a profit greater than the interest. As the Bank of England bears witness, bank notes can continue objects of desire and thus capital, even though the banks suspend payment; for the banks always receive in exchange for their notes an equal amount of private notes. Individuals desire this exchange because of the superior and more widely diffused confidence placed in the bankers' notes. In fact, the discount paid to bankers is not for any actual specie, but for the use of their name and credit. That the inconvertible Bank of England notes circulate is not because of the legal necessity of individuals' accepting them. If an article lacking value, such as a pint of water, were made lawful payment, credit operations would cease. Thus the legal-tender "continentals" immediately vanished from circulation when they ceased to be thought valuable. The Bank of England notes possess value because of their uses by individuals in liquidating their debts to the bank and in meeting the requirements of government. The only effect of the tender law is to prevent vexatious lawsuits. Thus in the United States if the banks were forced to suspend specie payments, the notes would not be depreciated, for bank debtors would gladly receive them as so much actual specie.

Government can easily meet the war costs by issuing loans equal to, or greater than, the loss of capital through abstraction of labor for war services and the consumption of goods by the abstracted labor. These loans are capital, for they are objects of value.

Government loans are in reality loans from government to the nation, for the money is not wanted for accumulation, but for expending. The borrowed money is immediately returned to the people, and in addition the people have the securities. Thus the national capital is increased to the amount of the government securities, and the nation may continue to use this borrowed capital by paying the stipulated interest which maintains its value. These securities in effect create the necessary aid for government by enabling the profitable issue of bank notes to prospective lenders to the government. So long as such "uses" are available—that is, uses paying a greater return than the bank interest—no depreciation can occur. Just as government loans increase the capital of a nation, so their liquidation—that is, a tax to redeem them—impoverishes people. But taxes to pay the interest are a necessary evil.

Johnson shortly afterward left the city, obtained a charter for an insurance company in Utica and tried to utilize it for banking, but was forced to cease operations by the authorities. He finally became the successful head of the Ontario Branch Bank in Utica, a respected authority among bankers throughout the country, and an entrepreneur with extensive interests.

Meanwhile, early in 1814, Astor warned fellow merchants, including Girard, that they would all be ruined unless there were a national bank with inconvertible notes and a capital composed of "bond and mortgages on good real security"—land. This land scheme was the best to "inspire confidence." Once it commences operations "property must come to its proper and fair value." [10] In April 1814 the New Orleans banks justified their suspension of specie payments on the ground that the contraband trade had drained their specie.

The advance of the British fleet up the Potomac late in August 1814 set off in Philadelphia, New York, and Baltimore a movement of bank suspensions of specie payments that eventually covered the entire country except New England. The *de facto* tender character of the notes was legally supported in various states by the stipulation that non-acceptance of the notes in payment of debts suspended the judgment.

As the Philadelphia banks prepared to suspend, Carey explained to them in a confidential circular that this action was preferable to the alternative of reducing discounts. Suspension is, of course, only justified by an extraordinary crisis, but it does "not wear the revolting features of novelty." It saved England from bankruptcy and has been recently found adequate to its object in New Orleans.[11]

The bank directors rephrased Carey's language somewhat and informed the public through the local press on August 30 that "the moment the vigorous blockade of American ports prevented the export of our produce, foreign supplies could be paid for in specie only, and as the importation of foreign goods [British] in the eastern [New England] states has been very large," it occasioned for many months a continual drain from the banks, aggravated by a trade in British government bills of exchange. "To meet this great demand for specie, the course of trade did for a considerable time enable us to draw large supplies from the southern states," but the unhappy situation there "has cut off this recourse, and circumstances having occurred, which have in a considerable degree occasioned alarm and distrust," the banks had to decide whether to continue to exert themselves to draw within their vaults the country's specie and thus facilitate its export, or whether to suspend specie payments to prevent further loss of their moneyed capital and thus be able to resume eventually with less difficulty.[12]

These arguments became standard for the commercial centers.

Short shrift was made of a proposal by Republican Congressman Bolling Hall of Georgia for the issue of legal-tender treasury notes to provide a uniform currency. The House refused to discuss the matter. Instead, the new Secretary of the Treasury, Dallas, proposed a national-bank scheme which had the endorsement of Astor, Girard, and other heavy holders of the "depreciated" government securities, along with former Congress opponents of the Bank of the United States, such as Senator Samuel Smith of Maryland.

Heretofore "the national faith, and not the national wealth, has . . . been the chief instrument of finance," said Dallas in his report to Congress in October 1814. But the government needs more money than would be politic even if practicable to raise by taxes. Credit must be utilized for a large share, but the public credit is depressed, and no hope of adequate aid can safely rest on it. To restore the public credit and establish a national circulating medium, a national bank operating on "credit combined with capital" should be chartered.

Under the Dallas scheme the bank would have a nominal capital of $50,000,000, with subscriptions payable primarily in public debt. Government would choose a third of the directors, receive a loan of $30,000,000 from the bank, and could order suspension of specie payments if such action were deemed necessary. But, whether the issue of a paper currency came either from the Treasury or a national bank, the acceptance of this paper must "forever be optional with the citizens," declared Dallas. "The extremity of that day cannot be anticipated when an honest and enlightened statesman will again venture upon the desperate expedient of a tender law."

Samuel Ingham, Pennsylvania manufacturer and Republican congressman, in defending the Dallas proposal explained that, by using the public debt for the bank subscriptions, we relieve the market of excessive issues, raise its price, and make possible eventual further government loans. The small amount of specie subscription is no hindrance. In ordinary times banking requires no specie except for settling balances between merchants in different cities and between banks, and for retail trade. The credit of a bank depends no more on the specie in its vaults than the credit of a merchant depends on the amount of money in his desk. The credit of the latter depends on his visible estate, income, and the like; and so does that of the bank. Its visible estate is the public debt and specie; its income is the dividends from the government and the interest from loans to government and individuals. Since the notes are a tender for taxes and other public dues, they cannot depreciate. England bears witness to the fact that suspension of specie payments would not hurt the country. The suspension in the United States may have been accompanied by the depreciation of bank notes, but this is because the local bank paper cannot, like specie before, pay balances between people of different states.

The journalist Hezekiah Niles argued that if the bank should pay specie, Britain would realize that the cheapest way of prosecuting the war would be to undermine the nation's credit by draining the basis of it.[13]

The Federalists said that they favored the right kind of a national bank. Gaston had already congratulated Congress because, at the same time that it was liberating commerce by repealing non-importation and export embargoes, "the fetters would also be loosed with which a narrow constitutional exposition had heretofore bound the government." But a proper national bank must approximate the size and character of the first bank. No bank can achieve its end unless the public has confidence in it. Such a belief keeps its bank notes in circulation. Furthermore, it enables the bank to do an extensive business without notes or specie, but merely by book transfer. Apparently forgetting his continual defense of inconvertible notes, state investment, and the like in North Carolina, he declared that practically all the provisions of the Dallas scheme, especially the government appointment of some directors, would excite distrust and injure the bank's credit. The Bank of England is not a good example, he said. It is more than a century old and is fairly rooted in public confidence. It is sustained "by ancient reverence, by universal interest and a stable government." But in spite of this it would have tottered on the suspension of specie payments, except for a prosperous commerce and most fortunate political occurrences. Webster added that a national bank would be an attack on the rights of the state banks, which were established on the ground that a national bank was unconstitutional. The advantages of any national bank are greatly overrated.

Calhoun agreed that government should have no power over the proposed bank. He ruled out government subscription, government directors, loans to government, and the suspension of specie payments. But subscription to its capital outside of the specie should be exclusively in new, interest-bearing treasury notes convertible by the government into public debt. To allow holders of the existing depreciated public debt certificates to participate would be giving them a large unearned gain. Ingham replied that Calhoun's proposal was a machine to squeeze a little depreciated money out of the people for the present by abandoning the great object of reviving the public credit.

Ingersoll was aghast that Republicans should support the Calhoun proposal. Why not come at once to the resolution of "honest Hall" and issue treasury notes without the unnecessary, unwieldy machinery of a bank? The proponents of the Calhoun plan perhaps feel that the public will occupy themselves in examining the mill without examining the material. But "those moneyed men whom you hitherto have looked to for support though now you seem ready to discard them . . . are a sharp sighted animal, who will pierce through your projects at a glance, however you may wrap and fold them up from common observation."

Secretary Dallas agreed. He informed Congress that discrimination between old and new creditors would lead to distrust by capitalists.

Girard wrote Ingersoll, apropos of Calhoun's opposition to the Dallas plan, that it was to be regretted that "jealousy or some other sinister cause against that class of wealthy citizens who have loaned their money to government, will induce gentlemen to reject the best mode of consolidating the credit of the United States, an event which alone can force an honourable peace." [14]

Almost all the Federalists voted for the Calhoun scheme. T. P. Grosvenor of New York was an exception. He supported the Dallas proposal. He claimed "no particular knowledge of the practical rules of banking." Like other gentlemen, he had studied the works of the great masters of the science of political economy. "But . . . many of their dogmas had been refuted, and most of their rules have been exposed to doubt, if not to subversion, by the experience of modern times." In this important science, it is not degrading to receive the lesson of experience even from an enemy. Pitt, realizing that wars cannot go on without loans, never lost the confidence of the capitalists.

Samuel Farrow, Republican of South Carolina, expressed the general sentiment. He was not acquainted with the principles of banking, and "this Hall is not a place to acquire any knowledge on the subject, for those who understand it best, differ the most," but he was for a bank in peace or war, provided it "wear the complexion of a commercial bank on banking principles."

A compromise was made. It provided for the separation of the bank and government, as Calhoun proposed. The capital was $35,000,000. Government would subscribe $5,000,000 in public debt; of the remainder, $5,000,000 would be specie, $10,000,000 public debt, and $15,000,000 treasury notes convertible into public debt.

Madison, on the advice of Dallas, vetoed this "emaciated" measure. The subscription of public debt was too small, and the obligation to maintain the specie payment would prevent the bank from supplying a national medium. But, as experience testifies, the bank's notes, resting on good pledges though not on specie and performing the uses of specie in tax payments and other public transactions, would "qualify the Bank to supply at once circulating medium and pecuniary aids to the government."

The vast amount of Bank of England legal-tender paper, Madison wrote Jefferson, has depreciated little if any because of its use in the large mass of government and private transactions. The difference in value between the notes and specie arose from the rise of the latter, not the depreciation of the former, and this is proved by the fact that the notes, in spite of a great increase in quantity, have been rising to a par with the metal in consequence of a favorable balance of trade which diminishes the demand for them in foreign markets.[15]

Federalist Senator Rufus King, formerly of Massachusetts but now of New York, agreed that the bank would be of little use during the war; but in peace it would be "invaluable. in the recovery and re-establishment of the credit and finances of the nation."

In the interlude, in accordance with Dallas's request, an act was passed to issue $25,000,000 in treasury notes. Those under $100 were non-interest bearing, fundable at option of holder into 7 per cent stock, and the others bearing 5⅖ per cent interest were fundable into 6 per cent stock. But peace came before the measure was passed.

At this time domestic manufactures came in for some attention through the publication in 1814 of Coxe's *Statement of the Arts and Manufactures of the United States.*

The great secret of the advantage of manufactures is labor-saving machinery, he said. It effects with an "exactness and promptitude beyond the reach of manual power and skill, a great variety and number of manufacturing operations." These wonderful machines "working as if they were animated beings, endowed with all the talents of their inventors, laboring with organs that never tire, and subject to no expense of food, or bed, or raiment, or dwelling, may be justly considered as equivalent to an immense body of manufacturing recruits enlisted in the service of the country." Aiding the development in the United States has been the utilization of otherwise idle children, the greater employment of females in general, the supply of funds to manufactures by sound banks, and especially the state enactment of general incorporation laws for manufacturing enterprises.

The physical, moral, and political evils hitherto associated with manufactures are eliminated by the use of machinery and allied processes. The ancient methods of hand production of the old manufacturing system created various classes of "morbid and decrepit persons." But the use of machinery in cotton manufactures has abridged and softened the labor of women and allowed the male weavers to employ themselves in superintendence, instruction, superior or other occupations and promote their health by occasional attention to gardening, agriculture, and the improvement of their farms.

The system adopted at the manufactory of Humphreysville shows how the American people may quicken and increase the virtue of the rising generation and reform the degenerate of later years by manufactures. The asylums of the poor and unfortunate, the aged and decrepit, and the penitentiaries for indiscretion and immorality are improved and aided by the employment and profits of labor-saving machinery.

This growth of manufacture should not conflict with the interests of commerce. The richest object of commercial enterprise for American merchants is the trade of non-manufacturing countries in selling them our manufactures and taking their raw materials, for this increases the nation's specie holdings and thereby facilitates our commercial and banking institutions and brings an increasing number of nations into our debt.[16]

But as for granting any "protection" to manufactures beyond what was given by the double duties for revenue purposes, the general attitude of both parties was summed up in Taylor's denunciation of such advocates as belonging in the category of the parasitic, aristocratic paper jobbers, who, by means of their law-created privileges, filched their gains from the industry of the sole productive class of farmers, and made them in effect slaves.

At the same time, he defended slavery as making for the love of virtue and liberty among freemen. Vicious and mean qualities become despicable in the eyes of freemen from being associated with the character of slaves. "Qualities, odious in themselves, become more contemptible, when united with the most degraded class of men, than when seen with our equals. It may be thus that personal slavery has constantly reflected the strongest rays of civil liberty and patriotism."

But the slaveholders have been deterred from making agricultural improvements and establishing any tolerable system of police for managing slaves by the foolish notion that the destruction of their lands and the irregularities of their Negroes were incurable consequences of slavery. The first error is occasionally detected by the rare effort of individuals, but these can never make a wide and lasting impression while they are defeated by the second. This obstacle of a bad police can only be removed by the legislative power. Existing legislation does not effectively prevent thievery by slaves, especially runaways, of the property of other than their masters.

A law providing that every slave who should run away or be convicted of theft must be sold out of the state or at a considerable distance from his place of residence, might be effective at only slight retrenchment of the prerogatives of ownership.

Another prerequisite is the elimination of the free Negroes. Cut off from most of the rights of citizens and from all the allowances of slaves, they are driven into every species of crime for subsistence. At the same time their existence tempts slaves to seek freedom and engage in insurrections. Thus they are an unproductive class living on agriculture, like stock jobbers or a capitalist class.[17]

Poor relief still was a problem. A committee of ladies of gentility in New York City informed the authorities that the problem would be solved if only "a fair proportion of the money, indefinitely expended on the poor" by private benevolence should be placed under the care of an institution to supply work for the indigent and pay them only for their labor, as they put it. The city should provide a "habitation or work house" to be called the "House of Industry," and private gentlemen should supply the operating funds. The town fathers applauded the scheme as ideal, for it would greatly relieve the pressure on the public charity and eliminate the "pretexts to mendicity and . . . idleness." They gave as a home the top floor of one of the town's charity schools—the "Economical School"—made a small donation for materials, appointed the ladies for "their respectable characters and benevolent lives" the managers of the establishment, and called on the people to contribute heartily.[18]

Some opposition was voiced against immigration, especially English, as threatening the interests of native labor, but the arguments came generally from the anti-war Federalists. As usual, the complaint was not that the immigrants were undesirable as laborers, but that they should not be allowed to become citizens and participate in the political life of the nation. Naturalized or not, they were those "worthless foreigners" who, along with the inhabitants of the western states, were charged with being among the primary causes of the war. Federalist Daniel Sheffey, attacking the Administration's Loan Bill in the House, said that he would not permit those who hereafter migrate here to meddle with the concerns of government in any manner. They do not know how "to use or appreciate the rights and duties of a citizen possessing a portion of the political power of his country," for their "habits have been formed in an opposite state of things."

Findley, who was an Irish-born Revolutionary War officer, observed: "When I look around me in the House, or in whatever company I happen to be, I see none but immigrants, or the descendants of immigrants, who at no very distant period have expatriated themselves."

CHAPTER XVI

The Era of "Good Feeling"

THE peace shattered the mighty Federalist Party. Most of its members gradually joined the Republican Party. But its social philosophy by no means disappeared. The most distinguished exponents of that philosophy, notably Calhoun, became the very men who led the Republican Party. Calhoun was a man of high intellectual caliber. Like Madison a generation earlier, he had visions of America, with the South in the lead, developing into a mightier England.

As Administration leader in the House, he proclaimed the policies of high Federalism, though the Federalists deprecated these policies at that time.. Of the two fatal extremes to which nations may go, military violence is more dangerous than feebleness, he said. That the country endures insults from foreign nations is not the fault of any administration nor of the two great political parties, but must be attributed to the people's reluctance to resort to arms and bear the financial burdens.

Nations "have heads but no hearts." The statesmen and patriots of every important nation are jealous of the progress of others. Since we are growing faster than any other country and rapidly developing in the very particulars in which England excels, it cannot be expected that England will permit the United States to achieve its great destiny. Therefore the country must have a substantial navy and a good army on a draft basis. To pay the heavy costs the country should develop a system of internal taxes, primarily excises.

But the general opinion of Congress was that, if this were the meaning of a vigorous government, they preferred the old-fashioned "feeble" kind.

The great immediate problem remained that of the monetary system as the suspension of specie payment continued and bank notes had varying rates of depreciation depending on the bank and area. There was no lack of sentiment in mercantile centers for continuing this situation. Condy Raguet, merchant, promoter, journalist, and Federalist member of the state legislature, declared in a series of Philadelphia newspaper articles that, even if desirable, specie payments cannot be restored because of the unfavorable balance of trade. The different rates of discount on bank notes between commercial centers or between city and country are due likewise to differences in the balance of trade between them. Even if the national bank, which he admitted he had supported for recharter in the 1810 dispute, were in existence, its notes would have become inconvertible and subject to varying rates of discount from region to region for the same reasons that bank notes had. Inconvertibility, as the Bank of England's suspension of specie payments shows, cannot adversely affect the nation's interest because the banks have the same means of meeting their notes as before—namely, their debtors' notes. While the latter cannot pay in specie, they can do so in merchandise of equal value. Only one evil, in fact, need be apprehended from inconvertible bank paper. Because of the absence of the check of specie redemption, banks may be tempted to overtrade in order to increase their dividends. But if they follow the principles of honest, prudent directors and issue no more notes than they would have under specie-paying conditions, they will always be solvent.[1]

The very conservative Republican *Analectic Magazine* commented that Raguet had uttered some sensible remarks but wondered how banks could fail which "make their payments (as they are miscalled) only in their own notes. Unless there should be a failure of copper, paper, and engravers, such banks cannot be in danger of bankruptcy." [2]

The magazine had its own scheme of allowing the banks to issue inconvertible notes but maintain them at a par with specie. This was presented by another adventurous figure, James Workman, a former English lawyer, Louisiana judge, member of the unsuccessful "Burr Conspiracy," and at the moment a hack writer for Philadelphia journals. Workman said that critics of inconvertible bank paper erroneously assert that a depreciated paper has always continued to depreciate until it was worthless, unless its credit was redeemed by its becoming the representative of specie again. Bank of England notes varied during the last seven years from 3 to 30 per cent, according to the state of commerce and political events. They fell with Napoleon's triumphs and rose with his disasters. Since his second abdication they have risen to par, but at no time were they the representative of specie.

The notes of the banks, especially the leading banks in Philadelphia, are not really worthless rags, for the capital of the banks consists chiefly of public stock and so cautious are the bank directors that other (private) lenders have more bad debts. Through the utilization of the public debt, the parity of bank notes with specie could be retained without the notes' being redeemed in specie.

Under Workman's scheme, the banks would stand ready to redeem their notes in public-debt stock with the 6 per cent stock as the standard. The government would pay the interest on the debt in specie, and this would impart to the bank capital, in so far as it was composed of public debt, a specie value. That capital would become a solid foundation for a paper currency, which "would mark an improvement in political economy." Whereas when notes were convertible into specie, banks could only circulate safely four times as much in notes as their specie reserves, under the new scheme one dollar would circulate sixteen dollars in notes.[3]

Secretary of the Treasury Dallas, however, now favored completely convertible notes. The English experiment, which has given rise to a contrary doctrine is not conclusive, he informed Calhoun in

1816, because the difference in situations, including governments, makes the experiment a bad precedent. Dallas justified the government's acceptance of the inconvertible notes at par during the war and the postwar period. True, such issues constituted a usurpation of the sovereign power to coin money, but the suspension had been generally accepted under the exigencies of extreme necessity. Had the government refused to accept them, it could not have raised the necessary loans and taxes, and at the same time such action would have destroyed the only adequate medium of exchange; in short, refusal would have shaken the very foundation of private property.

But at present the suspension continues because the banks have no interest to reduce their excessive issues. A proper national bank with convertible notes is the basic remedy. It would have a capital of $35,000,000 of which the government would subscribe $7,000,000 in public debt, and private parties the remainder in the proportion of three-fourths public debt and one-fourth specie. Government was to appoint five of the twenty-five directors. At the same time legislation should be passed providing that at the end of approximately a year (December 1816) notes of non-specie-paying banks should be deprived of government deposits and the acceptance of their notes for government dues. Should these measures fail, a graduated tax should be imposed on inconvertible notes.

As on most economic issues, the ensuing controversy cut across party lines and involved conflicting commercial and financial interests.

Calhoun guided the bill through the House and enthusiastically supported provisions of the bank he had formerly deprecated. The ultimate cause of the suspension, he said, was that the banks had undertaken business foreign to their nature in making long-term loans to government not as brokers but as stockholders. The banks, however, will not voluntarily sell these holdings to reduce their excessive note issues and obtain specie because this would reduce their great profits under the existing system.

Representative Henry St. George Tucker, the Virginia Republican, later professor of law at the University of Virginia, added that the self-evident truth of the impossibility of excessive issues under convertibility "has been happily illustrated by the celebrated author of *The Wealth of Nations*."

As for the most direct measure for resumption of the taxing proposal, however, Clay summed up the overwhelming sentiment of both parties in stating that neither Congress nor the community was prepared for its application.

A large segment of the pro-bank Republicans even sharply opposed the other proposal for resumption as poor requital to banks for their patriotism during the war. The gainers would be the hard-money men of New England, who combined to cripple the war effort and ruin the Administration by withholding their money in the hour of the nation's peril. Banks should pay in specie, but at some more distant date which they did not specify. Samuel Smith, one of the leaders of the group, added that he had never been able, with "all his practice and experience, to understand the subject of money fully." Therefore government meddling in such delicate subjects would cause business stagnation with its disastrous consequences.

On the Federalist side there were similar splits. The pro-bank Grosvenor of New York said that the Federalists should not complain of the government appointment of bank directors. Federalists, tolerating such appointments in New York banks, find the directors have little influence. But Webster thought Grosvenor and other bank Federalists should be read out of the party for their "compromise of principle on a great moneyed institution." Webster bemoaned that "though young . . . he possessed antiquated notions, and that to be useful he ought to have been with generations that had gone by," with the "hard-money men" who established the Constitution and the first bank. Timothy Pitkin added that this new monster would, like the first bank, use its enormous capital concentrated in few hands oppressively.

Joseph Hopkinson, aristocratic Pennsylvania Federalist, littérateur, and jurist, agreed that the bank would create a privileged moneyed aristocracy; but, unlike Webster and the New Englanders, he was against forcing the state banks to resume specie payments. The suspension had not been caused by excessive issues, but by the gloomy state of public affairs and consequent loss of confidence, he stated.

Federalist Senator William Wells of Delaware also appealed to laissez faire. "The science of banking, connected as it is . . . with . . . the great interests of society . . . is a science like all others" which progressively improves. It is only imperfectly understood by those who have studied it most. Could "this science now call to her aid, the justly celebrated author of the Wealth of Nations—even this, her favourite son, would be obliged to confess that much of this theory, which the world has so long adopted, was but like 'the clouds that gather round the setting sun, and seeming only to form a part of the brightness, by which they are illumined.' Who then, among us, is entitled to hold the 'lamp of truth' to this subject?" Surely the intelligent and enlightened people do not expect relief in this matter from the legislature. "They look not to us for health who have medicined them, into sickness. All they ask of us is to desist, 'to let them alone.' " It is far time for "the merchants—the Morrises and the Fitzsimonses—to take their seats among us, to assert their own character and maintain their own interests" against these former advocates of resumption.

The measure establishing a second Bank of the United States was finally passed, and so was Dallas's second proposal in the form of Webster's resolution that all government dues after February 1, 1817, were to be paid in specie, treasury notes, or convertible bank notes. The measures by no means meant the resumption of specie payments by the state banks.

Of course, there were a few old-fashioned Republicans like John Taylor who, in their academic manner, were still preaching against funding and banking systems as giving rise to a paper aristocracy which would destroy the liberty and property of the people. But the mass of good "Republicans" were of a different opinion; at least those who were in office and wrote in the journals. Said the Republican *Analectic*: Taylor's doctrine is in open "defiance of Adam Smith . . . and the whole host of our orthodox economists. . . . His work should be answered by some able advocate of the moneyed interest. It is quite foolish to talk, as some do, of despising such attacks: less powerful ones have sometimes shaken interests as firmly established as those of the stockholders of the United States, and that too in countries where the debtor part of the community (the larger majority of course) was not invested with the supreme power of the state." [4]

All the while Mathew Carey was busily denouncing the various measures in so far as they threatened a reduction of loans and discounts. The state banks instead of reducing notes and discounts should issue a new form of inconvertible notes called "bank credits" or "receivables," which had grown up during the war and were being pushed in the New York City *Columbian*. These notes are payable for debts due the issuing banks.

In effect the system is merely a change in form, not in substance, of the present system. The great mass of bank business in commercial cities is done without the use of specie or specie notes, but by check; and even if various banks are used it amounts to the same thing because the banks exchange them.[5]

So distant did resumption look at the end of the year and so much at odds were various financial interests as to when general resumption should occur, that Governor Wilson Carey Nicholas convened the Virginia legislature ahead of time, in November 1816, in order to prevent the state's Resumption Act from going into effect. If Virginia resumes specie payments before other states, he declared, the state banks will lose their specie, to the damage of the state's commerce and thus ultimately of its agricultural interest. A new state of things exists here and throughout the world "that baffles the theories of the political economists. It is not now so much an enquiry, how came we into the present difficulties, as how we can get out of them." [6]

Specie payments were resumed by the banks in February 1817, but toward the end of 1818 they were again suspended by many state banks throughout the country and even restricted by the Bank of the United States.

A demand was made in Congress that the bank's charter be revoked for failure to achieve the objects of its establishment—namely, furnishing a uniform currency throughout the Union, preventing excessive issue of bank notes, and bringing about specie payments. Instead, the bank had helped to bring on inflation and a consequent depression. Supporters of the bank quickly justified the mother bank's refusal to accept branch notes at par on the basis of Raguet's argument of differences in the balance of trade between offices.

The able Republican William Lowndes of South Carolina, who claimed that Adam Smith was the highest authority on monetary as well as other matters, found that the rate of exchange with the commercial countries—England, France, and Holland—had been relatively steady since the bank's establishment. So he argued that the amount of bank discounts must be in the aggregate nearly right and not excessive.

More dogmatic was the defense of John Sergeant of Pennsylvania. He was a graduate of the University of Pennsylvania, reared in the Federalist tradition, deeply interested in various philanthropic movements, and one of the most distinguished lawyers in the country. Though he had opposed the chartering of the bank, he became a director and its agent in negotiating a heavy specie loan abroad to commence operations.

The charge that the bank loaned little on good commercial paper is irrelevant, he said, for the loans were made on the best security —bank stock. Furthermore, to expect bank directors to discriminate among borrowers is not only to measure them by a higher moral standard than that demanded by the law of the land, but also to vest them with an arbitrary power over the borrowers' lives. The whole question of "speculation" is irrelevant too. "Real value is a matter of conjecture, depending upon a thousand considerations, and among the rest, at the present moment, depending upon the decision of the House."

The law not only does not, but should not, bar directors and officers from dealing in bank stock. Men whose daily occupation is to deal in stocks and money are deemed best qualified to be directors, but can they be expected on becoming directors to surrender their occupations, to purify themselves from the love of gain?

Congress itself certainly has no right to revoke the charter any more than it can legislate away the life of a national being. "Chartered rights are sacred things," as Pelatiah Webster said. Of course, the charter can be brought before the judiciary, but even if the charges were such as to work forfeiture according to the charter, the question of the expediency of such court action must be taken into account. The mere bringing of the action would dangerously wound the bank in its living principle, its credit. "This artificial being, though it has not precisely the same sort of susceptibility as the natural being, is nevertheless exquisitely susceptible."

The politicians and the learned searched everywhere for wisdom. Members of Congress looked at McCulloch's review of David Ricardo's *The Principles of Political Economy and Taxation* in the *Edinburgh Review*, discovered on the first page that he was the outstanding authority on money and banking; that he had written, just before the appearance of the famous Bullion Committee report in favor of a return of specie payments, a study containing a concise, satisfactory, and "luminous exposition of the principles regulating the distribution of the precious metals"; and that his work had done more to improve the principles of political economy than any single writer, with perhaps the exception of Adam Smith. They thereupon urged its reprinting in the United States and, along with government officials, made possible an American edition by subscribing for half the proposed edition.[7]

But even those who saluted Ricardo as the great authority on cur-

rency read his essentially hard-money views in the light of what
they considered the peculiar circumstances of America and came to
conclusions that somewhat puzzled Ricardo. Raguet, whose large
investments in coal lands and city lots were swept away by the depression, informed Ricardo that in reports he had prepared for the
legislature on the crises and the means of preventing them, he had
pointed out the evils resulting from the injudicious expansion and
contractions of paper. But the banks, instead of adopting a policy
of gradual reduction as advocated by all intelligent people, sharply
contracted, and this instantly paralyzed all industry and commerce.[8]

Raguet's friend Carey, who was again a state director of the Bank
of Pennsylvania, informed the Bank of the United States directors
in another printed confidential circular that their systematic, reprehensible reduction of discounts was the cause of the crisis.[9]

From the state-owned State Bank of South Carolina came one of
the most skillful attacks on the Bank of the United States as the cause
of the trouble. This report was signed by its president, Stephen
Elliott, who had a Yale training and was a wealthy plantation owner
and eminent botanist.

He was quite adept at manipulating the concepts of current economic theory. All prices, he said, had risen with cotton because the
value of labor employed in cotton regulated its value in other occupations. He was willing to grant that the market was unnaturally high
during the last two years, but no one could foresee the hour, much
less anticipate the rapidity or extent, of the fall. That decline had
been caused by the machinations of the Bank of the United States
in reducing the circulating medium.

The "foreign," private profit-making national bank has reduced
its issues and employed the government deposits to acquire the specie
of the state banks and force them to reduce their paper. The reduction of money might not be ruinous if it merely altered the general
price level and thus the relative value of all property. However, it
changes the situation of debtor and creditor. The necessary altera-
tions do not speedily occur in rents on long leases and in fixed fees
for various services, nor would the interested parties acquiesce in
the new state of things without a struggle.

As a consequence of a general scarcity of money, Elliott pointed
out, families cannot maintain their accustomed expenditure. A universal diminution of consumption arises. Cultivators and manufacturers of perishable articles will first feel the pressure. Unable to wait

for prosperity's return, they must sell at any price. But even with reduced prices they do not find the former consumption for their goods, and they are compelled to produce less. Their reduced incomes become insufficient for their usual expenditures. They withdraw their children from school or forego medical attention because the fees are still regulated by former practice.

Those continuing to charge the old prices suffer from reduced employment. They feel their embarrassments, but they know not where, or when, or how to yield. The producer of imperishable articles faces similar difficulties. Endeavoring to maintain the price of his labor, he withholds his production from a falling market and struggles until his capital and credit are exhausted. Thus the wealth of the country is engrossed by the opulent few.

A uniform national currency should be issued by government and be based on land as the least liable to fluctuate, the most permanent in its value, and bearing the most steady relation to labor and consequently to property.

Though Elliott's land-bank theory was denounced by other South Carolinians as heretical, he apparently knew how to lend money, for later conservative historians in their general indictment of any state participation in banking and of banks in general viewed Elliott's management of the bank as a conspicuous exception.[10]

The outstanding exponent of a national paper currency at the time was no westerner or wild-eyed radical but a learned, cultured Washington gentleman with the best of antecedents and a flair for promoting anything from a private national bank to a learned society. He was the Englishman, Thomas Law (1756–1834).[11] His wife was related to George Washington, and his brothers held high positions in church and state in England.

He proposed a national board to issue a limited amount of notes though, as in Blodget's scheme, his limit was never precisely defined. The notes were to be used by Congress for subscriptions to canal, road, and bridge companies and other "public improvements," especially companies in which he had interests. The notes could also be lent to subscribers to such companies at 3 per cent. The notes were to be receivable in payment for public lands and taxes and convertible by the holder into 4 per cent stock.

If any new kind of enterprise came along that attracted interest, Law could quickly bring it under the category of "public improvement" and proclaim the advantages of the national currency for its development. Thus he added manufacturing companies and railways when they began to be talked about. He even proved that the scheme could provide for the eventual emancipation of the slaves, with a board of emancipation to handle the notes of this operation.[12]

Law's connections, if nothing else, got him a respectful hearing. Madison doubtless summed up the general opinion: He is a genius, but his plan would not end the evils of an unfavorable balance of trade and the fluctuations of an exportable currency. A public board always involves the danger of an excessive issue of paper, which, instead of reducing the rate of interest, would depreciate the principal. As he urbanely wrote to Law, "The practicability of a paper emission, equal in value to specie cannot be doubted, provided its circulating quantity be adapted to the demands for it, and it be freed from *all apprehension* of undue augmentation." [13]

With public sentiment holding "overissue" or "overtrading" by the banks as the main cause of the depression, the House of Representatives in 1819 ordered Secretary of Treasury William Crawford to report measures for procuring and retaining sufficient specie for a circulating medium, or plans of a national circulating medium adapted to the exigencies of the country's depressed state. But Congress was hardly to be blamed for finding Crawford's reply of little use. He reported in 1820 that "the sufferings which have been produced by efforts to resume and continue specie payments have been great," but they must continue until the value of property and the price of labor assume that relation to the precious metals "which our wealth and industry compared with that of other states enable us to retain." [14]

Churchill C. Cambreleng, wealthy New York merchant, entrepreneur, and Republican congressman, amplified the idea by asserting that no "cheap money" device could work, for the rate of interest depends on the state of trade. To prove this, he set up a cyclical theory of trade on the basis of the last thirty years' experience of the many fluctuations in the market rate.

"Overtrading produces a reaction, business is dull. Capital may appear ample, but there is little use for it"; consequently circulation is dull and the interest rate is low. However, the "existence of a calm in trade" inspires confidence, which is gradually restored. Profits increase and business augments. The demand for money advances with the same pace, until all the actual capital of the community is employed. Business still increases and calls into action the use of fictitious capital or credit which is based on confidence. The rate of interest now advances, because business is active and there is a demand for money. This brisk state of trade sometimes will be disturbed by political events; and in any event by "a natural reaction." The amount of borrowed capital is inevitably swelled beyond all moderate bounds, confidence is destroyed, bankruptcies follow, the community is suddenly left in the same dead calm from which it started, and interest is again low. "Such are the revolutions, which capital, trade and interest are continually performing in this community."

This "proved," he felt, that people mistakenly accuse the banks of all calamities, and they should refrain from restraints on sound banks. Credit instruments are both essential and inevitable, and banks with convertible notes provide the safest. Whenever trade is profitable the ingenuity of the country will supply its wants and enlarge its business by the use of credit in various ways. Legislatures might as well attempt to confine the winds in an aviary as to encircle credit with legal restrictions, for there can be no limit to personal notes or to bills of exchange.[15]

States appointed investigating commissions to look into the evils of banking. These provided useful information on the manipulations and the promotional character of many of the banks, but their recommendations were vague. A New York legislative committee declared in 1826 that a sound discretion ought to be exercised in the increase of banks so that the banking capital might be located in commercial cities and villages only, and not where commercial business did not require it.

Closely connected with monetary and banking problems was the question of internal improvements, both national and local. The question of broad schemes of internal improvements ran up against the familiar complications of local and individual viewpoints or interests in commerce, taxation, land values, and even manufactures, within and between states and regions.

Calhoun proposed in 1817, as part of his program for building a great imperial power, that the bonus and dividends the government would receive from the national bank be devoted to a grand scheme of internal improvements. The first great object would be to perfect communications from Maine to Louisiana; the second to connect all the great commercial points on the Atlantic—Philadelphia, Baltimore,

Washington, Richmond, Charleston, and Savannah—with the western states; and the third to perfect intercourse between the West and New Orleans.

He maintained that this scheme, like other parts of his program, would prevent the breakdown of the vital currency system during wartime. In wartime the country must depend for its revenue on internal duties. Since the taxes are paid in money and since the expenditures are confined to the scene of military operations, the circulating medium is drained from one part and accumulated at another. Unless it returns through the operations of trade, the part constantly drained must be impoverished ultimately. But the road-canal scheme would provide the necessary easy commercial intercourse.

New Yorkers were willing to support the measure if restricted to canals. They frankly admitted their interest in the Erie Canal project, but this would so connect East and West that no Hartford Convention could ever dissolve the Union.

Cyrus King, Massachusetts Federalist and brother of Rufus King, insisted that it was preferable to remove the tax burden from the impoverished people rather than to build the internal improvements. But John Ross, Pennsylvania Federalist, said that he could not see how the defeat of the measure could relieve the poor, for he had heard no proposition to distribute the profits among the needy. In reality the bill would benefit the poor by providing employment for the thousands unemployed.

Clay, in amplifying this position of government aid, took to task the critics for following the visionary "let alone" principle of the political economists and asserting that when the condition of society is ripe for internal improvements—that is, when capital can be invested in them with a prospect of adequate remuneration, associations of individuals will execute them without government aid. But this general maxim, Clay insisted, holds without exception only for old countries possessing a great accumulation of surplus capital. Greatest of the gainers from government aid for internal improvements would be the farmers, in cheaper transportation for their produce to market.

Lowndes accepted the general principle that the private direction of industry and capital would generally conform to the public good, but he did not admit that all public improvements must be supported exclusively by private subscription: Canals and roads are in every civilized country the object of government. Roads are usually supported by taxes. The policies flow from the general position that a public improvement would be profitable to the public, though not sufficiently profitable to private parties unless they receive government aid. The profits of a turnpike road are distributed among the stockholders, landholders, and travelers; and, though a company constructing it might make only 5 per cent, the country might gain 10 per cent.

The general measure was passed by Congress both in 1817 and 1818, but it was successively vetoed by the two Virginia Presidents, Madison and Monroe, who now read the Constitution a little differently and more strictly than they had on previous occasions. They both expressed great sympathy for internal improvements but thought that Congress would have the power only through a constitutional amendment. Calhoun, on the other hand, said that he "was no advocate for refined arguments on the Constitution. The instrument was not intended as a thesis for the logician" on which to exercise his ingenuity. It ought to be "construed with plain good sense," and he found accordingly that the power to raise money is not limited to the enumerated powers but to the achievement of the general welfare.

In New York the Erie Canal project was now being pushed most actively by De Witt Clinton, another Columbia graduate. He came of a family powerful in the related fields of politics and highly speculative business. His political allegiance was ever-shifting. He was first a Jeffersonian, but, like Morris, he was a peace man during the war and could even court Federalist support in the struggles for political preferment which were often complicated by pecuniary considerations. But his learning, zeal, and political maneuvering were extremely useful in pushing through the Erie project.

The promoters presented almost the whole catalogue of familiar arguments in defense of canals, and even added some. The Erie Canal, by uniting the ocean with the trade of the Great Lakes, will prevent the only sectional struggle that might arise—that between the Atlantic and western states. Specifically, the canal would end the evil of smuggling and the sale of goods from Montreal at our borders at 15 per cent under New York prices, thus robbing New York merchants of their legitimate profits and supplanting our mercantile establishments with those of foreign countries. To the complaint of farmers that its construction would damage them by increasing the scarcity and price of labor, Clinton replied that, since population like "a snowball gathers in a geometrical ratio," the lengthy period of construction cannot seriously affect the price of labor. More relevant was the answer that the present is the time to begin because the disbanding armies and the convulsions in Europe make available cheap labor.[16]

In Pennsylvania Carey, pleading the necessity of the state to maintain its standing, had the legislature order the Bank of Pennsylvania to make a substantial contribution to canal companies.[17] And Condy Raguet, among his remedies for preventing the abuses of banking and resulting economic crises, had included the prohibition of investment by banks in any companies except those for internal improvement.

In North Carolina, as elsewhere, the state had done much for navigation companies, with the usual dismal results. But the movement was renewed right after the peace. Leading it was Archibald Douglas Murphey (1777–1832), a graduate and former teacher of the University of North Carolina, a member of the legislature, and a judge. Though nominally a Republican, his sympathies and many of his actions were with the Federalist Party of his good friend Gaston, whom he helped to elect to Congress in 1812. His financial operations included internal improvements companies, land in the affected areas and in Tennessee, and bank stocks.

In 1816 he supported the movement for canals on the ground that only through improving her navigation could North Carolina end her economic dependence on other states, especially Virginia. This dependence, he said, is due to the lack of at least one great commercial city in the state. Great commercial cities, through concentrating wealth, are the animating force of agriculture, industry, and science. Most of the state's agricultural produce, he said, goes to markets in Virginia for ship transit because the present impassable river navigation prevents the rise of a great commercial city. But if the legislature gives liberal aid, one of the greatest commercial towns of the Union will arise at the mouth of the Roanoke. True, the development of the Roanoke will require the aid of Virginia and thus increase land values there, but "we should remember we belong to the same political confederacy." A company was chartered by both states, and "liberal aid" bestowed.[18]

When the country went into a depression in 1819, Murphey prepared a *Memoir on the Internal Improvements Contemplated by . . . North Carolina*, which of course stressed the need of further state aid. In this day when "political economy has attained the rank of a science," he wrote, "statesmen will not seek to promote a country's agriculture by bounties and premiums," but to provide means whereby agriculture can find a good market and the profits of that market be made to contribute to this state's rather than other states' wealth.

He pointed to Virginia, which with her "customary liberality" has invested more than North Carolina in the stock of the Roanoke Canal project. Virginia will certainly succeed in directing the trade of this fine river to Norfolk if North Carolina does not increase her contributions. Worse, if North Carolina hesitates, she will lose all her enterprising citizens, each of whom is worth more to the state than 500 ordinary men. They are so disgusted with the poverty of the state that they are migrating to the western wilderness, especially Tennessee, and building up new states to outstrip North Carolina. Murphey was even willing now for the state to prosecute all the projects on its own account, although some years ago he thought otherwise. But anyhow appropriations should be made to companies already incorporated, for otherwise projects would not be completed. He admitted that they had been highly speculative ventures prosecuted on a shoestring and had not even waited for engineering supervision. But these were bygone mistakes, and if the state provided technical and financial assistance, all would be well.

The state provided much of the aid sought, but with the same results; as the companies sought more aid, Murphey was feverishly trying to meet his debts. He bitterly complained in 1821 that though he had a great estate he was threatened with ruin because he could not convert part of it into money. He had been one of the leaders in obtaining a branch of the Bank of the United States for Fayetteville, and he had also complimented the state at the time for taking effective steps to eliminate the "vicious" paper money and restore a convertible currency. But now he bewailed the fact that the Fayetteville Branch of the Bank of the United States was unjustly pressing him.

He informed an old Federalist friend and fellow enterpriser, Colonel William Polk of the State Bank, that he would like to publish a pamphlet calling on the people to eliminate the branch but, being indebted to it, he feared to proceed unless the State Bank agreed to "protect" him. The branch is the greatest curse on the state since the day the first Bank of the United States was established. Until this monster is eliminated, the local banks as well as individuals will be pressed if not ruined.

The state's true interest—and this does not mean that of the merchants trading to Petersburg, New York, or Philadelphia—is a bank paper a little below par. With convertible notes the whole community is inconvenienced so that "our merchants can deal in other states without much loss." The vaults of the state banks should never have been opened. Their paper, like that of the Bank of England, after a little fluctuation would have settled down at a fixed value and answered the state's commercial needs.

True, the idea prevails that the circulating medium of the state is too small to enable the local banks to make reasonable profits and that consequently their notes must be pushed out into distant states. The answer is simple. The legislature could and should throw money into circulation in the execution of public works, to the amount wished for by the banks; and in this way "give a guaranty to the nation, that the banks shall prove solvent." The banks might not trust the state on other subjects, but this does not hold for "money stipulations," for no state for over a century has "ventured to trifle with its pecuniary credit," and surely this state is too "far advanced in morality" to listen to such an idea.[19]

But just how devious the issue of internal improvement might be was illustrated in the case of Robert Mills, the eminent architect and engineer. He was born and raised in Charleston, South Carolina, became a protege of Jefferson both in architecture and politics, and was rather successful in obtaining contracts throughout the Union, ranging from penitentiaries to monuments to Washington. While temporarily located in Baltimore in 1820, in connection with constructing the city's water works, Mills wrote a *Treatise on Inland Navigation* calling on Marylanders to push a canal connecting the city with the Potomac and Susquehanna Rivers and thereby with the country west of the Allegheny Mountains and its valuable trade. Such an enterprise, he pointed out, can become a link in a system of canals and roads that will give Baltimore the benefit of the traffic of the possessions of the Union on the Pacific Coast and from them, of the valuable East Indies trade. But if Baltimore does not hurry, New York or Philadelphia will win the prize.

Returning to his native South Carolina in 1821 to become a member of her Board of Public Works, Mills was soon shifting the details but utilizing similar arguments to show why South Carolina should engage in a far-flung internal improvement program. He informed the public, through his *Statistics of South Carolina* in 1826, that its exports directly and through northern states exceed those of any state. But, though South Carolina's commerce merits great consideration from the general government, she has been treated almost like a slave. Among other things, she lacks a single naval depot, while millions are expended in fortifying the northern cities and in building navies. The general government collects $1,000,000 in revenue annually at Charleston, but less than $50,000 is disbursed there through salaries. Thus $950,000 is drained from the state to the advantage of the northern states in accomplishing general national objects and to the crippling of the commercial facilities of South Carolina. The obvious course for the government is to substitute Charleston for Key West, Florida, as a naval rendezvous.

More specifically, his scheme included improving the channels of entrance from the sea; and of course Mills, as an engineer-architect, had the plans. If Charleston improved her natural advantages, only New York perhaps would exceed her share of the foreign and domestic commerce of the Union. In fact, she could become the great commercial emporium of the southern states and might command nearly all the trade of the Carolinas, Georgia, and Florida. What would hold back Charleston would be lack of permanent capital. To attract European and northern capitalists, her bad climate must be rectified. This flowed from the 200,000 acres of unreclaimed swamp lands of the Charleston district which were held in great estates. The reclaiming could be achieved by the state's making a huge loan for the purpose of buying and hiring slaves to do the work. The state would reap millions in addition to her investment through an arrangement whereby she bought the swamp lands on credit and resold them at their high value as drained land.

In 1816 Virginia authorized the scheme of private companies and state subscriptions. The state would subscribe two-fifths of the stock of public-works companies and forego her share of the dividends until the private subscribers first received legal interest on their investment. The subscription of the state, said Tucker, is a moderate insurance against loss to private adventurers, who are expected to be attracted to all such enterprises by the hope of gain. The state regards herself as amply remunerated for the temporary suspension of her returns "by the accomplishment of a public work calculated to replace the interest at some future period and to augment in the interim her wealth and population." By including in the structure "the cautious sagacity, persevering industry and increasing vigilance of private interest," the state is assured the faithful and economical completion of public works.

At the same time, in Congress, on behalf of a House committee dealing with unincorporated banks in the federal districts, he denounced such banking associations as flooding the country with paper at their discretion and violating the principles laid down by Dallas. But he was willing to grant charters to the six unincorporated ones in the District of Columbia if they would lend and invest substantial parts of their capital in specified canal and turnpike companies connecting with Virginia and the great road and canal projects of Calhoun.

But in 1824 the dominant Virginia leaders were fighting government aid whether state or federal. Virginia's national leaders, with Philip Barbour in the van, declared that federal aid to internal improvement was for the sole benefit of the western states. Such expenditures, he declared, violate the principle that the locale of the collection of the public contributions and the locale of their distribution should be the same, lest the East be unjustly deprived of money for circulation.

Clay, then a Kentucky congressman and also attorney for the Bank of the United States, was not loath to defend federal aid on Barbour's premises. The national revenue is expended in the great northern commercial centers. There the interest on the public debt is paid and the fleet built and repaired. No just cause of complaint can be made against this concentration of expenditures, however, because it necessarily results from the accumulation of capital, the state of the arts, and other circumstances belonging to our great cities. But the poor West has more right than any other section to complain against this transfer of the circulating medium from one quarter of the Union to another. There is a perpetual drain of its circulating medium from that highly distressed portion of the country to the East. Only a few insignificant public works are found there. Vast sums are annually transferred for the public lands alone, and "almost every dollar goes, like him who goes to death—to a bourne from which no traveller returns." If this debilitating and exhausting process were inevitable, it must be borne with manly fortitude. But the federal government, by pushing internal improvements, could mitigate the evils.

In Virginia proponents of public aid for canals declared that, as a result of the effective Virginia opposition both to the state and federal scheme of internal improvements, "commerce, that inconstant handmaid of fortune has turned her helm from our ports to the favoured harbour of New York." While the people of Virginia quarrel over internal improvements, "New York has swallowed up the commerce of America. Drawn from us by unkindness it has gone where it was courted by wiser councils." [20]

The railroad was beginning to appear on the horizon. Most active of the early promoters was John Stevens of Hoboken, New Jersey. He had been an officer in the Revolutionary War and considered himself capable of writing on any topic, from metaphysics to government and economics. He was engaged in practically every important type of enterprise, including land speculation and banking. At the time the Erie Canal began to be promoted seriously in 1812, he informed the canal commissioners appointed by the state that they should build a railroad instead of a canal since it would be cheaper in the long run and more useful. With railroads not needing locks to pass and similar delaying and disturbing factors, "every one, whether travelling for business or pleasure, can calculate with certainty . . . when he will arrive." Because of their speed as compared to canals, the farmer will save three days out of four, and the traveler get farther in a day by a railroad than in a week by a canal.[21]

He also appealed to Congress to promote railroads. The revenue the railroads could produce would far exceed the total duties on imports because interstate commerce is vastly greater than external commerce. The farmer's transportation cost to market would be reduced four-fifths. There would be nothing to prevent a speed of a hundred miles an hour. Armies could cover a greater distance in a day than in a month of marching. It would be not only a means of guarding against an enemy, but would also quickly quell internal commotions.[22] He got charters for railroads in New Jersey and Pennsylvania, but capital was not forthcoming despite his appeals to state patriotism in each case to maintain and advance the state's commercial position.

As the Erie Canal neared completion, Stevens demanded that the government promote railroads connecting the Atlantic and western states, especially between the Ohio and Potomac, to prevent the vast Union from breaking apart because of general fear of New York. The Erie Canal would divert a large portion of the Atlantic commerce of the lakes to New York. Was it sound policy to acquiesce in giving a still greater preponderancy to the present commercial supremacy of that great and growing state? Already, he exclaimed, that aspiring state, or rather a faction, was seeking to elevate Clinton to the presidency by means of the Erie Canal.[23]

It was in the South, however, that definite construction was first successfully begun, with Charleston taking the lead. The promoters argued that Charleston is losing her great commercial position, and consequently her landed estate has within eight years depreciated in value to one-half. Industry and business talent, driven by necessity, have sought employment elsewhere. Many of her houses are tenant-less, and "the grass grows uninterrupted in some of her chief business streets." But a railroad to the border of Georgia would recapture the interior trade and, above all things, the value of city property. It would, of course, afford a speedy and safe retreat during the sickly season and provide quick transportation for troops and supplies to the city in time of war.

The South Carolina Canal and Railroad Company was formed and a charter received with valuable privileges, including the right of eminent domain, an exemption from taxation, and a monopoly of railroad and canal building and operation between Charleston and the specified points for thirty-six years. Its rates were fixed at a "liberal" level, and it was even empowered to farm out its privilege of operation or open its railroads and canals to public use for tolls, provided the company's net income from such tolls were not greater than 25 per cent on the investment.[24] It received the aid of the federal government in the use of federal military engineers for the survey, but Congress would not grant it direct federal aid or let in its iron duty free.

Though railroads began to be projected everywhere, respectable opinion held that they would merely be accessory to canals. The railroads would only be preferred when time became an important consideration.

Fed by the monetary controversy, the tariff during this period grew from merely a question of revenue and incidental protection to a problem of definite national policy, with all the struggles that surround an emerging interest. Hardly had the war ceased than Niles dedicated a whole volume of his *Weekly Register* in 1815 to the "Manufacturers of the United States whose labours are eminently calculated to build up a National character, and insure the real independence of our beloved country." If Congress does not speedily give additional assistance, the great investments of capital will be wiped out and the nation ruined; whereas if manufactures are allowed to mature, America's cotton and woolens will be produced more cheaply than those of England. Extortion is prevented, said the tariff spokesmen, by the competition which reduces prices to a "living profit." [25]

Calhoun proclaimed in Congress in 1816 that the question of manufactures must not depend "on the abstract principle that, industry left to pursue its own course, will find in its own interest" all the necessary encouragement. A program of encouraging manufactures along with the development of the Navy will prevent the drain of specie and consequent derangement of currency that almost defeated the nation in the war. On the other hand, the war prosperity poured vast amounts of commercial capital into the country which only a navy and domestic manufactures program could fully employ. But Calhoun, aside from the polemics to catch northern votes for the Republican Party, seemed to have in mind the needs of revenue and the encouragement of such manufactures of cotton and wool as would keep the Army and Navy adequately and cheaply clad at all times. This tied up with the interest of southern cotton planters in a tariff that would reduce the importation of East Indies cotton manufactures made of "foreign" cotton and could be used as a weapon to compel England to lift her discriminatory duties on American cotton.

The two outstanding statisticians and congressmen, Republican Dr. Adam Seybert of Pennsylvania and Federalist Timothy Pitkin, might differ in their politics, but both agreed with Thomas Mun's defense of the East India Company in the seventeenth century that, though the direct trade was unfavorable, the ultimate balance was favorable through the sale of the imports to Europe and elsewhere. In fact, Pitkin in his *A Statistical View of the Commerce of the United States of America* reached the conclusion that, considering the method of valuing exports and imports, the profit on freight and the like, the amount of re-exports, "paradoxical as it may appear, it is, nevertheless true that the real gain of the United States has been nearly in proportion as their imports have exceeded their exports."

Secretary of the Treasury Alexander Dallas, like President Madison, expressed great admiration for manufactures but argued that all the interests of the country must be considered.

Congress finally agreed in 1816, after what was called a deal between proponents of the bank measure and the tariff, to levy duties slightly lower than the wartime double duties, primarily for revenue purposes. A twenty-five cent duty was to be levied on cotton and woolens. East Indies cottons were hit by the provision that no cotton goods were to be estimated as having cost less than twenty-five cents a yard.

By 1817 another foreign factor furnished ammunition for the protectionists in their appeal to farmers. England began to invoke strictly her Corn Laws of 1815, which provided that if grain fell below a certain price its importation should be prohibited.

On the other hand, New York protectionists informed New England that she should support a tariff because her population was excessive and she was losing people to the West. If "she consulted the treatises on population," she would find that they said, "open new channels of industry, new sources of subsistence, in other words, introduce and extend manufactures." Only in this way could she maintain her high rank in the Union.[26]

New England replied with another edition of Adam Smith's *The Wealth of Nations*. However, Humphreys in his reforming zeal, suggested to President Madison that his manufactory establishment would be one of the most eligible sites "to found an Institution for extending the benefits of a military and manufacturing education to the orphan or other poor children of soldiers or other citizens, at the least possible expense to the public, . . . at the same time that the National government is so judiciously paying attention to the Academies and Institutions more peculiarly adapted to the education of the sons of the more wealthy." [27]

With the widespread suspension of specie payments by the banks in 1819, the cry for protection found a better hearing than ever. The cause was fortunate in having the services of Carey. In the spring Carey flooded Congress and the country with the *Addresses of the Philadelphia Society for the Promotion of National Industry*. The Philadelphia Society was composed of only eight other members besides Carey and his collaborator on the addresses, Dr. Samuel Jackson, linguist and physician, who later taught at the University of Pennsylvania. But Carey was indefatigable in the distribution of his writings and in the organization of societies.

The woeful state of the country, which he had been constantly picturing in connection with banks and which he still used occasionally against any restrictive discount policy by banks, he now blamed on a lack of a tariff to keep out East Indies goods and competing European manufactures of cotton and woolens, along with iron and coal. The effect of unrestrained trade is to drain the nation's specie and all valuable objects, and still leave a pressing foreign debt that brings with it everything from suspension of specie payments and vast unemployment of labor and capital to soup kitchens and danger-ous relief legislation. All prices fall disastrously, and men of capital are deprived of liberal profits.

The fate of the manufacturing capitalists is much worse here than in any European monarchy. Czar Alexander, the wisest monarch in Europe, raised Russia to eminence because he disowned the principle of letting trade regulate itself, which is really regulating trade for the benefit of foreign agriculture and industry. The Russian govern-ment not only excludes foreign competition, but also gives the manu-facturer bounties and thereby supports thousands of subjects and makes the country independent.

The distress cannot be blamed on the transition from war to peace because in the immediate postwar era our markets increased. But the transition did bring the distress in the sense that it tore down the protection the war provided.

Those blaming banks are mistaking effect for cause; in fact, the banks are more sinned against than sinning. The extravagant im-ports, by causing a drain of specie and increasing foreign indebted-ness, force the curtailing of discounts and depression.

Carey claimed that before he had written the *Addresses* he had never devoted three days to the study of political economy. So he gave the major part of his attention to "exposing" the fallacies of Adam Smith's "abstract" *The Wealth of Nations* as the exponent of the "new school of political economy," of unlimited freedom of trade, of unrestrained commerce, and took his stand with "the old school of political economy" of qualified restrictions of commerce, which had raised England to the pinnacle of her power.

He was well aware that mankind holds tenaciously to the tyranny of theory, but American citizens will scorn to abdicate their reason to the authority of a great name; instead, they will demand that the policy be supported not by closet speculations of visionary theorists, but by established fact. The most cogent and conclusive facts bear testimony against Smith and his school, including Ricardo.

One of the "grossest" errors in Smith which Carey attempted to refute was, strangely enough, one that heretofore had been used to show Smith's preference for home trade over foreign trade—namely, that the merchants knew how foreign trade enriched themselves, but how it enriched the country they never considered except when "they had occasion to apply to their country for some change in the laws respecting foreign trade." People realize, wrote Carey, that the great mercantilist writers and the great Philadelphia merchants such as Robert Morris and thousands of others know the process by which foreign commerce enriches the country without the aid of *The Wealth of Nations*. Every sensible person, whatever his trade, could instantly explain the process—namely, by selling more than is bought.[28]

Centering his energies primarily on the tariff proved fortunate for Carey and his group. Late in 1819 came the splitting up of the House Committee of Commerce and Manufactures into two separate committees, evidence that henceforth the tariff was to be a permanent interest rather than an incidental matter.

Carey and Jackson got busy as soon as it was announced that the Federalist, Henry Baldwin of Pennsylvania, later an iron master, was chairman. They wanted Condy Raguet to go to Washington as a spokesman for their Pennsylvania Society for the Promotion of National Industry. Raguet was willing to do so while the Pennsylvania Senate was in recess during the Christmas holidays, provided his expenses were reimbursed and his connection with the Society not made public, on the ground that in this status he could be more persuasive with congressmen, especially from Pennsylvania. His conditions were met, and Raguet spent a week in Washington giving Baldwin, who alone knew his mission, the views of the Pennsylvania friends of the manufacturing cause and discussing the matter with other congressmen. Raguet informed Carey and Jackson that a "confidential well-informed individual," a "private not a publicly declared agent," should be sent to continue the work, to help the chairman on detail and obtain from home such particulars from various branches of manufactures as are necessary in drafting the tariff bill.[29]

In Congress Baldwin presented a comprehensive tariff bill which ostensibly would view protection as a national system, with hemp, molasses, iron, cotton, and woolens especially given large increases and the East Indies goods increasingly burdened. The shrewd and able Lowndes, in opposing the higher tariff, proposed that the Committee on Manufactures present for the industries it felt required the higher tariff, the data on wages, other costs, and profits in the most efficiently conducted plants, to test the allegation of the manufacturers that they faced ruin under present duties. Baldwin replied that the committee neither had the data requested nor was it necessary, for the revision of the tariff had been proposed from considerations of national policy, not from the minute investigation of details. The great opponents of the tariff, he said, are the great monopolizing merchants, the wealthy capitalists organized in secretive chambers of commerce.

Clay, then Speaker of the House and leader of the tariff forces, exclaimed: "The maxim of let alone" is everywhere proclaimed but nowhere practiced. It is truth in the books of European political economists, those visionary theoretical writers, but it is error in the practical code of every European state. While Clay was singing the virtue of a "self-contained nation," he was also pleading for the recognition of the independence of South America on the ground of free trade. That area's great resources, population, and need of foreign goods offer the greatest inducement to commercial enterprise, once she is free from the restraint of despotism. Fear that Spanish America would be the nation's rival in agricultural production is groundless. Since it mostly produces articles more valuable than those raised here, it is not probable that they would abandon this more profitable culture for one less advantageous just to compete with us. That the United States produces little that Spanish America wants is irrelevant because the value of a commerce is not to be judged in terms of old-fashioned, particular balance of trade between two nations. Under this conception, our greatest trade, that with Great Britain, would be judged ruinous, but this so-called unfavorable balance is covered by the profits of trade with other nations. Besides, the United States already exports large amounts of manufactures to South America. Best of all, America would get the specie of the mines and, since the nation which commands the precious metal commands almost all the resources of the world, America's position would be pre-eminent.

On the other hand, Lowndes declared, friends have already shown that the industry affording most profit to the individual conduces to the state's wealth, and that a duty or prohibition which would direct any part of a country's industry to a business in which it would not otherwise engage, usually meant the substitution of a less profitable for a more profitable employment. These positions they hold in common with every political economist to whose words time has given sanction. The ills of manufacturers are really due in good part to failure to adopt the latest machinery as well as to over-expansion through credit inflation. But the "protectionists" want an exclusive indemnity against the depression which has affected all interests. Reasonable protection is very fine, but the manufacturers are now getting more than their patron saint, Hamilton, had advocated and then only for the stage of infancy which they had long passed.

To oppose buying in the cheapest market is the same thing as opposing the introduction of machinery which lessens cost. The appeal to the farmer is nonsense. Would the tariff advocates be willing to dispense with all tariffs if England dropped her Corn Laws?

If duties or prohibition on manufactures could raise the price of agricultural goods, manufacturers would not gain because they would face increased costs. But such duties cannot raise agricultural prices because the price of export commodities is fixed by the surplus exported. So far as laying duties on agricultural goods is concerned, this is a joker for the same reason. Gentlemen might lay duties on cotton, wheat, and tobacco, but this would change nothing except the words of the statute book.

The issues got more complex as Lowndes defended the East Indies trade. The fabrics from the East Indies are peculiarly suited to the wants of the poorest class. The great profits of the trade have paid for the great consumption of luxuries from the Orient. At the same time, it has helped to provide a navy, and the profits of freight have further increased the nation's capital. Finally, it is incomprehensible that the purchase of merchandise either in India or anywhere else, of which we keep only a part and sell the remainder for more than the whole cost, could lessen the country's specie. True, exclusive advantages were given the navigating interest, principally in the coasting trade; but this was done for national defense, not for profit.

Ezekiel Whitman of Massachusetts was the first to raise the constitutional question. He thought it strange that Congress should have a standing Committee on Manufactures, for the general government was not constituted with a view to manufactures. The Constitution grants no specific delegation of power for the object. Hitherto we have been content to do what the Constitution explicitly authorized Congress to do—namely, to regulate commerce. This was the prime force which pushed the Constitution into existence. In favoring commerce the general government is doing only what the Constitution requires.

John Taylor wrote another elaborate disquisition, *Tyranny Un-*

masked, to prove that the proposed tariff, being destructive of the freedom of commerce, is a tyrannical invasion of the natural rights of man. The science of political economy is founded on the unalterable laws of commerce. If we drop the equivocal idea of the balance of trade and ask whether commerce has made for national wealth and prosperity, the evidence is instantly intelligible and the conclusion certain, for commerce has brought about the great improvement in agriculture and manufacturing, the vast building of homes and ships, and the rise of cities.

Protection to merchants is not a bounty to merchants, as the pro-tariff forces claim, for the benefits from commerce are obviously reaped primarily by the owners and consumers of the commodities which it is the merchant's occupation to exchange. Commerce and capitalist occupations are thus quite different. The business of one is to exchange property and coincides with the "good soul" of money in regulating exchanges by free will, while the other coincides with the "bad soul," by promoting the transfer of property without giving an equivalent, as in excessive payments extorted by government or the holders of exclusive privileges.

With the defeat of the tariff in 1820 and 1821, Raguet turned to the other side. He informed Ricardo late in 1821 that the country was divided into two great parties. One wants the system of restrictions and prohibitions; the other stands for "the natural course of things" without any artificial excitement for manufactures. The latter, comprising the rice, cotton, and tobacco planters, almost all the merchants, and a considerable part of the economical manufacturers of the New England states, is "strongest both in number and talents."

Colonel Clement C. Biddle, a former Federalist, merchant, and littérateur, brought out an American edition of J. B. Say's *A Treatise on Political Economy* in 1821 for the cause of free trade. Say, Clement Biddle declared, rigidly pursuing "the inductive method of investigation" as against the hypothetical method of Ricardo, has succeeded in presenting a complete analysis of the simple and general laws on which the production, distribution, and consumption of wealth depend. Any statement of Say's that might not be forthright on the free-trade stand Biddle and his group had taken, was "corrected" in appropriate footnotes. Thus he found Say, like Smith, in error in declaring that internal commerce is most advantageous, though foreign trade should not be restrained. Capital, whether in home or in foreign trade, is equally productive, said the editor; for, if home trade realized a greater profit, capital would leave foreign trade and enter the former.

In 1824 another great battle began over the issue. Carey time and again cited former President Madison as a supporter of the tariff and tried to get a definite statement. But Madison wrote Carey, in his customary urbane manner, that he dissented from both sides on the tariff question. He believed in *laissez faire* with exceptions, "but to illustrate the generality of the rule and at the same time specify and explain the just exceptions is a task not yet perhaps adequately performed by political economists." [30]

In Congress Clay acknowledged his indebtedness to Carey, who merits "the public gratitude, for the disinterested diligence with which he has collected a large mass of highly useful facts and for the clear and convincing reasoning with which he generally illustrates them." Clay added that the protective system has the sanction of one of·the best and wisest men in all ages in all foreign countries as well as our own—namely, Napoleon. He was an authority even higher than those illustrious admirers of the system at home— Franklin, Jefferson, Madison, Hamilton—for his "was the master spirit of the age. Whether he was seated on the imperial throne, deciding the fate of nations, and allotting kingdoms to the members of his family, with the same composure if not with the same affection, as that with which a Virginia father divides his plantations among his children, or on the miserable rock of St. Helena, to which he was condemned by the cruelty . . . of his unworthy victors," he was equally an object of the most intense admiration. He comprehended with the "rapidity of intuition" the true interests of the state. Napoleon rightly held that the economists are mere systematizers; their principles correct in theory but erroneous in practice. His "continental system" was the true conception, for it was based on agriculture as "the soul of empire," on industry as "the comfort and happiness of the population," and finally on "foreign trade as taking care of the superabundance of agriculture and industry."

The so-called evils of the factory system Clay now viewed as blessings. "The poor rates, the theme of so much reproach without England, and of so much regret within it, among her speculative writers," really vindicate the prohibitory system. What other nation can dispense as much in regulated charity?

New England's Webster complained that the tariff agitation came from the improvident West with its vicious relief laws and depreciated paper. McDuffie of South Carolina declared that the West's complaint of hard times and the demand for a tariff had arisen from the excessive amount of public land thrown on the market; and henceforth he would oppose bringing more public land on the market unless there was a "fair and natural demand for it."

Harvard's professor of Greek, the Reverend Edward Everett, defended the "theorists" against the protectionists through the columns of the respectable *North American Review* as he prepared for his successful candidacy for a seat in Congress. He asserted that the men derided as theoretical should be considered the only really practical economists. Thus Ricardo "was a man who, from being an indigent Jew, of Portuguese descent, raised himself to a princely fortune, to a seat in Parliament, to respectability in the best English circles." He had the reputation of being the best versed man in all Europe "in the really abstract subject of money; and his opinions in the House of Commons, on this subject, were received with proportionate respect." [31]

But New England was beginning to shift to a tariff policy that would not too sharply interfere with her interest in foreign commerce. This was shown by the appearance in 1825 of a series of newspaper essays which the following year were brought together as the *Summary of the Practical Principles of Political Economy*. Their anonymous author was Caleb Cushing, friend of Everett, member of an old and powerful New England family and former Harvard tutor who was then beginning his main lifework as a politician. As "a friend of domestic industry," he denounced Smith and Say and bemoaned the use of Say as a textbook at Harvard.

The government must extend its protecting hand over industry, for without rewards in the shape of profits, industry will not be stimulated, Cushing wrote. But the government should never fix maximum prices because experience has "shown there are no more injurious restraints to individual and national interest than those on the free disposal and export of any of the products of human industry." Just as it would be unfair to insist that individuals with greater abilities, talents, resources, and advantages should be asked to share equally with those less fortunate, so nations with superior advantages should not be open to the products of other nations. Since in every nation the capital must inevitably belong to one set of persons, and the labor to another, allowing importation of foreign manufactures is permitting American capital to support the cheap degraded labor of Europe. Even if the imports were obtained free, the country would suffer because the domestic manufacturers would cease producing; unemployment would cause restricted demand for other goods and thus a general depression. Rising prices are beneficial, for the increasing profits cause the employment of more labor and augment production. Low prices depress production to the mere advantage of fixed incomes.

With the assembling in 1827 of the famous convention at Harrisburg, Pennsylvania, for the purpose of agitating a rise in the woolens tariffs, came a definite change in the attitude of leading New Englanders, including both Webster and Everett. Webster, now a senator from Massachusetts, claimed that the act of 1824 had encouraged the people of New England to invest in woolen manufactures. But with the fall in the world price of wool, England now had an advantage which would destroy New England's heavy investments in plant and equipment unless the tariff were raised. "They come here asking for relief," he informed the Senate in 1828, but "they are met with a volley of hard names, a tirade of reproaches and a loud cry against capitalists, speculators, and stock jobbers." Webster, however, did not like the proposed high tariffs on molasses and hemp. The shipping interest requires only an open field and fair chance, but these duties will destroy it. Colonel Richard Johnson, Kentucky protectionist, wrathfully exclaimed that Webster was "theoretically magnanimous," but he embraced only his own section. Webster left out, he added, western produce and western manufactures.

Webster by now gave up "what is called the 'science of political economy.' There is no such science. There are no rules on these subjects so fixed and invariable as that their aggregate constitutes a science." He had just recently run over twenty volumes, beginning with The Wealth of Nations and, he said, if he picked out with one hand "the mere truisms, and with the other hand the doubtful propositions, little would be left." [32]

On the other hand, with protection having gone further than leaders of southern sentiment had ever in reality deemed "reasonable," Calhoun dropped his old "national" position on this question—though not on others—and asserted that the protective tariff was an invasion of states' rights, an act of tyranny of the naked majority over the minority. The tariff, wrote Calhoun, makes the staple states of the South the serfs of the manufacturing North. The duties are in fact paid by the southern producers from their exports. The north-ern consumers recoup whatever higher prices they are charged by virtue of the tariff, but the southern cotton producers have no such possibility because they sell in an international market. The object of the protective tariff is to eliminate foreign competition and give the northern manufacturer a monopoly of the domestic market. But the southern staple producers, being compelled to pay higher prices for manufactures, have higher costs. This reduces their ability to com-pete in the markets of the world. The state of South Carolina there-fore has the duty to "interpose," or nullify to prevent the violation of the compact.

When Whitman of Massachusetts had presented the constitutional objection to a protective tariff in 1820, little attention was paid it; but now that New England's dominant sentiment embraced such a tariff for certain goods, and naturally dropped the doctrine, Cal-houn made it a fighting principle for the South.

Forced to abandon a pursuit to which our soil, habits, and peculiar labor are adapted, at an immense sacrifice of property, we would be compelled without capital, experience, skill, and labor to attempt to become the rivals instead of the customers of the manufacturing states, Calhoun wrote. Even if we succeeded in manufacturing, then those waging war on our gains would wage war on our labor lest we take the bread from their wives and children.[33]

The nullificationists claimed the authority of Madison, who, as the author of the famous Virginia Resolutions of 1798 against the Alien and Sedition Acts, had set forth a doctrine of state interposition. But Madison indignantly protested that his doctrine was being misin-terpreted and went on to insist that a protective tariff was not only constitutional but also economically desirable, provided, of course, the protection could be defended with one of his numerous excep-tions to the universal principle of free trade.

Calhoun's fellow South Carolinian, George McDuffie, used a some-what different technique to reach the same opposition to a higher tariff, especially on cheap woolens. "I will not . . . say that we might not be tempted to join this plundering expedition if the tariff could be so regulated as to raise the price of cotton," he exclaimed in the House of Representatives. But the position of the cotton plant-ers allies them naturally with the mass of the farming states. "The wealthy cotton planter of the South fights by the side of the small farmer, the mechanic, the merchant, and the laborer, in New York and Pennsylvania," because of their mutual interest in opposing a system which benefits the manufacturers at their expense. "This accounts for the fact notorious in our political history that . . . the aristocracy of the Southern States, has always been found on the same side with the democracy of the Northern States in all the political controversies" which have divided the country.

Northern protectionists saw no sense in the South's complaint that slavery was an insuperable bar to manufactures in the South. Slave boys and girls under twelve years of age could be hired at a third of their cost in the North, they said. Besides, manufactures would train the slaves to habits of industry and business which would tend to prepare them for a state of freedom and thus "pave the way for the gradual removal of the entailed evil," which cannot be directly or suddenly touched without committing a monstrous injustice to both parties.[34]

The upshot, however, was the famous "Tariff of Abominations" of 1828, which John Randolph so aptly described as referring to no manufactures "except the manufacture of a President of the United States."

Southern critics of the protective tariff, however, agreed with their opponents that trade unions were vicious. Francis Walker Gilmer, graduate of William and Mary, a lawyer, and later Jefferson's agent in selecting the original faculty of the University of Virginia and himself its professor of law, argued that both in enacting usury laws and in repressing combinations to raise wages the state justly overrides natural rights for the social welfare. Men, he said in his *A Vindication of the Laws, Limiting the Rate of Interest on Loans* (1820), have a natural right to do collectively what each is admitted to have a right to do separately, but the restraint on journeymen must be borne, for otherwise the great manufacturers could not exist and society would consequently be deprived of many useful and necessary fabrics.

Whatever meaning the ancient doctrine of the just price might have other than as a brute market price was being stripped from it by the students of "morals of trade." This was best presented by Gulian C. Verplanck, graduate of Columbia, littérateur, representative of New York in both the state and national legislature, and professor for a time at the General Theological Seminary. In 1825 he undertook to lay down the principles of the "morals of trade" as the outgrowth in New York City "of one of those seasons of wild commercial speculation . . . which like epidemics, from time to time without any perceptible cause, visit and afflict the mercantile world." The clue to solving the question of fairness in buying and selling, he declared in *An Essay on the Doctrine of Contracts*, is not to be found where the old lawyers and moralists of the just price alone sought it, in metaphysical definitions or logical distinctions, but in the "modern science" of political economy. Its truths are but those of morality viewed under another aspect.

"The acute and profound analysis of Ricardo has resolved all exchangeable value into its original elements of human labour, directly applied or accumulated in capital; and he has clearly traced the few simple, but universal and beautiful laws which govern its operation." But these considerations unfortunately do not immediately enter into the common reasoning by which men are governed in matters of traffic. Successful calculations of market prospects fall in the category of "superior skill." This hard-earned knowledge forms the most valuable acquisition and perhaps the most costly part of the successful trader's capital. Therefore the profits from utilizing the knowledge is as much the dealer's as the interest on his money or the rent of his house. Should the purchaser of real estate refund his gains from having, with more foresight than his neighbor, bought for a trifle, but at the "current market price," land which the increase of trade and population has since made worth millions? Suppose a merchant at great expense and risk ascertained that some unfrequented port in India offers a most profitable market for some articles in no special demand at home—for instance, opium. "Cannot he honestly purchase his opium . . . at the current rate" without informing the seller that it is not in his interest to sell it at that price but to ship on his own account to the newly discovered market? These advantages, on whatever scale they may occur, "from the profits of the fruiterer . . . to those of the gigantic capitalist who controls the price of the staple commodities of nations, in the great market of the world, are the necessary . . . stimulants of that activity which, in the search after private profit, opens a thousand springs of prosperity and plenty for the use of all."

But the doctrine of the just price, of equivalent values, merely confuses the discussion. Bargains and sales are not made with a view to giving and receiving equal values. All contracts in trade, all purchase of things to sell again, are "expressly and avowedly made with a view to profit." The merchant sells his cotton for cash and buys copper because he estimates that cotton is worth less money and the copper more. So in the petty retail traffic every man judges for himself whether or not the object he is about to buy is not worth more to him in use or in pleasure than the money asked for it. If he does not think so, he does not buy. In short, "when we make a bargain, I transfer my money to the seller on the condition of receiving what I judge more useful, valuable, or more agreeable to me than my money. I may judge erroneously but the correctness of my judgment as to my tastes or interests form no part of the contract and cannot affect it."

The imaginary doctrine of equality can hardly be reconciled with the confessedly fair profits of a monopoly price—as where a patent or peculiarities of soil of a certain vineyard give the possessor the sole power of supplying any large demand. The equivalent would be the cost of production, including ordinary profit, but no one doubts the justice of the producer's getting as much for his articles as the competition of buyers will give. Those attempting to reconcile the monopoly price with the just price by imputing a value to the patent or monopoly are engaging in specious arguments, for that value is nothing else than the very power of selling for more than the cost without being disturbed by other rivals whose underbidding would reduce the price to the market rate. The same reasoning applies to any rise of price from scarcity. A man's cost of production of flour, including "reasonable profit," may be four dollars a barrel; but if the foreign demand more than doubles it, "where is the immorality of my taking the market price? And how unjust and impolitic would be the law that prohibited the receiving it!"

Of course, there were certain prices still generally fixed in all the states for such transportation services as ferries, canals, bridges, roads, and the like. The usual justification was that the recipients had a legal monopoly. But Gilmer, in attempting to justify usury laws, introduced the argument that these prices were fixed because they were "natural monopolies"—that is, nature has limited the number of places fit for them. It is foolish to say that if the toll is excessive, other turnpikes will be opened. Even if a new toll road were started, the owners of the old and new roads might "run the race of a vindictive competition for a while," but when they have discharged the "acrimony of their gall, they will find underbidding a losing game," and they will then unite and double their profit. The result is that both will be badly kept, and there will be two extortioners instead of one. Eventually they may arrange that one will receive a certain remuneration for completely closing down. The community thus loses so much ground, labor, and capital employed to build the second road, and the first will be worse than it had been originally.

In the last analysis, he said, these prices are regulated because certain emergencies might arise inducing the passenger to pay almost any price. How much would a man pay who by being in New York by a certain day stands to make $100,000? The tolls should not be regulated by what the passengers can afford to give, but "by what the keeper on a fair estimate of the labour and capital expended in reference to other employments of each can afford to take." The assize for bread is proper because of the relative ease of combination of bakers. Those talking about the miracle of competition forget there is also a principle of combination. Perhaps Gilmer should have noted that the assize of bread was disappearing.

Loud complaints were heard about the burden of public poor relief. Hailed as the ideal solution by the most liberal in both the South and the North was the kind of voluntary society promoted by the respectable leaders of New York, involving establishment of "houses of industry" managed by the subscribers and with involuntarily unemployed women and children as its inmates.

To prevent pauperism, as distinct from relieving it, the New York society recommended the establishment of savings banks, Sunday schools, and churches in the outskirts of the city, and the reduction of the licensed shops for retailing spiritous liquors.

But the most prolific source of pauperism next to intemperance were the poor laws borrowed from England. By offering "a certain relief, a sure asylum, a comfortable support" to all indigents, and by setting aside a fund for public alms, with "fixed and legal claims on it," they "throw away all the salutary restraints upon improvidence, idleness and vice," produce an overgrown "glutted population," and render insolent all the claimants who thus eat the bread of charity. The society's plan, however, avoids these evils because it promises "no certain support of the poor." [35] Given these houses of industry, there should be no other relief of poverty or distress except the hospital, the asylum for orphan children and the aged.

In the South, Robert Mills, as he pleaded for federal and state aid for internal improvements, supported a similar scheme, though with less blunt arguments. He said in *Statistics of South Carolina* that we may assume as true that nine out of ten of those soliciting alms are capable of earning twelve and a half cents a day by their labor, which "we know is more than equivalent for their support"—in fact, ten or twelve cents is sufficient. Since charity is a religious duty, the fundamental guiding principle of poor relief should be voluntary charity. Those kind attentions which are so necessary to "reclaim the vicious and comfort and encourage the despondent" cannot be commanded by force—that is, by a tax for poor relief. At best all that the legislature should do is to initiate "houses of industry for the poor" with subscriptions from all classes. To create "public confidence," administrators of the poor should publish detailed accounts at stated periods. These should include, among other things, an alphabetical list of all recipients of alms and the amount of weekly or monthly aid given. Though day laborers and others in indigent circumstances may be able to give only a little, yet they ought to be encouraged to subscribe, for they "will be rendered doubly careful to avoid the humiliation of becoming an object of charity."

Grimly prophetic of the greatest struggle the nation was to witness since the Revolutionary War was the bitter controversy that broke out in 1819 over whether Missouri should be allowed to enter the Union with a constitution not prohibiting slavery. The great debates on the floor of Congress foreshadowed the Civil War. The northerners were split, with the great majority against the extension. The southerners were unanimous in opposition to any ban, and more than one southern speaker hinted that, if need be, this position would be defended by recourse to arms.

Leading the forces of slavery was Clay, who had begun his political career in Kentucky with an unsuccessful attempt to obtain legislation to end slavery in the state.

The speakers devoted most of their time to the constitutional issue of Congress's right to prohibit slavery in the territories. The defenders of the prohibition fell back on Congress's power to regulate commerce; the opponents appealed to states' rights. Each side could cite enough precedents to convince itself. But neither side was completely satisfied with merely presenting the constitutional question, for every speaker discussed the "expediency" of the measure.

For the most part, no open eulogy of slavery as an ideal institution was presented. The general opinion of the southerners was that it was a necessary evil for which no plausible remedy had yet been found, though "wisdom and benevolence united have increasingly brooded over the question." Randolph claimed that the greatest evil that had ever befallen him was being born a slaveholder, but he and all slave-holders must bear their heavy burden for the good of society and the black man, even if it might necessitate a resort to arms to keep outsiders from interfering with the question. Some did go so far as to argue that the institution made the South the land of true white democracy and equality. Colonel Richard Johnson, a senator from Kentucky, said this was so because in the South slaves do the servile labor, while in the North white men serve as menials. The white liveried servant of the northern rich master is in reality as much a slave as the black man under the command of his southern master. But the northern master must act coldly toward his menials; whereas in the South he can be friendly to his slaves because he has no fear that the slave will mistake this kindliness to "call him fellow-citizen or act improperly."

The economics of the question pivoted around the Malthusian doctrine of population. There was general agreement on the validity of the doctrine, but there were bitter disputes as to how it would operate in the specific case under discussion: whether extension would increase or decrease the number of blacks. Significant was the emphasis on statistics of population growth, as revealed by Seybert's statistical volume; but here again bitter disputes occurred as to their interpretation. Northerners pointed to the increasing rate of growth of slaves over whites and free blacks in the South, but southerners found no difficulty in reconciling these phenomena with their case. The ending of slavery, they argued, will inevitably come through the workings of the traditional principle of wages and the law of population. As the white population increases, the wages of white labor will fall until it will no longer pay to have black slaves. But until this time a diffusion of slavery would ameliorate the condition of the slave. Taken to the fertile soil of Missouri, he would naturally obtain better subsistence from his master. This, of course, would also ameliorate the condition of the slaves at home since they would be fewer. At the same time, with few slaves compared to whites in the old states, masters would not fear insurrections and would be more inclined to emancipate. The tendency would be accelerated by the fact that spreading of the slaves would spread the cost of manumission.

The spectacle of men who called themselves democrats using arguments that they denounced as aristocratical on other issues, was

too much for northern ex-Federalists. They reminded the southerners that their arguments were the shopworn stock in trade of aristocracy and "legitimacy" through all the ages. Nothing could be
more strange than the spectacle of a polished Massachusetts bearer
of the name of a leading Pilgrim father, Joshua Cushman, reminding
that son of the "frontier West," Clay, that though "Kentucky may
justly boast of her orators, statesmen and political economists," she
could imbibe some useful notions of liberty.

Hardly an argument used before or afterward was not heard in
the defense of slavery. They ranged from a blunt defense of property rights, including anticipated gains, to the uplifting of the blacks.
The true philosopher on this question was held to be John Taylor,
and his *Arator* was the authoritative treatise. The very men who
at the same session of Congress had fumed at the denunciation of the
"abstract truths" of the political economists by the protectionists,
now dismissed the Declaration of Independence in precisely the same
way. Congressman John Tyler of Virginia declared that he would not
deny as an abstract truth the "lovely and beautiful principle" that all
men are by nature equally free, sovereign, and independent. But every
walk of life evidences its fallacy. Distinctions will always exist because of virtue and vice, wealth and poverty, industry and idleness.
Human power cannot destroy the distinctions, for society itself en-
genders and gives birth to them. Liberty and equality are captivating
sounds, but they often captivate to destroy. England had her Jack
Cades and Levellers, and he pointed also to Revolutionary France.
To assume that the slaveholding states would have ratified the Constitution if they had not thought they were secure in their slave property would be assuming that they would "overlook that great and
almost exclusive motive to human action, self interest." The framers
of the Constitution, as sound practical men, could not be led away
by idle theories.

The learned senator from South Carolina, Charles Pinckney, who
in the Constitutional Convention had successfully opposed the immediate prohibition of the foreign slave trade, pointed to the depressed condition of the lower class of England. "Ask . . . their
economists . . . the numbers of millions daily fed by the hand of
charity." And he pointed to the miserable condition of the free
blacks politically, socially, and economically in the North. But the
slave during his whole life is free from care, "that canker of the
human heart, which destroys at least one-half the thinking part of

mankind, and from which a favored few, if indeed any, can be said to be free."

The great rate of increase in their growth that northerners deprecate is evidence of their happy and comfortable condition. Finally, the North apparently does not realize the value to her of southern slaves. If they were lost, he concluded, the value of southern lands would be diminished at least one-half if not to nothing, and the northerners would lose the great gains from shipping the South's bulky, valuable articles and bringing in return the manufactures and merchandise of Europe.

With most of the northerners the question was basically whether slaveholders were to have increasing political and economic power. Generally speaking, the northerners no more than the southerners favored a free black population in the country. In so far as northerners seriously thought of what was best for the black, the general logic was based on exportation from the Union. The critics of slavery thought exportation might possibly prove unworkable. They suggested that the southern slave owners, for their greater profit as well as safety, should emancipate those "most exemplary for industry and fidelity, and make them tenants of the wastelands of their plantations." The difference of color must, of course, be a perpetual barrier to a mixture of blood and "will therefore leave to the master superior respect, the right of protection, and the voluntary service and labour of a grateful and happy race."

Perhaps the speech on either side least tainted with the spirit of gain, irresponsible dominion, and partisan politics was that of the Quaker Thomas Forrest of Pennsylvania. He had served in the Revolutionary War under Washington. A son of a Virginia comrade-in-arms had just finished the customary southern speech calling for a resurgence of the spirit of '76. Forrest recalled that he and the speaker's father and their starving comrades in the darkest hour of '76 had fought on to victory with cries even carved into their belts of "liberty or death"—"united we stand, divided we fall"—" 'tis for posterity we die." Exclaimed Forrest: "Posterity! What, posterity perpetuate slavery! How shall I express myself? Oh *pour un mantel pour couvrir les faces de ceux qui sont les fils de mes compatriots*, who with me in battle fell, whose death I then regretted as premature and unfortunate, snatched, as I then thought, from a participation in the blessings of a happy independence, in the full enjoyment of every civil and religious liberty. But now I . . . rejoice . . . that

they were not like me, permitted to live to see posterity outgrow
the remembrance of the patriotic virtues of their fathers." If this
act for extension of slavery passes, "I shall think the small share I had
in the Revolution was the blackest part of my life."

The issue was temporarily settled by the famous Missouri Compromise. Missouri came in without a restriction, but the territory north
of 36° 30", exclusive of Missouri, was to be barred to slavery. However, since southerners like Madison interpreted the ban to apply to
the area as territories and not as states, trouble was in the offing.

Some of the most ardent southern Republicans opposed the compromise. John Taylor wrote a treatise, *Construction Construed*
(1820), to show it had been engineered by the banking octopus
intent on establishing an aristocracy: It all goes back to the era of
the formation of the government and the "corrupt squadron." Pecuniary favors granted to certificate holders begot banking, which
begot bounties to manufacturing capitalists, which begot an oppressive pension list. All together begot the Missouri project, and this
begot the idea of using slavery as an instrument for effecting a balance of power, which in turn will beget new usurpations on personal
liberty and property and eventually bring about the dissolution of
the Union. So heated was he on the question that he came forth with
the most rigid defense of property, a defense that denied even to the
states themselves any right to "interfere" with "property," and of
course slaves were property.

From the "old dominion" state, which had sent forth some of the
greatest expositions in defense of freedom, came a definite movement
to repress the growth of democracy. Its great national leaders opposed
not only white manhood suffrage, but also revision of the system of
apportionment of the state senators whereby the eastern slaveholding
seaboard retained a heavy preponderance over the western part. Majority rule, or "king numbers," would be the worst despotism, for
a majority without slaves would oppress slave owners through taxation. The voice of the legislature ideally should represent a "majority
of interests" of property as well as majority of white men, for the
moment property is separated from power, property will go in search
of power and power in search of property, said John Randolph. The
president of the state constitutional convention, Philip Barbour, who
in Congress denounced Massachusetts' stand on slavery and the tariff,
said: If he must have guide and precedent, he would not look toward
the new turbulent western states, but to the "steady habits of Massa-

chusetts," where the experiment has successfully operated for forty years in its apportionment of state senators in proportion to the public taxes paid.

Critics sarcastically commented that the "old dominion" has long been celebrated for producing men that can split hairs in all abstruse questions of political economy, but when they come home from Congress, they have Negroes "to fan them to sleep." A New York or western Virginian statesman, however, removes his coat on returning home "and takes hold of the plough. This gives him bone and muscle and preserves his Republican principles pure and uncontaminated." These same critics went on to say that the "unfair" apportionment fails to accord with the basic economic truth that labor is the source of value, be it performed by white men or black. But "the black labourer is represented through the person of his master," whereas "the white labourer is not represented at all." [36]

A new political phenomenon appeared with the victor of New Orleans—the "popular" candidate for the presidency. Andrew Jackson was supposed to be a man of the "people" and from the "radical" West, but no one in 1828 could have seriously said that his support came preponderantly from any one group. The complexity of the situation was no better illustrated than in a speech in Congress in 1828 on "Retrenchment and Reform" by that erratic genius, John Randolph. Randolph berated the incumbent, John Quincy Adams, who had been professor of oratory at Harvard, "as belonging to a class which combined great learning with inveterate professorial habits." These fitted one to be a good dialectician, making out irrefragable cases for every new client. Jackson, he said, might not be able to sign his name, but as a great military leader he was fit to be President. Randolph then went on to bemoan letting the West enter the Union on a basis of equality and to assert that the great advantages of free enterprise require excluding of the mass from the franchise. The productive powers of a people like the English, where property is perfectly secure and left free to act, and where the industrious classes are shut out from almost any participation in public affairs, are almost without limit. Two individuals discovered two mines, more precious and productive "than the most valuable mines of specie, and these furnished the means for Pitt's prodigality to such a degree that even he was astonished." They were Sir Richard Arkwright's spinning machine and Mr. James Watt's steam engine. But the imbecile and blundering Pitt "has been complimented with what is due to the unrivalled ingenuity and industry of his countrymen. So . . . in like manner, the young Hercules of America, who, if we can keep him from being strangled by the serpents of corruption, must grow to gigantic strength and stature."

Jackson called himself a Jeffersonian, but then practically everyone in politics did, even those who had fought Jefferson to the death. All had been marching under the banner of nominally one party, Jefferson's Republican Party, after the re-election of Monroe in 1821. Splits had since occurred, and in the election of 1828 Jackson marched at the head of the Democratic Party, while John Quincy Adams led the National Republicans; but every faction and party considered itself the only true Jeffersonian party.[37]

But precisely what were the ideals and views of the man whose spirit was invoked? This calls first for examination of the views of Alexander Hamilton and John Adams, in opposition to whom the traditional Jefferson developed.

CHAPTER XVII

Social Philosophies of the Founding Fathers

THE IMPERIAL DESIGN OF ALEXANDER HAMILTON

ALEXANDER HAMILTON was one of those great minds thrown up by wars and their aftermath.[1] The fluid state of affairs gave him a magnificent opportunity to shape the course of events. Blessed with tenacity of purpose and integrity of character, Hamilton helped to steer the development of the nation along lines that are still distinct. No man asserted more vigorously that he was a traditionalist opposed to all innovation, yet no man of the era was as great an innovator of financial expedients to expand "profitable commerce." But Hamilton definitely was a traditionalist, in so far as tradition meant an aristocracy of wealth and learning and a great respect for the accumulation of money, both by the individual and the nation, as the source of power and prosperity.

In his origins there was much that portended his development. He was born in 1755 in the British West Indies, the most aristocratic of Great Britain's American possessions.[2] Slave labor was the basis of that society, and expressive of its culture was the notorious magnificence and power of the host of absentee planters in London. Hamilton's mother came from the planter class, but his father, though of "good" English family, was shiftless and unsuccessful. At the age of fourteen Hamilton was clerking in a general mercantile store in the Danish West Indies. But three years later, in 1772, he managed to obtain funds to come to the continent for an education, and after a year at a private grammar school he applied successfully for advanced standing at King's College. There President Myles Cooper gave lectures in composition, disputation, theology, moral philosophy; Samuel Clossy, M.D., taught natural philosophy; and the remaining member, the assistant tutor, John Vardill, helped Clossy. But the academic halls were not open long in the midst of the stirring events leading to the Revolution. Vardill had long been writing in defense of Church and Crown. In 1773 he went to England to be ordained and was appointed Regius Professor of Divinity and Natural Philosophy at the College. Instead of returning, however, he joined the intelligence service of the British government. Clossy, disgusted with the outbreaks in the colony, returned to England in 1774. In the following year Cooper, with a mob at his heels, was forced to follow.

Hamilton's college career was cut short, but while still a student he had already sufficiently matured to enter the political controversy as a pamphleteer. Like his teachers, he took his stand on the immutable eternal natural laws, based on the whole volume of nature itself, but came to opposite conclusions from them by finding that the British regulations were null and void because they ran counter to the fundamental principle of no taxation without representation.

Compared to the defense of this doctrine by Moore, who had joined the Loyalists, Hamilton's defense was the relatively liberal standpoint of a belief in the democracy of property owners. He would grant that in England taxes were levied by representatives of the nation, though the mass of Englishmen, bereft of the necessary property qualification, lacked the franchise. A property qualification was essential; for otherwise, as Blackstone taught, the masses would be dependent on their masters and employers in selecting representatives. Still, they could obtain the franchise by industry and good fortune. But in America the propertied class was in the posi-

tion of the English masses. They had no representatives because they
selected none.

Hamilton did not hesitate to apply this criticism in full force to
government in the colonies. A strong executive was necessary, but
that instability was inherent in popular government was merely the
mouthing of politicians. A legislature with a senate of superior wealth
to check the assembly chosen by the people must end in convulsions.
"A representative democracy, where the right of election is well secured and regulated, and the exercise of the legislative, executive,
and judiciary authorities is vested in select persons, chosen really
and not nominally by the people" will be the most regular and durable government.[3]

He lashed out fiercely against members of Congress who used
their office for private profit. Samuel Chase, he publicly charged in
1778, was motivated by the love of power and pecuniary gain. The
spirit and practices of monopoly of such avaricious Congress members, he complained, caused the depreciation of the currency and the
exorbitant prices.[4]

But as the war progressed and the confusion increased, he began
to lose his faith in "popular rule," or, more accurately, the democracy
of property owners. He began moving in circles that had no doubts
that the country's ills flowed from democracy. He had ambitions,
both in the Army and the state. As secretary and aide-de-camp to
Washington, with the rank of lieutenant colonel, he was thrown into
intimate contact with men of wealth and position. The penniless
youth of illegitimate birth made a brilliant marriage. His wife was
a daughter of the wealthy and politically powerful General Philip
Schuyler of New York. This meant the necessity to make much
money to maintain his position in society. Also, he was surrounded
by a speculative group who were just beginning to exploit western
lands and enterprises. The group included Colonel William Duer,
afterward a great entrepreneur; Colonel Aaron Burr, grandson of
Jonathan Edwards; and Gouverneur Morris.

But if his position and his own sense of rectitude forbade mixing
in private ventures, there was nothing to prevent him from using his
pen and abilities to present schemes of financial regeneration that
might attract attention from the people in power. He was a youth
of twenty-four in 1779 when he began to present his ideas to military superiors, acquaintances in Congress, and not least of all to
Robert Morris. He now knew that the only way the country could

be saved was through the adoption of financial schemes that would be profitable to the financial and business world. His ideas shifted in detail, but he always held closely to the mutual support between business and government. The depreciation of the currency was not caused altogether by its excessiveness, he declared, since the moneyed people had found depreciation profitable. But this merely meant that the moneyed class must have a direct financial incentive to maintain the public credit.

His ideas shifted somewhat from time to time. At one stage he even favored a land-bank scheme. But the last product during his army years was a proposal for chartering an exclusive bank under government auspices but controlled by private stockholders with limited liability. It outdid even the scheme for the Bank of North America. The general government and the state were to deposit with it their specie and the proceeds of foreign loans. It was not only to perform the functions of discount and deposit, but also to coin money, issue paper currency, and have allotted to it all the contracts for supplying the armies and fleets. Its notes were to be acceptable in payment of all public dues.

The issue of notes in excess of specie reserves, argued Hamilton, would make possible loans to the government for which the customary market interest of 8 per cent would be paid. Furthermore, this additional paper, by creating business prosperity, would increase the amount of taxes which might be levied and so render the public debt secure. Since people are influenced by such things, the name of the new currency is to be changed. Even if the war should be lost, England would retain the bank because of its manifest advantages, and the shareholders would not be endangered. Of course, the support of the moneyed classes would be forthcoming only if a solid confederation, vigorous administration, and a permanent military force were established.

Similarly, bounties to promoters of domestic enterprise would be beneficial along with tariffs and other favors. Those who demand that the sovereign should leave trade absolutely alone are opposing the teachings of experience and common sense. Such views had arisen from the antipathy to wartime price-fixing and from the misreading of Hume's essay "Of the Jealousy of Trade." But neither Hume, "that ingenious and sensible thinker," nor any other authority questions that government interposition is one of those moral influences often necessary to rectify an unfavorable balance of trade and to restore commerce to the natural, invariable laws of profitable activity.

But the most important function of import duties is to provide the fund that would make the public debt fully negotiable; it could then serve as a circulating medium and as capital. Incidentally, this would also allow its holders to incorporate as a bank. The national debt would be a blessing for a further reason: the masses would be forced to work harder in order to pay the necessary taxes. Thanks to popular maxims, he thought, we labor less than any people of Europe. About the public debt he had strong views always; he suggested seriously in the closing days of the war a "combination between public creditors and the army" to compel Congress to take steps to meet the arrears of both; but Washington felt that such attempts would cause convulsions.[5] Still, Washington and Robert Morris were impressed with the ability of the young man.

After the victory at Yorktown, Hamilton left the Army. Five months of intensive study of the law proved sufficient to obtain him admittance to the bar, and after a fling as a member of Congress in 1782–1783, he settled down as a lawyer in Wall Street.

But Hamilton could never forget that he also had a role to perform in educating the community as to the wisdom of allowing the expansion of great enterprise and profitable commerce and achieving as essential thereto a strong national union.

Restrictions on capital, he knew from current economics, would only damage trade. As the New York legislature moved in 1784 to place restrictions on British merchants here, Hamilton successfully warned that this action, by reducing capital, would reduce trade and seriously damage local artisans, contrary to their expectations. "The only object of concern with an industrious artisan, as such, ought to be, that there may be plenty of money in the community, and a brisk commerce to give it circulation and activity. All attempts at profit, through the medium of monopoly, or violence, will be as fallacious as they are culpable." As it is, labor has plenty of employment at high wages, and the effect of establishing barriers would be to attract workers from other areas or employers would make other shifts to avoid labor's exorbitant demands.[6]

No man worked harder to achieve the Constitutional Convention. In those secret sessions Hamilton was blunt, too blunt even for those who fundamentally agreed with him. He seems, for instance, to have wanted a hereditary monarchy with so much power that no advantage would ever be found in obtaining more: In this way corruption would be made impossible. A House of Lords for the wealthy would create a permanent interest to check the inherent radicalism of a House of Commons, prone to pass paper-money acts and stay laws. Wealthy men at least indicate that they are enlightened as to their interests; the propertyless are irresponsible and moved by immediate rather than long-run interests; otherwise they would not be poor. Liberty is freedom to acquire and keep wealth; equality is nonsense.

If Madison might allow for a variety of interests in the community, to Hamilton there were only two. There must always be the rich and the poor, nobles and commons, creditors and debtors. The advance of industry and commerce would only widen these disparities; wealth would become more concentrated, and virtue would be its graceful appendage. All this might be deprecated as a departure from strict republican principle, but it could not be prevented. It is inherent in a human nature, which is self-interested and especially so in pecuniary affairs. Moreover, if the influence of the wealthy should be circumscribed by law, they would secure the same effect by corruption. Too much democracy would, through the rise of demagogues, lead to a despotism which must be less intelligent than that of the wealthy. In pursuing this thought, Hamilton cited Hume's Tory *History of England* in which Hume showed that the bribery of Parliament by the Crown was, under the circumstances, a wise way of maintaining an equilibrium. It brought out the dominant traits of self-interest and ambition, but it secured their energies for the public benefit.

In effect, the whole lesson of history is that "popular" government cannot last long, and that while it does last it makes misery. Therefore we should set up a President and a Senate chosen for life by an electorate restricted to substantial property holders, and center most of the power in these as against the necessary Chamber of Commons or small property holders—the "turbulent people." But he felt that even this would scarcely be enough: The states should be reduced to administrative units of the central government, within each of which a representative of the national authority would have veto power over its legislative assembly.[7]

With the adoption of the Constitution came Hamilton's great opportunity. Though only thirty-four at the time, he was appointed Secretary of the Treasury by President Washington, at the suggestion of Robert Morris. To help him, as Assistant Secretary, there was first Duer and then Coxe. But Hamilton needed little help as he set to work to put into practice a series of financial proposals which would yield to America the treasure or claims on treasure that made England such a mighty power.

Hamilton, like all the great figures of his day, was a mercantilist, but he had his own way of handling the logic. The "intrinsic value" of goods depends on the price of raw materials and the expense of fabrication, but without sufficient money, goods would fall below their "intrinsic value." [8] This defect of a supply of money is not to be remedied by issuing legal-tender paper, for specie is the only real money. Instead, Hamilton proposed a set of devices that would attach the financial community to the government. These were presented in a series of extraordinary state papers.[9]

The funding of the debt was the first problem. All holders were to be paid in full. Any question of discrimination between holders was not to be thought of, for aside from the host of other arguments, discrimination would destroy negotiability, and negotiability made the debt capital. Anything which can be converted into money is capital, said Hamilton. So strongly was he impressed with the need of maintaining negotiability that he argued not only against taxes being laid on the principal, income, or transfer of public securities, but also that even in times of war holders in enemy countries were to be paid the interest and principal when due. To violate any of these terms, he insisted, constitutes in effect a breach of the contract between the government and its creditors.

Related to this, of course, was the scheme for a national bank. This corporation was to have limited liability, and it was to be backed by the government's participation in ownership and by the acceptance of its paper for public dues; but it was to be privately operated, and its profits were to go elsewhere than to the Treasury.

Finally came the *Report on Manufactures*, Hamilton's most famous state paper. The encouragement of manufactures was a policy which would increase the national wealth. As for those who were inclined to weigh the farm against the factory, he had kind of answer. Agriculture, he said, would gain an increasing market for its products, and as a result of this land values would rise and proprietors would be benefited. The agricultural nations are cheated by the drain of their specie into the countries from which they buy the higher-priced manufactures. As for the Physiocratic idea that manufacturing is incapable of producing any surplus, as rent is produced by land, this is fallacious; even rent is really the profit produced by capital invested in the land, not something produced by the land itself. From this generalization Hamilton triumphantly concluded that manufacturing is a more desirable activity than agriculture since it yields higher profits.

The scarcity of labor could be remedied not only by introducing machinery, but also by using the labor of women, of children, and of immigrants. Adequate capital is available from foreigners and from the establishment of new banks, but, most important, from the use of public debt. English businessmen and sagacious theorists alike are agreed, said Hamilton, that the public debt has been the great animating agent of enterprise; this is proved by the universal inability otherwise to explain how England could become the world's fiscal agent and the center of its industry on so small an amount of specie. The linking of the public debt as capital with private enterprise would have certain subsidiary benefits also. The collection of taxes with which to pay it would force the people who pay them to be more industrious; they would therefore produce more and set the country forward in that way. It needs also to be said that, if manufactures are not encouraged, public debt repayments would involve exporting specie to foreign creditors; if this is not enough, it could be added that it takes good hard money to pay for the importing of useless luxuries which a wholly agricultural class would demand even though it does not make them.

It might be argued that if these enterprises really have a prospect of profit, self-interest alone would lead to their expansion; but, aside from the objection of competition from entrenched foreign enterprises, it has to be remembered that man, being a creature of habit, only tardily makes changes which are profitable to himself and to society. Consequently, to secure the confidence of sagacious, cautious capitalists, government must give guarantees against initial losses. Such aid might take the form of heavy duties on imports of manufactures, but much lower ones, if any, on raw materials. These would raise prices only until the domestic enterprise has matured. But better still are bounties and premiums. For the constitutionality of bounties is inherent in the general welfare clause of the Constitution. But, of course, this does not mean that the government could manufacture on its own account, with the possible exception of military supplies. It might, however, purchase stock in privately incorporated societies for manufacture. Finally, as a further aid to industry, no taxes on profits or capital should be allowed, since exposure of such secrets to a tax collector is contrary to the genius of liberty and the maxims of industry.

The reports of Hamilton in 1790 and 1791, taken together, constitute a theoretical plan which is just beginning to be appreciated. The economic organization logically involved was grand and imperial in scope. A fully negotiable funded debt, drained originally from the small-property classes and met by taxes paid by the masses, was to be used by an emerging moneyed class to create profitable speculative enterprises in lands, industry, and finance. This was the intent. However, after the funding and bank bills became law, a vast uproar began, complicated by the personal antagonism between Jefferson and Hamilton. Holders of the·debt in Congress, including the president of Columbia College, had voted for the bills, and some had become directors of the bank. Press and platform rang with denunciations of the "corrupt squadron of stock jobbers" and "paper jobbers": The bills had been passed by an insolvent majority. By the funding, soldiers were robbed; a hopeless debt and endless taxes were fastened on the country; the real property in the nation, the property of agriculture and industry, was taxed by the bank and the funding and placed at the disposal of gamblers in the stock market. Vast inequalities had been created overnight by jugglery in mere paper, by lending shadows and receiving substance. Formerly this new corrupt, barren, idle class were in effect paupers; now they constituted a "paper aristocracy" of rich and well-born. This great disparity in wealth could only lead to the destruction of liberty. Had not Hamilton shown by his use of the welfare clause to support bounties that all power and wealth would be usurped eventually by a select class, and the people reduced to poverty and distress, republican institutions overthrown, and despotic monarchy established?·[10] Hamilton was no more than a West Indian adventurer.

Even Washington became disturbed and called on Hamilton for an explanation. He gave his answers with customary facility. The public credit, of course, might be misused; but the true ground of safety must be the prevention at all times of attempts to defraud creditors. Governments as well as individuals must maintain their contracts. Unless the arrangements already made are upheld, private property and government would certainly fall, and Washington was warned again that the confidence of the moneyed class must not be alienated. They are the only solid support for government.

Challenged by bitter invective, Hamilton was hardly to be blamed for retorting in kind. Since the French Revolution was known to have the sympathy of his opponents, he was not averse to charging them with all the crimes which might be attributed to revolutionists. Those who oppose his ideas are "empirics" and "speculative thinkers" influenced by pernicious French doctrines, he told Washington. Criminally ignorant of human nature, they entertain the dangerous hope of man's perfectibility when a sound suspicion of his depravity is the only secure basis for public policy. Extending their principles of liberty toward licentiousness, they are at war with religion, morality, government, and property. To "the vain reveries of a false and new-fangled philosophy" they sacrifice all that is sacred, revered, enduring, and substantial in society. They worship "the idol of popularity" and propagate errors to be found only in the cottages of peasants.[11]

The battle went on in the press at great length and with the expenditure of vast energy, but his opponents had the advantage. They could utilize the rhetoric of democracy. Hamilton, much as he tried, could do so only haltingly.

Hamilton finally resigned in 1795 to turn to law and money making, but his financial policies and ideas were secure with his faithful friend Oliver Wolcott as the new Secretary.

His period of constructive statesmanship was over, and the subsequent period, so far as national policy was concerned, consisted merely in defending Washington's Administration. The Jay Treaty he appears to have viewed originally with as much distaste as the Jeffersonians. He called it an "old woman's treaty," but apparently it was enough that the Jeffersonians attacked it for him to take up his pen and vigorously support the treaty with arguments that generally ran counter to his own bent. It became to him one of the "fruits of adherence to reason left to its own light." With one doubtful exception, every article is of benefit to the nation. See, for instance, the advantage of securing a share in the trade with India. Opponents have said this is an empty privilege in the face of the great capital of the East India Company. But Hamilton, forgetting his hitherto consistent belief in the growing usefulness of the corporate device, insisted "that experience has proved (outside of banking) the superior strength and enterprise of individual effort." It is similarly erroneous to argue that allowing the British traders equal access to the Indians in the West overlooks the influence of the large capital of the British, for little capital is really needed to be successful in the Indian trade.

Finally, bordering territories should have free intercourse in the natural course of things. Heretofore the maxims of the United States favored a free intercourse with all the world. They have conceived they had nothing to fear from an "unrestrained competition of commercial enterprise" and have only desired to be admitted to it on equal terms, and to end colonial monopoly. But new ideas have suddenly arisen. The extremes of commercial jealousy are inculcated. Regulations and exclusive rights and privileges are demanded. Instead of feeling pleasure that new avenues of trade are opened, a thousand mischiefs are pictured. Free trade with all the world seems to have dwindled into trade with France and her dominions.

The English Navigation Acts are essential to England to protect her interests. They are merely regulating measures to provide her with a fleet and seamen. We never really objected to them while we were colonies, but only when they were used to raise revenue. We wisely follow England's policy in excluding foreign competition from the coasting trade and the fisheries.[12]

One of Hamilton's ventures had an unhappy outcome, though it conformed to his logic. He joined with his financial and political competitor, Aaron Burr, to obtain a charter for another bank from the New York legislature, though he had denounced a previous attempt by others as monstrous because it would result in creating excessive paper. Subterfuge was used to obtain the charter. It happened that the city of New York was seeking power from the legislature for a city waterworks system. Burr and Hamilton convinced the city authorities in 1799 that it would be financially impossible for the city to erect the works on its own account. The requisite taxes would be too heavy, and the work would not be zealously pushed. A private company in which the city would buy shares could easily and quickly accomplish the task. So a bill was passed by the legislature ostensibly providing for a private corporation, the Manhattan Company, to supply the city "with pure and wholesome water," but a clause was inserted which provided that it "may be lawful to employ surplus capital in the purchase of public or other stocks or in any other moneyed transaction or operation." Once the charter was obtained, the incorporators dug a well in the most thickly settled part of the city and pumped a little impure water. The city obtained no water supply, but the company entered its real business, which was banking. In the process Burr froze out the Hamilton interests, and Hamilton then described the bank as "a perfect monster in its principles, but a very convenient instrument of profit and influence." It was now ostensibly a Jeffersonian Republican bank and Republican spokesmen shouted that they now could prevent Federalist banks from coercing borrowers at election times.[13]

Meanwhile the Federalists were losing control of the government. The foreign-born particularly were rabid Jeffersonians, and their anti-British and pro-French sympathies made them doubly obnoxious to Hamilton. He felt that the proposed Alien Act giving President Adams arbitrary power to deport any undesirable foreigners should be administered with an eye to deporting the mass of foreigners— except, of course, the merchants among them and the "few whose demeanor amongst us has been unexceptionable." [14] Furthermore, he said, the Administration should appoint more judges. This "salutary patronage" would increase the government's influence. The people would grumble at first, but they would eventually become docile. On the other hand, the Federalists should establish a society for giving premiums for new inventions, discoveries, and improvements in agriculture and the arts. Such a society would "speak powerfully to the feelings and interests of those classes of men to whom the benefits derived from the government have been heretofore the least manifest." [15] He began to perceive also that the sources of the higher learning ought to be protected from common contamination. Commenting on the standard which ought to be used in choosing a president for Columbia in 1800, he wrote that the candidate must "be a gentleman . . . as well as a sound and polite scholar, [and] . . . his politics be of the right sort." He prevented Benjamin Rush from obtaining a post in the medical division.[16]

In the national presidential campaign of 1800 Hamilton was unrestrained in his partisanship. The Republican ticket of Jefferson and Burr had to be defeated at all costs. He unsuccessfully begged his political ally, Governor John Jay of New York, to overturn arbitrarily the election procedure in the state. The atheistical Jefferson, he wrote, is too earnest about democracy and would destroy the substantial interests of society. "From indubitable facts, not from conjectures or inferences," he knew that a revolution was planned with Jefferson as Napoleon.[17] The Republicans won, but Jefferson and Burr having both received the same number of votes, the law required the House of Representatives to determine who was president and who was vice-president. Federalist representatives, it seemed, might throw their support to Burr. Hamilton promptly transferred his invective to Burr, however much it must have hurt to support his old enemy, Jefferson. Burr, he shouted, is a potential dictator—a Godwin! [18]

With Jefferson in the White House, Hamilton found it increasingly necessary to defend the constitutional and fiscal structure he had labored to erect. Jefferson proposed to repay the public debt rapidly. The result would be an excess of money, said Hamilton. This, experience showed, would lower the morality and industry of the nation. In addition, specie payments to foreign holders of bonds and the importation of luxuries would create a defective circulation and less industry. The proposed elimination of the excise duty would be disastrous—it would destroy equality of burden; and if this revenue could be really spared it should be used for the benefit of commerce and navigation. Jefferson's statement in his inaugural address that industry prospers in proportion as it is left to the exertion of individual enterprise is preposterous, for "practical politicians know that [industry] may be beneficially stimulated by prudent aids and encouragements on the part of government."

Nothing was as terrifying, however, as the proposed reduction of the number of federal judgeships. This, he said, violates the sacred principles of contract and vested interest. It is based on the pernicious doctrine that no legislature can bind its successor; in other words, that no rights can be vested in an individual or collection of individuals whether of property or any other description which cannot be canceled at pleasure. This doctrine would prevent the making of any valid pledge of public faith.[19] To fight this "democratic frenzy," he and his friends founded in 1801 the New York Evening Post, which, according to the prospectus, was "to diffuse among the people correct information on all interesting subjects, to inculcate just principles in religion, morals, and politics, and to cultivate a taste for sound literature." But Hamilton soon found that a newspaper was not the most effective instrument to win the people to his side. He complained in 1802 that the Federalists had not heretofore pursued the wisest tactics. They had always appealed to the ignorant people on the basis of reason. But "men are rather reasoning than reasonable animals, for the most part governed by the impulse of passion." His opponents, he now saw, are aware of this. They praise democracy and equality; they give lip service to the reason of men; but their appeal is really to the most powerful of passions—vanity. This gives them the great advantage of having the vicious on their side. Since mankind is governed more by vices than by virtues, the Federalists must now and then depart from the path of absolute rectitude to win the support of those they despise. The best way to accomplish their ends, he thought, would be to organize a Christian Constitutional Society devoted to upholding the Christian religion and the Constitution. It should promote charitable societies for the relief of immigrants. Federalist-manned charitable science schools for mechanics and artisans should also be established to check the influence of the Jacobins in the populous cities.[20]

Hamilton's duel with Burr, in 1804, cut short his career, but not his broad scheme. Could he have lived the space of Jefferson's life, he would have realized that he had built more permanently than he appreciated, for the Jeffersonians took over his policies. His philosophy remained a basic ingredient in American tradition, though the idiom was to change from time to time: The mass was turbulent, ignorant, and poverty-stricken. With the growth of wealth, inequality and class antithesis must increase. Therefore the stability of the social order and the security of person and property can only be maintained by a strong government in the hands of the wealthy and intelligent. To these classes, government at all times should render financial aid for the sake of attaching them to the government by the strongest bond—interest—thus increasing national wealth and maintaining the employment of the mass.

Agreeing with Hamilton in political theory but differing with him in economic theory was his fellow Federalist, John Adams.

THE REGAL REPUBLIC OF JOHN ADAMS

Adams stands out not only as a president, politician, and statesman, but also as a political philosopher of authentic power and range. It is hard to think of anyone who has analyzed with equal directness and thoroughness the essential principles of man in society.[21] Certainly few systematic treatises in the field approach the level of those of Adams in objectivity and the determination to dig to the root of problems. To this intellectual quality, he added a political one and has contributed the best statement of the "conservative" position.

In approaching Adams, the reader becomes aware of a certain duality running through all his reflections. There is a hard core of judgment regarding man's nature and the destiny of society. He sees material forces as dominant in actual life and as summing up all other forcer and tendencies of man—the ethical and spiritual as well as the material. This basic attitude becomes explicit and articulate at the zenith of his career, but interlaced in that long and distinguished career are the vacillations, adaptations, and variations characteristic of the philosopher who is also a man of affairs. Different phases of his own life as well as that of his country are reflected in his radical propaganda in the colonial struggle with the mother country, in his attempt to consolidate the new government, in his defense of that government against "subversive democracy," and, finally, in his apology for it against what to him were shortsighted reactionaries and naïve democrats.

Adams was born in 1735 of orthodox Puritan parents in Massachusetts. The family proudly traced its descent from the founding of the colony, but it had little wealth. Adams's father was an independent artisan, a shoemaker, but he determined that his son should go to Harvard to prepare for the ministry.

He entered Harvard in 1751 and, according to the official classification of students by "dignity of birth, or . . . rank of parents," he was fourteenth in a class of twenty-four. He was properly inculcated in the classics, Calvinist theology, and the truths laid down by Locke, the authority in philosophy and social sciences. Though deeply religious and at all times a believer in the public support of the ministry, he felt that the heated theological disputes of the day were not for him. After graduating, he prepared for the law on the ground that the law was consistent with the bonds of religion and morality.[22]

Adams became not only a successful lawyer, but one of the ablest students of jurisprudence in a colony known for its scholars in the law. He soon obtained minor public offices, and his practice steadily increased as wealthy merchants came to appreciate his talents. He found that his "obstinate industry" not only in his legal practice, but also in extending loans on notes and mortgages and in borrowing for his own real-estate investments, was resulting in the accumulation of a comfortable capital.

Adams's background, temperament, and training fitted him not only for his business, but also for his role of pamphleteer, essayist, and political leader. He soon became active in the struggle between the mother country and the colonies. The argument of his writings during the Stamp Act controversy of 1765, an argument which he repeated with slight change through subsequent phases of the struggle, was for political home rule and economic freedom. Rulers, he argued, are after all merely agents. If they misuse their authority, the people may select better "attorneys" to carry out their will. The ordinary check on the rulers is the jury trial and the local colonial assembly. It was natural, therefore, for Adams to reject the jurisdiction of Crown-appointed admiralty courts to try cases of the infringements of Trade Acts, and the enactment of these acts or any act of taxation, in distant London, as contrary to fundamental rights. These demands for colonial autonomy and economic liberty were couched during this tense period not only by Adams, but also by more conservative revolutionaries—indeed, by all revolutionaries—in the exalted language of democracy. The British government became a "foreign" ruler whose officers fattened on the oppression of the poor and incidentally diminished the income of all other colonials. The Stamp Act in particular was sheer extortion of the least privileged, and in addition it embarrassed business, threatening to bring on economic convulsions by draining the country of its scanty cash.

In Adams's philosophy these political and economic arguments flowed from a grand postulate of human nature. It is that men love power and domination. This passion, properly restrained, is useful, the source of all good; unrestrained, it leads to tyranny. Adams saw this principle exemplified in the most remote origins of the Massachusetts colony. The unchecked love of power gave rise to the tyranny of the canon and feudal law, which deprived men of—in Locke's phrase—"the right of life, liberty and property."

The Reformation, the struggle against Charles I, and the peopling of the American colonies were related attempts to remove the corruptions of this passion. The leaders of the migration to New England appealed to the political wisdom of antiquity. They approved of monarchy and a publicly supported clergy, but they also saw the need of "popular" power as a balance to the monarch and the priest; for otherwise the government must degenerate into one of fraud, violence, and usurpation. But once again King and Parliament were overriding the "fundamental rights" of the "people" with tax and trade legislation and thereby were reviving the inequities and servilities of feudal and canon law.[23]

As the dispute over local autonomy developed into a struggle for national independence, Adams and his comrades found opposition from men of solid wealth who had little sympathy for revolution.

The "patricians," especially the political leaders in the South and Pennsylvania, Adams believed, were lukewarm to independence because of their wealth, not because of any idealistic loyalism. But immediately after the Declaration of Independence he also felt that the states should not drop these men from leadership, for their wealth and connections were essential cement for the Union.[24]

Fomenting popular revolutions was one thing, but making societies was another. Adams, like any respectable colonial of his generation, thought of "people" in two rather distinct senses—the spiritual and the civil. In the former, every human being is, in the sight of God, equally worthy. And it is this view which at one stroke excludes slavery, oppression, autocracy, arbitrary exactions, and every form of inequality. But in a practical civil society, account has to be taken not only of man's spiritual rights, but of his actual potentialities and inadequacies. Driven by the "passion for superiority," man seeks to distinguish himself above his fellows. Failures become envious of their betters. How then organize a civil society which will on the one hand guarantee considerable spiritual freedom, and on the other insure effective resistance to the dangers of tyrannical ambition and democratic anarchy? A society, to be stable, must be based on property, which breeds responsibility. But property should be relatively widespread in order to prevent too narrow an aristocracy. The "people" in civil society, therefore, does not include everyone but only those, preferably as many as possible, who can be trusted with political and economic rights. This, Adams felt, is exemplified in the freehold franchise of colonial Massachusetts. Now that the people have declared themselves free of "foreign" control and monarchy, they must organize a society based on property holders. If the "people" do not restrain themselves, the wise and honest may be driven to reintroduce monarchy, for even despotism is preferable to the factionalism of corrupted popular government.[25]

There was a certain mechanical quality in Adams's conception of a proper order, for he assumed that, given a sensible structure of government, not only political but also economic problems would automatically take care of themselves. But the economic problems which he was forced to face as a member of the Continental Congress and as a diplomat were peculiarly obstinate. With his customary candor, he confessed in his letters his ignorance of "coin and commerce." He blamed his narrow New England education for not giving him that comprehensive knowledge, including the knowledge of the commerce of the world, which apparently every British statesman had.

His only armor in this fight was the time-honored notion of national prosperity as dependent on the increase of commerce and money. But would these concepts meet the drastic necessities of war? Adams's puzzlement took the form of self-cross-examination. Should we confine our trade with other nations "to our own bottoms, which alone can lay a foundation for great wealth and naval power?" If America eliminates commerce, must not the mass of unemployed become either "a large discontented party" or too large a burden for the rest of the country to support? He did not question that, as far as necessaries and conveniences are concerned, the nation could dispense with foreign trade and be happier; but the people do not "have virtue enough to be mere husbandmen, mechanics and soldiers" for any length of time. "Is their temperance, fortitude, perseverance to induce such a mortification of their appetites, passions, and fancies" as the deprivation of elegancies entails? Finally, are not all interests, including the landed, so connected with the mercantile interest as "to produce general impatience under such severe restrictions?" [26]

As the war proceeded and confusion increased, Adams resorted to the old reliable: unrestrained "freedom of trade." He was against all shackles. "Let the spirit of the people have its own way, and it will do something." Massachusetts attempted to enforce embargoes and stop privateers in order to restrain prices and obtain soldiers. But Adams denounced these measures as ruinous to the war effort. If the privateers have "fair play"—that is, free trade—the state would obtain many prizes and hundreds of seamen. South Carolina, with a superior spirit of enterprise in trade, gets plenty of goods though at dear prices and can export her staples; for vessels, even from the enemy's colonies, find it profitable to come there. With the other states following a similar policy, "trade will soon be brisk in every state except Massachusetts." [27]

In the same spirit Adams emphatically disapproved of price-fixing from the start. It can offer only a partial, temporary remedy, for "after a time the evils will break out with greater violence. The waters will flow with great rapidity for having been dammed up for a time." Speaking of the Massachusetts price-fixing act, he declared that if it were not quickly repealed, civil war in the state would follow. "Rascally upstarts in trade" have made great fortunes by monopoly and oppression, but this evil can only be cured by people refusing to buy their goods.[28]

More perplexing than trade questions was the problem of government finance and credit. Like everyone else in the Congress, Adams approved of the first issue of the famous "continentals." However, after two years of war and extended issues, Adams was blaming all the evils of high prices, speculation, and extortion on the depreciating currency. It will destroy morals, he said, for many are forced to think extortion and injustice are necessary for their own security. The basic remedy is now loans, foreign and domestic.[29] By 1779 Adams, while trying to raise loans in Europe, in desperation called for a devaluation of the "vile paper" and recourse to taxation because the depreciating paper, being taken as a sign of losing the war, heartened the Tories and disheartened the Whigs more than it ought.

The remedy suddenly seemed "simple and obvious." Taxation alone must provide all future government revenues. Unfortunately people are still given to extravagance, except for a few wise and virtuous ones who struggle against the torrent of follies and frivolities and the mercantile speculators, gamblers, and stock jobbers.[30]

Congress sharply devalued the paper in 1780, but our French ally protested on behalf of holders of the paper that the action violated the sacredness of contract. Adams informed the French authorities that, on the contrary, the devaluation accorded with sound economics and morals. By straining the quantity theory of money he "proved" that the possessors were paid the real worth of their money: A certain sum of money is necessary to circulate a nation's business. "The precise sum is discoverable by calculation and reducible to certainty." The issue of more paper decreases the real worth of the money—that is, its value in the market. Besides, the receiver of paper takes it for goods and services, not at its nominal value, but at its market value. Consequently the devaluation act is not a breach of faith, but an attempt to restore a stable medium.[31]

But if America's allies—the French and Dutch governments—as well as European individuals should grant loans to the American government, the economic problem would be solved, especially if at the same time they would grant favorable commercial treaties. He informed the Dutch that a loan would give stability to money, invigorate Army enlistments, accelerate privateering, and expand foreign trade, especially with the Dutch. As for American postwar competition, the lending nations need not fear that an independent United States would become a great manufacturing nation because America's interest would be for centuries centered on agriculture. The true profit of America, Adams argued in the spirit of Physiocratic doctrine, must come from the rise in land values. "A day's work, worth two shillings upon wild land, not only produced two shillings in the crop, but made the land worth two shillings more. Whereas a day's work of the same price, applied to manufactures produced only the two shillings." But loans being lacking, necessity forces the United States to follow the less profitable route of manufactures.

The country's resources are more than adequate to meet the war costs eventually. Heavier taxes could not be imposed at first because of obstructions to trade. But the ability to pay taxes is increasing with the increase of population, cultivated lands, commerce, and successful privateering. In fact, retrenchment of the prevalent luxury alone would enable the country to prosecute the war. But at present, import duties, aside from reducing the market for European goods, would be dangerous to liberty.

At the same time America is acquiring considerable specie to meet loans and further increase trade. Everywhere the English Army goes it must leave specie behind for expenses and clandestine trade. Did not the British general, Howe, suspect that General Washington connived at the American people's supplying British-held Philadelphia in order to obtain for his country large sums of money and thus bring England to defeat? The addition of a French force helping the American fleet and Army will increase the supply. The more troops and ships France and England send, the more resources America will have.[32]

For all its inadequacies and inconsistencies, this argument was common coin not only in the contemporary world of commerce, but also in the world of statesmanship. Fortunately for the United States, the enemy operated on the same pecuniary logic.

The cessation of hostilities intensified the problem of debts and taxes. Any attempt to tamper with the American public debt Adams viewed as undermining justice. The demand for its devaluation seemed to him a sign of corruption, destructive of peace, order, decency, and industry. Creditors have an inalienable right to the full or "real value" by the fundamental principles of society.[33]

The rumbling of discontent in Massachusetts early in 1786 only gradually shocked Adams, then minister to England, into a realization that the people were still grossly ignorant of sound economics. His merchant friend and a leading political figure of Massachusetts, James Warren, wrote him that the Algerine pirates in the Mediterranean, the lack of markets for whale oil, the steady drain of specie to pay for English baubles had ruined commerce and trade, and consequently people could not pay debts or taxes. The upshot of Warren's complaint was that government must step in to help the harried businessman through "relief" legislation. This struck Adams as showing a lack of faith in individual enterprise. Wherever a lamp is burned, the oil could find markets "if our merchants will take pains by samples and experiments" to show its superior qualities. As for the Algerine piracies, he was surprised that the merchants had not calculated that a loan to repress them would cost only £18,000 a year in interest, while the piracies cost the country £1,000,000 a year. If Congress were given the power, heretofore refused, to levy a duty on exports and imports to pay the interest, the loan would be quickly forthcoming.

Everything must be done to restore public faith and confidence, otherwise business would stagnate. This means that the public debt must be funded immediately, the interest paid, and all fear of paper knavery annihilated.[34] The funding will end the enormously gainful speculation in public paper, and the capital released from speculation will produce a circulation that will relieve the commercial distress. Adams, of course, was hoping that the matter would right itself in the natural course of events. But he soon heard from Warren, who was witnessing the beginnings of Shays' Rebellion, that affairs in Massachusetts were getting worse, indeed bordering on civil war. Now, instead of castigating the leaders for timidity in business, Adams charged them with supineness in politics.[35] He had noticed before leaving America in 1779, he said, that there was need for vigorous leadership, for the "people" were ever on the watch to spread economic heresies. The county conventions with their resolutions calling for "relief" were evidence that the people "were running wild."

This economic situation, Adams said, had led him to prepare a political disquisition against proponents of extreme "democracy," whether in America or Europe.[36] His treatise, the famous *A Defence of the Constitutions of Government of the United States of*

America, must be understood in the context of his role as minister to England. It was his task, as it was of any envoy, to obtain favorable commercial arrangements from England and to encourage foreign investments and migration. But on one hand many respectable foreigners viewed the "democracy" of America as unsafe for property, while others felt that the state constitutions were not as free as they should be. On the other hand, Adams was forced to defend them as making for security of liberty and property, and at the same time, true to his bent, he was forced to admonish the states that they must perfect a "balance" against the "popular" power in order to provide that security which was the essence of liberty.

The principles of government, he declared in the treatise, could only be known on the basis of a knowledge of the history of mankind. Adams's comprehensive selected survey of history revealed that the English constitution was the only scientific government. But the peculiar conditions in America had to be taken into account: Since the American people are primarily agricultural and scattered over an extensive area, they are not subject to "those contagions of madness and folly" characteristic of densely populated countries with their "people in daily fear of perishing of want." Thus at present, he wrote, the people can live and increase under almost any form of government, even without any government. But foundations must be laid to fit the near future when the country will have 100,000,000 people, when the present states will be rich, powerful, and luxurious, and the lands will be held in few hands and the mass will be propertyless.

Of course, in America, as elsewhere, men love equality when they look up to higher ranks, and they love distinction when they look downward. This tendency to "superiority" must be supported by a hierarchy of officers and ranks. The Americans have avoided a legal nobility, but no well-ordered community has existed for long without one. Society will always be divided into plebeians, the "simplemen," obscure, ignorant, mean, and poor; and the patricians, the rich and well-born, the gentlemen who always administer government. In America as elsewhere wealth and good birth exercise dominance *de facto*. The poor are dependent on the rich for their subsistence; many of smaller fortunes will be in debt or under obligations to the wealthy. Still others, such as men of letters and the learned professions, will from acquaintance, "conversation," and expectation be connected with them. Finally, among the wisest people there is a degree of admiration, subtracted from all dependence, "which accompanies splendid wealth, insures . . . respect, and bestows . . . influence."

A few, having all the advantages of birth and fortune, constitute the "natural aristocracy," the greatest collection of virtue and abilities in a free government. This was again, of course, the theory of natural dominion. It found its socio-psychological aspect in Adams's theory of luxury. There were two traditional objections to luxury: moral—luxury corrupts; and political—the aristocrats are a wasteful, parasitic, luxurious class. In Adams's view luxury is industrially and commercially necessary, an inevitable accompaniment of man's vanity and thirst for distinction. In the circumstances, luxury is relative. In a sense the lower classes are responsible for what appears to be increasing luxury in the upper ranks. The higher ranks must maintain distinction between the lower classes and themselves lest they fall into contempt and ridicule. If the poor and the middle ranks reduce their luxury, then their superiors can do so safely.

On the other hand, "popular" democracy is most exposed to the evil of luxury. No subordination can exist to restrain it, since one citizen cannot bear another to be better than he. "A universal emulation in luxury instantly commences." So far as restraining luxury among the lower orders is concerned, monarchies and aristocracies may be more effective than democracy. In a completely aristocratic government, luxury is simply forbidden to commoners by sumptuary laws. In "simple"—that is, absolute—monarchies, luxury is generally only restrained by the means of gratifying it, but since the difference of ranks is established by law and universally known, the lower ranks are not tempted to imitate the splendor of the higher. A government in which distinctions have play can preserve liberty in spite of a great degree of "luxury, dissipation, and even profligacy of manners."

Such being the vices of man, the problem is how to make them subserve his aspirations to virtue (good). The answer is the "balanced" government. Of course, there must be a recognition of the principle that "the original and fountain of all just power and government is in the people." This recognition takes the form of a lower house, or "popular" assembly. The "people," as we have noticed, are the responsible propertied mass, organized by freehold suffrage or its equivalent. But just as order and property must be protected against the jealous passions and ignorance of the propertyless, larger accumulations must be secured against the more restrained, but no less dangerous, jealousy of the small-propertied. Most people are too indolent and irrational to work hard to acquire some property when they have none or to increase such property as they do have. But they powerfully envy it. Give them complete power, and they will rob the more foresighted and rich. By abolishing debts, imposing heavy taxes on the rich, and other ways, they will seek constantly to redistribute wealth. If the rich and powerful resist, as they inevitably will, the way is cleared for a new despot. To check the "popular" assembly, therefore, a senate becomes necessary. It becomes the guardian of liberty and property and prevents a thoughtless process of leveling. It is also necessary, of course, in order to achieve the blessings of a natural aristocracy.

At the same time an independent executive with an absolute negative and the sole power of appointing officers, civil and military, is essential as a response to that kingly tendency of domination in human nature which can only be controlled, not cured, and prevents factional disputes among the aristocrats or between the house and senate. The latter must be on its mettle in order to be given lucrative offices. And at the same time it acts as a check on the executive as well as the house. The jealousy between the executive and the "gentlemen" forces him to protect the "common people" and to humble any senator or other state officer who may become too powerful for the laws or the spirit of the constitution. This motivates the executive to look for merit among commoners and promote those capable of public employment. Therefore, to preach enmity against kingly government—that is, a powerful executive—is a vicious aristocratical device, a "conspiracy against the rights of mankind" and against that equality between the gentlemen and the commoners which "nature has established as a moral right and law should ordain as a political right" to preserve liberty. The American common people, he hoped, are too enlightened "to be seduced by this hypocritical snare; the gentlemen too, it is hoped, are too enlightened as well as too equitable ever to attempt such a measure because they must know that . . . after suffering all the evils of contests and dissensions, cruelty and oppression from the aristocratics, the common people will perjure themselves and establish an unlimited monarchy instead of a regal republic." In fact, the fatal defect of the Continental Congress springs from this source. Being selected by and responsible to the state legislatures, it is naturally composed of members of the aristocratical bodies in every state. Thus its tendency is to restrict the prerogatives of government and the privileges of the "people" in order to augment those of the aristocracy.

But Adams felt that his scheme provided an automatic, perfect balance or equilibrium. Each "order" balances the other and compels it to be guardian of the laws which restrain their rivalries, so that all can enjoy their liberty and property. By providing "constitutional liberty" it produces the opportunities for commerce which other types of government obstruct.

Adams thought that the publication of the *Defence* would make him the most unpopular man in America, but instead he was chosen Vice-President in the new government. The constitutional provisions for a divided sovereignty, a limited instead of an absolute executive veto, and senatorial participation in executive appointments, he thought, were serious defects; but the enlightened part of the community would gradually remedy these imperfections.[37] All the states were to some degree guilty of forgetting that the "defense of property" and the "freedom of commerce" were the substance of the liberty and justice for which they had waged war with England.[38] States that had enacted paper-money acts and other "relief" legislation, or had refused to grant the Continental Congress the power to levy an impost to pay the public debt, or had levied duties on the trade of other states, were "lawbreakers" as Adams understood the term. Thus Adams explained to friends that the American people "have smarted under a total oblivion of the two first principles of liberty and commerce, that laws are the fountain of freedom and punctuality the source of credit." He feared that they had "not enough of the spirit of Union to insure obedience to the laws nor enough of shame and scorn of evasion" to provide that revenue on which punctuality will depend.[39]

Hamilton's measures of funding the debt and establishing the Bank of the United States met his general approval as necessary evils, not as positive blessings. Debts meant taxes, and taxes contained the threat of revolution. The bank meant paper money, and paper enabled debtors to defraud creditors. The real evil was the increase in state-chartered banks with the note-issue privilege. As a consequence he considered himself taxed one-half of his salary and one-half of "all the interest of my money to support banks and bankrupts." [40] Issues of the paper money, he asserted later, caused a rise in the price of labor, land, and goods to the defrauding of creditors and the ruin of commerce. But so many people lived on the banks that little could be done.[41]

Just as Adams became Vice-President there came the ominous note of the French Revolution, the creation of the Supreme National Assembly with the threat to eliminate the king and the nobility. Adams saw more in it: the danger that the United States might return to the "democracy" of the days of the Confederation. Unfortunately, while America had yet to perfect the balance, the French, he said, had copied the American errors which cost America dear.[42] That a reformation was necessary in France he admitted, but the evils flowing "from the great and perpetual distinction" between the few rich and the many poor could be avoided only by a retention of the king and nobility.[43] So he strove through the newspapers to educate the American people on the wisdom of the "balance" for all countries and the dangerous tendencies of France.

Although his treatise, *Discourses on Davila* (1790), does not add any new ideas, it presents the clearest and most consistent exposition of the views already surveyed. These views appear with an emphasis and pointed quality which give the *Discourses* a certain starkness. A passionate pessimism pervades them. And they ring with the tone of a homily on human depravity and vanity and a reluctant reconciliation to the sad forces of society. The love of dominion now becomes a pervasive exaggerated love of esteem.

The theory becomes severely psychological. Men have pride of birth because an illustrious descent attracts notice. Noble blood, more so in republican than in other types, is more highly esteemed because benevolence, sympathy, "congratulation" have been so long associated with those names in the people's minds that they become national habits. Because men love ostentation and dread the shame of poverty, contempt, and inattention, they are dissatisfied with working for a simple subsistence, avoid the humble occupations of farmer, mechanic, and laborer, and run to the ends of the earth to accumulate useless wealth.

Every reflective individual, of course, realizes that he must be industrious and respect the rights of others. But this simple reasoning is too much for most men. So nature entices man by instilling in him a desire for esteem and admiration. This desire is as real a want of nature as hunger; neglect is as severe as pain or disease. The result of this vanity is that men of all sorts, even those with the least reason, virtue, or beneficence, are "chained . . . to an incessant servitude to their fellow creatures." Man is forced to play the role assigned him in "the system of the world and the society of mankind."

But suppose through the diffusion of knowledge most men become reflective, would this not dispose of the pessimistic picture? To answer this question Adams turned from a psychological to a materialistic interpretation. The great question will forever remain: "Who shall work?" Only the few men of property can have the leisure for study, for the indispensable wants of all require the incessant toil of 99 per cent of the people. Since rest is rapture to the weary man, those laboring little will be envied by those laboring much, though the latter are in reality the most to be envied. Consequently the increase of knowledge intensifying the rivalry between rich and poor renders it increasingly indispensable that "every man should know his place, and be made to keep it." So "let the rich and the poor unite in the bands of mutual affection, be mutually sensible of each other's ignorance, weakness and error" through separate chambers, and unite "in concerting measures for their mutual defence against each other's vices and follies, by supporting an impartial mediator."

As Adams looked forward hopefully to a second term as President, the group which he felt contained most of the "natural aristocracy" doubted that he was suited for the honor. This was the faction which regarded Hamilton rather than Adams as the leader of the Federalist Party. They were annoyed somewhat by Adams's lack of enthusiasm over Hamilton's great financial measures. Much more serious, however, was his peaceful settlement with France of the difficulties arising from French "interference" with American commerce, and his refusal to engage in a war of conquest which might have brought Hamilton military glory. So in the campaign of 1800, though Adams was the party candidate, some Federalists openly attacked him and thus assured his defeat. But this political dispute within the party Adams seemed to view as merely personal. More disturbing to him was the victory of Jefferson and the "awful spirit of democracy." As he was about to surrender the presidency, he appointed John Marshall as Chief Justice so that the courts might provide "the firmest security . . . against . . . visionary schemes ·or fluctuating theories." [44] Applying his political philosophy to his own political fate, he could calmly write that, although his Federalist critics had knifed him, they possessed "so much wealth and so great a portion of the talents of the country, and at the same time so many virtues, and good principles, and are so nearly right . . . that . . . without them" anarchy must result.[45]

That Adams was a philosopher and statesman rather than merely a conservative politician and partisan was demonstrated in his attack on irresponsible Federalist maneuvers. In office the Federalists had argued for a powerful executive; out of office they were toying with the idea of undermining Jefferson by the opposite process of strengthening Congress. Adams would have none of it. To the specious Federalist argument that, since we have no natural aristocracy, we should have no strong executive, Adams replied that we did have "a material which actually constitutes an aristocracy governing the nation," namely, great wealth.[46]

Applying his rigorous standards, he found that Jefferson and Madison, in retaliating against English restrictions on American trade, exhibited sounder views of the nation's commercial interest than his own party. In 1812 he thought that the government under Madison so closely approached his "balanced" scheme that he would vote for Madison's re-election. Among other considerations, the government is restoring the taxes—the excise and the like—which ought never to have been repealed, and is providing a navy, he said.

During the War of 1812, for a moment he lost his faith in the "natural aristocracy," or at least that part of it which in New England was talking of secession. In that region the upstart Higginsons by "a profligate system of Funds and Banks and by an immense credit from Great Britain," exercised a domineering power.[47]

Having parted company with the extreme Federalists who would play havoc with the federal government and its foreign policy, Adams found himself thinking that his views approached the position of Jefferson, or at least his own interpretation of it. Therefore, when John Taylor, taking his stand as a Jeffersonian democrat, attacked Adams as an "aristocrat," the latter pointed simply to the fact that no one could be more aristocratic than a southerner who, like Taylor, owned much land and many slaves to boot. It was not that Adams felt that the slaves should be freed: The ex-slaves would become criminals or, living a precarious existence, would beg their masters to return them to slavery. But the slave owner dominates the lives of his dependents, as a few rich men dominate Boston. In fact, the gentry are not only aristocrats but Tories. Only commerce, manufactures, navigation, and naval power supported by a moneyed interest prevent their erecting the worst oligarchies.[48]

Property naturally creates, indeed is, aristocracy. It will accumulate in individuals and families despite provisions for alienation of estates and divison of intestate estates, for the industrious must gather the wealth of the profligate. If, as the Jeffersonians grant, superior genius, talent, strength, and activity obtain superior wealth, and if superior wealth naturally influences society, why not call the possessors a natural or actual aristocracy? The view of Jeffersonians that increase of knowledge will destroy aristocracy was still nonsense to' Adams. Adams now had the benefit of Malthus's teaching to buttress his old argument that the mass can never have the leisure to acquire learning.

In illustrating the evils of aristocracy, Taylor had pointed to the abuses and monopolies fostered by government grants, charters, and tariffs. But Adams asked, how can they be prevented under the present political structure, "when the few are craving and the many mad for the same thing," when democrats and aristocrats unite with few exceptions in urging these monopolies and incorporations, and when every man opposing them is sure to be ruined?

In short, if the aristocracy of Federalism had led to "democratic" deviations, and if, on the other hand, the "democracy" of Jefferson had not prevented obnoxious aristocratical developments—like charters for banks and other monopolies—the trouble seemed to Adams to stem from the imperfection of government.

The philosophy of Adams is essentially a "political philosophy." Economic problems arise only because of a defective political organization. Hence there is no need for detailed inquiry into economic problems as such. Their solution lies in the mechanics of government. Given the automatic balancing of "orders," unrestrained freedom of enterprise can work no harm. The leaders of industry will control the aristocratic senate; yet if they overstep their bounds they will instantly be checked by the other branches. Therefore they will have no interest but to act for the good of the community, stripped of any possibility of perverting their wisdom to their selfish interests at the expense of others. By setting up a perfectionist criterion, Adams ascribed the greatest evils of an aristocratic system to the lightest admixture in it of democratic elements.

Furthermore, Adams's procedure of arguing at one and the same time that the leadership of a "natural aristocracy" of wealth is both actual and virtuous achieves the same purpose by two methods that appear at first sight to be extreme opposites: fatalistic economic determinism on the one side, and religion and morals on the other.

Adams's political theory was not unlike that of Hamilton, but ironically enough his views on economic matters were the kind that Hamiltonians labeled "agrarian." Adams disliked banks with the note-issue power and public debts and had little enthusiasm for protective tariffs. In his own eyes and in the tradition he had inherited, he was eminently conservative; and he saw in his later years that it was the Hamiltonian policies that were subversive. In this the aristocratic Adams saw eye to eye with his and Hamilton's political enemy, Thomas Jefferson.

THOMAS JEFFERSON: COMMERCIAL AGRARIAN DEMOCRAT

Jefferson is the great American radical. For a century and a half his name above all others has been invoked in support of democratic and progressive measures.[49] He has been revered as a humanitarian statesman; as an agrarian democrat suspicious of great wealth and enterprise; as a devotee of the simple life of the farmer; and as an opponent of the evils of cities and industrialism.

He was indeed a great man and too complex for easy generalization. His life span covered several generations of extraordinary change in the domestic and the international scene. Of course, as a political leader he often changed his mind, but there was a certain consistent pattern to which his thinking and actions conformed.

Like all the humanitarian figures of the modern era of Western civilization, he was heir to two traditions. There was the moral-religious attitude of secular Christianity that deprecated material greed, worshiped simplicity and the "natural" life of the tiller of the soil. But on the other hand every statesman was well aware that commerce was the source of "wealth and power." The moral tradition was ever present, but the claims of commerce interposed the basic realities of the material world. While their reconciliation was no less a problem to Jefferson than to others, his task was infinitely complicated by the various roles he played for more than fifty years: a leader in Virginia and in the Continental Congress during the American Revolution; minister to France on the eve of the French Revolution; President Washington's first Secretary of State; leader of the opposition to the Federalist Administrations; President of the United States; and, finally, elder statesman.

Jefferson, son of a Virginia planter, had eminently respectable if not aristocratic antecedents. He studied at the Crown-chartered College of William and Mary. He always remained deferential to the classic seats of learning, whether in the Tory North or in Great Britain, "the land of our own language, morals, manners and habits." [50] Law was the road to political preferment, and Jefferson became a lawyer as well as a planter. He was always a gentleman farmer and quite naturally occasionally loaned money on mortgages and engaged in commercial enterprises. However, his intellectual and political interests so absorbed his time and attention, that he ended up deeply in debt and almost impoverished.

Jefferson was an extraordinarily cultivated man even in an age in which politicians and statesmen were generally men of learning, and vice versa. His knowledge was wide, and his intellectual contacts spanned the whole Western world. In the realm of philosophy, he enjoyed the friendship of the great Common Sense philosopher, Dugald Stewart, Adam Smith's biographer and professor of moral philosophy at Edinburgh. Only a man who had absorbed the classic treatises on government could have penned the Declaration of Independence, that keen summary of the best of English liberal thought of the seventeenth and eighteenth centuries. His interest remained unflagging as he ran up bills with booksellers for the latest treatises. He himself translated his friend Count Destutt de Tracy's *A Commentary and Review of Montesquieu's Spirit of the Laws*. He was closely acquainted with the standard literature of political economy and found in it an armory for controversy on public issues. He was a friend and correspondent of such leading contemporary figures of authentic stature in the science as J. B. Say and Dupont de Nemours. He supervised the translation of Destutt de Tracy's *Treatise on Political Economy* from the French manuscript.

His views, like those of any classic or representative figure, were of a piece with his character and his background. Solid citizen that he was, Jefferson believed in the importance of a sound public credit, the sanctity of contracts, and of course the right of property. For property is founded "in our natural wants, in the means with which we are endowed to satisfy these wants, and the right to what we acquire by those means without violating the similar rights of other sensible beings." [51]

In a very substantial sense he was an agrarian. The Virginia society of his day seemed on the whole ideal. The sensational manifestations of poverty so characteristic of the Old World seemed to him to be absent. The extant beggars, which of course in the eighteenth century were a conspicuous feature of the European landscape, were foreigners in the towns. The agricultural people were God's chosen people. They were incorruptible, since they were not dependent on the caprices of customers. The moderate but sure income of husbandry begot permanent improvement and an orderly conduct in private and public life. As a liberal agrarian Jefferson was opposed to the feudal remnants of entail and primogeniture. Slavery, of course, was a moral blot. He expected that it would eventually though gradually disappear in one fashion or another. In his early days he proposed concrete plans to the Virginia legislature for the abolition of slavery. But the problem, he came to feel, was inextricably tangled with other issues and the general laws of property, and hence touched what he conceived to be the foundations of the Union. And so, though he never relinquished the hope of erasing this blot, he became extremely cautious—so cautious that he opposed the demand for the prohibition by Congress of the extension of slavery into Missouri.[52]

Commerce was, to Jefferson, the great multiplier of national wealth and the disposer of agricultural surpluses. Jefferson was no doctrinaire Physiocrat or Socialist or homespun radical. Commerce had a crucial place in his attitude. He did, however, deprecate the greedy and aggressive spirit which so frequently accompanied commercial enterprise and excessive commercial ambition: Merchants are often deficient in virtue and *amor patriae*. Unless kept within rein, they promote a heady fashion of gambling. It was this moralistic view that has been misinterpreted as opposition to commerce and commercial development.

On manufactures, Jefferson was, in the nature of things, ambiguous. I say in the nature of things because manufactures and crafts of the home and village seemed to him not only desirable, but also necessary to the ideal of a complete and interesting society; but he deprecated the large-scale factories and their concentrated, turbulent, "starved and rickety paupers and dwarfs."

The higher or more modern reaches of banking and finance that were so congenial to Hamilton were objects of suspicion to Jefferson. They seemed to be in the nature of stock-jobbery and gambling, far removed from the "real" values of agriculture and commerce. But, since they were the outworkings of, and bound up with, commerce and the maintenance of the public credit, he found it just as hard to get along without them as with them. Consequently he had some'difficulty in differentiating the legitimate aims of commerce and industry from the illegitimate.

Such were the general views to which Jefferson adhered more or less throughout his life. But they must be placed, and occasionally discounted, when in the context of a wider activity, in his successive political roles, he faced the conflicting forces of the commercial political world.

As revolutionary leader he took a commercial point of view whether dealing with the restraints of the mother country or with the specific interest of his own state. The colonists, it seemed to him, had taken up arms to defend their freedom and property "acquired solely by the industry of our forefathers and ourselves." [53] At the same time, in accordance with the accepted notion that draining the enemy of specie was one of the most effective means of warfare as it was of profit, Jefferson felt that the sale of Virginia's tobacco and foodstuffs to the enemy was eminently desirable. The increased circulation of money created prosperity and made possible the payment of heavy war taxes.[54]

Shortly after hostilities with England ceased, Jefferson urged Washington to revive the Virginia–Maryland canal project for joining the Ohio and Potomac, lest other areas, by developing alternative waterways, win the great prize of supplying the West with European merchandise. "All the world," Jefferson wrote to the General, "is becoming commercial. If we could isolate our empire from the rest of the world, we might indulge ourselves in speculating whether commerce contributes to the happiness of mankind," but since "our citizens have too fully tasted of the comforts furnished by the arts and manufactures to be debarred their use . . . we must in our defence endeavour to share as large a portion as we can of this modern source of wealth and power." [55]

This was a characteristic of Jefferson's inner struggle with respect to the values of the simple life and the rich economy. The struggle was to be repeated again and again. Very soon thereafter he wrote his greatest eulogy of the agrarian ideal in his famous *Notes on Virginia* in 1784. The ink was hardly dry when, as the newly appointed minister to France, he assumed the' task of promoting and developing the commercial interests of the country. And that involved commercial intercourse not only with European countries, but especially with their colonies and notably the West Indies at our own door. He wrote home on the eve of the French Revolution that, if the American government would pay off its war debts to the financially pressed King, American commerce might legally penetrate into the French West Indies.[56]

He felt that commercial privileges might be obtained more easily from the European powers if the public credit of the United States were better, because public credit is a barometer of national strength and wealth. Therefore the public debts should be paid in full even though original holders have been forced to sell to speculators at a considerable discount. The proposed import duty to pay the debts is sound, for the funds thus obtained would make the securities desirable for investment by raising their value. Foreign creditors, and thus foreign nations, would be further impressed with the strength of the Confederation if creditors were given instantaneous recovery against debtors on pain of imprisonment.[57]

Jefferson, who was abroad during the discussion and adoption of the Constitution, in general approved of the strengthened national government as being in the commercial interest of the country. He hoped and expected that the federal government would have absolute power over the commerce of the states and such control of all credit and taxation as would maintain the national credit.[58]

Summoned home by President Washington to be his first Secretary of State, Jefferson continued to be absorbed by the problem of expanding our foreign commerce. He suggested to American consuls that they impress upon foreign powers the fact that this country would be satisfied to remain an agricultural country provided it were able to sell its agricultural surpluses. If our trade were interfered with, as was wont to happen especially during European wars, we should be forced to consider seriously turning to manufacturing.[59]

European wars must not be allowed to interfere with American prosperity, especially with the "golden harvest" of a policy of neutrality. The government, he said, could not stand idly by as industry was suspended and unemployment created by the interference of foreign powers with the "country's natural rights" of trading. England's interference with American exports of food and military supplies to the enemy violated the right of neutrals to sell in the best market they could find. Suppression of the traffic would violate the right of every man to follow his lawful calling.[60]

In the same spirit Jefferson sought from Spain the right of free navigation of the Mississippi for American commerce. The surplus production of the western farmers demanded, in his view, an easy access to foreign markets. The interests of eastern merchants and ship owners were, of course, as much involved if not more.[61] Of this Jefferson could not be unaware, but it was always his predilection—a predilection of mood as well as style—to put an issue in agrarian terms. The right to navigate would, however, be nugatory unless the territory at the mouth of the river were in American hands. Spain must cede New Orleans and the territory on the lower east bank of the river. The United States would then guarantee her possessions on the western side, and she would for ages have no interest in crossing the river. Should Spain waver, our government would not be responsible for the actions—traditionally precipitate—of its western citizens.[62]

It was during his tenure as Secretary of State that Jefferson's feud with the Secretary of the Treasury broke out. To the proud Virginian, Hamilton was a young upstart of uncertain origins. President Washington was placing increasing confidence in Hamilton, but the more Jefferson saw of Hamilton's financial and economic programs, the more he became convinced that the Hamiltonians embodied that excessive commercial spirit that he time and again deprecated. The expedients proposed seemed to him to be the brain children not of the substantial men of the country, of planters and real merchants, but of penniless, irresponsible adventurers in high finance, aiming to get rich overnight. They were really paupers seeking to monopolize the wealth of the nation through privileges and grants from government. If such a class of people became predominant, the result would be an absolute monarchy; and, to the mind of the eighteenth-century liberal, the greatest abomination was the union of political privilege with economic ambition which "monarchy" represented. But such objectives as payment of public debts and extension of commerce Jefferson also wanted. It is only in the light of this complex consideration that Jefferson's "tacking" in the Hamiltonian controversy can be understood.

Jefferson felt that Hamilton's National Bank Act, providing for a privately managed institution with its capital primarily in funded debt and with its notes alone receivable for government dues, placed the circulating medium of the country at the mercy of the speculative interests which controlled the bank. The value of specie, Hume had taught him, was fixed by the natural laws of commerce, and the supply varied in each country according to its commercial needs. The bank notes would inevitably be overissued. The paper, by raising labor costs and prices, would destroy the foreign markets. Specie would be drained from agriculture for use in speculation, thus upsetting the former.

Similarly, Jefferson felt that Hamilton's plan for bounties to great "company enterprises" in manufactures was unconstitutional and oppressive. Hamilton had appealed to the clause empowering government to promote the general welfare, but Jefferson and his supporters argued that the clause could only apply to the more specific powers granted the federal government and that if Hamilton's interpretation were accepted this power would be great enough to destroy the states themselves. Moreover, the socio-political effects of such subsidies would be disastrous. The government subsidies would not only inordinately enrich a few privileged individuals, and press heavily on the citizenry because of the heavy taxation involved, but would also strengthen governmental power to a dangerous degree. This would again raise that bugaboo of the unholy union between great wealth and great power which spelled despotism. The road to a great aristocracy of wealth would be opened.

In the heat of the conflict, Jefferson was drawn into some sharp inconsistencies. He had, for example, more than once approved of the basic features of Hamilton's Funding Act, but now he attacked it. Both the Bank and Funding Acts, he declared, were passed by a corrupted legislature for the benefit of stock jobbers who were making a lottery of the real property of the country, the property of the agricultural class. Debtor South would be arrayed against creditor North, destroying the Union.

Behind such radical rhetoric Jefferson, though not legalistic, was an upholder of the validity of government no less than of private contracts and obligations. For example, he emphatically stated when he became President, and indeed always believed, that the public debt was the first charge upon government revenues.[63] The measures enacted by his opponents, whether referring to public credit or banking, must be rigorously observed. The Acts might not be renewed when they expired, but until then they were sacred obligations and tampering with them would threaten the national credit.

Later, in the War of 1812, when a revival of the bank was demanded as a war financing measure, he stood on his old opposition. Paper money was vicious and unnecessary in general; and this was certainly true of paper money of small denominations, for the ordinary citizen could use specie for his petty needs. He continued to oppose the issue of paper money by the ordinary private bank. And even when pressed by necessity, he would not willingly agree to allowing a private national bank to do so. As a last resort, if paper money had to be used, the government Treasury should issue it during the emergency. This would prevent manipulations of public and private credit and the rise of financial oligarchies. In order to manage credit, Jefferson definitely approved of commercial banks which restricted themselves to the proper functions of discount and deposit.

Thus Jefferson, anti-Hamiltonian out of supreme office, became in good part Hamiltonian as President. This is the judgment of a large segment of posterity. And indeed the evidence is impressive. In his own estimation, however, Jefferson took a larger view of these matters than his critics did. The difference between him and the Hamiltonians was not merely a formal one. The Hamiltonians conceived of an increasing domain to be exploited by the few daring "rich and well born." Jefferson's vision was that of an ever-increasing domain, both geographic and social, for the flowering of opportunity, if not exactly for everyone, at least for an increasing proportion of an increasing population.

Jefferson was no Socialist or proponent of economic equality by fiat. The use of the taxing power to correct inequalities of wealth violated, he said, the first principle of society, "the guarantee to everyone of a free exercise of his industry and the fruits acquired by it." Such taxation robbed the virtuous of the fruits of the industry of themselves and their fathers for the benefit of the less virtuous.[64] But he was confident that the existing policy of taxation of imports, which fell proportionally on the rich, and the equal division of intestate estates [65] would bring about a relatively equal distribution of wealth in a free economic society with abundant resources.

This democratic theme Jefferson clearly enunciated as he took office. The "Tories," he said, were the wealthy, nerveless, and corrupt who sought security in a strong executive; the sound Republicans were the virtuous, healthy, and enterprising who wanted government confined to preventing men from injuring one another. Enterprise throve best when left free to individual initiative, and government should protect the enterprises only from casual embarrassment.

This rising nation possessed a "chosen country with room enough for our descendants to the hundredth and thousandth generation." [66] And on all questions relating to the expansion of this "room" Jefferson was aggressive and, if we may dare use an invidious term, imperialistic.

Indian tribes had complained in 1802 that the government was forcing the sale of their lands by chiefs, which was a questionable procedure under tribal law; Jefferson answered, perhaps irrelevantly, with the cliché: "The right to sell is one of the rights of property." Forbidding sale "would be a wrong to your nation." [67] He informed American agents among the Indians that their objectives should be peace, the encouragement of agriculture, and the transfer of lands to our government. If an agent failed in the last, he would be regarded as being more friendly to the Indians than to the United States.[68] But it would be to the advantage of the Indians themselves to exchange "surplus lands" for agricultural implements. Antiquated habits and customs, however, unfortunately prevented the Indians from adjusting themselves to a new policy from which they could profit.

In tune with his expansionist policy, Jefferson sent the Lewis and Clark Expedition, in the guise of a scientific survey, to examine fur trading opportunities for private enterprise in the West and incidentally to look over any other commercial features of the intervening territory.[69]

On Jefferson's shoulders fell the task of securing, once and for all, "the absolute freedom" of the Mississippi for American commerce. Learning in 1802 that Spain was transferring New Orleans together with the rest of Louisiana and Florida to France, he warned that this would not be tolerated, since the produce of almost half the territory of the United States passed through New Orleans. Spain's weakness, he said, would soon force her to cede the territory to us, but powerful France was another story. Besides, permanent peace between the United States and France would be impossible if the two countries were such close neighbors, since the French were reckless and impetuous. Therefore, the moment France occupied the territory, the United States would join England in order to control this continent and rule the seas.[70]

When Napoleon made the astounding offer to sell all Louisiana to the United States, Jefferson called on Congress to supply the funds. The Constitution, he argued, does not provide for holding foreign territory or incorporating a foreign nation into the Union, but Congress must overlook "metaphysical subtleties"—as the President himself was overlooking them—and expect the assent of the people to what the people themselves would do. The new territory would provide opportunities for uplifting uncivilized groups. Indians, dispossessed of their lands on the east side of the Mississippi, could be exported to the territory to begin a sedentary agricultural life; free Negroes and rebellious slaves could also be sent there under a system of indentured servitude.[71] And if the country should be involved in war with the great territorial empires, as seemed likely more than once during the Napoleonic struggle, why should this country desist from protecting itself by acquiring more territory? In a war with Spain, for example, the Regular Army might seize Mexico with its rich mines, privateers would prosper by plundering the commerce and coasts of the Spanish possessions, and Cuba, valuable for her sugar, would likely enter the Union. Canada might be the fruit of a war with England. By acquiring Canada and Cuba, the United States would have natural protection without the need of a navy, and further expansion of the country would be unnecessary. "We should have such an empire for liberty as she has never surveyed since the creation." [72]

During his presidency Jefferson continued to press for his ideal of a mixed agrarian-commercial planter society. This ideal implied free enterprise at home and also free exchange and shipping in the world, in particular the freedom of the oceans. The struggle for world supremacy between France and England placed that ideal in jeopardy. American commerce was already being increasingly subjected to restraints by the warring powers. It was the immediate aim of his embargo and other "restrictions" to "persuade" the rivals to lift their restraints on the "neutral" commerce of Americans. He would thus safeguard his preference for an agrarian-commercial society.

In making his striking public concessions to a more vigorous manufacturing nation, therefore, Jefferson had two fundamental reasons: first of all, it was part of his policy to force the emancipation of American commerce without the costly and dangerous resort to war; second, it was a hedge against the failure of such a policy.

The Federalist opposition to Jefferson in general and to his famous embargo in particular included both merchant and manufacturing capitalists. It was in order to split this opposition that Jefferson coyly suggested to the manufacturing element that the cessation or lessening of foreign trade presented a great opportunity for large-scale manufacturers.[73] In other words, he made an immediate compromise with manufacturing for the greater glory of commerce.

In the unlikely and unfortunate event that one or the other of the great contending powers should as an outcome of the war secure supreme commercial control, America would really have to become a manufacturing power if she did not wish to become the slave of the victor. Jefferson's doctrine, no less than any other statesman's, can be measured against the law of necessity. That this was his view was demonstrated by his attitude immediately after the War of 1812. The ending of the war hardly ended our trade difficulties with Great Britain and, as a club for freer conditions of trade as well as a source of greater revenues, Jefferson went along with a tariff policy which was mildly protectionist in character.   •

This strategic position underlay the public correspondence in 1815 and 1816 between himself and Benjamin Austin, ardent Republican leader of Boston. Austin had asked for Jefferson's sentiments on manufactures, since the "friends of England" were citing his early "abstract remarks" in *Notes on Virginia* to advocate American dependence on "foreign workshops." He hoped that Jefferson as a patriot would wish to protect the manufactures which had grown during the war to a respectable state of maturity and improvement.[74] Jefferson replied that circumstances had changed since he wrote the *Notes on Virginia*. Then peace reigned in the world. Commercially speaking, agriculture was and still is the most profitable occupation for Americans, and it also yields employment to American commerce. But since "we have experienced what we then did not believe, that there exists both profligacy and power enough to exclude us from the field of interchange with other nations: that to be independent for the comforts of life we must fabricate them ourselves. We must now place the manufacturer by the side of the agriculturalist. . . . If those who quote me as of a different opinion, will keep pace with me in purchasing nothing foreign, where an equivalent of domestic fabrics can be obtained without regard to difference in price, it will not be our fault if we do not have a supply at home equal to our demand, and wrest that weapon of distress from the hand which wielded it."

In short, it appears again and again that Jefferson's concessions to manufacturing were made in emergency conditions: the continuing commercial friction with England, the discontent of New England, and the immediate need for revenue. On a permanent policy of converting America into a nation which should supply the world as well as itself with manufactured products, Jefferson was far more conservative. Here he persisted in the position of the *Notes on Virginia:* Is it better to employ the surplus labor in agriculture or in manufactures? The question need not be answered for some time, and the maxims to be applied will depend on the then existing circumstances, "for in so complicated a science as political economy, no one maxim can be laid down as wise and expedient for all times and circumstances." [75]

By 1819 the situation had changed radically. The danger of domination by a great imperial power was banished. "Normal" commercial relations had returned. On the other hand, the manufacturing interest had perforce been encouraged during the emergency and, having smelled blood, now came forth with a demand for a prohibitory tariff. Jefferson had been driven far enough; he turned at bay and revealed he was truly a commercial-agrarian free trader. He denounced all the protectionists as Federalists in fact though they might be Republicans in name. The new Federalists, he exclaimed wrathfully, looked to an aristocratic government "founded on banking institutions, and moneyed incorporations under the guise . . . of their favoured branches of manufactures, commerce and navigation, riding and ruling over the plundered ploughman and beggared yeomanry." They stretched the power to regulate commerce to include unlimited control over manufactures and agriculture in order to take the earnings of the most depressed interest and give them to the most flourishing. [76]

These views on economic matters might be said to comprise his economic theory. But to obtain a complete sense of his position, we must examine his conception of the place of education and the nature of republican government.

Jefferson's society was not composed exclusively of economic men, but of an increasingly educated population giving forth a natural aristocracy of talent. In order to make such an aristocracy democratic, he would encourage, even through subsidies, educational opportunities for the poor. Classically rooted in English cultural, though not imperial, traditions, Jefferson conceived of education in the English pattern. His University of Virginia would teach the subjects and inculcate the doctrines of liberal Englishmen, or Anglo-Americans.

To the enlightened, cultured gentleman of the eighteenth century, what men today call democracy or popular rule was mob rule and naturally not an object of admiration. Jefferson always opposed "demagogic radicalism." In a republican government the "people" ruled, but it always was the "people" in their organized political capacity, in a "balanced" government. In the heat of bitter political controversy, Jefferson would appeal to the "people" in the rhetoric of radicalism, but in his day the "people" generally had to have property to be "people" with a voice in government. Of course, when he was setting up invidious comparisons between the mass of Americans and the *canaille* of Europe, he could easily imagine that anyone in America could have a voice because property could, he felt, be easily obtained by the frugal and industrious, thanks to available land. The drift toward manhood suffrage, especially in the new states, did not therefore disturb Jefferson, as it did some of his disciples. He simply felt that as long as men had opportunity to acquire a competence there would be no danger of anarchy or despotism. Such opportunities existed and could be further multiplied, provided they were not monopolized through legally created privileges for a few..

Men in the mass are not bad in themselves, said Jefferson; but a mass of people whose livelihood depends on the favor and caprice of avaricious and power-mad employers, and who are ignorant and illiterate besides, cannot be expected to exercise sound judgment on matters of public policy. It is only those men who have attained a modicum of economic independence and welfare—that is to say property—who can rise to their rational task in a republican society. Ideally such men should form an increasing proportion of the population, and then and only then would democracy be tantamount to a counting of heads. Properly conceived, he found, a democratic and republican government is one which gives a greater guarantee of security to private enterprise and competence than a capricious absolute monarch or a demagogic legislature could. Even during the period of his aggressive revolutionism, from the Declaration of Independence to the formation of the Constitution, there is a note of deprecation of the supremacy of the "popular"—the legislative—organ and a correlative note of respect for an independent judiciary. In the very year that he wrote the immortal Declaration of Independence, he called for giving Virginia judges "estates for life in their offices." [77] The right of the state judiciary to void acts of the legislature would thus be safeguarded.[78]

He said that he would have liked the federal Constitution better if the judges had been given a veto power like that of the President over the legislature. The tyranny to be feared was that of the legislative branch. Since in his eyes the state judiciary in Virginia was under the thumb of the "tyrannical" supreme state assembly, he was enthusiastic over what he thought to be an accepted feature of the Constitution—namely, the supremacy of the federal over the state judiciary.[79] Such supremacy would secure property rights, especially of foreigners, against the designs of state legislatures.[80] Legislatures, prone to infection with an overdose of "patriotism," especially when it coincided with the immediate pecuniary interests of members as in the case of Virginia debts to British creditors, were likely to act contrary to the long-run requirements of commerce. But an independent judge, subject, of course, to impeachment for bad behavior, had a healthy appreciation of the sanctity of contract and obligation for the stability and progress of free government and commerce.

It is plain, therefore, that Jefferson's political doctrine of a proper balance of government may be reduced to the fundamental position that though society should as far as possible be free, its foundations must rest on a few rigid principles: security of property, maintenance of the public credit, and freedom of commerce.

To understand the ambiguity and duality of Jefferson's mind is to penetrate the inner meaning of the greatest tradition in America. Jefferson was characteristically the sanguine, forward-looking, imaginative American. He was sentimentally attached to the land; he morally deprecated the habits and spirit of commerce. To him American commerce, if linked to agricultural surplus, was the handmaiden of agriculture, and as such was moderated by the only virtuous class, the independent farmers. But the independent exigencies of commerce increasingly asserted themselves and, while related to the agricultural economy, occasionally tended to dominate it. In a mixed fashion both commerce and agriculture combined to usher in a great territorial empire.

Jefferson paid a high compliment to commerce by calling the seaport towns the torchbearers of civilization as well as the centers of wealth. The history of man's progress could be seen by starting with the Rocky Mountain savages in a state of nature. Then came "our semi-barbarous citizens, the pioneers of the advance of civilization," followed by gradual stages of improving man until "his as yet most improved state in our seaport towns." The march of civilization advanced from the seaport towns, passed over the country like a cloud, increased the people's knowledge, and improved their condition.[81]

If civilization sprang from the sea and commerce, commerce and also land empire had increasingly become infected with the virus of Hamiltonian finance and manipulation. And so Jefferson ended up willy-nilly much more a Hamiltonian than when he had started out. It is ironical and yet also symbolic that his eulogy before the American Philosophical Society in 1826 was delivered by that good "Jeffersonian" who was President of the Bank of the United States—Nicholas Biddle.

Those immediate, direct disciples of Jefferson who moved across the international scene more completely exemplified the fusion in the economic realm.

CHAPTER XVIII

The International Commercial Mind

THE COMMERCIAL REPUBLIC OF THOMAS PAINE

AMERICANS have thought of the generation of the Revolution as essentially involved in a desperate struggle between conservatives and democrats. But when most of the significant figures are placed in the context of their own concerns, they appear, and quite irrespective of their differences of political philosophy, as economic men with the characteristic stamp of the late eighteenth century. Each was a combination of business speculator, land agent, statesman, politician, and philosopher. Generally of respectable middle-class origin, they were refined and sophisticated men. They were Americans, of course, but no more so than the English were Englishmen and the French were Frenchmen, for all were self-conscious citizens of the Western world. They moved with ease in the social and economic life of their respective nations and across national boundaries, for the economy of the world was then cosmopolitan to a degree. Its dominant note was foreign commerce and speculation, and this of necessity made them adept at manipulating —and cross-fertilizing—politics and finance. Often the distinction between these activities became dim; indeed, at times there was none.

The shrewdness of a Benjamin Franklin was the shrewdness of this type brought to its supreme development.

Less successful in acquiring wealth or political position, but of far more dramatic significance, was Thomas Paine (1737–1809).[1]

On the eve of the Revolutionary War, Paine, a failure in England, landed in America and threw in his fortunes with the revolting colonists, fighting "for the security of their natural rights, and the protection of their own property." [2] Then began a career which made him one of the most powerful pamphleteers of the eighteenth century. He played a prominent role not only in the American Revolution, but also in that of France; and many English authorities feared that he might instigate one in his native land.

However, Paine was more than a pamphleteer, more even than a revolutionary. Though reflecting utterly the commercial enlightenment of his age, the creative force and the enormous influence of his writing gave stimulus and point to the intellectual and economic aspirations of his century.

In *Common Sense* and other writings during the American Revolutionary War, Paine justified independence on the ground of natural right and economic interest. Government should be distinguished from society. Men by a natural gravitation associate in order to satisfy their wants; society consists of the bonds created by exchange and contracts. Government, on the other hand, is a necessary evil. Security of property is the more specific end of government. Men surrender a part of their property to protect the rest.

Inequality of wealth is natural, for it arises from differences in "industry, superiority of talents, dexterity of management, extreme frugality, fortunate opportunities." It is not due to oppression and avarice. Oppression may be the consequence of riches but is seldom the cause, and avarice generally makes men too timid to be wealthy.

On the other hand, the distinction between king and subject cannot be termed natural. It is a violation of the mutual compact and is the result of oppression and conquest. People remain blind to this interference with natural right and pecuniary interest through the force of fear, superstition, and prejudice. Hereditary monarchy has the least justification, for no generation has the right to bind future generations to any particular government.[3]

By eliminating commercial restraints and the expense of maintaining a useless royalty and aristocracy, Paine argued, American independence will promote the security and increase of property.

England's protection is unnecessary, for America's "plan is commerce," and since it is to Europe's interest to have access to American trade, America will enjoy the friendship of Europe. Independence will even benefit the important classes of the English nation, the merchants and the manufacturers, because the increased commerce will enhance their profits. At the same time, America's commercial rights must be extended, for independence without commercial prosperity is hollow.[4]

The cause of America stands on "the broad foundation of property and popularity," and the latter depends on the former. True, a country's valor is evidenced by the character of its inhabitants and the bravery of its soldiers, but confidence of success is best evidenced by the support of men of substance. In this way a war becomes really popular.

The costliness of the war is only apparent. The creation of a national debt would be beneficial, for it would bind the people into a whole. Since taxes are distributed within the country, they are a spur to industry; consequently in the absence of tax levies the country would be poverty-stricken, just as without commerce people would be indolent. An import duty is the best type of taxation, for it keeps foreign trade in the hands of Americans and forces foreigners to contribute to the national defense.[5]

In the midst of his efforts in behalf of the revolutionary cause, Paine illustrated his philosophy of contract by publishing a pamphlet, *Public Good* (1780), denying Virginia's claims to western lands. He supported the contentions of land companies, with ambiguous titles, that the lands belonged to the Confederation, which alone could decide their disposition. Effective government, which Virginia could not possibly furnish to these frontier areas, would result in a rapid appreciation of land values. Land rather than trade is the real source of riches, he now argued. The riches of other countries, based on industry and trade, are fictitious. They are matters of convention, subject to risk, but lands constantly increase in value with the growth of population. He advocated that Congress organize the territory with a view to creating new states. The new states were to have but limited congressional rights for seven years. Paine felt that such states would at first require more aid from the Confederation than they could give to it, and that the inhabitants, being largely composed of immigrants, would require further tutelage. After the appearance of this pamphlet the Virginia legislature voted down a proposed land grant for Paine. Hę did receive 300 shares as "public relations counsel" from one of the companies, but they turned out to be valueless because of the non-recognition of the company's titles.[6]

Of a more elevated though substantially similar character was his attempt in 1782–1783 to convince recalcitrant Rhode Island to ratify the request of Congress for a 5 per cent import duty. After conferring with Robert Morris, then financier general, and his assistant, Gouverneur Morris, as to how he might be useful, Paine in 1782 signed an agreement with Robert Morris, George Washington, and Robert Livingston, Secretary of Foreign Affairs. He was to receive $800 a year from the secret service fund for employing his pen to prepare the people for "such restraints and such taxes and imposts as are absolutely necessary." [7]

In line with his assignment, he had published in the *Providence* [Rhode Island] *Gazette* and in Philadelphia newspapers a series of letters on the impost, signed "A Friend to Rhode-Island and the Union." These presented practically every argument that could be thought of to convince all classes in the state that each would benefit from the measure. He especially stressed that the opposition was led by selfish merchants. "The richest men in the state," he exclaimed, "are making tools of the poorest." [8] Rhode Islanders showed their gratitude by labeling the author mercenary. The anonymous writer denied that he "ever sought from any man, or body of men, any place, office, recompense or reward, on any occasion," for himself. "I have had the happiness of serving mankind, and the honour of doing it freely."

The end of the war left Paine without his position, but not without his pen. It was not idle for long, as he joined the Morrises in 1785–1787 to defend the Bank of North America, which he had helped to promote. The first product was a pamphlet in 1786 which urged that the Pennsylvania Assembly repeal the act revoking the bank charter and refrain from issuing paper money of any kind. In *Dissertations on Government; the Affairs of the Bank; and Paper Money*, Paine maintained that the citizens should be aware of certain self-evident truths not because the bank is concerned, but because constitutional rights and privileges are involved. If the legislature has the power to repeal the charter or in any way interfere with the bank, then the laws of the land and the courts of justice are useless. When people form a republic, which means a government for the public good, rich and poor mutually pledge themselves to the rule of equal justice. This gives security to the rich and consolation to the poor, for it permits every man to have his own possessions and protects him from the despotism of the majority. Since the people renounce as unjust the tyrannical right to break contracts, the assumption of this right by their representatives, the government, destroys the sovereign principle of the republic and installs despotism. Like contracts between individuals, contracts by the legislature, as a representative of the public, with a person or persons cannot be broken or changed without the consent of both parties. A legislature is prohibited from voiding a contract not only by legal and constitutional restrictions, but also by "natural reasons, or those reasons which the plain rules of common sense point out to every man." If such prohibition did not exist, a government of established principles administered by established rules would become a government with discretionary powers during the existence of one legislature, and a new revolution would occur with the election of every new legislature. The charter of the Bank of North America, established by "the enterprising spirit of patriotic individuals," constitutes a contract.

In answer to the objection to a perpetual charter, Paine admitted that no generation has a right to bind a future generation. Future generations may do as they see fit in accordance with the pecuniary canons of justice. Unfortunately, however, Paine did not determine when a new generation begins, or how the contract may be broken. He rejected the assertion that government should exercise some control over the bank, since the citizens who compose the bank will not be free if they are dependent on every new legislature. This would be exercising an authority over them which the legislature does not exercise over other citizens and thereby would destroy the equality of freedom which is the bulwark of the Constitution. Purchase of bank stock by foreigners is a good instead of an evil, for where their money is, there are their hearts, and so we obtain a stronger influence over them than they can exercise over us.

Instead of monopolizing the money of the country, the bank is merely a steward, a useful depository for its real owners—the holders of bank notes and deposits. By making available otherwise idle money, the bank quickens business and creates employment. True, discounts have been stopped and loans have been called, but this was done either to settle accounts or to prevent exportation of specie.

Paine bitterly denounced the issuance of the non-legal-tender paper by the state. The Pennsylvania constitution contains nothing which gives the assembly the power to issue paper money. Those urging paper emissions on the fictitious ground of scarcity of money are base debtors, hoping to defraud their creditors through depreciation. Paper causes the exile of specie. The value of specie is determined by the quantity nature made, and man has no share in its value whether it bears a government stamp or not. The love of specie may produce covetousness, but covetousness is not properly a vice but "frugality run to an extreme." Paper, however, costs only a trifle and thus inevitably becomes too plentiful. Since its value depends on caprice and accident, the value varies greatly and thus becomes the object of jobbery and schemes of deceit. Every principle of justice is violated, and the bond of society is dissolved. An act to suppress the issuance of paper money is really an act to suppress vice and immorality. To make the paper legal tender is a violation of contract, destroying morality and undermining freedom, security, and property. "The punishment of a member [of the assembly] who should move for such a law ought to be *death*."

Bank notes, however, are not of this character, for they are redeemable in specie. For the restoration of credit Paine proposed an ingenious scheme whereby the bank would more effectively control the finances of the government and the wealth of the community. Instead of having the state issue paper, he suggested that the government borrow from the bank sufficient bank notes for its financial needs, and the bank and related mercantile interests would bring in money to pay the notes, since the interest on the loans would be a bounty to import specie. Such combining of authority with usefulness is the distinguishing characteristic of a republican system, he said.

On the floor of the Pennsylvania Assembly his old "radical" friends denounced him as a mercenary writer, and naturally enough Robert Morris defended him. Paine did not let the charge go unchallenged. He replied through a series of letters in the Philadelphia newspapers under his familiar pen name, "Common Sense." He claimed, of course, that he had no personal interest in defending the bank, but was seeking to instill the true principles of free government and commerce.

Who are the opponents of the bank? he cried. They are in the first place the usurers and great moneyed men who know that if the bank were destroyed they could charge extortionate rates, buy country produce cheaper, and eventually monopolize the wealth of the state. Joined with them are the shiftless frontiersmen who, unlike the hard-working substantial farmers of the settled areas, have nothing to sell and are looking for such devices as paper money to relieve them of the hard labor of converting the wilderness into cultivated farms.

He reiterated that "public banks"—that is, chartered, incorporated ones—are the "offspring of free countries," for "where the people . . . live under the continual apprehensions of the power exercised over them, the rich secrete their money, and the bulk of the people, from the want of its free . . . circulation are kept poor."

But "free countries" meant to Paine, as before, countries where the state exercised only nominal, if any, control over its chartered corporations. So, he argued, it is of little consequence or interest to the generality of the people how the stockholders of the bank conduct their private concerns or regulate their elections. Since the stockholders know their own business best and have their money at stake, they know best how to manage it. Therefore the bank should be rechartered along the line of its original charter as far as possible. Of this we have had an "experienced security, to which innovations may . . . be fatal."

Paine thought the bank needed additional safeguards besides its old charter. The abrogation of the charter showed the crying necessity to change Pennsylvania's government of a practically supreme single assembly into a bicameral legislature. The single assembly which he had originally supported had been necessary during the war because such a simple structure made for dispatch. But now "things are done too rashly." In fact, a single supreme assembly with all its members elected at the same time "is capable of becoming a complete aristocracy." The majority will be made up on the ground of party prejudice or fitted to be the dupes thereof; and thus the government becomes that of "party favour and oppression."

The bank received a modified charter, but Paine temporarily lost his reputation among his old "democratic" friends. Leaving his $1000 bank stock in the care of President Willing, he set off for Europe in 1787 to obtain wealthy or at least influential patrons for his bridge invention.[9] While there he continued to pamphleteer and became something of an intelligence agent for Jefferson, then minister to France. For a while he shuttled between France and England.

The French Revolution proved to be another great opportunity for Paine's talents. When he arrived in England, reform was in the air. Burke's bitter denunciations of the French Revolution were at first coolly received, and Paine replied to him with his finest work, *The Rights of Man*, which in large part recapitulated the arguments of *Common Sense*.

The origin and continuation of monarchy, aristocracy, and church establishments, Paine insisted, are due to force and fraud. Their beneficiaries are beggars. Heavy taxation, needed to support them, causes riots and disturbances. If primogeniture is abolished, estates will be left equally among the heirs, and there will no longer be any need for sinecures in church and state for the younger sons of noble families.

Paine demanded removal of property qualifications for voting. He laid special emphasis on the fact that under present arrangements limiting voting to freeholders and "freemen" of the incorporated towns, important business classes are disfranchised. In some places, he remarked, the lowest characters without visible means of support can vote; in other places, great merchants, manufacturers, and tenant farmers with heavy capital investments cannot.

Paine strongly advocated less "government" and more "society." The landholder, farmer, merchant, and trader prosper by mutual aid. "Common interest regulates their concerns," and the usages growing out of this intercourse are more influential than the acts of government. Society really performs almost everything attributed to governments. The more civilized man is, the less need there is for government. The laws of trade and commerce are laws of nature, or of society, and they are obeyed regardless of government. In the trading associations, where men act on the principles of society, the units combine naturally. Governments follow precedent and oppose enterprise, but improvements in agriculture, arts, and commerce are due to the enterprise of individuals and private associations. The promoter asks only that the government leave him alone. The government functionaries are merely stewards with the duty to maintain the property and freedom of the people. The need of government is limited to the fact that every man wishes to pursue his occupation and enjoy the fruits of his property. Consequently combinations of laborers to raise wages are unlawful, and the practice of fixing maximum prices, though famine prevails, causes the greatest distress.

Commerce, Paine asserted, is the great civilizing force. Nature has made commerce the means of eliminating war, for it is cheaper to obtain commodities through commerce than through war. Since commerce is fostered only by the reciprocal interest of nations, attempts to control commerce by navies and conquest are a futile waste of resources, and the heavy cost involved leads to domestic oppression. Therefore, Paine reasoned, the combined reduced fleets of England, Holland, France, and the United States could force Spain to give South America her independence and thus open countries of immense wealth to world commerce. This area would provide a ready market for English manufactures, whereas England at the moment was drained of specie to pay for the imports of competing manufactures from India.

Paine's suggestions for financial reform would relieve the business classes of heavy taxes. The support given to useless government establishments could be directed toward eliminating the poor rates. The discontent of the poor would be allayed and poor relief abolished by such measures as education, old-age pensions, and work barracks for the unemployed. Education was to consist of "reading, writing, and arithmetic." Thereby the children could obtain a profitable living and cease to be a drain on the industrious. Old-age pensions were to consist of small annual payments of £6 to those between the ages of fifty and sixty, and £10 thereafter. Taxes paid by the consumer, such as the excise and customs taxes, should be retained so that trade would not be disturbed. Taxation of land and land incomes was to be arranged to encourage division of the estates and thereby eliminate the institution of primogeniture. However, "it would be impolitic to set bounds to property acquired by industry."

The English financial system, as one of credit, is based on paper rather than real money. Credit is the child of credulity and, if the holders of Bank of England notes were to demand specie, the entire system would collapse. The contradiction between his views on the Bank of North America and those on the Bank of England was somewhat resolved in his mind by the argument that, to the extent that the Bank of England issued paper, based on discounted bills growing out of commercial transactions, it was engaged in legitimate business.

In fact, Paine would tamper but little with the debt. Its origins might be shady, but it was not the crime of the present holders. Furthermore, the interest should not be touched, for it might affect adversely legitimate credit and commerce. As the interest was paid in Bank of England notes, it kept alive a capital useful to commerce and thereby neutralized to a considerable degree its own burden. Since the amount of specie was inadequate, it would be bad policy as well as unjust to eliminate a capital that met the defect of the circulating medium. Still, in view of the discontent over the national debt, it would be good policy for the holders to allow a slight tax on the interest.[10]

As a result of attacking monarchy in his *Rights of Man*, Paine was ordered to stand trial. At first this did not disturb him because reform had been a popular cry, and a trial would give wide publicity to his works. However, when the British government became intent on ruthlessly suppressing even mild demands for reform, Paine left the country to take a seat in the French National Convention.

In France, as in England, he suggested reforms which would relieve the poor without disturbing trade. The unsuccessful communist revolt led by Babeuf against the reactionary French government in 1796 prompted him to publish *Agrarian Justice*. Paine denounced the leaders for attempting to overthrow society instead of waiting for the customary elections or proposing useful measures. But he was willing to go a considerable way in meeting the social problem. Of course, the great mass of poor are ever increasing and have become a hereditary race. In the natural state poverty did not exist, but civilization has created splendor and wretchedness side by side. This paradox has been caused by the rise of ownership of land, whereas in the original state every man was a joint proprietor in the products of nature. Increasing population necessitated private cultivation, and since it was impossible to differentiate private improvement from the land itself, the latter became private property also. To obtain for the dispossessed poor their share in the common or natural property, a fund should be raised by levying·a death duty of 10 per cent. Personal property should be subject to the tax because it is the effect of society, not that the individual owes society the property, but that without society an individual cannot acquire it. According to Paine's plan, the fund was to provide the rather small amount of £15 for each individual, rich or poor, on reaching the age of twenty-one, and a yearly pension of £10 after the age of fifty.

The scheme would have many beneficial results. The national lands would sell at better rates. The masses would see that the more riches a man acquires the better it is for the poor.

On his return to the United States in 1802 Paine found that the prevailing sentiment was hostile to him. Jefferson, who was in his second presidential year, had praised *The Rights of Man* as the orthodox doctrine of American political theory, but the Federalists regarded Paine as a regicide. In religious circles·he was denounced as an atheist for his *Age of Reason*, which had expounded Deism. He had written that God was known through nature and that the laws of science were the formulations of the laws of inscrutable, beneficent nature. Therefore, if men would be happy and moral, they should follow the ways of nature as expressed in the "wise and economical sayings" of Franklin. The devout, however, only noticed his diatribes on organized religion and his characterization of the Bible as an obscene document.

Jefferson sought Paine's advice on important questions but made little effort to aid him. Paine wrote the President that when Napoleon had conquered England the United States should seize Canada and the Bermudas. In another communication he expounded views which were later expressed in the Monroe Doctrine. He thought that the United States should mediate between France and rebellious Santo Domingo and guarantee the settlement. This would give the United States great political and commercial influence in Santo Domingo. Paine advised Jefferson on how Louisiana could be obtained from Napoleon. He suggested that Jefferson propose to purchase the territory and then inform Napoleon that the inhabitants of the western territories were growing so powerful and restive that it was impossible to restrain them from seizing New Orleans, and that it was equally impossible for France to prevent them.

Jefferson was worried over his constitutional right to make the purchase, but Paine informed him that the Constitution had nothing to do with the matter since its framers could never have foreseen the occasion. The transaction was within the President's jurisdiction. It was a sale and purchase similar to any financial transaction. The object was an increase of territory for a valuable consideration.

Concerning the government of the territory, Paine recommended a period of tutelage for the French inhabitants, since they were not acquainted with democratic institutions. At the same time, he asked Jefferson about the acquisition of lands in the territory by individuals, for he had friends in the British Isles who had funds to purchase unlimited amounts.

To promote the sale of lands and settlement, government should encourage and financially support a system of indentured servitude in the newly acquired territory. On the expiration of their service, Congress rather than their masters should give them a few acres which would serve as an incentive to purchase more at a later date.

Paine pointed to the good done by the Quaker merchants of Pennsylvania. They went extensively into the business of importing indentured servants, for it was consistent with their moral principles of bettering the condition of the poor and ending Negro slavery. Free Negroes might also be imported into the territory through government financial aid. Congress should supply the passage to New Orleans; and the Negroes, after working for the planters for a few years, should be made share croppers.[11]

When the inhabitants of the Louisiana territory petitioned for self-government, they advanced Paine's political philosophy of the rights of self-government in accordance with "the laws of nature." The colonial arguments against England were cited. Paine replied in a public letter that the Louisianians were not experienced in the representative system, that the colonies had obtained their rights by an expensive war, that it was not the duty of the United States to fight the world's battles for the world's profits, that the territory was not a contracting party to the cession but had merely been purchased. Congress was the guardian of this valuable property for all the United States, and repayment of the purchase price must come from the land sales. It was better for the inhabitants that Congress govern, since its effective government would encourage increased population and thereby raise the land values.

The fear of the inhabitants that governors with no interest in the welfare of the territory might be appointed was unfounded. True, despotic governments, like those of their former masters, might do so; but their references to practices of their old rulers revealed that the inhabitants did not understand the principles or interest of a republic, or the difference between governments distant and despotic and those domestic and free.[12]

During this period Paine's views regarding banks underwent a change to a more democratic philosophy. Scandals had occurred in connection with bank charters, particularly in Pennsylvania. He now asserted in Constitutions, Governments, and Charters (1805) that neither the Pennsylvania constitution nor that of any other state gave the government the right to grant charters or monopolies. The spirit of the times was against all such speculations. Furthermore, long-term charters were a violation of the principle of annual election of the legislature. Charters for more than one year meant that one legislature could pass measures beyond the power of succeeding legislatures to correct. Paine did not suggest that incorporation should be forbidden, but rather he proposed a device which he had originally suggested to prevent the revocation of the charter of the Bank of North America. Extraordinary matters such as incorporations should be passed by two successive legislatures. If the citizens disliked a measure, they could refuse to re-elect those who had supported it.

As a whole the works of Thomas Paine present a scheme of things closely resembling that of the Benthamites, which came a generation later. His views foreshadow Herbert Spencer's philosophy of a sharp distinction between a system of status and one of free contract. Abolition of church, aristocracy, and royalty would solve all social problems by leaving individuals to the natural play of free contracts. Just as *Common Sense* advocated independence on the ground of eliminating unnecessary expense and the restrictions on commerce and property, and thus on personal rights, so on the same basis *The Rights of Man* called for the abolition of royalty and aristocracies, and *The Age of Reason*, for the abolition of organized religion.

The elimination of all institutions, except those involving property and its security, would, he appeared to feel, make for that expansion of business enterprise that he and the enlightened men of his generation almost completely identified with free government.

Paine succinctly summed up his economic philosophy when he said in *Agrarian Justice:* "I am a friend of Riches," and in *The Rights of Man:* "In all my publications, wherever the matter would admit, I have been an advocate of commerce." His was the luckless fate of the general run of pamphleteers, to live precariously and die in poverty.

It was the more practical-minded friend of Paine, the distinguished American poet of the Revolutionary and post-Revolutionary era, Joel Barlow (1754–1812), who gave concrete meaning to the "revolutionary" social philosophy of Paine.

JOEL BARLOW: TRAFFICKER IN TRADE AND LETTERS

Barlow's itinerary of his life reads like the pilgrim's progress of the commercial cosmopolite. Born in New England, active in American politics and speculation, busy in economic and imperial ventures in England and France, pursuing commercial opportunities over the whole of Europe, negotiating in Africa, he finally died in Poland on a routine mission of trade and diplomacy.[13]

Barlow received the typical respectable education of the day. Of Connecticut Puritan yeoman stock, he was trained at Yale in the customary mixture of Calvinist theology, Lockian philosophy, and classical literature. He began life by trying in quick succession, and sometimes jointly, a variety of occupations for which his poverty and versatility were equally responsible.[14] After serving as an army chaplain during the War of Independence, Barlow was lawyer, publisher, printer, storekeeper, and agent for discontented ex-army officers. Throughout his life he wrote the poems which, peculiarly enough, became the foundation of his fame.

Land speculation, the dominant enterprise of the developing country, inevitably attracted him. Lack of capital was no bar if one were adventurous enough and had the talent of a negotiator and publicist. It was in keeping with his character and the nature of the business that Barlow should presently appear on the administrative board of a company that threatened to maintain its land claims against state authority by force of arms and, if need be, to establish a separate state. All means, apparently, were fair. In 1786 he joined several associates, all recipients of the Master of Arts degree from Yale College, in writing a series of anonymous satires in the newspapers attacking competitors and critics of his concerns. The objects of the satire were in fact substantial, highly conservative citizens, but they were described as "anarchists" and demagogues, who raised the "DEMOCRACY of hell!" and threatened civil war.[15]

These bold ventures, however, brought him little pecuniary success; but a "constructive" epic poem, *The Vision of Columbus*, in 1787 revealed talents that fitted him for a larger role in finance and politics. It portrayed the great development and prospects of America as part of God's plan of making "the spirit of commerce" the civilizing agent of the world. The seraph informs Columbus in the "vision" that after him will come Cortez and other "ruffians" who, allured by gold, wreak destruction on peaceful peoples, but

> Such impious deeds, in Heaven's all-ruling plan,
> Lead in disguise the noblest bliss of man.

*   *   *   *

> And buried gold, drawn bounteous from the mine,
> Give wings to commerce and the world refine.

The poem's authorized dedication to Louis XVI, its impressive list of subscribers, headed by the King with twenty-five copies and

George Washington with twenty, and its British edition attested to Barlow's great gifts of salesmanship and diplomacy. Although the epic brought him little money, it gained for him something of an international reputation as a literary figure. This made him especially useful to a group of speculators who were in need of a foreign agent; and he quickly attracted the attention of the Scioto Associates, one of the manifold promotions of the greatest enterpriser of the day, Colonel William Duer.[16]

As secretary of the government board disposing of public lands, Duer arranged for the sale of 3,500,000 acres of western lands to his own Associates at approximately sixty-six and two-thirds cents per acre in specie or in the heavily depreciated continental certificates of debt at par. But until the payments were made the grant remained merely a pre-emption right. Duer expected to pay the government through sales to wealthy Europeans abroad, who held large quantities of the debt certificates. Such foreign operations were considered legitimate by enlightened Americans, for anything that brought money and men to America would develop the nation's resources and increase its commerce.

Barlow, then a minor official of the Ohio Company, was just the man for the job, or so at least thought the Reverend Manasseh Cutler, Duer's influential fellow promoter of both organizations. The poet was given a sizable share in the Scioto company, armed with letters from General Washington to prominent Frenchmen, and sent abroad during the summer of 1788.[17] In Europe Barlow faced stiff competition; so in 1789 he obtained the assistance of William Playfair of Edinburgh, scientist, engineer, statistician, and follower of Adam Smith.[18] Barlow had sized him up as "a bold and enterprising spirit," with good imagination and the advantage of some years in business in Paris, where he had become acquainted with many people of property.[19] Together with prominent French officials and merchants, the two men organized an incorporated subsidiary—*Compagnie du Scioto* —to raise funds for the purchase of the mother company's lands. They issued a glowing prospectus which omitted the pertinent fact that the Scioto Associates so far owned not land, but merely pre-emption rights.

For a few months the new company enjoyed prosperity—on paper. Barlow wrote home, in the winter of 1789–1790, that the company had great expectations since prosperous Europeans would migrate to America in order to escape the disorders of the Revolution.

"Many respectable and wealthy families are . . . making their purchases and are going in the spring; among them are several noblemen and members of the National Assembly." Should the first hundred people be happy there, "the stream of immigration would be irresistible." Business is good, and a profit of $1,200,000 might be expected in a short time.[20]

Barlow, however, sent no funds, and this first business expedition was a fiasco. When the stranded nobility began sending back complaints, Barlow even feared for his life. He had already appealed to Duer to have Alexander Hamilton, then Secretary of the Treasury, ease the terms of sale to the Scioto Associates. Hamilton, desiring to advance large enterprises, recommended in his first *Report on the Public Credit* that the price for public lands be reduced to twenty cents an acre. At the same time he granted an indefinite leave of absence to the naval officer of New York, Colonel Benjamin Walker, to investigate Barlow's activities in Paris in behalf of the Duer group. The upshot was that both Playfair and Barlow decided in 1791 to leave France temporarily, each accusing the other of causing the debacle.[21]

Although he held land claims in America, Barlow was now penniless in London. His next step was to join a group of reformers in London, "composed in good part of American citizens who for commercial or political traffic or both" were "sometimes resident in England and sometimes in France." [22] To one of that group—Thomas Paine—he was especially attracted. There seemed little doubt that the man who had stirred the American people to independence with his *Common Sense* would now with his *Rights of Man* stir England and the rest of the world to follow the example of revolutionary France. He was the idol of all English reformers; and soon the French Assembly would award him French citizenship, and four departments of France would vie with one another to elect him a deputy to the National Convention.

From Paine, Barlow could learn much, and he did. *The Rights of Man* became his political bible. Barlow hailed Paine as the greatest man of the age. He was much impressed, too, by the rise to power in France of two fellow Duer agents, Brissot de Warville, the politician and journalist, and Etienne Clavière, the learned refugee Swiss banker and economist.[23] This inseparable team had the gift of giving projects of commercial expansion and conquest the fair appearance of peace and universal liberty. Paine, after all, was primarily a pamphleteer who announced the grand political philosophy of a commercial civilization. Brissot and Clavière were shrewd politicians and hard-headed businessmen able to turn that philosophy to practical ends. Before the French Revolution they had been engaged in schemes for developing interest in American trade and investment along with republican political reforms.[24] To this end they had issued in 1787 *De la France et des États-Unis*, describing the effects of the American Revolution on Europe in general and France in particular, and especially the new commercial prospects, including financial operations, which the Revolution opened to Frenchmen.

In the summer of 1788 a group of Dutch and French bankers, and their resident American associates, sent Brissot to the United States to investigate the possibilities of speculation in the public debt and lands. After making arrangements with a Duer group, he hurried back in less than six months to attend to business and to witness the historic opening of the Estates General that marked the beginning of the French Revolution. Brissot quickly rose to political power as head of the revolutionary faction (Girondists) representing the upper middle class, which opposed government interference with business. With him rose Clavière, who had suggested the issue of assignats and later became minister of finance. Through all their feverish political activities, they did not lose sight of their business ventures. Late in 1791 the team issued a revised edition of their first treatise and a new book, *Nouveau Voyage*, on American conditions, in the form of a series of letters from Brissot to Clavière. The material consisted chiefly of familiar American promotional and advertising literature written for European consumption.[25]

Barlow immediately translated the latter book under the title *New Travels in the United States of America* (1792). Judging by his appraisal of Brissot in the introduction as an accurate, sober observer, he was pleased with the praise of Scioto Associates. That company had been accused of selling lands it did not own, of giving exaggerated accounts of their fertility, of deceiving emigrants, and of sending them where they might be butchered by Indians. This, Brissot argued, was false. Of course, French aristocrats who emigrated with the foolish idea of forming a monarchy would be sadly deceived. Seeking to fly from the equality of rights in France, "they would fall into a society where this equality is consecrated even by the nature of things; where every man is solicited to independence" by the very ease of supplying his wants.

Some foolish critics of investment and migration to the United States, so ran the argument, warn that the West may separate from the Union. As a matter of fact, the two sections are bound together by a common interest in opening an extensive commerce with South America and in pushing beyond the Mississippi. Spain, in adhering to the narrow policy of preventing this expansion, has acted unwisely. It fears the communication of those principles of independence which the liberty-loving Americans preach wherever they go. But already an American commercial settlement west of the Mississippi, though under Spanish auspices, marks the beginning of the conquest of Louisiana. Within the next century the whole continent will be united "under the reign of liberty which leads to universal harmony."

This prospectus was but the practical elaboration of the economic-political doctrine of commercial individualism set forth in *De la France*, which Barlow also translated under a new title, *The Commerce of America with Europe* (1794). Monarchical government must become enlightened on the "science of commerce," heretofore neglected because of aristocratic prejudice. This "science" teaches that prosperity and national glory rest upon commerce, that monarchies must refrain from arbitrary interference, including price-fixing, and must establish entire liberty of commerce, both externally and internally, so that merchants may have the hopes of prosperity which "in republics incline them with ardour to every kind of commercial enterprise." In short, the authors contended that commercial liberty is the very heart of liberty. Liberty is "the choice which everyone may make of that which is most agreeable to him."

All this and more Barlow could appreciate thoroughly, for he was about to embark on the most critical period of his career in politics and finance, a phase which embraced simultaneously the activities of pamphleteer and political adviser on the one side and merchant and soldier of fortune on the other. With the methods and success of Paine and the two Frenchmen to inspire him, he sent forth in 1792–1793 his famous *Advice to the Privileged Orders*. Its guiding premise is—again—that human liberty is based on free commerce. The "spirit of commerce," by making nations advantageous to each other, eliminates war and induces people to "change the form of their governments, that society may be restored to its proper foundation." Like Paine's *Rights of Man*, the *Advice* calls for the elimination of all feudal vestiges interfering with "nature's plan." Barlow regards as "feudal" anything that interferes with "freedom of trade," whether it be cumbrous legal procedure or undesirable trade acts. "Feudalism" destroys man's emulative instinct to obtain the good opinion of his fellows by exercising his physical and moral power in accumulating wealth.

Along with Brissot and Clavière, and all the other Physiocratic writers, Barlow argued that since land is the productive element, taxes should be derived directly from it. Excise, customs and similar levies are "surreptitious" and destructive. The middle class, as embodying the men of commerce, is the class in which "the semblance of nature most resides." That class must force the extremes in the "wretched scale of rank"—the improvident mass at the bottom and the idlers at the top—to conform to the system of free commerce. The author pointed to America, where government had been stripped of its impurities by the Revolution. The Americans believe that the state should be managed as simply as a family, except that it requires more hands. The states decide boundary claims on the basis of simple convenience; all questions of land are settled as merchants might settle the course of exchange between two commercial cities. But in "feudal" Europe agriculture and commerce are considered degrading, lest idle nobles forget themselves and engage in "contaminating" occupations to the destruction of all social distinctions.

France, the *Advice* goes on, by destroying "feudalism" has exalted the idle duke to a useful merchant. Wealth is now devoted to enterprise, which becomes honorable in its own right. To safeguard this system, all that is needed is an elementary education, which implements man's natural right to the means of subsistence. Barlow pointed as proof to the inexpensive public-supported schools of Connecticut. Neither extreme poverty nor extraordinary accumulations existed there, and the few criminals are Europeans.

These arguments of the *Advice*, which, of course, the privileged orders of Europe were in no hurry to accept, are applied to colonies in an eloquent public letter to the French National Convention in 1792. Beginning with Adam Smith's individualism, based on the distinction between society and government, Barlow proceeds to the conclusion that the French do not need a king. He then gently transfers the argument to the desirability of France's surrendering her colonies. Though the mother country may desire their welfare, it cannot know their wants as well as they can. Whatever solid advantage may flow to her from their controlled trade will necessarily flow to her from free trade. The cost of maintaining the trade monopoly will always exceed the profits.[26]

The French Convention accepted Barlow's philosophy of individualism but not in its application to the colonies. It showed its appreciation of his sympathetic attitude toward the Revolution by making him a citizen of France, and he in turn accompanied a French commission for organizing the annexed Duchy of Savoy. From this vantage point he called on the people of near-by Piedmont, in a public letter, to overthrow their King and welcome the French armies of "liberation" on pain of fearful slaughter. France, armed with the "panoply of reason," was waging a war in "defence of human nature." It was a horrible lie that the French Revolution threatened the destruction of private property; on the contrary, so sacredly did the French regard property, that they assumed the burden of the immense debt contracted by the wicked court. What then did the French armies bring as the principles of the French Revolution? They brought to the freed peoples the essentials of happiness—namely, security against war, control of the fruits of their labor, and "a free circulation of the objects of commerce." Barlow pointed to the depressed situation of Savoy under its royal master. The province had good river communications with France, but the King shackled its commerce and thereby discouraged its agriculture and other industrial pursuits.[27]

This appeal to the people of Piedmont was no more directly effective than his *Advice to the Privileged Orders*. Nor did the people of Savoy show their appreciation of his presence, for they refused to elect him a deputy to the National Convention, although he was the "administration" candidate. But he had a role to play in schemes of colonial expansion dear to Brissot and his friends. These were the spectacular ventures to seize the great Spanish colony of Louisiana. The imperial promoters were a motley group and included a number of prominent English reformers, such as Thomas Cooper and Barlow's close friend, Mary Wollstonecraft, and her faithless lover, Captain Gilbert Imlay, who had served as an officer in the Revolutionary War and who advertised the potentialities of the West with fine maps and a romantic novel.

The "reformation" of Louisiana would be of enormous advantage to France and the Revolution. The familiar arguments of the great benefit of colonies to a nation's commerce and industry were sketched. New Orleans would provide an excellent haven for privateers preying on enemy commerce. American citizens should execute the coup, and this would bring the United States to the side of France in the war for universal liberty against universal despotism. Barlow was to take general direction of the plan and manage the funds supplied by the French government, as he was "a true friend of liberty, a philosopher, and pure in his morals."

The execution of Brissot on charges of counter-revolution and the suicide of Clavière resulted in some changes in the project. Barlow and Mark Leavenworth, another Yale graduate, frankly referring to themselves as "entrepreneurs," proposed to the new government of Robespierre that they seize Louisiana. They would take care of expenses in return for the property of the Spanish Crown in the colony. After France had accomplished her revolutionary mission, her soldiers, who otherwise might become turbulent, could be given lands in the country. Both troops participating in the expedition and some discharged later in France might have the opportunity to share in the distribution.[28]

But the French government, sensitive to the attitude of the United States, was not seriously interested. Barlow showed no nationalistic scruples in assigning Louisiana to France rather than to America because from his commercial, cosmopolitan point of view it made no difference. Was he not a citizen of both countries?

In the meantime, despite these setbacks, Barlow was rapidly accumulating a large fortune from "commerce and speculation." He had hardly finished the *Advice* when he was off to the Continent on a mysterious trip involving, it appears, wartime smuggling and similar operations on a grand scale. Henceforth he was constantly moving through the ports and cities of war-torn Europe on obscure "business." There were substantial rewards waiting for those who could bring supplies through the British blockade or, for that matter, flout French regulations. Robespierre's government might think Barlow's prices higher than those of other "importers," but it did a large business with him.[29] Since he viewed filibustering expeditions as an aspect of commerce, it is not surprising to find him associated in these more peaceful ventures with his collaborators of the Louisiana schemes. He had interests even in privateering ventures.

It appears also that he did well in purchasing commercial claims of American citizens against the French government.[30] The result was that, while in 1792 Barlow lived in poverty, four years later he was worth $120,000.[31] He was a made man. So close was he to the

French Directory that Washington's Administration decided to take advantage of his double citizenship, and of the good relations between France and Algiers, to have him negotiate the ransoming of American seamen enslaved by the Algerians.[32]

Beginning in 1798, however, Barlow found his principles and interests jeopardized by the strained relations between his two countries over French "interference" with American commerce, especially the carrying trade. It was no easy task to placate both sides. In pamphlets to the American people and letters to American friends, he attempted to place the blame on the United States and England. France had vindicated her principle of commercial and civil liberty, but England's interferences with neutral trade, especially her utilization of the tyrannical doctrine of contraband, had forced France to take retaliatory measures. Since America unfortunately acquiesced in British actions, France sought to affect America's vital pecuniary nerves so that she would assert her own rights against England. The United States, however, had an instrument for forcing commercial law and peace on the world without a navy—namely, by taking advantage of its debtor position to seize the private debts owed abroad as a fund to compensate her citizens damaged by the English regulations.

At the same time, though with less warmth, Barlow and his business associate, Fulwar Skipwith, the American consul general in France, appealed to the French authorities to follow the principle of free trade by prohibiting French privateering and by respecting all neutral flags. If France allowed neutrals to be the carriers of English commerce, England's wealth would be reduced through loss of the profits of freight, and she would be weakened in her marine by the encouragement of foreign shipping. Since France could not effectively carry her own goods, she should let neutrals do so. Besides, the drain of manpower for ships and privateers weakened France's agriculture and manufactures, which were the real sources of her wealth.[33]

An even better way of handling England was suggested by Barlow's versatile friend Robert Fulton. The inventor had been living with him since his arrival in France in 1797, and Barlow not only invested his money and time in Fulton's various inventions, but seconded his friend's efforts to obtain government aid. Among these inventions was the "submarine bomb" or "torpedo," more properly described as a mine. Enough of these placed conveniently in the waters frequented by the British Navy would end the tyranny of Britain. Napoleon tested it and found it unsatisfactory. So did the British government, on trying to neutralize it by enticing Fulton with sufficient pecuniary rewards. Such sad experiences, along with an accumulation of approximately $200,000, induced Barlow to leave for his native land. France had become unsupportable "from the follies of the many and the rogueries of the few." [34]

Barlow built the first magnificent estate in the environs of Washington; turned out poetry and anonymous articles in support of President Jefferson and his political heir, President Madison; became a bank president and gave considerable attention to Fulton's interests as well as to his own, in fine arts, canal construction, steamboats, and in the "torpedo." His assets continued to mount rapidly. In 1812 he listed among his holdings $115,540 in bank and corporate stocks and estimated land claims at $175,000.[35]

Many of his activities, artistic and pecuniary, Barlow found worthy of government encouragement, even if this meant some modification of his earlier formulation of the doctrine of freedom of commerce. In oration and pamphlet, for example, he preached that, though the duties on imports had been originally established to meet the public-debt charges, the redemption of the public debt should not necessarily entail the reduction of the duties. Surplus revenues should be devoted to public works and higher education. The funds should first be used for roads and canals to connect the interior with the sea. Such expenditures would increase the value of public and private property. They would directly stimulate the sale and value of public lands. Not the least of the public works that the government should promote is Fulton's "torpedoes," for "God has given them to us as a weapon to free the seas from naval tyranny and the attacks on American commerce."

All such government activities should be guided by a publicly supported, but not governmentally controlled, National Institute or University to be established in Washington, with—incidentally—Barlow at the head. It would manage a host of activities—from the Army and Navy officers' training schools to the operation of the mint. Fine arts were to be encouraged as favorable to republican manners and discipline. By multiplying people's wants and diversifying objects of emulation, the arts would stimulate industry. To repeat the statement of the earlier epic, "imaginary wants must be increased in order to inspire a passion for commerce." Of course, gross sensual luxuries were undesirable, as leading to poverty and other ills, but these could not be checked by direct governmental action without running the danger of restraining wealth and civil liberty. Government might indirectly achieve the desired effect by encouraging a taste for the more elegant luxuries—the fine arts—for these excite passions which the means of each individual prescribes.

Finally, the "moral sciences," especially economics, should receive considerable attention. No one denies their importance, but "the science of political economy as well as the whole science of government is in its infancy." Researches in this field "are so vague in their nature and have been so little methodized as scarcely to obtain the name of science." [36]

How true this was Barlow himself soon illustrated in negotiations with Napoleon's minister of foreign relations, the Duke of Bassano. President Madison had sent him to France in 1811 as special envoy to induce the Emperor to remove restraints on the freedom of American merchants and reduce, if not abolish, customs duties on American goods. Barlow tried to convince the Duke that such actions would not interfere with Napoleon's "continental system," but on the contrary would give activity to neutral capital, with all its manifold blessings. With the confidence of American merchants restored, France and her allies would be able to obtain food supplies and be relieved of their accumulated stores of export commodities. The Duke, however, was equally adept in the manipulation of the concepts of economics. He even returned Barlow's own arguments in the *Advice*. The author-businessman had denounced customs imposts as burdens borne ultimately by the depressed mass of consumers. The Duke blithely argued that the duties, which covered mainly colonial luxuries, simply raised their price without affecting either profits or the amount of trading.[37]

After months of disputation in Paris on what constituted "perfect reciprocity," the discussion was interrupted when Napoleon left on his proposed conquest of Russia. He found time to invite Barlow to meet him in Vilna for further negotiations. Barlow hastened to Vilna. Napoleon soon was too busy retreating from the Russian winter to attend to this matter. Barlow joined the retreat and took ill. As he lay dejected, whatever admiration he may have had in the past for the modern Cortez, Barlow was in no mood to view him as an agent of Providence. Then it was in December 1812 that he penned his best poem, "Advice to a Raven in Russia." The scavenging bird is the "best friend" of the tyrant: one feeds on the other's destruction. Winter has frustrated both.

> The [soldier's] frozen orb, preserving still its form,
> Defies your talons as it braves the storm,
> But stands and stares to God, as if to know
> In what curst hands he leaves his world below.[38]

Barlow died on Christmas Eve, near Cracow. The American poet-adventurer found a lonely grave in the soil of Poland.

The character of Barlow, as it emerges from the story of his practical affairs, is unclear and complex. It is not, however, the complexity of the pioneer thinker who struggles with problems too fundamental for simple solution or even simple statement. It is the complexity that comes from constant and resilient adjustment to changing circumstance. In the nature of things, speculative enterprise in an age of social upheaval partakes of the discrete and opportunistic. And the attempt to articulate such interests in terms of a more or less consistent set of principles must lead to watering and tacking. We need not be surprised that such an attempt will reveal the nature of the immediate interests rather than the philosophy used to defend them.

Yet Barlow, although not a profound man, was not a dishonest one. Sanguine, able, industrious, he was surely avid for power, competence, and position. He moved in circles where prestige depended upon material success and a cultivated ability. To attain success he strained ability to the utmost. As a sophisticated and cultivated man, he found a convenient correspondence between his economic ventures and the climate of opinion. His living experience made it habitual for him to think of "natural society" as being essentially in the words of the *Advice* "a company of merchants" writ large. He never ceased to be the literary man; he never gave up his avocation of poet and publicist. And, what is socially and politically significant, he somehow fitted his enterprises into the spirit of the age. Hence, running through all his "philosophy" and explanations, there is a broad acceptance of the prevailing doctrines of natural rights; the natural rights of man and the natural rights of the businessman.

ROBERT FULTON AND THE ECONOMICS OF INVENTION

Robert Fulton has achieved immortality as the inventor of the first financially successful steamboat.[39] But fame is always narrower than life, and in life Fulton was promoter, pamphleteer, and businessman; a businessman, moreover, whose locus of activity spanned the Atlantic. Inventor, economic pamphleteer, and Jeffersonian partisan, he shuttled between the United States, England, and the Continent to promote his inventions, using the best political and economic arguments that the climate of opinion of his time, as well as circumstances, placed at his disposal. In England he tried to promote the building of canals, arguing that they would develop the economy; in France he sought to sell the submarine "torpedo" which would end the dominance of the British Navy; and later in the United States he promoted the steamboat, which finally brought him great renown.

Robert Fulton was the bright young man who left his humble home to make his fortune in the world; and his experience echoes Paine's and that of many others. In 1786, at the age of twenty-one, he left Pennsylvania to study painting in London; he became a garret painter. From painter to craftsman inventor seems a great distance today, but in the eighteenth century it was not. Specialization was not so advanced in any of the branches of learning and endeavor; and the relation between the arts and crafts was much closer. Painting, drawing, architecture, a little chemistry, and construction belonged together. Like so many others, he had been artist and mechanic at the same time at home. Besides, Fulton's was a versatile and lively mind. For a while he painted portraits and miniatures without shining success. It is hardly surprising, therefore, to meet him in 1796 trying to "sell" to the British government and private men the idea of cheap canals to provide "easy communication with the marts of trade." In a book published in that year he elaborated an economic analysis drawn from Adam Smith and other more or less popular writers to show how his particular schemes would promote the wealth and power of England. His argument was familiar and for that very reason an effective weapon for his cause.

It is natural to find him arguing that cheapening communication would promote enterprise and thus increase the common stock of the nation and fully develop its resources. The main argument was that canals, as compared with roads, save manual labor in construction, maintenance, and use. But, while reducing labor costs, canals multiply produce and thus in turn increase population, which, by creating a greater demand, pushes improvement to a higher spiral.

It so happened that England had been developing large-scale lock canals. Fulton's scheme stressed the use of small canals, requiring relatively little capital and only small boats, and carrying traffic not only between great trading areas, but also between local communities; in short, the ancient road eventually was to be abolished. Of course, the great lock canal companies, he argued, would immediately fly to Parliament and demand restrictions on the ground of protecting their investments and the value of affected mill and land property. A wise legislature, however, knows that competition is "the true polish of society." It always takes as little profit as it can afford, but "monopoly as much as it can draw." Competition, therefore, should be encouraged, restrictions should be as few as possible, and "circulation [should] be as free as the air we breathe."

Typically casting his net in several directions, Fulton addressed the governor of Pennsylvania, a state which was then a center of interest for canals. His argument here was based on the peculiar necessities of a vast inland and undeveloped area. The state, he maintained, must provide the capital, and the returns would not only repay the cost with a profit, but increase the value of land by increasing profitable commerce. Whereas in England the role of Fulton was that of promoter, constructor, and operator, in Pennsylvania it became that of contractor, engineer, and perhaps operator of a government enterprise. The functions varied only in form, and Fulton was not a stickler for form, for a year later he was willing that a private corporation should undertake such construction in the United States, which he knew generally meant substantial financial aid from the government.[40] But his canal schemes, though they had some financial support from Robert Owen, made no headway in either country.

Despairing of success in England, Fulton betook himself in 1797 to Paris, where he lived with Joel Barlow. The two men formed an excellent combination. Barlow's command of both French and English proved invaluable in preparing commercial addresses and memorials. Both were active friends of the French Revolution and all its successive governments, and both were particularly concerned with businesses in which official friendship was useful. In this period of unending wars, with their blockades and restrictions on commerce, Barlow's constant preaching of complete freedom of external sea trade fitted in neatly with Fulton's water projects. So Fulton became an ardent disciple of Barlow, and Barlow invested in Fulton's ideas.

They were soon engaged in showing the authorities how the revolutionary movement could be fostered through promoting their specific enterprises. Fulton suggested to the French Directory, as "the friends of mankind," that it should abolish tariffs on imports, give up colonies and all restrictions on external commerce, and thereby promote trade. Let the government collect its revenue from the operation of a network of small canals to cover all France. The argument that such free trade would expose France to ruinous competition from English manufacturers, Fulton answered in a number of usual ways. First, France would maintain her competitive position and full employment by specialization in fine fabrics and wine and any agricultural goods which would find a market in England. Second, if full employment could not be provided by agriculture, subsidies from the profit of canals might be used to encourage home manufactures and induce ingenious foreigners to establish their plants in France. Finally, there is no way to stop the "importation" of cheaper goods anyway.[41]

Fulton urged these doctrines of free trade and canal construction on other influential men, including General Bonaparte. He wrote his fellow engineer and republican that the "system of exclusive commerce and distant possessions" makes for war not only among monarchies but also among republics. Instead of restricting external trade, government should devote itself to "internal improvements." When France conquers England, she should therefore still further extend freedom of trade.[42] While this argument might seem Utopian, Fulton and more so Barlow, might hope for at least a slackening of the mercantilistic practices which impeded the free flow of commerce and profits.

Fulton passed from this effort to liberalize the commercial policy of France to an attempt to liberalize sea trade in general by destroying the naval supremacy of England. In this he was in his favorite sphere of inventive engineering. He developed a "torpedo" and "submarine." The "torpedo" was a submarine mine, not a projectile. It was intended to be anchored, dragged by a boat, or allowed to drift with the tide and to explode by concussion. The submarine was an underseas boat, or "plunging boat," to carry these bombs to their destination unobserved.[43]

His devices, Fulton wrote the Directory, would destroy the British Navy and facilitate a French invasion to bring about a revolution in favor of republican government there. With England republicanized, the seas would be free. The liberty of the seas in turn would become a guarantee of perpetual peace to all maritime nations. France, because of her superiority in resources and population, would then hold the balance of power in Europe. The instrument might appear revolting, but "it is certainly the gentlest and the least bloody method that the philosopher can imagine to overturn this system of brigandage and of perpetual war . . . and to restore men to their natural industries."

At this point Fulton passed easily to the novel trade of naval *condottiere*, for he proposed no less a measure than that the naval might of England should be met by an instrument of destruction wielded by a commercial company. Under his proposal the French government would pay his company a handsome amount for every naval ship sunk. All prizes of British vessels and cargoes taken by the company would become its property, and the company would have the exclusive right to use the invention from all the ports of France, except when the government wished to do its own construction, in which case the government was to pay the company 100,000 livres in specie for each vessel built. If war with England ceased within three months, the company was to be reimbursed for its expenses. "I hope it may be stipulated," wrote the inventor, "that this invention, or any similar invention, shall not be used" against the United States unless the United States shall "first apply the invention against France."

Fulton stressed also that, since "fire ships or any other unusual means of destroying navies are considered contrary to the laws of war, and persons taken in such enterprise are liable to suffer death," the government must give the company's agents commissions in the French Navy, specifying that all persons captured on these expeditions shall be treated as prisoners of war, or a fourfold retaliation would be taken against British prisoners.[44] The Directory turned down this and subsequent offers. The minister of marine held that commissions could not be given, for men practicing such means of warfare could be considered no better than pirates. Besides, retaliation would not be effective since England had three times as many prisoners as the French.[45]

With the overthrow of the Directory in 1799 and the rise of Napoleon to supreme power, Fulton's hopes became brighter. Napoleon encouraged him until he became convinced that the engines were not practicable, at least immediately.

Following his now ingrained habit of peddling his projects from government to government, Fulton tried the Dutch, but with no greater success. The English government, however, stirred by the reports of such a terrifying invention, entered negotiations in 1803 for his naval devices. Under a contract made the following year, Fulton was in a position to make at least £40,000 if his scheme proved successful. He now felt that he was already engaged in destroying the "tyrannic principles of Bonaparte . . . [who] should be hunted down as the enemy of mankind." [46] However, the British government eventually agreed with Napoleon concerning the impracticable nature of the invention. Fulton conducted an arduous campaign with the British ministry in which he contended that he had performed his part of the bargain and that the government had not properly tested his device. In the end he received, for two years' work of experimentation, the not inconsiderable sum of £15,000. [47]

By this time Fulton was on his way to America in order to put into practical operation an invention which he had developed while in France—namely, a steamboat. But he never forgot the "torpedo." It remained the invention dearest to his heart and through letter and pamphlet he pushed for government encouragement, with some success. The Republican Administrations of Jefferson and Madison were friendly to schemes that might destroy what they considered the oppressive power of the British Navy over the commerce of neutrals.

England's enterprising and commercial people, argued Fulton in 1810 in his *Torpedo War, and Submarine Explosions*, have taken full advantage of the great technological advance in "chemistry and mechanism" that has developed immense resources and multiplied the produce of productive labor, but the profits of this superiority, instead of being devoted to internal improvements, have gone to enable England to build an ever larger navy to oppress commerce. America lacks adequate pecuniary resources to build an effective navy, but the "torpedo" is much cheaper. Best of all, the "torpedo" is "republican," because every order of things tending to remove oppression and to ameliorate man's condition by directing his ambition to useful industry is republican. Every system nourishing war, with its consequent thousands of idlers and oppressors, is aristocratic.

Under the circumstances Napoleon became again a hope of republicanism; he, too, was trying to destroy the British Navy, and the United States was edging toward a rupture with England. Many people have a foolish fear, Fulton said, that if Napoleon gets command of the seas, he will reduce London to ashes and utterly destroy the civilization and economy of England. But Napoleon well understands that Europe benefits tremendously from English arts and industry. He is not opposed to England's making profits from her skills, but to her devoting these profits to building a navy and interfering in continental affairs. If Napoleon had the "torpedo," he would use it to destroy England's Navy and give "so ingenious, industrious, enterprising, and estimable a people, a perfect liberty of commerce." But Fulton claimed that he himself was "wholly attached" to his country. He got some government aid for tests and the ardent support of the most radical Republican organ, Duane's Philadelphia *Aurora*, but the experiments again showed poor results.

Fulton also did not forget his old love, canals. The savings which would be effected by disposing of the need for navies (through the use of "torpedoes") might well be turned into canal improvements. In the running controversy over this type of waterway Fulton played a public, rather than a strictly commercial, role. It is interesting to note that in urging extensive canals he developed the vision of a great united nation knit by trade and transportation connections against all possibility of division and disintegration, but in pressing for the steamboat he relied on the existing instrumentality of states and privileges which rested on an extreme form of states' rights.

When Secretary of the Treasury Albert Gallatin sought his advice in 1807 in developing a program of government aid for canals, Fulton responded enthusiastically. The canals would forever end the intrigues for a separate government in the West. Some irresponsible leaders had argued that, since the inhabitants beyond the mountains were cut off from the Atlantic seaboard, they should use their resources to divert communications southward (on the Mississippi) instead of eastward, and that they were too remote from the government seat to enjoy fully the advantages of the Union. Others held (as did Montesquieu) that the country was too extensive to remain a republic. But these had taken their examples from the European monarchies. Such states had arisen out of the feudal habits of warriors whose minds were bent to the absolute power of the few and the servile obedience of the many.

All the critics, Fulton believed, had failed to appreciate that men are creatures of habit, and that their habits as well as their interests may be so combined as to make separation impossible. England, once seven petty kingdoms, had by habit been combined into one. Scotland had become united to England by hereditary succession, and was bound to her by habit, turnpike roads, and canals. The United States likewise could be consolidated by canals, by cheap and easy access to markets in all directions.

The Union must engage the interest of "every man to sell the produce of his labour at the best market, and purchase at the cheapest." This accorded, he said, with David Hume's notion "that the government of a wise people would be little more than a system of civil police; for the best interest of man is industry and a free exchange of the produce of his labour for the things which he may require." [48]

Yet later, when he joined with Gouverneur Morris and others in advocating and pushing state construction of the Erie Canal, Fulton employed arguments that brought him closer to a state than a national position. A canal is in effect a great labor-saving machine owned "by a prudent and skillful manufacturer, the economy and profits of which are applied to extending his works and increasing his capital." The Erie Canal would be an immense object of glory and a vast and noble example to the sister states. It would be a source of abundant revenues obtained by the economy of labor and consequently a clear gain to the state. It would consolidate population. It would prevent the immense trade of the West from going by way of the St. Lawrence and Canada, to New York's injury. It would draw forth revenues into and through this state. Tolls would quickly repay the cost of $10,000,000 and would not only obviate the need of any state taxes afterward, but also provide funds for other internal improvements. [49]

But the direct object for which Fulton had returned to America was the steamboat. Of course, the history of the steamboat goes back to earlier years and involves a good many figures besides Fulton. In fact, the great interest in the steamboat appears to have been aroused by the work of the two other Americans, John Fitch and James Rumsey, who, while Fulton was in Europe, had been engaged in fighting in the public prints and legislative halls over priority, exclusive state grants, and franchises. Fulton developed his idea in France while engaged on the "torpedo." He was fortunate in obtaining the financial assistance in 1802 of his fellow Republican, Robert R. Livingston, who had just come to France as Jefferson's minister. This step was crucial, for the whole Livingston influence was thrown behind the project.

Livingston, by virtue of his family and wealth as well as early services in the American Revolutionary War, was one of the most powerful figures in the political and economic life of New York state. He was one of the authors of the extremely conservative constitution of New York and held the leading judicial position in the state, that of chancellor. His economic interests ranged from sheep raising to banking. Livingston had also long been interested in the steamboat. In 1787 John Fitch had obtained from the New York as well as other state legislatures a fourteen-year grant for the exclusive manufacture and operation of steamboats. Though this luckless inventor and promoter had built steamboats, they had not been successful, and he committed suicide in Kentucky in 1798. Thereupon Livingston persuaded the New York legislature to transfer to him Fitch's exclusive right. He received a twenty-year grant with the stipulation that he must produce within a year a boat with the speed of four miles an hour. He joined with a brother-in-law, John Stevens of Hoboken, New Jersey, and another inventor of means, Nicholas Roosevelt of New York. However, their attempts did not immediately prove successful, and Livingston thought that Fulton might have the answer.

Livingston easily enough obtained a further renewal of the grant, this time in Fulton's name as well as his own. A boat, the "North River Steamboat of Clermont," was placed in operation in 1807, and the.following year the legislature provided that the exclusive charter of Livingston and Fulton was to be extended for every boat they produced.

But no sooner had the Fulton boat made its first run than there began a long war between rivals, not only over franchises and profits, but also over the relative merits of various inventions and subsequent improvements. Most notable among these controversies was that between Stevens, who now was engaged in independent efforts, on the one hand, and Livingston and Fulton on the other. At various times the parties, being more interested in business than in constitutional law, tried to reach an amicable settlement to their mutual advantage and profit and to the exclusion, incidentally, of other competitors. They reached an agreement between themselves at one time for division of territory throughout the country, but this was short-lived. Livingston complained that "everyone" seemed to want to go into the steamboat business, and that, "should our patents be out of the way, steamboats would ruin many proprietors and enrich none."

The controversies shaded off easily from ordinary business competition into the social aspects of invention and then into the constitutional issues of the scope of the federal powers to grant patents and regulate commerce.

Briefly stated, Stevens's position, like that of other rivals of Livingston and Fulton, was derived from a "loose" and liberal construction of the Constitution. The right of patent—which is a federal right—should enable him to employ his boat in New York waters, as indeed in the waterways of any state. If a state could convey exclusive rights to one of several alternative patents, then most patent rights were in effect nullified. This brought up the question of national against state powers, but it also brought up another issue which, from a practical point of view, was much more important—free trade versus monopoly. If Fulton's federal patent or state grant could exclude all other patents and also later improvements, the progress of society and the increase of trade through competition would be impeded. It would, moreover, establish and maintain the privilege of the first lucky patentee and monopolist.

Except for the monopoly given Livingston and Fulton, Stevens argued, the waters of New York would be full of steamboats, and improvements would be carried to a surprising degree. If a person should find a better way of performing the same thing, why should he not enjoy the benefit; does not the patent law state that its object is to "promote the progress of science"?

It is interesting to watch the somersaults of Livingston and Fulton in asserting the right of a state to choose one patent from several alternatives and also to prevent any patent from being exploited in its jurisdiction. The basic concept used here was the power of the state to prevent activities detrimental to the general welfare. "Suppose Connecticut so fully peopled as with difficulty to support labouring classes by the manufacture of linens and woolen cloth. Suppose a patent granted for a labour-saving machine by which one man might . . . do the work of 500. . . . Virginia might encourage it as a useful invention, and Connecticut prohibit it as injurious."

Stevens's argument that subsequent patentees and improvers might be hurt was turned around neatly by Fulton and Livingston, who argued that, unless the first practice was protected against subsequent ones, the incentive to invention would be destroyed. The state, considering the undertaking was expensive and hazardous, properly thought Livingston and Fulton should be encouraged by particular privileges. "Would it not be . . . unjust to rob the inventors of the reward held out to them merely because another person had later . . . found . . . another mode of doing the same thing? . . . Surely the last comer would have no complaint if his invention be not taken from him but merely prohibited where it is not wanted, or where prior engagements interfere with it." [50]

Of course, on the issue of whether their rights were monopolistic, Fulton and Livingston, as Jeffersonians, were bound to be sensitive. So sensitive were they, as well as the state legislators, that it was basic to their defense to contend that their right was, properly speaking, no monopoly. On this issue even a stanch Federalist would flinch. Their Federalist attorney, Cadwallader Colden, argued that "monopolies" are the offspring of despotism. "In such the monarch may grant, for his own private emolument, or to gratify the cupidity of favourites, exclusive privileges." Such monopolies are justly odious. "But can a grant, made upon good consideration by a free representative body, exercising its delegated power in a manner that will, in its opinion, best promote the interest of the community, be identified with a grant, emanating from the will or caprice of a sultan or king?" Those who contend that such a grant violates the right of property by interfering with the use of the property ignore the distinction between the title and the unlimited use of a thing. If the state, for example, should grant fishing rights on the Hudson exclusively to an individual, there is no destruction of property.[51]

However the language might be strained, monopoly was still monopoly, and people did not like it. The Federalist Gouverneur Morris warned Livingston that "the word *monopoly* is of dangerous efficiency. That envy of wealth and talents which exists everywhere is a prime mover in States, where popular power is unrestrained by political organization. It may turn the current of opinion against you, and it is too much the fashion of our day to swim with that current." [52]

The legal upshot was that during their lifetime the Fulton-Livingston monopoly was upheld by the state legislature and state courts headed by the ultra-Federalist chancellor, James Kent. It was ironic justice that Fulton's own idea of an integrated nation based on free trade was vindicated after his death by the great Federalist Chief Justice Marshall. who voided the grant, to the financial detriment of Fulton's heirs. The idea won out against private interest.

With characteristic ingenuity Fulton began to apply the steam-boat idea not only to commercial transportation, but also to larger realms of finance and war. For example, in 1814 he and his associates elaborated a complex enterprise which involved obtaining a charter for a bank with note-issuing power, the raising of funds for exploit-ing coal mines, and the transportation and supplying of coal for various uses in New York. But the legislature, by this time wary of the inflationary dangers involved in the creation of more banks, and for other reasons as well, did not accede to the request.[53]

On the outbreak of war between the United States and Great Britain in 1812, Fulton came forth with a scheme of steam frigates to serve in effect as batteries against an invasion force. He argued that a large number of frigates would be as effective as, and much cheaper than, a land force against invasion. The enemy's potential forces of 15,000 would require the maintenance of 100,000 defending Americans. This would embarrass the Treasury and cause loss of labor to farmer and artisan. As a "political economist," he calculated the loss to the country of this "productive" labor at 60 cents a day for 300 working days for 100,000 men, or $18,000,000, plus 7 per cent interest on the sum paid the same men at 50 cents a day in the Army, or $1,277,500, totaling $19,277,500 a year.

On the other hand, if the government built instead twenty frigates at $250,000 each, the annual interest charges would be, at 7 per cent, $350,000; add to this the wages of $1.00 a day for 300 men on each vessel ($2,190,000 a year) and the loss of their labor in merchant service at 60 cents a day ($1,080,000 a year), and you have a total cost of only $3,620,000 instead of $19,277,500—a saving, in short, of more than 80 per cent. In view of the brilliant successes scored by the less money-minded American naval commanders, it was perhaps fortunate that President Madison did not accept Fulton's suggestion that he be made Secretary of the Navy to put his novel plan into operation.[54]

Robert Fulton was a businessman, promoter, and engineer, but he was something more. He was also an artist and social philosopher. He was not untypical of the enterprising spirit of his era. It was an age of magnificent opportunities for men of talent with a sense of ad-venture. Rising to manhood in the troublous times of the aftermath of the American Revolutionary War, and maturing in the surround-ings of the epoch of the French Revolution, he developed great ability to adjust himself to the sudden turns and developments that were constantly occurring.

That he had great technical and inventive skill is not to be questioned. He would have liked, at least in his early days, nothing better than a substantial government pension—what government little mattered—that would enable him to devote his time exclusively to invention. But he also learned that government ministers and individuals of wealth and influence were not given to thinking in terms of the significance of inventions to progress, let alone to social welfare. Persuasion and bargaining and the promise of profit were essential elements of the situation. The contrast of his early poverty with the splendor of the English aristocracy was brought home to him sharply when he sought commissions for painting and later patronage for his canal schemes. The atmosphere of wars, Revolutionary and Napoleonic, with its sudden overnight fortunes, was capable of calling forth the highest idealism, but it also furnished opportunities for the emergence of sordid traits.

It became easy for Fulton, as he sought a place for himself, to see his inventions, useful and destructive alike, in the glowing light of human welfare and gently to convert all values into personal, money values. The "submarine" and the "torpedo" stood on the same level of civilization with the canal and the steamboat. In fact, the instruments of destruction might, in his mind, acquire an even higher value than the tools of peace. Since the wealth of England depended on commerce and her Navy protected her commerce, the real worth of his military instruments, which in the hands of another power would destroy her Navy, was obviously the profit of that commerce. He felt that he was being reasonable when he asked the British government for a minimum of £100,000, the cost of only one first-class British naval ship. By the same token the "torpedo" was just as valuable to the countries whose commerce was suffering from the "oppression" of British naval power.

Fulton was a republican patriot. In a sentimental way he loved the land of his birth, but he could convince himself and attempt to convince others that the sale of his military engines to foreign powers was not disloyal. Indifference to the great value of his services and engines by the home authorities provided a handy excuse. "Will any American or liberal-minded man call such actions sordid and wish me to abandon years of industry to the public good while neither he nor the government has offered one shilling to promote so glorious an enterprise?" [55] This attitude was not unusual for the inventor-businessmen of the day. Thus Stevens, in attempting to sell the Russian government his own plan of steam frigates and anticipating the question of why he did not sell to his own government, declared that "the indecision and procrastination which naturally pervades . . . a republican government" prevented it.[56]

To Fulton, as to all other enlightened men, monopoly was a great bugaboo. But a mind that could view the "submarine" and "torpedo" as the harbingers of perpetual peace was hardly strained to regard his steamboat privileges, which even some Federalists thought was a monopoly, as simply the reward of industry. Fulton was responding, though perhaps in an exaggerated fashion, to the old notion that great enterprises stand in need of great privileges for encouragement and protection. All too frequently, however, the contest was over who was to get the privileges, and men of all parties easily condemned in others what they themselves, when the opportunity offered, as arduously practiced and as vehemently defended as did Fulton.

Fulton was concerned with the welfare of the mass only in so far as he felt that the great leaders of industry, the technicians and inventors of all sorts, through their labor-saving devices, made possible an ever-increasing population and greater national wealth and power; for a populous and developed nation "can of course sell cheaper than her neighbour." [57]

Fulton was a republican, but he was a living example of that definition of republicanism which he gave while seeking American governmental aid for his "torpedo": "Republicans are those who labour for the public good." [58] Outright anti-Republicans among the learned gentlemen of business might, however, have much the same cast of economic mind.

JUSTUS ERICH BOLLMANN: ARTIFICER OF MONEY AND EMPIRE

Justus Erich Bollmann was a man of ability and learning. He was essentially rooted in his age, but he was no mere synthesizer or mere reflector of its fashions. He was original not only in the choice of his business activities, but also in the formulation and use of his ideas. What made him so striking a figure was the wide range, both in geographical area and in occupation, of his interests.

Bollmann was born in 1769 in Hanover, whose ruler was King of England. He received a Doctor of Medicine degree at Göttingen, and always used the degree in his signed works. He moved around the political and social centers of southern Germany and France, presumably to acquire medical knowledge. When he arrived in Paris early in 1792, he claimed that he had already been "much shaken in his professional faith from the great diversity of medical opinions, and proceedings, which he had observed among celebrated practitioners" in various places. His travels and the excitement of the Revolution whetted his appetite for adventure. He hoped to acquire success and distinction by some sudden spectacular exploits, some "romantic effort," rather than by "steady labour in a beaten track." [59] A contemporary felt that his countenance, manner, and address possessed "every qualification to engage the warmest interest in his favour as a scholar, a gentleman, or perhaps a gallant." [60]

Bollmann was soon active in a new business of the age—the smuggling out of France of the potential victims of revolutionary justice. "His facilities were so versatile," an American Republican was later to complain, "as to render him useful to the *royalists* as well as the *republicans*." Many monarchists indeed owed their lives to his "boldness and enterprise." [61]

In 1794 Bollmann was on his way to what promised to be a crowning achievement. Lafayette, protesting against the suspension of Louis XVI, had abandoned his post in the French Army. For his trouble he was imprisoned by the enemies of France in an undisclosed fortress. Bollmann, as the agent of sympathizers of Lafayette, went through Germany under the guise of "a traveller in pursuit of instruction and knowledge," discovered where Lafayette was incarcerated, and with the help of an American effected his escape from the dungeon at Olmütz. However, all were subsequently captured.[62] Bollmann served eight months in prison and was released on condition that he never again enter Austria.

He came to the United States in 1796 with plans for another attempt at Lafayette's rescue and with expectations of rewards for his previous activities. Hamilton thought highly of him, but President Washington rightly prophesied that Bollmann will be a "troublesome guest." He asked Hamilton to inform Bollmann that Lafayette's friends here would be willing to raise sufficient money to enable Bollmann to leave the country.[63] Bollmann instead decided to settle in Philadelphia, where he opened an extensive mercantile house to deal primarily with the north German states.

He engaged in almost every operation, from dealing in colonial goods to attempting to induce wealthy acquaintances in Germany to invest in the United States through him. After several years of this relatively prosaic life, Bollmann's business failed in 1803, but he was by no means completely impoverished. Critics were unkind enough to say that he had failed not from "any natural inaptitude" for the life of a merchant, but through his "excesses in speculation and intrigue." [64] Bollmann turned from the staid business of a merchant to the more spectacular and adventurous enterprises of Spanish treasure and frontier empires. For a while, according to his story, he held a license from the Spanish Crown to trade with Spain's American colonies, which involved not only trading in goods, but also returning treasure from the mines of Spain. However, his and all other licenses were revoked in favor of a Philadelphia house from which the Spanish Ambassador to the United States, in the old-fashioned mercantilist spirit, drew "prodigious gains."

Then Bollmann turned to land speculation on the frontiers, operating especially in recently acquired Louisiana. He naturally found himself functioning alongside the great speculators, including the most famous of them all, Aaron Burr. His talents and his supposed influential contacts in Europe made him useful to Burr in his schemes for a western empire—ostensibly at the expense of Spain, but by no means precluding the possibility of getting American western territory. Bollmann became one of Burr's most important agents. In 1806 he was arrested by the American military authorities in New Orleans. He claimed he was a "mere land speculator" and told a tale of a conspiracy for President Jefferson's ear which, whether true or false, is a tribute to his imagination.

Burr and his friends, it seems, had planned to establish a monarchy in Mexico, for the Mexicans were "not fit for a republican government." It was not the "conspirators," but France, the "scourge of Europe and humanity," and her then equally detestable ally, Spain, who were scheming to regain Louisiana. Bollmann's role in the adventure was to obtain recognition and help for the new empire, at first from the American government and eventually from interested European powers. True, Burr and his agents had treated with the Spanish Ambassador, but merely in order to hoodwink the Spaniards. If they had also negotiated with the British Ambassador, it was because the British were friendly to the United States, and both countries had a strong interest in overthrowing Napoleon, whose despotic power was threatening to engulf the world.

Jefferson had earlier tried to show appreciation of Bollmann's services to Lafayette by offering him various public appointments. But now he was convinced that Bollmann had compromised himself and could not be trusted. The President nevertheless hoped that Bollmann would testify against Burr in exchange for a pardon. This Bollmann shrewdly refused to do and thus, it is thought by many students, helped materially to acquit his chief; if it is assumed that he expected Burr to be acquitted anyway, he was merely playing safe.[65]

By a new permutation of the elements in his life, Bollmann now turned—it is hard to say how seriously—to medicine. While Burr went to London for another attempt on Spanish territories, his former agent returned to New Orleans. But not for long. He soon complained that westerners had little interest in seizing Spanish possessions, and that too many doctors were there and the Americans shunned him. He decided to visit France because an old friend was now high in Napoleon's favor, and with Napoleon taking Spain over completely there might be an opportunity for him in the Spanish possessions. With this change in his hopes he naturally changed his attitude toward the Emperor. But, ironically enough, he could not leave the United States because of the embargo. Meantime, as though clearing the decks for business under Napoleon, especially when he heard erroneously that Burr had interested Napoleon in his schemes, he was glad to recall that he was to have been the personage who would make Burr's peace with Napoleon. "Does he [Napoleon] remember me?" Bollmann asked plaintively.[66]

Stranded in Philadelphia, Bollmann's main source of income now came from arduous "literary" work. If he couldn't make money from his own speculations, he might turn a penny in defending those of others, and the best opportunity lay in taking the Federalist side of the great issue of the privately controlled Bank of the United States. While the "radical" wing of the Republican Party threatened to end the institution dear to Federalism, conservative Republicans like Albert Gallatin, Madison's Secretary of Treasury, were for rechartering. Bollmann defended Gallatin's recharter proposal in his *Paragraphs on Banks* in 1810.

Carefully examined, Bollmann's publications seem to disintegrate into a mass of inconsistencies and errors. But his writings were like his character, which we cannot construct simply by describing his activities in the proper order. In addition to presenting a realistic appreciation of advanced business practice and economic theory, especially of banking. Bollmann somehow managed to develop a coherent general theory of banking and credit. Even his opponents acknowledged this.[67]

Bollmann made an impressive case for a national institution which controls the issue of paper money. A country cannot rely exclusively on a specie medium or it would be at the mercy of international fluctuations of trade and bullion, he wrote. When a bank first arose to facilitate commerce, its operations were limited by its specie holdings. But the managers soon realized that the customers made their large payments to one another by "bank credits"—that is, by checks which drained no specie from the bank but merely transferred sums from one customer's account to that of another on the bank's books. This applies only, of course, to the internal exchanges of countries which have large banks. But for international exchanges specie is still needed to settle balances because the world does not have a large bank.

The specie takes on the character of merchandise for payments of government debt abroad, East India goods, or the like—in short, for transactions where domestic produce will not be accepted, or will be less profitable than the specie, in exchange for goods wanted here. The bank, in return for the useless disgorged specie, receives interest-bearing public debt and merchants' promissory notes. The bank is thus a mint because by its loans it creates the primary circulating medium of bank credits or deposits. The loans are regulated not so much by the amount of capital or specie as by the soundness of the security in the sense of the borrower's ability to pay the required interest; and, as in the case of merchants of good credit, the bank's danger lies not in exceeding its capital, but in poor knowledge. Thus if they loan on good security, the bank can make great profits though it charge low interest and will always satisfy the community's need for circulating medium.

Now suppose the Bank of the United States were forced to wind up. The bank notes and specie of the other banks are carried to the closing bank to pay obligations. Thus they are forced to reduce their discounts, and credits in all banks are annihilated. As with the closing bank, these banks had granted credits whereby they contracted debts which "in the regular course of business they would never be called upon to discharge." As a result, since the medium essentially consists of the balances which the banks owe their customers, the calling of loans starts a cumulative fall in the price of all property that brings general desolation to all, including the stockholders. In short, the issue of the recharter involves not only the Bank of the United States, but the whole financial system of the country. In this system all the banks, large and small, share in one grand series of operations, and specie becomes quite rightly but a fraction of the circulating medium. "The banks are like a fleet," buoyed up by confidence and credit and gliding down the spacious stream of trade and prosperity, each just *comfortably ballasted with specie*, and all of them *linked together* by a mighty chain of debtors and creditors, fastened to that ballast." Should any of them, and particularly the big battleship in the middle, be forced to retard her course and anchor, the rest must do the same, "otherwise the chain begins to *pull*, and they become top heavy and upset, or else sway around and dash to atoms against each other."

But the Bank of the United States is not simply a bank which is larger than others. It also prevents excessive credits, to which banks are particularly addicted. So long as judicious industry can turn money to yield a profit above interest on the loans, there can be no excess of circulating medium; but a multiplicity of banks leads all to discount risky paper or discount notes among themselves to speculate with the proceeds, at the expense and often to the destruction of their banks; whereas the national bank's small losses on loans evidences its adherence to the canon of good security.

The ideal scheme would be one bank with branches in various states, for then all the payments would be made on the same bank, and the call for specie or its equivalent, bank notes, would be at a minimum. But, since Congress seemingly has no power to suppress the many existing banks, the proposed increased capital of the national bank which Gallatin was recommending would work toward the desired end by forcing the paltry ones into liquidation and controlling the conduct of the others. Such a bank, with its state branches, would unite the diverse areas and interests, for they would be sensible that "if you touch the banks, you touch them." The national bank is so important that it should be secured, like the judiciary, in the fundamental structure of the country and be independent of the executive and legislature.

The issue of constitutionality provoked Bollmann into the most unorthodox angle of his theory. The Constitution gives Congress the power of coining money, he argued. Now the paper of the banks has become the money of the country, especially for large transactions, in the sense of being the actual circulating medium. This makes the banks "mints." Hence Congress, in order fully to control money, must resort to the intermediary of a national bank.

Underlying Bollmann's discussion was the notion that the currency should be inconvertible and be issued by a privately operated central bank similar to the Bank of England. In a public letter addressed to Alexander Baring, head of the great financial house of Baring, he attacked the Parliamentary committee's famous *Bullion Report* which recommended that the Bank of England resume specie payments. Bollmann might have been exaggerating in claiming that Baring, who had signed the *Bullion Report*, had sent him a flattering answer after seeing the manuscript; but Bollman's letter did accord with the policy of the British government. Bollmann had intended to publish the letter in a British publication, but Robert Walsh had just started his Federalist pro-British *American Review* and was willing to pay for the article. Bollmann added an introduction explaining that America could also profit by the advice.

Had it not been for inconvertible currency, he argued, England would long since have been defeated by Napoleon. Her experience since 1797, when the Bank of England suspended specie payments, proves that such a currency supplied by a central bank is possible and desirable. In a similar crisis or war, the United States would be in greater and more imminent danger. With hundreds of independent scattered banks, and no bank to control the flow of specie, it would disappear overnight, to the ruin of the country. Of course, Bollmann continued, "excessive" issues depreciate the currency. His remedy was that the Bank of England should be limited to its present amount of notes. But Parliament should allow the bank to increase its issues whenever the mercantile public needs money or when a considerable fall in prices occurs! However, to return to the specie method would lead to unfortunate fluctuations in prices which would frustrate the rational calculation so essential to business. It would also give creditors an unfair gain.[68]

Congress refused to recharter the bank, and the owners sought a charter in Pennsylvania, the home of the mother bank. The other banks and financiers, fearful of the power of the larger institution, were opposing a charter. They were emphasizing the danger by pointing to Bollmann's own defense of the disparity between credits and issues on the one hand and specie holdings on the other. This held the great danger of huge issues by the new bank.[69] Thereupon the bank officials invited Bollmann to write an anonymous pamphlet in return for a "satisfactory compensation."

Bollmann showed that he knew how to answer his own formal arguments better than his enemies had done. Quite suddenly he stressed the importance to Pennsylvania of keeping a bank with as formidable a specie treasure as the Bank of the United States had. The state with the greatest amount of specie, he wrote, will be the most prosperous and make the rest of the Union tributary to its wealth by the great advantage of its resulting large-scale business establishments and operations. With the old bank's immense treasure, Pennsylvania would become the Holland of America; but if Pennsylvania refuses a charter, it will be in a deplorable state. The stockholders will transfer the capital intact to any state that will appreciate the opportunity. Should no state show this intelligence, a great share must be returned to the stockholders abroad. Furthermore, payment of the still outstanding claims of the bank against other banks and individuals will drain practically all the specie from the state. This argument on specie differs sharply from his previous argument for complete inconvertibility. He further contended that the bank's great size was no threat to the smaller banks. On the contrary, it was extremely useful to the smaller banks because, acting like opulent traders toward smaller traders, it gives them financial aid in emergencies and checks them when they run wild.

Turning to political arguments, Bollman showed that he was as good as the next man in using democratic arguments when the occasion suggested. He had acknowledged in *Paragraphs on Banks* that large moneyed institutions, like great disparities in wealth, have anti-democratic tendencies which are inevitable in the nature of things. He now argued that a republic resting on the sovereignty of the people need have no fear of a large chartered bank. All state officers are responsible to the people. The daily political history of the people "proves the absolute *insignificance of wealth* in the regulating of its public concerns!" How can a bank meddle in the politics of a country where four-fifths of those who solely and ultimately decide on men and measures, "*never ask for a discount or draw a check*—nay would not know what either means?"

But as he was completing the pamphlet, notice of rejection by the legislature appeared. He challenged the claim that the legislature had used its own "free and unbiased judgement. . . . The South of the

United States is jealous of the prosperity of the North—the republican zeal of our representatives has been abused." [70]

As President Madison informed Congress in 1812 of the futility of peacefully forcing England to forego the "monopoly of commerce" and the impressment of American seamen, Bollmann, now the economic expert on Walsh's *Review*, deprecated "the thirst for conquest" against a country fighting Napoleon, who had shown "enmity to popular institutions and popular governments." Repeating a frequent practice, he used economic arguments on the political battlefield. He attacked the Republicans for not having built up the nation's economy to make a war possible, and at the same time he opposed the war altogether on economic grounds. The nation lacks a navy and army, a national spirit, an adequate revenue, and public credit. It abounds in wealth, but not in money. But Bollmann was ready with the proper system for both peace and war. The firm establishment of public credit on the basis of an ample revenue and good faith is required to obtain funds. Sufficient revenue requires a good system of taxation. The tax he proposed was a direct tax, and at the time the strategy of the Federalists, in opposing the Administration and war with England, was enthusiastic support of direct taxes. The tax most correct in principle and congenial to our Federal republic is "a direct personal tax" proportioned to income. It should be called a "Union Tax," for its fund is for permanently maintaining the Union. However, the tax was to be paid merely on the oath of the payer and without investigation, in order to avoid interfering with business affairs. Honest returns will be made not only because of conscientiousness and the ease of acquiring subsistence here, but above all because of the emulatory drive to avoid making a "shabby appearance" in the collectors' book. People will consequently generally overrate their income.[71]

Laborers' wages should not be exempt, for the faculty of earning is a productive estate. Before introducing the system, a general political catechism ought to be prepared for all citizens and schools, so that everyone will understand why they ought to pay the "Union Tax honestly." Finally, every year, just before announcing the percentage of income to be taxed, the government should distribute freely among the people an annual report of its operations. Thereby the people, "particularly the poorer description, would receive something tangible in return" for their contribution, "something to take home; to be read and talked of; something to illustrate the catechism." [72].

At the same time, an adequate medium of circulation must be provided to raise the taxes and animate industry, and this was naturally Bollmann's main interest. Of course, this should be his old central bank with no direct government "interference," its notes legal tender, and state bank notes redeemable in specie or in the national bank notes. "Should a Bonaparte be at our door, and thereby cause a great export of specie, our machinery of credit [without specie payments] could continue the ordinary operations." [73]

This was followed by a criticism of the embargo preparatory to war with England, both of which steps he viewed politically as evidence of the Administration's incurable habit of truckling to Napoleon. Though the embargo and the war were undertaken to assert the freedom of foreign commerce against British "interference," the Administration, seeking to split the opposition of New Englanders by wooing the manufacturers, contended that foreign commerce was the cause of war and national distress, and that domestic manufactures made a nation truly independent. Bollmann argued with equal skill and logic that not only the mercantile and agricultural interests suffer from an embargo, but also the manufacturers. Since the principal support everywhere for manufactures is domestic consumption, the diminished national income from trade by reducing consumption must reduce the demand for domestic manufactures as well as foreign goods. [74]

In opposing the embargo Bollmann was espousing his customary doctrine of free trade. To the argument that Britain's policy represented a constraint of trade, he had the easy answer that Napoleon's success would impose a much greater constraint; and that England, in fighting him, was to that extent promoting freedom. He therefore turned his attention to demonstrating the paramount importance of international trade. Both views were elaborated on the outbreak of the war in a lengthy article which was to supply America's need for a simple statement of his "favourite science of political economy."

The concept of value is fundamental. When stated without qualifications, it means commercial value, which is fixed in any given place and period. But what causes people to trade? Some, like Adam Smith, have sought it in a peculiar propensity to truck and barter—that is, in a sort of commercial instinct; others have sought it in a certain prevailing vice of mankind. But they all have a defective psychology. The universal passion of every living creature is the desire to experience, multiply, and prolong agreeable sensations; in other words, to improve his condition. This gives rise to the concept of relative value which underlies exchange value. It is value with regard to those who actually have or need possessions. It depends entirely on 'the individual's habits, circumstances, and feelings. Consequently it is never fixed, but is constantly changing. The constantly changing difference in the relative value of commodities—in other words, "the different degree of consequence attached by various individuals to the possession of a commodity"—is the prompter of all commercial intercourse.[75] The thing acquired, therefore, is always preferred by the receiver to the thing parted with in exchange, to the mutual gain of both parties; otherwise the exchange would not be made. The amount of each party's gain is in exact proportion to the degree of difference in the relative value of the things exchanged. To a manufacturer the relative value of the commodity he brings to market is simply the expense of the raw material, the quantity of labor bestowed, and interest on the capital employed—that is, the cost. Since the object is made for sale, he can attach no particular importance to its possession. But if its relative value to consumers is very great, he obtains an excellent price. Thus a manufacturer or trader, aiming to exchange his goods with those for whom the relative value is the highest, benefits both himself and his nation by his great gains. Since diversity of habit, talent, and skill are greater between countries than within a country, the difference in relative value will be greater in foreign than in domestic trade. Therefore, abstractly considered from the standpoint of gain, foreign commerce is more beneficial than domestic commerce.[76]

When war broke out, Walsh's *Review* found it undesirable to continue publication, and Bollmann's meager income was suddenly cut. He turned more to practicing business than writing about it. The public was soon informed by Bollmann that he had succeeded in making platinum into bars, wires, spoons, and crucibles. This metal might prove a rival of gold, since it was suitable for art work and even for coinage. But he would not reveal a process which had cost him so much to develop; in short, he invited the investment of capital.[77]

In 1814, on the eve of the American peace conference at Ghent and the momentous Congress of Vienna, Bollmann was off to Europe, ostensibly on private ventures. He left bemoaning to his brother in a letter in German that the pervasive influence of "Jeffersonianismus and Jacobinismus" had debased the nation.[78] He warned his Federalist acquaintance among the commissioners, Senator James A. Bayard, that the country must make peace quickly or face utter collapse. for the drain of specie in the absence of a central bank dominating all the others must destroy confidence in bank paper.

He next informed Bayard that the British Treasury authorities, already acquainted with his published "Letter to Alexander Baring," had invited him to a conference where he had urged that England agree to liberal terms of peace with the United States. Such a course would overthrow the Republican Administration party "and cause Democracy, and Jacobinism in the United States . . . , since no longer countenanced in Europe, to die a natural death."

In Paris Bollmann likewise tried to impress William Crawford, the American minister to France, who had been a supporter of the recharter of the Bank, with his "patriotic" efforts. But Crawford warned the American commissioners that Bollmann was probably a British agent and was still in contact with "the restless and unprincipled Burr." Certainly his explanation of the private ventures that brought him to Europe made little sense. "This philosophic and science-loving man," it seems, has come "to impart to the Chymists and mechanicians of Europe, his discoveries in rendering zinc malleable, and is going to Austria, which he has been forbidden to enter, and where patents have never been granted, to establish steam-boats on the Danube." Having become a respectable businessman, he was evidently welcome in Austria.

In Vienna Bollmann felt thoroughly at home. The Congress swarmed with crowned heads, journalists, intellectuals, merchant-adventurers, and opportunists of all sorts. At the center of affairs was Metternich's right-hand man, the brilliant and ambitious Friedrich von Gentz. Another one of the group was Adam Müller, the "economic theorist" of the German romantics, who was secretly in the pay of Metternich. Both of them had an authoritarian social philosophy that somehow included support of Adam Smith and inconvertible currency. Bollmann naturally got along well with them and with others of the same kind. They were all men of intellectual ability who were busily carving out careers and incomes for themselves by taking advantage of the great opportunities in the scarcely distinguishable fields of high finance, diplomacy, and business promotion.

"My essays, though hardly attended in the United States," Bollmann wrote Bayard in a mixture of sulkiness and sanguine hope, "have been read . . . here and brought me in contact with most of the characters . . . of the Congress." The Austrian government wished him to remain to execute his monetary ideas, but he was loath to surrender his American allegiance, though a temporary residence would be useful and agreeable. For Bollmann planned to establish consular relations between Austria and the United States. He convinced Metternich, or at least he thought he did, that a highly profitable trade could be built up between the countries if only agents were appointed to supply commercial and political information. With Metternich's blessing, Bollmann left for the United States to obtain the American post to Austria for himself and attempt to sell the American government some French battleships recently acquired by Austria.[79] But President Madison could hardly be expected to have forgotten so soon Bollmann's American activities, and his mission failed.

Before returning to England for a "visit" to prosecute some "new project for manufacture," he tarried in the United States and participated in the struggle over chartering a second Bank of the United States. He was not a little exasperated at the treatment of himself and his financial schemes. In his last treatise published in the United States he explained that, "owing . . . to the natural hardness of character of all republicans, and to the peculiar frigidity of the inhabitants of this north western continent," he was, after a residence of twenty years during which he had endeavored to serve the country, nearly as unconnected with it as if he "had just dropped from the moon."

Yet he would make one last attempt to teach the Americans the truth about banking and currency—namely, that the existing inconvertible bank currency would work wonders if his scheme of a national bank were accepted. Depreciation is an evil, true enough, but appreciation—which would result from the lack of sufficient money—is worse, since it further impoverishes the poor and enriches only tne receivers of fixed incomes. Reliance upon specie, which it is not easy to increase or control, is especially unfortunate for young and growing countries.

A properly chartered central bank, led by respectable directors elected by the stockholders and reporting the general state of the bank to the government every two years, could avoid overissue and hence too sharp depreciation. If loans are limited to short-term though renewable commercial bills and the ability of the borrower to pay the interest, then the amount of inconvertible circulating medium will be adapted to the demands of the social body. By adhering to these tests the Bank of England paper preserves the value of money; while the precious metals, like other commodities, fluctuate around this standard. This system has proved so successful that most of the zealous bullionists now doubt the wisdom of the bank's resuming specie payments.

But since there existed a strong prejudice for convertibility, he proposed a compromise arrangement. This was an elaboration of the scheme proposed by another of the men involved in the "Burr conspiracy," James Workman. The government would pay the interest on the public debt in coin, and the notes of the national bank would be payable on demand in 6 per cent public-debt stock at par or in specie at the option of the bank. The payment of the interest in specie would give a specie value to the debt, and thus a par value to the notes. Thus, without the use of much metal, a connection would be established between specie and paper money.

But in any event—and here we leave economic theory for business promotion—inconvenient, dirty, disease-carrying small bank notes —those under five dollars—used by the public would be replaced by platinum token coinage which Bollmann had recently attempted to convince the Bank of England to use in place of its silver token coinage.

Both theory and promotion soon went up in smoke as Congress moved to establish a central bank issuing convertible notes and having some government-appointed directors. Bollmann, of course, was horrified at this "abortion of authority and art." [80]

Back in London, Bollmann continued to occupy himself busily in inventing, experimenting, speculating, and pamphleteering. As Parliament in 1819 prepared to follow the advice of Ricardo and the example of the United States and order the Bank of England to resume specie payments, Bollmann in two pamphlets once more pleaded for the retention of the old system, secured only by a vague "maximum" amount of inconvertible notes.

The *"popular* party" in Parliament, he said, has taken the *"aristocratic* side of the question,"* while the ministerial party defends the interests of the public at large, for resumption means an appreciating currency. This increases the burden of debt and taxation, oppresses the larger, poorer, industrious, active part of the community for the unmerited gain of the rich fixed-income receivers. The whole nation must be distressed to maintain the parity of exchanges and thus enable capitalists to speculate more advantageously in foreign funds. "The natural order of things will be reversed. Instead of a steady currency and fluctuating exchanges, we shall have steady exchanges and a fluctuating currency."

This confusion Bollmann traced to Ricardo's "one great error" in his "admirable treatise on political economy," his doctrine that value is derived from the quantum of labor required by the production of the commodity, From this doctrine Ricardo derived the stability of specie. But the true doctrine, that of Adam Smith, is that value depends on the quantity of a commodity in proportion to its uses—that is, on demand and supply. Cost of production affects the value only through its effect on supply. All value springs immediately and directly from demand. Value is but "*a species of reaction of certain moral affections of men*, upon the objects with which [they] are surrounded." It "arises from the desire of possession which an object awakens—that is to say, from *demand*." Gold, too, owes its value "to the situation it holds among the mass of things . . . as an object of desire, as a commodity demanded, in reference to the existing facility or difficulty of satisfying the demand." The quantity of gold in the world depends on a thousand circumstances beyond control; but slips of paper—bank notes—can be conveniently controlled. In short, only bank paper can be stable.[81]

In the end the respectable British, no less than republican Americans, disappointed the preacher of the true gospel of money, and dreaded specie came back.

Bollmann was no mere adventurer. At his command was the learning of the English-speaking world and the Continent. From this vast armory he drew with ease arguments to suit the occasion. He used them jauntily. Consistency was much less important than convincing as many of the people who counted as possible. The stakes were high and called for a cavalier treatment of ideas. But it is an abiding testimony to a strong intellectual streak that he generally sought to give them a form worthy of attention by the leaders of economic theory. He was pleased to be told that his *Paragraphs on Banks* would have done honor to Adam Smith. He regarded himself as a "theorist," but this simply meant a franchise to choose the facts that suited his argument. The "theorist," he said in his article on "Political Economy"' must proceed from speculative grounds, for "facts [are] always difficult to collect correctly and extremely difficult correctly to understand." Yet he must verify the conclusions by an appeal to the huge and vague area of "experience," which all too frequently turned out to be mere assertion rather than examined history. "Theory" after all was to Bollmann an instrument in the game of persuasion, and he would shift from one "school" or authority to another, even within the same discussion. But back of all his winding ran a thread of consistency: the adherence to orders in society and traditional authority for which Burke had brilliantly set the fashion and which βollmann's German brethren who swarmed around the Congress of Vienna elaborated over and over again.

This doctrine Bollmann did not state in authoritarian terms; on the contrary, he presented it as the idea of freedom—the freedom not of democracy, but of that "rational independence" which was vouchsafed only to Britons and their descendants in America. Such Anglo-Saxonism was but a detour from Germanism, for the enterprising love of independence is traceable to the "woods of ancient Germany." The primitive Germans were first to conceive that love of liberty which was later refined by wise men and then incorporated in British institutions and woven into British custom. Freedom cannot be "established"; it is attained only by a long historic process which develops the "habits of freemen in those to be governed. . . . *What they have been*" rather "than *what they wish to be*" determines the character of nations. France, who thought it was "only necessary to *know* and to *will*, in order to *grasp* and *possess*" these sources of political happiness, produced only "the tyranny of unprincipled demagogues and military leaders." [82]

Liberty, which leads to inequality of wealth, does not connote democracy. For there is a natural clash between the generously propertied and the large moneyed institutions on the one hand and the jealous populace on the other. In the last analysis, the inevitable growth of economic inequality spells the doom of the republican form of government. Freedom can only mean the ability of the adventurous to move spontaneously in the search of distinction and the good things of life. The social contract itself, Bollmann once observed, is after all made for the accumulation of wealth.

Bibliographic Notes

The spelling for the earlier period of this study generally has been modernized; a few quoted passages are given in the original in order to help convey to the readers the flavor of the times. The Congressional debates referred to in the text are to be found for the appropriate dates in the *Annals of Congress* and its successors, the *Register of Debates in Congress*, and the *Congressional Globe*.

CHAPTER I

1. *The Clarke Papers*, edited by C. H. Firth, London, 1891, I, 301-302.
2. "Court Book," February 6, 1635, in Ethel Bruce Sainsbury, *A Calendar of the Court Minutes, etc., of the East India Company, 1635-1639*, Oxford, 1907, p. 18.
3. Edward Misselden, *The Circle of Commerce*, London, 1623, p. 17.
4. "Instructions Touching the Bill for Free Trade," 1604, in *English Economic History; Select Documents*, edited by A. E. Bland, P. A. Brown, R. H. Tawney, London, 1921, pp. 443-449.
5. *Political Arithmetick*, 1690; reprinted in *The Economic Writings of Sir William Petty*, edited by C. H. Hull, Cambridge, 1899, I, 275.
6. Dudley Digges, *The Defence of Trade*, London, 1615, pp. 32-33.
7. Milton, *Of Reformation Touching Church-Discipline in England*, 1641, reprinted in *Milton's Prose*, edited by Malcolm W. Wallace, London, 1925, p. 51.
8. "A Justification of Separation from the Church of England," 1610, in *Works*, edited by Robert Ashton, London, 1851, II, 140, 212, 223, 314-315; "A Just and Necessary Apology," 1625, *ibid.*, III, 42-43.
9. For a definitive discussion of non-Separatist Congregationalism, see Perry Miller, *Orthodoxy in Massachusetts, 1630-1650*, Cambridge, 1933, pp. 86-90.
10. "Common Grievances Groaning for Reformation," 1624, in *Winthrop Papers*, Boston, 1929, I, 302, 307.

CHAPTER II

1. Robert Johnson, *Nova Brittania*, 1609, reprinted Rochester, New York, 1897, pp. 10-13, 23-24; Patrick Copland, *Virginia's God Be Thanked*, London, 1622; Alexander Whitaker, *Good Newes from Virginia*, 1636, reprinted New York, 1936, pp. 1-2; "A True Declaration of the Estate of the Colony of Virginia," 1610, reprinted in *Tracts and other Papers*, collected by Peter Force, Washington, 1844, III, 17; "Laws Divine, Morall and Martiall," gathered by William Strachey, 1612; reprinted in *Tracts*, III, 12.
2. *The Records of the Virginia Company of London*, edited by Susan M. Kingsbury, Washington, 1906-1935, III, 221, 457, 489, 505; IV, 108, 235, 268, 269.
3. J. P. Baxter, *Sir Ferdinando Gorges*, Boston, 1890, I, 223; II, 37.

4. *Records of the Virginia Company of London*, II, 148; III, 473, 486–487, 496, 557–559, 666, 690; IV, 49–52, 262–266, 478–479.

5. *Records of the Virginia Company*, II, 256–258; III, 606; IV, 69, 194–195. *Statutes at Large of Virginia*, edited by W. W. Hening, I, 230–238. *Travels and Works of Captain John Smith*, Arber edition, 1910, II, 610–620. Wesley Frank Craven, *Dissolution of the Virginia Company*, New York, 1932, pp. 220–291.

6. Samuel Fortrey, *Englands Interest and Improvement*, 1663, reprinted Baltimore, 1907, p. 35.

7. *Calendar of State Papers, Colonial Series, America and West Indies*, 1681–1685, p. 152.

8. *Statutes at Large of Virginia*, I, 308.

9. *Calendar of State Papers, Colonial Series, America and West Indies*, 1681–1685, pp. 691–694; *ibid.*, 1685–1688, p. 362.

10. *Calendar of Virginia State Papers*, I, p. 53.

11. H. Hartwell, J. Blair, and E. Chilton, *The Present State of Virginia and the College*, 1697; first printed, 1727; reprinted, with an introduction by H. D. Farish, Williamsburg, Va., 1940, pp. 8–20.

12. *Statutes at Large of Virginia*, I, 336.

13. Charles Molloys, *De jure maritimo et navali*, London, 1690 edition, p. 356.

14. William B. Weeden, *Economic and Social History of New England*, Boston and New York, 1890, I, 339–340.

15. "Speeches of Students of the College of William and Mary," delivered May 1, 1699, *William and Mary College Quarterly*, 1930, 2nd series, X, 327.

16. "Lord Baltimore to the Lords of Trade and Plantations," March 26, 1678, in *Calendar of State Papers, . . . America and West Indies*, 1677–1680, p. 227.

17. C. M. Andrews, *The Colonial Period in American History*, New Haven, 1937, III, 223.

18. T. Ashe, "Carolina," 1682, reprinted in *Historical Collections of South Carolina*, edited by B. R. Carroll, New York, 1836, II, 67–84.

CHAPTER III

1. William Bradford, *History of Plymouth Plantation*, Massachusetts Historical Society edition, Boston, 1912, I, 109, 115, 301–302, 324, 372, 373, 449–456; II, 8, 348. Robert Cushman, *A Sermon Describing the Sin and Danger of Self-Love, Preached at Plymouth in New England*, 1621; Stockbridge, 1822, pp. 29, 32–33; John Winthrop, *History of New England*, Savage edition, Boston, 1853, I, 156.

2. "General Observations for the Plantation of New England," 1629, in *Winthrop Papers*, Boston, 1931, II, 110–149.

3. "John Cotton to Lord Saye and Sele," 1636, in Thomas Hutchinson, *The History of the Colony and Province of Massachusetts-Bay*, 1764, L. S. Mayo edition, Cambridge, 1936, I, 414.

4. John Cotton, *The Keyes of the Kingdom of Heaven*, 1644, reprinted Boston, 1852, pp. 41, 44, 52.

5. Cited in Williston Walker, *A History of the Congregational Churches in the United States*, New York, 1894, p. 46.

6. *The Happiness of a People*, Boston, 1676, pp. 8–10, 33.

7. "John Cotton to Lord Saye and Sele," 1636, in Hutchinson, *op. cit.*, I, 415.

8. Reply to Winthrop, 1638, in *Collections of Connecticut Historical Society*, Hartford, 1860, I, 11.

9. "Two Sermons," *ibid.*, I, 21.

10. "A Sermon Preach'd at the Election of the Governour, at Boston in New England, May 19, 1669," printed 1670, facsimile in *Transactions of the Colonial Society of Massachusetts, 1904-1906*, Boston, 1907, X.

11. "A Declaration of the General Court Holden at Boston, 4, (9), 1646," in *Hutchinson Papers*, Albany, 1868, II, 227.

12. Cotton, *A Briefe Exposition With Practicall Observations Upon the Whole Book of Ecclesiastes*, London, 1657, p. 92.

13. Cotton, *A Practicall Commentary, or An Exposition With Observations, Reasons, and Uses Upon the First Epistle Generall of John*, 2nd edition, London, 1658, p. 132.

14. *New England's First Fruits*, London, 1643, p. 23.

15. "A Discourse Concerning the Danger of Apostasy," delivered in 1677, in *A Call from Heaven*, Boston, 1679, p. 108.

16. *A Sermon . . . Wherein is Shewed that Excess in Wickedness doth bring Untimely Death*, 2nd edition, Boston, 1685, p. 27.

17. *Massachusetts Colonial Records*, I, 109.

18. *Ibid.*, I, 109-111, 223, 226.

19. Given in Richard B. Morris and Jonathan Grossman, "The Regulation of Wages in Early Massachusetts," in *The New England Quarterly*, II, (September 1938), 481-488.

20. *Massachusetts Colonial Records*, V, 62-63; *Laws*, 1660, p. 236.

21. *Plymouth Records*, IX, 81.

22. "To John Winthrop," 1645, in *Collections of the Massachusetts Historical Society*, 4th series, Boston, 1863, VI, 65.

23. "Governor William Leete to the Lords Committee of the Council for Trade and Plantations," July 15, 1680, in *Calendar of State Papers, . . . America and West Indies, 1677-1680*, pp. 576-577.

24. John Winthrop, *The History of New England*, I, 377-382.

25. "The Last Will and Testament of Me, Robert Keayne," in *A Report of the Record Commissioners of the City of Boston, Containing Miscellaneous Papers*, Boston, 1886, pp. 30, 34.

26. "Winslow to Winthrop," 1640, in *Collections of the Massachusetts Historical Society*, 4th series, Boston, 1863, VI, 166.

27. *Massachusetts Colonial Records*, I, 307.

28. Bradford, *History of Plymouth Plantation*, II, 311.

29. "William Pynchon to Roger Ludlow," January 19, 1637/1638, *Proceedings of the Massachusetts Historical Society* (1924-1925), LVIII, 388.

30. "Statement," *ibid.*, XLVIII (1914-1915), 47-48.

31. Samuel Eliot Morison, "William Pynchon, Founder of Springfield," *ibid.*, LXIV (1930-1932), 67-111.

32. *Plymouth Records*, IX, 172-173, 176.

33. *Massachusetts Colonial Records*, V, 200.

34. "Essay on the Ordering of Towns," 1635, in *Winthrop Papers*, Boston, 1943, III, 182.

35. "A Reply to Mr. Williams," 1647, in *Publications of the Narragansett Club*, Providence, 1867, II, 46-47.

36. S. S. Crosby, *The Early Coins of America*, Boston, 1875, pp. 104, 421.

37. "The Diaries of John Hull," in *Transactions and Collections of the American Antiquarian Society*, Boston, 1857, III, 211, 300-309.

38. "The Necessity of Reformation, with the Expedients Subservient thereunto agreed upon by a Synod in 1679," in *The Results of Three Synods*, Boston, 1725, p. 110.

39. *Calendar of State Papers, . . . America and West Indies, 1685-1688*, pp.

266–267; C. P. Nettels, *The Money Supply of the American Colonies Before 1720*, Madison, Wisconsin, 1934, pp. 171–173.

40. "Subjects for Masters Degree, 1655–1791," in *Proceedings of the Massachusetts Historical Society*, 1880–1881, Boston, 1881, XVIII, 129–130.

41. *Thirty Important Cases, Resolved With Evidence of Scripture and Reason*, Boston, 1699, p. 27.

42. *A Compleat Book of Divinity*, Boston, 1726, pp. 634–635.

43. *The Great Blessings, of Primitive Counsellours*, Boston, 1693, p. 19.

44. "The Bostonian Ebenezer," 1698, reprinted in *Magnalia Christi Americana*, 1702, Hartford, 1820, I, 94–95.

45. *Rules for the Society of Negroes*, 1693, reprinted New York, 1888, p. 8.

46. "The Selling of Joseph," 1700; "Computation that the Importation of Negroes is not so Profitable as that of White Servants," 1706, reprinted in *Historical Magazine*, June 1864, pp. 194–199.

47. Andrew McFarland Davis, *Colonial Currency Reprints, 1682–1751*, Boston, 1910, I, 150.

48. John Saffin, "A Brief and Candid Answer to a Late Printed Sheet, Entituled, the Selling of Joseph," Boston, 1701; manuscript transcript in New York Public Library, pp. 1–5.

49. "Letter Book of Samuel Sewall, I," in *Collections of the Massachusetts Historical Society*, 6th series, 1886, I, 332, n.

CHAPTER IV

1. "Experiencia," 1607, in *Winthrop Papers*, I, 162–163.

2. *Winthrop Papers*, II, 125–126.

3. Appendix in Robert C. Winthrop, *Life and Letters of John Winthrop*, Boston, 1867, II, 430.

4. John Winthrop, *History of New England*, I, 138, 182; II, 29, 269–270, 280–282.

5. R. C. Winthrop, *op. cit.*, II, 237.

6. "To Lady Barrington," May 2, 1629, in the *New-England Historical and Genealogical Register*, XLIII (July 1889), 319

7. *New-England's Sence, of Old-England and Irelands Sorrowes*, London, 1645, p. 27.

8. *Massachusetts Colonial Records*, I, 160, 161.

9. "Letters of Roger Williams," in *Publications of the Narragansett Club*, Providence, 1874, VI, 3–6.

10. "Mr. Cotton's Letter Lately Printed, Examined and Answered," 1644, in *Publications of the Narragansett Club*, Providence, 1866, I, 322.

11. "Queries of Highest Consideration," 1644, in *Publications of the Narragansett Club*, Providence, 1867, II, 262.

12. To Mr. Daniel Abbott, January 15, 1680/1681 in "Letters of Roger Williams," *Publications of the Narragansett Club*, Providence, 1874, VI, 401, 402.

13. "To Winthrop," July 31, November 10, 1637, *ibid.*, pp. 54, 105.

14. "To the General Court of Massachusetts Bay," October 5, 1654, *ibid.*, p. 276.

15. *Experiments of Spiritual Life & Health, and Their Preservatives*, 1652; 1863 edition, p. 15.

16. "A Key into the Language of America," 1643, reprinted in the *Publications of the Narragansett Club*, Providence, 1866, I, 245.

17. "To John Winthrop, Jr.," May 28, 1664, in "Letters of Roger Williams," p. 319.

18. "George Fox Digg'd out of his Burrowes," 1676, reprinted in *Publications of the Narragansett Club*, Providence, 1872, V, 5, 248, 307, 309.

CHAPTER V

1. "Additional Observations on the Preceding Petition," 1649, in *Documents Relative to the Colonial History of New York*, edited by E. B. O'Callaghan, Albany, 1858, I, 263; "The Magistrates of Gravesend to the Directors in Amsterdam," September 14, 1651, *ibid.*, II, 155-156; Alexander C. Flick, *History of the State of New York*, New York, 1933, I, 337.
2. Joel Munsell, *The Annals of Albany*, Albany, 1871, IV, 78-79.
3. Notes appended to Daniel Denton, *A Brief Description of New York*, 1670, edited by Gabriel Furman, New York, 1845, pp. 42-43.
4. Cornelis Van Tienhoven, "Answer to the Representation of New Netherland," 1650, reprinted in *Narratives of New Netherland*, edited by J. Franklin Jameson, New York, 1909, p. 365.
5. *Calendar of State Papers, . . . America and the West Indies*, 1697-1698, pp. 456-459.

CHAPTER VI

1. "Some Fruits of Solitude," 1693, reprinted in *The Peace of Europe, Some Fruits of Solitude and Other Writings*, edited by Joseph Besse, Everyman's edition, p. 61.
2. "Just Measures," 1692, in *The Select Works of William Penn*, 3rd edition, London, 1782, IV, 440-446.
3. *The Spirit of Alexander The Copper-Smith, Justly Rebuk'd*, London, 1673, p. 12.
4. "No Cross, no Crown," 1669, in *Works*, II, 121.
5. "Penn to the Lords Justices of Ireland," July 1, 1698, in the Historical Society of Pennsylvania.
6. "England's Present Interest Considered," 1675, in *Works*, III, 209; "An Address to the Protestants of all Persuasions," 1679, *ibid.*, IV, 178; "England's Great Interest in the Choice of this New Parliament," 1679, *ibid.*, IV, 245-246.
7. "One Project for the Good of England," 1679, *ibid.*, IV, 262.
8. "Fragments of an Apology for Himself," 1668-1695, copied from the original autographs in the Library of the American Philosophical Society, printed in *Memoirs*, Historical Society of Pennsylvania, Philadelphia, 1736, Vol. III, Part 2, pp. 237-238.
9. *The Protestant's Remonstrance*, London, 1681, pp. 13, 14, 25-26, 33-34.
10. "Some Account of the Province of Pennsylvania in America Made Public for the Information of Such as are or May be Disposed to Transport Themselves or Servants Into Those Parts," 1681, in Hazard, *The Register of Pennsylvania*, May 17, 1828, pp. 306-308.
11. Daniel B. Shumway, "A Rare Dutch Document Concerning the Province of Pennsylvania in the Seventeenth Century," in *Pennsylvania Magazine of History and Biography*, 1925, XXXIX, 99-140; Gabriel Thomas, "An Historical and Geographical Account of Pennsilvania and of West-New-Jersey," 1698; Penn, "A Further Account of the Province of Pennsylvania," 1685, in *Narratives of Early Pennsylvania, West New Jersey, and Delaware, 1630-1707*, New York, 1912, pp. 259-279, 307-352.

12. *Proceedings and Debates of the British Parliaments Respecting North America*, edited by Leo Francis Stock, II, 200.

13. *Colonial Records of Pennsylvania*, I, 98.

14. "To Nicholson," December 31, 1700, in the Historical Society of Pennsylvania.

15. "To James Harrison," October 25, 1685, in the Historical Society of Pennsylvania.

16. William Hull, *William Penn, and the Dutch Quaker Migration to Pennsylvania*, Swarthmore, Pennsylvania, 1935, pp. 294-299.

17. Prospectus reprinted in Hazard, *Annals of Pennsylvania*, Philadelphia, 1850, p. 551.

18. "To Logan," February 20, 1702/1703, in *Correspondence Between William Penn and James Logan*, with notes by the late Mrs. Deborah Logan, edited with additional notes by Edward Armstrong, Philadelphia, 1872, I, 164.

19. "To the Council of Trade and Plantations," March 6, 1701, *Calendar of State Papers, . . . America and West Indies*, 1701, pp. 110-111.

20. "To Harley," 1701, in *Historical Manuscripts Commission*, 15th Report, Appendix, Part IV, *Duke of Portland Manuscripts*, p. 30.

21. *Documents Relative to the Colonial History of the State of New York*, edited by E. B. O'Callaghan, IV, 757.

22. "To Logan," September 14, 1705, in Armstrong, *Correspondence*, II, 74.

23. "To the Council of Trade and Plantations, April 21, 1703, *Calendar of State Papers, . . . America and West Indies*, 1702-1703, p. 369.

24. "To Logan," December 4, 1703, Armstrong, *Correspondence*, I, 248.

25. *Colonial Records of Pennsylvania*, II, 27.

26. *Acts of the General Assembly Hitherto Unprinted*, 1694-1722, in *Archives of Maryland*, Baltimore, 1918, XVII, 9.

27. *Documents Relative to the Colonial History of the State of New York*, IV, 33.

28. "To Charles Lawton," December 21, 1700, in the Historical Society of Pennsylvania.

29. "To Logan," March 9, 1705/1706, Armstrong, *Correspondence*, II, 105.

30. "To Roger Mompesson," February 17, 1704/1705; "To Logan," July 12, 1704; *ibid.*, I, 305, 374.

31. "To Harley," February 9, 1703-1704, in *Historical Manuscripts Commission, op. cit.*, p. 81; "Proposals to the Lords Commissioners for Trade and Plantations about the Surrender of the government of my province of Pennsylvania," June 18, 1703, and "Report of the Commissioners of Trade and Plantations," December 16, 1703, in *Proceedings and Debates of the British Parliaments*, III, 16-17.

32. "Penn's Instructions to his Commissioners," in *Memoirs*, Historical Society of Pennsylvania, Vol. II, Part 1, pp. 220-221.

33. "Sir Robert Southwell to Petty," September 19, 1685, in *The Petty-Southwell Correspondence*, edited by the Marquis of Lansdowne, London, 1928, p. 155; "Petty to Southwell," September 26, 1685, *ibid.*, p. 168.

34. "To Jasper," February 5, 1682/1683, in the Historical Society of Pennsylvania.

35. M. D. Learned, "From Pastorius' Beehive," *Americana Germanica*, Vol. I, No. 4 (1897), p. 98.

36. For a general discussion of Penn's social philosophy, see Edward Beatty, *William Penn as Social Philosopher*, New York, 1933.

CHAPTER VII

1. Cotton Mather, *Magnalia Christi Americana*, I, 542-543.
2. Frederick J. Shepard, ed., *Good Order Established in Pennsylvania and New Jersey*, Cleveland, 1902, Introduction.
3. "To Robert Turner," no date, in "Letters of William Penn," *Pennsylvania Magazine of History and Biography*, XXIII (1909), 311.
4. *The Petty Papers*, edited by the Marquis of Lansdowne, London, 1927, II, 114.
5. *Calendar of State Papers, Domestic Series*, 1690, p. 201; *Calendar of State Papers, Ireland*, 1660-1662, pp. 433-436.
6. John T. Hassam, "The Bahama Islands," in *Proceedings of the Massachusetts Historical Society*, 2nd series, XIII (1899-1900), 26-27.
7. *Calendar of State Papers, Ireland*, 1663-1665, pp. 645-646.
8. Robert N. Toppan, "Dudley Records," in *Proceedings of the Massachusetts Historical Society*, 2nd series, XIII (1899-1900), 255.
9. *Colonial Currency Reprints*, edited by Andrew McFarland Davis, Boston, 1910, I, 8-14, 137, 146-151.
10. Andrew McFarland Davis, "Was It Andros?" in *Proceedings of the American Antiquarian Society*, New Series, XVIII, 346-360.
11. "Letter from Penn," September 24, 1688, in Hazard, *The Register of Pennsylvania*, August 15, 1829, p. 105.
12. *Colonial Records of Pennsylvania*, I, 236.
13. "To Penn," January 25, 1688/1689, *Pennsylvania Magazine of History and Biography*, LXIX (July 1945), 233-237.
14. "To Penn," June 24, 1689, *ibid.*, VI, 363-364.
15. Penn to Blackwell, September 25, 1689, *ibid.*, XXXIII (1909), 314. Another letter of same date in the Historical Society of Pennsylvania.
16. Quoted in Arthur Pound, *The Penns of Pennsylvania and England*, New York, 1932, p. 217.
17. Cited in Andrew McFarland Davis, "Currency and Banking in the Province of the Massachusetts Bay, Part I," in *Publications of the American Economic Association*, 3rd series, I (1900), 8-15.
18. *Collections of the Massachusetts Historical Society*, 2nd series (1846), III, 260.
19. *Diary of Cotton Mather II*, *ibid.*, 7th series, VIII (1912), 296.
20. *Calendar of Treasury Books*, Vol. X, Part I, p. 179.
21. *An Essay Towards Carrying on the Present War Against France and Other Publick Occasions*, London, 1695.
22. "A True and Exact . . . Inventory of . . . Sir Lambert Blackwell, Bart. . . ." London, 1721, p. 8, in *Accounts of the Estates of the Directors of the South Sea Company*, 1721-1723, I.
23. "Penn to the Council of Trade and Plantations," March 6, 1701, in *Calendar of State Papers, . . . America and West Indies*, 1701, p. 111.
24. "Penn to Logan," April 30, 1703, Armstrong, *Correspondence*, II, 15.

CHAPTER VIII

1. Verner W. Crane, "A Lost Utopia of the First American Frontier," in *The Sewanee Review*, XXVIII (January 1919), 48-61.
2. Cited from the will of Mrs. Anne Beckham, 1736, in Mrs. Philip Wallace

Hiden, "The Money of Colonial Virginia," in *Virginia Magazine of History and Biography*, LI (January 1943), 52.

3. Alexander Cowie, *Educational Problems at Yale College in the Eighteenth Century*, New Haven, 1936, p. 5.

4. William Smith and James Jay, *An Humble Representation*, London, 1762.

5. *An Inquiry Into the Human Mind, on the Principles of Common Sense*, Hamilton's edition of *Reid's Works*, 8th edition, Edinburgh, 1880, I, 118; *Essays on the Intellectual Powers of Man, ibid.*, p. 434.

6. Cited in V. L. Collins, *President Witherspoon*, Princeton, 1925, I, 141.

7. *A Brief State of the Province of Pennsylvania*, London, 1755, p. 6.

8. "Observations on the Balance of Power in Government"; "Address to the Freeholders and Freemen," *Cadwallader Colden Papers*, IX, 252-253; III, 328; "An Account of Governor Clinton's Administration," MS. in the New York Historical Society.

9. *Boston Evening Post*, January 4, 1762.

10. *Boston Gazette*, January 11, 1762.

11. See his 1764 edition of William Wood's *New England's Prospect*, p. 90 n.

12. "The Rights of the British Colonies Asserted and Proved," 1764, reprinted in Charles F. Mullett, "Some Political Writings of James Otis," Part I, in *The University of Missouri Studies*, IV (July 1, 1929), 308.

13. *The Good of the Community impartially considered*, Boston, 1754, p. 45.

14. Maurice Moore, "The Justice and Policy of Taxing the American Colonies in England," 1763, in *Some Eighteenth Century Tracts Concerning North Carolina*, edited by W. K. Boyd, Raleigh, N.C., 1927, pp. 165-174.

15. "Publius Agricola," in *Maryland Gazette*, December 23, 1746.

16. "An Addition to the Present Melancholy Circumstances of the Province Considered," 1719, in *Colonial Currency Reprints*, I, 373-374.

17. "Address to the Freemen and Freeholders of the City of New York," in New York *Weekly Journal*, May 23, 1737. The style is that of Colden.

18. "Logan to Penn," August 22, 1705, in *Correspondence*, II, 54.

19. "Letter of 'A.B.' to the printer" in *Maryland Gazette*, November 16, 1769

20. The Reverend Thomas Barnard, *A Sermon Preached in Boston . . . Before the Society for Encouraging Industry, and Employing the Poor*, Boston, 1758, p. 19.

21. *Doct. Gale's Letter, to J. W. Esquire*, Hartford, 1769, pp. 21-23.

22. *The Correspondence of James Logan and Thomas Story*, edited by Norman Penney, Philadelphia, 1927, p. 87.

23. "To James Tilghman, Jr.," February 17, 1774, in *The Writings of George Washington*, edited by John C. Fitzpatrick, Washington, 1931-1941, III, 187.

24. Pat. Tailfer, Hugh Anderson, *et al.*, *A True and Historical Narrative of the Colony of Georgia in America*, 1741, reprint of 1897, pp. 24-25, 89.

25. L. Tyerman, *The Life and Times of John Wesley*, New York, 1872, II, 132.

26. "Votes and Proceedings of the House of Representatives of the Province of Pennsylvania," 1722-1723, *Pennsylvania Archives*, 8th series, II, 1477.

27. "Observations On and Answers to the Foregoing Report," 1772, in *The Writings of Benjamin Franklin*, edited by Albert Henry Smyth, V, 518. This report has been generally attributed to Franklin in the past, but for Wharton's authorship see Clarence Walworth Alvord, *The Mississippi Valley in British Politics*, Cleveland, 1917, II, 134.

28. Samuel Sewall, *Diary*, II, *Collections of the Massachusetts Historical Society*, Boston, 1889, 5th series, VI, 281.

29. "The Board of Trade to Sir William Johnson," July 18, 1764, in *Cadwallader Colden Papers*, VI, 327.

30. "An Answer to Some Cases of Conscience," 1722, reprinted in *Magazine of History with Notes and Queries*, Extra Number 55, 1917, pp. 14–15.

31. Benjamin Colman, *Some Reasons and Arguments Offered to the Good People of Boston and Adjacent Places, for the Setting up Markets in Boston*, Boston, 1719, pp. 8–9, 11–12.

32. "A Brief Account of the Rise, Progress and Present State of the Paper Currency of New England," 1749, reprinted in *Colonial Currency Reprints*, IV, 392–393.

33. Letter to the editor, signed "A Planter," in *Virginia Gazette*, week of October 27–November 3, 1738.

34. *Calendar of State Papers, . . . America and the West Indies*, 1731, pp. 47–50, 57; *ibid.*, 1732, pp. 93–98.

35. *Maryland Gazette*, May 30, July 12, 1753.

36. Letter signed "Philopatris," in *Virginia Gazette*, week of April 28–May 5, 1738.

37. *Maryland Gazette*, February 25, 1762.

38. "An Essay on the Means of Improving the Trade of Maryland," in *Maryland Gazette*, December 9, 16, 23, 30, 1747.

39. *Maryland Gazette*, February 11, 1762.

40. "Washington to Thomas Johnson," July 20, 1770, in Washington's *Writings*, III, 17–20.

41. "Mason to Washington," February 17, 1775, in Kate Rowland, *The Life of George Mason*, New York and London, 1892, I, 187.

42. "To Jefferson," March 29, 1784, in Washington's *Writings*, XXVII, 374.

43. *Maryland Gazette*, March 11, 1762, in *Boston Weekly News-Letter*, September 2, 1762.

44. "An Impartial Relation," 1770, reprinted in *Some Eighteenth Century Tracts Concerning North Carolina*, p. 318.

45. "Publius Agricola," in *Maryland Gazette*, December 16, 1746.

46. "Pastorius' Essay on Taxes," with an introduction and notes by Henry J. Cadbury, in *Pennsylvania Magazine of History and Biography*, LVII (1934), 258.

47. Original manuscript, *The Second Part of the Interest of the Country in Laying Duties*, printed in *Cadwallader Colden Papers*, IX, 267–279. *The Two Interests Reconciled* has heretofore not been attributed to Colden or to any other person, but a comparison of it with the manuscript of *The Second Part* reveals a substantial similarity.

48. See Colden's "Comments on Government in General," MS. in the New York Historical Society.

49. *Boston Weekly News-Letter*, June 20, 1754.

50. *Some Observations on the Bill* and Samuel Cooper, *The Crisis*, Boston, 1754.

51. *A Plea for the Poor and the Distressed Against the Bill for Granting an Excise Upon Wines and Spirits, Distilled, Sold by Retail, or Consumed within this Province*, Boston, 1754.

52. *Boston Weekly News-Letter*, June 27, 1754.

53. *Pennsylvania Archives*, 8th series, V, 3819.

54. *A Report of the Record Commissioners of the City of Boston Containing the Boston Records for 1729 to 1742*, Boston, 1885, p. 123.

55. "Dissertation II," in *Four Dissertations, on the Reciprocal Advantages of a Perpetual Union between Great-Britain and Her American Colonies, Written for Mr. Sargent's Prize-Medal*, Philadelphia, 1766, p. 71.

56. Cadwallader Colden, "Of the Trade of New York," 1723, in *Documents Relative to the Colonial History of the State of New York*, V, 688–690.

57. "Memorial to the Council of Trade and Plantations," in *Calendar of State Papers, . . . America and West Indies,* 1720–1721, p. 473.

58. *Ibid.,* 1731, pp. 257–262, 383–384.

59. John Ashley, *The British Empire in America, Consider'd,* London, 1733, p. 26; *Proposals Offered for the Sugar Planters Redress, and for Reviving the British Sugar Commerce,* London, 1733, p. 28.

60. "The Rights of the British Colonies Asserted and Proved," pp. 339, 341–342; "Considerations on Behalf of the Colonists," 1765, in Mullett, "Some Political Writings of James Otis," Part II, in *University of Missouri Studies,* IV (October 1929), 372.

61. "Dissertation I," in *Four Dissertations,* pp. 16, 22, 23.

CHAPTER IX

1. Samuel Sewall, *Diary,* II, 365–366.

2. "A Letter from One in Boston to his Friend in the Country," 1714; "A Vindication of the Bank of Credit," 1714, in *Colonial Currency Reprints,* I, 264–292, 296–312.

3. *Diary of Cotton Mather,* II, in *Collections of the Massachusetts Historical Society,* 7th series, VIII, 295–297.

4. "The Present Melancholy Circumstances of the Province Considered," 1719; "An Addition to the Present Melancholy Circumstances of the Province Considered," 1719, in *Colonial Currency Reprints,* I, 351–396.

5. "Burnet to the Council of Trade and Plantations," November 21, 1724, in *Calendar of State Papers, . . . America and West Indies,* 1723–1724, pp. 409–411; "Messages to the House," September 17, 23, 1728, in *Journals of the House of Representatives of Massachusetts,* 1727–1729, Boston, 1927, pp. 327, 340.

6. "The Distressed State of the Town of Boston, etc., Considered," 1720, in *Colonial Currency Reprints,* I, 398–408.

7. *The Boston News-Letter,* April 18, 1720; "A Letter from One in the Country to his Friend in Boston," 1720; "A Vindication of the Remarks of One in the Country Upon the Distressed State of Boston," 1720; "A Project for the Emission of an Hundred Thousand Pounds of Province Bills," 1720, in *Colonial Currency Reprints,* I, 409–412, 416–442; II, 20–40, 139–156.

8. *Colonial Currency Reprints,* III, 29–46.

9. "To Warham Mather," January 20, 1734/1735, *Belcher Papers,* Part II, in *Collections of the Massachusetts Historical Society,* 6th series, VII (1894), 187.

10. "Committee Report of April 28, 1736," in *A Report of the Record Commissioners of the City of Boston Containing the Records from 1729 to 1742,* Boston, 1885, pp. 145–146.

11. *Proceedings and Debates of the British Parliaments Respecting North America,* V, 97–98.

12. "Some Observations on the Scheme projected for emitting £60,000 . . . ," 1738; "An Inquiry into the Nature and Uses of Money," 1740; in *Colonial Currency Reprints,* III, 181–312, 366–474.

13. *Boston Weekly News-Letter,* week of March 23–30, 1738.

. 14. "An Essay Concerning Silver and Paper Currency," 1738; "Discourse Concerning the Currencies of the British Plantations in America," 1740; "Postscript to a Discourse Concerning the Currencies," 1740; "A Letter to . . . Merchant in London," 1741; "A Second Letter to . . . Merchant in London," 1741; in *Colonial Currency Reprints,* III, 217–250, 307–356; IV, 45–80, 113–130.

15. "To Douglass," January 4, 1739/1740, New York Historical Society.

16. "Governor Shirley to the Board of Trade," March 19, 1742/43, in Columbia University Library.

17. Mr. Turell's *Brief and Plain Exhortation to his People, On the Late Fast*, January 28, 1747/48, Boston, 1748, p. 5; Nathanael Hunn, *The Welfare of a Government Considered*, New London, 1747, pp. 11–13.

18. *Civil Magistrates must be just, ruling in the Fear of God*, Boston, 1747, p. 22.

19. *Acts and Resolves . . . of the Province of Massachusetts Bay*, Boston, 1878, III, 373.

20. *Boston Weekly News-Letter*, November 25, 1748.

21. Hutchinson, *The History of . . . Massachusetts-Bay*, II, 299, 333-334, 342, 393, 410; Douglass, *A Summary, Historical and Political of the First Planting, Progressive Improvements, and Present State of the British Settlements in North-America*, London, 1760, II, 88.

22. "A Word in Season to All True Lovers of Their Liberty and Their Country," 1748; "Massachusetts in Agony," 1750; "Appendix to Massachusetts in Agony"; in *Colonial Currency Reprints*, IV, 353-371, 437-485; *Boston Weekly News-Letter*, July 7, 1748.

23. "Proposals Regarding the Government of the Colony," in *Samuel Johnson, His Career and Writings*, edited by Herbert and Carol Schneider, New York, 1929, I, 148-151.

24. *The Correspondence of the Colonial Governors of Rhode Island*, edited by Gertrude S. Kimball, Boston and New York, 1903, II, 130-131.

25. Hutchinson, letters in *Boston Evening Post*, December 14, 1761; January 4, 11, 1762; Bowdoin, under signature of "Y.Z." in *Boston Evening Post*, January 11, 1762; Otis, letters in *Boston Gazette*, December 21, 28, 1761; January 11, 1762; Thacher, *Considerations on Lowering the Value of Gold Coins*, Boston, 1762.

26. Act printed in Washington Augustus Clark, *The History of the Banking Institutions Organized in South Carolina Prior to 1860*, Columbia, 1922, pp. 13-19.

27. "Petition of Merchants and Traders to South Carolina to Council of Trade and Plantations," May 22, 1723, in *Calendar of State Papers, . . . America and the West Indies*, 1723, p. 261.

28. *The Report of the Committee of the Commons House of the Assembly of the Province of South Carolina on The State of the Paper Currency of the Said Province*, London, 1737.

29. "An Address to the Inhabitants of North Carolina," 1746, in *Some Eighteenth Century Tracts Concerning North Carolina*, pp. 57-106.

30. *Proceedings and Acts of the General Assembly of Maryland, 1733-1736*, in *Archives of Maryland*, Baltimore, 1919, XXXIX, 92-113.

31. *Pennsylvania Archives*, 8th series, II, 1474-1477.

32. *Ibid.*, II, 1469-1472, 1486-1496; III, 1876.

33. Richard Lester, *Monetary Experiments: Early American and Recent Scandinavian*, Princeton, 1939, p. 85.

34. *A Dialogue Shewing What's therein to be found*, Philadelphia, 1725, pp. 14-15, 29-30.

35. *Ways and Means for the Inhabitants of Delaware to become Rich*, 1725, reprint of 1878, pp. 13-65.

36. *Pennsylvania Archives*, 8th series, IV, 3520; V, 3818-3826.

37. Extract from a treatise intended to be published on the "Nature and Advantages of a Paper Currency," *American Weekly Mercury*, week of February 11-18, 1741/1742; "An Essay Toward Explaining the Nature of Money in General and of Paper Money in Particular," *American Magazine*, March 1741/1742, p. 86; *A Discourse Concerning Paper Money*, Philadelphia, 1742/43. MS. petition of

Webbe "To the Honourable Representatives of the Freemen of the Province of Pennsylvania in General Assembly Met," in the Historical Society of Pennsylvania. This petition is attached to the copy of *A Discourse* in the Society's possession.

38. Tench Francis, "Considerations on a Paper Currency," first published in Pownall, *The Administration of the British Colonies*, London, 1768, pp. 190–226.

39. Cited from the Report of the Board of Trade, February 9, 1764, in Benjamin Franklin, "Remarks and Facts Concerning the American Paper Money," 1764, reprinted in Franklin's *Writings*, Smyth edition, V, 1.

40. "The Late Regulations Respecting the British Colonies On the Continent Of America Considered," 1765, in *Political Writings*, Wilmington, 1801, I, 56–58.

41. "Letter of 'A.B.' to the printer," in *Maryland Gazette*, November 16, 1769.

42. "Johnson to Washington," May 10, 1772, January 24, 1775, in Edward S. Delaplaine, *The Life of Thomas Johnson*, New York, 1927, pp. 73, 79–80.

43. Hildreth, *History of the United States*, New York, 1863, II, 295.

44. A Supplement to *The New York Weekly Journal*, March 28, 1737. The style is that of Cadwallader Colden.

CHAPTER X

1. "The Busybody," No. 8, 1729, reprinted in *The Writings of Benjamin Franklin*, edited by Albert Henry Smyth, New York, 1905-1907, II, 131. All references are to this edition of Franklin's collected works unless otherwise noted.

2. "To Jared Eliot," July 16, 1747, *ibid.*, II, 313–314.

3. "To Richard Jackson," May 5, 1753, *ibid.*, III, 134–138.

4. "Report of the Committee of Aggrievances of the Assembly of Pennsylvania," 1757, *ibid.*, III, 370–377.

5. "To Mary Stevenson," March 25, 1763, *ibid.*, IV, 194.

6. "To William Franklin," January 9, July 2, 1768, *ibid.*, V, 90, 142–146.

7. "To William Franklin," April 16, 1768; "To Joseph Galloway," May 14, 1768, *ibid.*, V, 121–122, 134–135.

8. "On the Price of Corn and Management of the Poor," 1766, *ibid.*, V, 534–539.

9. Franklin, *Political, Miscellaneous, and Philosophical Pieces*, collected by Benjamin Vaughan, London, 1779, p. 52.

10. "To John Ross," May 14, 1768, in *Writings*, V, 133.

11. "Remarks on The Plan for Regulating the Indian Affairs," 1766, *ibid.*, IV, 469–470.

12. Plan is published in William Renwick Riddell, "Benjamin Franklin and Colonial Money," in *Pennsylvania Magazine of History and Biography*, LIV (1930), 60–63.

13. "To Galloway," August 8, November 27, 1767, in *Writings*, V, 43, 44, 72.

14. "To Cadwallader Evans," February 20, 1768, *ibid.*, V, 102–103.

15. "To Samuel Cooper," April 27, 1769, *ibid.*, V, 205.

16. "To Lord Kames," January 1, 1769, *ibid.*, V, 189.

17. "To Joshua Babcock," January 13, 1772, *ibid.*, V, 362–363.

18. "To Thomas Percival," September 25, 1773, *ibid.*, VI, 139.

19. "A Conversation . . . on . . . Slavery," 1770, reprinted in Verner T. Crane, "Benjamin Franklin on Slavery and American Liberties," *The Pennsylvania Magazine of History and Biography*, LXII (January 1938), 1–11.

20. "On a Proposed Act of Parliament for Preventing Emigration," 1774, in *Writings*, VI, 293.

21. For "formal" studies of Franklin's economics see W. A. Wetzel, *Benjamin Franklin as an Economist*, Baltimore, 1895; and L. J. Carey, *Franklin's Economic Views*, New York, 1928.

22. Biographical material and citations are from Amelia Mott Gummere's excellent edition of Woolman's works, *The Journal and Essays of John Woolman*, New York, 1922.

CHAPTER XI

1. Edward Wigglesworth, *Calculations on American Population*, Boston, 1775.

2. "To Price," October 5, 1772, April 10, 1775, in "Price Letters," in *Proceedings of the Massachusetts Historical Society*, 2nd series, XVII, 266, 285.

3. [Thomas Bradbury Chandler], *The American Querist*, New York, 1774.

4. *Journals of the Continental Congress*, Library of Congress edition, I, 78.

5. "A speech delivered by dr. Benjamin Rush," March 16, 1775, in *American Museum*, V (June 1789), 584.

6. *A Letter from A Virginian*, Boston, 1774, pp. 26-31.

7. *Free Thoughts, on the Proceedings of the Continental Congress*, New York, 1774; *The Congress Canvassed*, New York, 1774.

8. *Considerations on the Present State of Virginia*, 1774, reprint of 1919, pp. 15, 31-32.

9. "Hampdén," in *Virginia Gazette*, reprinted in *Maryland Gazette*, May 23, 1776.

10. "Address To the Natives of Scotland Residing in America, appended to Sermon, The Dominion of Providence over the Passions of Men," 1776, in *Works of the Reverend John Witherspoon*, edited by John Rodgers, Philadelphia, 1802, III, 55-58.

11. Reverend William Gordon, "The Doctrine of Transubstantiation Considered and Refuted," 1781, in Sister Mary Augustina Ray, *American Opinion of Roman Catholicism in the Eighteenth Century*, New York, 1936, p. 379.

12. "To Samuel Chase, Esq." in *Maryland Gazette*, August 23, 1781.

13. February 25, 1777, *Archives of the State of New Jersey*, 2nd series, Trenton, N.J., 1911, I, 305.

14. "Jones to Madison," December 8, 1780, in *Letters of Joseph Jones of Virginia, 1777-1787*, Washington, 1889, pp. 63-64.

15. "Washington to Laurens," April 10, 1778, in Washington's *Writings*, XI, 237.

16. "Nathaniel Ramsay to Otho Williams," August 4, 1781, in *Calendar of the General Otho Holland William Papers*, Baltimore, 1940, p. 48.

17. "Decius," in *New England Chronicle*, reprinted in *Maryland Gazette*, November 23, 1775.

18. "Jones to Madison," November 5, 1780, in *Letters of Joseph Jones of Virginia, 1777-1787*, Washington, 1889, pp. 41-42.

19. "To Mazzei," July 7, 1781; "To Pendleton," September 18, 1781, in *The Writings of James Madison*, edited by Gaillard Hunt, New York, 1900-1910, I, 145, 154.

20. "Information to Those Who Would Remove to America," 1782, *Writings*, VIII, 609-612.

21. *Connecticut Courant*, June 8, 1779.

22. Jared Sparks, *The Life of Gouverneur Morris*, Boston, 1832, I, 13, 38; Edmund Cody Burnett, *The Continental Congress*, New York, 1941, p. 81.
23. Willard O. Mishoff, "Business in Philadelphia During the British Occupation," 1776–1778, in *Pennsylvania Magazine of History and Biography*, LXI (April 1937), 177–178.
24. "An Essay on the Danger of Too Much Circulating Cash in a State," 1776, reprinted in *Political Essays*, Philadelphia, 1791, pp. 6–7.
25. Rush Diary, February 14, 1777, in *Letters of Members of the Continental Congress*, edited by Edmund C. Burnett, Washington, 1921–1936, II, 252–253.
26. "On the Proposed Market in General Washington's Camp," in *Works of the Reverend John Witherspoon*, IV, 359–362.
27. *Public Records of the State of Connecticut*, edited by Charles J. Hoadly, Hartford, 1895, I, 62, 592–597, 604, 614–618; "Nathanael Greene to Gov. Nicholas Cooke," July 1777, in "Revolutionary Correspondence," *Rhode Island Historical Society Collections*, Providence, VI, 194.
28. "Morris to Washington," October 26, 1778, in Sparks, *The Life of Gouverneur Morris*, I, 175.
29. "To James Warren," March 31, 1779, in Washington's *Writings*, XIV, 313.
30. "To Stephen Sayre," March 31, 1779; "To Samuel Cooper," April 22, 1779; "To Thomas Ruston," October 9, 1780; "Of the Paper Money of the United States of America," 1774, Franklin's *Writings*, VII, 275, 294; VIII, 151–158; IX, 234.
31. "To Price," May 20, 1779, in "Price Letters," p. 320.
32. "Nathaniel Scudder to Richard Harry Lee," December 9, 1778, in *Letters of Members of the Continental Congress*, III, 524.
33. "To Benjamin Trumbull," August 18, 1778, in Lewis Henry Boutell, *The Life of Roger Sherman*, Chicago, 1896, p. 106.
34. "Observations Upon Continental Money," in *Virginia Gazette*, March 19, 1779.
35. *Journals of the Continental Congress*, September 13, 1779, XV, 1052–1062.
36. "Daniel Jenifer to the Governor of Maryland," May 24, 1779, in *Letters of Members of the Continental Congress*, IV, 232.
37. *Pennsylvania Gazette*, May 26, June 2, 1779; *Maryland Gazette*, June 11, 1779; *Virginia Gazette*, July 24, 1779.
38. *Political Essays*, pp. 9–127.
39. "Observations Written Posterior to the Circular Address of Congress in Sept. 1779, and Prior to their Act of March 1780," in *Letters and Other Writings of James Madison*, Congress edition, Philadelphia, 1867, IV, 460–466.
40. *Acts and Resolves of the Province of Massachusetts Bay*, Boston, 1922, XXII, 352.
41. *4 Statutes at Large of South Carolina*, Columbia, S.C., 1838, pp. 563–564.
42. "Proceedings and Observations of the Committee of Finance, November, 1780"; "Witherspoon to the governor of New Jersey," December 16, 1780, in *Letters of Members of the Continental Congress*, V, 464–472, 488.
43. "Robert Morris to John Jay," July 13, 1781, in *The Diplomatic Correspondence of the American Revolution*, edited by Jared Sparks, Boston, 1830, VII, 439.
44. "Madison to Edmund Pendleton," January 8, 1782, Madison's *Writings*, I, 169.
45. "Hugh Williamson and William Blount to Governor Martin," October 22, 1782, in *State Records of North Carolina*, XVI, 434–435.
46. "Speeches of Witherspoon," in *Letters of Members of the Continental Congress*, VI, 415–420, 464–467.
47. "Franklin to Morris," December 25, 1783, in Franklin's *Writings*, IX, 138.
48. "A Dissertation on the Political Union and Constitution of the Thirteen

United States of North America," 1783; "A Sixth Essay on Free Trade and Finance," 1783; "An Essay on Credit," 1786, reprinted in *Political Essays*, pp. 215–219, 235, 443.

49. For general biographical material on Gale, see Benjamin Hall, *History of Eastern Vermont*, Albany, 1865, II, 643–650; Lorenzo Sabine, *Biographical Sketches of Loyalists of the American Revolution*, Boston, 1864, I, 452–453; J. B. Wilbur, *Ira Allen, Founder of Vermont*, 1751–1814, New York, 1928, I, 48–49.

50. "American Loyalists, Transcripts of the Manuscript Books and Papers of the Commission of Enquiry Into the Losses and Services of the American Loyalists," in New York Public Library; see *Commission Reports*, XI, 154–155; *Examinations in London*, XLV, 487–493; *Calendar of Original Memorials, Vouchers*, III, 321–322.

51. "Gale to John McKesson," February 29, 1776, April 12, 1776, in *Journals of the Provincial Congress*, Albany, 1842, II, 120, 184.

52. "To Duane," March 2, 1785, MS. in the New York Historical Society.

53. *Monthly Review*, LXXI (November 1784), 365–368; LXXIII (November 1785), 418–422; LXXIV (June 1786), 430–431; LXXVII (October 1787), 302–306.

CHAPTER XII

1. "Thanksgiving Sermon," 1783, in *Works of the Reverend Witherspoon*, II, 472.

2. "Williams to William Lewis," June 15, 1786, in *Calendar of the General Otho Williams Papers*, p. 133.

3. Howard C. Rice, "James Swan: Agent of the French Republic 1794–1796," in *The New England Quarterly*, X (September 1937), 464–486.

4. *A Dissuasion to Great-Britain and the Colonies, from the Slave Trade to Africa*, Boston, 1772.

5. "A Seventh Essay on Free Trade and Finance," January 10, 1785, in *Political Essays*, p. 291.

6. *American Museum*, I (May 1787), 405–409, 414.

7. Rush, *Essays, Literary, Moral & Philosophical*, Philadelphia, 1798, p. 17.

8. "To R. H. Lee," July 6, 1785; "To James Monroe," August 7, 1785, in Madison's *Writings*, II, 150–151, 156–157.

9. *A Letter from an American, Now Resident in London, to a Member of Parliament, on the Subject of the Restraining Proclamation*, London, 1784, pp. 23–24, 31, 42–43; "Bingham to ——," October 14, 1783, cited in Margaret L. Brown, "William Bingham, Eighteenth Century Magnate," in *Pennsylvania Magazine of History and Biography*, LXI (October 1937), 397.

10. "King to Elbridge Gerry," June 4, 1786; "Monroe to Governor Henry," August 12, 1787, in Edmund Cody Burnett, *The Continental Congress*, New York, 1941, p. 656.

11. "To Jefferson," August 20, 1784; "To Lafayette," March 20, 1785, in Madison's *Writings*, II, 73, 120.

12. "To the President of Congress," August 22, 1785; "To Henry Lee," June 18, 1786, in Washington's *Writings*, XXVIII, 231, 461.

13. "To Jefferson," August 20, 1784; "To James Monroe," June 21, 1785, in Madison's *Writings*, II, 64–66, 147.

14. "Address of Governor Alexander C. Martin, April 20, 1784, to the General Assembly," in *The State Records of North Carolina*, XVII, 38.

15. "To Jefferson," March 29, 1784; "To Governor Benjamin Harrison," October 10, 1784, in Washington's *Writings*, XXVII, 373–377, 473–474.

16. "To Morris," February 1, 1785; "To Lafayette," July 25, 1785, *ibid.*, XXVIII, 49–55, 206–207.

17. "Johnson to Washington," September 1785, in Corra Bacon-Foster, *Early Chapters in the Development of the Patomac Route to the West*, Washington, 1912, p. 70.

18. "The Letters of Sylvius," in *American Museum*, II (August 1787), 117–120, 129.

19. "An Address to An Assembly of the Friends of American Manufactures," 1787, reprinted in *A View of the United States of America*, Philadelphia, 1794, pp. 38–41.

20. George Clymer and Tench Coxe, "Report to the Board of Managers of the Pennsylvania Society for Promotion of Manufactures and Other Useful Arts, On the Report of the Committee for Manufactures," in *Pennsylvania Gazette*, November 12, 1788.

21. *Pennsylvania Statutes at Large*, XXXIII (1787–1790), 239.

22. "To Jefferson," February 13, 1789, Washington's *Writings*, XXX, 199.

23. "To Jefferson," August 12, 1786, in Hunt, Madison's *Writings*, II, 257–267.

24. "Extract from the presentments of the grand jury of the district of ninety-six, in the State of South Carolina . . . ," November 26, 1788, in *American Museum*, V (May 1789), 444.

25. Philip A. Crowl, *Maryland During and After the Revolution*, Baltimore, 1943, p. 84.

26. "An Address of the House of Delegates of Maryland to their Constituents," in *Maryland Gazette*, January 25, 1787.

27. *Remarks on the Proposed Plan of an Emission of Paper, and on the Means of Effecting It*, Annapolis, 1787.

28. N. S. B. Gras, *The Massachusetts First National Bank of Boston, 1784–1934*, Cambridge, 1937, p. 212.

29. *Debates and Proceedings of the General Assembly of Pennsylvania, on the Memorials Praying a Repeal or Suspension of the Law Annulling the Charter of the Bank*, edited by Mathew Carey, Philadelphia, 1786; Pelatiah Webster, "An Essay on Credit," 1786, reprinted in *Political Essays*, pp. 427–464; Gouverneur Morris, "An Address on the Bank of North America," 1785, reprinted in Jared Sparks, *The Life of Gouverneur Morris*, Boston, 1832, III, 437–465; James Wilson, "Considerations on the Power to Incorporate the Bank of North America," 1785, reprinted in *Selected Political Essays of James Wilson*, edited by Randolph G. Adams, New York, 1930, pp. 125–149; Janet Wilson, "The Bank of North America and Pennsylvania Politics: 1781–1787," in *Pennsylvania Magazine of History and Biography*, LXVI (January 1942), 11.

30. Editor's introduction to Collins's edition of Witherspoon's *Lectures on Moral Philosophy*, Princeton, 1912, p. xv.

31. "The Internal State of America," in Franklin's *Writings*, X, 117.

32. "To Price," October 27, 1786, in "Price Letters," *Proceedings of the Massachusetts Historical Society*, 2nd series, XVII, 354.

33. James M. Varnum, *The Case, Trevett Against Weeden*, Providence, 1787.

34. "James Warren to John Adams," April 30, 1786, in *Warren-Adams Letters*, Boston, 1925, II, 271–273.

35. Thomas C. Amory, *Life of James Sullivan with Selections from His Writings*, Boston, 1859, I, 193.

36. "To Edmund Pendleton," January 9, 1787, in Hunt, Madison's *Writings*, II, 307.

37. "Bowdoin to William Shephard," January 21, 1787, in *The Bowdoin and Temple Papers II*, in *Collections of the Massachusetts Historical Society*, 7th series, VI (1907), 130.

38. *The essential requisites to form the good Ruler's Character*, Hartford, 1788.

39. "To Edmund Pendleton," April 12, 1787, in Hunt, Madison's *Writings*, II, 354.

40. "To Bowdoin," March 15, 1787, *The Bowdoin and Temple Papers II*, 173–183.

41. "Camillus," 1787; reprinted in *The Works of Fisher Ames*, Boston, 1809, pp. 8–19.

42. "To Price," June 3, 1787, in "Price Letters," pp. 367–368.

43. "Observations," MS., April 1787, in Hunt, Madison's *Writings*, II, 362.

44. *The Records of the Federal Convention of 1787*, edited by Max Farrand, New Haven, 1911, I, 422–423; II, 284, 304, 370–371, 440, 451, 452, 631.

45. *Thoughts Upon the Political Situation of the United States of America*, Worcester, Mass., 1788. The authorship is disputed. It has been attributed to Sullivan among others.

46. The authors and writings cited are from Paul Leicester Ford's two collections of contemporary documents: *Pamphlets on the Constitution of the United States*, Brooklyn, 1888; and *Essays on the Constitution of the United States*, Brooklyn, 1892.

47. The authorship has in the past been attributed to Coxe, but among the facts that throw doubts on this attribution is the lack of emphasis on labor-saving machinery, which is a characteristic of Coxe's comprehensive essays. My guess is that the author was Swan. He was at the time in France, but this does not rule him out because years later, while in a French prison, he was having pamphlets published in America telling the American government what policies it should pursue.

CHAPTER XIII

1. Tench Coxe, *A View of the United States*, pp. 361–362.

2. "Observations on the . . . Duration of Human Life, and the progress of Population in the United States," March 18, 1791, in *Transactions of the American Philosophical Society*, III (1793), 25–55.

3. Dr. Nicholas Collin, "An Essay on those Inquiries in Natural Philosophy, which at present are most beneficial to the United States of North America," April 3, 1789, *ibid.*, p. xiii.

4. Louis Morton, *Robert Carter of Nomini Hall*, Williamsburg, 1941, pp. 266–267.

5. "John Breckinridge to Isaac Shelby," March 11, 1798, cited in Bernard Mayo, *Henry Clay, Spokesman of the New West*, Boston, 1937, p. 66.

6. Jonathan Edwards, *The Injustice and Impolicy of the Slave Trade, and of the Slavery of the Africans*, New Haven, 1791.

7. Morton, *op. cit.*, pp. 258–259.

8. *Ten Letters to Dr. Joseph Priestly*, New Haven, 1800, pp. 24–25.

9. Harry R. Warfel, *Noah Webster, School Master to America*, New York, 1936, pp. 209–210.

10. *Political Inquiries: to Which is Added a Plan for the General Establishment of Schools Throughout the United States*, Wilmington, 1791, p. 98.

11. Noah Webster, *A Collection of Essays and Fugitiv Writings*, 1790, Hartford, pp. 304–316, 336.

12. *Observations on the North-American Land-Company, Lately Instituted in Philadelphia*, London, 1796, pp. xiii–xiv.

13. Rush, *Essays*, pp. 213–224.

14. [William Smith], *A Historical Account of the Rise, Progress and Present State of the Canal Navigation in Pennsylvania*, Philadelphia, 1795.

15. "James Bowdoin to Lady Temple," October 31, 1793, in *The Bowdoin and Temple Papers*, pp. 205–206.

16. "Bingham to Hamilton," November 25, 1789, in James Wettereau, "Letters from Two Business Men to Alexander Hamilton on Federal Fiscal Policy, 1789," in *Journal of Economic and Business History*, III (August 1931), 672–683; Price, "Observations on the Public Debt of America," in *American Museum*, VI (November 1789), 387–389.

17. "Reflections on the State of the American Union," 1792, reprinted in Coxe, *A View of the United States*, p. 333.

18. "A Brief Examination of Lord Sheffield's Observations on the Commerce of the United States," 1791; *ibid.*, pp. 165–167.

19. "To Jefferson," April 15, 1791, in Jefferson Papers, Library of Congress.

20. J. S. Davis, *Essays in the Earlier History of American Corporations*, Cambridge, 1917, I, 386.

21. "Petition against Excise," 1792, in *The Writings of Albert Gallatin*, edited by Henry Adams, Philadelphia, 1879, I, 2–3.

22. Manifesto of August 1792 Pittsburgh meeting, in H. M. Brackenridge, *History of the Western Insurrection in Western Pennsylvania*, Pittsburgh, 1859, p. 37.

23. "A Plan for Encouraging Agriculture, and Increasing the Value of Farms in the Midland and More Western Counties of Pennsylvania," reprinted in Coxe, *A View of the United States*, pp. 384–402.

24. "To Alexander Hamilton," in John C. Hamilton, *History of the Republic*, 2nd edition, Philadelphia, 1864, IV, 74.

25. Editorial note in Webster, *A Collection of Essays and Fugitiv Writings*, p. 378.

26. "Rush to Madison," February 1790, cited in Abbot Emerson Smith, *James Madison*, New York, 1937, p. 165.

27. *To the Stockholders of the Bank of North America*, by a Citizen of Philadelphia, 1791.

28. "Reflections on the State of the American Union," in Coxe, *A View of the United States*, p. 352.

29. *Fourteen Agricultural Experiments*, Philadelphia, 1797.

30. Hildreth, *History of the United States*, New York, 1863, V, 218.

31. *Letters Addressed to the Yeomanry of the United States*, Philadelphia, 1791; *Five Letters, Addressed to the Yeomanry of the United States*, Philadelphia, 1792; "Address by the President of the Germantown Society," 1792, in *American Museum*, XII, Appendix II, pp. 22–23.

32. *Memoir of Dr. George Logan of Stenton*, edited by Frances A. Logan, Philadelphia, 1899, p. 99.

33. "Observations on the Preceding Letters," in *American Museum*, XII (September–November 1792), 167–170, 217–221, 272–278.

34. *Debates and Proceedings of the General Assembly of Pennsylvania, on the . . . Charter of the Bank*, edited by Mathew Carey, Philadelphia, 1787, pp. 12–13.

35. "Petition of Merchants of Alexandria," 1792, in *William and Mary College Quarterly*, 2nd series, III (July 1923), 206–207.

36. *An Enquiry into the Principles and Tendency of Certain Public Measures*, Philadelphia, 1794; *Definition of Parties; or, the Political Effects of the Paper System Considered*, Philadelphia, 1794; *An Inquiry Into the Principles and Policy of the Government of the United States*, Fredericksburg, Va., 1814, p. 51.

37. Hildreth, *History of the United States*, 1863 edition, New York, IV, 548.

38. "A Sketch of the Finances of the United States," 1796, reprinted in Adams, *The Writings of Albert Gallatin*, III, 73-168.

39. James Bowdoin, *Opinions Respecting the Commercial Inter-course Between the United States of America, and the Dominions of Great-Britain*, Boston, 1797.

40. Rice, *op. cit.*, pp. 469-482; "Jefferson to Swan," August 4, 1789, Jefferson Papers, Library of Congress; "Monroe to Madison," June 30, 1795, in *The Writings of James Monroe*, edited by S. M. Hamilton, New York and London, 1890, II, 313-314.

41. *Ten Letters to Dr. Joseph Priestly*, New Haven, 1800, pp. 19-21.

42. "Logan to Citizen Merlin," September 9, 1798; and "To the Citizens of the United States," 1799; in Frances Logan, *Memoir of Dr. George Logan*, pp. 99, 129-130.

43. Webster, *Miscellaneous Papers, on Political and Commercial Subjects*, New York, 1802, p. iv.

44. Coxe, *Strictures upon the Letter Imputed to Mr. Jefferson, Addressed to Mr. Mazzei*, Lancaster, 1800, pp. 7-8.

CHAPTER XIV

1. "A Letter to the President of the United States," in *Miscellaneous Papers, on Political and Commercial Subjects*, pp. 1-76.

2. Curtius, *A Defense of the Administration of Thomas Jefferson*, from the *National Intelligencer*, Washington, 1804.

3. "Virginian Supremacy," No. 5, in *Freeman's Journal and Philadelphia Mercantile Advertiser*, October 10, 1810.

4. "An extract of a note from Mr. Dupont de Nemours to the Consul Le Brun," in *American State Papers, Foreign-Relations*, II, 547.

5. "Livingston to Madison," March 11, 1803, in *American State Papers, ibid.*, p. 545.

6. "Political Review," 1802, in *The Works of Fisher Ames*, pp. 265-268.

7. "Ames to Thomas Dwight," October 31, 1803, *ibid.*, pp. 484-485.

8. "Gallatin to Jefferson," April 13, 1807, in Adams, *The Writings of Albert Gallatin*, I, 332.

9. *Memorial of the Merchants of the City of New-York*, January 1806.

10. "To Thomas Dwight," November 27, 1805, in *The Works of Fisher Ames*, pp. 490-496.

11. Webster, "On the Rights of Neutrals," in *Miscellaneous Papers, on Political and Commercial Subjects*, pp. 78-214.

12. "A Memoir, Containing an Examination of the British Doctrine," in *Letters and Other Writings of James Madison*, II, 229-391.

13. "Gallatin to Jefferson," December 18, 1807, in Adams, *The Writings of Albert Gallatin*, I, 368.

14. Hildreth, *History of the United States*, VI, 87.

15. *A Free Enquiry into the Causes, Both Real and Pretended for Laying the Embargo*, by a citizen of Vermont, Windsor, Vt., 1808, p. 13.

16. "Abigail Adams to Abigail Adams Smith," December 8, 1808, in "Abigail Adams, Commentator," edited by A. B. Forbes, in *Proceedings of the Massachusetts Historical Society*, LXVI (1936-1941), 150.

17. Francis Blake, *An Examination of the Constitutionality of the Embargo Laws*, Worcester, 1808.

18. *A Circular Letter from the General Republican Committee of the City*

and County of New York, . . . In Vindication of the Measures of the General Government, New York, 1809.

19. "Abigail Adams to William Stephens Smith," August 28, 1811, in "Abigail Adams, Commentator," *op. cit.,* p. 153.

20. "Madison to William Pinkney," December 5, 1808, in *Letters and Other Writings of James Madison,* II, 427–428.

21. *Arthur Mervyn* (1799–1800), *Jane Talbot* (1801), in *Collected Writings,* Philadelphia, 1887, II, 209; V, 87.

22. *The British Treaty,* London, 1808, pp. x–xvi.

23. "Madison to the House of Representatives of the State of South Carolina," January 8, 1812, in Hunt, *Madison's Writings,* VIII, 175.

24. "Madison to Jefferson," March 18, 1811; "Madison to Barlow," November 17, 1811, *ibid.,* 134, 170.

25. *Message from the President of the United States, Transmitting Copies and Extracts from the Correspondence of the Secretary of State, and the Minister Plenipotentiary of the United States at Paris . . .* Washington, 1812; "Madison to Barlow," February 24, 1812, *ibid.,* VIII, 180.

26. "Madison to Jefferson," May 25, 1810, *ibid.,* p. 102.

27. "Memorial of the Artists and Manufacturers of Philadelphia," 1803, Appendix to *An Essay on the Manufacturing Interest of the United States,* Philadelphia, 1804.

28. *Annals of Congress, Eighth Congress, First Session,* pp. 946–949.

29. *An Essay on the Manufacturing Interest of the United States,* Philadelphia, 1804, pp. 25–26. The essay has been generally attributed to Coxe, but Coxe at the time held a federal appointment. Of course, this would not have prevented Coxe from writing the essay, but it is hardly likely he would have sharply denounced a Congressional committee.

30. "The Military Establishment," in *Aurora,* January 18, 1812.

31. *Annals of Congress, Eleventh Congress, First Session,* pp. 363–365.

32. Frank Landon Humphreys, *Life and Times of David Humphreys,* New York and London, 1917, II, 365–366, 417–420; Leon Howard, *The Connecticut Wits,* Chicago, 1943, p. 242.

33. "The Trial of the Journeymen Cordwainers of the City of New York for a Conspiracy to Raise their Wages," 1810, reprinted in *Documentary History of American Industrial Society,* edited by John R. Commons *et al.,* Cleveland, 1910, III, 330.

34. *American Register,* XII (Part I, 1810), 339–356.

35. Henry Banks, *Sketches,* Richmond, 1811.

36. "Introduction to the Collection of Laws, Treaties, and Other Documents Having Operation and Respect to the Public Lands," 1810, in Adams, *The Writings of Albert Gallatin,* III, 225–226.

37. "Sullivan to Monroe," May 9, 1806, *The Writings of James Monroe,* IV, 482–483 n.

38. "To the Congress of the United States," by "Popillius," in *Aurora,* March 9, 1812.

39. Joseph Howard Parks, *Felix Grundy,* University of Louisiana, 1940, pp. 21–30; Bernard Mayo, *Henry Clay,* pp. 163–177.

40. Elmer C. Griffith, "Early Banking in Kentucky," in *Proceedings of the Mississippi Valley Historical Association,* II (1908–1909), 176–177.

41. *Propositions to Establish a Mechanic's Bank in the City of Richmond, Connected with Some Objects of Benevolence and Public Utility,* Richmond, 1812.

42. D. H. Gilpatrick, *Jeffersonian Democracy in North Carolina, 1789–1816,* New York, 1931, pp. 149-152, 236.

43. *The Letters of Common Sense Respecting the State Bank and Paper Currency,* Raleigh, N.C., 1811, reprinted from the *Raleigh Star.*

44. Griffith, *op. cit.,* p. 174.

45. *Nine Letters to Dr. Adam Seybert, On the Subject of the Charter of the Bank of the United States,* 2nd edition, Philadelphia, 1811.

46. *Debates of the Legislature of Pennsylvania, in the Session of 1810–11,* reported by William Hamilton, Lancaster, 1811, pp. 9-35, 47-50.

47. *Propositions by the Trustees of the Late Bank of the United States,* Lancaster, 1812.

48. Kenneth L. Brown, "Stephen Girard's Bank," in *Pennsylvania Magazine of History and Biography,* LXVI (January 1942), 32–36.

49. Dixon Ryan Fox, *The Decline of the Aristocracy in the Politics of New York,* New York, 1919, p. 228.

CHAPTER XV

1. Elijah Parish, *A Protest Against the War,* Newburyport, 1812, p. 16.

2. "Humphreys to Madison," February 19, 1813; "Madison to Humphreys," March 23, 1813; "On the Necessity of State and Self-Defence," June 22, 1813, in Frank Landon Humphreys, *The Life and Times of David Humphreys,* New York and London, 1917, II, 392-407.

3. *Proceedings of a Convention of Delegates . . . Convened at Hartford, . . . Dec. 15, 1814,* Hartford, 1815.

4. *Speech . . . at the Celebration of the Recent Triumphs of the Cause of Mankind, in Germany. Delivered at Annapolis, January 20, 1814,* Alexandria edition, 1814.

5. *An Oration, Delivered . . . June 29, 1814 . . . In Celebration of the Recent Deliverance of Europe from the Yoke of Military Despotism,* New York, 1814; "Morris to William Hill Wells," November 1, 1814, in Sparks, *The Life of Gouverneur Morris,* III, 318.

6. "Logan to Jefferson," December 9, 1813, in Frances Logan, *Memoir of Dr. George Logan,* pp. 137-139.

7. *National Intelligencer,* February 3, 1814.

8. *Laws of the State of New York,* Vol. 6. Webster and Skinner edition, Albany, 1812, VI, 509.

9. "The memorial & Remonstrance of Stephen Girard," 1814, in John Bach McMaster, *The Life and Times of Stephen Girard,* Philadelphia and London, 1918, II, 257.

10. Kenneth Wiggins Porter, *John Jacob Astor,* Cambridge, 1931, II, 959–960.

11. Circular "To the Presidents and Directors of the Different Banks of the City of Philadelphia," August 29, 1814, reprinted in Mathew Carey, *Miscellaneous Essays,* Philadelphia, 1830, pp. 248–249.

12. Letter "To the Public," August 30, 1814, in *Aurora,* September 1, 1814.

13. *Niles' Weekly Register,* January 21, 1815, VII, 335. On Niles see Richard G. Stone, *Hezekiah Niles as an Economist,* Baltimore, 1933.

14. "Girard to Ingersoll," November 25, 1814, in McMaster, *op. cit.,* p. 285.

15. "Madison to Jefferson," October 10, 1814, in Hunt, Madison's *Writings,* VIII, 313-315.

16. *A Statement of the Arts and Manufactures of the United States of America*

for the Year 1810: Digested and Prepared by Tench Coxe, Esquire, of Philadelphia, Philadelphia, 1814.

17. *Arator; Being a Series of Agricultural Essays, Practical and Political*, Georgetown, 1814, pp. 57–67, 260–262.

18. *New York Commercial Advertiser*, July 1, 1814.

CHAPTER XVI

1. *An Inquiry into the Causes of the Present State of the Circulating Medium of the United States*, Philadelphia, 1815.

2. "Domestic Literature and Science," in *Analectic Magazine*, VI (December 1815), 523.

3. "On Banks and Paper Currency," *ibid.*, pp. 489–517.

4. "Domestic Literature and Science," *ibid.*, VII (May 1816), *Analectic Magazine*, 459–462.

5. *Essays on Banking*, Philadelphia, 1816, pp. 163–184.

6. *Journal of the House of Delegates . . . of Virginia*, session of 1816–1817, p. 6.

7. "Joseph Milligan to Jefferson," January 18, 1819, Jefferson Papers, Library of Congress.

8. "To Ricardo," September 20, 1820, April 19, 1821, in David Ricardo, *Minor Papers on the Currency Question*, edited by Jacob Hollander, Baltimore, 1932, pp. 199–203.

9. "To the Directors of the Bank of the United States," June 30, 1818, in *Miscellaneous Essays*, pp. 262–266.

10. A. Barton Hepburn, *A History of Currency in the United States*, New York, 1915, p. 103.

11. For the biography of Law, see Allen C. Clark, *Greenleaf and Law in the Federal City*, Washington, 1901, pp. 219–336.

12. *An Address to the Columbian Institute on a Money System*, Washington, 1828; *An Address to the Columbian Institute on the Question "What Ought to be the Circulating Medium of a Nation,"* Washington, 1830.

13. "To Doctor Cutting," December 7, 1822; "To Law," January 1827, in *Letters and Other Writings of James Madison*, III, 289–290, 549.

14. *Report of the Secretary of the Treasury, in Relation to the Bank of the United States*, in *Sixteenth Congress, First Session, House Documents* No. 86 (1820).

15. *An Examination of the New Tariff*, by one of the People, New York, 1821, pp. 191–193.

16. *A Serious Appeal*, by a Friend to his Country, New York, 1816; *Memorial of the Citizens of New-York in Favour of a Canal*, New York, 1816.

17. Kenneth W. Rowe, *Mathew Carey: A Study in American Economic Development*, Baltimore, 1933, pp. 83–84.

18. "Mr. Murphey's Report to the Legislature of North Carolina on Inland Navigation," 1816, reprinted in *Papers of Archibald D. Murphey*, edited by William Hoyt, Raleigh, N.C., 1914, II, 35–47.

19. "To Colonel William Polk," July 24, 1821, in Hoyt, *Papers of Archibald D. Murphey*, I, 216–217.

20. Charles F. Mercer, in *Proceedings and Debates of the Virginia State Convention of 1829–1830*, Richmond, 1830, p. 178.

21. "To Livingston," March 16, 1812, in Archibald Douglas Turnbull, *John Stevens*, New York and London, 1928, p. 369.

22. *Documents Tending to Prove the Superior Advantages of Railways and Steam Carriages over Canal Navigation*, New York, 1812.

23. Turnbull, *op. cit.*, pp. 465-466.

24. U. B. Phillips, *A History of Transportation in the Eastern Cotton Belt to 1860*, New York, 1908, pp. 132-166.

25. "Communication to Editors," signed "Civis," in *National Intelligencer*, February 24, 1816.

26. Review of Bristed's *Resources of the United States*, in *American Monthly Magazine and Critical Review*, III (June 1818), 105.

27. "Humphreys to Madison," May 16, 1816, in Humphreys, *Life and Times of David Humphreys*, p. 421.

28. *The New Olive Branch*, Philadelphia, 1820; *Essays on Political Economy*, Philadelphia, 1822.

29. "To Carey and Jackson," December 17, 30, 1819, in Daniel J. Ahearn, "Condy Raguet," unpublished master's thesis, Columbia University, 1938, pp. 10-12.

30. "To Mathew Carey," March 10, 1824, in Madison Papers, Library of Congress.

31. Edward Everett, "The Tariff Question," in *North American Review*, XIX (July 1824), 227.

32. "Webster to Dalton," May 9, 1830, in *Writings and Speeches of Daniel Webster*, edited by Fletcher Webster, Boston, 1903, XVII, 501.

33. "The South Carolina Exposition," 1828, in *Works of John C. Calhoun*, edited by Richard K. Crallé, New York, 1851-1856, VI, 1-59.

34. Thomas P. Jones, M.D., "On the Progress of Manufactures and Internal Improvement in the United States," address delivered in the Hall of the Franklin Institute, in Philadelphia, *National Gazette*, November 23, 1827.

35. "Society for Industry," in *American Monthly Magazine and Critical Review*, II (April 1818), 469-473.

36. *Proceedings and Debates of the Virginia State Convention of 1829-1830*, Richmond, 1830, pp. 119, 145.

37. Hugh Swinton Legaré, "Diary of Brussels," entry of September 16, 1833, in *The Writings of Hugh Swinton Legaré*, edited with a memoir by Mary Legaré, Charleston, S.C., 1845-1846, I, 90.

CHAPTER XVII

1. For a general survey of Hamilton's social philosophy see Rexford Guy Tugwell and Joseph Dorfman, "Alexander Hamilton: Nation-Maker," in *Columbia University Quarterly*, XXIX (December 1937), 209-226; and XXX (March 1938), 59-72. For a formal study of Hamilton's economics, see E. C. Lunt, "Alexander Hamilton, as a Political Economist," in *Journal of Political Economy*, III (June 1895), 289-310.

2. Recent researches have somewhat reduced Hamilton's precocity by revealing that he was born two years earlier than the date usually given (1757). See Harold Larson, "The Birth and Parentage of Alexander Hamilton," *American Genealogist*, XXI (January 1945), 161-167.

3. "To Gouverneur Morris," May 19, 1777, in *The Works of Alexander Hamilton*, edited by Henry Cabot Lodge, New York and London, 1904, IX, 71-72.

4. "Publius," 1778, *ibid.*, I, 199-209.

5. "To Washington," March 17, 1783, *ibid.*, IX, p. 326.

6. "Letters from Phocion," 1784, *ibid.*, IV, 244-246.

7. "Propositions for a Constitution of Government," and speeches in the Federal Convention, *ibid.*, I, 347-428.

8. "On the Establishment of a Mint," 1791, *ibid.*, IV, 28.

9. The reports included in *Papers on Public Credit, Commerce and Finance, by Alexander Hamilton*, edited by Samuel McKee, Jr., New York, 1934.

10. "Jefferson to T. M. Randolph," March 16, 1792, and "Jefferson to Washington," September 9, 1792, in *The Works of Thomas Jefferson*, edited by P. L. Ford, New York and London, 1892-1899, V, 455, VI, 101-109.

11. "To Washington," August 18, 1792, in Lodge, *The Works of Alexander Hamilton*, II, 455.

12. "Defense of Mr. Jay's Treaty," 1795, *ibid.*, V, 283, 292, 483, 487, VI, 44; Henry Cabot Lodge, *Alexander Hamilton*, Boston and New York, 1899, p. 186.

13. *Minutes of the Common Council of the City of New York, 1784-1831*, New York, 1917, II, 514-515, 517-521; W. B. Lawrence, "The Croton Aqueduct," in *The Merchants' Magazine*, XI (May 1844), p. 435; "To Bayard," January 16, 1801, in Lodge, *The Works of Alexander Hamilton*, X, 415; James Cheetham, *Remarks on the "Merchants' Bank*," New York, 1804, p. 33.

14. "To Timothy Pickering," June 7, 1798, in Lodge, *The Works of Alexander Hamilton*, X, 293-294.

15. "To Jonathan Dayton," 1799, *ibid.*, X, 331-333.

16. "To Bayard," August 6, 1800, *ibid.*, X, 385; H. A. Good, *Benjamin Rush and His Services to American Education*, Berne, Ind., 1918, p. 92.

17. "To Jay," May 7, 1800, in Lodge, *The Works of Alexander Hamilton*, X, 371-374.

18. "To Bayard," January 16, 1801, *ibid.*, X, 415.

19. "Examination of Jefferson's Message to Congress of December 7, 1801," *ibid.*, VIII, 246-373.

20. "To Bayard," April 1802, *ibid.*, X, 433-437.

21. This section, except for minor revisions, was originally published in the *Political Science Quarterly*, LIX (June 1944), 227-247.

22. "To Charles Cushing," April 1756, in *The Works of John Adams*, edited by Charles Francis Adams, Boston, 1850-1856, I, 32.

23. "A Dissertation on the Canon and Feudal Law," 1765; "Instructions of the Town of Braintree to Their Representative," 1765; "The Earl of Clarendon to William Pym," 1766; *ibid.*, III, 448, 466, 481.

24. "To Mrs. Adams," April 14, July 10, 1776, in *Letters of John Adams Addressed to His Wife*, edited by Charles Francis Adams, Boston, 1841, I, 95, 135-136.

25. "To James Sullivan," May 26, 1776, in Adams, *The Works of John Adams*, IX, 375-377; "To Mrs. Adams," May 22, 1776, in Adams, *Letters of John Adams*, I, 229; "To Mrs. Adams," July 3, 1776, in Adams, *The Works of John Adams*, IX, 418; "To Joseph Hawley," August 25, 1776, *ibid.*, p. 435.

26. "To James Warren," July 23, October 7, 19, 20, 1775, in *Warren-Adams Letters*, Boston, 1917, I, 88, 128, 146, 156.

27. "To James Warren," April 6, 1777, *ibid.*, I, 312-313.

28. "To Mrs. Adams," February 7, September 8, 1777, in Adams, *Letters of John Adams*, I, 183, II, 6.

29. "To James Warren," October 29, 1777, in *Warren-Adams Letters*, I, 377.

30. "To James Warren," February 25, 1779, *ibid.*, II, 90-91; "To Mercy Warren" [Sept. 1779?], *ibid.*, p. 120.

31. "To Count de Vergennes," June 22, 1780, in Adams, *The Works of John Adams*, VII, 193-197.

32. "To Calkoen," October 26, 1780, *ibid.*, VII, 294-298, 299-301, 311.

33. "To Robert Morris," July 11, 1783, *ibid.*, VIII, 92–93.
34. "To James Warren," July 4, 1786, in *Warren-Adams Letters*, II, 276–277.
"To Jefferson," August 25, 1787, in Adams, *The Works of John Adams*, VIII, 447.
35. "Warren to Adams," October 22, 1786, in *Warren-Adams Letters*, II, 278.
36. "To James Warren," January 9, 1787, *ibid.*, II, 280–281.
37. "To Richard Price," May 20, 1789, April 19, 1790, in Adams, *The Works of John Adams*, IX, 559, 564.
38. "To Henry Marchant," August 18, 1789, *ibid.*, IX, 560.
39. "To Mercy Warren," March 2, 1789, in *Warren-Adams Letters*, II, 305–306.
40. "To Mrs. Adams," May 5, 1794, in Adams, *Letters of John Adams*, II, 158.
41. "To John Trumbull," January 22, 1791, in Adams, *The Works of John Adams*, IX, 373; "To Mrs. Adams," January 9, 1793, May 5, 1794, in Adams, *Letters of John Adams*, II, 117, 158; "To F. A. Vanderkemp," February 16, 1809, in Adams, *The Works of John Adams*, IX, 610.
42. "Discourses on Davila," 1790, in Adams, *The Works of John Adams*, VI, 279.
43. "To Alexander Jardine," June 1, 1790, *ibid.*, IX, 563; "To Thomas Brand-Hollis," June 11, 1790, *ibid.*, p. 571.
44. "To William Cunningham," March 14, 1804, in *Correspondence Between the Hon. John Adams . . . and . . . Wm. Cunningham*, Boston, 1823; "To John Jay," December 19, 1800, in Adams, *The Works of John Adams*, IX, 91.
45. "To Benjamin Waterhouse," August 7, 1805, in *Statesman and Friend: Correspondence of John Adams with Benjamin Waterhouse, 1794–1822*, edited by Worthington C. Ford, Boston, 1927, pp. 28–29.
46. "A Review of the Propositions for Amending the Constitution Submitted by Mr. Hillhouse to the Senate of the United States in 1808," in Adams, *The Works of John Adams*, VI, 530.
47. "To Waterhouse," March 11, 1812, March 31, 1813, in Ford, *Statesman and Friend*, pp. 17, 96.
48. "Letters to John Taylor, of Caroline, Virginia, In Reply to His Strictures on Some Parts of the Defence of the American Constitutions," in Adams, *The Works of John Adams*, VI, 507, 508, 511, 516.
49. This section, in a somewhat different form, appeared originally as "The Economic Philosophy of Thomas Jefferson," in the *Political Science Quarterly*, LV (March 1940), 98–121.
50. "To Dugald Stewart," April 26, 1824, in *The Writings of Thomas Jefferson*, edited by A. E. Bergh, Washington, 1907, XVIII, 332. All references to Jefferson's writings are to this edition unless otherwise specified.
51. "To Dupont de Nemours," April 24, 1816, *ibid.*, XIV, 490.
52. "To John Holmes," April 22, 1820, *ibid.*, XV, 249–250; "To Jared Sparks," February 4, 1824; "To Edward Everett," April 8, 1826, *ibid.*, XVI, 8–13, 163, 239.
53. "Declaration by the Representatives of the United Colonies of North America," 1775; reprinted in *American Archives*, 4th series, Washington, 1839, II, 1870.
54. "To Patrick Henry," March 27, 1779; "To Benjamin Harrison," February 7, 1781, in Bergh, *The Writings of Thomas Jefferson*, IV, 48–51, 352.
55. "To Washington," March 15, 1784, Ford, *The Works of Thomas Jefferson*, III, 420.
56. "To John Jay," September 19, 1787, in Bergh, *The Writings of Thomas Jefferson*, VI, 310.
57. "To N. and J. Van Staphorst," July 30, 1785; "To David Hartley," September 5, 1785; "To A. Stuart," January 26, 1786, *ibid.*, V, 45, 122, 259.

58. "To James Madison," June 20, 1787; "To George Washington," December 4, 1788, *ibid.,* VI, 132; VII, 224.

59. "Circular to the American Consuls," May 30, 1792, *ibid.,* VIII, 352; "To Colonel David Humphreys," June 23, 1791, in Humphreys, *Life and Times of David Humphreys,* II, 112–113.

60. "To Madison," March 1793; "To George Hammond," May 15, 1793; "To Thomas Pinckney," September 7, 1793, in Bergh, *The Writings of Thomas Jefferson,* IX, 34, 90–91, 221–223; "Report on the Privileges and Restrictions on the Commerce of the United States in Foreign Countries," December 16, 1793, *ibid.,* III, 275–283.

61. A. P. Whitaker, "Reed and Forde: Merchant Adventurers of Philadelphia," in *The Pennsylvania Magazine of History and Biography,* LXI (July 1937), 262.

62. "Heads of Consideration on the Conduct We Are to Observe in the War Between Great Britain and France," and "Heads of Consideration on the Navigation of the Mississippi," August 22, 1790, in Bergh, *The Writings of Thomas Jefferson,* XVII, 299–307; "Report Relative to Negotiations with Spain to Secure the Free Navigation of the Mississippi and a Port on the Same," December 22, 1791, *ibid.,* III, 164–198.

63. "To Albert Gallatin," April 1, 1802, *ibid.,* X, 307.

64. "To Joseph Milligan," April 6, 1816, *ibid.,* XIV, 466.

65. "To Dupont de Nemours," April 15, 1811, in *The Correspondence between Thomas Jefferson and Pierre Samuel du Pont de Nemours, 1798–1817,* edited by Dumas Malone, Boston and New York, 1930, p. 133.

66. "Inaugural Address," March 4, 1801; "First Annual Message," December 8, 1801; "To Joel Barlow," May 3, 1802, in Bergh, *The Writings of Thomas Jefferson,* III, 320, 337; X, 320–321.

67. "To Brother Handsome Lake," November 3, 1802, *ibid.,* XVI, 395.

68. "To Andrew Jackson," February 16, 1803, *ibid.,* X, 357–359.

69. "Confidential Message Recommending a Western Exploring Expedition," January 18, 1803, *ibid.,* III, 493.

70. "To Robert R. Livingston," April 18, 1802, *ibid.,* X, 312–313.

71. "To John Breckinridge," August 12, 1803, *ibid.,* X, 411.

72. "To Pierre Samuel Dupont de Nemours," July 14, 1807; "To James Madison," August 16, 1807; "To James Monroe," January 28, 1809; "To James Madison," April 27, 1809, *ibid.,* XI, 274, 326–327; XII, 241–242, 276–277.

73. See the correspondence between Jefferson and Humphreys in Humphreys, *Life and Times of David Humphreys,* II, 375–380.

74. "To Jefferson," December 11, 1815, in Jefferson Papers, Library of Congress.

75. "To Benjamin Austin," January 9, 1816, in Bergh, *The Writings of Thomas Jefferson,* XIV, 387–392.

76. "To William B. Giles," December 26, 1825, *ibid.,* XVI, 147, 149–150.

77. "To George Wythe," July 1776, *ibid.,* IV, 258–259.

78. Jefferson took for granted that the state courts had this right. See "To James Monroe," January 8, 1811, *ibid.,* XIX, 181–182.

79. "To James Madison," December 20, 1787, March 15, 1789, *ibid.,* VI, 387; VII, 312.

80. "To James Madison," June 20, 1787; "To George Washington," December 4, 1788, *ibid.,* VI, 132–133; VII, 224.

81. "To William Ludlow," September 6, 1824, *ibid.,* XVI, 75.

CHAPTER XVIII

1. This section in a somewhat different form originally appeared as "The Economic Philosophy of Thomas Paine," in the *Political Science Quarterly*, LIII (September 1938), 372–386.

2. "The American Crisis," No. 10, 1782, in Moncure C. Conway, *The Writings of Thomas Paine*, New York and London, 1894–1896, I, 334.

3. "Common Sense," 1776; "Dissertation on the First Principles of Government," 1795, *ibid.*, I, 70, 75–84; III, 268.

4. "Common Sense," "The American Crisis," No. 3, 1777, No. 4, 1778; "Peace, and the Newfoundland Fisheries," Nos. 1 and 3, 1779, *ibid.*, I, 88, 204, 287; II, 3, 14.

5. "Common Sense," "The American Crisis," No. 9, 1780, No. 10, 1782, *ibid.*, I, 102, 305, 321, 340.

6. Shaw Livermore, *Early American Land Companies*, New York, 1939, p. 119 n.

7. Frank Smith, *Thomas Paine, Liberator*, New York, 1938, p. 94.

8. "On the Five Per Cent Duty," No. 6, 1783, reprinted in *Six New Letters of Thomas Paine*, with an introduction and notes by Harry H. Clark, Madison, Wis., 1939, pp. 57, 58, 60.

9. M. C. Conway, *The Life of Thomas Paine*, New York and London, 1892, I, 213, 215, 265; "Dissertations on Government; the Affairs of the Bank; and Paper Money," 1786. in Conway, *The Writings of Thomas Paine*, II, 132–187; *The Pennsylvania Gazette*, April 5, 12, 19, June 21, September 20, November 8, 1786, March 7, 1787.

10. "Prospects on the Rubicon," 1787; "The Rights of Man," 1791–1792; "Address to the Addressers," 1792; "Letter to Danton," 1793; "The Decline and Fall of the English System of Finance," 1796. in Conway, *The Writings of Thomas Paine*, II, 214, 312–512; III, 88–89, 137, 286–312.

11. "To Jefferson," December 25, 1802, *ibid.*, III, 379–380; Conway, *The Life of Thomas Paine*, II, 319–320, 332–333, 344–351.

12. "To the French Inhabitants of Louisiana," 1804, in Conway, *The Writings of Thomas Paine*, III, 430–436.

13. This section, except for minor revisions, was originally published in the *Political Science Quarterly*, LIX (March 1944), 83–100.

14. For Barlow's beginnings, see Theodore Albert Zunder, *The Early Days of Joel Barlow*, New Haven, 1934.

15. Robert Morris, who was with a competing group of Pennsylvania speculators, was included among the "anarchists." *The Anarchiad*, edited by Luther G. Riggs, New Haven, 1861, pp. 69, 77. For relevant material, see Leon Howard, *The Connecticut Wits*, Chicago, 1943, pp. 172–177; Julian P. Boyd, *The Susquehanna Company*, New Haven, 1935, pp. 43–47.

16. For the company's operations, see J. S. Davis, *Essays in the Earlier History of American Corporations*, Cambridge, 1917, I, 124–150, 213–253.

17. "Letters to Lafayette *et al.*," Washington's *Writings*, XXIX, 503–504, 506–508.

18. Playfair prepared an annotated edition of *The Wealth of Nations*.

19. "To Benjamin Walker," December 21, 1790, in "Selections from the Gallipolis Papers," edited by Theodore T. Belote, in *Quarterly Publications of the Historical and Philosophical Society of Ohio*, II (April–June 1907), 72.

20. "To Mrs. Barlow," January 1, 1790, in M. Ray Adams, "Joel Barlow, Political Romanticist," *American Literature*, IX (May 1937), 115; "To Duer," November 29, 1789, in Belote, *op. cit.*, pp. 58–60.

21. Playfair continued an adventurous career including journalism in support of the British government's policy of opposition to the French Revolution. Though a sympathizer of the Revolution during the company's operation, he turned to denouncing the movement in general and Paine in particular. He accused Paine of being irreligious and seditious. Worst of all, Paine was guilty of bad arithmetic in his calculations of the eventual financial bankruptcy and downfall of England. *Playfair's Answer to Thomas Paine's Decline and Fall of the English System of Finances,* London, 1796.

22. Charles Burr Todd, *Life and Letters of Joel Barlow,* New York and London, 1886, p. 87.

23. From Clavière's extensive library, J. B. Say, who was his secretary, first learned of *The Wealth of Nations.*

24. Eloise Ellery, *Brissot de Warville,* Boston and New York, 1915; also Frederick L. Nussbaum, *Commercial Policy in the French Revolution,* Washington, 1923.

25. Compare Letter XXVIII of *Nouveau Voyage,* Vol. II; and Benjamin Rush, "An Account of the Progress of Population, Agriculture, Manners, and Government in Pennsylvania, in a Letter to a Friend in England," in *Essays,* pp. 213–225.

26. "A Letter to the National Convention of France," 1792, in *Political Writings,* New York, 1796, pp. 194–195.

27. "A Letter Addressed to the People of Piedmont," 1792, *ibid.,* pp. 212–214, 221, 228, 234.

28. "Imlay's Observations," in *Annual Report of the American Historical Association,* 1896, I, 953–954; "Documents on the Relations of France to Louisiana, 1792–1795," in *The American Historical Review,* III (April 1898), 491–510; *Four New Letters of Mary Wollstonecraft and Helen M. Williams,* edited by Benjamin P. Kurtz and Carrie C. Autrey, Berkeley, 1937, pp. 61, 67.

29. *La commission des substances de l'an II. Procès-verbaux et actes,* edited by Pierre Caron, Paris, 1925, pp. 88, 102, 662–663.

30. It was charged though never clearly substantiated in 1803 that Barlow had received "advance" information of the inclusion of the settlement of such claims in the treaty ceding Louisiana to the United States. "Monroe to Madison," December 17, 1803, in Hamilton, *The Writings of James Monroe,* IV, 120.

31. "To Mrs. Barlow," July 8, 1796, in Todd, *op. cit.,* pp. 110, 297.

32. "Timothy Pickering to Colonel David Humphreys," June 18, 1796, in Humphreys, *Life and Times of David Humphreys,* II, 247.

33. *Letters from Paris to the Citizens of the United States,* London, 1800; Hildreth, *History of the United States,* V, 56.

Skipwith, after suffering financial reverses, went to West Florida, then under nominal Spanish authority, to recoup his fortunes. He participated in the insurrection of 1810, and when the insurgents, mostly American and British citizens, proclaimed an independent state, he became the head. This independence was short-lived, for the American government, which also claimed the territory, ignored Skipwith's pronouncements on the rights of man and revolution and sent troops to restore order. Isaac J. Cox, *West Florida Controversy, 1798–1813,* Baltimore, 1918, pp. 433–434.

34. "To Abraham Baldwin," 1804, in Leon Howard, "Joel Barlow and Napoleon," *Huntington Library Quarterly,* II (October 1938), 37–38.

35. M. R. Adams, *op. cit.,* p. 141.

36. *Oration Delivered at Washington, July 4, 1899, at the Request of the Democratic Citizens of the District of Columbia,* Washington, 1809; *Prospectus of a National Institution to Be Established in the United States,* Washington, 1806; *The Vision of Columbus,* Hartford, 1787, p. 243.

37. *Message from the President of the United States, Transmitting Copies*

and *Extracts from the Correspondence of the Secretary of State, and the Minister Plenipotentiary of the United States at Paris,* Washington, 1812.

38. The poem is printed in Leon Howard, *op. cit.,* p. 50.

39. This section, except for minor revisions, was originally published in the *Political Science Quarterly,* LIX (December 1944), 528–543.

40. *A Treatise on the Improvement of Canal Navigation,* London, 1796, pp. 112–113, 136–138; "To President Washington," February 5, 1797, in H. W. Dickinson, *Robert Fulton, Engineer and Artist,* London and New York, 1913, p. 57.

41. "Thoughts on Free Trade," October 9, 1797, English manuscript copy in Columbia University Library. The French manuscript has been published in the *Bulletin of the New York Public Library* (August 1901), V, No. 8.

42. "To Bonaparte," May 1, 1798, in Dickinson, *op. cit.,* pp. 68–70.

43. William Barclay Parsons, *Robert Fulton and the Submarine,* New York, 1922, pp. 151–152.

44. "To the Executive Directory," December 13, 1797; "To P. J. N. F. Barras," October 27, 1798, in Dickinson, *op. cit.,* pp. 74–75, 90–91.

45. Dickinson, *op. cit.,* p. 77.

46. "To Lord Melville," cited in Cadwallader Colden, *The Life of Robert Fulton,* New York, 1817, pp. 48–49.

47. *Letters Principally to the Right Honourable Lord Grenville, on Sub-marine Navigation and Attack,* privately printed, London, September 23, 1806; "To Joel Barlow," September 1806, in Todd, *op. cit.,* p. 209.

48. "Mr. Fulton's Communication," in Albert Gallatin, *Report of the Secretary of the Treasury, on the Subject of Public Roads and Canals,* Washington, 1808, pp. 108–123.

49. "To Gouverneur Morris," February 22, 1814, in Colden, *op. cit.,* pp. 284–287.

50. Correspondence in Turnbull, *op. cit.,* pp. 241, 245, 249, 262.

51. *A Vindication of the Steam-boat Right Granted by the State of New York,* New York, 1819, pp. 9–10, 55.

52. "To Livingston," October 21, 1811, in Jared Sparks, *The Life of Gouverneur Morris,* III, 273.

53. *Plan for Supplying the City of New York with Fuel,* by the New York Coal Company, New York, 1814.

54. "To Madison," November 5, 1814, MS. letter in Columbia University Library.

55. Cited by Parsons, *op. cit.,* p. 143.

56. Turnbull, *op. cit.,* p. 400.

57. "Fulton's Projected Letter to Pitt," in Samuel Bernstein, "Robert Fulton's Unpublished Memoir to Pitt: Science in the Service of Liberty," in *Science and Society,* VIII (Winter 1944), 59.

58. "Torpedo War, and Submarine Explosions," in *Magazine of History with Notes and Queries,* 1914, Extra number 35, p. 53.

59. Bollmann, "An Account of an Attempt, Made by Dr. Bollmann . . . to Liberate M. de la Fayette . . . , in *The Port Folio,* 4th series, II (August 1816), 94, 100.

60. "Private Journal of Blennerhassett," November 7, 1807, *Blennerhassett Papers,* edited by William H. Safford, Cincinnati, 1864, p. 484.

61. Duane, "Quid Statesmen," in *Aurora,* January 24, 1807.

62. Bollmann, "An Account of an Attempt," p. 100.

63. "Washington to Hamilton," May 8, 1796, in Washington's *Writings,* XXXV, 41–42.

64. *Blennerhassett Papers,* p. 484.

65. Madison, "Substance of a Communication . . . by Dr. Bollmann to the President," in *Letters and Other Writings of James Madison*, II, 393–401; "Jefferson to Lafayette," July 14, 1807, in *The Letters of Lafayette and Jefferson*, edited by Gilbert Chinard, Baltimore and Paris, 1929, pp. 260–261; "Bollmann to Duane," June 24, 1807, in *Aurora*, July 8, 1807.

66. "To Burr," August 11, 1808, November 12, 1808, June 24, 1810, in *The Private Journal of Aaron Burr*, edited by Matthew L. Davis, New York, 1838, I, 29–30, 84; II, 17–18.

67. Duane, "Review of Pamphlets on Banking," Nos. 4, 5, 6, in *Aurora*, January 1, 4, 7, 1811.

68. "A Letter to Alexander Baring" in *The American Review*, II (October 1811), 243–295.

69. *Debates of the Legislature of Pennsylvania in the Session of 1810–1811, at Lancaster*, reported by William Hamilton, Lancaster, 1811.

70. *Concise Observations on the Propriety of Incorporating New Banks*, Philadelphia, 1812, pp. 20–21, 31. This pamphlet is listed in catalogues without an author, but *The Private Journal of Aaron Burr* (II, 443) reveals Bollmann's authorship and the circumstances of publication. It also reveals that Bollmann was the author of at least six articles on politico-economic questions in *The American Review*, whereas heretofore only two which he mentioned in a signed publication have been attributed to him.

71. Jonathan Swift used this analysis before. See *Gulliver's Travels*, "Laputa," Chapter 6.

72. "Thoughts on a Financial System adapted to the present circumstances, and future prosperity of the Union," in *The American Review*, III (April 1812), 221–260.

73. "Outlines of a Plan for the Regulation of the Circulating Medium of the United States," *ibid.*, pp. 275–293.

74. "A Cursory Inquiry into the Embargo Policy of the American Government," *ibid.*, pp. 306–332.

75. This embryonic "Austrian" theory of value seems to have been the outgrowth of his experience in the Austrian prison. He later recalled that, though he was not allowed candlelight or books, was limited in food to what four cents a day would procure, and was attacked by "millions of famished vermin," still he was far from unhappy. "We always overrate the sufferings experienced under similar circumstances. When deprived of almost everything, the value and importance of what is left rises in proportion. A sharp bone discovered in a piece of meat, and hid; a pin found in a chink; a piece of charcoal, of chalk, happily secreted, are so many hoarded treasures, which feed hope, impart elasticity to the mind, and give rise to endless combinations." Bollmann, "An Account of an Attempt," pp. 109–110.

76. Bollmann, "Political Economy," in *The Emporium of Arts and Sciences*, New Series, II (December 1813), 119–167.

77. Cooper, "Miscellaneous"; "Bollmann to Cooper," June 6, 1813, *ibid.*, I, 181, 344–345.

78. "To Ludwig Bollmann," July 14, 1814, in Friedrich Kapp, *Justus Erich Bollmann*, Berlin, 1880, p. 372.

79. "Bollmann to Bayard," August 24, September 13, October 9, 1814, January 9, 1815, in "Papers of James A. Bayard, 1796–1815," edited by Elizabeth Donnan, in *Annual Report of the American Historical Association*, 1913, II, 318–319, 330, 339–340, 372–376; "Crawford to the Commissioners," September 13, 1814, in "Letters relating to the Negotiations at Ghent, 1812–1814," in *The American Histori-*

cal Review, XX (October 1914), 118–119; Paul Sweet, "Erich Bollmann at Vienna in 1815," *ibid.*, XLVI (April 1941), 585–586.

80. *Plan of an Improved System of the Money-Concerns of the Union*, Philadelphia, 1816; see also reprint of a Bollmann article under "Coinage" in Thomas Cooper's edition of Willich's *Domestic Encyclopaedia*, 1821.

81. *A Letter to Thomas Brand* and *A Second Letter to the Honourable Thomas Brand*, London, 1819.

82. "Letter to Alexander Baring," p. 249, "An Account of an Attempt," p. 95.